THE ABSOLUTELY INDISPENSABLE MAN

THE ABSOLUTELY INDISPENSABLE MAN

RALPH BUNCHE, THE UNITED NATIONS,
AND THE FIGHT TO END EMPIRE

KAL RAUSTIALA

OXFORD

UNIVERSITY PRESS

OXFORD
UNIVERSITY PRESS

Oxford University Press is a department of the University of Oxford. It furthers
the University's objective of excellence in research, scholarship, and education
by publishing worldwide. Oxford is a registered trade mark of Oxford University
Press in the UK and certain other countries.

Published in the United States of America by Oxford University Press
198 Madison Avenue, New York, NY 10016, United States of America.

CIP data is on file at the Library of Congress
ISBN 978-0-19-760223-2

DOI: 10.1093/oso/9780197602232.001.0001

1 3 5 7 9 8 6 4 2

Printed by Lakeside Book Company, United States of America

CONTENTS

FOREWORD

I N 2006, I entered my new office in Bunche Hall for the first time. I had been a professor at UCLA for six years and had often been inside the tall North Campus tower. On its eleven floors are an array of social science departments and classrooms, and, at the very top, is housed the center that I now direct, the Ronald W. Burkle Center for International Relations. Over the coming years I would spend many days in Bunche Hall.

As I settled into my new office, I realized I did not really know much about Ralph Bunche. I knew he had been an accomplished leader at the United Nations, an institution I had studied for years. I knew he had won a Nobel Peace Prize. And I knew he was one of the very few Black men prominent in midcentury diplomacy. But beyond that, I knew almost nothing about how he had stitched together such a strikingly unusual and illustrious career. Curious, I began to explore Bunche's life, reading the now almost three-decade-old biography written by his deputy and friend, the late Brian Urquhart, and subsequent works by excellent scholars such as Charles Henry, Ben Keppel, Pearl Robinson, and Ed Keller. Among other things, I discovered that Bunche spent much of his adult life in Kew Gardens, Queens, about a mile from where I had lived as a young child and my grandparents had lived out their lives after immigrating to the United States. Indeed, Bunche and I lived in Kew Gardens at the same time, though he was by then an elder statesman and I was a toddler.

During this period I was teaching a course on the UN for UCLA students. Each July, for a month, I would take twenty-five students to New York City. We would tour the UN, meet with officials and ambassadors, and visit some of the nongovernmental organizations that work closely with, and sometimes sharply criticize, the UN. As I walked by the long line of fluttering national flags on First Avenue, I would sometimes think of the early decades of the organization and the role Bunche had played. When he began, at the time of the UN's founding, there were about fifty member states; today there are nearly 200. That huge growth in flags was in turn a huge story—a transformation of the international system and an often peaceful revolution in human self-determination, in which dozens of former colonies gained their independence.

Over time, I began to think of writing my own book about the UN, one that would focus on the momentous change of postwar decolonization and how it transformed world politics, and I would tell that story of transformation through the life and work of Ralph Bunche. I learned that UCLA possessed an enormous trove of his papers—some 200 linear feet of boxes—and that sealed the deal. I dove in and soon became immersed in Bunche's remarkable life. As I did so, the focus of the book evolved, becoming less a history of the UN and decolonization and more a biography of one of the organization's greatest and most influential figures.

Still, I have not written a conventional biography and I do not try to tell the full story of Ralph Bunche's life. Rather, this is a political or professional biography that engages primarily with his career in diplomacy, especially during his UN years. Other authors, better placed to explore the personal or other sides of him, I hope, will write different books. I have focused on my expertise—Bunche the diplomat and policymaker—and so I spend only enough time on his childhood and family life to give context and texture to his impact on the postwar world.

As the focus of the book fell into place, I struggled with what aspects of his story I could tell. As an international lawyer with a PhD in international relations, I felt very comfortable with Bunche's career at the State Department and at the UN. This was terrain I had studied for decades. Yet Ralph Bunche was more than a diplomat. He was a Black man with a lifelong commitment to racial justice. That story, too, had to be acknowledged, if the book was to be at all truthful to his spirit and legacy. With the guidance of friends and colleagues at UCLA such as Anna Spain Bradley and Robin D. G. Kelley, I read widely on 20th-century Black internationalist thought and tried to understand the intellectual milieu in which Bunche lived. I reached out to the extended Bunche family, and, thankfully, they welcomed my project and offered me much wise counsel and recollection. In particular, Ralph Bunche III, his grandson, and Ronald and Peter Taylor, his cousins, gave me access to materials, personal insights, and family lore that improved the book immeasurably. I cannot claim to have done justice to all dimensions of his life, or to understand the experience of a Black man born at the high point of Jim Crow. Instead I have tried to be sensitive to how he saw the world and, as much as possible, to tell that story through his own words. In this regard, I was lucky that Ralph Bunche was an inveterate note-taker and journal-scribbler. He recorded many thoughts in detail, especially toward the end of his life, musing on issues ranging from the prospects for peace in the Middle East to the future of American race relations to the crucial influence of his grandmother on the arc of his life.

I also struggled with how to accurately portray a man who was born almost 120 years ago. Our language and expectations have changed, in some cases dramatically. Words and their meanings are always evolving and are often contested. How much should I directly quote Bunche, even when his words might trouble some readers today? Even more, what about quoting contemporaneous newspapers, books, and the like? This book often deals with war, hate, and prejudice. Is quoting a prewar news report that is imbued with racism giving the reader a frank description of the reality of the times, or is that outweighed by how it may amplify hateful voices from the past? I ultimately decided that there was no way to truly understand these aspects of his life and times without appreciating how different politics and social thought was. I have at all times tried to put such ideas and quotations in context. I also have endeavored to show respect to Bunche and his life by quoting him in his own voice, such as in his almost universal use of the word "Negro,"* and by presenting with clarity but also concision the ideas, often abhorrent, that he was fighting.

---

* By contrast, in my own voice, I use the word "Black."

I have come away with tremendous respect for the accomplishments of Ralph Bunche. As a Black man in the very white world of Cold War diplomacy, he faced insuperable odds and often crushing oppression. Despite this, he and his ideas helped change the world for the better. He led an extraordinary life, but in the end he was a human being, with all the attendant foibles. I have tried to write a book that illustrates his life and legacy in full, while also telling the story I began with, a story that to Bunche was absolutely essential—a story he cared so much about he devoted his life, and arguably his health, to it. That is the story of the transformation of the global order from one of war and empire to one of a diverse constellation of independent and sovereign states living—usually—in peace and collaborating, albeit unevenly, through the United Nations. The UN was an organization he believed in, fought for, and even loved. The values Ralph Bunche stood for—mutual respect, multilateralism, equality—are values he thought the UN also stood for. And he was not wrong. The UN has, of course, many failings and infirmities, as he knew only too well. But he always believed the organization did and could do much good and that the alternatives were far worse.

Were Bunche alive today, it is hard to say what he would make of the world of the 2020s. But he would surely be pleased to see the continuing demise of empire, even as it tenaciously persists in many places. He would likely be troubled by the frequent talk of a new Cold War between the US and China, by the brutality of Russia's invasion of Ukraine, and even by the implications of the rising climate crisis. He would certainly find the continuing conflict and suffering of the people of Congo (now the Democratic Republic of Congo) and of the Middle East—places in which he spent some of his most significant moments—upsetting. And he would undoubtedly be thinking, writing, and speaking about what racial justice means in a globalized world.

As I think Ralph Bunche would want, I dedicate this book to the unsung civil servants of the organization he devoted his career to. The UN is a vast place, and anyone who has worked for it, as I have, knows that there are many kinds of people there. Some, to be sure, do little, and at times even seem to labor to undermine the purposes of the organization. But in my experience most UN staff are true believers, as Bunche was himself. They work hard to try to make the world a more peaceful and more just place. They do this not only for us, but especially for future generations. I am confident Ralph Bunche would be very pleased that this part of his legacy continues.

A BOOK OF THIS MAGNITUDE REFLECTS many debts. For helpful reads of aspects of this book, I want to thank Jose Alvarez, Tony Anghie, Asli Bali, Gary Bass, Elad Ben-Dror, Peter Blake, Anu Bradford, Anna Spain Bradley, Ralph Bunche III, Anthony Tirado Chase, Michael Doyle, James Thuo Gathii, Oona Hathaway, Charles P. Henry, Lise Howard, Viva Jeronimo, Miles Kahler, David Kaye, Ben Keppel, Robin D. G. Kelley, Blanca Montejo, Luis Moreno Ocampo, Bob Orr, Anthony Pagden, Tom Plate, Stuart Reid, Angela Riley, Pearl Robinson, Loraine Sievers, Richard Steinberg, Lara Stemple, Jeffrey Stewart, Peter Taylor, Ronald Taylor, Barbara Walter, Dov Waxman, Adrien Wing, and Adam Winkler. The librarians and archivists at the United Nations, UCLA, and the Schomburg Center for the Study of Black Culture at the New York Public Library all were invaluably helpful to my research. In particular, I want to thank Rachel Green, Kevin Gerson, and Neil Hodge for their assistance. Many research assistants helped out with this book, in particular Matt Galla, Alexander Fay, Simon Ruhland, and David Silverlid. I gave presentations of aspects of the book at a number of places, including the State Department, Columbia Law School, the National War College, the Nazarian Center for Israel Studies at UCLA, UCLA Law School, and the Geffen Academy at UCLA. My long-time editor at Oxford, Dave McBride, was, as always, a source of sage advice and encouragement. My agent in New York City, Chris Calhoun, helped me think through what this project was really about. I want to add a special note of gratitude to the late Darryl Roberts, of Tuskegee and Duke universities, whose suggestion that I consider graduate school during his seminar many decades ago put me on the path to this book, and indeed to my entire career. I appreciate very much the feedback from all these sources, and I apologize for any omissions.

O N MARCH 29, 1951, AT THE PANTAGES THEATER on Hollywood Boulevard, hundreds of actors, directors, and entertainment moguls gathered for the 23rd Academy Awards. The crowd—and the many listeners on the radio nationwide—waited for the final and biggest award of the night: Best Picture. Among the films in the running were the Spencer Tracy comedy *Father of the Bride*; *Sunset Blvd*, the classic saga of old Hollywood decline; and *All About Eve*, the Broadway drama starring Bette Davis.

As the excitement built, the host for the evening, the dapper, slim Fred Astaire, leaned into the podium. "For the presenter of the final award," Astaire said,

> We've stepped outside the industry. We've stayed true to our Los Angeles roots, however. I'd call him the town's most distinguished son. He achieved the miracle of peace in Palestine; he won the Nobel Prize; he is now one of the large figures in the United Nations organization. It's an honor for all of us to hear from Dr. Ralph Bunche.[1]

Ralph Johnson Bunche, a forty-seven-year-old official at the then-new United Nations, walked across the broad stage wearing a white tie and tails and clutching some papers. Abundant applause and a fanfare of trumpets rang out. Bunche, who had grown up in Los Angeles, paused at the lectern to look out at the sparkling crowd. Speaking at first a bit stiffly and slowly, he thanked Astaire and began his speech.

Quickly striking a serious tone, and invoking the Cold War context of 1950s America, Bunche declared that it is "imperative to our way of life that this great medium be kept fully free." Freedom, he continued, brought "sober responsibilities." As a result, it was vital that the American film industry reflect democracy and "be directed toward democratic objectives." As the audience listened respectfully, he discussed the new United Nations organization, which just five years before had held its first meetings in London. The Cold War had already shattered many hopes about peace and cooperation in the postwar world; the Korean War was well underway as Hollywood's glittering stars and powerful moguls listened to Bunche's remarks. That very morning, in a courtroom in New York, Ethel and Julius Rosenberg had been convicted of spying for the Soviet Union and would soon be sentenced to death.

Despite this chilling global context, Bunche remained optimistic. The UN looked to Hollywood, he explained, for aid in achieving a world of peace and brotherhood. Bunche (or perhaps his speechwriter) tried to leaven this sober message with a few weak jokes about comedy and drama among diplomats. But he soon circled back to the main point he wanted the audience to take home: through the UN, "honorable peace can be achieved and secured."

His address complete, Bunche turned to the pressing matter at hand: the winner of the Oscar for Best Picture. After being handed a small white card—envelopes were not yet used in those days—he brought the heady evening to a close, announcing that *All About Eve* had triumphed. As legendary producer Daryl Zanuck bounded up to the podium, Bunche smiled broadly as he offered him a golden statuette and shook his hand.

Ralph Bunche's turn on the Academy Awards stage was emblematic of the extraordinary celebrity he enjoyed in midcentury America. His fame was not just recognized by Hollywood. Throughout the 1950s and 1960s, he was bombarded with speaking invitations, job offers, and appeals for his appearance. His Nobel Peace Prize, awarded the year before he spoke at the Pantages Theater, recognized his groundbreaking mediation between the new state of Israel and its Arab neighbors. The Nobel Prize made Ralph

Bunche a household name for many Americans. He received a ticker tape parade down Broadway's Canyon of Heroes and became the subject of an inspirational ABC docudrama. Presidents sought his advice; world leaders his attention; visionaries and activists—including Martin Luther King, Jr.—his advocacy. Bunche had enjoyed abundant professional success, but relatively little personal fame, until his landmark efforts in Palestine brought him to popular attention.

The mediation in the Middle East changed his life—and, but for a delayed plane, would have surely caused his death. He was soon on a first-name basis with presidents from Harry Truman to Richard Nixon. His impressive and inspirational life story became grist for the mill of American progress. The *Nation* called Bunche "a symbol throughout the world of the American Negro's increasingly effective struggle for equality."[2] The *New Yorker* described his life as "exhilarating" and "marvelously bound up in the fabric of everything we love about this country."[3] As a high-ranking Black man in the very white world of diplomacy, numerous administrations sought to bring him back to Washington, DC, from the UN, where he remained until his untimely death in 1971.

Once "the most honored African American in America," Ralph Bunche is largely forgotten today; remembered by some as a master of international diplomacy, by others as an "icon of racial equality," yet little known to the public at large.[4]

Bunche merits renewed recognition both for his extraordinary American life and for the lens he provides on two significant features of the 20th century—the creation of the postwar international order and the struggle for racial equality—that are rarely joined but deserve to be, and that he himself married in the realm of ideas and in his own person. As a scholar, he helped produce the landmark book, *An American Dilemma: The Negro Problem and Modern Democracy*. As an advocate, he marched arm in arm with Dr. Martin Luther King, Jr. from Selma to Montgomery. Yet he spent most of his career as a diplomat at the United Nations. His hands lay behind some of the signal features of the postwar order, from peacekeeping to conflict mediation to his most significant and lasting legacy, the one that made both peacekeeping and mediation so often necessary: the dismantling of European empire.

Bunche saw no dissonance in this pairing of diplomacy and civil rights. He fought to make both America and the world more just, more free, and more fair. During his lifetime—and in part due to his efforts—nearly a billion people of color gained independence from foreign rule.

The titanic global conflicts of the 20th century, from the Great War to the Cold War, are rarely viewed today through the lens of race and rights. Yet for much of the 20th century race was arguably *the* central principle in international relations, and colonialism—which generally meant the domination by Europeans of Africans, Asians, and others—the key connective concept. To Bunche racial justice was a global, not merely national, issue. Empire was one of racism's most potent and perilous guises, and the fight to end it provided a throughline in his career. Ralph Bunche was born into the heyday of colonial rule. By his death, the number of independent nations in the world had tripled. From the white-dominated world of early-20th-century empires came our world today: one of large power disparities, to be sure, but also one of sovereign, independent states led by governments of all races and religions.

This change did not come easily. At the end of the Second World War, European leaders like Winston Churchill fought to keep their prewar empires alive. Yet they quickly found they could not. In the early years of the UN, Bunche spoke before the NAACP at the Hollywood Bowl and declared: "The age of colonialism is in its twilight."[5] And he was right. In 1960 alone, a year he famously dubbed "The Year of Africa," seventeen new states gained their independence. Though it would take many years and much struggle to win, the battle between Churchill's vision of empire and Bunche's vision of equality was ultimately no contest.

A modest man, Bunche did not and could not lay claim to this vast transformation in geopolitics. The systematic retreat of empire was driven by a complex mix of charismatic liberation leaders, powerful ideas about self-determination and nationalism, the interests of the new postwar superpowers, and sometimes violent struggle. But as a prominent scholar, advocate, and policymaker, he played a critical role in fostering the decolonization of the globe. While the high hopes of some new nations were soon dashed against the rocks of realpolitik, Bunche always saw that the larger issue was a moral question: in his words, whether "the white man could ever accept darker peoples as equals."[6]

The end of European empire that he championed transformed the global order. In its wake came the rise of what was once called the Third World,[†] with implications for everything from the Vietnam War and the OPEC oil shocks of the 1970s to the contemporary rise of China. It also, in important ways, coincided with what some consider a new and more subtle form of empire: the United States' informal version, which generally eschewed territorial control in favor of less overt forms of hegemony. As a patriotic American, Ralph Bunche rarely questioned the postwar dominance of the US, and, as his Academy Award remarks showed, he largely accepted— even as he himself experienced the brutality of segregation—the Cold War consensus of a titanic global struggle between freedom in the West and oppression in the East.

He was, of course, far more critical of traditional empire, and not only propelled forward its unraveling but helped to devise ways to blunt its sharper edges. Traversing the globe in the 1950s and 1960s, Bunche was present at the creation of many new states, managing the often-turbulent politics that resulted from nation-building. This work occurred at the UN, his professional home for twenty-five years. He helped build the organization from its wartime origins in Franklin Delano Roosevelt's State Department and then spent the remainder of his life as one of its best-known officials. As a result, his story is closely, even inextricably, aligned with the story of the United Nations.

From nearly its opening moments until today, the UN has been castigated for failing to end the world's tragedies. Yet as the legendary American diplomat Richard Holbrooke once said, blaming the UN for failing to create

---

[†] Today "Third World" is seen by some as pejorative, with terms like "Global South" preferred. Still, Third World remains the most common term today, though its peak usage was in the 1980s. For historical accuracy I use Third World in many contexts throughout this book.

peace is like blaming Madison Square Garden for the Knicks failing to win.[7] Holbrooke was not wrong, but sometimes a different setting *can* change the outcome. Bunche was a true UN believer, and during his career he saw the UN manage, dampen, and even avert crises. He also witnessed its evolution into an organization that was as much about the needs and interests of the emerging Third World as it was a tool of the victorious great powers of the wartime Allied coalition. In particular, he was a key player in two under-appreciated UN-led developments that helped build the global rules-based order that emerged from the ashes of war.

The first development, the one that Bunche was most proud of, was the rise of UN peacekeeping. Colonialism may feel like a dusty relic of the past, but its legacy is still felt today. In much of the world, national borders—often drawn by 19th-century Europeans in gilded conference rooms—bear little relation to ethnic, religious, or linguistic divisions. The fight to end empire was a just cause, but it bore some bitter fruit. Since 1945, three-fourths of all civil wars have been concentrated in formerly colonized nations. UN peacekeeping was largely developed as a response to these challenges, born of necessity but ultimately proving surprisingly successful.

The notion that foreign militaries could police and deter conflict was not unknown in world history. Contemporary peacekeeping, however, is a radical departure from the power politics of the past. Peacekeeping began as an experiment in the early years of the UN. Bunche played a key role in developing it in the Middle East in the wake of the 1956 Suez Crisis, when Gamal Abdel Nasser's Egypt suddenly seized control of the vital Suez Canal, and Britain, France, and Israel secretly conspired to attack in response. Peacekeeping reached a controversial apogee in Congo in the early 1960s. After decades of brutal rule by Belgium, the huge colony suddenly achieved liberation. Bunche was there, on the ground, for the chaotic early months of independence. As Congo began to rip apart, the young, fiery liberation leader Patrice Lumumba was assassinated and the Cold War seemed ready to swallow up the new nation. The world looked to the UN to maintain control. Bunche remained a key figure in that struggle, especially after the tragic—and to this day, mysterious—death of UN Secretary General Dag Hammarskjold in a plane crash in the Rhodesian jungle in 1961.

Bunche and his UN colleagues developed the basic principles that define contemporary peacekeeping. And for the remainder of his career, knowing it was often essential to secure a stable process of decolonization, he paid close attention to peacekeeping, shaping policy in New York and flying around the world visiting troops in tense standoffs from Kashmir to Congo to Gaza.

The second key development Ralph Bunche influenced was conflict mediation. Peacekeeping and mediation go hand in hand; both aim to keep a lid on war in a world riven with potential conflict. Bunche's popular fame stemmed from his mediation of one of the most unfortunately enduring of conflicts: that between Arabs and Israelis. After the first UN mediator, Swedish Count Folke Bernadotte, was brazenly gunned down in an ambush on a Jerusalem street—an attack that Bunche, in a twist of fate, only narrowly missed—he took over the reins of the process. Months of table-pounding, charm, strategy, and billiards games produced, in Fred Astaire's now sweetly naïve words, "the miracle of peace in Palestine." Bunche's armistice between Israel and its enemies, achieved while sequestered in a shuttered hotel on the Mediterranean island of Rhodes, seemed to prove that the new UN could do what traditional great powers such as Britain could not.

For the next two decades Ralph Bunche was a towering figure in foreign policy circles and an icon of peace and probity to many Americans. Hailed as a modern-day Horatio Alger—literally; he won the Horatio Alger prize in 1952—many Americans looked to him as a powerful symbol of racial progress. (Though later, as the civil rights movement grew more radical, he was occasionally disparaged as a token. Malcolm X called him "a black man who didn't know his history.")[8] Even after the initial ticker tape parade and flurry of invites to speak, Bunche continued to operate at the highest levels—negotiating with presidents and prime ministers throughout the world, having dinner with Hollywood stars and European royalty, and attracting fan and hate mail on a regular basis.

Bunche's uncompromising beliefs and sharp analytical mind, his personal charm and unassuming manner, and his comfort and familiarity with establishment figures and thinking explain why Harry Truman, John F. Kennedy, Lyndon Johnson, and many others sought his counsel and commitment. Bunche often resisted his image as a symbol of racial progress. Yet he never lost faith in America. Indeed, he saw America as a model for the diverse societies arising elsewhere: "The very fact of racial diversity in our society makes of our nation throughout the entire world a unique symbol of the promise, the unlimited possibilities for strength and greatness, the spiritual depth and the virility of democracy as a way of life," he declared.[9] As one of his UN colleagues recollected, he was "absolutely American and the best of America."[10]

It has been fifty years since Ralph Bunche's untimely death. World politics in the 2020s is at a hinge point. The continued diffusion of economic growth and political power has led to increasing uncertainty about who stands where in the global order. Large numbers of Europeans and Americans again fear the rising political, economic, and cultural power of nonwhite peoples. Political leaders around the world have brazenly made exclusionary racial, ethnic, and religious appeals to their followers. The world, once open, seems to be drawing closed. Against this backdrop stand a set of ideas that date back to the destruction and distress of the 20th century—equality between peoples, the virtues of diplomacy, and the value of a rules-based multilateral order. While no pacifist, Bunche believed that if the xenophobic impulses that too often led one people to oppress another could be defeated, the world could be a better place.

And though he saw up close how corrupt and pointless politics in the UN could be, he believed the alternatives were clearly worse. In the late 1960s, Richard Nixon toured the UN headquarters with Bunche at his side. Turning to him, Nixon remarked that "it must be discouraging for you to work here." Never discouraging, the ever-optimistic Bunche said, but often frustrating. Nixon, who knew a thing or two about frustration, looked at him knowingly and repeated his words back, as if appreciating their larger significance: "never discouraging, but often frustrating."[11]

Bunche's optimism was tempered by a realism born of hard experience. He was driven to make the UN work because he saw—or knew—that an international organization *could* be a force for good in a violent world. When the Vietnam War seemed to make a mockery of the UN, Bunche maintained the faith even as the war challenged his belief in America's benevolent role in the postwar era. As Lyndon Johnson increasingly grumbled about Secretary General U Thant's rising criticism of American intervention, Bunche became, as he often had been in the past, a key interlocutor between Washington and New York. Visiting the White House in 1966, US Ambassador to the UN Arthur Goldberg brought Bunche and Thant, who was up for reappointment for a second term, upstairs to meet privately with the president.

"Ralph is one of the two absolutely indispensable men at the UN," Goldberg told LBJ—quickly adding that Thant was the other. Downstairs, Secretary of State Dean Rusk told Bunche the real deal: "You will just have to stay on whether U Thant does or not."[12]

At his death in 1971, the *New York Times* called Ralph Bunche "the personification of the United Nations."[13] His was an incredibly rich life of both struggle and success—for peace and justice; against racism and oppression—fought out in the glare of celebrity. And it was a life, especially in its second half, devoted to internationalism. Whatever its faults, the UN possesses one unique quality. It remains, in President Dwight D. Eisenhower's words, "man's best organized hope to substitute the conference table for the battlefield."[14] Bunche shared Ike's belief. He also knew that a new, more equal postwar order was of a piece with the pursuit of civil rights at home. Once freed from the oppression of colonialism, nations would not necessarily coexist peacefully. Without that freedom, he knew they never would.

CHAPTER 1

WEST AND EAST

How may permanent peace be best attained? By world leagues? World courts? By
world conference, pacts, treaties?
  —Ralph Bunche, "That Man May Dwell in Peace," Speech at UCLA, 1926

On July 29, 1927, a Gala Benefit Frolic and Carnival, billed as "One Night
of Joy," was held at the Bronx Palm Gardens nightclub near downtown
Los Angeles. It was a warm night, coming at the end of a long late-July hot
spell, and the club was steamy. Admission, for .75 cents, offered the music
of Curtis Mosby and His Dixieland Blues Blowers and dancing by Mildred
Washington and Her Creole Cuties. The Friday night event benefited the
Ralph Bunche Scholarship Fund. Someone, perhaps Bunche himself,
scrawled $50 in pencil on a flyer from the event that he held onto, likely the
night's take and a reasonable one at that: about $800 in 2022 dollars.[1]

The scholarship fund had been set up by a local neighborhood group
known as the Iroquois Friday Morning Civic and Social Club. The aim
was to assist Bunche, who had just graduated from UCLA (then known
as the University of California's "Southern Branch"), to head east to attend Harvard for graduate school. Less than 4 percent of Americans had a
college degree in 1927, and far fewer went on to graduate school. Only a

vanishingly small number of Black Americans entered any form of higher education, let alone Harvard. In short, what Ralph Bunche was doing was almost never done—especially from small, far away Los Angeles—and it placed him in a very rare cohort.

The gala at the Bronx Palm Gardens nightclub was a big event, but there were other efforts and contributions to help him make his way east. In the end, the scholarship fund totaled some $570, a sum sufficient to cover much of his living costs while in Harvard's doctoral program in political science. Bunche, who came from a family of modest means, was very grateful for these efforts. He profusely thanked the generous women behind the Iroquois Friday Morning Club, declaring them to have a fine spirit which proved that "the elders heartily endorse a program of education."[2] A few weeks after the gala, money safely in hand, he excitedly boarded a train for the long journey from the West Coast to Cambridge, Massachusetts. He had never been to New England; indeed, though he had moved often as a child, he had never set foot on the East Coast at all. Harvard would be a new and challenging experience, one matched to his large ambitions and competitive spirit. At the railway station downtown he declared to those waving him goodbye, many of them friends from UCLA, "Tell all Angelenos, for me, it matters not what great things the future may hold, nothing can cause me to ever forget the summer of '27 and the good friends that helped me."[3]

Ralph Bunche was coming off four very successful years in college. While his decision to study colonial rule came later, while at Harvard, UCLA was where he began his intellectual journey into international affairs and where he first explored a more public-minded side of his personality. Bunche loved UCLA and spoke of it often throughout his career—far more than he ever spoke of Harvard. "UCLA was where it all began for me; where, in a sense, I began; college for me was the genesis and the catalyst," he said, some four decades later, at the dedication for UCLA's Bunche Hall.[4]

RALPH JOHNSON BUNCHE ATTENDED THOMAS JEFFERSON High School in Los Angeles, which had been built just a few years before he began as a freshman. A high school class photo taken in 1922 shows sixteen students,

Photo 1.1 Bunche in high school, Los Angeles

all white except for one. The Bunche family had moved to the growing city of Los Angeles in 1917 from Albuquerque, New Mexico, and before that Cleveland, Knoxville, and Detroit, where Ralph Bunche was born.[5] His year of birth is a matter of some dispute; some sources credibly insist on 1903, including a private Johnson family history; others use 1904. Bunche himself wrote an essay in the 1950s citing 1904.[6] (This book uses 1903.)

In Detroit, at the time a small metropolis populated by many German immigrants, young Ralph developed his lifelong love of baseball and music, spurred by Ty Cobb, the Detroit Tigers, a musical family, and the many street bands that once roamed the city. An avid athlete, he loved to skate and sled in winter, and to play street hockey with tin cans in summer, sports that would fall out of his life once he moved to California. While Bunche later described his Detroit neighborhood as white and working class, and claimed to have "never experienced any unfriendliness from our white neighbors," in particular at the local YMCA, later research suggests that in fact the neighborhood had many Black residents—and an "openly segregationist YMCA."[7] Whether Bunche's memory was faulty, which was certainly plausible, or whether he was simply strongly prone to see the racial glass as half-full—maybe even three-quarters full—is difficult to say. It may well have been both.[*] Whatever the true state of affairs, he and his family soon left the Midwest for the more healthful climate of the Southwest. In Albuquerque, then a small town of less than 20,000 inhabitants, Bunche experienced a different and far more rural life. He would explore the abundant open countryside and hunt with his uncle for rabbits and quail. ("Is there anything more delicious than fresh quail broiled in butter?" he later reminisced.)[8] There were timber wolves and mountain lions on the nearby peaks, and brisk air and open skies everywhere.

Bunche was a good but not necessarily focused student as a child. A family history notes that in elementary school he loved books and school but also liked to talk in class and would sometimes get "a few licks over the knuckles with a ruler."[9] His father, Fred, was often on the outskirts of family life. He left in 1916 to look for better fortunes, never really to return. (Bunche later claimed his father phoned the family in Los Angeles in 1929 but was not welcomed back.)[10] In 1917 his mother, Olive, whose persistent health problems had precipitated the move to the dry desert air of New Mexico, suddenly died of tuberculosis. Ralph Bunche, only 14, was now raised by his grandmother, Lucy Johnson.

The family soon headed further west, as far as they could go, to California. At the time somewhat off the beaten track of the mainstream of American life, Los Angeles provided a new start. They moved into a modest house near Central Avenue just south of downtown. Bunche enrolled at 30th Intermediate School. He seemed to thrive on the West Coast, but his mother's tragic early death haunted him. Toward the end of his life, after attending a funeral, he wrote in his diary that "now, more than ever I seem to regret that I lost my mother when both she and I were so young. I feel cheated to have been deprived of her. . . . I can never get it out of my mind

---

[*] Charles P. Henry, in his 1999 *Ralph Bunche: Model Negro or American Other?*, reads this disjuncture as reflective of the "old Black elite's optimism about race relations." Bunche was certainly an optimist on many issues, as later chapters will reveal.

that on that night of her death in Albuquerque she had asked for milk and there was none in the house because I had drunk it up."[11]

Having effectively lost both his parents, Bunche was under the care of his grandmother, Lucy Johnson. In later years he would speak often of her tremendous influence, saying no one could owe more to one person than he owed her. She was, he said, the "literal matriarch of our 'clan.' "[12] A small woman of fierce will and high expectations who seemed to brook no nonsense or disrespect, she made a lasting impression on him and others around him. She taught him to guard against excessive pride, he once explained, but also to stand up for himself.[13] Bunche described her as "indomitable in spirit." A former teacher of his agreed, remarking many decades later that while she had met his grandmother just once, she never forgot "the emanation of power from that tiny figure."[14] When his school's principal suggested to his grandmother that Bunche be steered toward a trade program, she was steadfast: "My grandson is going to college."[15]

Lucy Johnson was strict but loving, and a deeply religious Baptist. Liquor, smoking, card games, dancing, movies or plays on Sunday, "even coffee" were taboo in the household, Bunche later recounted.[16] There is little evidence that her religious fervor stuck with him, however. Offered the chance to be baptized by his grandmother's favorite preacher in Detroit as he headed to Harvard, he at first demurred. Protesting that he did not hear "the call," he tried to get out of the ceremony, but the preacher insisted that doing a good deed for her was both call *and* response. Bunche acquiesced, the ceremony took place, but he felt it was not the sort of call she had in mind. Occasional brushes with divine intervention did not change his somewhat areligious views. One Sunday as a child, violating a cardinal rule of his grandmother's, he sneaked into a play. When, during a dramatic moment, the theater's chandelier began to shake disturbingly, the audience realized a minor earthquake was striking. As he bolted out in fear, he ran directly and shockingly into his Aunt Ethel in the aisle. Ashamed at their mutual transgression, the two dutifully confessed when they returned home. Lucy Johnson assured them they had only gotten out alive because it was God's will. Bunche remained skeptical—no one was hurt in the incident— but it was a sign of his grandmother's seriousness.[17]

Looking back, he described his childhood as poor but proud. "We bowed to no one, worked hard, and never felt any shame about having little money."[18] He held a number of jobs in his early years, and indeed worked almost continuously through high school, college, and even into graduate school. In California in the 1910s and 1920s, those jobs included working as a paper boy for the *Los Angeles Times*, in the paper's printing press rooms, in the kitchen in resort hotels, on board a ship, in the home of a silent film star, and even laying carpets. When the new governor of California, a former head of the Screen Actors Guild named Ronald Reagan, proposed tuition at the University of California in 1967, Bunche, now famous and an elder statesman, invoked his carpet-laying job when he spoke out in opposition. It is an obligation of society, he argued, to make education available to all. If it had not been for UCLA's free education, he would likely still be laying carpets. That's an honorable job, he explained, "but not as exciting as what I'm doing."[19]

Throughout his life, colleagues remarked on Bunche's drive, determination, and capacity for hard work. Edward R. Murrow would later introduce him on national television as a man who likes to work, and indeed could not "remember when he didn't have to work."[20] But Bunche also was fun-loving and found many moments to enjoy life, especially theater and sports. His family was musically inclined, indeed sometimes performed publicly, and in Los Angeles in the 1920s he saw his first real stage musical. "I loved it and have a been a musical buff ever since," he later wrote—though at some point in his childhood, playing in hay, a piece of straw became stuck in his ear and damaged his hearing. Years later that would be one factor that kept him out of active duty in the Second World War.[21] Bunche's own musical skills were concededly minimal. His grandmother once implored him, for the sake of the family's good name, to "never let anybody hear you try to sing."[22]

Los Angeles had a relatively small Black population in the early 20th century, but it was growing.† (The first Black representative to the California State Assembly was elected from South Central Los Angeles in 1918,

---

† W. E. B. Du Bois, in 1913, said of Los Angeles that it was "wonderful" and nowhere else in the nation was "the Negro so well and beautifully housed."

around the time Bunche arrived.) It was there that he began, as he later put it, to develop "a real racial consciousness."[23] Once, when he was working at the *Los Angeles Times*, the paper took all the newsboys out to the amusement pier at Venice Beach. Bunche had a wonderful time riding the roller coaster, eating ice cream, and playing games. But when the group went to swim in the "Venice Plunge," he was told that only the white employees could enter the water. The incident made a deep impression on him. Later, speaking of segregated pools before a local audience, he declared that "any Los Angeles Negro who would go bathing in that dirty hole with that sign 'For Colored Only' gawking down at him in insolent mockery of his race is either a fool or a traitor to his kind."[24]

Ralph Bunche's grandmother had instilled in him a strong sense of racial pride, and he more frequently began to see himself in competition with the white classmates around him. "I was the only Negro in the class," he remarked later, "and I was determined to show I was as good as the white kids."[25] How segregated his early life was became a matter of some dispute, even within his family. In 1969, interviewed on ABC television by Sam Donaldson, Bunche said: "I grew up in a ghetto . . . the apparent ghetto of Watts." His Aunt Nelle, watching the broadcast, immediately dashed off a letter. "Where did you ever get the idea that you grew up in the black ghetto? When you were growing up this street of ours was almost entirely white."[26]

Bunche began to do very well in school, yet he nonetheless described himself as an "apprehensive and not very confident youth" with no burning desire to go to college.[27] He often happily roamed Central Avenue, the hub of Black life and music in 1920s Los Angeles, and went to the gallery at the Orpheum to see vaudeville shows. ("We were wilder than was good for us," he said of his high school friends, though Prohibition was in full force at the time.) A quite successful student by high school—chosen as valedictorian of Thomas Jefferson High—it was his grandmother who stressed that he had to go to college, insisting he would not regret it. "I can't really be happy till you get there," she told him, having seen early glimpses perhaps of what others would later see in Ralph Bunche. His boss at his high school carpet job also saw something early on: he offered to send Bunche to Cal Tech to study the chemistry of dyes. Bunche consulted his grandmother, who was against it, telling him it was "important to be free."[28] Despite being valedictorian, he was not admitted to the city's academic honor society because he was Black. This cut deeply and almost dissuaded him from continuing his education. But once again his grandmother intervened and pushed him toward college. It was only her insistence that he continue his education "as Johnson forebears had done," that allowed him to "break out of the iron ring of the ghetto."[29]

In 1922 he fulfilled her wishes by entering UCLA. At that time the university was not yet in its grand, tree-filled Westside location, but instead on Vermont Avenue, much closer to downtown. UCLA was quite small in this era. He and other students had a remarkable degree of freedom and access to faculty and administrators—something, he surmised decades later, that was likely no longer true on the "huge Westwood campus" with its "teeming masses." He found UCLA a "new world, an exhilarating environment, and I enjoyed it immensely." He mentioned the university often in speeches in the 1950s and 1960s, usually by joking about a man who became a friend and, in a way, a rival: "And then I went on to UCLA which is, as you know, Jackie Robinson's school."[30]

EARLY ON AT UCLA, RALPH BUNCHE showed an interest in and aptitude for public debate. In one of his first speeches, he criticized what he saw as the complacency of older Black Angelenos in the face of rising racial injustice. The local Black community was growing in size, and Bunche believed they needed to push back harder against discrimination. If we did not do so now, he asked, would we soon see "separate, inferior schools, parks, and who knows, perhaps even Jim Crow cars forced on us?"[31] Perhaps the blatant racism of the Venice Plunge incident was still fresh in his mind. If segregation was not fought to the "bitter end," he continued, only one conclusion was possible: "that the Los Angeles Negro is cowed—that he lacks racial pride and racial consciousness." Reflecting his grandmother's influence, he offered education as an all-encompassing solution. Education, he argued, is the "keynote" for the advancement of Black people in America—the "panacea for [our] ills."

Bunche himself certainly took education seriously. Once at UCLA, he enrolled in courses in political science, law, philosophy, economics, and history. At a time of comparatively little grade inflation, he received mostly As, with an occasional B (philosophy, administrative law, Spanish) thrown in. Although he never spent much time studying economics, in his first course his professor awarded him an A, embellished with a note: "Best record of anyone in the course, so I'll have to forgive you that morning you were sleeping."[32]

Ralph Bunche may have been sleeping in his economics class because he was unusually active in so many pursuits. The Vermont Avenue campus of UCLA had ivy-covered buildings, and, because everything grows well in Southern California, the ivy often overwhelmed the windows.[‡] Among his jobs was regularly trimming it back. In addition to that, and occasional janitorial duties around the buildings, he worked on the school newspaper, was president of the debating society, served as sports editor of the yearbook, and attended UCLA on an athletic scholarship. He played basketball, which he took up after his first love, football, left him sidelined with a leg injury. Many years later, in one of the notes he would often jot down in a spiral notebook or even stray piece of paper, he reminisced about what UCLA basketball meant to him:

> When a few years ago I came home one evening to be told by my wife and the police that we had been burglarized, my first words after expressing relief that my wife had not been hurt were: Did they leave my 3 gold basketballs? I was referring to the awards I cherish for playing on the championship varsity basketball teams at UCLA in the years '24–'27. They are my most prized possessions, and I would not trade them for any award I know of. I mean that.[33]

Bunche enjoyed life at UCLA and was by all accounts outgoing and social. Yet he soon began to focus more and more on serious matters. Indeed, he was such an excellent student that he graduated as valedictorian of the class of 1927. A fundamental aspect of his personality seemed to take root

---

[‡] The site today is home to Los Angeles Community College.

in this period. He discovered that he thrived in a setting where he could prove himself, whether on the basketball court or, more critically for his future, in the classroom. "I've been asked what my main drive has been," he later said. "And I think it is one thing: competitiveness. I have the pride of a competitor. I like to win."

An early interest in war and peace also seemed to take root. In an oratorical contest in 1926, he gave a speech entitled "That Man May Dwell in Peace." The speech was florid and dramatic, punctuated with strong statements about the aftermath of the First World War, which then was still in recent memory. Bunche spoke of the "unholy sacrifice" to a "bestial wargod" this brutal European conflict had entailed. He addressed the many conventional reasons given for the outbreak of what was then known as the Great War: to make the world safe for democracy; to affect disarmament; to protect minority rights; and even to end imperialism. (The great W. E.

Photo 1.2 Bunche playing basketball, UCLA

B. Du Bois, propounding a view close to Bunche's own, had said the First World War was in fact fundamentally about racial dominance: "the jealous and avaricious struggle for the largest share in exploiting darker races.")[34] Bunche saw the war as an abomination, yet rightly foresaw that any future war would be even more horrific.

He then proposed a solution to the enduring problem of conflict, one that is striking in light of his later quarter-century career at the United Nations:

> But how may permanent peace be best attained? By world leagues? World courts? By world conference, pacts, treaties? Though such measures may be truly significant considerations in the growth of international osmosis, they are insufficient— something more profound is needed if man is to solve this gigantic problem. The proposal which I would present as an antidote for world "war-poisoning" is centered about two basic principles, essential, I believe, to any rational peace plan. These are International Organization, involving every nation of the world; and the full development of the "International Mind or Will."[35]

The speech went on to presciently describe some of the challenges that would later vex Bunche and the UN in the decades to come. In the development of this cooperation, what is to become of the "sentiment of nationality?" Must we altogether condemn nationalism and "race pride," he asked, in favor of some kind of universalism? In raising these questions, he was foreshadowing a key challenge of the postwar international order: how to balance national interest with multilateral cooperation, in a world soon to be threatened with total annihilation.

In 1926 Bunche, of course, knew nothing of the coming and horrific Second World War, nor did he recognize that the war would usher in a golden age of international organizations. Yet in making the case for a form of international organization, he argued that nationalism and race pride need not be condemned. Pivoting to the early American experience, he described how the original thirteen colonies were full of division and rivalry, yet still found common bonds sufficient to allow a political union to develop. His sense of the political cleavages in colonial America may have been a bit off—he called them comparable in many respects to the differences among the nations of the world—but he was not wrong to look to federal structures for *national* governance as a model for future *global* governance. Still, he recognized that federal systems, treaties, international organizations, and the like were merely tools. Without the will to use them and the normative basis to rely on them, conflict could and would recur. As a result, he argued, the world must also cultivate a cooperative will and a "spirit of world brotherhood."

Ralph Bunche's commitment to an institution that joined every nation of the world would only grow in the decades to come. Even as he spent the bulk of his working life at the UN, he never lost his early belief in the power of cooperation to contain war and promote peace. Chastened by years of bearing witness to humankind's capacity for death and destruction, however, he would later renounce his youthful enthusiasm for world brotherhood in favor of more modest goals. "May I say a word or two about brotherhood?" he asked in one interview late in his life. "I used to make speeches about brotherhood but I never mention it any more. Brotherhood is a misused, misleading term. What we need in this world is not brotherhood, but coexistence."[36]

INTERVIEWED IN 1962, WHEN HE WAS the highest-ranking American at the United Nations, Ralph Bunche was asked if he had any idea as a college student what direction his life would take. "I can't say that I really did," he replied. "I enjoyed [UCLA], but I didn't have much sense of direction." Law had always been an assumption on his part, but he soon realized he was not actually all that interested in being a lawyer. "I went into graduate school not really knowing just where I was going," he told his interviewer.[37] But he deeply believed in education, and his grandmother had instilled a sense that he had no real limits other than those he himself imposed. Offered two fellowships for graduate school, one at Stanford and one at Harvard, Bunche chose Harvard.

As he was preparing to leave Los Angeles, he took a moment to pen a letter to W. E. B. Du Bois, perhaps the most prominent Black intellectual of the day. Du Bois had written his landmark *The Souls of Black Folk* the year

Bunche was born. Du Bois was a hero to Bunche, as he was to many ambitious young Black Americans of the time. "Since I have been sufficiently old to think rationally and to appreciate that there was a 'race problem' in America, in which I was necessarily involved," he wrote the older man, "I have set as the goal of my ambition service to my group."[38] He had met Du Bois before, though he assured him that he was "sure you do not remember me." Nonetheless, he continued, he had long felt the need to meet with and connect with the "leaders of our race." That, Bunche explained, was why he was anxious to come East and attend Harvard. Perhaps there was something he could do at the NAACP, he inquired. He politely closed the letter by stressing that he hoped Du Bois would not "think me presumptuous in taking this liberty."

Du Bois sent a brief, noncommittal reply. But he took notice of Ralph Bunche. In the August 1927 edition of the NAACP's magazine *The Crisis: A Record of the Darker Races*, Du Bois, who was the editor, included Bunche's UCLA graduation photo. It was presented as part of an annual spread of photographs of "The College Educated Negro"—a forum Du Bois deployed to highlight the group he famously called the Talented Tenth of the Black community in early 20th-century America.

Du Bois was a man of myriad talents and interests and a towering figure in political and social thought surrounding race. He saw the question of the color line as a global, not merely national, issue. Bunche came to share this global view of race, and as he rose to prominence in academic and activist circles in the 1930s and began to work seriously on the question of race and empire, he would encounter Du Bois again and again. Both men were active in the NAACP and deeply interested in how racial dynamics played out in America and abroad. Yet much later, when Bunche was at the height of his fame, he and Du Bois were no longer on speaking terms. Du Bois publicly attacked him as anti-Jewish in a 1948 speech in Madison Square Garden during Bunche's historic mediation of the postwar Palestine conflict. Bunche, wounded and irate at what he considered a wholly unfounded critique, wrote Du Bois out of his life. In the 1920s, however, this was all far in the future, and Bunche, as supplicant, was writing to Du Bois to seek advice but surely also to simply place himself on the great man's radar, to let him know that even in distant Southern California there were young Black men, educated and ambitious, who were headed to Harvard and beyond.

Arriving in Cambridge, Bunche moved into an apartment just east of Harvard Square. It was a quick five-minute walk to campus. His official Harvard photo shows him on a sun-dappled day, a broad, searching smile across his face and a sense of energy and engagement radiating outward. One of his housemates, Robert Weaver, who would go on to become Secretary of Housing and Urban Development under Lyndon Johnson, recalled a man who was "extremely attractive, quite vocal, articulate, and approachable."[39] Charming and charismatic, Bunche made friends easily and was fun to be around. Even then one of his signature traits was apparent. "What impressed me most about Ralph in those days," said Weaver, was his optimism. This, Weaver explained, was an optimism rooted not in wishful thinking, but in the experience of working hard and overcoming obstacles: confidence as much as optimism.

Photo 1.3 Bunche at Harvard

Decades later in Cyprus, Bunche would speak about his optimism when attempting to mediate the long-running dispute between Greek and Turkish Cypriots. At the airport in Nicosia in the 1960s, a reporter asked if he was optimistic about the deadly conflict. "I am a professional optimist," he replied.

> If I were not a professional optimist through 21 years in the United Nations service, mainly in conflict areas—Palestine, Congo, here, and in Kashmir—I would be crazy. You have to be optimistic in this work or get out of it. . . . That is, optimistic in the sense of assuming that there is no problem—Cyprus or any other—which cannot be solved and that, therefore, you have to keep at it persistently and you have to have confidence that it can be solved. . . . And so, personally, I am always inclined to pessimism, but professionally I am inclined to optimism.[40]

This optimism would serve him well during the turbulent years of the Cold War. And it seemed deeply rooted. At UCLA, in a philosophy course, he had written a paper with the memorable title "Is Man Naturally Low and Despicable?" In it, he debated Thomas Hobbes's famous claim about life in the state of nature (nasty, brutish, and short, Hobbes had argued.) Bunche disputed this viewpoint, calling it quite pessimistic and unwarranted. Yes, there were many base motives and instincts in humankind. But, he maintained, he had a deep-set conviction that "man *must* have an inherent notion of right and wrong." Toward the end of his life, despite having witnessed much hatred and suffering, and having grown somewhat more pessimistic himself about many issues, he still maintained much of this basic view. As he told the *New Yorker*, "I've always had faith in the essential goodness of people. I think that basically man is good. He can be misled, but he's *good*."[41]

When Bunche began his studies at Harvard in 1927, neither diplomacy nor international relations seemed clearly to be in his academic trajectory. Indeed, his plans were vague. In a letter to his former professor, Charles Rieber, he told Rieber of his Harvard professors and the small network of UCLA "Bruin brethren" he was spending time with as he adjusted to life in New England. Most importantly, he explained that he had decided to cast his lot in the "realm of the scholarly rather than the purely legal." From now on, he pledged, he would "bend every effort toward the attainment of the Ph.D."[42] Rieber replied that he was very glad he was turning to the life of a scholar.[43] Bunche had great respect for Rieber, and this supportive letter must have pleased him. In 1966 Bunche recalled with some nostalgia that he and Rieber were quite friendly; Rieber, he said, had a profound mind and could use words "as a rapier." Bunche, who could be tart and did not suffer fools gladly, noted that he "may have borrowed something of that from him, come to think of it."[44]

Bunche was familiar with the discipline of political science from UCLA and came to his graduate work well prepared. Although the field in a sense was centuries old, dating back to Machiavelli, Hobbes, and even Aristotle, political science was a somewhat new term in the 1920s. The American Political Science Association, of which he would become president many years later, had been founded only in 1903.§ At Harvard he explored various and sometimes arcane corners of the field. He wrote his master's thesis on the political theory of Sir Robert Filmer, an obscure 17th-century English royalist. (His future colleague and mentor at Howard, Alain Locke, called Filmer's work "glib nonsense"; this was an intellectual foray Bunche did not return to.) He also ranged closer to home. He wrote papers on "The Negro in Chicago Politics" and "Negro Political Philosophy," both of which suggested a growing academic interest in the intersection of race and politics.

In "Negro Political Philosophy" Bunche urged a greater focus on participation in local, rather than just national, elections. He criticized what he saw as a basic political conservatism in Black communities, which led to timidity in embracing new ideas. With regard to socialism, for instance, he asked "can we not at least intelligently investigate what it has to offer us for our sufferings?"[45] In "The Negro in Chicago Politics," Bunche argued that no racial group in the country save the Irish "is more manifestly 'political' in its everyday life than the American Negro." He was generally

§ When Bunche arrived there, Harvard used, and today still uses, the term *Government* rather than *Political Science*.

positive about the political impact of the Black vote in prewar Chicago.[46] Yet he did not ignore the obvious injustice found elsewhere—and surely in Chicago as well—concluding that the Black vote was far too often arbitrarily denied.

Bunche received his master's degree from Harvard in 1928. He intended to stay on in Cambridge to begin his PhD coursework the following year. But Howard University, a historically Black college long seen as the center of Black academic life in America, was seeking to establish a political science department and offered him a position as a professor straight away. Only twenty-five and barely out of college himself, he seized the opportunity and relocated to Washington, DC. Though he would return to Harvard repeatedly, Howard became Ralph Bunche's intellectual and professional home for the next decade.

HOWARD UNIVERSITY IN 1929 WAS THE premier Black university in the nation. A product of the post–Civil War effort to improve the lives and education of Black Americans after emancipation, Howard was created in 1867. Despite being an historically Black institution, in the late 1920s Howard still had a mostly white faculty. The university had also been run by white administrators until Mordecai Johnson was appointed president of the university in 1926. Johnson made it a point to actively recruit promising Black faculty to Howard.

At Howard, Ralph Bunche joined a burgeoning group of influential Black intellectuals, led by the famed Alain Locke, the "father of the Harlem Renaissance" and author of the influential *The New Negro*. Howard in the 1930s was a unique Black institution, a sort of "black Athens."[47] Washington, DC, was still heavily segregated in this era, and Howard served as an intellectual oasis for Bunche and his colleagues. Still, he did not always like the atmosphere there, and it is perhaps telling that he spent relatively little time there during the 1930s. He later expressed dissatisfaction with the university, in particular with Mordecai Johnson's leadership. Bunche was perhaps not really suited to the quiet academic life. "I guess I was always hardheaded and independent," he once said. "I always felt I wanted to do what I *wanted* to do. I liked adventure, and I was willing to gamble, to take chances."[48]

Howard was nonetheless a formative place for him, and it was there that he developed his full sense of the interplay of politics, race, and history. Alain Locke sometimes spoke of Bunche's "athleticism," a quality Bunche took to mean that "intellectually, I was aggressive and competitive and differed from the pure intellectual in that respect."[49] Bunche also loved teaching and taught a strikingly wide array of courses while on the Howard faculty: Constitutional Law; American Political Thought; Feudalism and the Feudal State; International Law; Colonial Policy; and Leading Decisions of International Tribunals were just a few. He was in addition the frequent host of an informal Saturday night salon at his house. There Howard faculty would gather to discuss and debate social change, the Black experience, and, especially after the great stock market crash of 1929, the future of capitalism. The social scientists at Howard tended to focus on Bunche "not only because he was an attractive (that's not really the word) personality but also because he was one of the few faculty members who lived on campus."[50] His early years at Howard also had great personal significance; he was there when his grandmother died, in November 1928. Bunche, who had lost both his parents, had now lost the most significant influence in his life. Her final letter to him contained a warning to dress warmly to avoid the flu and a burning question: "Will you finish at Harvard this year?"[51]

In his first semester at Howard, at a party, he met a young woman in the night program named Ruth Harris. The two quickly hit it off and soon enough were romantically involved. Ruth was still a student—in this era faculty–student relationships were not uncommon or especially frowned upon—and at one point she even enrolled in one of Ralph's courses. Unhappy with the B he gave her, she visited his office to challenge her grade. Ralph, a stickler, stood firm. Still, the relationship passed this particular test and the two continued to date. ("I admired her spirit" in fighting for the better grade, he later explained.)[52] Less than two years later they married.

From the beginning their relationship was marked by extensive absences. Ralph shuttled between Cambridge and Washington, still working to complete his PhD. Though he assured Ruth that his extensive absences would soon end, in fact they never did. Indeed, over the coming decades, and almost right up to his untimely death in 1971, Ralph would spend long

Photo 1.4 Ruth Bunche

stretches of time away from Ruth and their children, often in distant overseas locales such as Palestine, Cyprus, Gaza, Congo, and Kashmir, where
mail was slow and communication difficult.

Bunche was a popular professor at Howard, and he liked to be around
students. He even kept up some of his younger pursuits, such as playing basketball on the Howard Faculty Men's team.[53][**] Years after he left for the federal government and the UN he continued to visit Howard. Stopping by
the men's dormitory, known as Cook Hall, dressed in a jacket and tie with
cigarette in hand, he would sit with groups of students and discuss politics
and policy. The personable, down-to-earth nature that would endear him
to many of his negotiating partners in future years was evident to Howard
students. As one alumnus recalled, he was warm, open, and approachable: "I could say to him exactly what I was thinking." He was skilled at

[**] He also won the Howard University Faculty Men's Tennis Championship in 1931.

putting students at ease. Bunche was "not intimidating . . . I can assure you we would not have approached W. E. B. Du Bois the same way."[54] As part of his commitment to straightforward conversation unencumbered by formality, he would tell students "Don't call me Dr. Bunche."

Though a professor at Howard, at Harvard Bunche was still a graduate student. After completing the necessary coursework for his PhD, he had to choose a dissertation topic. Brazil, which had a legacy of African slavery and a domestic racial dynamic not unlike the American one, appears to have been an early idea he explored.[55] Another idea related to the League of Nations; in a letter to one of the deans at Howard in late 1930, he wrote that his intended dissertation topic was the League and its work on the suppression of slavery. Ultimately, he veered away from these ideas, though he kept the League of Nations connection. Encouraged by Alain Locke, he chose to write a dissertation about a different sort of racial dynamic, one that would come to serve as a throughline in his long and varied career.

The topic was the political structure of empire. Bunche became interested in how colonialism really worked on the ground, in particular in Africa. He proposed to his Harvard professors to analyze the administration of colonial Africa via a comparison of the governance of two quite similar—in fact, literally adjoining—territories that were nonetheless legally and politically distinct: the French colony of Dahomey (now Benin) and the French-administered "mandate" of Togoland (now divided between the states of Togo and Ghana). "Mandate" referred to a League process that assigned the empires of defeated states in the First World War to the supervision of the victors in that war.

His choice of PhD topic was an unusual one for the time, yet it was important. In the 1930s much of Asia and Africa was under European control, and imperialism was a central feature of prewar world politics. Understanding how empires operated and what systems of colonial governance worked best were his immediate goals. Bunche thought this issue was of potentially huge significance given the vast expanse of empire. And, like many at the time, he expected colonialism to persist for decades. For that reason studying colonial administration was important: Africa would likely remain colonial for quite some time.

He also felt that Americans, especially Black Americans, did not pay enough attention to Africa. It was, he wrote in his PhD proposal, "deplorable" that the "American Negro has seen fit to ignore" the question of colonial rule in Africa, and instead, "ostrich-like . . . bury his head entirely in the sands of relatively petty local problems."[56] His project would help rectify that, he thought, and begin to fill out the knowledge, in American universities at least, of how the governance of much of the globe operated. This, too, was encouraged by Locke. In Bunche, Locke saw "an earlier version of himself, a rebel against the notion that Negro intellectual thought should be confined to the small, the narrow, and the segregated American mindset."[57] Bunche and Locke did not always agree—for example, Bunche was strongly attracted to Marxist analyses in this era, and Locke was not—but Locke took Bunche under his wing and gave him substantial guidance in the new world of academia. That Locke, gay, also found the handsome Bunche very attractive has been offered as one reason for the deep interest Locke took in him.[58] But their scholarly interests also aligned. Locke had likewise studied the League's mandates system in the late 1920s and had even prepared a report on it for the New York–based Foreign Policy Association. But Locke had not really done much fieldwork—even Geneva proved too much for Locke to visit with any regularity—and Bunche's proposed project would go much deeper.

Bunche's PhD project also demonstrated an interest in a closely related question that would ultimately consume his professional life: how colonized societies best transitioned to independence. In this he was influenced by several people, but perhaps most by Raymond Buell, a former Harvard professor and research director of the Foreign Policy Association (the very same organization that had sponsored Locke's research on the mandates system). In Bunche's opinion, Buell, who had done fieldwork in Africa, was the author of the best work to date on the European colonies there, a book called *The Native Problem in Africa* and published in 1928. Like many at the time, Buell saw world politics in racial terms. As he wrote that same year in *Foreign Affairs*, for centuries "the world has been confronted with interracial problems." But, suggesting change was afoot, he noted that the ascendence of "primitive peoples" was creating a conflict, unique in history, between "the will of the European invaders and the needs of the native." Buell lent Bunche materials, assisted him in clarifying his research design, and—perhaps with Locke in mind—impressed upon him the importance of getting into the field, to Africa.[59]

By focusing on the French West African mandate of Togoland and comparing it to ordinary parts of the French Empire, Bunche would explore the details of colonial rule. And he would see firsthand the process, such as it was in the 1930s, for bringing formerly colonized states into self-governance that had recently been developed by the League. And that, in turn, would shape his thinking when, a decade later in the US State Department, he found himself drafting the provisions in the United Nations Charter that addressed decolonization and created the postwar concept of "trusteeships."

In short, the choice to study colonial governance in French West Africa was a fateful one. It would launch him on a path he could never have imagined, one that would ultimately put him at the center of the single most dramatic and momentous change in the governance of the lives of hundreds of millions of people in Asia and Africa, a change that would radically reshape world politics in ways that continue to reverberate today.

CHAPTER 2

MANDATES AND COLONIES

All the nations that have power that can be mobilized are going to be members of this League, including the United States. And what do they unite for? They enter into a solemn promise to one another that they will never use their power against one another for aggression; that they never will impair the territorial integrity of a neighbor; that they never will interfere with the political independence of a neighbor; that they will abide by the principle that great populations are entitled to determine their own destiny and that they will not interfere with that destiny...
— President Woodrow Wilson, speech at Pueblo, Colorado,
September 25, 1919

Created in 1919, the League of Nations was the precursor to the United Nations and the brainchild and passion of President Woodrow Wilson. Despite Wilson's exhortations, however, the United States never joined the League, due in large part to enduring American isolationism and to the fact that the First World War had been a much less intense and shocking experience for Americans than for Europeans. Wilson was so fixated on his project for a world organization that he spent an astonishing five months in Paris negotiating with the other great powers.[1] The U.S. Senate nonetheless refused to ratify the resulting Treaty of Versailles. Flawed yet groundbreaking, Wilson's vision for the League was never truly realized.

Now often denigrated as ineffective and a failure, the League of Nations had many revolutionary and influential features. Among them was its treatment of captured colonies. The French system of rule over the West African territory of Togoland that Ralph Bunche chose to study was the product of a set of provisions in the League Covenant that reflected concern with the perils of imperial competition, but it also embodied the great powers' nascent and unevenly held belief in the moral and political case for self-determination for all peoples. The new system, known as mandates, was based on a principle Bunche would later characterize as "no spoils of war." Those vanquished in the First World War (primarily Germany and the Ottoman Empire) were stripped of their colonies under the terms of the Treaty of Versailles. But rather than simply take these territories as prizes, as had often been done in the past, the victorious powers created an agreed set of rules about how they would be governed. "Mandatory powers" were assigned to rule these territories as temporary stewards and, in theory, to prepare them for eventual independence.[2] League mandates were typically granted to one of the two leading imperial nations of the day, Britain or France—though Wilson at one point contemplated an American mandate over Armenia, the Dardanelles and the Bosporus.[3] The choice to create the mandates was one of the Paris Conference's "most bitterly contested decisions."[4]

The mandates system reflected the fact that empires were a defining feature of the international order in the early 20th century. Europeans of the time widely believed that overseas empires sustained yet also reflected national power. The political and economic utility of empire was sometimes debated, but its ability to confer status was not. Many also believed that empires were just and natural: prevailing ideas of the survival of the fittest drew from Darwin's theory of evolution and applied the basic mechanism of natural selection to societies. Europeans were also enamored of a related legal concept based as much on prestige as on power: that there was a single "standard of civilization."[5] Many in the West thought it self-evident that some societies were civilized and others were not. They believed that not only were *they* civilized; they also had the authority to decide *who else* was civilized. White Christian nations were de facto civilized; others, such as Japan, could possibly be deemed civilized if they too met the legal standard.* The standard of civilization reflected the nakedly racial theories of the day, which posited that some races (e.g., the "Nordic") were on the top of a hierarchy of humankind, and others were arrayed below in a descending order—a view that would soon reach its zenith, or nadir, in the Nazi ideology of a white, Aryan master race.

These theories had profound impacts on the hierarchy of colonialism. Some early colonial thinkers even saw white society as the natural predator of Black society. "Is it any more unjust," Frenchman Jules Virey asked in 1841, "for the lion to devour the gazelle?"[6] In a somewhat less brutal view, non-European peoples were often analogized to children who needed supervision from the West. Self-styled liberals were not immune; indeed, the Anti-Slavery Society, an early human rights organization, literally used the phrase "child races of the world."[7] Ideas like these made colonialism seem almost altruistic, enabling the West to justify the conquest that its technological mastery made so easy.

Europe's domination of the globe was at a political and ideological highpoint in 1919 when the League of Nations was created. (Indeed, some in Europe, sensing a peak, had already begun to fear that the supposed vigor of Western civilization was fading; German historian Osvald Spengler published his highly influential *The Decline of the West* on the eve of the First World War.) Much of the world was under the yoke of a European power; just before the onset of the war, the British Empire alone comprised nearly a quarter of the world's population. Europe at large controlled about 85 percent of the world's territory. Rising pressures of nationalism and growing moral and political qualms about colonial rule, however, were slowly beginning to push in the opposite direction.†

---

* As a Japanese diplomat observed in 1905, after Japan had defeated Russia on the battlefield, "We show ourselves to be at least your equal in scientific butchery and we are at once admitted to your council tables as civilized men."

† Perhaps pushing things along from a different direction, Lenin's *Imperialism: The Highest Stage of Capitalism* was published in 1917, presaging an enduring, if often hypocritical, Soviet critique of European colonialism.

The League's mandate system that interested Ralph Bunche so much in the early 1930s embodied this tension. It was based in part on the idea that, eventually, all peoples ought to rule themselves. Yet the system also extended colonial rule and, arguably, legitimated it by giving the mandatory power the imprimatur of the international community. It formalized—even legalized—their dominance. For this reason, Bunche's future Howard University colleague, Alain Locke, memorably called the mandates "a new code of empire."[8] The League Covenant described its approach this way:

> To those colonies and territories . . . inhabited by peoples not yet able to stand by themselves under the strenuous conditions of the modern world, there should be applied the principle that the well-being and development of such peoples form a sacred trust of civilization. . . . The best method of giving practical effect to this principle is that the tutelage of such peoples should be entrusted to advanced nations.

A key point was that this "tutelage" was exercised on behalf of the League. Indeed, Woodrow Wilson referred to the League as the "residuary trustee" of the mandates.[9] Under the mandates system, imperialism was internationalized, not destroyed. Yet the language of trust and tutelage suggested a degree of benevolence and a trajectory toward self-determination—someday. One can readily see the connection between this system and the trusteeship system Ralph Bunche later developed, in 1945 in San Francisco, for the new United Nations Charter.

ARTHUR BALFOUR, WHO REPRESENTED BRITAIN AT the Paris Peace Conference in 1919, articulated the view of racial equality that many Europeans held at the time. Balfour commented that it was "true in a certain sense that all men of a particular nation were created equal; but not that a man in Central Africa was created equal to a European."[10] Reflecting this disturbing mindset, the League's mandates were divided into three categories: Classes A, B, and C. These categories were broadly based on perceived levels of political and social development, but they had a clear racial cast. The Class A mandates were former Ottoman territories of the Middle East such as Syria and Palestine. Togoland, like most African colonies, was classified as a Class B mandate; Class C mandates were in Southwest Africa (now Namibia) and in the Pacific islands such as New Guinea and Samoa.

The concept of mandates as a way for the powerful to rule the weak in trust for the international community was not an entirely new idea even in the 1920s. Europeans had long couched their conquest and rule of other peoples as a civilizing mission that flowed from their supposedly nat-ural dominance. Even the specific language of "trust" had precursors that dated to the 19th century.[‡] An influential 1898 book titled *The Control of the Tropics* argued that "the tropical region occupied must be held to be the fulfilment of a *trust* undertaken in the name of civilization."[11] Later, as the League process began in the 1920s, Lord Frederick Lugard, the former gov-ernor general of the British colony of Nigeria, wrote of "the immense re-sponsibility of governing the backward races which people the tropics." The so-called advanced nations, Lugard declared in *Foreign Affairs*, the house journal of the then brand-new Council on Foreign Relations, are "trustees for civilization" on behalf of peoples dependent on outside guidance.[12] This, in Rudyard Kipling's infamous phrase, was said to be the White Man's Burden.

These ideas of colonial trusteeship were perhaps a step up from naked plunder. They nonetheless permitted the West to exploit its colonies, at times ruthlessly. Lugard's ideas were influential (his 1922 book *The Dual Mandate in British Tropical Africa* was called the definitive defense of British colonial rule by its "most eminent practitioner") and the basic thrust of the mandates system followed them.[13] Trusteeship perhaps sounded benevo-lent, but as one writer later put it, it was perhaps better thought of as the "old liberal colonial project," now brought under the aegis of an international organization.[14] Indeed, even as early as 1921, some called the mandates system a farce in which the Allied powers used the League "simply as a Doctor Jekyll—a false front to shield their Mr. Hyde doings."[15]

[‡] This idea had been broached even in the 18th century. Edmund Burke, in response to British rule in India in the 1780s, used the language of trust to argue that "all political power which is set over men" ought to be exercised ultimately for their benefit.

Bunche began his colonial research in French West Africa against this backdrop of widespread and troubling ideas about race, power, and human destiny. His goal was to see whether, in fact, the League's philosophy and rules made a difference in how the local African populations were actually governed.

Bunche would ultimately adapt the League's approach for the United Nations. But in part because he had carefully studied how the mandates actually worked, his later goal was to ensure that these postwar trusteeships were supervised far more closely than the League mandates had, and that the peoples involved in fact moved to independence with some momentum. A pragmatist, he believed that whatever traditional forms of governance had existed previously in precolonial Africa, survival in the 20th century as truly independent nations would require a very different set of political structures. These structures happened to be largely alien to the political traditions of the continent, and therefore the shift would require substantial assistance. As the Kenyan legal scholar Makau Mutua, writing some six decades after Bunche began his research, has noted, "the concepts of sovereignty and statehood, as developed and used in traditional international law by a handful of European powers, were historically crafted without precolonial Africa in mind. Yet it is precisely these concepts which have been the basis for the creation of scores of modern states in Africa."[16]

The same was true for many other former colonies around the world. The European system of territorially defined sovereign states, stemming from ideas enshrined in the 17th-century Treaty of Westphalia, did not independently arise outside Europe. Rather, the process of developing and extending the sovereign state system globally was fundamentally—and forcibly—driven by the spread of European empire.[17]§ To be sure, not all states that accepted European ideas of sovereignty and statehood had been colonized. Still, the vast majority of the states that became independent during Ralph Bunche's lifetime were former colonies whose shape and size came not organically but imposed.

§ In a widely noted speech in the wake of Russia's invasion of Ukraine in early 2022, Kenya's ambassador to the UN declared, in defending the sanctity of borders, that "almost every African country was birthed by the ending of empire."

This process of embracing a foreign political system was, as he saw up close during his UN career, challenging and often violent. But African societies had no real choice. As Makau Mutua arrestingly put it, the "imposition of the nation-state through colonization balkanized Africa into ahistorical units and forcibly yanked it into the Age of Europe, permanently disfiguring it."[18] Bunche would not live to see all the myriad ills that resulted from this "disfiguring," but his career would, in large measure, be defined by efforts to address those ills. As the devastating effects of civil war and internal conflict that plagued so many postcolonial states in the postwar era consumed the attention of the new UN, Bunche found himself at the heart of these conflicts again and again.

THE EUROPEAN CONQUEST OF AFRICA HAD largely occurred in a burst that began in the wake of the Industrial Revolution. In 1870, only 10 percent of Africa was under European control. Some fifty years later nearly all of it was. Europeans, in what came to be known as the late 19th century "Scramble for Africa," believed the continent contained huge amounts of gold, diamonds, rubber, and other natural wealth, and they competed with one another to claim as much of it as possible for themselves. Famed Welsh explorer Henry Stanley, whose reports in some respects sparked the Scramble, remarked that the speed with which Europeans carved up Africa reminded him of how his porters "used to rush with gleaming knives for slaughtered game during our travels." The imagery of carving was evocative and common.

> In the rhetorical metaphor of imperial jingoism, [Africa] was a ripe melon awaiting carving in the late nineteenth century. Those who scrambled fastest won the largest slices and the right to consume at their leisure the sweet, succulent flesh. Stragglers snatched only small servings or tasteless portions; Italians, for example, found only deserts on their plates.[19]

Of the many societies in West Africa, the most easily accessible coast for European ships, the Kingdom of Dahomey attracted attention both for its warlike reputation and its unusual use of female soldiers. Yet in a series of attacks in the 1890s French forces conquered Dahomey, and in 1894 France declared it a colony. A decade later France incorporated it into French West Africa, a vast federation of colonial territories. Then in the wake of the First World War, Togoland, an adjoining German colony, was seized and divided into British and French mandates. The French portion was known as French Togoland.

For his doctoral research, Bunche chose a comparison of the governance of Dahomey and French Togoland, the former a colony and the latter a League mandate. The two territories shared a long border, a common history, and the same European ruler. In his dissertation proposal, Bunche argued that there "is scarcely a more vital problem in the entire study of government than that of colonial administration."[20] Noting that almost a billion people lived under foreign rule (at a time when the global population was roughly 2 billion), he argued that many of the world's most serious problems have "arisen out of the contact of the white with the dark races through the medium of this political relationship." Understanding this relationship—its politics, its history, its administration, and above all its future—seemed essential.

At this point, Bunche had not yet set foot in a colony. But, like many in the 1930s, he was skeptical of how ready most colonies in Asia and Africa were for independence. His dissertation, he proposed, would be governed by two assumptions: that "racial consciousness" will remain a powerful force in politics and, most crucially for his later experiences at the United Nations, that European withdrawal from Africa was "neither possible nor desirable within a long period of years to come; at present it could only result in hopeless chaos."[21]** He made another noteworthy statement in his proposal, one that had an interesting resonance for his future as a mediator in the Middle East. In emphasizing the importance for the Black diaspora of understanding colonial rule, he stated that "the Negro, like the Jew, is practically without a real national home."

In June 1932, Bunche headed to Europe and then onto West Africa itself. Just before leaving, he had what was perhaps his first serious exchange

---

** His dissertation was supervised by Arthur Holcombe, chair of the Government Department at Harvard.

with the US State Department, which would become his professional home during the Second World War. He met with Assistant Secretary of State James Rogers to discuss his planned overseas research. As he memorialized in a letter to Rogers after the meeting, he was seeking the imprimatur of the State Department so that he "might make all possible progress" in his meetings with French and other officials.[22] He may have been concerned about progress in part because his Howard colleague, Alain Locke, who had recently studied the mandates system, had run into some difficulty. Locke did not do any actual fieldwork in Africa, but he did visit the League headquarters in Geneva and prepared a report for the Foreign Policy Association, an organization founded in 1918 to catalyze American attention to foreign affairs. (The Association was unhappy with Locke's work and declined to publish it.)[23]

Bunche journeyed first to Paris and then to Geneva to interview French and League officials and to study records about governance, economics, and education in the two territories. In Paris he traveled with Locke and some others from the Howard faculty. Surviving photographs show the men in suits and ties relaxing in the sidewalk cafes of Paris, sometimes deep in reading and debate.[24] Locke, a bit infatuated with the younger Bunche, even considered joining him on the Geneva leg of the trip but in the end stayed back. Bunche was handsome and charming, and Locke's biographer has speculated that Locke may have hoped to have a more intimate relationship with him, though seemingly to no avail. Indeed, Bunche often attracted sexual attention. As a columnist for the *Pittsburgh Courier* wrote in 1952, at the height of his fame: "Take that Ralph Bunche, the number 1 man. When his cigarette dangles from his lips, when his eyes sparkle and he looks like he's going to wink but he doesn't, a gal reporter has a tough time concentrating on weighty United Nations problems."[25] (There is no evidence he was anything but a devoted husband in this regard.) Ralph and Ruth Bunche had married just two years before he headed to Paris with his Howard colleagues, and, shortly before leaving for his fieldwork on the thesis, their first daughter, Joan, was born. Soon after arriving in Europe Bunche begged Ruth and the six-month-old Joan to join him for this portion of the trip, which they did—an early indication that though he was a loving, if often stern, fixture in the family, work nearly always came first. In his diary he bemoaned that Ruth picked "the slowest boat" from New York but wrote, "Boy, I'll be happy to see them!"[26]

Bunche found the diverse mixture of prewar Paris fascinating. "Race inter-mingling everwhere—and what contrasts! Jet-black Senegalese boys and blonde French girls. Better keep Americans home—must be terribly shocking to see such crimes all around them. And yet they frequent the places and like it—in Paris!"[27] He discovered what he deemed the absence of the color line to be a huge breath of fresh air, and, like other Black Americans who had journeyed to the City of Light, he was surprised at how indifferently everyone in Paris treated him and his family. Being able to go to restaurants, theaters, and the like without much restraint was a relief. France may have been imperial, but it seemed tolerant and open.

One day he stumbled upon a communist rally protesting the Scottsboro Boys case.[28] The Alabama Supreme Court had just months before upheld the convictions, by an all-white jury, of a group of Black teenagers falsely accused of rape. A thoroughgoing miscarriage of justice, the case attracted substantial attention. The rally he witnessed in Paris featured the mother of two of the defendants, who, Bunche thought, gave a well-rehearsed version of the events. Perhaps the only other Black American there, he spoke with her about the case after her speech, but he came away concerned that her grief was being used for political ends: "I met her afterwards and found her to be exceedingly ignorant. She doesn't seem to know what it's all about."[29]

The Parisian Scottsboro rally was an example of how the fight for racial justice has long had global dimensions. Yet it was also an indication of how communism, anti-imperialism, and racial oppression intersected in the prewar era. Throughout the 1930s, Bunche would encounter many Black Americans (and Africans) who saw communism, then ascendant, as a helpful ideology and political movement for the liberation of Black people. In Paris that day, he was less than impressed with the communist effort, though he certainly saw the convictions as a farce and an example of the depths of racial oppression in the South. He would later describe the Scottsboro trials as a "puppet show" and castigate the all-white jury as "degenerated descendants of pure American stock . . . who live like peasants in the Balkans" with "white superiority" all they've ever had.[30] This more fiery Bunche would soon develop his own flirtation with the Marxist analysis of race and empire as well. Along the way, he would gain an "unrivaled understanding" of European colonialism.[31] The Marxism would eventually fall away; his colonial knowledge would remain. It was this expertise—once the Second World War began—that would launch him on a new and consequential path in the administration of President Franklin Delano Roosevelt.

———

CARRYING A BORROWED MOSQUITO NET, BOOTS, a "sun helmet," and a dinner jacket with cummerbund, Ralph Bunche traveled alone by ship, on board the *Foucald*, to begin his fieldwork in French West Africa.[32] Ruth and Joan had just returned to New York. Upon arrival in Africa, he spent his days touring colonial offices, interviewing locals, and exploring the villages and countryside. In doing so he was almost unique; only one other political scientist in America had ever studied colonial governance on the ground in Africa.[33] Most of what was known, or thought to be known, about how colonialism really worked came from men like Lord Frederick Lugard, the British author of *The Dual Mandate in British Tropical Africa*, who had a vested interest in perpetuating and valorizing the system and Britain's role in it.

The light-skinned Bunche was surprised to discover he was sometimes treated as a European in French West Africa. This afforded him some small luxuries, such as seats up front in vans; it was an experience that foreshadowed his treatment in Congo decades later, where, as he wrote to his son Ralph Jr during the chaotic violence in the summer of 1960, "wouldn't it be ironic though if I should now get knocked around here in the very heart of Africa because of anti-white feeling."[34] He found Africa alien yet fascinating. Having grown up largely in 1920s Los Angeles, and then having lived in Cambridge, Massachusetts, and Washington, DC, he had spent most of his life in cities surrounded by white people. The experience of being in a Black-dominant population in a largely rural setting was new.

Bunche enjoyed his time in Togoland and Dahomey. He was genuinely impressed by the "lack of open racial prejudice and easy social mixing" he found in the French colonies.[35] And, most important for his scholarly agenda, he discovered that the legal distinction between mandate and colony—though perhaps important in Geneva—made little practical difference on the ground. France seemed to govern both territories much the same way; there was no real evidence that the mandate fared better than the colony. Before the officials and members of the League of Nations, France portrayed its role as mandatory power for Togoland in a positive light. But Bunche did not believe the official reports were accurate. "To the Togolese, the French in Togo are merely some more colonial administrators with a new and strange language and a knack for collecting taxes," he wrote in this thesis. "In truth, this new status means little to them now and will continue so for many years."[36]

By nature an optimist, he believed African societies would eventually rise above their current plight. Yet he was troubled by the grave poverty and political inequities he observed in both Togo and Dahomey. He did not see a bright future for the region looming on the horizon, and, as he wrote in his dissertation, he believed that independent statehood was "many generations removed from the present day."[37] Still, he found Togo and Dahomey intriguing and even charming:

> Sitting out here on the veranda of the Hotel de France under a brilliant tropical sky and with the lazy rumble of the tropical Atlantic in my ear. . . . This is a marvelous country and after seeing a bit of it and its people, one is apt to become more puzzled than ever as to what is to become of it, or even what *should* become of it.[38]

Bunche was captivated by the diversity of French West Africa, which was partly the result of encroaching Western norms and practices. He was particularly struck by the Africans who had begun to adopt European ways. In the coastal towns, he later wrote, are "thousands of natives who have become detribalized, who have picked up many European customs and forgotten many of their own." They wore Western clothes, spoke French or English, and some even sent their children to school in Europe. Yet, he wrote, "they may worship fetishes, marry several wives, eat without cutlery and sleep on the floor."[39] He found these "transitional," and clearly upper class, West Africans paradoxical, but also a sign, he believed, of the direction the entire society was taking. French colonies in particular seemed to encourage a sort of liminal status for some locals; Bunche noted that while France had many Africans or individuals of African descent, perhaps from Martinique or elsewhere, in the Colonial Service, the British did not.[40] Alain Locke had similarly been surprised that French troops in Europe in the '20s were often integrated. Black officers even could be found commanding white troops—"something unheard of in American or British armies."[41]

Seeing colonial rule in Africa up close in this way was profoundly impactful. It set Bunche on an intellectual and professional trajectory that would guide the rest of his career.[††] In his thesis he made a key argument that would resonate in his later work at the United Nations. It was the importance of keeping local people and their preferences central in governance decisions. "Too often," he wrote, "in the earnest consideration of Africa and her myriad problems, sight is lost of the African. . . . The solution of the problem of the future of Africa is to be found in the determination of the eventual relationships that will prevail between the Africans and other peoples."[42] This sentiment seems obvious today, but it was uncommon in the 1930s.

Later, as the pace of African decolonization sped forward in the 1950s and 1960s and Bunche had risen to be a key figure in the process, some argued that he was insufficiently interested in the desires of "the African" and too measured in his pace. For some he was even characterized as "an enemy, rather than an ally, of worldwide black liberation."[43] But later still, as the problems of postcolonial states deepened, his careful and cautious approach elicited more praise. As a Ghanian interlocutor put it some three decades after Bunche's death,

> Even though I disagreed with him at the time, even though a lot of Africans were impatient about his strategy, in retrospect Bunche may have been right that the politics of the situation demanded that we adopt a more, how should I put it, a slower pace and maybe a more deliberate pace in the whole decolonization process.[44]

[††] For this project Bunche won the Robert Toppan Prize for the best dissertation at Harvard in political science.

Back in the early 1930s, however, Bunche was on the forefront of those pushing for a faster process and one that respected African views and needs as much—or more—than European ones. Yet in part because he was so busy doing so many different things, he never published his doctoral dissertation as a book. As he was writing it, however, he did author an article in the *Journal of Negro Education* in 1934 drawn from his research. Titled "French Educational Policy in Togoland and Dahomey," the article highlighted both the failings of colonial rule and the promise he believed Africa represented.

In this essay Bunche made another key argument about colonialism, one that, like his focus on the perspective of Africans, would guide his later work as a diplomat and policymaker. Africa, he argued, was "one place in this troubled world where mistakes previously committed may be corrected; where, indeed, a new and better civilization may be cultivated." This view— that Africa was in some sense a political blank slate that ought to be cultivated by the international community—would prove even more significant and would animate his later efforts at the UN to welcome and guide newly liberated states into sovereignty. As his 1934 essay on education shows, however, it had deep roots.

To Bunche, Africa in the colonial era was a place where two ways of life crashed into one other, with somewhat unpredictable results. Whether or not there was a formal education process in African colonies (and by this point there generally was), the key fact, he believed, was the intensity of the colonial encounter. The technological divide between Europe and most of Africa in the early 20th century was overwhelming. The complex paraphernalia of modern industrial life, he wrote, have been "paraded before the startled eyes of the African" with "kaleidoscopic rapidity." It was "astonishing" that the African has not been "completely dazed by it all."[45]

This created a challenging climate for education. Still, he was critical of what colonial education looked like, noting that the primary result was solely "practical utility, for the French first and for the native second."[46] He agreed that education in a Western manner was essential for progress. At the same time, he critiqued the French practice of teaching entirely in French, reflecting its failure to meet the local residents on their own terms. He again returned to the importance of local conditions. Done right, education would provide the path to liberation; done wrong, it would cement inequality:

If education in Togo and Dahomey is to make anything of the native other than a robot and rubber-stamp, it must be adapted not only to the local conditions of native life but must afford an opportunity for transcending those conditions as well . . . only in this way can the African be expected to cultivate that spirit and articulateness necessary to the development of a national and racial soul, which alone will justify his ultimate right of self-control in his own country.[47]

Bunche's work on education and governance in this period was smart, straightforward, and not especially ideological. But his interest in Marxist analyses of world politics and of imperialism continued to grow. This was not unusual for the time, as the Scottsboro Boys rally he stumbled upon in Paris illustrated. For example, soon after returning from French West Africa, he presented a paper at a Howard University conference on the broader trajectory of imperial rule. In it, he traced, if at times implicitly, the links between capitalism and imperialism that Vladimir Lenin had famously drawn out decades before in his influential *Imperialism: The Highest Form of Capitalism*. Bunche argued that only if capitalist society was transformed could there be any possibility of developing a new international order, one that could "promise the subject peoples of the world genuine surcease from the burdens of imperialistic domination."[48]

Ralph Bunche's belief in the relevance of Marxist theory to the future of the colonial world peaked in this period, however. It would soon be eclipsed by what he came to see as a much more threatening set of ideologies: fascism and Nazism.

BUNCHE RETURNED FROM HIS FIELDWORK IN Togo and Dahomey to Howard and life with his growing family (Ralph and Ruth soon had a second daughter, Jane). He spent significant time writing up his thesis research, ultimately submitting it to Harvard in 1936. The year before he had published an article in the UCLA alumni magazine.[‡‡] The *Southern Alumnus*

[‡‡] The "magazine" was a simple mimeographed collection called "the Southern Alumnus," stuffed into the main alumni magazine of UCLA's sister and soon to be rival campus to the north, Berkeley. UCLA was at first simply the "Southern Branch" of the University of California.

magazine identified him as "the most distinguished Negro graduate of the University and one of the finest scholars among the entire alumni body." Entitled "Light on the Dark Continent," Bunche's essay sought to describe to the overwhelmingly white alumni of UCLA what was happening in Africa. The dominant force in modern Africa was change, he announced at the outset of his essay. Africa, he wrote, has been "subdued" by Europeans, but the contact with the West also created a powerful new set of desires and even politics. "Native society is disintegrating" under a "steady onslaught of impatient Western forces." He repeated his blank slate argument about Africa. The continent's greatest significance, he claimed, centered on its possibilities "as a fine proving ground in human relationships." Africa was a place where "mistakes previously committed may be corrected; where, indeed, a new and better civilization may be cultivated, through deliberate application of human intelligence and understanding."[49] Africa, in a sense, offered a new beginning, much like Europeans had seen in the New World centuries earlier.

Bunche's language in "Light on the Dark Continent" certainly reflected the times, or perhaps his intended readership: he referred to the people of Africa as "natives" and "black primitives." But his arguments were also ahead of the times. He stressed that Europeans made little effort to understand African life; if they did, they would understand the sophistication and depth of African society. He also laid down a forthright conclusion: this "great continent and its sweltering population," he wrote, "are mere sacrificial offerings on the altar of world imperialism."

Bunche's interests in this period were not solely international: he also debated Black politics with his rich array of Howard colleagues. Unhappy with the NAACP and other mainstream Black organizations, which tended to focus more on civil rights and legal strategies than on economic improvement, he helped launch a new body, the National Negro Congress (NNC). At first Bunche was very excited about the project, declaring that the NNC's equal "has never been seen in the history of the American Negro."[50] Within a few years, however, the NNC would become more radical and more influenced by communist doctrine, reducing it, in Bunche's view, essentially to a communist front. Over time he increasingly distanced himself from the organization, though his association with it would later come back to haunt him. By 1941, he would write that "the Negro had been misled and duped by many groups, the Communist especially."[51]

Meanwhile, his interest in European colonial rule continued. In 1936, for example, he organized a major conference on "The Crisis of Modern Imperialism in Africa and the Far East." To truly understand the colonial relationship and political future, however, Bunche felt he needed a better understanding of the intricacies of African societies. His training in political science was excellent for its day, but it had not emphasized social or cultural practices. Sensing the limits of what the discipline of political science could offer, and encouraged by others such as Carter Woodson, editor of the *Journal of Negro History*, Bunche considered further study in adjacent fields. (Woodson had suggested that Bunche find some "educated natives" to inform him of the "anthropological and ethnological phases of life in their tribes.")[52] Bunche reached out to a prominent anthropologist, the Polish-born Bronislaw Malinowski, asking for help. "I feel the need of additional preparation in the field of anthropology," he wrote in a letter to the London-based professor.[53] Malinowski agreed to the idea of the promising young scholar studying with him at the London School of Economics.

To pursue this plan, Bunche received funding from the Social Science Research Council for a two-year project that would combine further fieldwork in colonial Africa with academic training in anthropology. Some of this training occurred at Northwestern and the University of Chicago. But much of it would take place abroad, with Malinowski in London, and when it was finished he would return to Africa for some time. Ruth Bunche, who had continued to hope that Ralph's frequent absences from home were coming to an end, reacted with trepidation and even dread to this new idea. "The next two years seem like a nightmare to me," she told him. "I hate to think of it."[54]

CHAPTER 3

A WORLD VIEW OF RACE

Africa is imperialism's greatest and most characteristic expression.
—Ralph Bunche, *A World View of Race* (1936)[1]

In February 1937, the Bunche family boarded a ship named the *Berengaria* in New York harbor and headed across the frigid Atlantic to London. The ship had been seized from the Germans during the First World War and was now part of the Cunard Line. It had originally been named the *Imperator*— a Roman word that served as the source of the word "emperor." London, the Bunches' destination, was the heart of what was still the world's largest empire and a buzzing, cosmopolitan city in the 1930s—the most populous in the world after New York City. Ralph Bunche found London immensely stimulating but also shabbier and gloomier than he had imagined. (Despite a life of significant travel in Europe, he was often unhappy there.) The Bunches took in the London sights and scenery and even attended the coronation of George VI in May of 1937. But most of Ralph's attention was focused firmly on the London School of Economics and Professor Bronislaw Malinowski and his circle of students.

Malinowski, an intense-looking, bespectacled figure, had published leading works of anthropology such as *Crime and Custom in Savage Society*, which explored the legal system of the Trobriand Islanders of New Guinea. Taking a seminar with the renowned scholar, whom he had first met in 1933, Bunche came to know many prominent young African intellectuals who had gravitated to the center of the British Empire for their education. Among them was Jomo Kenyatta, who would ultimately become independent Kenya's prime minister and president.* In his red fez, Kenyatta stood out at the school; later he would provocatively pose wearing animal skins and caressing the tip of a spear for his book, *Facing Mount Kenya*.[2]

While Malinowski's focus was Melanasia, he had studied South Africa as well, where Bunche would soon visit; he saw the origins of this "deeply divided society" in the process of "world expansion of imperialism and colonialism."[3] Malinowski was sympathetic to African societies but thought they were "too fragile, too fragmented," to accept rapid or dramatic change. He believed the role of the anthropologist was to instruct governments on "how to make the best of these delicate social worlds and to coax them into the European-dominated future, without destroying them in the process."[4] Bunche generally agreed, though he was at times critical of Malinowski, who had something of a Rasputin-like effect on his students. "There's never been a primitive religion so demanding as 'Malinowski' is here. But I ain't converted," he breezily wrote in his diary.[5] Malinowski was vain and dogmatic, he thought, but he also appreciated the anthropologist's sharp and able mind.[6]

Bunche's London experience was eye-opening. And it put him on a first-name basis with many who would become key figures in postcolonial Africa. In London he observed at close range the developing group of liberation-minded Africans who would assist and, as in the case of Kenyatta, even lead their nations to independence in later years. Many were interested in the burgeoning ideas of Pan-Africanism, a position Bunche rejected then and would continue to do so when in position of power and influence. Also in London during this period was a famous Black American whom Bunche

---

* Kenyatta also became Bunche's Swahili instructor.

got to know well, Paul Robeson. Robeson was a phenomenal prewar polymath: a former football star turned lawyer turned singer and actor and, eventually, political activist. At the time Bunche met him, Robeson was successful in London theater and film, yet despite his very busy life somehow found the time to enroll in classes in Swahili at London's School of Oriental and African Studies.

The Bunches and the Robesons hit it off immediately. Robeson was "anti-white and all out for the USSR," Bunche wrote in his diary, yet a fascinating figure and someone who lived a life of celebrity, style, and luxury.[7]* At one point Bunche and Essie Robeson, along with a young former missionary named Max Yergan, who would later become head of the National Negro Congress, jumped in the big Robeson family Daimler to see Paul on the set of his latest film, a First World War drama named *Jericho*. During the ride, Yergan, whom Bunche would tangle with in the coming decades, impressed upon Bunche his fervor for communism; Bunche was less enthusiastic. Eventually, the conversation turned to more prosaic matters: prize fights and who should win them.[8] Bunche was dazzled by Robeson's sophisticated English life and was soon drawn into his circle. The London sojourn, however, was merely a prelude to his next journey, one on which Ruth and the girls would not join him: a return to Africa, and this time, a trip to South Africa and East Africa, followed by an around-the-world journey by ship through Asia to California.

MUCH AS BUNCHE ENJOYED LONDON AND having his family with him, he was eager to return to fieldwork, especially now that he was armed with new theories and tools drawn from the burgeoning field of anthropology. His first planned stop was South Africa, which had recently been granted independence from Britain as one of the (typically white-ruled) British "dominions."

---

* Robeson would later be branded "the Kremlin's voice in America" during the House Un-American Activities Committee hearings of the 1950s and have his passport revoked. Under pressure, Jackie Robinson and even the NAACP denounced the political views of Robeson, who some were then calling the "Black Stalin."

Photo 3.1 Ralph Bunche and daughters

While the formal policy of apartheid would not be instituted until after the Second World War, South Africa in the 1930s was nonetheless highly segregated. Bunche was understandably concerned about how he would be treated there. His London circle contained some prominent African activists who were known to the British government and likely to be deprecated by the South African leadership. Ideologically adjacent to his immediate circle at the London School of Economics were communist sympathizers such as Robeson and Yergan. Association with communism and Marxist thinking generally did not carry the same valence in the 1930s that it would in the 1950s, when Bunche would defend himself before an American government "loyalty board" and find his political views attacked by prominent right-wing columnists such as Walter Winchell. (By 1949 Bunche would say of Robeson, who argued that Black Americans would never fight the Soviet Union, "Paul should stick to singing . . . I think he's radically wrong.")[9] Yet even as Bunche continued to embrace variants of Marxism in his scholarship in the 1930s, he was already sensing that too close an association with the actual application of communist and other radical ideas could be troublesome.

Bunche's instincts on this point proved correct. A few months after he arrived in London, a British official wrote to a South African colleague. While in England, the official wrote, Bunche "has apparently been pushed into touch with some of our black undesirables." We do not know the full extent of his sympathies, the letter continued. "It is quite on the cards that he has simply been led astray by names . . . but I pass this on to you."[10] Despite this warning Bunche succeeded in receiving the necessary clearance to continue on to South Africa. But he resisted South Africa's racial separation. When filling out the immigration form, he ignored the categories offered— European, Hebraic, Oriental, African—and wrote in "American" by hand.[11]

The Bunche family left for the Netherlands together in late July, with Jomo Kenyatta seeing them off at the train station. After a few weeks holiday in prewar Paris and Brussels, Ruth and the girls headed back to New York, and Ralph, standing on the dock, waved as they headed home across the Atlantic. Setting sail for Cape Town in late September, Ralph played ping-pong on deck during the long voyage and read extensively. He was impressed to see Black travelers in first class and at the Captain's table, and a Black priest presiding over mass on the ship. The trip, involving many days at sea, was at times dreary. "Last day on board ship—thank the Lord!" he penned in his diary as they finally approached port.[12]

Bunche found South Africa both fascinating and infuriating. The state of race relations and the fine parsing of racial differences were disturbing, even as he himself, who locals struggled to fit neatly into the available categories, was often treated well as an American of some prestige. While French racial practices in colonial Africa were strikingly similar to what he saw in Paris, the British colonies such as South Africa were different. The British had much the same attitude as the Americans on race, he thought— though they were "more genteel about it perhaps."[13] South Africans were different: Bunche would later write that the white population appeared to suffer from a "group 'fear psychosis' almost approaching hysteria."[14]

Friends and acquaintances in London had offered him advice on navigating the tricky racial waters. A South African historian had even suggested he "'pass' for white wherever he could."[15] Bunche's race was in fact a matter of frequent confusion in South Africa. Buying a railway ticket to Durban, a clerk mistook him for Filipino. In Johannesburg, he was mistaken for Portuguese. Later, on a train, the conductors huddled to figure out where to place Bunche, eventually choosing the white coach. "They first started to put me in a double compartment with a white man. I still don't know whether I'm 'passing' or not on this train," he wrote in his diary.[16]

The anthropological training he received in London took root, and he spent substantial time meeting with South Africans of all stripes and observing social and political gatherings. The mix of people intrigued him. "More swarthy, frizzy-haired, 'suspicious-looking' 'white' people here than any place I've ever seen," he wrote at one point; at another he simply jotted down, "Negroes so mixed up here the place looks like Harlem."[17] Bunche later said that in South Africa he found "so many problems that struck me, as an American Negro, as interesting and familiar."[18]

He spent many weeks in the former British colony. With his journey drawing to a close on New Year's Eve, he departed for Kenya and Tanzania. Boarding the SS *Tasman* to head north up the eastern shore of Africa, Bunche woke up with a slight hangover from what he described as (one can only assume with some exaggeration) "last night's 'orgy.'"[19] With a three-berth stateroom to himself, the voyage on the *Tasman* to Mombasa, on the warm Indian Ocean coast, was peaceful and restful.

In Kenya, he was welcomed with honors thanks to Jomo Kenyatta and his other powerful friends from London. His connections permitted him to witness a number of striking events, one of which, a traditional genital cutting ceremony, allowed him to fully immerse himself in his newfound ethnographic methods. Bunche even filmed the ceremony, which involved both boys and girls, later publishing an academic article on it.[20] Presaging future debates over female genital mutilation/cutting and human rights, he argued that the social importance of the ceremony had risen as European encroachment into Kenya had destroyed many aspects of traditional life, such as long-standing systems of land tenure. As Western missionaries and colonists tried to stamp out such ceremonies, their seeming importance only grew. The rite itself had become the central symbol of "tribal chauvinism" and the "rallying cry of their cultural loyalty," he wrote; an "emblem of their national self-assertion and a recompense for lost power."[21] In this analysis, which would become more common in the postwar era, Bunche was again ahead of his time.

Leaving Kenya by ship, he headed to Singapore, then a British colony, and the Dutch East Indies, now Indonesia. He found the Dutch colony, a vast archipelago of distinct island societies, refreshingly liberal racially compared to what he had seen in Kenya and South Africa. His voyage next took him to the Philippines (then still an American colony) and Hong Kong (another British colony). He even saw Japanese soldiers outside of Shanghai. Asia provided a fascinating contrast to Africa, though it, too, reflected a shared experience in colonial rule and exploitation. Arriving back in the US, he landed in San Francisco and then headed home, to Los Angeles. He very much missed his family, but otherwise was ambivalent about returning to the US. "First thing I saw on the front page of the S.F. Chronicle was a report of a lynching of a Negro in Mississippi," he wrote in diary.[22] But in Los Angeles Ruth and the girls were there to meet him, and they visited with cousins and aunts he had not seen in some time. He was home.

By the time he returned to California, Bunche was one of the most preeminent Africanists and colonial experts in the nation. His journey through the prewar colonial world seemed to cement a view he already held, that race relations in America were not unique but rather a species of a larger genus. "We tend to regard our problems as peculiar to our own country," he wrote to a Howard colleague in 1938. "My view is that, our problems are merely a part of a universal pattern which applies to minority groups and to non-European peoples throughout the entire world. My plea is, of course, for an international approach to the problems of the American Negro."[23]

As Charles P. Henry has written, Bunche's thinking underwent subtle shifts during this era, as reflected in three basic orientations: "(1) a belief in the feasibility of the modernization of 'backward' societies; (2) a normative commitment to egalitarianism; and (3) an affective commitment to African peoples."[24] Later, at the UN, Bunche would largely follow these principles in his quest to facilitate the unwinding of European empire. He remained focused on the decolonization of Africa throughout his life. Yet he also saw weaknesses in African political structures. In later years, he did not hesitate to assume, or argue, that newly independent African states were not always able to rule effectively on their own. That did not mean they needed further colonial rule, however. The process of self-determination was complicated but urgent, and these societies would simply need extensive assistance, he believed, from the international community.

BUNCHE'S INTERESTS IN THIS PERIOD REMAINED fixed largely on empires and their administration. Yet at times his research drifted closer to home. He faced some pressure at Howard to do so; early on, Howard President Mordecai Johnson had complained to the Howard faculty that "Bunche is going all the way to Africa to find a problem."[25] Bunche was irritated by this jibe; he was well aware of the many problems at home, but he was consistently drawn to what he saw as the most interesting and important problem: that of empire.

Bunche's most significant domestic work during this period was his participation in a major, multiyear project funded by the Carnegie Corporation. He worked closely with Swedish economist Gunnar Myrdal on the project, the aim of which was to better understand domestic race relations in the US. The Myrdal study, which involved extensive fieldwork in the South, was ultimately published in 1944 as *An American Dilemma: The Negro Problem and Modern Democracy*. Later called a "monumental achievement in the annals of social scientific reporting on race relations," *An American Dilemma* was influential in its treatment of racial injustice in national life.[26] Often credited with advancing the civil rights movement in the ensuing decades, the book spurred President Harry Truman to set up the first-ever presidential commission on race relations and to desegregate the armed services in 1948. Perhaps most famously, it would help shape the Supreme Court's landmark 1954 school integration decision in *Brown v. Board of Education*.

Myrdal, a prominent Swedish academic, was an odd choice for this endeavor. Selected mostly for his distance from American politics and society, he knew little about American society or its racial dynamics. As a result, the

Carnegie project deployed an extensive research staff with greater local expertise. A rising star in Black academic circles, Bunche was invited to be one of these project members.

Bunche accompanied Myrdal in his travels around the Jim Crow South in the late 1930s. Myrdal found him "extraordinarily intelligent, open-minded, and cooperative."[27] Together they conducted interviews with Black and white residents and compiled social, economic, and political evidence about race relations. For Bunche, having been raised mainly in California, this was a disturbing experience. The entire process was an object lesson in the pervasive and crushing oppression of Jim Crow. The trip through the South also made clear to him that while they were both successful social scientists, he and Myrdal would never be treated as equals. The indignities were constant. Each evening, after dropping Myrdal off at the leading local hotel, he would seek accommodations for himself, "usually at the home of the local black clergyman or some other black professional." Finding such accommodations was not always easy in the rural South. On one occasion, after substantial searching, Bunche finally found a place to sleep: "on a slab in a black mortuary, separated from a cadaver by a screen."[28]

Throughout the process he worked at a feverish pace. His many memos for the project totaled an astonishing 3000 pages. Bunche also acted as a sort of protector and guide for Myrdal, who did not always appreciate the vehemence of Southern racism or its specific hazards. At one point in their travels, a warrant was even issued for Myrdal's arrest. Interviewing a prominent white woman in Atlanta who expressed concern about the alleged sexual appetites of Black people, Myrdal "intervened to ask whether she had a subconscious desire" for interracial sex. He then mused whether she herself perhaps had mixed blood. Myrdal and Bunche made a quick exit after this exchange. With the Atlanta police in pursuit, the two fled across state lines to Tuskegee, Alabama.[29]

An American Dilemma provided Bunche with the opportunity for academic immersion into domestic race relations. Yet much like his dissertation, his huge memos for the project were never published. Some included ideas he may have not have intended to be published; for example, he strongly criticized the NAACP in one memo for its lack of an economic program and its upper-class tendencies and approach. NAACP leader Walter White offered Myrdal a lengthy rebuttal to Bunche's attack, arguing that if Bunche could only "forget that he is a college professor" and better identify with the people, he would be less "naive."[30] (Despite these fairly sharp differences, Bunche and White would work together in the future in a friendlier way, and both, eventually, would find a common antagonist in W. E. B. Du Bois.)

Bunche did later distill some of the Myrdal work for a broader audience, however. In a 1941 article in the *Journal of Negro Education* titled "The Negro in the Political Life of the US," he explored some of the themes that grew out of his unusual fieldwork. As he would throughout his life, he strongly defended American democracy. But he also argued that the "political status of the Negro in America is itself a record of glaring imperfections in American democracy."[31] In this regard, he focused especially on the South. As he wrote the article, the US had not yet entered the Second World War. But the likelihood that it would do so was looming. "There is something ironical," he argued, "in the fact that this South which thus grossly denies an elemental right to a vast population within its midst is more enthusiastic than any other section of the country over the fight to defeat Hitler and pre- serve democracy in the world."[32]

In making this statement, Bunche foresaw a challenge that the US foreign policy establishment would recognize and fixate on during the Cold War:

> [T]the ability of this nation to protect its interests is now seriously affected by the traditional imperfections in the democratic process. In an hour of great need the nation reaps the harvest of racial disunity it has sown and cultivated. . . . There can be no maximum unity in a military establishment that fosters a white army and a black army; in an economy that recognizes employment and wage differentials be- tween white and black workers; in a political system that extends political privilege to some and withholds it from others.[33]

The view that racial oppression at home could have deleterious effects on American national security was not widely held in 1941. His argument was again far-sighted. And after the Second World War was won and the Cold

War took root, the problem of home-grown American racism took on another insidious dimension for national security. The Soviet Union repeatedly pointed to the overwhelming oppression of Black Americans as a way to divide the newly independent states of Asia and Africa from the US and nudge them toward the Eastern bloc. Lynchings, Jim Crow, and the entire panoply of white supremacy in the US provided ample fodder for Soviet efforts.[†] As the Soviets tarred the US in the global sphere in the late 1940s and 1950s, American leaders from the secretary of state on down began to push for greater integration at home. That push, of course, was many years away when Bunche published his essay. But he perceptively foreshadowed not only the connection between racial equality and national security, but the fact that connecting the two would, as a political matter, ultimately bolster both.

Bunche would return to this linkage many times in the future. But for the most part he would leave domestic issues behind. And just as his account was being published in the *Journal of Negro Education*, he would enter government service, a transition that would eventually lead him away from scholarship and academia and into diplomacy and politics.

────────────

DURING THIS SAME PERIOD WHEN BUNCHE worked on *An American Dilemma*, he published a book of his own entitled *A World View of Race*. The slim volume, which came out in 1936, honed his developing theories of the intersection between geopolitics and race, as encapsulated in the pervasive phenomenon of empire. The book was part of a series, known as the *Bronze Booklets*, edited by his Howard colleague, Alain Locke.

Locke, a generation older than Bunche, also saw empire as a central feature of prewar world politics. Writing in 1927, Locke had declared that the basic causes of the First World War were "extra-European."[34] Rivalries of economic imperialism "molded the alignments and oppositions of the Great Powers and along with these the underlying issues of the conflict."

[†] The highlighting of American racism by foreign adversaries continues today. China's Foreign Ministry, after the State Department's criticism of its treatment of Hong Kong in 2020, tweeted back, invoking a notorious instance of American police brutality, "I can't breathe."

This viewpoint, that imperialism was *the* central feature of international relations in the interwar period, was common in the 1920s and 1930s. The "vital crux of world politics" today, Locke continued, and most of the latent threats to world peace, point in the same direction, and "the extra-European rivalries of the imperialistic world powers, America included, still dominate international relations."[35] Locke was right to emphasize the role of imperialism in great power conflict: one later view of the Second World War was that what united the Axis powers was that they all had failed to amass or maintain large overseas empires. Indeed, empire was arguably a central cause of the war. By the 1930s, the Allies held 1500 percent more colonial territory than did the Axis powers. The war, as one historian has described it, was largely "a conflict between incumbent and insurgent imperialists."[36]

Bunche picked up on these themes in his book for Locke's series. At this point, there is no indication that he envisioned any sort of life of public service; academia was his home, and, it appeared, was destined to be his life's work. Yet he already was thinking about issues that would connect deeply to his later career in diplomacy. *A World View of Race* began by noting the hypocrisy of Western powers, who professed belief in equality and yet ruled over others they deemed inferior. The ruling classes of the West found it expedient, Bunche argued, "to hark back beyond Locke, Rousseau and Jefferson to the more limited and comforting philosophy of 'equality' advanced by the Greek philosopher Aristotle—'some men are born to serve and some to rule.'"[37] This point had obvious resonance for a Black man living in the 1930s. But Bunche went further: racial discrimination was a geopolitical issue as well as a civil rights issue. It was impossible, he claimed, to understand world politics interpreted merely in "simple terms of nations." He argued that European imperialism reflected a distinctive politics grounded in race. Racial distinctions were a convenient device for imperialism:

> Imperialist propaganda has taught the world to regard certain peoples as helplessly backward . . . [and] this classification is not a mere theoretical one. It is used as the basis for justifying conquest and exploitation and for dividing the world into

dominant and subordinate peoples. . . . Powerful industrial nations have raped Africa under the false pretense of shouldering "the white man's burden."[38]

A World View of Race had a strongly Marxist thrust. Reflecting the thinking widely associated with Lenin's famous analysis of imperialism as the highest stage of capitalism, Bunche saw empire as a largely economic enterprise that was, at bottom, motivated by greed. The poorer, weaker parts of the world were simply a source of wealth to be taken by the more powerful. Imperialism is an "international expression of capitalism," he wrote.[39] Racial distinction provided a justification for dominance that was skillfully deployed by Europeans to divide, conquer, and make oppressive rule easier to maintain.

Bunche's draft of A World View of Race caused some consternation. Its "decidedly Leninist bias . . . greatly distressed" Alain Locke.[40] Locke gave Bunche extensive notes in an effort to tone down what one early reader called its "doctrinaire tone."[41] Bunche may well have gone overboard in his enthusiasm for Marxist thinking; while class was seen as the key cleavage in the 1930s, it was not self-evident (and history would suggest otherwise) that race was secondary and would fade away as a category in a classless society. His views on the centrality of economics to empire, however, and on the way racial divisions primarily served economic interests, would be echoed as well as challenged by others in the era. Writing in 1945, for example, Hannah Arendt argued that Lenin had "[laid] bare the purely economic motives" of imperialism but failed to reveal its political pattern: imperialism's "attempt to divide mankind into master and slave races, into higher and lower breeds, into colored and white men."[42]

To Bunche, who was well acquainted with the American racial caste system, this system was all too familiar. Indeed, in his earlier fieldwork in French West Africa, he had found the attitudes of colonial officials very much akin to those of the white Southerners he met on his travels with Myrdal. "Like the typical white American from the South," he wrote, "these men know the African."[43] Imperial leaders such as Lord Lugard had long seen colonial rule as a way to "teach" hard work to the Africans they had conquered, whom they viewed as primitive and not to be trusted without white supervision. Tutelage in the ways of modern life in turn provided a convenient and allegedly humanitarian justification for empire.

In keeping with the focus on economics as the primary driver of political behavior, and perhaps in some tension with the title, Bunche in *A World View of Race* foresaw class, and not race, as the true dividing line of the 20th century. In this sense, the book reflected its times, in which ideology trumped identity. "The titanic conflicts of the future," he wrote, will yield "uncompromising struggles" between those who have and those who have not. Class, he declaimed, "will someday supplant race in world affairs."[44]

This analysis was arresting and, in its polemical tone, at odds with his later reputation as a consummate diplomat and establishment insider. Indeed, years later, when the YWCA requested copies of *A World View of Race* in the wake of his Nobel Peace Prize, he disavowed the work. It was a hastily written manuscript, he wrote in reply, "and I am not at all proud of it."[45] By this point—only a dozen years away—Bunche had transitioned to a more establishment way of thinking. He would go on to embrace the Cold War liberal consensus and, though he was an international civil servant, would with some justification be seen as closely aligned with the upper echelons of American foreign policy. His radical past became an albatross to this new Bunche, one he tried to distance himself from as much as possible.

These more conventional views were still in the future, however. And *A World View of Race*'s marriage of race and international politics was not far out of mainstream thinking in the prewar era. The early 20th century was obsessed with racial hierarchy. World politics in this era fundamentally rested on imperialism, and imperialism fundamentally rested on a race-based view of international relations. Indeed, some viewed the First World War as an unfortunate internecine war among white people; a distraction from the looming rise of nonwhite peoples who, rapidly growing in number, would eventually battle for supremacy with Europeans. In 1920, the best-selling *The Rising Tide of Color: The Threat against White World Supremacy* by Lothrop Stoddard reflected the widely held view that global racial conflict was inevitable: the only real question was who would end up on top. (Stoddard's book was obliquely invoked by the character of Tom Buchanan in *The Great Gatsby*: "Have you read 'The Rise of the Colored Empires' by this

man Goddard? . . . If we don't look out the white race will be—will be utterly submerged.")

For Stoddard and his acolytes, the then-recent war between Japan and
Russia, in which an Asian nation defeated a white power and emerged as
a "civilized" state, was a cause for alarm. White supremacy appeared to be
in jeopardy. Stoddard's book was a bestseller and, for the most part, was
praised by the American mainstream. According to the *New York Times*:

> Lothrop Stoddard evokes a new peril, that of an eventual submersion beneath
> vast waves of yellow men, brown men, black men and red men, whom the Nordics
> have hitherto dominated . . . with Bolshevism menacing us on the one hand and
> race extinction through warfare on the other, many people are not unlikely to give
> [Stoddard] respectful consideration.[46]

To be sure, many in the 1920s and 1930s still saw geopolitics in traditional
terms: the conventional wisdom was that great power competition had
been at the heart of the First World War. But Stoddard's viewpoint, and
the perspectives of others like him, such as Madison Grant, author of *The
Passing of the Great Race* (1916), placed racial difference front and center
in foreign affairs.[‡] This included not only the supposed economic and political opportunity offered by white domination of the tropics, as espoused
by men like Lord Lugard, but also—and perhaps more importantly—the
threat these regions posed to white supremacy as they developed. There
was a "persistent dread" that it was only a matter of time before Europeans
themselves would be outnumbered and defeated.[47] These viewpoints justified colonial rule in many of the same terms used to justify segregation and
oppression at home.

Indeed, in 1921 President Warren Harding spoke in Birmingham,
Alabama, before a huge crowd and favorably cited Stoddard's *Rising Tide of
Color*. "Our race problem here in the United States," Harding said, "is only a
phase of a race issue that the whole world confronts."[48] It was not only white

---

‡ In a published debate with Alain Locke Stoddard argued, for example, that segregation was essential not because whites were necessarily superior to Blacks but simply
   because the races were different.

thinkers who thought like this in the prewar era; in the wake of the Great War, W. E. B. Du Bois himself wrote of the "fight for freedom which black and brown and yellow men must and will make unless their oppression and humiliation and insult at the hands of the White World cease." The "Dark World," Du Bois's favorite term for the non-white world, "is going to submit its present treatment just as long as it must and not one moment longer."[49]

Nazism, of course, made racial conflict an overriding obsession. Herman Goering, the Third Reich's highest military leader, called the Second World War "the great racial war."[50] Yet some who were proud believers in white supremacy, such Jan Smuts of South Africa, opposed Nazism precisely because it distracted from what they saw as the true racial conflict. Smuts, an influential South African leader—who would later draft the stirring pre-amble to the UN Charter—thought, in a Stoddard-esque manner, that the problem with Nazi ideology was that it divided *white* civilization on racial grounds. As a result, Nazism "constituted a grave threat" to white world su-premacy.[51] In a way, Du Bois saw things in a similar way. When speaking of the Second World War, Du Bois argued that "it would be a grave mistake to think that Africans are not asking the same questions that Asiatics are: is it a white man's war?"[52] These were all different takes on the racial dimensions of world politics, but they shared a common core: race was a master key to understanding the struggle for global dominance in the 20th century.

Against this backdrop, Ralph Bunche not only wanted to understand the mechanics of colonial rule, but also, as *A World View of Race* illustrated, fun-damentally challenge its racial bases. Bunche was not alone in his criticisms of colonialism, of course. Anticolonialism would prove a central pillar of Franklin Delano Roosevelt's approach to the postwar order. Criticism of European empire could be found on the right as well as the left in the US before the Second World War. This reflected a traditional American dis-taste for old world power politics, but also partly a rising sense that the eco-nomic implications of empire were bad for the rapidly industrializing US. In 1939, for instance, the prominent conservative Frank Hanighen published an essay in the progressive *New Republic* titled "No Colonies for Anybody." In this work, Hanighen castigated the European powers: "Every last one of them, in its colonial administration, shows an almost unbroken history of cruelty, greed and stupidity sufficient to make the angels weep."[53] Bunche, far to Hanighen's left, undoubtedly agreed.

The postwar study of international relations would soon obscure, if not erase, empires and their racial underpinnings from Bunche's chosen discipline of political science. The Cold War and the nuclear standoff between the superpowers ushered in a new approach that aspired to scientific principles built around arid and neutral concepts such as bipolarity. In the process, race and empires were largely relegated to the musty past. Bunche, having left the academic life by then, did not engage much with the new midcentury theories of international relations. But he continued to press scholars to study empire's lasting effects.[§] In 1953, while still serving in the UN, he became president of the American Political Science Association. He used his presidential address to urge greater attention to the study of colonialism, particularly African colonialism. Political scientists, he said, were still "regrettably slow in grasping fully the world significance of this problem."[54]

ONE OF THE LAST SCHOLARLY WORKS on empire Bunche published before leaving academia for government service was an essay called "Africa and the Current World Conflict." At the time he wrote *A World View of Race* in 1936, the Nazi Party had established the Third Reich, but Germany's threat to Europe was not fully apparent. Japan was at war with China from 1937 onward and had invaded Manchuria years earlier, though here, too, the implications for the US and the rest of the world were not widely appreciated. By contrast in 1940, when he wrote "Africa and the Current Conflict," the Second World War was well under way, Germany had conquered large swaths of Europe, Japan was set to dominate East Asia, Italy had conquered Ethiopia, and the threat posed by fascism was uppermost in the minds of many Americans. Ralph Bunche was no different.

In his essay, Bunche decried the likely fate of Africa in the emerging global conflagration. In times of peace, he argued, Africa had been subjected to brutal commercial exploitation. And in times of war, the continent "is

---

§ Years later, Bunche would shift from Marxism to neoliberalism in his assessment of Africa, referring to it as "a growth continent, to borrow Wall Street language."

converted into a bloody battlefield on which the great 'civilized' nations of Europe fight each other like mad dogs over a bone."[55] Africa was not just a bystander or a by-product of European war, however: "world wars and African imperialism are closely linked." Bunche catalogued the ills that plagued Africa under white rule, and, again marrying the twin issues of racial oppression abroad and at home, he noted that the justifications of African colonialism were of the same sort "often employed to justify the enslavement of the Negro in America."

At this point in the essay, however, he pivoted. Progress, however slow, was occurring in colonial Africa:

> The ability of the African to make this sort of slow but steady progress under the harsh rule of European imperialism has been in large measure due to the fact that the imperialist governments represented in Africa from the end of World War I to the present, excepting only Italy in North Africa and Ethiopia, have been democratic governments.[56]

To be sure, these democratic governments were, in his words, "imperialistic democracies." But they at least paid lip-service to ideals of freedom and the newer idea of self-determination. (Some feared the result: Robert Lansing, Woodrow Wilson's secretary of state, had thought that self-determination was an idea "loaded with dynamite" and "bound to breed discontent, disorder, and rebellion.")[57] Moreover, Bunche argued, the democracies had over time extended some of the key elements of democratic practice to their colonial subjects. As a result, slowly—too slowly, to be sure—conditions were improving. "The African in Africa, therefore, is much like the Negro" with regard to democracy: unable to share in its full fruits but "given some of the peelings from the fruit."[58]

Because of this slow but undeniable progress, Bunche argued, the political future of Africa and the African diaspora fundamentally rested on the outcome of the war. Nazi Germany or Fascist Italy would never offer Africans the opportunities or freedoms that the imperialistic democracies had. He drew comparisons with experiences on the Myrdal project. The Jim Crow South was terrible. Yet Germany embraced a "racial theory more severe and more brazen than any the modern world has known—more formal, more deliberate even than that found in our own Deep South." Invoking Adolf Hitler's *Mein Kampf*, he described how Nazi ideology divided humanity into Aryans and "something less than humans." For Bunche, there was no contest: a Nazi-ruled world was a disaster too horrible to countenance.

This essay marked a departure. As one later writer noted, Bunche's position in 1940 stood "in sharp contrast" to the view of colonialism in his dissertation and marked "a remarkable change in tone from the polemics of *A World View of Race*."[59] Bunche was pivoting sharply to the threat posed by Nazi Germany, and, seeing more menacing dangers abroad, he put slightly to one side his then-standard attacks on Western imperialism. In many ways this pivot was one he never reversed. Although his academic career came to an end in 1941, his speeches and public positions (as well as private notes) throughout the rest of his life adhered to the basic position laid out in "Africa and the Current World Conflict." He knew Western imperialism was fatally flawed and deeply oppressive. He fought it throughout the postwar era. But he believed that things could be worse.

Bunche's apprehension about Germany, and his ultimate support for American intervention in the war, were in contrast to some prominent views among Black intellectuals of the time, none more so than W. E. B. Du Bois. Du Bois, who revered the deep roots of German culture and also saw much to like in Soviet Russia, had a less fearful view of Nazism. He had also spent time in Japan, a place that greatly impressed him despite its colonial foray into Manchuria, in part because he saw it as an assertive and powerful Asian nation challenging white world supremacy. Indeed, shortly after Japan's incursion into mainland Asia, Du Bois had approvingly written that "Clearly, this colonial effort of a colored nation is something to watch."[60] In the months before Pearl Harbor, Du Bois had laid out the case for US abstention from the war in clear and unwavering terms. He even went so far as to speculate that the ultimate outcome of Nazi-Japanese cooperation might well be "increased freedom and autonomy for the darker world, despite all theoretic race ideology."[61]

Ralph Bunche, by contrast, had no particular interest in Japan and saw Nazi Germany as an absolutely grave threat to African peoples. As a later wrote a friend, a "Hitler victory" would mean "the end of me and my people."[62] He was no great fan of the Soviet Union either and puzzled at the fervor for communism of friends such as Paul Robeson. At the same time, it was becoming clear to Bunche that colonial rule in Asia and Africa was ultimately doomed to fail. Because of the democratic basis of rule they enjoyed at home, and the driving need to use every source of power they had in the apocalyptic struggle of the growing war, the colonial powers— at least most of them—had little choice but to slowly move toward greater freedom and, eventually, the liberation of their colonies. This was a position that he would encourage and fight for and that even Winston Churchill, the ardent defender of British Empire, would grudgingly come to acknowledge in years to come.

CHAPTER 4

THE WAR

This Imperialist War

—Headline in the *Spectator*, March 29, 1940

Ralph Bunche arrived at the White House by cab on May 15, 1940. Hopping out of the car, he announced to the liveried doorman that he was there to see Eleanor Roosevelt. Bunche had written to Mrs. Roosevelt twelve days before requesting a meeting; surprisingly, she invited him to lunch. The meeting was part of his final research for the *American Dilemma* project on race relations. As he explained in his letter to the First Lady, he was seeking her input on a project that was "strictly a scholarly one," though he rightly surmised it would have broader impact in a world in which "racial theories and hatreds assume increasing prominence."[1]

Bunche entered the Red Room of the White House, taking in the large paintings of Theodore Roosevelt and Grover Cleveland. A strong breeze flowed through an open door, ruffling the heavy red drapes. He had arrived early, and as he waited he thought about the fact that it was, as he put it, considered "so much more significant that a Negro would be sitting in the Red Room waiting for lunch, than should a white person." Indeed, he was unsure whether Eleanor Roosevelt knew he was Black when she issued her invitation. (She did not, he discovered, but right away she told him it made no difference to her.)

Eventually Mrs. Roosevelt walked in, saying immediately, "How do you do, Mr. Bunche?" and extending her hand.[2] The two stepped out to the South Portico, where a table had been set. As the May sun shone, they sat together, chatting informally over their chicken salads, sliced tomatoes, and cornbread. "I don't believe I have interviewed anyone about whose sincerity I am more impressed," Bunche later said of the First Lady.

Over the next hour and a half, Bunche and Roosevelt discussed race relations in America, but also the situation in Europe and the looming perils of Nazi Germany. Just days before their lunch, German forces had invaded Belgium, the Netherlands, and France. They both shared a deep concern about the Nazi threat. The war in Europe was growing in intensity, and Bunche thought that Nazism, with its unrelenting focus on racial hierarchy and fetishization of Nordic imagery and traits, was clearly ominous for Black people. Eleanor Roosevelt agreed. She also thought that the dire situation abroad might help push Congress to take bold steps toward racial justice at home, in order to "present a united front against the Nazi menace."[3] Interestingly, she intimated to him that the allied states had already made feelers to Hitler for peace and had been turned down. The situation appeared very bleak.

In the months that followed their White House lunch, Eleanor Roosevelt and Ralph Bunche continued to correspond. Over the ensuing years the two would talk and meet often: on the *Queen Mary*, en route to London for the opening session of the United Nations in 1946; at a black-tie dinner at the Waldorf Astoria in 1949; and on Roosevelt's radio show in 1950, shortly after Bunche's Nobel Peace Prize was announced. He would even appear on her short-lived PBS talk show in 1960, "Prospects for Mankind." Roosevelt, a champion of human rights in the postwar years who played an important role in crafting the landmark 1948 UN Declaration on Human Rights, seemed to find him a stimulating and likeable interlocutor. He in turn found Eleanor Roosevelt, despite her fame and (indirect) power, to be approachable and engaging.

Bunche's trip to the White House that May afternoon was his first brush with the very apex of American power. It would not be his last—nor would it be his last meal at the White House. In May 1940 he was still deeply invested in his academic career at Howard University. He had devoted enormous effort in the preceding years to his research for the Carnegie book project, but he was also working on his continuing passion: the future of Africa and the rolling back of European empire. Bunche was writing at a blistering pace, and he was already an academic success and someone who had a high profile at Howard.

As the 1940s dawned, the threat Nazi Germany and Imperial Japan posed to world order led President Roosevelt, cognizant that the US would eventually enter the war, to create the Office of the Coordinator of Information. Roosevelt and his national security team wanted to better analyze incoming intelligence about the progress of the war. This new federal bureau would soon grow and morph into the famed Office of Strategic Services; after the war was over, it was reorganized and renamed the Central Intelligence Agency.

In the summer of 1941, almost exactly a year after his White House lunch with Eleanor Roosevelt, the new Office of the Coordinator of Information began seeking an Africa specialist. Few Americans had expertise on the continent, which had now become an important front in the rapidly expanding war. Earlier that year, Germany had created the Afrika Korps, and the North Africa campaign of the war had taken the battle to Libya and Egypt. Many feared that British and French colonial possessions would be targeted next. Germany, unlike the allied democracies, had no territories in Africa, having lost them as part of the peace settlement after the First World War. German leaders deeply resented the loss of their African empire and sought to regain a foothold— or more—on the continent. The Roosevelt administration needed a plan. Faculty at Harvard, asked to propose a suitable Africa expert for the new intelligence bureau, suggested Ralph Bunche of Howard University.

RALPH BUNCHE'S EXPERIENCE RESEARCHING COLONIAL GOVERNANCE in French West Africa, his extensive tours of South and East Africa, and his general knowledge of African politics made him an unusual figure in America.

The State Department had no Africa division at this time; there were only a handful of independent African nations in 1941. Understanding African politics in this era essentially meant understanding colonial rule and rivalry. When the Roosevelt administration made Bunche its overture to join the new intelligence office, he was of course already living in Washington, and so the transition to government service was not disruptive to his wife or to their family life. While it was the start of a major career change for Ralph, he was surprisingly receptive to the idea. Despite his many justified critiques of American democracy, he believed the American ideal was well worth defending and was even a model for the larger world. The very fact of racial diversity in our society, he would later declare in an NAACP speech, "makes of our nation throughout the entire world a unique symbol of the promise, the unlimited possibilities for strength and greatness, the spiritual depth and the virility of democracy as a way of life."[4]

Nazi ideology and power represented a direct threat to this way of life. In December 1940, a few months before his move into government, Bunche spoke to the Association of Colleges and Secondary Schools for Negroes on "The Negro's Stake in the World Crisis." His core message was that the "complacency" and narrow, local focus that he believed too often characterized the Black community had blinded it to the fact that the "gravest problem today"—indeed, he believed the gravest since Emancipation—was the threat posed by Nazism:

> Never since the Civil War has a conflict meant so much to the Negro and his future as this one which now engulfs the world. For this is more than a world conflict: it is a world revolution that is in progress; a revolution that is determined to blot out all of the very values that we have lived by. . . . If this world revolution which Hitler and his regimented minions strive for succeeds, it promises to enslave all non-white peoples and a good many who are white as well. Its fruition would make the three-fourths century of qualified freedom which Negroes have enjoyed since emancipation little more than a strange interlude.[5]

Bunche's clarion call exposing the dangers of German fascism was aimed at a mindset he characterized as having two parts: (1) "it doesn't make any difference to the Negro who wins the war," and (2) "the Negro has been subject to fascism all along anyway."

However bleak his fears of fascism were, Bunche was acutely aware of the depths of racial injustice at home, even as the nation geared up to fight the Axis. One day in 1941, not long before the US entered the war, he penned a brief note. "There's a lot of irony in this American racial situation. I'm sitting up in a Pullman from Raleigh, NC, en route to Wash. DC—from one cap-itol to another—writing notes in defense of the American democracy." Yet, he continued, he could only get on the train "through deception." He had to have a former student "who can 'pass'" retrieve the ticket for him. Bunche had been at Shaw University, a historically Black college, speaking about why "the Negro had to support the struggle of the American and British 'democracies' against the Nazi world revolution."[6] Bunche's scare quotes around the word *democracy* demonstrated his awareness of American hy-pocrisy; still, the fact that the "most bigoted and intolerant persons feel it necessary to pay lip-service to [democratic] principles is itself an important fact." Insincere or incomplete or even hypocritical democracy was better than none at all, Bunche felt, "when the only alternative is Nazism."[7]

Joining the Roosevelt administration's burgeoning war effort fit well with these beliefs. (Bunche even tried to join the Army directly, but various physical ailments meant he was rejected from active service.) He had long focused on the ills of race-based thinking in politics. That one could draw a line from the Scramble for Africa that began in Otto von Bismarck's Berlin drawing room in 1884 to Nazi notions of Untermenschen was not readily apparent to most Americans, but many Black Americans could identify the path. Indeed, the starting point was probably a few centuries earlier. As the *Chicago Defender* put it in an editorial during the war, in turn criticizing an editorial in the more mainstream *Chicago Tribune*, the *Tribune* "would have us believe that the age of hate began with the triumphal entry of Herr Fuehrer into Vienna. The age of hate began with the slave trade and the in-tensification of prejudice which followed the liberation of the slaves."[8]

Seen in this context, aiding the war effort was less a break with Ralph Bunche's past than a continuation of his life's work. But as a matter of quotidian routine, it heralded a huge change. As he later described this period in his life,

> Unexpected opportunities kept punctuating my career. In September 1941 I was at my desk at Howard ready to start the fall term. . . . Suddenly, the phone rang. A man named Conyers Read, whom I didn't know, wanted to see me. Mr. Read turned out to be a history professor at the University of Pennsylvania, who was now working for Col. William Donovan in the agency later to be called the Office of Strategic Services. Read needed a man to head up the colonial aspect of their intelligence work.[9]

Bunche happily agreed to this unexpected offer. Indeed, he may have been pushed as much as pulled; a few months before the opportunity to work for the federal government arose, Bunche complained to a colleague about his fatigue with academic research. "I am trying to drag myself back to the African field notes," he wrote, referring to his lengthy trip to Africa a couple of years before, "but I have developed such a revulsion toward work since my sentence on the Carnegie project expired that it is very difficult."[10] Seemingly exhausted by that experience, in which he wrote thousands of pages, Bunche was perhaps more than ready to exit the scholarly rat race and take a detour into the policy world. And once there, his desire to compete and win in the white world; his generally moderate, reasonable temperament; and his apparent comfort in establishment settings allowed him to rise within, and to some degree even embody, the sort of Cold War liberal consensus that marked the late 1940s and 1950s.

Once in the novel setting of government, his immediate assignments were a very practical set of issues: preparing American troops for battle in Africa by explaining the political and social terrain in European-ruled colonies. His initial focus was the British colonial possessions, which at the time included Kenya, South Africa, North and South Rhodesia, Uganda, and other territories—places he had the rare distinction of having actually visited. Bunche threw himself into the task with his usual work ethic and rigor. He wrote reports on Liberia, on North Africa, on South Africa, and on Pan-Africanism as a movement—a movement he was skeptical of throughout his career. (Indeed, at least one historian alleges that he used his position at State to delay plans for a war-time pan-African conference in favor of broader colonial coalitions that would tie Asians and Africans together.)[11] He drafted memos making the case for Africa's importance to the war, and for America's interest there. In a memo to Conyers Read, for instance, Bunche argued that it was in the national interest to "cultivate cordial relations" with Africans. In doing so, special efforts should be made to "preserve carefully the native legend of America as a liberalizing force in the world."[12] And he put together guides for Allied soldiers, such as *Union of South Africa Soldiers Guide: What Americans Should Know about South Africa.*

Regarding North Africa, a key early battleground, he stressed that the region was an important part of the "broad strategy to smash Hitler's armies and thereby liberate the long-suffering peoples of Europe from the Nazi yoke."[13] (Liberation of North Africa's peoples from colonial rule was not, however, invoked as a goal—though Bunche had more to say on that topic later.) His field guide supplied a brief analysis of North Africa and French colonial policy. Current French policy, he wrote, appeared designed to "arouse considerable apprehension in democratic quarters." The French had made little effort to improve conditions in these territories, and there was "profound native dissatisfaction" with French rule. Prophetically, he suggested that French North Africa might well prove a "testing ground of the United Nations' democratic pronouncements."

Bunche's use of the term *United Nations* at this point referred to the then-common phrase for the Allied powers, not the organization that would come later. But either way, he got it broadly right. The Nazi threat and the framing of the conflagration as one of ideology as much as territorial or political dominance led to many stirring statements about freedom and democracy that would, soon enough, come back to haunt the colonial powers of the West.

Bunche's work on Africa was crucial to the war effort. Many Americans of the time, even those in the upper reaches of the national security establishment, knew little of the continent and had outdated and highly negative views of Africans. The American consul in Lagos, Nigeria, claimed at the time that "West African natives are 500 years behind the American Negro." Sumner Welles, the under secretary of state, thought Africans were "in the lowest ranks of human beings" and did not actually want autonomy. Against this backdrop, Bunche's knowledge of Africa took on great importance.[14] Aware from his London days of the political movements afoot across the continent, he stressed that nationalism was a growing force. Of Tunisia, for instance, he wrote in a secret memo that the absence of any real effort by France to move toward autonomy was arousing resentment which would, coupled to what he described as "an enormous discrepancy" between the pronounced ideals of the Allies and actual colonial practice, likely only end in conflict.[15]

Bunche also had been struck in his earlier fieldwork by the way, in French colonies at least, local and white soldiers had trained "shoulder to shoulder."[16] And he believed that Black soldiers from the US would be better received in colonial Africa than white ones. He had personally witnessed both the wide differences between American Blacks and Africans and the sometimes-powerful ties of racial affinity. During his fieldwork in Kenya he

> found the tribal elders assembled in a field to bid me welcome. Through an inter-
> preter, I made a short speech. I told them about my African background, how my
> ancestors were carried across the water, enslaved in a strange land, how they had
> later been freed and begun to prosper. I ended with an expression of my happiness
> in being back in the land of my fathers.[17]

A "grizzled elder" then stepped forward. He told Bunche excitedly about the stories he had heard as a youth of relatives in distant times taken across the "big water," never to return. The elder gave Bunche the name Karioki, which meant "he who has returned from the dead." The name stuck, and everywhere Bunche went children called out "Karioki!" "This degree of ac-ceptance," he observed, "greatly aided my research."[18]

Shortly after Bunche joined the Roosevelt administration, the Japanese attacked the American naval base at Pearl Harbor. In the wake of the at-tack, the US formally entered the war, and the intelligence work he and his colleagues were doing took on greater urgency and secrecy. Bunche took

seriously the need for confidentiality. Interviewed years later, he told a reporter for the *New York Amsterdam News* that his work for the Office of
Strategic Services (OSS) was "highly secretive, as you know." Members of
the press as well as personal friends were "eager to know what I was doing,
but at the time nobody dared breathe a word about preparations for the
invasion of North Africa."[19] Bunche turned out to be a very good intelligence officer. An excellent analyst and prodigious writer, he was immediately recognized as a rare asset. Under Secretary of State Edward Stettinius,
with whom he would work closely in the negotiations over the planned
United Nations in San Francisco at the end of the war, wrote that the men
who received his African guides have expressed "great appreciation for your
work."[20] Conyers Read, his supervisor at the OSS, wrote him a sterling recommendation for a promotion. Bunche has done brilliant work, Read advised; "His knowledge of Africa is unique, his diligence in research very
remarkable, and his tact in personal contacts outstanding."[21] Read noted
that he was now sought after by several other agencies within the federal
government. Bunche got the promotion.

Then, even as battles raged in North Africa between the Allied forces
and the German Afrika Korps, Bunche attended a conference that would in
many respects change his life. The Institute of Pacific Relations Conference,
held in December 1942 in the snowy resort city of Mont Tremblant near
Quebec, Canada, brought together many Allied officials and experts in an
early effort to begin to think through a postwar system of peace and security.
While the war was far from over, the failures of the League of Nations had
led President Roosevelt—who had been a strong supporter of the League
in the 1920s—to push for a renewed effort at some kind of postwar international organization.* The Institute of Pacific Relations was one of several bodies that existed in the interwar period focused on relations among

---

* Roosevelt's interest in a world organization long predated the Second World War. In
the election of 1920, running as the vice presidential candidate for Democrat James
Cox, FDR sought to resurrect American participation in the League of Nations, calling
it "the dominant issue of the campaign" and giving many speeches on the League's
importance.

peoples—or, as it was commonly viewed then, relations among races. The focus was on the Pacific and Asia, but inevitably discussions ranged more broadly.

The notion of a successor organization to the League was not a new idea in 1942. In fact, the much-maligned League was in many ways the first draft of what would become the UN. And as the war raged on, the League was actually still operating in neutral Switzerland, if largely pointlessly. (In December 1944, the *New Yorker* noted, somewhat tongue in cheek, that "Practically everybody you meet these days has a plan for a permanent world organization but almost to a plan none of them takes into account the fact that we already have a permanent world organization in the League of Nations.")[22] Hobbled from the beginning by American absence and great power dissension, the League was unable to effectively constrain the rush to hostilities that followed. The Allied governments increasingly came to believe that an entirely new world organization, with a different structure, was necessary.

This idea was helped along by various private groups who were pushing for the development of a more potent postwar international organization.[23] One of the more prominent organizations, with which Bunche was tangentially associated, was the Commission to Study the Organization of Peace. Led by James Shotwell of Columbia University, an historian and international relations specialist, the committee enlisted Bunche a couple of years after the Mont Tremblant meeting to prepare a report called "The United States and the International Trusteeship System." This report later fed into American views on the details of the trusteeship system for former Axis colonies that emerged as a key component of the UN Charter.

Bunche called the Mont Tremblant conference "the best international conference I've ever attended."[24] Despite the deep cold of a Quebec winter, it attracted many important leaders with whom Bunche would work throughout his career. Mont Tremblant was also the place that, at least in his own estimation, launched him on his career as a diplomat. In an address before the conferees, he declared that plans for international organization "are all means and not ends." The real objective "must always be the good life for all people." That good life included the obvious—peace, security, education—but "above all, the right to walk with dignity on the world's great boulevards."

This last point, no doubt born of bitter personal experience, underscored how Ralph Bunche saw the importance of racial equality in international affairs. It was, at bottom, an issue of morality, equality, and respect. In his view it was this speech in Quebec, and the abundant attention from the delegates it garnered, that set him on a path that would lead him to the highest levels of the future United Nations Organization.

THE MONT TREMBLANT CONFERENCE WAS THE first of many Ralph Bunche would attend that would grapple with the thorny issue of how to unwind European colonialism in a manner that was principled, practical, and politically realistic. European nations may have "raped Africa," as he had written in the 1930s, but they now possessed title to much of it.[25] Moreover, these states were wartime allies. They could not easily be forced, but rather had to be persuaded—somehow—to give up their overseas territories. Many Europeans felt African and Asian societies might eventually become independent, but not just yet. Further European rule was necessary, even if they agreed that self-determination over the long run was appropriate.

Bunche was one of the few who had seen firsthand what European domination in Africa and Asia looked like, and he strongly favored self-government over European notions of colonial good government. He was a pragmatist at heart. Yet he nonetheless believed that waiting for the right moment for freedom was morally wrong and politically difficult. He agreed that some colonial societies could not take the political reins immediately without risk of disorder and even civil war. But others were ready now. Either way, he felt that when a people demanded self-government, they ought to get it. The Quebec conference helped him recognize that difficult political struggles lay ahead, and governments would inevitably be forced to take sides on this looming issue.

The backdrop for the conference was an early Allied declaration known as the Atlantic Charter. Negotiated somewhat combatively in 1941 between British Prime Minister Winston Churchill and President Franklin

Roosevelt, the Charter was signed off the coast of Canada aboard the battle cruiser *Augusta*. The Charter spoke of cooperation between the two English-speaking nations, and also of their shared values and opposition to the perils posed by the Axis. The US had not yet entered the war when the two leaders met on the *Augusta*, and Churchill desperately wanted a commitment from Roosevelt to do so. A wide swath of American public opinion was still opposed, however, and Roosevelt could not yet guarantee America would aid the British. Roosevelt in turn sought assurances from Churchill that Britain did not have secret treaties to dispose of foreign territories after the war.[26] He also pressed Churchill to agree to disband the system of British imperial preferences, which essentially created a free trade zone within the British Empire and higher tariffs for those outside of it. Churchill, an avowed imperialist, resisted what we saw as American meddling in internal affairs. This early jockeying over the future of empire would consume substantial attention in the years to come.

On board the *Augusta*, the two men also discussed the notion of a postwar international organization. Despite his long-standing support of the League, Roosevelt was uncertain about the utility of revamping the League or using it as a model. As a result, the two leaders simply agreed on a call for disarmament, "pending the establishment of a wider and permanent system of general security."[27] Neither man was completely happy with the Atlantic Charter negotiations. But the resulting communique kick-started the process toward Allied collaboration. Of particular interest to Bunche, the Charter spoke of the long-standing question of the self-determination of peoples. It declared that the parties "desire to see no territorial changes that do not accord with the freely expressed wishes of the peoples concerned."[28] The signatories also announced their respect for the right of all peoples to choose the form of government under which they will live.

These principles were written in a sweeping and general manner. Roosevelt, seeking to cement their significance, publicly asserted in a 1942 radio broadcast that the Atlantic Charter and its statements reached "to the whole world." Back in England Churchill contradicted his partner, quickly clarifying that the Charter "was not intended to deal with the internal affairs of the British Empire."[29] Churchill's "correction" received substantial notice in the Black press in the US. The *Chicago Defender* editorialized that "Black America is truly shocked by the bold and brazen stand by Churchill. We have never known or believed him a friend but we hoped that he as well as the world is learning about democracy from the very 'blood sweat and tears' of war."[30] A skeptical W. E. B. Du Bois put it more succinctly: "I do not like the Roosevelt-Churchill manifesto."[31]

Bunche, who helped author a 1942 report titled *The Atlantic Charter and Africa from an American Standpoint*, nonetheless saw promise.[32] In *The Atlantic Charter and Africa*, he and his colleagues—a diverse and influential group that included both Du Bois and John Foster Dulles, later to be secretary of state—declared that the Charter's fundamental points had "vital implications" for the "full development of the native African peoples." (The insertion of "native" suggests early concern with the possible domestic blowback from international statements related to race.) Still, they seconded the common view that any process of African independence would have to proceed carefully. Self-determination could be dangerous, they warned, "if complete self-government is provided before the people are qualified through education and experience to make use of it wisely and effectively."[33] With this caveat in mind, Bunche's goal was to ensure that the language of self-determination would not merely pertain to the conquered peoples of Europe, as had been the case after the First World War, but also to colonized peoples the world over. It would take time, but this vision would eventually prevail.

Meanwhile, the Americans and the British continued to warily engage each other over the possible contours of the postwar order. The two nations shared many common aims. But as Roosevelt's tangles with Churchill presaged, there were significant differences around the issue of empire. Over dinner in 1942, Roosevelt told Churchill that there were many kinds of Americans, "but as a people, as a country, we're opposed to imperialism—we can't stomach it."[34] Roosevelt was reflecting an important strand of thinking in American politics. Yet the situation was not quite that simple. On the one hand, as citizens of a former colony, Americans did like to see themselves as naturally anticolonial. Yet the US also possessed a huge land empire of its own, and at the very end of the 19th century had even colonized far-flung islands. Victory in the Spanish-American War of 1898 had led the US to acquire the Philippines, Puerto Rico, and other island territories; the US had also annexed the Hawaiian Islands.

The late-19th-century burst of American interest in becoming a colonial power quickly proved politically contentious. Elites argued over the legal implications of absorbing colonies into a republic, and soon the American people did too. The Supreme Court was forced to rule repeatedly on the many novel legal questions this posed.[35] Opposition to colonialism ran the gamut from philosophical objections to racial fears. The presidential campaign of 1900 reflected these views. "The Filipinos," the Democratic Party platform declared, neatly encapsulating both the racist and republican objections to empire, "cannot be citizens without endangering our civilization; they cannot be subjects without imperiling our form of government."[36] William McKinley, the Republican incumbent, nonetheless defeated William Jennings Bryan, the Democratic anti-imperialist firebrand, temporarily preserving America's incipient overseas colonial empire.

By the onset of the Second World War, the Bryan wing of thinking had largely taken over, however. While the US would retain several colonies of its own, such as Puerto Rico, rhetorically and politically it evinced more open opposition to formal empire. By the onset of the Second World War, Americans increasingly saw formal imperialism as contrary to their national values. And as the world's largest economy, it was free trade, not imperial preference schemes, that best served America's interest. The war gave the US leverage to pursue these goals. In 1942, Under Secretary of State Sumner Welles would declare that "our victory must bring in its train the liberation of all peoples." The "age of imperialism," Welles baldly stated, "is ended."[37]

The British, of course, were not so sure. Churchill in particular was a committed believer in empire. While he is conventionally seen, by many Americans at least, as a heroic foe of fascism, within the former British Empire Churchill's reputation is more complicated. Indeed, while George W. Bush prominently placed a bust of Churchill in the Oval Office, Barack Obama—whose Kenyan grandfather was imprisoned without trial and tortured on Churchill's watch—had it removed.[38] Even for his time Churchill was an outlier in his faith in the merits of colonial rule and in his unvarnished racism: he famously called Indians "a beastly people with a beastly religion" and reveled in the British military's power over native forces.[†] At the same time, Churchill was justly renowned as one of the great orators of democracy. His many speeches during the war provided, as Bunche himself could have predicted, powerful ammunition for those seeking liberation from foreign rule. Kwame Nkrumah, the first prime minister of independent Ghana, later noted this effect, declaring that "all the fair brave words spoken about freedom that had been broadcast to the four corners of the earth took seed and grew where they had not been intended."[39] Even Churchill acknowledged as much in later years. At the age of eighty, discussing the challenge posed by Mau Mau rebels in British-controlled Kenya in 1954, someone referred to the rebels as "savages." Churchill interjected. "Savages? Savages? Not savages. They're savages armed with ideas—much more difficult to deal with."[40]

Churchill's efforts to save the British Empire were also challenged from another corner. The central importance of the Soviet Union to victory in the war added a second future superpower to the mix. The Soviet Union, like the United States, also possessed a huge land empire and was ideologically opposed to formal imperialism. Indeed, as far back as 1917, Lenin had identified imperialism as the highest stage of capitalism. Still, Stalin did not make dismantling imperialism a priority in the wartime planning in quite the same way that Roosevelt did, though the Soviets would do so with far more fervor after the war. With Soviet support, Roosevelt began to insist to Churchill more strongly that the postwar order would need to dismantle the colonial world. In short, American power, European weakness, rising nationalism, and the prospect of creating a new postwar international organization all began to break down resistance to the unraveling of empire. The combination ultimately proved fatal. Ralph Bunche, sitting at the intersection of these trends, not only saw it transpire but drew new motivation in his work in government.

RALPH BUNCHE REMAINED AT THE OSS through 1943, even as Africa as a battleground receded in importance during the war. (He was offered

---

[†] Churchill particularly despised Gandhi, calling him a "malignant subversive fanatic" and "a seditious Middle Temple lawyer, now posing as a fakir of a type well known in the East, striding half-naked up the steps of the Viceregal palace."

a position at the Institute of Pacific Relations, which had hosted the Quebec conference, but he chose to stay in government.)[41] During the same period, his third and last child, Ralph Jr., was born. Early that year he was consulted by the State Department, which had a small team beginning to explore the contours of a comprehensive postwar settlement. He was asked for advice on a "colonial charter" that could be a part of the envisioned settlement. This was the seed of what would evolve into the UN Charter's treatment of "non-self-governing" territories and trusteeships.

Bunche was concerned that the US was behind the ball with regard to postwar colonialism. He noted to a colleague that the British and others had been "working feverishly" on the topic and that as a result, the US was "ill-prepared to cross swords."[42] To fix this problem, he suggested that an intelligence mission be sent to discover what Britain, in particular, was planning with regard to postwar Africa. In an oblique, yet fairly transparent, way Bunche proposed himself for this task. After describing his close connections to many key British officials and his experience in African colonies, he suggested that if the person to be sent on this mission was "carefully selected" along the lines he suggested (lines that pointed almost directly at himself), "it would scarcely be necessary to invoke any elaborate cover." If some cover *was* thought necessary, he proposed to use the Phelps-Stokes Fund, which funded research on Africa. In short, Bunche, who seemed to have imbibed fully the mission of the proto-CIA he was now working for, was proposing to use his academic past and stature to disguise an intelligence mission aimed at ensuring that the US was not outflanked by the British in the postwar game.[‡]

Within a year, Bunche would transfer from the OSS to the State Department (in July 1944). This move brought him closer to the diplomatic path that would form the core of his career. His first post, as Area Specialist and expert on Africa and dependent territories in the Division of Territorial

---

[‡] There is no evidence that this plan ever came to fruition.

Studies, led to a set of promotions and, eventually, appointment as Acting Chief of the division in July of 1946.[§]

At first the move did not go smoothly. Behind the scenes, some officials at State blocked his appointment on the grounds that he was Black. But he had strong supporters as well. The conflict eventually went all the way up to Secretary of State Cordell Hull. As Bunche later recounted, Hull, a Southerner, was angry about the whole affair. "A man's color, he insisted, made no difference to him. He wanted qualified men in the department. . . . And so I was appointed—the first Negro ever to hold a 'desk job' at the State Department."[43]

At State Bunche was increasingly drawn into the planning for a postwar peace organization. His role in developing this still-amorphous body was limited, at least initially, to the question of what should be done about Germany and Japan's colonies. Small at first, this issue grew in importance. As Roosevelt and then Stalin came around to a more comprehensive view of postwar international organizations, they moved further in a direction Churchill did not like. Bunche would later say that Roosevelt, buoyed by rising American power and influence, liked to "needle" the British, and later the French, about their empires.[44] Churchill pushed back, declaring, to his fellow ministers at least, that "'Hands off the British Empire' is our maxim."[45] Still, as the Allies headed toward victory, it was becoming clear to London that its insistence on retaining a large empire clashed directly with the anticolonial attitudes of the Soviets and Americans. This situation threatened the global status which British leaders "valued above all else."[46] Forced to choose between empire and status, Britain chose status.

The French had a similar dilemma. French power was at a very low ebb in the war years. France's defeat and occupation by Germany meant it was largely left out of the planning for the postwar world. De Gaulle and other Free French leaders nonetheless believed the nation would quickly return

---

[§] Although Bunche's tour of duty was relatively brief, the State Department makes the most of it today. The department's library in its Foggy Bottom headquarters is named the Ralph J. Bunche Library.

to greatness and, along the way, resurrect its empire. Bunche, summarizing a 1944 Free French conference held in Brazzaville, the capital of French Equatorial Africa, wrote that the French essentially offered "no compromise with the basic principle that French West Africa belongs solely to France."[47] Moreover, he discerned no recognition that France owed any accountability to the international community in the conduct of its colonial affairs.

In May 1944 Bunche had helped advise the American delegation to a conference of the International Labor Organization (ILO), held in Philadelphia. The ILO was a League-era organization, still extant today. With US support, the conference delved into colonial politics, not an obvious step for a labor organization but an important one. Bunche himself had no particular background in labor issues, but in Philadelphia he helped negotiate a set of Minimum Standards of Social Policy in the Dependent Territories that the ILO adopted. In doing so, the ILO reinforced the idea that the Atlantic Charter's principles applied to all territories, colonial or not. Bunche was increasingly warming to the idea that the path to freedom for colonial peoples ran through multilateral cooperation. That is, rather than simply seek liberation individually—or violently rebel—a more collective approach to decolonization was likely to be more effective. The international community could guide the move to independence and assist the protagonists, and in the process blunt the objection that the colonies were not yet ready or prepared to be independent. The ILO standards reflected this basic concept. To his relief, the notion that the international community (though tellingly the words actually used in the declaration were "the civilized world") had an interest in the treatment and ultimate disposition of colonies was becoming further entrenched.

BY LATE 1944, THE MOMENTUM OF the war was decidedly moving in the Allies' direction. The D-Day invasion occurred in June of that year; the Japanese were now in retreat across the Pacific; and the Soviets were marching steadily westward, retaking Eastern Europe. Within the State Department the effort to map out a postwar organization took on greater urgency. Bunche was increasingly devoting his time to this planning process and was now tasked with thinking about what the US position on colonies should be in the upcoming set of closed door negotiations set for August 1944.

The erosion of colonial rule was but one, admittedly small, part of the bigger picture the State Department was seeking to paint. While the global order that followed the defeat of the Axis had many elements—some of which were neither intended nor necessarily anticipated—at its core was the goal of a new world organization that would, it was hoped, decisively reallocate authority over the security of the world. The proposed organization was intended to be a permanent, standing body. It would be stronger and more effective than the moribund League and would incorporate all the leading powers in a novel collective security arrangement. The new organization, formed by the Allied nations, would be called the United Nations.

At this point in history, the phrase "United Nations" had only recently come into use. Roosevelt, during a visit from Churchill in December 1941, had pondered at length what to call the Allied states, then denoted somewhat anodynely as the "Associated Powers." Suddenly struck one morning by the phrase "United Nations," he went to find Churchill, who was in the midst of taking a bath. Roosevelt called out, and in the door leading to the bathroom, his assistant later recounted, appeared the Prime Minister, "a pink cherub (FDR said) drying with a towel and without a stitch on! FDR pointed at him and exploded: 'The United Nations!' 'Good!' said WSC."[48]

The phrase first appeared officially on New Year's Day 1942, when the Allies signed a declaration of cooperation entitled *Declaration by United Nations*.[49] Soon the "United Nations" became a synonym for the Allied powers. In the dark days of 1942, years before the UN Charter was signed, the Declaration was meant to signal resolve and to tie together the efforts of each of the twenty-six signatories. Through the declaration each signatory pledged to use all available means to defeat the Axis powers. Most importantly, each also pledged to remain united and not enter into any separate peace with the enemy states. This issue became live when, in April 1945, with the Red Army rapidly advancing on Berlin, Heinrich Himmler sought to negotiate with the West.** Himmler was desperate to escape the coming Russian onslaught. After a rush of telegrams across the Atlantic, Truman, Churchill, and Stalin refused. They reiterated that any surrender had to be unconditional and "simultaneous to the three major powers."[50]

The preface of the *Declaration by United Nations* reflected the total, almost apocalyptic struggle represented by the Second World War. The document announced that the parties were

> convinced that complete victory over their enemies is essential to defend life, liberty, independence and religious freedom, and to preserve human rights and justice in their own lands as well as in other lands, and that they are now engaged in a common struggle against savage and brutal forces seeking to subjugate the world.

Nothing less than the future of civilization was at stake. When the declaration was drafted in 1942, the focus of the "United Nations" was still on winning the war. Soon enough the focus would shift to winning the peace.

** Conveying Himmler's last-minute offer to the West was the Swedish Count Folke Bernadotte. Bernadotte, just a few years later, would become the UN's first mediator for Palestine—with Ralph Bunche by his side as deputy.

CHAPTER 5

REBUILDING THE WORLD

Today as we try in anticipation to rebuild the world, the propositions of Dumbarton Oaks center their efforts upon stopping war by force and at the same time leaving untouched, save by vague implication, the causes of war, especially those which lurk in rivalry for power and prestige and race dominance.

— W. E. B. Du Bois, *Color and Democracy* (1945)

The bombs were still falling in Europe and Asia as the delegates from the United States, the Soviet Union, and the United Kingdom assembled at a leafy estate in Washington, DC, on August 21, 1944. While Germany and Japan had not yet ceased fighting, the outcome of the war was increasingly clear. General George Patton and the US Third Army were steadily advancing through France. Within days of the conference's start, Paris was liberated, and soon after Allied troops entered Belgium. In the Pacific Theater, American forces had retaken Guam and were closing in on the Japanese home islands.

The representatives from the "Big Three" great powers sat around a horseshoe-shaped table in the stately brick mansion near Rock Creek Park, in a room bedecked with parquet floors and intricately detailed beamed ceilings. (In a perhaps not-coincidental twist, the iconic United Nations Security Council table would also be a horseshoe, albeit a more stylish,

curved version.) Among the American delegates was John Foster Dulles, the future secretary of state, hobbling about on crutches due to a foot injury; Cordell Hull, the current secretary of state; and Ralph Bunche, newly working at the State Department. The goal of the meeting, which began on a sunny summer morning, was to begin to hammer out a new charter for a postwar international organization. Known forever after as the Dumbarton Oaks Conference (officially, "Conversations"), the gathering was named after the estate at which it was held, recently bequeathed to Harvard and formerly the home of an American diplomat—and also of John C. Calhoun, the notorious proponent of slavery and former American secretary of war.*
Bunche was at Dumbarton Oaks watching and absorbing the proceedings, which occurred at a high level, and thinking about the implications for the nearly 750 million people still under the yoke of colonialism.

While highly significant, the discussions at Dumbarton Oaks were but one piece of the larger puzzle of the postwar order. What would emerge from the ashes of the Second World War was one of the great remakings of the global system. On par with the Treaty of Westphalia in 1648, the Congress of Vienna in the 19th century, and the Paris Peace Conference of 1919, which followed the First World War, this remaking was a great power conclave first and foremost. But the new order the great powers were sketching out in the quiet of Dumbarton Oaks would have major implications for the rest of the world. In many respects. this recasting of the international system would be much more profound than that of 1919, its nearest predecessor, and certainly more enduring.

Ralph Bunche had transitioned into the new International Security Organization working group just weeks before the Dumbarton Oaks talks commenced. The administration of President Franklin Delano Roosevelt had been contemplating a new international organization for years. With the war effort going well, the planning for what was being called the United Nations Organization took on a new urgency. As one of the nation's only

---

* A young State Department official named Alger Hiss, later to be accused of spying for the Soviet Union, had suggested the estate to his superiors as a secluded, yet nearby, site for the conference.

experts on colonial governance, Bunche was an important player on the postwar planning team. It was also a role that would transform his life. His doctoral research on the League of Nations' mandates had given him expertise in a central aspect of the now moribund League. Yet aside from that revolutionary feature, he had paid only limited attention to the small but growing field of international organization. That changed dramatically in the wartime years. Indeed, Bunche would spend the remainder of his professional career immersed in the topic of international organizations and their powers and responsibilities.

The focus of the negotiations in the summer of 1944 was over what the Allies were calling the Security Council. Within this body the great powers would cooperate to police the postwar world. At Dumbarton Oaks the role and responsibilities of the Security Council were in fact essentially the sole topic of discussion. The future of colonialism, the topic that most animated Bunche, was left for later meetings. This troubled Bunche, as it troubled others concerned with racial equality around the globe. (As W. E. B. Du Bois wrote of the plans that emerged, "There are those of us who see in the rifts of race many and multiplying causes of war, and therefore scan the proposals made at Dumbarton Oaks with misgiving.")[1]

How the new organization would treat European empires was nonetheless a subject of great, if for the moment muted, contention among the Allies. Looked at today, "the transition from empire to nation in the twentieth century appears inevitable."[2] Yet at the time this transition was hardly clear. Nearly the entire continent of Africa was still under the domination of foreign powers. Much the same was true of parts of Asia and the Pacific. Now, with the war nearing its end, growing movements of national liberation were destined to reshape the globe yet again. Many in Europe, however, still believed empire would and even should be an enduring feature of the postwar world.

Bunche saw the issue of colonial rule as not just one of power. It was also, or even mainly, a question of morality. In a speech in Cleveland, Ohio, six months after Dumbarton Oaks, he declared that the modern world "has come to the realization that there is a great moral issue involved in the perpetuation of colonial systems." That issue, "stated boldly," is whether any people "are morally good enough to rule permanently over another."[3]

\He acknowledged that colonialism had brought change to many non-Western societies. Some of it, he said, was even laudatory. "It cannot be questioned," he argued, that colonization has brought "much progress to the dependent peoples of the Far East."

The problem was that colonialism was wrong. As a result, Bunche thought it would be—indeed, was overdue to be—unwound. Political pressure needed to be brought to bear, but just as important, concrete mechanisms needed to be developed and put in place to assist formerly colonized societies in achieving self-determination. His aim was to create such mechanisms in a way that would both prepare societies for self-governance and ensure accountability in the interim. Having seen during his own research how colonial rule actually worked on the ground, he was uniquely situated to shape—and, as it eventually transpired, to administer—such a system of transition.

Meanwhile, the leading European states resisted the notion that the imperial age was ending. In late 1942, British Prime Minister Winston Churchill famously declared that "I have not become the King's First Minister to preside over the liquidation of the British Empire."[4] (Harlem Congressman Adam Clayton Powell, Jr. would later retort: "We did not fight to make the world safe for Churchill.")[5] Yet Churchill's bombast could not stop the tides of change. Britain ultimately did liquidate its empire, quickly shedding its most prized possession, India, in 1947 and, in the years to follow, nearly all of its remaining colonies. The same was true for France, Belgium, the Netherlands, and other imperial powers. Each of these European empires rapidly disintegrated, leaving only small and usually sunny vestiges—Gibraltar, Bora Bora, St Barts—behind. European colonialism, which had begun centuries before, would come to an end in a few decades.

The demise of empire mostly occurred in the 1950s and 1960s—years when Bunche was at his height of power and influence on the world stage. But the foundation for much of that effort was laid down during the closing months of the war, when the Allies, led by the small State Department team of which he was now a member, drew up the blueprint for a new world organization.

HISTORIANS HAVE LONG DEBATED THE CAUSES of the "Twenty Year's Crisis" between the end of the First World War and the start of the Second.

From 1919 to 1939, trouble broke out around the world, cascading toward chaos, and the fragile peace that followed the Great War crumbled. In a bitter but prophetic take on President Woodrow Wilson's claim that it was the war to end all wars, Alfred Milner, the British colonial secretary, called Wilson's jewel, the Treaty of Versailles, "a peace to end peace."[6] Yet the Treaty of Versailles cannot take all or even most of the blame for the ensuing disorder: this was a world that was in many ways prone to violence, one of empires and subjugation, in which European (and Asian) powers dominated other societies, racial hierarchies were widely accepted, and war was viewed as a legitimate and even valorized tool of nations.

Given this backdrop, and the violence wreaked by the Axis powers, it was not surprising that the fundamental problem facing the planners of the postwar order was aggressive war. Efforts to renounce war had occurred earlier, most famously with the 1928 Kellogg-Briand Pact.[7] In late 1944 the approach was similar, yet expanded: war was to be renounced in the United Nations Charter, but the key innovation, the Security Council, was premised on the great powers policing the globe while protecting their fundamental interests. The notion of a club of great powers was in fact the core, and to a degree even the peel, of the original Allied plan. When in 1941 Churchill and Roosevelt met off the coast of Canada, onboard the *SS Augusta*, Churchill had raised the idea of a postwar, reworked League of Nations–style assembly, and Roosevelt rejected it.[8] Roosevelt preferred something much more dictatorial, led by the Big Three of the UK, US, and Soviet Union.

By 1944, Roosevelt had come around to the idea of a broader, more inclusive international body. A few months before Dumbarton Oaks, with a simple "OK FDR," he had signed off on the proposal for such an organization that had been drawn up in the State Department, titled Plan for the Establishment of an International Organization for the Maintenance of International Peace and Security.[9] Once onboard, the Roosevelt administration took the idea seriously. The US brought over thirty delegates to Dumbarton Oaks to begin the discussions; Ralph Bunche was officially listed as "assistant secretary." He was also the only Black man in the negotiations room, one lavishly festooned with grand artifacts from Europe.

Secretary of State Cordell Hull began the proceedings that day in Washington by declaring that "we meet at a time when the war is moving toward an overwhelming triumph for the forces of freedom." It is our task, he continued, to help lay the foundations "upon which, after victory, peace, freedom, and a growing prosperity may be built."[10] Hull noted nonetheless that the talks they were about to commence were "exploratory and non-committal." Hull sought to create an effective postwar peace organization, but the devil was in the details and he was cautious about setting expectations. To achieve their goal, the US officials believed the organization must rest on a strong commitment from the great powers. As a result, the meetings at Dumbarton Oaks involved only a few governments: at the first session only Britain, the Soviet Union, and the US. In a second phase of the process, China briefly joined the discussions.

At the end of the first day, Bunche walked past the cordon of military police, pistols dangling from their holsters, and left with the other participants out the grand entry gate of the nearly 250-year-old estate. Reporters thronged just outside. Pressed by one to comment on what had transpired inside, Bunche, a junior member of the team not authorized to comment, at first refused. Then he offered a small insight. "Look," he said, "there's a motto in that mansion, carved in marble. *Quod Severis Metes*. As you sow, so shall you reap! You can say we're keeping that motto very much in mind."[11]

The negotiators pressed on over the next weeks. Substantial disagreement arose over matters of membership and voting. These and new rifts would continue to plague the process through to the end of the proceedings. President Roosevelt, meeting with the delegates at the White House, pressed them to try to find common ground. Desperate to break the ice, at one point Edward Stettinius, the under secretary of state, took a number of delegates to New York for a weekend junket. In addition to watching the Rockettes dance at Radio City, the group took in *Dragon Seed*, a war film set in the Pacific theater starring Katherine Hepburn. They then stayed out till 2 a.m. at Billy Rose's Diamond Horseshoe, a former burlesque house turned nightclub famed for its tall showgirls, known as the Long-Stemmed Roses. The next day the presumably sobered-up delegates attended a number of Broadway shows. Tickets, the *New York Herald Tribune* reported, "were 'on

Photo 5.1 Bunche at Dumbarton Oaks

the house,' according to an American delegate, but he wouldn't identify the 'house.' "[12]

Stettinius's effort to use social settings to break down barriers and encourage compromise was in a way an old idea. But Bunche would learn from it, and he used it to his advantage a few years later when negotiating with Arabs and Jews over Palestine. (Bunche subbed in snooker for the showgirls.) In the case of the Dumbarton Oaks meeting, it was not initially clear that Stettinius's gambit helped matters. The Soviets certainly seemed to enjoy the drinks and shows. Yet by late September Russian intransigence—soon to be a running theme in UN affairs—appeared to doom the effort. Bunche, like many participants, was unsure of what would come next. At home, his young daughter Jane asked him one night, "Daddy, what do you do there all day?" He replied "yesterday we played Pass the Buck. Today we played Musical Chairs."[13]

"Pass the Buck" may have seemed apt to Bunche, but the phrase that was on more minds at this juncture was "League of Nations." The *Los Angeles*

Times, in an assessment in late August 1944, reported that "an organization which it may be difficult to distinguish from the League of Nations appears to be shaping up" in the discussions at Dumbarton Oaks.[14] While the newspaper was correct to note the similarity, the new organization being constructed would have some significant differences with its predecessor. The League had lacked a strong inducement for great power participation and also fell down on enforcement. The UN would attempt to rectify that by being far less reticent to acknowledge power and hierarchy. The five biggest powers gained enormous privileges in the proposed Security Council, something that rankled many smaller nations at the later, much larger, planning conference in San Francisco—and, indeed, continues to rankle them today.

At Dumbarton Oaks the delegates focused on how to achieve lasting peace through collective strength. Alongside this overarching concern was another set of topics that, many believed, were formidable obstacles to a more stable global peace. Chief among them was the question of the future of empire. Imperialism had long rested, at least as a matter of justification, on racial distinction and hierarchy. It was this notion that animated many Black intellectuals in the 1940s to increasingly focus on the plight of Africa and the colonial question. And it was that same notion that drove the one non-Western power at Dumbarton Oaks—Chiang Kai-shek's China—to seek to obtain some commitment to racial equality in the planned peace and security organization. China was not the first non-Western state to tackle the issue of race in world politics and to challenge the European belief that they alone set the standard for civilization. Japan had likewise attempted to insert a racial equality clause at the Paris Peace Conference of 1919, to no avail. Aware of Japan's failure, Chiang Kai-shek, in response to Roosevelt's invitation to participate at Dumbarton Oaks, replied that "I am particularly grateful to you and Secretary Hull for the insistence on the necessity of China being represented at the conference." Noting that Asians represented half of humanity, China then put forward an official proposal that the new organization rest on a fundamental principle: "The principle of equality of all states and all races shall be upheld."[15] After backdoor discussions among the Soviet, American, and British foreign offices, however, the Chinese racial equality provision was quietly killed. The notion of racial equality was seen as simply too inflammatory.

Despite its importance to the postwar order, the related question of the future of colonial rule did not end up on the Dumbarton Oaks agenda either. The State Department wanted it to be, and certainly Ralph Bunche hoped it would be. News reports discussed it as a likely topic and even floated the idea—radical at the time, and ultimately not adopted—to have multiple states, rather than just one, act as trustees for existing and future colonial mandates.[16] Bunche strongly believed that the new UN ought to have a robust system of governance and accountability for the colonies of the soon-to-be defeated Axis powers. Colonies needed to be shepherded to self-governance, and not merely allocated to the winners of the war like so many prizes. Ultimately, the system he would help devise would be dubbed "trusteeship."

Trusteeship meant that former Axis colonies would be governed by Allied states, but, like the League's system it was modeled on, only temporarily. They would then be placed on a path to eventual independence. The new UN system, Bunche hoped, might even go further than the League had and ensure that the trust powers were collectively supervised and closely monitored.

But just before the conclave began, Bunche and his team were told the topic of colonial rule would be omitted. His State Department colleague Ben Gerig said bluntly: "we've lost—there is to be no mention of trusteeship."[17] The War and Navy departments—the joint Defense Department had not yet been created—were by this point opposed to any binding provisions on the disposition of captured enemy territories.† Bunche and his colleagues would eventually find a way to satisfy both sides of the American government, however. Indeed, his reply to Gerig, in keeping with his spirit of optimism, was "we've lost the first battle, but not the war." But for the moment, the views of the military establishment prevailed.

---

† The change in name from Department of "War" to "Defense" after the Second World War reflected political shifts in how war was viewed, but also a profound change in how international law treated armed conflict. For centuries, war had been normal and

The source of the military's objection was its goal of lasting security in the Pacific. The Navy was committed to ensuring that the nation would never again experience an attack like the Japanese surprise assault on Pearl Harbor. The many Pacific islands captured from Japan were seen as an essential first line of defense against any future strike from Asia. This was also the origin of a momentous new national security orientation for the US. Rather than retreating behind the oceans, as it had done after the Great War, America would become "forward-deployed," with an unparalleled network of alliances and bases strung across the globe like so many Christmas lights.[18]

Henry Stimson, the secretary of war, agreed with the Navy on the importance of the islands. A Republican whom Roosevelt appointed in a stab at bipartisanship, Stimson argued that the American acquisition of the distant islands did not represent an attempt at colonization or "exploitation." Instead, the US was merely claiming the bases for the defense of the Pacific. To serve such a virtuous purpose, the islands "must belong to the United States with absolute power."[19]

The State Department, taking a broader view, believed a path of independence for all colonies was in America's long-term economic and political interest. Stettinius would later refer to this clash of views as "warfare between the 'Hottentots and Crusaders' in the State Department and 'hard-boiled realists' of the Navy and War Department."[20] Indeed, the State Department—in particular Secretary of State Cordell Hull—was quite anticolonial. Hull, for example, personally wrote a policy memo on France's North African possessions in this period. As Ralph Bunche later described,

> I had thought I was an advanced thinker on colonial questions, but when I sat there and read Mr. Hull's paper, I realized how conservative I was, because this paper was an incitement to rebellion in North Africa. . . . Our job in the committee was to tone down the paper from the Secretary of State himself. That was one of my first assignments in the State Department, and it always struck me as amusing, because

legitimate. After 1945, war was no longer an acceptable tool of statecraft; in pride of place now was "self-defense."

I thought I was going to have to go in there and fight my way; that if you mentioned liberation of peoples you would be very much in the minority.[21]

The internal stalemate between these conflicting views, and perhaps, too, concerns about opening the door to discussions of racial equality, kept the topic of decolonization off the agenda at Dumbarton Oaks. Bunche, showing his facility with the often anodyne language of diplomacy, later detailed in a State Department report that "discussion of this subject was temporarily postponed, however, pending completion of studies of the many complex factors involved."[22] Winston Churchill, his gimlet eye spying an opening, was more blunt: "If the Americans want to take Japanese islands they have conquered, let them do so with our blessing and any form of words that may be agreeable to them."[23]

This impasse meant the issue of how to create a new system to assist overseas colonies in achieving independence was kicked down the road to the much larger, and more significant, postwar planning conference set to start in April 1945 in San Francisco.[‡]

IN JANUARY 1945, RALPH BUNCHE MADE his first major proposal. He prepared a "Draft Secret Memorandum to the President" that argued that the planned postwar organization should have a system of "international trusteeship" for existing League of Nations mandates as well as other territories "which may be detached from enemy states."[24] In this sense he was suggesting a partial continuation of the League approach. But as Bunche knew from his PhD research, the mandates approach did not work well; a new, more focused system was required. Indeed, Bunche's draft memo went further and recommended that "colonial peoples . . . should be given full independence in accordance with a fixed time schedule." These proposals seem fairly anodyne in hindsight, but they arguably entailed overturning centuries of European domination.

[‡] In response to the failure of the Dumbarton Oaks talks to address colonialism, W. E. B. Du Bois organized a "Colonial Conference" in New York City in the spring of 1945. Kwame Nkrumah, future leader of independent Ghana, was among the attendees; Bunche, invited, did not attend.

As Bunche and his colleagues at the State Department drilled down on the emerging plans for the postwar world, the Allied leaders had already sorted out many features of the planned organization. In particular, some absolutely key issues—such as the question of a great power veto on the Security Council—were discussed not only at Dumbarton Oaks but also at the famous summit meeting of Roosevelt, Churchill, and Stalin in Yalta, Crimea, in February 1945.

The idea of the great power veto was twofold: to protect the most vital interests of the great powers and thereby ensure they joined the new organization. The veto was unquestionably and unabashedly exclusive. The question at Yalta was less who would get the veto than what the veto could be used for. Stalin, who sought the strongest possible veto rules, prophetically declared to Churchill and Roosevelt that "the greatest danger is conflict among ourselves."[25] After much discussion, Stalin acceded to a compromise position: a veto on all matters of substance but not on procedure. What this meant was that no permanent member of the Security Council could block *debate*, though they could block *action* by vetoing any resolution put up for a vote. The distinction between substance and process sounded clear, though in practice it could be opaque. (Years later, asked by a diplomat of a small state how to discern the difference, the Soviet representative to the UN replied: "we will tell you.")[26] Yalta was also where the invitations to come to San Francisco were agreed upon and drafted, to the indignation of French leader Charles De Gaulle, who was left out of the process.

The progress at Yalta nonetheless left a number of important topics still to be negotiated. Chief among them was the critical question of how captured colonies and existing empires would be treated. On this issue, which would occupy Bunche for countless hours in the months to come, the traditional European powers would ultimately find themselves simply outmatched by the US and the USSR, two states that saw little advantage in prolonging the imperial age. The phrase "superpower" had only recently come into use by the time of the conference.§ Yet it was rapidly becoming

§ The 1944 book *The Super-Powers* by Columbia professor William T. R. Fox, often credited with popularizing the term, had a subtitle that was rapidly eclipsed by events

clear that the US and the Soviet Union stood far above the rest of the Allies. China, still desperately poor and weak and in the midst of a civil war, was added to the original Big Three at the insistence of the Roosevelt administration, partly because it believed that the huge nation would be supportive of American views on decolonization. France was added later, as a kind of geopolitical lagniappe to a once-great European power. Brazil, to its bitter regret, was briefly considered for permanent membership but was ultimately dropped.[27] Despite these additions to the privileged club at the heart of the new global order, it was clear that the center of political gravity had decisively shifted to the US and the USSR, and the consequences for the world would prove momentous.

In the runup to San Francisco, the British were increasingly wary of American pressure about their empire. They had begun to push back more aggressively on the US, in part by using domestic race relations against it. One British official asked whether the US would seek self-determination for its fifteen million Black citizens. Bunche, who spoke from personal experience, quickly dismissed the comparison:

> There is utterly no connection between the two problems . . . the Negro is an American, and his struggle is directed exclusively toward one objective: the full attainment of his constitutional rights as an American citizen. Unlike the colonial peoples, the American Negro, who is culturally American, has no nationalist and no separatist ambitions.[28]

Though he was right to reject the comparison, "separatist ambitions" among Black Americans were not unknown. Liberia had been settled in the 19th century by free Black Americans, forging a new society on the west coast of Africa. The Jamaican-born Marcus Garvey had espoused a popular version of Black nationalism in the 1920s. Later, in the 1960s, notions of Black separatism, such as that of the Nation of Islam, again became more mainstream.

---

but perhaps underscored how perceptions of British power lagged behind reality. Fox's full title was *The Super-Powers: The United States, Britain, and the Soviet Union— Their Responsibility for Peace.*

Throughout his life Bunche viewed these ideas as folly, indeed a trap. In a 1956 speech, for instance, he referred to the idea of Black nationhood as the "worst perversion of Wilsonian doctrine of self-determination: in the late 20s and 30s, [the] communist party line of 'self-determination for the Negro in the black Belt'" posed the issue as a form of colonial rule. This, he declared, was an "incredible misreading of history."[29] A decade later, his views had not budged: he wrote toward the end of his life that the promise of "an all-black Elysium is, of course, an escapist dream."[30]**

British attempts to equate colonial rule and Jim Crow failed to blunt American pressure over colonialism in 1945. In the decades to follow, however, the Soviets (and others—in particular China) would adopt a similar strategy and berate the US for its domestic racial oppression in order to degrade American standing among newly independent African states. This effort would prove more successful.

In the spring of 1945, three recent and significant changes were most relevant for the future of empire. One was that, as wars often do, the Second World War had reshaped domestic politics, including the issue of racial equality. Two, the idea that Europeans should rule non-Europeans no longer seemed to be the natural, let alone just, order of things. Indeed, after the horrors of Nazism, racialist politics were widely perceived as abhorrent. Last, there were now two superpowers astride the world stage who, for different reasons, believed continued colonialism was against their interests.

The First World War had already proven the power of war to spur political change in European colonies. In British Honduras, for instance, martial law was declared in 1919 after returning war veterans rioted for greater equality at home. "The participation of West Indian Negroes in the war," the colony's governor wrote to London, had given rise to a "strong and

---

** In a handwritten note from the 1960s in his files, Bunche wrote of the rising calls for Black separatism: "What can be said about the complete separation of the races in this country? .... It is an expression of the complete loss of hope and faith in the American society, its promise and its dream of equality and integration, motivated also by animus against whites and a virulent black racism." He then expressed his belief that as long as Black America was economically dependent on white America, no such separation, only a terrible form of apartheid, was truly possible.

dangerous ill-feeling" against white rulers.[31] This experience was a warning. (Indeed, in a report for the OSS in 1942, Bunche had noted that England had tried to avoid the militarization of its colonies as long as possible for this reason.)[32] Yet, faced with an existential threat in Nazi Germany, the colonial powers again reached out to their imperial domain for much-needed manpower. Liberation movements had for decades existed in many colonies; emboldened by the war, they now fought harder than ever for independence. Indeed, in 1946 Bunche would argue that the war had "intensified the nationalist aspirations of most of the colonial peoples."[33] The result was a decisive acceleration of the drive toward colonial freedom by the time of the San Francisco conference—and beyond.

Notions of racial hierarchy, so widespread and unquestioned in the early 20th century and so essential to the colonial project, also seemed wrong to more and more people by 1945, and not just in the colonies themselves. The extreme views of white supremacists such as Lothrop Stoddard were still popular in some quarters. But they were fading as a justification for white rule in Africa and Asia. China may have been outmaneuvered, or simply outgunned, in Dumbarton Oaks, but things were soon to change. In San Francisco, many states outside Europe saw a commitment to racial equality in the proposed UN Charter as not only right, but in their interest. Carlos Romulo of the Philippines,[††] in a speech to the assembled delegations a few months later, declared that "[b]efore this war broke out I toured the Asiatic territories and I learned from the leaders and from the people of the flame of hope that swept the Far East when the Atlantic Charter was made known to the world. Everywhere these people asked the questions: Is the Atlantic Charter also for the Pacific? Is it for one side of the world and not the other? For one race and not for them too?"[34]

This view was growing stronger within the US, too. *One World*, an improbable travelogue and paean to internationalism by the failed 1940 Republican nominee for president, Wendell Wilkie, had been a runaway bestseller in 1943. *One World* supported the basic vision of the United

---

[††] Four of the original members of the UN were not, at the time they joined, fully sovereign: India, the Philippines, Ukraine, and Belarus.

Nations. But Wilkie's book also declared that "[t]he moral atmosphere in which the white race lives is changing." Colonial peoples were "no longer willing to be Eastern slaves for Western profits."[35] Widely read and followed, Wilkie reflected, and fed, an increasingly common viewpoint among Americans—who certainly had their own reasons to want to focus on the racist practices of other nations.

In his memoirs Harry Truman wrote, with exaggeration but with an element of truth, that colonialism "in any form is hateful to Americans." The US fought its own war of liberation against colonialism, and "we shall always regard with sympathy and understanding the desire of people everywhere to be free of colonial bondage." Truman explained further that he hoped that by making the Philippines "as free as we had made Cuba, it would have an effect on British, Dutch, and French policy in their Far Eastern affairs."[36]

Truman's statement reflected the fact that Americans, having largely left their burst of direct empire-building behind in the early 20th century, had begun to embrace the ideology of anti-imperialism with greater fervor. The American public may well have had a principled belief in self-determination and independence. But the US also had economic motives to press for greater decolonization around the world. The 1930s had been a world of beggar-thy-neighbor economic policies and comparatively little free trade. Even at the time, some believed this economic strategy, with its zero-sum mindset, was dangerously prone to war. A prominent British commentator wrote in 1935 that an economically closed empire would "gratuitously create economic causes for war where none need exist."[37] (And, indeed, the US complained about what was sometimes termed Britain's "Closed Door" policy in its African territories.) Nonetheless, imperial preference systems were the dominant approach in the interwar period, and in an insular world without extensive free trade, large empires offered significant advantages. For Britain, for example, it was undoubtedly beneficial to be at the center of a "vast sterling bloc" with a common currency and tariffs.[38] Smaller states, such as Belgium or the Netherlands, likewise had ready and exclusive access to invaluable natural resources via their colonies.

The US now sought to use its overwhelming power to dismantle this economic system: to eliminate preferences, roll back colonialism, and introduce a much more open global order. Such an order would, many believed, promote prosperity. Above all, it would be less prone to armed conflict. Perhaps equally important, it would also favor the most dynamic and successful national economy. In 1945, this was without question the American economy.

That the envisioned postwar order would place America firmly in the driver's seat of a new form of hegemonic power was not lost on either Britain or France. In many ways, the new postwar system simply ushered in a historically unprecedented form of empire, one that was informal but, arguably, nearly as powerful. At Churchill's death in 1965, the prominent British historian John Grigg wrote that, although Churchill hoped to retain the British Empire, he "presided, in fact, over the inauguration of the American empire."[39] Many would come to agree. The postwar US did not control vast far-flung territories the way the British or French had. But by encircling the globe with its military, leading the Western alliance, and dominating the global economy, the US achieved many of the ends of empire without the form.

With both principled and pecuniary reasons to seek to wind down the age of European empire at a moment of American triumph, the views of the US carried substantial weight. The Soviet Union's objections to imperialism were different—the Soviets did not want an open economic order; quite the opposite—but they, too, saw political advantage in dismantling the great European empires. Reducing the wealth and power of the West through decolonization only helped the USSR. Colonialism also drove a welcome wedge through the West, dividing them rather than uniting them. Stalin's domination of Eastern Europe, moreover, was superficially presented as a consortium of like-minded governments. While flimsy, the pretense was sufficient to allow the Soviets to position themselves in the Cold War as champions of colonial liberation.

The two superpowers thus shared a common aim of dismantling colonialism, albeit for different reasons. The key issue was how to achieve that aim and how hard to push it.

———

FRANKLIN DELANO ROOSEVELT DIED IN HIS home in Warm Springs, Georgia, on April 12, 1945, just before the San Francisco talks began. Harry

Truman, now rushed into the presidency, sought to faithfully implement Roosevelt's vision for the United Nations as the San Francisco conference approached. Despite being a Midwesterner of mostly local political experience, Truman was a true believer in the basic concept of global governance. For years, he had carried several stanzas of Lord Tennyson's prophetic "Parliament of Man" poem in his wallet:

> For I dipt into the future, far as human eye could see; Saw the Vision of the world, and all the wonders that would be;
>
> Saw the heavens fill with commerce, argosies of magic sails; Pilots of the purple twilight, dropping down with costly bails;
>
> Heard the heavens fill with shouting, and there rained a ghastly dew; From the nations' airy navies grappling in the central blue;
>
> Far along the world-wide whisper of the southwind rushing warm; With the standards of the people plunging through the thunderstorm;
>
> Till the war-drum throbbed no longer, and the battle-flags were furl'd; In the Parliament of Man, the Federation of the World;
>
> There the common sense of most shall hold a fretful realm in awe; And the kindly earth shall slumber, lapt in universal law.[40]

In short, Truman was already committed to the vision of a peace organization before he became president. And now he was willing to use America's unprecedented power to achieve it. In an address to Congress shortly after Roosevelt's death, Truman called upon Americans, "regardless of party, race, creed or color," to support the efforts to build a strong and lasting United Nations.[41]

On April 18, 1945, Bunche and many other members of the large American delegation headed west by special train. They embarked on a four-day nonstop journey to San Francisco—the first-ever, coast-to-coast nonstop train in American history. The State Department had requisitioned the train, one among many, to carry foreign delegations, reporters, and others to the West Coast—partly, it appeared, as a strategy to make clear just how big the United States really was.[42] The timing of the San Francisco conference proved propitious. Germany was near defeat; the Allied forces were closing in on Japan, and President Harry Truman was weighing an invasion—or the use of a shocking new secret weapon (so secret that even he himself had only learned of it upon assuming the presidency) that was soon to be tested at the Alamogordo Bombing and Gunnery Range in New Mexico. While the path to victory was still to be determined, victory itself was nearly at hand.

Aboard the train, which stopped in Los Angeles and briefly allowed Bunche to see his family, the State Department team worked vigorously on the planned UN Charter text.[43] The US was not only the host of the conference; it was also in many ways the agenda-setter. From the runup to Dumbarton Oaks onward, American officials had drafted the key provisions. Bunche's role—he had just been named head of the Division of Dependent Area Affairs at State—was particularly important at this juncture, given how prior talks had almost entirely sidestepped the question of colonialism.

The looming colonial question at San Francisco drew the attention of the Black press. The *New York Amsterdam News* reported, under the headline "Race Issue Raised at Frisco," that W. E. B. Du Bois, Mary McLeod Bethune, and other Black intellectuals and luminaries were attending the UN parley. Through this conference, the paper quoted McLeod Bethune as saying, "the Negro becomes closely allied with all the darker races of the world, but more importantly he becomes integrated into the structure of the peace and freedom of all the people, everywhere."[44] McLeod Bethune was echoing an important view of the time, that racial oppression was a global phenomenon that ought to be tackled via global forums. This was a view Bunche had long held as well. While he had harangued the Black community at times for what he saw as its overly insular focus, now, in San Francisco, he was pleased to see so many civil rights organizations and leaders engaging with the UN effort.

Meanwhile, on the train to the conference, Bunche strategized with colleagues about how to move toward a postwar world of African and Asian independence. It was exciting to be participating in this effort, and at this crucial juncture in history, it afforded him an unusual opportunity to apply many of the ideas that had been percolating in his scholarship and thinking for years. Ever pragmatic, he knew that liberation for the hundreds of millions of people living under colonial rule was not coming fast. Nor did he necessarily believe all these societies were ready to rule themselves ably. The key, he would come to believe, was that the international community serve as a bridge to modernity. With the assistance of what would become the UN, these new states would gain expertise, aid, and legitimacy. While at the San Francisco conference, he would have the opportunity to push this principle forward and, if he was successful, develop mechanisms that would prod and propel the inevitable process of independence.

Bunche was of course just one member of a big team, dominated by an array of often outsized personalities. The delegation was led by Edward Stettinius, now the secretary of state. Stettinius was a former General Motors executive from Chicago who first entered government service in 1939. He was new in the role of secretary when the UN talks started. Just months before, Cordell Hull had retired, and Stettinius was unexpectedly elevated.[‡‡] A few years older than Bunche, Stettinius had mainly handled economic issues, such as the Lend-Lease Program that aided Britain in the early days of the war, before joining the State Department. Bunche was not impressed. In a letter home to his wife he was unsparing in his assessment: "Stettinius is a complete dud, whatever the press may say about him. He is simply in a job for which he has utterly no qualifications and about which he knows nothing."[45] Along as well were a few future legends of American foreign policy, like John Foster Dulles and Averell Harriman, and some lesser known but highly influential staffers, such as Leo Pasvolsky, a rotund, bespectacled man who knew more about the draft UN Charter— largely because he had helped to draft it—than anyone else on the planet. The unassuming Pasvolsky was a marked contrast to the far more glamorous Stettinius, who *Time Magazine* called "impressively handsome."[46]

In a shrewd gesture to the experience of Woodrow Wilson and the League of Nations a generation before, Roosevelt had also included some important members of Congress in the delegation, whose disposition back on Capitol Hill would make or break the entire effort. In particular,

---

[‡‡] Hull was and remains the longest serving secretary of state in American history and would win the Nobel Peace Prize in 1945 for his efforts to create the United Nations.

Roosevelt had invited Senator Arthur Vandenberg, a professorial-looking but powerful Republican and a long-time isolationist, to join the effort. Vandenberg had a unique credibility on the issues at stake in San Francisco. In a dramatic and influential speech on the Senate floor, given just months before the conference opened, Vandenberg had effectively renounced his formerly avowed isolationism:

> I have always been frankly one of those who has believed in our own self-reliance. I still believe that we can never again—regardless of collaborations—allow our national defense to deteriorate to anything like a point of impotence.
>
> But I do not believe that any nation hereafter can immunize itself by its own exclusive action. Since Pearl Harbor, World War II has put the gory science of mass murder into new and sinister perspective. Our oceans have ceased to be moats which automatically protect our ramparts. Flesh and blood now compete unequally with winged steel. War has become an all-consuming juggernaut. If World War III ever unhappily arrives, it will open new laboratories of death too horrible to contemplate.
>
> I propose to do everything within my power to keep those laboratories closed for keeps. I want maximum American cooperation, consistent with legitimate American self-interest, with constitutional process and with collateral events which warrant it, to make the basic idea of Dumbarton Oaks succeed. I want a new dignity and a new authority for international law. I think American self-interest requires it.[47]

Our oceans have ceased to be moats which automatically protect our ramparts. In a sentence, Senator Vandenberg encapsulated the new reality that he and so many Americans felt—and the reason that Roosevelt, and then Truman, put so much effort into creating the UN even as the war continued. The result would not only be a new organization of all the world's powers. It would also be a new US: one with an unquestioned position of hegemony and leadership in the West. Vandenberg's strong support was absolutely critical to Roosevelt's plan for the postwar order, since the Senate, of which Vandenberg was a central player, was absolutely critical to approving American participation. To be sure, the prospects on Capitol Hill looked good in the spring of 1945. The basic notion of a postwar international security organization was very popular: some 80 percent of Americans supported the Dumbarton Oaks blueprint.[48]

Ralph Bunche, too, had long been committed to this vision of international organization. While still a student at UCLA he had given a speech, now almost two decades old, titled "That Man May Dwell in Peace." In it, the young Bunche, who had been a teenager as the First World War ended, spoke of the need for permanent peace. But, he had asked his audience, how may such peace be best attained? After considering the various options— treaties, leagues, and so forth—he had argued that they were all insufficient, that something more profound was needed. "The proposal which I would present as an antidote for world 'war-poisoning' is centered about two basic principles, essential, I believe, to any rational peace plan. These are International Organization, involving every nation of the world; and the full development of the 'International Mind or Will.'"[49]

While the idea of an international mind or will never really took root— nor was it especially clear what Bunche meant at the time—the first principle, that of a truly universal international organization, was now about to reach fruition.

CHAPTER 6

SAN FRANCISCO

We fully realize today that victory in war requires a mighty united effort.
Certainly, victory in peace calls for, and must receive, an equal effort.
—President Harry Truman, address to the United Nations Conference on
International Organization, April 25, 1945

The San Francisco negotiations opened on a rainy April day in the grand Beaux-Arts opera house downtown, with its huge entrance hall and beautifully barreled, coffered ceiling. The assembled delegates, from some fifty nations, noted President Franklin Delano Roosevelt's recent death with a minute of silence, but the schedule did not change. All the participants worked with intensity. Even the surrender of a devastated Germany on May 7, 1945, only received another brief minute of silence before the negotiations resumed.

The delegates at the conference came from all over the globe, ranging from Belarus to Belgium to Bolivia. All major regions of the world were represented, though only three states were from Africa: Ethiopia, Liberia, and South Africa. From Asia were China, India, and the Philippines.* Of the

---

* The Middle Eastern participants in San Francisco—Egypt, Iran, Lebanon, Syria, Saudi Arabia, and Turkey—could technically be counted as Asian or African, or even European in the case of Turkey; but then, as now, they are generally seen as composing a politically distinct region.

Asian nations present, only China, in the midst of a civil war with a communist insurgency led by a charismatic rural leader named Mao Zedong, was in fact an independent state in April 1945 when the proceedings opened in San Francisco. The Philippines was still an American colony; the islands became independent a year later, in July 1946. India likewise was still under British rule when the talks began, though its participation was predicated on looming independence. During the darker days of the war, desperate to shore up imperial support, Winston Churchill had promised India it would become a "dominion," a status, previously enjoyed by white settler communities such as Canada, which entailed independence and free association in the "commonwealth of nations." Two years after the signing of the United Nations Charter, India would undergo a violent partition. It emerged as two states, India and Pakistan, joined in an enmity substantial enough that the UN would, at times under Ralph Bunche's watchful eye, be forced to patrol key parts of the border between them for decades. The remainder of the world was still under the colonial yoke of the European powers or, as with Germany and Japan, were treated as "enemy states."

San Francisco was a huge event: over 3500 delegates and advisors from nearly fifty nations, many private organizations lobbying for this or that cause or provision, and several thousand journalists to cover the proceedings. A far cry from the quiet, intimate diplomacy of Dumbarton Oaks, the conference was intended not only to be a negotiating forum but also a coming out party for the new world organization that was virtually guaranteed to emerge at the end of the conclave. The negotiations were on a scale that had never been seen before in foreign affairs. The closest analogue, the Paris Peace talks of 1919, had been far smaller. The mix of nations, private interest groups, and foreign and domestic media was unprecedented as well. This was the future of diplomacy, not the past: multilateral and multilingual, with a wide and diverse array of actors weighing in. On average, the participants consumed a staggering half a million sheets of paper a day.[1]

The conference drew attention from all quarters of life. An amazing array of midcentury figures were in attendance. Among the journalists—which numbered almost 2500—were heavyweights such as Walter Lippmann and James Reston, but also a young Navy veteran named John F. Kennedy.

It even attracted Hollywood stars and entertainment figures, from Rita Hayworth and Orson Welles to Paul Robeson. Among the interpreters was Isaiah Berlin, who would go on to become one of the leading philosophers of the 20th century. Officially called the United Nations Conference on International Organization, it lasted over two months. Ralph Bunche called it "the hardest working conference I have ever attended."[2]

FRANKLIN DELANO ROOSEVELT HAD MADE THE creation of the United Nations his overriding focus toward the end of the life. He feared that once the war ended Americans would quickly forget the horror and lose interest in a new postwar system.[†] The United States, by this point wholly committed to the outcome, spared no effort to ensure success. The State Department distributed over 1 million copies of the basic UN proposal around the nation in advance of the opening of the conference in April. Nearly thirty governors declared the week before San Francisco "Dumbarton Oaks Week."[3]

Many Americans—and others around the world—were riveted by the proceedings in the California city, which began on April 25, 1945. (Bunche, revealing the sad state of racial diversity at the conference, wrote to Ruth after the first day's opening event: "I did feel a bit proud this afternoon at being the only Negro who sat on the first floor."[4]) ABC even offered a number of radio broadcasts discussing the negotiations for interested listeners. One of the commentators was James Shotwell, a Columbia University professor whose 1944 book proposing a UN-like body, *The Great Decision*, sold half a million copies and introduced the American public to the proposed organization. (Shotwell optimistically argued that, with the right approach to a postwar body, the Allies could enjoy victory not only over the Axis "but over war itself.")[5]

Major newspapers offered extensive and generally supportive coverage of the proceedings. The *Washington Post*, for example, reported early on that already "the most dangerous 'banana peels' have been swept away" by the

---

[†] *The New York Times* on April 29, 1945, bemoaned the fact that the late President Roosevelt drew all the attention in San Francisco; "But has the world so soon forgotten Woodrow Wilson?" "It would not be hard to call this ingratitude," the *Times* continued.

assembled delegates in California. *The Christian Science Monitor* argued that the conference was fleetly moving toward success and, identifying a key political vulnerability to be avoided, declared that "the significant fact is that the political errors of Versailles are not being repeated at San Francisco."[6] It was certainly accurate that San Francisco was not Versailles. And the sense of optimism there, while at times perhaps unwarranted, was bolstered by the fact that the key powers had already decided some of the most significant issues at Yalta and Dumbarton Oaks.

Bunche found the pace of the conference unrelenting—to Ruth he wrote "Stettinius is driving us at a terrific pace"—yet also exhilarating and fascinating.[7] It was a crash course in global diplomacy. Participating in the conference also accelerated his growing national profile. While he had occasionally appeared in the public eye before—his 1927 graduation photo from UCLA, for instance, had been published in *The Crisis*, the magazine of the NAACP—he was relatively unknown to the wider public at this time. With San Francisco as a focal point, the Black press began to run more frequent quotes by Bunche, and he became an important source for many Black reporters. Several Black papers ran profiles;[‡] the *New Journal and Guide*, for instance, under the title "Dr Ralph Bunche Advanced in State Department on Rare Merit," noted that he had risen with rapidity in the government since leaving Howard University and was "one of the best prepared authorities" in San Francisco.[8] The *New York Amsterdam News* similarly covered his upbringing, Howard years, OSS work, and State Department duties—the last deemed to be so little known to most readers that the paper described what the State Department did, noting that he was now "in the inner circle of policy-makers." Edward Stettinius, the secretary of state, was quoted describing Bunche as "our top man on colonial and African affairs."[9]

The delegates in San Francisco debated issues large and small, but the struggle over the Security Council was the most intense. This body would be able to make—and alter—international law with its decisions. Would

---

[‡] The *Afro-American* even ran a profile of Ruth Bunche, under the title *Meet the Missus.* "Even though my days and evenings are filled to capacity," she told the reporter, "I still find time to be interested in my husband's work and often read and correct some of his material."

the Big Five powers, each of which would have a permanent seat on the Council, also be able to veto any decision they chose? Small states naturally fought to limit the veto. But the great powers, with the League's failures in living memory, had made up their minds before the conference even began. At its core, the question of the veto was really a question of whether the new organization would be one of sovereign equals, or instead one that granted the great powers extraordinary privileges and power. It was, in a nutshell, about hierarchy versus equality.

From one vantage point, the design of the Security Council arrogated overwhelming powers to the biggest states—and legitimated, and preserved, those powers by building them into a standing international organization. This was the view, for instance, of prominent Yale law professor Edwin Borchard, who called the new UN "a thinly disguised military alliance of the three largest powers."[10] From another perspective, the notion of a Security Council with voting was a substantial improvement over the alternative, which the world had just witnessed. Indeed, during the war Churchill and Stalin at one point sat down over a map to sketch out potential spheres of influence in Eastern Europe. "Let us burn this paper," Churchill told Stalin as they wrapped up the meeting. "No, you keep it," Stalin replied.[11] Compared to this more traditional approach, a veto for great powers seemed a reasonable accommodation—one that reflected the reality of power, yet thankfully smoothed a bit of its often very rough edges.

Still, the small powers fought hard to rein in the privileges of the great powers. As the debate drew to a close, Senator Tom Connolly of Texas, another American delegate, grew frustrated. He theatrically declared, "you may go home from San Francisco, if you wish, and report that you have defeated the veto.... But you can also say, 'We tore up the Charter.'" Connolly then lifted up a copy of the draft UN Charter, literally tore it up, and threw the shreds of paper on the table before him.[12] The veto remained intact.

NEXT TO THE VETO, DECOLONIZATION AND trusteeship were, in Bunche's opinion, the "the star subject" at the San Francisco conference.[13] (A bit of hyperbole, perhaps, but the contrasts in view among the key players were certainly stark.) The basic contours of this issue had also been decided

Photo 6.1 Stettinius meeting with world leaders in San Francisco

beforehand but in a more cursory way. At Yalta, Roosevelt, Stalin, and Churchill had broadly agreed on the need to replace the League system of mandates. But exactly how they would do so was still to be determined.[14]

This gave Bunche an opening, and he quickly set to work. His immediate boss, Harold Stassen, was a rising political star from Minnesota who, reflecting the bipartisan cast of the American delegation, had sought the Republican nomination for president in 1944. (Stassen would famously go on to seek the nomination eight more times, right up until 1992—and never succeed.) Vaguely resembling Dwight D. Eisenhower, Stassen was a Navy veteran and, in Bunche's assessment, "an easy person to work with, provided you don't mind working."[15]

In the runup to San Francisco, Britain and France had spent considerable time strategizing about how to defang whatever colonial system Bunche and his team might devise. France, which had been excluded from Yalta, was particularly concerned. Two months before the opening of the conference, the French representative in Moscow asked the Soviet foreign minister, Vyacheslav Molotov, to assure him that French colonies were in no danger.[16] Molotov directed him to Washington, saying that the Truman administration was taking the lead on colonialism and no firm plans had yet been decided. France's head of the delegation to San Francisco, Georges Bidault, instructed his team that France would reject any plan to assert international control "over all or part of her colonial empire." To the Greek ambassador he said that US plans for a trusteeship system reflected America's selfish political and economic interests.[17] France, humiliated by Germany's military in the war, was eager to regain grandeur through its imperial prowess and deeply feared the Americans and their colonial plans.

The French concerns were known to the American delegation in part because the US military was spying on the foreign delegations in San Francisco. Thanks to an early version of National Security Agency eavesdropping—quite literally, in that the NSA's predecessor, the Army Signal Security Agency, had set up shop at the large Presidio base just a few miles from the meeting site to intercept diplomatic cables and phone calls—Stettinius and his team knew in advance many of the objections, alliances, and stratagems other nations were planning at the conference.[18] American spying did not end there. The FBI, tasked with investigating many of the private groups gathering in San Francisco, was especially attentive to those who sought to push the new UN to take a strong stance on racism, perhaps in the guise of anticolonialism. A particular focus was the New York City–based Council on African Affairs, an organization devoted to promoting Pan-Africanism and political liberation. Black Americans had become more deeply interested in Africa and African colonialism in the 1930s and 1940s. As Walter White of the NAACP noted at the time, "World War II has given the Negro a sense of kinship with other colored—and also oppressed—peoples of the world ... the struggle of the Negro in the United States is part and parcel of the struggle against imperialism and exploitation" around the globe.[19]

The Council on African Affairs reflected this new focus and brought together the internationally oriented Black elite of the day: its chairman was Paul Robeson, whom Ralph Bunche knew well from his days in London, and its vice chair was W. E. B. Du Bois, another familiar face. Among its other founders was Bunche himself. There is no evidence that he was aware of the FBI's spying on the Council, and he had moved on from the organization years earlier. But the FBI expressed substantial interest in how the group might attempt to influence the negotiation of the new UN Charter. The State Department had also been following the debate over colonialism within Black intellectual circles for some time. A 1944 report noted with concern that "leading Negro journals like *The Crisis*," the NAACP's magazine, long run by DuBois, "conduct a perpetual and bitter campaign against 'white imperialism.' "[20]

The FBI was also interested in the efforts of the National Negro Council, which Bunche had also founded years earlier but had resigned from over concerns with its increasing ties to communism. Max Yergan, whom Bunche had met in London, was an avowed communist and NNC leader who came to San Francisco. While there, Bunche discovered that Yergen had implicated him to the FBI in an effort to assist the Soviets in the negotiations. Bunche was furious and "railed that Yergan was nothing but a 'phoney' and a 'slicker who was milking nice old Quaker ladies for money.' "[21] Bunche was beginning to see his more radical past as more a danger than a source of pride. Quickly seeking to distance himself from Yergan, he refused to give Yergan access to the main parts of the San Francisco negotiations.

The FBI's concerns were additional signs that the push for decolonization was unevenly felt within the American government. From a geopolitical perspective, decolonization was good; from a domestic perspective, many members of the American government were unsure and fearful of the repercussions for segregation and discrimination and did not like the apparent ties to communism at all. The linkage between race-based rule abroad and white supremacy at home yielded intense politics. So, too, did the linkage between the more robust internationalism, as represented by the planned UN organization, and national sovereignty. Indeed, in years to come, conservatives in the US would resist the very notion of binding human rights treaties largely on this basis.

Against this backdrop of varied political pressures and swirling rumors and tactics, Bunche sought to forge a set of provisions about colonies that were ambitious and yet politically workable. Interested parties, such as

Du Bois, quickly recognized that Bunche was their key interlocutor in the American delegation. His years at Howard and his work with organizations such as the NAACP meant he was a well-known figure to the Black intelligentsia. As the only high-ranking Black official of the State Department, he was in a unique position to shape an issue that many believed was crucial. To Bunche, Du Bois transmitted language that he hoped to see appear in the UN Charter and that was "tantamount to an obituary for the British and French empires."[22] In an attempt to provide more ammunition, Du Bois also published a book during the conference, titled *Color and Democracy*, with the subtitle "Colonies and Peace" and an arresting aphorism: "Colonies are the slums of the world."

Other forces, however, pushed in the opposite direction. Historian Mark Mazower has argued that the UN's postwar embrace of anticolonialism "has tended to obscure the fact that like the League it was a product of empire and indeed, at least at the outset, regarded by those with colonies to keep as a more than adequate mechanism for its defense."[23] Many drafters of the UN Charter, such as Jan Smuts from South Africa, who was one of the most influential participants, firmly believed in the basic logic of empire and its foundation in racial inequality. To men like Smuts, ending fascism was one thing; ending imperialism was another. Du Bois pithily summarized the situation, commenting that "we have conquered Germany, but not their ideas."[24] (Earlier, Du Bois's sometime foe at the NAACP, Walter White, had argued that the "plain bitter truth" was that there was a powerful element at home that had "practiced Nazism long before Hitler was born.")[25] Both men had a point, yet in fact those ideas were steadily losing their political appeal, much to the consternation—and even amazement—of many European colonialists.

How to encourage this emerging trend toward self-determination was Ralph Bunche's overriding obsession. The outlines of the UN Charter made clear that territorial gains via aggressive war would no longer be permitted under international law. This meant the future expansion of imperialism was unlikely. Tearing down *existing* empires was another matter, however. It was wholly unrealistic to expect any system decided in San Francisco to guarantee the dismantling of the existing empires. But creating a process of trusteeship that would move some colonies toward independence would tend to discredit some of the arguments commonly given in support of colonialism, in turn facilitating and propelling forward the gradual unwinding of empire generally. Most importantly, the UN itself would provide a global forum for the expression of the basic principle of self-rule. It would provide the legitimacy of the UN—huge at this point in history—to the idea of freedom for all peoples.

The rough text of the trusteeship provisions Bunche, Stassen, and the others had compiled in San Francisco comprised over 400 pages. One of Bunche's main tasks was to distill down these varied proposals to a coherent and concise package that the delegates could digest.[26] This package would have to work with the existing League system of mandates and yet extend and strengthen the process of moving former colonies toward self-governance. Bunche quickly became the key figure in the process. Not only did he know more about mandates than anyone else; as one of the Chinese delegates later remarked, he "was the fastest draftsman I'd ever seen. He would listen to a discussion, no matter how complicated, and right away he would make a draft of it—adding his own ideas, which were always very good."[27] Bunche was coming to see the process of policymaking, with its give and take, stratagems and feints, and need for analytically grounded, pragmatic solutions as perhaps even more fascinating and suited to his skills and interests than academic life had ever been.

Within the American delegation, Bunche generally pushed for stronger language in the Charter, including overtly listing "independence" as a goal of the trusteeship process, something Harold Stassen resisted.[28] Indeed, for all its rhetoric about decolonization and equality, the American delegation at times backed its imperialist allies against efforts to make the UN Charter even stronger. When Ecuador, for instance, proposed that a 2/3 vote of UN member states in favor could lead to independence for a colonial territory, the proposal went nowhere.[29]

The final treaty text on colonies is dry and a bit opaque. It is not a radical rewrite of the League's system, nor a repudiation of empire generally. Yet read carefully, it makes clear that support for colonial rule was wilting. First, Chapter XI, which Bunche helped draft, addresses "non-self-governing territories." This was intended to be a sweeping provision that would cover all colonies, whether trust territory or not. States that have responsibility for such territories are required to, among other things, help them "develop self-government, to take due account of the political aspirations of the peoples, and to assist them in the progressive development of their free political institutions." The trusteeship system, covered in Chapter XII, was more detailed:

> The basic objectives of the trusteeship system . . . shall be:
> a. to further international peace and security;
> b. to promote the political, economic, social, and educational advancement of the inhabitants of the trust territories, and their progressive development towards self-government or independence. . . .
> c. to encourage respect for human rights and for fundamental freedoms for all without distinction as to race, sex, language, or religion, and to encourage recognition of the interdependence of the peoples of the world;

These principles, often declared in the past as universal but rarely so applied, set the stage. The trusteeship system then distinguished three categories of territories: former League mandates, such as Palestine; colonies of the "enemy states" defeated in the war; and territories "voluntarily placed under the system by states responsible for their administration"—that is, added to the system by the colonial powers. These trust territories would eventually include Togoland, the French mandate Bunche had studied in the 1930s.

Each trust territory would be subject to an agreement placing it under the trusteeship system, to be negotiated with the new Trusteeship Council. This agreement reflected the internationalizing of trusteeship that Bunche and others sought. (As he later pointed out to a reporter, this was especially true for former League mandates: the mandatory power "is but one of the states directly concerned" with the future status of these territories, which already had an international status simply due to their inclusion in the system of mandates.)[30] To solve the problem of the Pacific islands, the Navy and War departments insisted on a concept of "strategic trusts."

For an area designated as strategic, all agreements went instead before the Security Council, where the US wielded a veto over any decision. In this way, the American delegation protected its ability to retain key overseas territories—but at a price: now any other Big Five power, including Britain and France, could do the same. This clever solution saved the trusteeship debate from an uncertain end.

The Trusteeship Council, operating on a one nation–one vote system with no vetoes, would have jurisdiction over ordinary trust territories. The Trusteeship Council would have novel powers: the ability to visit the colonial territories in question, receive petitions from locals, and consider reports from the governing state. The petition process gave agency to local populations, something Bunche believed was essential. He considered the reporting system particularly useful because it forced the supervising state to explain its actions in the trust territory. His experiences in French West Africa had suggested that reporting under the League was often bogus. But Bunche hoped that a newly revamped system, with more intrusive review, would work much better. As he explained to a reporter, the UN Charter provisions spelled out the functions of governments far more specifically than the mandate system ever did and provided flexibilities that were "entirely lacking" before.[31] Moreover, he said, in Chapter XI the Charter provided "a unique statement" in international agreements since it applied to "all dependent territories," not just those taken from vanquished foes. Under Chapter XI, all colonial states had to report on the conditions in their colonies.

The reporting provision, as one later analysis put it, was the "most seemingly benign element" of the new system.[32] Yet it proved to be deceptively potent. Reporting soon became the subject of some of the most acrimonious debates in the UN, and the committee created to receive the reports became an important battleground over the future of empire. Bunche's instinct, born of his early research, was correct: reporting and review could at times be quite effective. He had managed to fruitfully apply his academic expertise to create a concrete and ultimately meaningful change.

Yet it was also true that the UN Charter expressly carved out a domain free from UN scrutiny: Article 2(7) of the Charter stated that nothing in the text authorized the UN to intervene in matters that were "essentially within the domestic jurisdiction" of any state. Much of the debate in the earlier years of the UN over colonialism circled around the tension, or conflict, between these twin provisions. Many colonial powers argued that their ordinary colonies—that is, nontrusteeship colonies—were matters of domestic concern that the Charter explicitly left in their control. The result was a process that, to be sure, left much colonial rule intact. Yet in forcing European states to justify their continuing rule over foreign peoples, the Charter system allowed liberation movements and local political leaders to make claims and challenge practices before the world's premier international body. This gave an important voice to many such groups. And it permitted a level of scrutiny over foreign rule that, while certainly building on the League system, had never before existed.

Despite its many weaknesses Bunche was proud of this system. He placed a copy of a diagram, showing the Trusteeship Council as a co-equal branch of the UN, in his suitcase to show his children when he got home. To his wife he wrote, "Stassen, Gerig and I received full credit for winning the toughest fight of the conference. We have a Trusteeship Chapter in this Charter, though many thought it could never be pulled off." It was, moreover, "a thrill even for your blasé old hubby to see his own writing in it—writing over which he struggled for long, long hours."[33] Bunche was excited about the chance to be part of the creation of the UN and sensed that his work there was more impactful than any he had done previously. Adding to his sense of satisfaction was the fact that it combined his academic expertise, forged over long periods of fieldwork and scholarship, with his political commitments to democracy. He acknowledged that international "machinery and principles, no matter how perfect, are not enough." But he felt the UN Charter resulted in an unparalleled opportunity for colonized peoples to realize "their true aspirations" and to exert an effective voice in shaping their future.[34]

Still, not everyone thought the new UN Charter system marked the advance Bunche thought it was. One African journalist even declared of the Charter that "new life has been infused into predatory imperialism." Rayford Logan, a Howard colleague, went so far as to call the Charter a "tragic joke."[35] It was true that the Charter, having been agreed to by the colonial powers, had been shaped with the goal (for some) of keeping colonialism alive—or at least on life support. Yet these views turned out to be overly pessimistic: trusteeship was not a joke, and the decolonization movement ultimately achieved "almost unbelievable successes" in the postwar era.[36] Indeed, the UN quickly became the political space where "imperialism and internationalism coalesced."[37] Soon, dozens of former colonies would gain independence and, sometimes as their very first act, seek membership in the UN.

This transformation was not always easy, however. In a speech he delivered in Nashville in 1956, shortly before Ghana's independence from Britain kicked off a huge wave of African liberation, Bunche noted what he termed the "UN Dilemma": "internationalism vs the encouragement to *new* nationalisms."[38] Here Bunche was identifying an important tension, one he had recognized as early as 1946. Throwing off colonial rule entailed the creation of new nations. Yet the spirit of the UN, as well as the need for international cooperation, required more globalism. To square this circle required careful guidance and a commitment to multilateral collaboration on the part of the new nations. Bunche believed the UN could provide the necessary guidance. As he had surmised as far back as the 1930s, Africa in particular became a sort of blank slate for this new model of statehood: an entire continent "launched on the road to cooperative success" by new leaders with the help and advice of the UN.[39] In the decades to come, this idea would be put to the test.

Decolonization in the years after San Francisco emerged alongside another critical development, that of individual human rights. Rather than the rights one enjoyed because of a national constitution or because of an ethnic identity, human rights transcended borders and protected all persons, everywhere. That was the tragic lesson of Nazi Germany: the older system of national sovereignty had permitted and arguably even enabled a horrific, stunning genocide to take place. The Nuremberg trials of Nazi war criminals helped to establish the principle that no longer could a state do what it wanted behind its borders, using its sovereignty as a shield. In different ways, the 1948 Universal Declaration of Human Rights, and the contemporaneous Convention on the Prevention and Punishment of the Crime of Genocide, were meant to enshrine that concept in international law.§

The world began to unevenly connect the new language of human rights to the battle for sovereignty. The UN Charter itself, in its very first article, notes the principle of equal rights and self-determination of peoples. The Charter also stresses the importance of promoting respect for human rights and for "fundamental freedoms for all without distinction as to race, sex, language or religion" (in short, a delayed victory for China). The Universal Declaration of Human Rights, passed by the General Assembly in 1948, extended these ideas, and laid out in a revolutionary fashion the basic freedoms every human being enjoyed. While it focused on individual rights—in contrast with the League's earlier, prewar rights system, which was more concerned with group or "minority" rights, and whose group-based approach was echoed in the postwar Genocide Convention—the Universal Declaration also spoke to questions of political rule. As the Declaration stated, "the will of the people shall be the basis of the authority of government; this will shall be expressed in periodic and genuine elections which shall be by universal and equal suffrage."[40]

While general and not easily enforced, these principles were also clearly in tension with colonial rule. As Bunche later noted approvingly, the international community was exhibiting a new concern for the "rights and dignity of individual" that had been spearheaded by the UN.[41] This concern made it increasingly difficult for proponents of empire, such as Winston Churchill, to maintain the fight, and increasingly easier, as Ghanian president and Pan-African leader Kwame Nkrumah later declared, for "all the fair brave words spoken about freedom that had been broadcast to the four corners of the earth" to take seed and grow "where they had not been intended."[42]

IN SAN FRANCISCO'S VETERANS WAR MEMORIAL BUILDING, seated alone at a very large, light-colored, and perfectly round table, Edward Stettinius

---

§ "Genocide" was a new word, though the act—the intentional killing of a group, with the aim to exterminate—was certainly not. The invention of a Jewish international signed the accord creating the new United Nations. President Truman, who had come all the way to San Francisco for the occasion, stood to his right, dressed in a dark double-breasted suit and gazing up at the gallery. Flags of the fifty nations present surrounded the stark table in a large semicircle, and behind that table were heavy dark curtains. Pen in hand, each foreign minister or leader took turns seated at the table. Members of the national delegations typically stood behind the signer respectfully observing. From the gallery, with a huge chandelier overhead, others watched the solemn proceedings.

On June 26, 1945, the day the UN Charter was signed, the Second World War was not yet over in the Pacific Theater. In six weeks the first atomic bomb would be dropped on Hiroshima. (In a twist of fate, the uranium used for the bomb came from mines in the Belgian Congo province of Katanga—a place that would consume Ralph Bunche's attention for years.) Hiroshima's devastation shocked the world. But it did not elicit surrender from Japan. Shortly after the bomb detonated, Truman, in his plainspoken, matter-of-fact style—a marked contrast to the elegant Roosevelt, whose mid-Atlantic accent and dramatic delivery had glued Americans to their radios for years—made a bold declaration: "The Japanese began the war from the air at Pearl Harbor. They have been repaid many fold. And the end is not yet. . . . If they do not now accept our terms they may expect a rain of ruin from the air, the like of which has never been seen on this earth."[43]

Three days after Truman's "rain of ruin" speech, a second atomic bomb incinerated much of Nagasaki. Hours before the Soviet Union had finally declared war on Japan. Truman waited. Then on August 15, 1945, at high noon, the Japanese people heard over the radio something almost none of them had ever heard before: the voice of the Emperor of Japan.

Speaking in a classical and rarely used form of Japanese, it was not easy for his listeners to follow Hirohito's words. He spoke elliptically, indirectly. But the ultimate message of surrender was comprehended. "Despite the best that has been done by everyone, the war situation has developed not

---

lawyer from Poland named Rafael Lemkin, who lost dozens of family members in the Holocaust, genocide became one of the signature international crimes of the postwar era, along with war crimes, crimes against humanity, and slavery.

necessarily to Japan's advantage," the Emperor said. Moreover, "the enemy has begun to deploy a new and most cruel bomb." Japan would accept the Allied terms of surrender, which were unconditional, bringing history's bloodiest war to a close.

The formal instrument of surrender was signed some two weeks later aboard the USS *Missouri*, anchored in Tokyo Bay.** Hundreds of American soldiers and sailors lined the decks to watch Foreign Minister Mamoru Shigemitsu, wearing a top hat and suit, walk to the small desk where the surrender document lay. At 9:04 local time, Shigemitsu signed the surrender document on behalf of Japan. Accepting the surrender for the Allied powers was General Douglas MacArthur.

Japan would spend the next several years under American occupation, ruled almost single-handedly by MacArthur. As an "enemy state" Japan would not be able to join the UN until 1956. Yet throughout the postwar era, and till the present day, Japan served as an outpost of what many soon considered a novel form of empire. Even after the end of the occupation the US retained control over the strategically placed islands of Okinawa. By the early 1980s Prime Minister Yasuhiro Nakasone would promise Ronald Reagan that Japan would serve as an "unsinkable aircraft carrier" for the US. Today Japan is the home of tens of thousands of American troops as well as the Navy's Seventh Fleet, and pays billions back to the US. to help cover the costs. Churchill, who lived to see some of this transformation, may well have shook his head in awe at what Truman and his heirs accomplished in the age of decolonization.

At the time Japan surrendered, Ralph Bunche was back at his desk at the State Department. The president had just appointed him the American representative to the Anglo-American Caribbean Commission, and he would shortly head to London for the preparatory meetings in advance of the first opening of the United Nations in January 1946. Bunche was already thinking about joining the staff of the UN. In a letter to Ruth from San

---

** Perhaps to remind Japan of American tenacity, on a nearby bulkhead was the flag flown by Commodore Matthew Perry in 1853, when the US forcibly "opened" Japan to the world after more than two centuries of isolation.

Francisco, he had noted that many colleagues were discussing the idea of working at the new peace organization. The UN's location had not yet been chosen, but many assumed it would be Geneva, the home of the League of Nations, which was surprisingly still operating at this point. Bunche mused "that's a decision we will have to make before long . . . if things go right. In many ways it would be great for all of us and especially the children—a new life, new surroundings, good schools, no ghettoes and no Jim Crow."[44]

CHAPTER 7

THE UNO

Empire and Peace are incompatible.

—George Padmore, "The Second World War and the Darker
Races," *The Crisis* (1939)

The Second World War had left entire cities horrifically incinerated; tens of millions were dead and many more injured and destitute in the fall of 1945. Safely in Washington, Ralph Bunche was far from the death and destruction that plagued so many, especially in Europe and Asia. Yet he was steeped in building a new and more peaceful postwar order. For Bunche, working on the UNO, as it was often called in those early days, was a compelling opportunity: a chance to help construct a new system of postwar security while furthering the vital mission of assisting oppressed peoples in their quest for self-governance. In a notebook he scrawled his thoughts on the new UNO. The security organization was not intended to be a "super-state," he wrote. But it did have a "policing function"—to check wars—as well as a "remedial function"—to eliminate the causes of wars.[1]

Bunche also believed the UN, especially the trusteeship process he had worked so hard to negotiate, could be a powerful vehicle for satisfying the aspirations for freedom and equality of the hundreds of millions of people still under colonial rule. And, he thought, no group had "a larger stake in the success of the proposed international organization than the Negro."[2] "Our progress," he wrote, "is tied up with the progress of the world." These ideas reflected the striking new terrain of the postwar world. At the same time they harked back to Bunche's early thinking at UCLA, where, in a speech as a student in 1926, he had proposed that an important part of the antidote to "war-poisoning" was the development of an organization encompassing every nation of the world.[3]

How race would fit into this vision was still unclear. Bunche was not alone in his belief that racism was a global phenomenon and colonialism a central component of white world supremacy. The creation of the new multilateral organization, with its paean to human rights in the preamble, seemed to promote a larger movement of postwar change in which people of color around the world might band together and begin to achieve greater justice. Indeed, in Madison Square Garden in New York City, W. E. B. Du Bois excitedly announced that "the dark world is on the move!"[4]* Du Bois was correct: liberation struggles in Africa and Asia had renewed energy in the wake of the war. They also had new ammunition in the form of powerful political rhetoric against fascism and for freedom that could not readily be cabined, as had happened after the First World War, to the white peoples of Europe. From the Atlantic Charter to the UN Charter the Western powers had endorsed a set of principles—sovereign equality, self-determination, human rights—that were crucial to the many independence movements around the globe.

These postwar liberation struggles would prove multifaceted. At times violent and bloody—Mozambique's flag has an AK-47 on it—but more often peaceful, they were diverse in their politics and strategies. Not all saw the new UN as essential or helpful to liberation. Yet in the years after 1945 the UN, even with its abundant talking and seemingly endless meetings, eventually became the primary site where "anti-colonial nationalists staged their reinvention of self-determination," in the process transforming a secondary

---

*   Du Bois went further that night in Madison Square Garden: "Whites may, if they will, arm themselves for suicide, but the vast majority will march over them to freedom!"

principle of the UN Charter into a human right.[5] In short, a major and often unsung accomplishment of the UN was to facilitate the transition from "the era of empires to the era of sovereignty."[6]

This shift at first seemed to have important ties with the American struggle over racial justice. Solidarity with colonized peoples was at a high point among Black Americans in the 1940s. Many believed, as Bunche long had, that the struggle against Jim Crow was of a piece with the struggles for independence taking place in Africa and Asia. In 1947, the NAACP even submitted a petition on racial discrimination to the organization. Largely crafted by Du Bois, it was titled *An Appeal to the World: A Statement on the Denial of Human Rights to Minorities in the Case of Citizens of Negro Descent in the United States of America and an Appeal to the United Nations for Redress.*[7] The effort ultimately proved fruitless, however: the UN Charter had been carefully drafted to ensure that domestic matters fell outside its purview, and powerful political currents pushed back against the very notion of international scrutiny of American racial practices. (Indeed, the struggle to combat racial oppression in the US would quickly abandon the internationalist language of "human rights" and focus instead on "civil rights.")[8]

But was colonialism itself a domestic matter? The UN Charter made clear that self-determination was a central principle in the new postwar order. And as Bunche himself noted in late 1945, the "problem of dependent peoples" had come to be widely accepted as a matter of "proper international concern."[9] The new power constellation in place after the war helped push this concern forward. In the fall of 1945, Harry Truman supportively declared that all peoples prepared for self-government should be permitted to do so, "without interference from any foreign source."[10]

Yet exactly how this would occur remained unclear. The Trusteeship Council, Bunche's first home in the new organization, was the one place where colonial rule was central to the international agenda. To be sure, most colonial territories were not under trusteeship and would never be. European powers nonetheless quickly found much to dislike about the trusteeship system and feared the implications of its activities. Even more dangerous from their perspective was the broader momentum toward decolonization that developed in the early postwar years at the UN General Assembly. Over the long run, it would be the General Assembly, not the Trusteeship Council, that would play the greatest role in decolonization. But the trusteeship process put forward many of the ideas and practices that would shape the General Assembly's approach over time, and trusteeship was where Bunche initially focused his efforts.

Soon he would witness decolonization in full flower. As European empires came apart, at first slowly and then rapidly, the global community ushered in one new state after another, until eventually the UN was no longer an enclave dominated by Western powers but instead the seat of a diverse array of sovereign states, many brand-new to the international system. The process of "liquidating African colonialism" was a critical one, Bunche would later say, and the job of the UN was "to show these people that their aspirations can be realized in a reasonable amount of time without resort to violence."[11] This was not only consistent with the Charter of the UN: it became a core mission. As he argued in 1950, upon receiving his Nobel Peace Prize,

> [the UN] exists not merely to preserve the peace but also to make change—even radical change—possible without violent upheaval. *The United Nations has no vested interest in the status quo.* It seeks a more secure world, a better world, a world of progress for all peoples. In the dynamic society which is the objective of the United Nations, all peoples must have equality and equal rights.[12]

In the view of some observers at the time, this was a radical restatement of the initial purposes of the organization. By the end of Bunche's diplomatic career, two decades later, it would be widely accepted.

ON DECEMBER 30, 1945, BUNCHE WAS on board the *Queen Elizabeth II*, ready to sail to London for the opening meetings of the United Nations. He had already visited London a few months before, as part of the preparatory team sent to get the process moving. Now the official start of the UN era was imminent. Flashbulbs burst as newsmen snapped shots of the various senators in the American delegation. Edward Stettinius, now the inaugural

US ambassador to the UN, came up the gangplank surrounded by an entourage, "like a prizefighter entering the ring," Bunche thought.[13]

At the State Department, Stettinius had been replaced by a new secretary, James Byrnes, who unlike the rest of the delegation went to London by air. Byrnes was a former Supreme Court justice and had taken office at State at the very end of the San Francisco conference. Bunche had been critical of Stettinius, whom he sometimes referred to as "Big Ed," but he was even less impressed with his replacement. Byrnes, he felt, was "no team man." (A Southerner, Byrnes was also a vocal supporter of segregation.) Bunche was no more enthusiastic about another luminary on the American delegation, John Foster Dulles. Bunche had served on the wartime Committee on Africa, the War, and Peace Aims with Dulles. Dulles, he felt, was a "ponderous, unconvincing guy who . . . couldn't carry [Harold] Stassen's duffelbag." He generally found the US position going into London to be weak and "vacillating."[14] All this troubled Bunche, who was excited about the opening meetings and feared the US would fumble the implementation of the new organization.

Also on board the ship as it steamed east across the cold North Atlantic were some familiar faces from San Francisco, notably Senators Arthur Vandenberg (R-Michigan) and Tom Connolly (D-Texas). Perhaps the most famous face in the delegation was Eleanor Roosevelt. Still wearing her widow's black feathered hat, dress, and white pearls, Eleanor Roosevelt stood out on the American team both as a living link to FDR and, increasingly, as a powerful voice in favor of human rights. Bunche had many conversations with her on board the *Queen Elizabeth*. The two would take what he described as "mammoth walks" around the deck of the ship; "that was the best way to talk to her."[15] For Bunche, who had sometimes felt Howard University was a small place with petty politics, it was exciting to be in such rarified company, en route to what he hoped, and indeed proved to be, a world-changing set of meetings.

One chilly afternoon on the crossing Alger Hiss, a fellow State Department official, came upon Bunche working in the lounge of the vessel. Hiss sat down to discuss some issues. He first mentioned that John Foster Dulles would probably be working on the topic of trusteeship. Bunche knew that Dulles was knowledgeable on the issue, though he found him "very legalistic." Hiss then asked whether, in the event the US was offered a personnel slot in the new Trusteeship Division, Bunche might be interested. Bunche, who was indeed interested, demurred, saying "first we'd better see if the job is open to us." Hiss nodded and added that he considered him to be the best qualified for the post.[16]

The ship docked in Southampton. Met by the mayor, who carried a massive gold mace for the occasion, the American delegation was quickly sped to the capital. Bunche found the return to London after nearly a decade away surprising and sobering. The weather was still bad. But other things had changed in the wake of the war. "London isnt the same when all of us saw it last in 1937," he wrote to his daughters Joan and Jane. "It is a badly battered city, living conditions are bad, food and fuel is scarce . . . there is no gaiety."[17] He thought the people looked grim and weary. Bunche tried to stay connected to his wife and children while there, but it was becoming clear to Ruth that his career—now moving in a new direction from what she had imagined when they first met at Howard—was going to pose a deep challenge to any semblance of normal family life. In a series of letters in the fall of 1945, when he first traveled to London as part of the US advance team, Ruth had expressed concern with the trajectory they seemed to be on. His new work was hurting the family, she argued: "achievement is a grand thing and I am very proud of yours but we shouldn't let it blind us to the values of life." In reply, Ralph underscored his "burning desire to excel" and his felt need to succeed in order to provide for his family.[18] There was no true resolution to this dilemma, then or later. Indeed, to Ruth's dismay, he continued to spend long stretches of time away from home, often in distant places with only the most limited means of communication.

The opening session of the UN, held in Central Hall, Westminister, began with a speech by Clement Attlee, the new British prime minister. Labor had recently prevailed in British elections, and Winston Churchill, to the surprise of many Americans, was suddenly out of power. The change in government left only Stalin still standing of the original Big Three that had met in Yalta to hone the contours of the UN Charter. In his welcome address, Clement Attlee made clear his commitment to the ideals of the organization. Britain's change in leadership had changed nothing about its foreign policy, Atlee took pains to convey. He noted that after the First World War there was a tendency to regard the League of Nations "as something outside the ordinary range of foreign policy."[19] Old habits returned, and ultimately the League altered little about world politics. Now, Attlee stressed, things were different. Strongly endorsing the new UN, he declared that "we must—we will—succeed."

The delegates in London quickly got to work on the difficult task of succeeding. Their goal was to erect an actual organization from the dry language of the treaty text negotiated six months before. Bunche remained skeptical as to whether the American team was up to the challenge. "This diplomacy by amateurs is appalling even to a neophyte like me," he wrote in his diary. Byrnes had presented a draft to British Foreign Minister Ernest Bevin which Bunche thought was "weak and ambiguous."[20] To make matters worse, Byrnes then accepted further changes from Bevin that made it even weaker. Bunche, time would show, was a skilled and careful diplomat in public, but privately he was often a tough and tart critic of those around him. In London Byrnes would often be in his line of attack.

There were many facets to address in London, but colonies were Bunche's central focus. The trusteeship provisions agreed to in San Francisco were both an extension of and a fundamental recasting of the system of colonial mandates that had been administered by the League. Yet the difference between trusteeships and mandates was not obvious, and many journalists and observers struggled with the distinction.

The trusteeship system shared with the mandates system the basic principle that captured territories should not simply be spoils of war. Yet it differed in some important ways as well. (In a brief article in the *New Republic*, Bunche, exaggerating a bit, called it a "completely new system of international responsibility.")[21] Trusteeship was in principle not limited to territories captured in the war from enemy states or existing League mandates. It could also include any territories that a party chose to place under the system. The key, as Bunche explained to reporters in early 1946, was that "before a territory—and this includes present mandates—can be placed under the trusteeship system . . . agreements on the terms of the trusteeship must be negotiated among the interested parties."[22] As a result, the new system was potentially far broader than that of the League: it reached not just territories of the vanquished but also, potentially, those of the victors. Trusteeship in this guise was voluntary: states *could* opt to place territories under the UN system, but they were not obligated to. This legal flexibility meant that norms of acceptable behavior were potentially of great importance.

Bunche was unsure which imperial powers would choose to embrace the new system. Already there was a push to put all foreign-ruled territories under trusteeship: Egypt, supported by India, pleaded in London that the UN members, "animated by the splendid spirit which inspired our work," immediately place all colonies, territories, and protectorates under the trusteeship system.[23] Unsurprisingly, this call was not heeded. To Bunche's relief, however, Bevin announced that Britain would put all the African mandates it held under trusteeship. Bevin also promised that Jordan, then called Transjordan, would become independent later that year. The French were more hesitant, and South Africa, which controlled the League mandate of South West Africa, now known as Namibia, declined to place it under trusteeship.[24] (South Africa's refusal to relinquish control of South West Africa—alongside its accelerating policy of apartheid—would eventually make it a pariah within the UN.)

The US itself gave conflicting signals on the new trusteeship concept. On the one hand, the US continued to support the system and took a generally anticolonial stance; on the other hand, at a press conference by President Truman, held while the first round of UN meetings were taking place in London, Truman announced that "the national defense necessities of the United States will not be sacrificed in arranging United Nations postwar trusteeships."[25] As in San Francisco, Bunche found that concern with the future independence of former colonies received rhetorical support, yet often could and did take a back seat to perceived national security imperatives. Indeed, some elements in the US government feared the trusteeship system might work *too* well. One American official explained to Bunche that the Europeans might take their overseas possessions and "dump them onto the UNO," thereby placing a great financial burden on the US, which was due to cover 25 percent of the organization's budget.[26] Bunche rightly discounted this theory, but it illustrated how little anyone really knew of what was going to happen to the colonial world.

IN THE COMING WEEKS, THE NEW peace and security organization slowly came into focus. One of the key issues for Ralph Bunche concerned the meaning of Chapter XI of the UN Charter, which was a declaration pertaining to all "non-self-governing" territories; that is, to colonies generally, not just trusteeships.

Chapter XI was a bit of a wildcard. Its language was sweeping and undefined. Colonial powers, Chapter XI read, must "recognize the principle that the interests of the inhabitants of these territories are paramount." The colonial states were also obliged to develop self-government and "take due account" of the political aspirations of the peoples of these colonies. These seem like obvious, utterly unobjectionable ideas, but for most of the 20th century they had not been. Colonialism in this era still had a thin veneer of good works to it—the *mission civilisatrice*—and putting actual commitments about governance into legally binding treaties spurred resistance. To be sure, there were no time limits on these commitments, nor were the obligations easily enforceable. To keep the process on track, Chapter XI required that the colonial powers regularly transmit to the UN statistical and other information "of a technical nature" relating to economic, social, and educational conditions in the territories they controlled.[27] The reporting mechanism was one of the only concrete obligations in the Charter with regard to colonies. Bunche had pushed for it based largely on his earlier research in French West Africa. It appeared relatively innocuous, yet it set in motion a process of collective review by the international community that, over time, helped spur reform and speed independence.

Providing impetus to these efforts was a newly forthright rejection of the racial basis of world politics, driven, in part, by the horror of Nazism. To be sure, many states, including the US, were sites of intense racial discrimination in the 1940s. But unlike in the League era, in which calls for racial equality, such as by Japan, were ignored, the new UN took a more critical stance toward racial discrimination, at least rhetorically. The UN

Educational, Social and Cultural Organization (UNESCO), founded in the fall of 1945, was a signal example. The UNESCO constitution declared that "the great and terrible war which has now ended" had been made possible by the denial of the democratic principles of dignity, equality, and mutual respect, and by the valorization of "the doctrine of the inequality of men and races."[28] The goal of eradicating this inequality "of men and races" would hardly be realized right away, nor is it fully banished today. (Indeed, some may argue that it is newly resurgent.) But the fact that it *was* a goal in 1945 was an important step forward.[†]

Bunche found the new antiracist rhetoric encouraging. But the issue of exactly how to supervise non-self-governing territories was tricky, and trusteeship soon became politically contentious in London ("Trusteeship Issue Rocks UNO," blared one early headline.) The colonial powers quickly jockeyed to blunt any further momentum toward decolonization or even monitoring. Many saw their empires as critical political and economic assets, but also essential features of their identity. France, for example, sought to restore French grandeur after the humiliating defeat and occupation by Germany in the war. France was attached to her empire and "her colonies are equally attached to France," an official from French Guiana proudly, if unconvincingly, told the delegates in London.[29] As a result, French Togoland, the subject of Bunche's PhD work, was not put under the trusteeship system. Other European states acted similarly.

Bunche was frustrated by this maneuvering, which at times seemed to hark back to attitudes of the 1930s. Yet while his focus was developing the trusteeship system, he occasionally worked on other issues in London. As he detailed to Ruth,

> Last night your husband sat as a delegate in a plenary session of the General Assembly! There was a night session beginning at 9 and all of our delegates, including Mrs. F.D.R., who has been the most conscientious of the lot, had

---

[†] UNESCO soon passed a resolution "proposing and recommending the general adoption of a programme of dissemination of scientific facts designed to bring about the disappearance of that which is commonly called race prejudice."

engagements or were ill. So Alger Hiss[‡] told Dorothy Fosdick and me to sit for the US in order that we should be represented. Ben Cohen joined us later, so I told Dorothy, it was "minorities night" on the US bench, with a woman, a Negro, and Jew representing the country.[30]

He closed his note to Ruth with a prophetic call: "I would certainly like a chance to address a plenary session of the Assembly some day!"

The days went by, meeting after meeting, amid the cold, dark, and fog of wintertime London. Far from home and family, Bunche would occasionally break from the routine with a movie at the nearby Odean Theater, which offered gratis tickets to the UNO delegates, or a glass of whiskey and a game of dice with his colleagues. But mostly he was consumed by work, and, a night owl when away from home, he would often stay up till 2 or 3 a.m. preparing memos on trusteeship or marking up proposed new language. He also had a chance to assess some of the key players who would dominate the organization in the years to come. Of Andrei Vishinsky, for instance, the Soviet ambassador to the UN—and the person who cast the very first veto in the Security Council—Bunche wrote that he was "a quick speaking, deadly serious, rosy-cheeked Russky" who nonetheless did not seem to be as blunt or forceful as the other Andrei, surname Gromyko, who had headed the USSR's delegation to San Francisco.[31]

The London meetings crawled forward. The US continued to press its anticolonial positions: John Foster Dulles, for instance, spoke of the importance of the "whole of the colonial problem," and not merely the 15 million persons or so who would likely come under trusteeship.[32] The day after Dulles's speech Bunche enjoyed a personal triumph: the General Assembly unanimously adopted a resolution recognizing that the problems of the non-self-governing peoples, wherever they were located, were "of vital

---

[‡] Hiss would later face charges that he was a communist spy. Bunche's association with Hiss was minor, yet their ties would be raised in later years when Bunche, like many Americans at the UN, would be accused of communist sympathies.

concern to the peace and well-being of the world." In his diary, he noted how pleased he was "to hear my words being used in this important international affair and also to see Chapter XI, which I had drafted to so large [an] extent, being effectively invoked."[33] He had always been a rapid writer and seemed to enjoy the process of scholarship during his academic career. But here was a chance to see his words actually enacted into law, a prospect that Bunche found much more satisfying. While colonialism would likely remain in place for a long time, language like this seemed to helpfully point to and encourage change. He felt the building blocks of colonialism's demise were slowly accumulating.

The colonial states nonetheless mounted multiple defenses of their empires in London, which they repeated and elaborated on during the coming years. The most common was that most colonies were simply not ready for self-governance. The very premise of trusteeship reflected how common and accepted this view was. Imperial powers also often argued that the economic and social conditions in their colonies were better than conditions in many similar independent states. As a result, colonialism was said to be generally salutory, and ending it was, by implication, a mistake that would only harm the inhabitants. A distinct claim was more conceptual: that there was in fact no "nation" in a given colony to give independence to. Instead, as Belgium later argued with regard to Congo, the very people whose self-determination was allegedly at stake in a colony were in fact simply a grouping of different peoples only joined together through colonial rule. With no true nation and no single people, self-determination made no sense. (This claim would take on a particular resonance when, in 1960, the wealthiest province of Congo, Katanga, tried to secede in the immediate wake of Congo's independence, a process that would lead Bunche into some of the most dangerous moments of his life.) Winston Churchill, as was often the case, went even further in this line of argument, declaring that India is "merely a geographic expression. It is no more a single country than the Equator."[34] Some colonial states, such as Portugal, tried a more frontal defense: they denied they possessed any non-self-governing territories. In a move that strained credulity, they instead claimed that distant overseas territories such as Goa and Angola were all equal parts of a single country.[§]

Perhaps the most interesting argument, however, was that the problem of non-self-governing peoples, the nomenclature used in Chapter XI of the Charter, was (or should be) far broader than colonies in the traditional sense. Many ethnic, racial, and Indigenous minorities were oppressed and denied political voice within the accepted borders of existing states. Why was that not also a problem of non-self-governance? Why did the notion of a colony, or colonialism itself as a concept, have to rest on a distinct territory?

Bunche had encountered an early version of this argument during the war, when British officials, in a transparent attempt to blunt American criticisms of their empire, had asked about the "self-determination" of Black Americans. And it went back even earlier, to Woodrow Wilson's concerns about self-determination on the part of Eastern European peoples trapped in sprawling multinational empires. The argument would resurface in various forms in the coming years. Some colonial powers used it to attack what was sometimes referred to as the "blue water" or "saltwater" definition of colonies: that only territories in far-off, overseas locales counted as colonies. The Soviet domination of Armenia, for instance, the Chinese domination of Tibet, or the American domination of the Navajo simply were not colonialism under the saltwater definition—which not coincidentally favored the new superpowers who, it was becoming increasingly clear, were dominating the postwar world.

In what later came to be known as the "Belgian Thesis," in 1952 Belgium argued that its intransigence on decolonization was not actually an objection to the premise of decolonization. Nor was it opposed to the international supervision of colonial governance itself. Rather, Belgium claimed it only wanted to see those worthy principles extended even more broadly— to include not only distant territories but also minority groups closer to home. Far from wishing to restrict these principles, Belgium's Pierre

---

[§] The US would also make this argument with regard to Puerto Rico, which was removed from the list of non-self-governing territories in 1953.

Ryckmans somewhat unconvincingly argued, "we wish on the contrary that they should be respected in their fullest meaning. Far from defending a restrictive interpretation we declare ourselves in favour of a wide interpretation in conformity with the humanitarian spirit which should dominate our Organization."[35] In other words, Belgium claimed to want to see *all* minorities, wherever they might be located, enjoy self-determination.

The Belgian Thesis was creative, but only mildly effective. It was a sort of political poison pill defense that many states were unwilling to swallow. Its implications—if taken seriously—were simply far too sweeping for it to gain much traction, its true goals too transparent, and thus it did little to blunt the efforts to chip away at colonialism in its traditional guise. The newly independent states (at times busily oppressing disfavored ethnic groups themselves), as well as the traditional critics of colonialism such as the US and Soviet Union, who had their own oppressed internal minorities to worry about, shared a strong interest in ignoring or disputing Belgium's argument. Yet the Belgian Thesis was not wholly wrong, and it foreshadowed the later focus of the UN and its human rights bodies on the rights of Indigenous groups. Indigenous peoples were often oppressed and subsumed into larger political entities—such as the US itself—and while they were not part of a "colony," they clearly had been colonized.

At an even deeper level, the very premise of the human rights transformation that unfolded in the coming decades was that equal treatment, nondiscrimination, and other principles of equality were every human's birthright, no matter their citizenship or territorial location. This suggested that whether there was water—salt or otherwise—between a government and an oppressed people really did not matter. In 1946, however, the provocative Belgian Thesis was still several years away. But already it was clear that the traditional European powers and the new continental superpowers had quite different views on the future of empire.

PERHAPS THE SINGLE BIGGEST DECISION IN London was to select the first leader of the United Nations. The position was to be called the secretary general. On the question of the first occupant, the two superpowers were divided. The United States initially sought to put Canadian diplomat Lester

Pearson in the seat. The Soviets resisted, believing he would be too close with the Americans. In late January, the new Security Council settled on a relatively little known Norwegian foreign minister, Trygve Lie, and the General Assembly quickly approved. Ralph Bunche, calling it a "big hurdle over," would later work very closely with Lie.[36] Lie would go down in history as a relatively minor figure in the UN pantheon. Bunche himself was no great fan; Lie, he later wrote, "never exerted himself very much, liked a siesta in the afternoon and rarely worked late. He was vain and self-centered, tending to appraise even important matters in terms of the impact on himself."[37] Lie nonetheless seemed a neutral choice for the inaugural leader of the UN, one that would not ruffle many feathers. The strategy of installing someone inoffensive from a relatively small nation as secretary general would prove to have enduring appeal, even though it often meant choosing a relative unknown. Indeed, the Norwegian was so little known in 1946 that when Stettinius gave his endorsement speech he first needed someone to point out who Lie actually was.[38]

It was in London that Bunche was first approached, as Hiss suggested he might, about working for the Trusteeship Division. With Lie in place, the UN's Secretariat now needed staff; while it took on some two hundred former staffers of the League of Nations, now in the process of finally winding down, many more were required.[39] Bunche was unsure of whether to accept, though he did stress to others around him the "importance of hiring qualified Negroes."[40] Indeed, he had long made this a priority, corresponding with friends and former Howard colleagues such as Alain Locke, seeking suggestions for Black candidates for the new UN.[41]**

The notion of a move to the UN's permanent staff was intriguing but potentially momentous. Bunche had departed Howard for the State Department largely out of patriotic duty (and some restlessness with his research agenda) and found that he very much liked being steeped in the policymaking world. Yet in leaving Howard—though he was careful at the time

---

** Locke, calling it "quite an assignment," speculated that eventually Bunche could compile "an adequate list." Locke then included himself as interested in the "African Section" of the soon to be formed Secretariat.

only to say his departure was temporary—he was not only trading academic for policy work. He was also leaving a small, Black institution for a massive white one. One of the very few Black Americans at the State Department in the 1940s, Bunche was no doubt stirred by the opportunity. In his own estimation, he was highly motivated by a spirit of competition—particularly, he later wrote, "when pitted against white people."[42] He speculated that this motivation might have stemmed from the tremendous influence of his grandmother, who constantly admonished him to let "white folks know that you can do anything." Howard, especially during Alain Locke's later tenure, had attracted an outstanding group of Black scholars. But the State Department, and later the UN, were far better places to compete against whites.

The feelers about the UN post continued in the coming months, until eventually, in the spring of 1946, he decided to take the plunge and move over to the new Secretariat, at first on loan from the State Department. Discussing the prospect with Ruth, he pointed out the implications: "this isnt just another mission, another meeting. If I took this job it would mean moving to New York. Selling the house here."[43]

Life in the Washington foreign policy establishment had been very interesting, and the work was clearly important. Bunche seemed to move into government with surprising ease. Although it had been a major change, he thrived in the policy world. Indeed, he later wrote that entering the field of diplomacy was "simply a process of natural evolution based on the relationship between educational background and my work experience during the war."[44] Whether true or not, Bunche grew to like the exercise of power and the impact he saw himself having. His profile was rising as well; the many stories about him in the press, the frequent reporters calling, all gave him attention that no Howard colleague could really match.

Still, Bunche's true intentions about his future at this point were unclear—they likely ebbed and flowed—and he often claimed he was only taking a temporary break from teaching. In a September 1946 letter to Mordecai Johnson, the president of Howard University, he requested additional leave and explained that the reason behind his annual requests for extension was his own disinclination to accept a permanent post in government. However, he added that his immediate goal was to see the work he had devoted so much energy and time to in the past three years come to fruition. Noting that he had numerous opportunities for a permanent position in the federal government, Bunche declared that he had declined them "for the simple reason that I have never intended to divorce myself permanently" from academia. My prime interest, he continued, "has been and remains in scholarship and teaching."[45]

Bunche may have meant what he wrote Mordecai Johnson in the fall of 1946. Yet despite many future offers of prestigious professorships—from Harvard, Princeton, and elsewhere—he never accepted any. He seemed to find working in diplomacy ultimately more rewarding. Moreover, his later comments about Howard were not always positive. When he began teaching at Howard, he told the *New Yorker* toward the end of his life, Mordecai Johnson "once openly criticized me in a faculty meeting. 'Bunche is going all the way to Africa to find a problem,' he said. Negro colleges are petty places. The horizon is very limited, very narrow."[46] His desire to leave this life behind was by no means limited to his unhappiness with Johnson or academic life or politics. Bunche chafed at the indignities of segregated Washington, DC, even more. Living in the nation's capital, he once remarked, "is like serving out a sentence. It's extremely difficult for a Negro to maintain even a semblance of human dignity in Washington."[47]

One example stands out, its very degradation and absurdity making it emblematic of his frustration with life in the capital city. Indeed, it was the one he chose to raise with Harry Truman years later when the president offered him the position of assistant secretary of state. During the war years, the Bunche family dog died. As Brian Urquhart, his former UN colleague, later recounted, "the children wanted it buried in the local cemetery. Bunche drove there to make arrangements and found that there was one section for white people's pets and another for black people's."[48] There were unfortunately many similar examples. Dean Rusk, who later served as secretary of state in the Kennedy and Johnson administrations, took Bunche for lunch one day during the war to the Officers Dining Room at the War Department. As the pair walked in, they drew a good deal of attention; no Black American had ever dined there before. "Our innocent stroll into the dining room was quite an incident for its day," Bunche later wrote. Years later, Rusk remarked that neither man knew the dining room was segregated; "we were just hungry," Rusk said.[49]

Work at the State Department, or Howard for that matter, could not make up for these oppressive experiences or the impact they had on his family. Ruth Bunche felt the same way. When Ralph later debated the UN's offer to become a permanent staff member in New York, he noted to a friend that "the fact that Ruth wants to get out of Washington is an influential factor, of course."[50] Moving to New York City was a daunting change, but the Bunches felt that the city, while hardly a racial paradise, would be a step forward.[††] In the meantime, Bunche excitedly devoted himself to representing the US government in London. "This conference gives me the very best opportunity I have ever had, since I am the sole US representative in my committee," he explained to Ruth.[51] In this capacity, as a result of overwhelming American power, he was able to wield great influence. At least that was the theory. In practice, the US seemed unsure of how aggressive to be at the new UN, a hesitation, it soon became clear, the Soviet Union did not share.

[††] The St. Louis Post-Dispatch offered an additional, more prosaic reason for Bunche's refusal to take up Truman's offer: "Bunche Can't Afford to Accept Offer of State Dept Job," the headline read on May 26, 1949, noting that Bunche earned $14,000 a year tax free at the UN but would only get $10,000, taxable, back at the State Department.

CHAPTER 8

THE STRUGGLE OVER TRUSTEESHIP

The colonial system ... has borne some very evil fruit.
—John Foster Dulles at the United Nations, 1947

Just days after the United Nations' opening session in London concluded in February 1946, a five-part telegram on the Soviet Union, running to some 8000 words, arrived at the State Department. Sent by George Kennan, the American *charge d'affairs* at the embassy in Moscow, what became known as the "Long Telegram" is a landmark in Cold War history. Kennan's deeply pessimistic appraisal of Soviet foreign policy argued that despite the Allied victory, the Soviets retained "an instinctive Russian sense of insecurity."[1] Josef Stalin, Kennan wrote, firmly believed that there could be no permanent peaceful coexistence with the West.

While the Long Telegram's fame arose mainly from its influential diagnosis of Soviet motivations, and its decidedly dour view of the prospects of continued cooperation after the war, Kennan also spoke about the new UN:

Russians will participate officially in international organizations where they see opportunity of extending Soviet power or of inhibiting or diluting power of others. Moscow sees in UNO not the mechanism for a permanent and stable world society founded on mutual interest and aims of all nations, but an arena in which aims just mentioned can be favorably pursued.[2]

That George Kennan had identified something central about Soviet aims and ambitions at the new UN had arguably been demonstrated just days before when Ambassador Andrey Vishinsky cast the first veto in the nascent Security Council. The vote was over a relatively minor issue involving a continuing French presence in the Middle East. After the president of the Security Council declared that the measure met the majority rule to pass, Vishinsky, who Ralph Bunche had characterized in his diary as "deadly serious," spoke up. First quoting the UN Charter, he stated: "I think a mistake was made. I did not vote in favor of this proposal, I voted against it."[3]

The existence of the veto had of course been deeply contentious in San Francisco. But the great powers saw it as absolutely essential to the consortium of power they envisioned the Security Council to be. While no one in San Francisco knew with any certainty how often the veto would be wielded, many believed it would be used quite sparingly. The Soviets did not agree. Vishinsky's veto was the onset of a cascade: in the UN's early years, the USSR vetoed liberally—on average, about a once a month through 1950.[4]*

Outside the Security Council, the growing chill of the Cold War was perhaps less immediately apparent, but robust political combat would ensue nonetheless. The European powers almost from the start aimed to ensure that the UN's powers with regard to colonies were as weak as possible. At times, Bunche wrote to Ruth, it was "a one man fight against the British, French, and Dutch."[5]

Bunche had substantial assistance in this fight, however. While still alive, Franklin Delano Roosevelt had used America's might to press Europe on

---

* In a sign of how sensitive and difficult the Soviets were already perceived to be, when lots were drawn for seating order in the first General Assembly in New York in 1946, the United Kingdom drew the first seat. Realizing that under the planned system of alphabetical order this meant the Soviets (formally, Union of Soviet Socialist Republics) would then have the last seat in the room, some unknown Secretariat official had a flash of creativity and decided to use "USSR" on the nameplate instead—thereby giving the Soviets the third seat.

the need to roll back their empires. In the war's aftermath, the United States was even more powerful. Spared little direct attack except for Pearl Harbor, it dominated the global economy to an unprecedented degree. This gave the nation enormous leverage, especially over its close ally, Great Britain. As historians William Roger Louis and Ronald Robinson bluntly described it, "During the eighteen months between the end of the hot war and the beginning of the cold, most Americans regarded empires as obsolete. British claims to world power seemed pathetic."[6] Weakened and broke, the once-dominant British needed American help desperately. Washington, with its vast influence, was willing to write off some of London's huge debt to save an important ally—but not to secure its empire.

A FEW MONTHS AFTER THE OPENING meetings of the United Nations in London, while still an employee of the State Department, Bunche delivered a speech in New York entitled "United States Responsibility toward Colonial Peoples."[7] He first emphasized that the issue of colonialism was a "matter of direct international concern." This viewpoint was accurate and even obvious, but it had a new valence given the UN's sweeping charter. Bunche told the audience that, while colonial territories varied, all of them desired a greater voice in their own affairs. In some cases, this desire took the form of what he called "virulent nationalist movements"; in others, it had more benign manifestations. Whatever shape the aspiration for self-rule assumed, it was a matter of historical record, he argued, that dangerous rivalries had typically developed over such territories. Colonialism, simply put, was an enduring source of international conflict.

In tying colonial rivalry to global conflict, Bunche was channeling arguments W. E. B. Du Bois and many others had made years earlier. Bunche was also tying the question of colonialism to the core purpose of the new UN: to ensure peace and security in the postwar world. This was an important attack on the notion that colonial governance was simply an internal affair, something the international community had no right to intrude upon or question. (Indeed, that argument had already been made by the Netherlands, with regard to Indonesia.)[8] If colonial rule led to international conflict, it followed that it was not a domestic matter, and the new UN needed to regulate it.

The traditional civilizing rationales for colonial rule, he continued, were at best romantic and "Kiplingesque," and were no longer acceptable. The US, he argued, had made the ultimate independence of the non-self-governing peoples a centerpiece of the postwar effort. Citing Woodrow Wilson's Fourteen Points and the League of Nations mandates system, Bunche claimed that a collective and rule-based approach to decolonization had long been the position of the American government. The intent of trusteeship was to "establish a *new* system, not merely a continuation, under different auspices, of the mandates system" the League had created. Among the key differences with the League, he stressed, were the ability of the UN itself to govern a particular territory; the role of periodic reviews and visits to territories under trusteeship; and the power of territorial inhabitants to petition the UN directly. Most importantly, he suggested, the new UN placed the interests of the colonial people themselves paramount.

Bunche, stretching a bit, made the trusteeship system sound like it was already a fairly significant step forward. The system itself had yet to formally get off the ground, however. In a September 1946 memo summarizing the state of affairs, he noted some positive steps toward operation. Five states— the UK, France, Belgium, Australia, and New Zealand—had declared their intention to place territories under trusteeship, and the General Assembly had unanimously passed a resolution on non-self-governing peoples.[9]

Bunche continued to focus his energies on these issues, even as he was diverted to other issues, such as a trip in the winter of 1946 to the Virgin Islands for a meeting of the Anglo-American Caribbean Commission. The chance to leave the cold of New York to visit a tropical island was welcome. But the Caribbean Commission also served as an early template for later efforts at the UN. Asked about the work of the Commission in September 1946, he argued that the Commission was designed to benefit colonies. By encouraging the colonial powers to work together rather than singly to address health, education, and development issues, the Commission helped to move the Caribbean colonies more expeditiously toward independence. Since "most of the problems of that area are regional, an effort will be made to find regional solutions," he explained.[10] In making this statement, he was previewing a view that would become central to his work at the UN in the coming decades. Colonies that lacked infrastructure and expertise or were simply very small could, Bunche conceded, struggle as independent nations. Indeed, he was often skeptical of their prospects and hardly a cheerleader for immediate independence. But by internationalizing the process, and providing assistance and aid through international organizations, the prospects for success would grow.

There was substantial anticipation of what would happen next in New York, in the first full session of the UN in the fall of 1946. On NBC's "University of the Air," a radio program that aired that fall, Bunche noted that the future of Italy's African colonies had already been discussed, as had some of the existing League mandates. It was only natural that the existing mandates should be the first to find their way into the new trusteeship system, he suggested, "and actually, that is the way it seems to be working out." The nations that had been in charge of these mandates had had years of experience in administering them, he noted on NBC's program, somewhat eliding the fact that his own research in French West Africa suggested that their track record was not all that impressive. "That experience makes them the natural ones to lead off in drawing up trusteeship agreements."[11]

FOR THE FALL 1946 MEETINGS, THE United Nations delegates moved on to the auspiciously named town of Lake Success, just over the New York City line in suburban Long Island. At this point Ralph Bunche was living in a hotel, taking the occasional train down to Washington to see Ruth and the children and working out of temporary offices. The issue of housing for Black delegates quickly rose to the fore. The Waldorf Astoria Hotel and a set of apartments, both of which had been rented out for incoming UN delegations, precipitated a crisis by refusing to allow diplomats from Liberia, Haiti, and Ethiopia to stay at their establishments. The State Department quickly intervened to secure housing, but it was an early warning that America's obsession with racial segregation was going to create foreign policy headaches for the US government.

Meanwhile, Bunche began to give more thought to the prospect of joining the UN permanently. Earlier that summer he wrote Ruth telling her that after a "tiresome ride up" on the train he really regretted having to leave. "I wish you would just write me and tell me frankly just what you think of my idea of transferring up here and making our home here."[12] Increasingly, Bunche seemed to be questioning whether he would ever return to his old academic life at Howard.

While in New York he strategized further about the system of trusteeship. One issue he took a particular interest in was who would possess legal title to the new trust territories. As he noted in advance of the New York meetings, the rights and titles to mandated territories were left uncertain under the League, and their location "has always been a subject of contention." (Indeed, this issue would later vex the question of Israeli occupation of the West Bank after the 1967 war; Israel's argument, in essence, was that the West Bank had never been under the legitimate sovereignty of Jordan.)[13] In other words, was the territory "owned" by the international community as a steward? Or was it owned by the state that ruled it as the trustee? Bunche suggested it would be "entirely within the spirit" of the new system to have each trusteeship agreement make clear that titles rested with the UN.[14] His suggestion reflected the fact that he was not thrilled by the early drafts of the trust agreements. The drafts were not "broad and imaginative," and he predicted that if they were not revised considerably they might engender protracted debate within the international community.

The trusteeship system was built on the premise of governance agreements that the "states directly concerned" would negotiate and the General Assembly would approve. From the beginning, the issue of who exactly was directly concerned arose. The Soviets felt the permanent members of the Security Council had an interest in everything; therefore they were always directly concerned. The US disagreed. In fact, John Foster Dulles argued to the assembled delegates that "it is said that in this world it is quite customary that to those who have shall be given and from those who have not shall be taken away. But I don't think that is a system which we need to incorporate in our trusteeship policies."[15] This issue of control bedeviled the new UN and showed how the politics of decolonization were rapidly growing in scale and scope.

There were other issues on the colonial agenda in 1946. (The first official meeting of the Trusteeship Council would occur in March 1947.) From the start India, presaging an approach it would champion in coming decades, sought a greater role for the General Assembly. Bunche observed this effort with mixed feelings. He was often frustrated with what he saw as the overreach of Indian officials, even if he shared their basic goals. In his diary he noted with annoyance that India seemed to think that the General Assembly was in charge of the trusteeship agreements, when in fact under the UN Charter it only approved them after they were negotiated.

India was prescient, however. In the years to come, the General Assembly would loom ever larger in debates on decolonialization. By 1960, when the General Assembly passed the landmark Declaration on the Granting of Independence to Colonial Countries and Peoples, the chamber had become the primary site of struggle between the colonial powers of the West and the newly independent and often nonaligned nations of what would become known as the Third World.[16] In the 1940s, however, most states did not have any inkling of the changes to come. The process was slow to get moving, and colonial powers still seemed to think that change was still far off in the future. Yet, as one prominent scholar later wrote, things soon changed with surprising speed. The UN fell into the hands of "the ex-dependent peoples," and, within a decade or two, the authority "to 'meddle' in colonial affairs would not only be asserted but exercised on a grand scale."[17]

Indian leaders had long set their sights on ending imperialism. (Gandhi, writing to Hitler during the war, said "We resist British Imperialism no less than Nazism. If there is a difference, it is in degree.")[18] They saw the UN as a new and potentially quite useful arena for this effort. India also had a particular interest in South Africa. South Africa had a large South Asian population that had moved there when both territories were part of the British Empire. As Bunche well knew from his fieldwork in the 1930s, South Africa was a society with a finely honed system of race-based discrimination. South Africa also wanted to annex the former German colony of South West Africa, thereby absorbing more territory and an even larger Black population. This was contrary to the spirit of the UN Charter and provided an opening, if more was needed, to attack South Africa's racially discriminatory domestic policies—an opening India grabbed with alacrity.

In a speech that fall, Maharaj Singh of India attacked South Africa for its proposed annexation of South West Africa. Jan Smuts, the influential leader of South Africa, counterattacked on the grounds that India's caste system was no different than racial discrimination. Singh, in response, asked why Smuts and South Africa were ignoring one of the basic objectives of the Charter, "namely, the political advance of dependent peoples and their progressive development toward independence?"[19] Smuts responded that the proposed annexation of South West Africa was merely a joinder of two similar territories and peoples, much like the merger of Scotland and England or Texas and the US. The debate continued; there was no immediate resolution. Yet in confronting South Africa, India was throwing down a marker: the language of the UN Charter was not going to be treated like the language of the League Covenant. Self-determination was a real goal and would be monitored and enforced.

The South West Africa question dominated the early meetings and was, in many respects, the first skirmish in the larger battle to come over decolonization. China, too, spoke out against South Africa's plans, stating that it would be a sad commentary on the Charter if the organization should now "turn backwards and lightly endorse a proposal to annex a mandated territory."[20] Speaking in support of annexation were the other colonial powers. The British claimed that the inhabitants of South West Africa had been surveyed and favored annexation: "the natives, by an overwhelming majority, have voted for incorporation . . . in the face of these facts, and in the face of the principle of self-determination, is the UN to gainsay the wishes of the people themselves?"[21] The Netherlands concurred. The Chilean delegate quipped that the debate demonstrated that the "democratic education of the natives consisted of teaching them to vote in favor of the whites."[22]

For the next four decades, the question of South West Africa was the subject of numerous General Assembly debates, Security Council resolutions, and even International Court of Justice disputes. (South West Africa successfully declared its independence only in 1990, becoming Namibia.)

In 1951, Bunche even telegrammed the chiefs of the Herero and other tribes in the territory, inviting them to present their petitions on govern-ance to the UN in person. The notion that local African groups had an im-portant voice in their own destiny was growing, even if South Africa barred the chiefs from traveling.[23]

South Africa's postwar intransigence and policies of apartheid earned it the opprobrium of nearly every nation on earth. But India's attacks on South Africa engendered a different set of politics. Fearful of the implications for the American South, the US delegation fretted over how to respond. Senator Vandenberg, who had been part of the original team negotiating in San Francisco, conceded that he could see little difference be-tween "Indians in South Africa and Negroes in Alabama."[24] If the new UN was going to be taking on such issues in South Africa, where would it stop? The result was a burgeoning American concern over the growing power of the General Assembly and trepidation about the nascent concept of human rights, one result of which was that the US did not ratify a UN human rights treaty until almost the 1990s.[25] Still, the General Assembly did manage to pass a resolution in the fall of 1946 declaring it was "in the higher interest of humanity to put an immediate end to . . . so-called racial persecution and discrimination."[26]

Meanwhile, in an early sign that it would try to grab the mantle of leading anti-imperialist, the Soviets pushed the Western powers to move forward more quickly on the UN trusteeship system, demanding "a stop to any fur-ther procrastination" with regard to setting up the Trusteeship Council.[27] On this particular point Bunche agreed with the Soviets. In the fall of 1946, the *New York Times* reported that the trusteeship process was advancing quite slowly. Only eight agreements were under consideration. (The story noted in passing a point about one League mandate that would soon loom large in Bunche's life: "The future status of Palestine," the *Times* wrote, "is unclear.")[28]

After the first eight trusteeship agreements were approved at the end of 1946, the Trusteeship Council was finally established. The eight ter-ritories were British Togoland; French Togoland; British Cameroons; French Cameroons; Tanganyika; New Guinea; Ruanda-Urundi; and

Western Samoa. Even in putting these cases forward, the colonial powers were quick to highlight the various obstacles they perceived to independence. Australia, for instance, suggested New Guinea was a special case, as "the bulk of the inhabitants . . . have progressed little beyond the stone age."[29] France pointed to a different challenge, one Bunche had given some thought to: how did nationalism fit into the trusteeship equation? France argued—as Belgium would later with regard to Congo and the Netherlands with regard to Indonesia—that there was in fact no superseding identity in these colonies. "There is at present no nationality such as Togolandese or Cameroonese," the French claimed.[30] This lack of a political conception of nationhood in many colonies, France suggested, made self-determination and independence hard to envision and maybe even dangerous.

France had ulterior motives in making this statement, but the concern it raised was not wholly without foundation. Yet, in many respects the problem—to the degree it existed—was of the Europeans' doing. Because the borders of so many colonies had been drawn decades earlier in European palaces, with no concern for the local populations, they often encompassed disparate peoples with differing histories, religious traditions, and even languages. Tying these varied peoples together in a single nation would prove challenging. Bunche himself puzzled over a closely related issue, which he dubbed the "UN Dilemma": that there was a tension between the need to develop nationalism in the newly independent states and the need to retain the internationalism inherent in the UN itself.[31] To Bunche the problem was less that former colonies lacked a cohesive national identity (on this particular point he often agreed); it was more that nationalism would sweep up political energy and focus politics inward. He thought it essential to ensure that, as decolonization took place, proper respect for international cooperation remained.

Initially, however, he did not fixate on this potential problem. He was most focused on simply seeing the trusteeship system come to fruition. When it did, in March 1947, it marked an important change in world politics. In an interview that spring, Bunche said he had "no illusions" about the power of the UN to confer self-government in Africa and Asia. "I am certain, however, that we can create a mechanism which will make self-government much easier."[32]

ONE OF THE MORE DIFFICULT SETS of territories to arise on the United Nations' agenda were the former Italian colonies of Libya, Somaliland, and Eritrea. None of these had been League mandates; Italy had acquired them through conquest and treaty. While Italy was a former Axis power, and therefore seemed to fall into the "enemy states" category within the UN Charter, to Ralph Bunche's surprise the State Department initially proposed that Italy itself administer the territories.[†] As troubling as this was on some level—returning the henhouse to the fox, as it were—he quickly grasped an opportunity. Italy's bargaining leverage was very weak given its Axis past, and so he and his colleagues had a chance to draft strong proposed agreements that the former fascist state would be hesitant to reject. He was given the task of drafting for Libya. As one colleague later wrote, "Bunche saw the instructions as a heaven-sent opportunity to design a model of what trusteeship should be."[33]

American views on Italy as a trust power soon shifted, however, and Bunche's specific draft was not used. Of Italy's former colonies, only Somaliland went under Italian trusteeship. Yet the drafting exercise proved useful down the road. And the Italian territories did in fact provide strong precedents for UN action. A few years later, in 1950, the General Assembly voted that Libya "shall be constituted an independent and sovereign state" by January 1, 1952.[34] As the New Yorker wrote in the wake of the vote, "Libya, Mussolini's former colonial show place in Africa, and a country almost three times the size of Texas, may go down in history as the scene of the United Nations' first successful effort to set up a brand-new independent federal state."[35] The decision to grant independence, the New Yorker continued, has "already created violent repercussions throughout French North Africa— Tunisia, Algeria, and Morocco—where the French have for many years been assuring the Arabs that they are not yet ready for independence." The

---

[†] Italy did not become a UN member until 1955. Japan joined the UN in 1956 and Germany, in part due to a stalemate between the USSR and the US, not until 1973.

New Yorker was highlighting a political truth: the General Assembly's move was surprising, and soon France, by 1954 already defeated in Vietnam in the battle of Dien Bien Phu, would face another bloody colonial war in Algeria.

In 1947, however, this was all a few years in the future. Yet the basic pieces of the postwar UN/colonial nexus were falling into line, and the eagerness exhibited by the General Assembly to move Libya to independence was another indication that in the struggle between the forces of empire and the forces of equality, equality was rapidly gaining the upper hand.

The first meeting of the Trusteeship Council finally commenced in March 1947. Bunche, drafting welcome remarks for Lie, threw in a wry comment about the growing intensity of the postwar trusteeship debate. The road to establishing this Council, Lie declared at the opening, "has been long and arduous." Along the road there have been many conflicts, he continued; on occasion, the "administering authorities"—that is, the Trust powers—"may have wondered whether they or the Trust Territories most needed United Nations protection."[36] Bunche's quip reflected the new reality: the European powers seemed to be taken aback by the focus and vigor of their opponents.

Meanwhile, Bunche was showing himself to be a skilled bureaucratic grappler. He early on recognized the power of process within UN bodies to nudge matters in his preferred direction. The UN Charter's clause requiring colonial powers to report on the conditions in their colonies was a signal example. Bunche and his colleagues helped the organization develop a questionnaire that ran to nearly 250 individual items.[37] This formed the basis of the reports from the trust powers to the Trusteeship Council. Reporting and review mechanisms are today a mainstay of many multilateral arrangements for cooperation. The essential notion is that the process of reporting on performance, and having that reviewed by other states, is both an effective information-forcing mechanism and a mode of collective performance review. Done right, it can shift the behavior of states in the desired direction by forcing them to explain their actions to others and subjecting them to pressure from their peers.[38]

Having witnessed firsthand the poor nature of European colonial governance in Africa, Bunche believed this process was essential. For the system to work effectively, however, the member states themselves and not just the Secretariat had to play some role in reviewing and responding to the reports. To the colonial powers, however, this scrutiny was unwarranted and even an affront. As one historical account argued, internal British documents from the era

> tellingly use the terms "interfere" and "interference," rather than "accountability" or "oversight," when discussing the trusteeship system, demonstrating the anti-colonial tenor with which British officials believed the UN was imbued. But because Britain could no longer defend colonialism with the older language of "civilization" and tutelage it resorted to other defences.[39]

As Bunche later said, his aim in elaborating this process was to "keep a steady fire burning under the powers whose colonies are not trusteeships. The UN members read our reports and resolutions and say to France or England or some other country: 'How about the health facilities in this colony?' or 'Let's do something about education in that territory.' "[40]

Photo 8.1 Bunche meets with member of the Wa-Meru people at the UN

The reporting system also highlighted some subtle but significant differences with the mandates system. The League had been forced to accept reports of the colonial powers as authentic because, "had their accuracy been questioned, the affected states would have been affronted." The UN, however, could make periodic visits to "see for itself how the territories are being administered."[41] By 1956, each trust territory had been visited multiple times.[42] These new forms of scrutiny reflected Bunche's effort to ensure the postwar system was a true advance. As he described it, the "prestige and authority" of the Trusteeship Council should certainly be greater than that enjoyed by the Mandates Commission, and its recommendations should correspondingly carry more weight.[43] These changes also reflected a broader change in the nature of international diplomacy, which had previously been obsessed with notions of sovereign dignity. These ideas did not die after 1945; there were still many instances in which international law reflected a somewhat antique concern with "affronting" sovereigns. But the basic idea of inspecting and even critiquing state behavior was slowly becoming more accepted.

Colonial powers, opposed to these steps and wary of their impact, argued that they were not required by the UN Charter. Indeed, they maintained that the procedures were violations of the Charter's provisions ensuring that domestic matters remained outside the organization's purview. The State Department also did not always agree with Bunche that such collective scrutiny was a good thing. It likewise was lukewarm about involving the General Assembly too much in colonial matters. Britain and France were important allies and the US needed their support. This tension between supporting allies and promoting decolonization would endure throughout the coming decades. The relative weight of each concern, however, waxed and waned. Initially, the US put substantial pressure on its European allies. Then, as the Cold War intensified in the late 1940s, "competition between the two superpowers came to the rescue" of empire.[44] Anticommunism took precedence over anticolonialism. Later, the pendulum swung yet again: Anticolonialism *became* a form of anticommunism, as the fear that the clutch of newly independent states entering the international system would be driven into the arms of the communists led the US, for example, in the late 1950s Suez Crisis, to humiliate the British and French in a show of overt power.

As his colleague Lawrence Finkelstein later described it, Bunche's views on the scrutiny of colonial governance prevailed in the end, but not because he persuaded the State Department brass. Bunche found a way to "work informally with the Chinese delegation, which introduced the proposal that led to the creation ... of the Ad Hoc Committee on Information from Non-Self-Governing Territories."[45] In so doing, he was able to initiate a process that, over time, would put the most vocally anticolonial chamber of the UN in a position to continue to discuss imperial matters—and harangue the imperialists.

PERHAPS THE MOST BASIC EARLY DEBATE in the new organization was where the United Nations' headquarters should be built. Reflecting its European focus, the League had been housed in the Swiss city of Geneva. The Truman administration very much wanted the new UN to be sited in the US, however. Various locations were considered, including San Francisco, Philadelphia, Atlantic City, and even South Dakota. The South Dakota boosters put together an impressive package, which included a rendering of what was essentially a purpose-built city in the high plains to house the Secretariat, the diplomats, and their families.[‡] Ultimately, New York City was chosen as the most convenient and desirable location. But where exactly in New York the UN complex would go was at first unclear.

For the second part of the UN's opening session, in March 1946, the delegates briefly met in temporary quarters at Hunter College in the Bronx. The conditions were spartan. As the *New York Times* reported, "diplomats met in a gymnasium. Reporters worked out of a broom closet. Wooden classroom seats served as chairs. And the likes of Eleanor Roosevelt and Andrei A. Gromyko mingled freely with clerks, secretaries and junior officers."[46] Then, after the Rockefeller family assisted with the purchase of

‡ The proposed South Dakota site later became "Reptile Gardens," at one time the world's largest reptile park. In 2015, the local mayor, declaring "United Nations and Reptile Gardens Location Day," proclaimed: "I would rather have Reptile Gardens here than the United Nations."

a tract of squalid but well-located land along the East River in Manhattan, the UN moved into larger temporary quarters out in Lake Success while the new headquarters was being built under the supervision of Robert Moses, the city's infamous construction coordinator. The new buildings would be sited in a neighborhood long known as Turtle Bay, a term that then became synonymous with the UN itself. (Moses, who called the UN headquarters project "interesting and unique," claimed the location had been chosen so that the diplomats and foreign leaders could be near "the restaurants, hotels, and the fleshpots" of midtown Manhattan.)[47]

To design the UN complex, a global dream team of architects was put together, including Le Corbusier and Oscar Niemeyer. The result was the striking, midcentury campus we know today with its iconic glass-walled tower and flags fluttering along First Avenue. (The building was initially panned by some; in the *New Yorker*, Lewis Mumford called it a blend of "the grandiose and the obvious.")[48] Yet even its design reflected the mindset of the time with regard to colonialism. The official report of the Secretariat to the General Assembly in July 1947 proposed the new complex be built to accommodate about seventy member states; in 1949, when construction began, the UN comprised fifty-nine states.[49] There was room for growth, but only a little. No one, in short, anticipated the rapidity of the wave of independence to come, which would swiftly swell the membership well past 70—indeed, to over 100 a decade after the UN headquarters' opening in late 1950.[§] Today the organization tops out at almost 200 states. Embodying the belief that colonialism was here to stay, the new UN complex was too small almost from the moment it opened.

There is no record that Ralph Bunche anticipated the size the UN would become or with what speed. But he was certainly more focused than most on the notion that the postwar system of states was going to expand. In the fall of 1946, at a speech at Wellesley College, he reminded the crowd that despite the great changes wrought by the war, there were still "several hundreds of millions of people . . . who have no direct voice in international

§ The Secretariat staff began to move in on August 21, 1950; the first General Assembly was held in the complex in 1952.

councils." The war, he explained, had "intensified the nationalist aspirations of most of the colonial peoples."[50] With Bunche's star rising, he made these points frequently in the addresses he was increasingly invited to give. The Black press was offering more profiles of him, and, reflecting the heightened interest in the global dimensions of racism, these articles, too, stressed the importance of decolonization. In 1946, for example, the *Pittsburgh Courier* ran an article titled "A Peep Behind the Scenes at the Work of Dr. Ralph Bunche." "Dr. Bunche is dead set against imperialism of all kinds," the *Courier* told its readers. "He wants to see all people politically free."[51]

It was in this period that the Bunche family finally relocated to New York City permanently. He had enjoyed his experience at the State Department. He had successfully journeyed from life as a Marxist-inclined academic to bureaucrat, policymaker, and diplomat. A pragmatist by nature, he had discovered that working from the inside could be very gratifying, and he came to see the value of incremental, reformist policy work that yielded concrete results on matters he had long cared about. His earlier radicalism seemed largely buried, certainly rejected in any overt form. In December 1946, he finally moved over to the UN Secretariat permanently. After the family sold the DC house, Ruth and the children moved up to an apartment Ralph had found in Parkway Village, a newly completed garden apartment complex nearby in Queens. He would spend the rest of his life in Queens, eventually moving with his family to the leafy neighborhood of Kew Gardens.

The UN position appealed to him for several reasons: for his children and what it would mean for them to live in New York; because of his growing belief in the mission of the UN; and perhaps because he perceived that a Black man like himself could only go so far in the State Department of the 1940s. It didn't hurt either that at the new UN salaries were tax-free—and higher than those at the State Department. Still, he thought the move to New York would be temporary, and he would soon return to his former life as a professor. As he explained in a letter to a friend in early 1947:

> and the deciding factor was really the well-being of the family. Ruth and I both felt strongly that the children would have much better educational and cultural opportunities in New York than in Washington. I felt also that a bit of experience on the

international side would not be at all harmful to me. I do not look upon it as a long-enduring proposition, as I am increasingly intent on getting back to the academic fold.[52]

Events, of course, have a way of getting in the way of the best-laid plans.

AS THE WORK OF THE UNITED NATIONS garnered greater attention, many Black Americans wondered whether the new organization and its lofty principles would impact discrimination at home. It was one thing to focus on the freedom of Africans; but what about the freedom of the African diaspora?

Speaking at the "Hungry Club Forum" at the Butler Street YMCA in March 1947, a venue intended to address race relations and allow whites and Blacks to mix in segregated Atlanta, Bunche addressed what the UN might achieve at home. He explained to the audience that the UN was centrally focused on world peace and would remain so. Conceding that one of the core principles of the UN was equality of all peoples, he nonetheless stressed what he saw as a basic political fact: the new organization was not going to have any immediate impact on the plight of Black Americans—or, he added, any other minority group in the world. "Don't look for any quick results in our domestic situation" from the UN, he warned the audience.[53] He closed by urging his listeners to pay more attention to international affairs, a point he had been making nearly since high school.

His speech reflected the growing interest in what the UN meant for minorities. Indeed, the NAACP, led by W. E. B. Du Bois, was planning to issue a petition to the UN that fall. Du Bois believed the UN Charter's language offered a unique opportunity to put racial injustice in America directly before the international community. While certainly sharing Du Bois's concerns about the state of domestic race relations, Bunche was skeptical of the strategy (though one NAACP board member, decades later, claimed Bunche encouraged the NAACP effort behind the scenes).[54]

Du Bois forged ahead and presented a fifty-five-page petition in October 1947. He was joined by a twenty-member delegation, which included his arch-rival at the NAACP, Walter White. The NAACP petition declared itself to be a "frank and earnest appeal to all the world for elemental justice against the treatment the United States has visited upon us for three centuries."[55] A copy was given to every UN ambassador. In their remarks at their press conference, Du Bois and White made clear that the concerns raised in the petition were not limited to American racial minorities: "Because injustice against black men in America has repercussion upon the status and future of brown men in India, yellow men in China, and black in Africa, we submit that no lasting cure of the causes of war can be found until discrimination based on race or skin color is wiped out of the United States."[56]

This plea to the UN in some respects foreshadowed the foreign policy case for racial justice during the Cold War. Within a few years, as the Soviet Union ramped up its critiques of Jim Crow as a way to drive a wedge between the US and the newly emerging states of Africa and Asia, the American national security establishment began to worry that the Cold War struggle for global hearts and minds would be irreparably harmed by Southern intransigence on race. As the *New York Times* reported of the NAACP's UN petition, Du Bois's presentation posed an important question: "When will nations learn that their enemies are quite as often within their own country as without?" The *Times* added that the effort highlighted "that it is not the Soviet Union that threatens the United States so much as Mississippi; 'Not Stalin and Molotov but Bilbo and Rankin.'"[57] Bunche himself would later echo this argument, saying in 1962 that "the greatest threats to democracy are internal," and, referencing Mississippi Governor Ross Barnett and John Birch Society co-founder Robert Welch, stated that "the Barnetts and the Welches do so much more harm than Mr. Khruschev ever can do."[58] Still, in 1947 Bunche was not convinced that directly petitioning the UN about American racism would work or was wise.

The NAACP's petition was not the first effort to tie injustice at home to the new peace organization. The National Negro Congress had presented a similar petition the year before. Arguing that they had no choice but to plead their case before the international community, the NNC document detailed how, despite the defeat of fascism abroad, millions of Americans remained "bound to the soil in semi-feudal serfdom . . . lynched . . . terrorized" and "segregated like pariahs." The NNC presented their plea to what they called "the highest court of mankind—the United Nations."[59]

The NAACP's petition was also not the last. In 1951, as the Cold War had fully taken root in American society, the Civil Rights Congress put forward *We Charge Genocide*, a 200-page document that cited the new Convention on the Prevention and Punishment of Genocide, which the General Assembly adopted in 1948. The petition was presented by Paul Robeson. Bunche and Robeson had stayed in touch since London; Robeson had written to Bunche the year before about issues relating to Africa at the UN.[60] At this point, Robeson, whom Bunche had thought was "all out for the USSR," was hugely controversial for his outspoken support for communism. Indeed, the State Department had canceled his passport in 1950 on the grounds that his speeches were a national security threat.[61] (Robeson petitioned for a special passport for the occasion of the petition.) Probably not helping matters politically, the *Daily Worker*, the newspaper of the Communist Party of the US, called the genocide petition an "irrefutable indictment against white supremacy."[62] *

Alarmed at the comparison of American racism to genocide, the State Department enlisted the NAACP's Walter White in condemning the Civil Rights Congress's effort.[63] The father of the Genocide Convention, Rafael Lemkin, also criticized the 1951 petition as a perversion of the true meaning of genocide. The petition was the product of communist sympathizers, Lemkin declared, meant to "divert UN attention from true genocidal crimes being committed against Soviet-dominated peoples, and perhaps discourage US ratification of the pact." The *Washington Post's* headline summed up the establishment view: "Charge of US Genocide Called Red Smoke Screen."[64]

UN officials were unsure how or even whether to react to these petitions. Some believed they were not empowered to accept them. Even if they could, they likely feared taking action that would alarm the government that was both their host and primary financial supporter. Moreover, even nominally sympathetic members of the US delegation to the UN, such as Eleanor Roosevelt—also a member of the NAACP board of directors—were not pleased with this approach. Roosevelt refused to introduce the

NAACP's petition, fearing it would harm the international reputation of the US. Indeed, a year earlier Roosevelt had opposed criticism of South Africa at the UN on the grounds that it could set a precedent that might allow the UN to investigate racial discrimination in the South.[65] The UN ultimately took no action on the NAACP petition. Eleanor Roosevelt in fact offered to resign from the NAACP, telling the board that the petition had "embarrassed her" and "embarrassed the nation."[66]

The various UN petitions on racial justice in America resulted in no concrete actions. Nonetheless, they illustrated the power of the UN to serve as a focal point for human rights claims. The petitions shined a harsh global spotlight on an ugly aspect of American democracy. Perhaps the new UN was powerless to change it, but it was an aspect the US foreign policy establishment, during the rapidly approaching Cold War, would begin to work to alter and, as much as possible, to obscure.

THE NAACP HAD CHOSEN OCTOBER 1947 to introduce their petition because that was when the UN General Assembly was meeting. The tradition of "UN Week," the opening of the General Assembly each fall, had already begun. The opening was a bit different in 1947 than it would be in years to come. Bunche and the rest of the UN staff and delegates were still ensconced in temporary quarters on Long Island. (Bunche's office in the old Sperry Gyroscope factory overlooked the parking lot.) In October Bunche headed out to a grand dinner at the Waldorf Astoria to commemorate the start of the fall session. Sitting on the dais, he watched Douglas Fairbanks Jr., the 1940s silver screen star, emcee the event. The presence of stars such as Fairbanks, the many celebrities who had come to San Francisco in the spring of 1945, the NAACP petition—these were all different, even highly disparate events, but they illustrated the hold the new UN had on many Americans in these early years.

At this point, the UN was still widely seen as a peace and security organization representing a (increasingly fractured) wartime alliance and implicitly focused on what was still seen as the center of international order: Europe. Soon, however, the UN would begin to evolve. The decolonization that followed in the coming decades did not merely represent a change in the number of UN member states. It also marked a major shift in the politics of the UN as a whole. Of the initial fifty members of the UN, only three were from Asia—India, China, and the Philippines—and three—Ethiopia, Liberia, and South Africa—were from Africa. (If one counted Egypt, there were four.) Over the coming years, this "Afro-Asian" group would grow markedly, and many challenges involving non-self-governed peoples would emerge. Of the first challenges that were put before the young UN, none proved more complex than that of the British-administered territory of Palestine. Ralph Bunche would soon learn more than he ever imagined—or wanted to know—about the small but highly coveted territory between the Eastern Mediterranean and the Jordan River.

CHAPTER 9

THE PROBLEM OF PALESTINE

I swear by all that is holy, I will never come anywhere near the Palestine problem once I liberate myself from this trap.
—Ralph Bunche, letter to Ruth Bunche, 1950

In the winter of 1949, on the island of Rhodes, Israeli and Egyptian negotiators listened as Ralph Bunche, acting as mediator for the United Nations, spoke before them. United in conflict and fresh from war, they had flown to the Hotel des Roses, set on a picturesque beach promontory overlooking the Mediterranean, in an effort to restart a nascent peace process and agree on some form of armistice. Bunche laid out the stakes, starkly pressing the delegates to rise to the occasion. The success of these talks is in your hands, he declared. "The lives of many people, and indeed, the peace of the Near East, hang in the balance while you meet. You cannot afford to fail. You must succeed. I have faith that you *will* succeed."[1]

Israel had been a sovereign state for less than one year when Bunche spoke these words. Israel's declaration of independence in May 1948 immediately ignited conflict in the Middle East. Arab forces attacked the new nation. As would occur again and again in decades to come, Israel's military power proved formidable to its enemies. Arab states, while numerically much stronger, were hobbled by disagreement, disorganization, and differing interests. Yet a lasting solution to the struggle between Arabs and Israelis was and remains ultimately a political, not military, matter.

In the brief period between the end of the Second World War and Israel's independence, the new UN, just a few years older than Israel itself, became the focal point of efforts to broker a peaceful settlement in Palestine.* Bunche, due to a tragic twist of fate, became the point person for much of those efforts. Over several months in Rhodes, with Bunche as their taskmaster and cheerleader, the two sides debated, argued, played snooker, and were by turns accommodating and disagreeable. The differences between the parties were large and sharp. Yet in the end, agreement came. Bunche's first accord, signed in February 1949 between Egypt and Israel, established an armistice, moved troops, and recast lines of control. (Related negotiations between Israel and Jordan would result in the famous "Green Line," still a focal point today for discussions over a potential two-state solution to the Israeli-Palestinian conflict.) Acting as UN mediator, Bunche cajoled and charmed the assembled delegates in the grand seaside hotel. But he was also firm and sometimes harsh in his assessments of the attitudes and tactics of both sides. Bunche's process was groundbreaking, and it created a template for the use of the UN as an "honest broker" in many future conflicts.

The success of the negotiations in the Middle East, a region he previously had had little experience or interest in, brought Bunche from relative obscurity to the height of fame. In an act that turned him into a household name, the Nobel Committee would award him the 1950 Peace Prize. The Peace Prize elevated him from a rising star in diplomatic circles to a national and even global phenomenon. And he used his newfound prominence to extol the virtues of the UN as a peace broker. As a committed internationalist, Bunche believed deeply in the need for peace among different nations and races and in the moral case for self-determination and independence. He reiterated these themes many times throughout his life. His Nobel

---

* I use the term *Palestine* throughout this chapter; at the time of the British mandate, and for the early UN, that was the term used for the area now more commonly known as Israel and the West Bank and Gaza.

Prize gave him a megaphone of the first order to do so. But to get there, the "Palestine problem" had to be solved.

PALESTINE HAS AN UNUSUALLY COMPLICATED HISTORY. Jerusalem was first settled at least 3000 years ago and has enjoyed, and endured, many rulers during the millennia. Throughout the 19th century, and nearly until the end of the First World War, Palestine and the surrounding territory were controlled by the Ottoman Empire. A fading power by the dawn of the 20th century, the Ottomans had sided with Germany in the war. Once defeated, the Ottomans faced the prospect of losing much of their empire, which comprised large parts of the Middle East.

Britain and France, the primary victors in the First World War, already had footholds in the region. But the two European powers craved more. Indeed, before the war was even over, they had negotiated a secret agreement to divide up the territories of the Middle East. Known as the Sykes-Picot Accord, it would later be vilified by nearly all factions within the region. As had been done for Africa decades earlier, the Europeans created colonial borders that suited their preferences, with little regard for local interests or peoples. As Robin Wright recounts,

> Borders were determined with a ruler—arbitrarily. At a briefing for Britain's Prime Minister H. H. Asquith, in 1915, Sykes famously explained "I should like to draw a line from the 'E' in Acre to the last 'K' in Kirkuk." He slid his finger across a map, spread out on a table at No. 10 Downing Street, from what is today a city on Israel's Mediterranean coast to the northern mountains of Iraq.[2]

Over a century later, the Sykes-Picot agreement, and the colonial politics it represents, is still infamous. When in 2014 ISIS conquered a vast swath of territory deep in the Middle East, leader Abu Bakr al-Baghdadi declared that "this blessed advance will not stop until we hit the last nail in the coffin of the Sykes-Picot conspiracy."[3]

Sykes-Picot perfectly reflected the politics of the early 20th century. European states had been swapping territories in postwar settlements for centuries; to do so in the rest of the world came naturally, especially when

European military power allowed them to conquer and dominate many foreign societies easily. Still, even under the Sykes-Picot framework, Palestine was seen as special—and was intended to be put under "international administration."

The secret wartime plans of the British and French did not come to fruition, however. The intervention of the US in the First World War and President Woodrow Wilson's vision for a new League of Nations transformed aspects of European colonialism. No longer would Europeans openly swap territory like so many poker chips. Wilson wanted a different approach, one more consistent with his call for self-determination. Britain gained its legal authority over Palestine as part of the League's system of mandates, and now was supposed to govern it in trust and, perhaps, shepherd it to independence. There was only one problem: Arabs and Jews thoroughly disagreed over whose land Palestine really was.

Arabs significantly outnumbered Jews in Palestine at the end of the First World War. But Zionism, the movement to build a Jewish national state in Palestine, had brought many more Jews to the region in recent decades and so the demographic gap was shrinking. Although Zionism seemed utopian to some and threatening to others, the belief in a Jewish homeland was gaining strength by the early 20th century. In awarding the mandate for Palestine to Britain, the League had favorably noted an earlier statement by the British government, known as the Balfour Declaration. In a 1917 letter to prominent Jewish leader Lord Walter Rothschild, Foreign Secretary Arthur Balfour had promised that "His Majesty's Government view with favour the establishment in Palestine of a national home for the Jewish people, and will use their best endeavours to facilitate the achievement of this object."[4] By awarding Britain the Palestine mandate, the League was essentially endorsing the Balfour Declaration and its call for the creation of a Jewish homeland. The difficult question was how—and where—to create it.

From the beginning the process was not smooth. The Arab nations in the region had significant stakes and strong opinions but little formal say. Of the founding states of the League, none were Arab. (Iraq, the first Arab member, joined in 1932; Egypt in 1937.) By the time the UN was created in

1945, there was substantial Arab opposition to the idea of a Jewish state and mounting tensions throughout the region. At the same time Jewish immigration was growing, Zionist groups were increasingly active, and there was rising sentiment around the world in favor of creating a Jewish state, especially in the wake of the defeat of Nazi Germany. How to square this circle was very hard to determine.

In fact, by the 1930s the struggle between Arabs and Jews was already viewed, in a way familiar to contemporary ears, as nearly intractable. In 1937, the British government said it was "driven to the conclusion that there is an irreconcilable conflict between the aspirations of the Arabs and those of the Jews in Palestine."[5] To many Jews in Palestine, it was in fact the British who were the primary obstacle—and perhaps even the primary enemy—of Zionism. (Some radical elements in Jewish society in Palestine hated the British so much they advocated collaborating with the Nazis against them.) To many Arabs, the notion of a Jewish homeland in Palestine was simply theft of their land. In this setting it was almost inevitable that both sides increasingly engaged in hostilities.

Soon the British were looking for an exit. Just after Germany's surrender, Churchill, tiring of American pressure over Zionist aspirations, wrote that Britain should not retain control over Palestine while "the Americans sit and criticize." Somebody else, Churchill thought, "should have their turn now."[6] As Churchill noted, there were "at least 100,000 men in Palestine who might be at home strengthening our depleted industry."[7] Adding to the pressure, in October 1946 President Harry Truman publicly announced American support for a Jewish state in Palestine. Exhausted from the war, Britain finally declared it had had enough: "His Majesty's Government are not prepared to continue indefinitely to govern Palestine themselves merely because Arabs and Jews cannot agree upon the means of sharing its government between them."[8] Seizing an opportunity, in 1947 the British conveniently referred the question of the future government of Palestine to the new UN.

Palestine was not the easiest problem for a fledging international organization to tackle. For good reason, one of the world's great powers had just washed its hands of it. Was the problem unfixable? Perhaps. But it also illustrated the advantages of having a functioning international organization. When powerful states wanted to shed responsibility for a problem, they could now hand it to the UN. And the UN was at least in principle an impartial body. Member states came from diverse regions, religious traditions, and cultural groupings, and the General Assembly, operating on a one-nation one-vote system, allowed them all a say. As a result, a UN-led process had at least a veneer of legitimacy.

This all made, and continues to make, the UN an attractive repository for the intractable problems of the world. The British could easily be blamed for putting their interests above those of the various inhabitants, whatever solution they imposed. This was certainly the view of radical Jewish paramilitaries such as the Irgun, who in 1946 killed ninety-one people in a terrorist bombing at the King David Hotel in Jerusalem, the site of the British Mandate Secretariat. It was less easy to blame the UN this way (but as events later proved, not impossible). A UN-led process for Palestine's future had at least a chance to be seen as more legitimate and, perhaps as a result, to be more successful.

RALPH BUNCHE HAD ONLY BEEN WORKING in the new Trusteeship Department of the United Nations officially, as a UN staffer, for a few months when in early 1947 the British announced they would toss the Palestine hot potato to the UN. This presented a fraught but significant opportunity for the new organization. Britain did not want to place it under the trusteeship system: that would likely mean it would remain the trust power, and the British preferred to get out altogether and have the UN directly decide the territory's fate.[9] Trygve Lie, the Norwegian secretary general, immediately called a meeting to discuss what the organization should do. Bunche, with his broad knowledge of colonies and interest in self-determination, was part of the small group Lie convened to strategize about how to handle this development. As a former professor might, Bunche told Lie that he thought it was essential to first have a dedicated team study the matter.[10] Only if the UN understood the true scope of the challenges in Palestine, he suggested, could they be addressed properly. In no-good-deed-goes-unpunished style, Lie promptly put Bunche in charge of the new study. (Bunche, who by this point had an attractive offer in hand from the University of Pennsylvania for a professorship, may have wondered if academia would give him more freedom.)[11] Known as the "Preparatory Committee," Bunche's UN team produced several volumes of facts, figures, and analysis of previously proposed solutions to the Palestine impasse.

In 1947 Bunche was no expert on the Middle East, let alone the thorny Palestinian question. He had never really studied the region or its complicated, layered, and often vicious politics. Still, he was staunchly against foreign domination and had strong views on anti-Semitism.[†] For Bunche, anti-Semitism was another form of racism and fundamentally un-American. Speaking years later in New York, Bunche declared that "racial prejudice, anti-Semitism, anti-Catholicism—these are all un-American attitudes and harmful to our national unity. They are seriously divisive influences which sap our national strength at the very moment in our history when we need our maximum strength."[12]

As the Palestine process at the UN developed, American newspapers often underscored the perceived connection between racial discrimination in America and the problems of the Jews in Palestine—a sort of inverse of the 21st-century connection, which far more often assimilates the Palestinians to the plight of racial minorities in the West. As the *Christian Science Monitor* put it in a representative analysis in 1947, Bunche "stands thus a distinguished member of a subordinated minority group given a key role in the working out of another minority people's problem."[13]

It is not clear that Bunche saw things that way. He was certainly sympathetic to the plight of the Jewish people and saw them, as many Americans did, as a beleaguered minority. Yet the notion that Bunche was somehow inclined, simply by being Black, to identify with Jews more than Arabs is not supported by either his public actions or his private writings. Both sides, as it turned out, saw Bunche as a friendly figure and courted him. He in turn

---

[†] Bunche nonetheless had enjoyed little contact with Jews growing up and was occasionally bemused by Jewish customs. In 1967, after attending a Jewish funeral, he noted that "I sort of like the yomulka [sic] custom but I dislike the men wearing their hats indoors usually with the front brim turned down and the hat at a jaunty angle. Somehow, it offends me."

was often put off by the intensely emotional politics of the region and the deception and cunning that he witnessed in the negotiations from both sides. Over the long run, however, he grew closer with Israeli officials than Arab ones, though the causes of that are hard to pin down and likely reflect, at least to some degree, the fact that the UN process, of which Bunche was a central figure, in the end worked more to Israel's relative advantage.

The UN Preparatory Committee worked fast, but it was just the beginning of the international community's process with regard to Palestine. A few months later the General Assembly held a special session on the topic. The question was whether to build on Bunche's early fact-gathering effort and create a special committee of inquiry into Palestine, with the goal of issuing concrete recommendations on how to proceed with a comprehensive political solution. The committee would travel to the region, meet with the antagonists, and assess the situation on the ground. The idea of the committee was approved. It was known, in what would become typically clunky UN style, as UNSCOP: the UN Special Committee on Palestine.

Almost immediately the US and the Soviet Union began jockeying over the composition of UNSCOP. The Cold War had barely begun in 1947. Yet already the two superpowers had found the UN an excellent arena for geopolitical jousting. President Truman wanted as much as possible to stay out of the limelight with regard to any decision over the future of Palestine. By contrast, the Soviets were eager to play a prominent role in the postwar Middle East and very much wanted to be on the UNSCOP committee.

To avoid this outcome, the US suggested that no great powers participate: only small or neutral states, with no particular interest in Palestine, ought to serve on the committee. (The US would use this tactic again a decade later to keep the Soviets out of Egypt during the Suez Crisis.) This proposal had the great advantage of empowering the numerous smaller states, who naturally supported it. Ultimately, eleven states were chosen as members, among them Canada, Guatemala, India, Iran, the Netherlands, Peru, and Yugoslavia. This group was given just three months to issue their recommendations.[14] To support UNSCOP, the UN Secretariat created a small staff. Ralph Bunche, fresh off his work on the Preparatory Committee and now one of the more knowledgeable members of the new

UN bureaucracy, was forced to cancel his planned summer vacation and head to the Middle East.

Bunche found a tense Jerusalem when he arrived in June 1947. The city was far smaller then, and the Old City, with its warren of narrow alleyways and calls to prayer and ritual, dominated even more than it does now. Jerusalem, Bunche wrote later, was like an armed camp: most of the main roads were mined, "there were constant kidnappings and assassinations in the towns and frequent sniping . . . barbed wire barricades were everywhere."[15] The British had been facing sporadic, but increasing, violence from Jewish insurgents. "The British are everywhere and they all carry guns," he noted. The situation was frightening, but also electric and exciting. Two radical paramilitary groups in particular were active against the British: Irgun, led by future Israeli prime minister Menachem Begin, and Lehi, led by Avraham Stern, and then known as "the Stern Gang." On the first working day for UNSCOP, five members of the Irgun were sentenced to death for terrorism.[16] Thrust into this volatile mix, Bunche was uneasy and unsure of what was to come.

The tension was exacerbated by the fact that from the beginning, Arab states and the local Palestinian leadership refused to participate in UNSCOP's work.[17] The Arabs adopted the position that there was nothing to debate in Palestine. The decision was a risky move that proved politically unwise over the long run. This was also a troubling start for UNSCOP, which wanted to ensure the legitimacy of its work by involving all stakeholders. But the committee felt it had no choice but to move forward anyway.

UNSCOP took its task seriously. Still, Bunche, a tough critic, was no more impressed with the committee than he had been with the initial US delegation to London in 1946. Indeed, he thought the UNSCOP members were a surprisingly poor team. To Ruth he wrote they were "just about the worst group I've ever had to work with . . . if they do a good job it will be a real miracle."[18] In particular, he found the Pakistani delegate, Abdur Rahman, to be "rabidly anti-Jewish," even "venomous." Of another delegate, Ivan Rand of Canada, Bunche would later say "Canada could not possibly have done worse."[19] They were also bumbling. At the Church of the Holy

Sepulchre, the Dutch delegate literally fell into the Tomb of Nicodemus, nearly breaking his leg. None of this boded well.

The many religious sites in Palestine were a particular focus for UNSCOP, in part because of their political relevance for people all over the world. The committee secretariat even prepared a special report on the "Holy Places."[20] The visits to Palestine were often rough—security checks were everywhere, the weather was sometimes broiling, and prices were high—but Bunche grew fascinated by the region and its ancient customs, marveling at Jews at the Wailing Wall as they prayed and stuck small pieces of paper in the cracks of the stones. Later, in Tel Aviv, he saw displaced Jews arriving from Europe, some of whom had just two years before been in concentration camps and bore blue tattoos on their forearms. Bunche learned that Jews were more diverse than he ever knew, including what he called "Black Jews," by which he meant Jews from the Middle East and even India.[21]

The UN team interviewed many leaders from various factions and interests. A small group went to meet with Chaim Weizmann, the Zionist leader, in what Bunche referred to as the "Jewish White House." Bunche even met with Irgun leader Menachem Begin in his secret Tel Aviv hideout—what he described as his "most exciting adventure" on the trip.[22] The UNSCOP members eventually visited Jewish refugee camps in Europe. But most of their time was spent in Palestine.

While on the ground, UNSCOP members were the subject of considerable interest and suspicion. With a political boycott in place, Arab journalists were warned to not cover the visits. British officials, still nominally in charge of the territory, also generally steered clear, wanting to avoid seeming to take sides in a problem they were hoping to rapidly leave behind. This left the Jews as UNSCOP's primary interlocutors—an advantage quickly capitalized on. In the political vacuum, "Zionist diplomats and spies were able to work unencumbered" to achieve their goals.[23]

[T]he entire intelligence service of the Jewish underground organization Haganah was put to work monitoring UNSCOP members. Microphones were placed in hotel and conference rooms. All phone conversations were tapped. The cleaning staff in the building in Jerusalem where the committee held daily hearings was replaced by female agents who reported back each day on its activities. The tactic did not go unnoticed. A member of the Swedish delegation complained that the women on the cleaning staff were "too pretty and educated. They are the eyes and ears of the Zionist leaders, who come to hearings with replies prepared in advance."[24]

Seemingly serendipitous but entirely manufactured encounters occurred with UNSCOP personnel, all with an eye toward shaping their disposition. The Dutch delegate, for example, somehow kept encountering Jewish emigrants from the Netherlands, who even farmed with Dutch-bred cows in the desert.

Largely unaware of how the Jewish leadership was shaping their fact-finding process, the committee toured settlements of various kinds. "The spirit in the kibbutzes is impressive," Bunche wrote in his journal, though he also found that the country generally had a "lazy tempo."[25] He was struck by the farmers trying to work the rocky, dry terrain in much of the land, next to hillsides often speckled with herds of sheep, goats, and even camels. Palestine in 1947 was very poor. To Bunche, who had been raised in a religious Baptist household as a teen, it sometimes seemed a trip back in time, with grain thrown in the air to thresh in the ancient manner and water carried around by hand. To add to the medieval feeling, there were reports of an outbreak of bubonic plague in Haifa during UNSCOP's visit. Even later, in 1948 when he returned as part of the UN mediation effort after Israel's declaration of independence, the region seemed barely developed. At one point, his plane had to fly low over a runway at the Jerusalem airport simply to scare off a goat herd grazing there.

UNSCOP's efforts to interact with Arab leaders generally went nowhere. Even its two Muslim delegates, from India and Iran, were unsuccessful.[26] Bunche was a minor exception. In an early sign of how he was able to gain trust in difficult negotiations, he found local Arab leaders and even ordinary people occasionally willing to open up—at least with him. "All the Arabs treat me like a long-lost brother—why, I don't quite know why," he wrote in his diary.[27]

UNSCOP did occasionally visit with Arab leaders. On July 24 the delegates headed to Amman to meet the king of Jordan. The visit was fraught, and it was unclear if it was being treated as "official"—as in UNSCOP visiting the king—or simply an assemblage of individual visits by the committee members. Arriving at the palace, Bunche was impressed with the exoticism of the encounter: the king in his turban and robes, the almond milk served with the coffee. The servants, Bunche noted, were Black, "probably from the Sudan."[28] The atmosphere was new and alien, yet alluring to Bunche's inner anthropologist.

Greeting the group, the king made clear that in his view there were already enough Jews in Palestine. Asked if he might accept some Jewish refugees in Jordan, he laughed and replied "that would be asking me to cut my own throat." The king took a particular interest in Bunche. At the end of the meeting, he "put his hand on my arm, pulled me back into the room to look at the picture of his father who, he had said in the meeting, is buried in Jerusalem and had told him to look after Palestine." He then asked Bunche where he was from. Hearing "America," the king looked surprised. He then made "some reference to my complexion and [said] that I might be taken for an Arab."[29]

The UNSCOP delegation declined the royal invitation for dinner and, after some further meetings in Amman, headed back to the airport. Meeting the prime minister of Jordan before their departure, Bunche learned from him that the Arabs were a highly individualistic people, a trait that (supposedly) justified the unrepresentative monarchies of the Middle East, on the grounds that individualism is expressed by extending loyalty to someone "above and better than them" such as a monarch. Bunche was unsure of this political theory, which certainly seemed self-serving. The prime minister told UNSCOP that while no new Jews should enter the region, the Jews currently in Palestine could remain as a minority with equal rights in a new Palestinian state. Self-determination, he said, was an essential right—but for the majority Arab population. The UN could perhaps guarantee that minority rights would be respected—a throwback to the League of Nation's approach—but partition into two states would violate the very principle of self-determination.[30] The discussion presaged debates that would often arise at the UN in the years to come, as many former colonies gained their independence yet, because they often comprised disparate ethnic and linguistic groups, faced difficult questions of *whose* self-determination was paramount.

UNSCOP's tour of the region seemed like a sensible attempt to untie the thorny knot of Palestine. Bunche, a seasoned social scientist who had done extensive fieldwork all over the world, knew how important it was to see things on the ground. The various tours certainly yielded insight into the often clashing viewpoints at stake. Yet like many visitors to the region, Bunche found the situation Byzantine and the solutions, such as they were, all deeply flawed. "The longer we stay the more confused we all get," he wrote home in a letter. "The only thing that seems clear to me after five weeks in Palestine is that the British have made a terrible mess of things here." Indeed, as far as he could see, the only area of agreement between the warring factions in Palestine was that "the British must go."[31]

Bunche puzzled over the problem of Palestine. He found the Jews in Palestine to be different from the Jews he had come to know back in New York; imbued with the zeal of Zionism, they struck him as having a distinct spirit and personality. He also saw early on that both Arabs and Jews "are here and intend to stay."[32] Indeed, more Jews were trying to come every day: while he was there the *Exodus*, attempting to ferry thousands of European Jews to Palestine, was famously attacked by the British at sea. Like virtually everyone since who has contemplated the conflict, he came to realize the aspirations of the two peoples could not be mutually satisfied. Abstract justice, he thought, would not solve the problem of Palestine: there was likely to be no solution at all, only varying degrees of unhappiness with the results. A chief danger, he believed, was that a caste system would develop, with the Arabs on the bottom. Although Bunche would later be lambasted for being too pro-Israeli, he learned to his surprise that in the local Hebrew language press he was being called anti-Semitic, on the grounds that he allegedly feared that creation of a Jewish state would "stir up demand among US Negroes for a state also."[33]

Now finished with its visit, the UNSCOP team began the journey back west, one that involved many sightseeing stops along with way, including

Athens and Rome. (Bunche quipped that the committee "may not write a good report on Palestine but ought to be able to do a good job on ruins.")[34] Arriving in Geneva near the end of July, they began work on their final report. Geneva was certainly pleasant in summer, ringing by the soaring snow-capped Alps and set on a lovely lake shore. Yet Bunche felt increasingly lonely and homesick for Ruth and his family. He was frustrated with the lax work ethic and shoddy drafting of his fellow committee members. Increasingly, it was Bunche who was rewriting aspects of the report, acting, in his wry words, as a "ghost-writing harlot."[35]

He also was struck by the way that several members now openly expressed their anti-Semitism. Surprisingly, this did not necessarily dim their view of partition or the creation of a Jewish state. In part, it disturbingly seemed, they actually preferred it as a way to create a permanent place to send Jews from their own nations. The Canadian delegate, Ivan Rand of the Canadian Supreme Court, said that the Jews must be given a state in Palestine "so we can dispose of them once and for all and they won't be bothering us all the time."[36] These comments, of which there were several, bothered Bunche. Yet they showed how the preference for a Jewish national home in Palestine drew fairly wide, if incongruous and differing, political support.

In early August, on a Geneva day marked by rain after a long heat wave, Bunche received a mysterious phone call: "a woman's voice with [an] English accent saying 'I have regards from Fred.'" This was the identification signal agreed on with an Irgun representative before he left Jerusalem. Bunche made an appointment to meet her in his office the next day. The Irgun contact visited him in the afternoon and arranged for Bunche to be picked up at 7 p.m. the next evening. After a cloak-and-dagger handoff to another Irgun member, Bunche was taken to see "Fred." Even in his private diary Bunche never revealed who this high-placed Irgun leader was. But the man he met told Bunche that Irgun would never accept partition in Palestine and attacked the other compromise-minded Jewish organizations that were open to it. Irgun, the nameless leader promised, will disband as soon as the state of Israel is born.

While in Geneva, the UNSCOP delegates also debated whether to visit the "displaced persons" camps still operating in Europe: legalese for mostly Jewish victims of Nazi Germany who, perhaps due to their liberation from death camps, were temporarily housed in the German countryside. Eventually, the UNSCOP members voted to visit the camps. In early August a subcommittee of members, Bunche not among them, headed to Munich, which was still occupied by American forces, to see the situation for themselves. Upon their return, the group vividly (and Bunche would later argue, decisively) described their shocking encounters to the rest of the committee. The Holocaust had not been uppermost in the minds of the members during their time in Palestine, but it was increasingly weighing on them as they pondered their report.

For the remainder of August the committee stayed in Geneva. The delegates were consumed by arguments over what a solution ought to look like. Finally, on September 1, 1947, the report was done. Bunche returned to New York after a twenty-hour flight. "Now to rejoin my family!" he wrote in his diary that day, somewhat hastily in light of subsequent events. "The Palestine episode is over."[37]

UNSCOP SUBMITTED A LENGTHY AND DETAILED report to the UN General Assembly. The report first carefully analyzed the history, politics, and economics of the region. The committee unanimously recommended that the British mandate in Palestine be ended. But it split over how to proceed beyond that.

The first proposal, and the majority recommendation, was for partition into two states. Here was an early version of the much-vaunted, and perhaps now dead, two-state solution.[38] The sole exception to this two-state approach was Jerusalem. As the site of so many holy places, a dizzying array of traditions and ethnicities, and ancient and intertwined streets and squares, Jerusalem was the most complex to apportion politically. It would consequently be held in "international trusteeship" by the UN itself—following, in essence, the plan in the notorious Sykes-Picot accord of 1916.

UNSCOP's second, minority, proposal was for a federal, binational state—in essence, the one-state solution, only with political guarantees for both peoples. The new state would have carefully apportioned political representation of Arabs and Jews; Jerusalem would be the shared capital. This kind of complex constitutional arrangement was not without precedent, but it posed many practical challenges and likely would satisfy no one.

UNSCOP's divided recommendations reflected not only the great difficulty of the problem, but also the limited time the committee had to sort out a solution. As UNSCOP's deadline had approached, the group was still in Geneva debating the way forward. Bunche implored the committee to find common ground; he believed they could make a real difference with the right proposal. As Bunche put it at the time, his principal goal was to "ensure that there should be no need for another commission." Bunche was a practical person when it came to diplomacy. That meant compromise, and he had pushed the group to compromise again and again. At times, proposals were killed if they were too controversial. As he later told a member of the American delegation to the UN, a majority had felt an Arab state in Palestine should be joined with Jordan, "but it did not include this idea in their report."[39]

Arab states nonetheless rejected both of UNSCOP's proposed solutions. For them, Palestine was self-evidently Arab and should remain so. On the Jewish side, by contrast, there was general acceptance of the UN partition proposal, even if many complaints persisted about details. (There was more pointed opposition—in particular with regard to the governance of Jerusalem—on the part of radical and religious elements in Jewish society in the region.) The task now fell to the UN General Assembly, the body that represented all fifty-six member states, to vote on a resolution dictating a final path forward.

Meeting in a renovated former ice-skating rink at the old World's Fair grounds in Queens that fall, the UN delegates debated the future of Palestine. Newspapers around the world followed the proceedings intensely. The UN, now just two years old, was still imbued with substantial hope. The Truman administration was supportive of the proposed resolution, and many delegations received telegrams from American senators encouraging them to vote yes. Zionist organizations were in high gear, encouraging wavering states to support the resolution. Arab states fought back strongly. The delegate from Lebanon gave a passionate speech before the General Assembly, declaring Jerusalem the center of his universe. Behind the scenes, fierce lobbying was underway on all sides. In his memoirs, President Truman wrote that

[t]he facts were that not only were there pressure movements around the United Nations unlike anything that had been seen there before, but that the White House, too, was subjected to a constant barrage. I do not think I ever had as much pressure and propaganda aimed at the White House as I had in this instance.[40]

With the British mandate set to expire in May 1948, General Assembly Resolution 181, endorsing partition was finally put to a vote. On November 29, 1947, thousands of anxious spectators crowded into the former skating rink. The final vote was easily over the bar: 33 in favor, 13 opposed, with 10 nations abstaining. The partition of Palestine was approved.

Many years later, in a speech in Dallas, Texas, Bunche would claim that the critical turning point in UNSCOP's decision process was their tour of refugee camps in battered postwar Europe. The committee members, he said, were undecided when we left Palestine. It was the visits to refugee camps in Europe "that proved decisive. . . . Hitler [was] really responsible for the partition decision of the General Assembly in 1947."[41] Whatever the cause—and of course the reasons for the votes of the General Assembly members may not have flowed directly from UNSCOP recommendations—partition into two states, with all the political fallout that encompassed, was the decision taken.

Fighting in the region commenced almost immediately in the aftermath of the UN vote. Arab leaders had made many public pronouncements opposing the prospect of partition and, now thwarted by events, felt they had little choice but to attack its approval. To Bunche it was unclear what would happen next. In the US, the newly formed CIA provided a summary of the situation to Truman. The UN plan, the CIA counseled, "cannot be implemented. The Arab reaction to the recommendation has been violent and the Arab refusal to cooperate . . . will prevent the formation of an Arab state."[42]

The US itself was somewhat divided about the way forward. While Truman, in former Secretary of State Dean Rusk's words, could be "schizophrenic about Palestine," many US officials saw the Arab side as the more strategically important.[43] They were ambivalent about partition and unsure of the wisdom of creating a new Jewish state. The Arabs were potentially important allies, not least because they controlled vast and newly significant oil fields. Indeed, in March 1948, just months before Resolution 181 was set to go into effect, US Ambassador to the UN Warren Austin spoke out in the Security Council chamber proposing that the plan be suspended. Predicting "heavy fighting and chaos" should partition go forward, Austin proposed that Palestine be put under the UN's trusteeship system. Historians debate the degree to which Truman knew, approved, or was blindsided by Austin's speech. But Bunche characterized it as a "US bombshell launched."[44]

Austin's speech sparked immediate confusion. Was America now reversing course on the first major issue to come before the world body? "As you can well imagine, we in the Trusteeship Department received the surprise US proposal on temporary trusteeship for Palestine with mixed emotions and not a little shock," Bunche wrote to a State Department colleague. "I thought you liked us." Having seen the situation firsthand, he knew the UN, young and untested, was not in a position to supervise the future of Palestine. Fortunately, from Bunche's perspective, Austin's surprising proposal ultimately went nowhere.

In addition to endorsing a two-state solution, Resolution 181 created a new UN Palestine Commission to oversee the process. The commission had delegates from five member states. The real work would of course be done by the UN staff. As principal secretary, Trygvie Lie chose the man who was rapidly becoming the UN's in-house Palestine expert. "Dr. Ralph J Bunche, forty-three-year-old Director of the United Nations Trusteeship Division, was understood today to be the U.N.'s first choice to fill the difficult post as head of the UN secretariat to accompany the five member committee that will oversee the partition of Palestine," ran a story in the *New York Herald Tribune* in late 1947. The Palestine assignment was "probably the most difficult one yet to develop under the progress of U.N. affairs." The *Palestine Post* reported that Bunche "is regarded by experts here as one of the most capable officials to deal with minority and colonial matters."[45]

The British authorities in Palestine wanted little to do with the latest UN body. They feared inflaming the situation on the ground, which was already moving from smoldering to burning. Both Arabs and Jews were increasingly perpetrating attacks on civilians that winter. The situation worsened as it rapidly hurtled toward the declared end of the British mandate in May 1948. In a March 1948 internal report, the Palestine Commission advance group noted that "Partition is already carried out, or being carried out, not only in Palestine as a whole but inside Jerusalem." The two zones were "fluid" but were "real war zones."[46]

In April, one month before the British would depart, the Palestine Commission reported that it had been stymied by "the armed hostility of both Palestinian and non-Palestinian Arab elements, the lack of cooperation from the Mandatory Power [and] the disintegrating security situation in Palestine."[47] The Security Council, which had passed various cease-fire resolutions, in response appointed yet another commission,

Photo 9.1 Bunche and the UN Palestine Commission

called the "Truce Commission." The young UN was pouring substantial effort into the Palestine problem, hoping that it could somehow move the volatile situation toward peace, but little was changing.

ON MAY 14, 1948, THE LAST British high commissioner for Palestine and Transjordan departed for London. The British mandate was now over. In a building on Rothschild Boulevard in Tel Aviv, David Ben-Gurion and other leaders of the Jewish community in Palestine gathered to proclaim the independence of the state of Israel. In their formal declaration, they set forth their claims to the land of Israel in historical terms. Yet the new Israeli leaders also repeatedly invoked the core role played by the UN. "Recognition by the United Nations of the right of the Jewish people to establish their State is irrevocable," they declared. "We appeal to the United Nations to assist the Jewish people in the building-up of its State and to receive the State of Israel into the community of nations." Diplomatic recognition of the new state soon trickled in, including from both the US and the USSR. Everyone at the UN was "startled" by Truman's rapid recognition, Bunche wrote in his diary—even the US delegation to the UN.[48]

For Palestinian Arabs, this was the onset of the "Nakba"—the catastrophe. Israel's independence declaration punctuated the armed conflict that had been ongoing for some time in Palestine. Yet it also dramatically intensified the fighting and the flow of refugees. The Arab world responded to the declaration with armed attacks. Israel's defense showed surprising strength, blunting the assault to a large degree. But the Arab states still seized substantial territory that, under the UN plan, was intended to be part of Israel.

With the conflict accelerating dramatically, the UN needed a new approach. On May 16, Secretary General Trygve Lie wrote to US Secretary of State George Marshall a "secret and personal letter" he nonetheless shared with all the permanent members of the Security Council. Lie implored Marshall to rally the Security Council to act, arguing that if the Council, "by slow and ineffective action," permitted the Egyptians to establish a de facto position in Palestine, the outcome for the region and for the UN would be terrible.[49]

Two days earlier, the Security Council had decided to establish a "UN Mediator in Palestine" in yet another effort to move toward a peaceful resolution. As mediator, Lie looked to a prominent fellow Scandinavian, Count Folke Bernadotte. Bernadotte was the grandson of the king of Sweden and a noted humanitarian. A high-ranking official in the Swedish Red Cross, during World War II he had rescued thousands from German concentration camps. (Sweden had remained neutral during the war.) Bernadotte's appointment was nonetheless controversial for two reasons.

First, late in the war Bernadotte had met directly with Heinrich Himmler, the Nazi Gestapo chief, in an effort to rescue prisoners held in Nazi camps. Himmler, knowing the end was near, sought to smooth his path to some kind of special treatment by allowing Bernadotte to retrieve prisoners and bring them back to Scandinavia. Meeting in great secrecy outside Berlin, Bernadotte found Himmler unimpressive and ordinary; he later remarked that Himmler looked "like a typical unimportant official ... one would certainly have passed him on the street without noticing him."[50] Although Bernadotte achieved a number of important goals from his meeting with Himmler, including the release of 13,000 Scandinavians held in Nazi camps, his encounter with such a notorious war criminal raised concerns. Later, in Israel, radical nationalists opposed to his mediation efforts would call Bernadotte a "Nazi agent."[51]

Second, Bernadotte had no real experience in the Middle East. "My knowledge of the situation in Palestine was very superficial," he confessed at one point.[52] If his mediation had any hope of success, he would need an able staff with substantial expertise. In his cable to Bernadotte confirming the appointment, Lie, along with accepting Bernadotte's request to bring along his personal doctor, secretary, and clerk, noted that a small Secretariat team would work with him.[53]

Ralph Bunche was out at a book party at the Park Avenue apartment of Marshall Field, the department store magnate, on the night of May 20, 1948. Returning home, Ruth told him the secretary general's office had been calling. He called back immediately. I've just talked to Count Bernadotte, Trygve Lie told Bunche, and he's agreed to become mediator. "I want you to take him to Palestine." Bunche listened uncomfortably but assented.

The next morning the two men discussed further how the new mission would work. Bernadotte would be mediator, and Bunche's title would be chief representative of the secretary general in Palestine. As Bunche later recounted, "This was on a Friday. Lie wanted me to fly to Paris on Sunday, meet Bernadotte, and accompany him to Israel on Tuesday. 'You'll be away three or four weeks,' Trygve Lie assured me."[54]

Bunche had hoped his Palestine days were behind him. The appointment as Bernadotte's deputy was a great shock. Three days later, with some apprehension, he was on a plane to Europe to begin his service with Bernadotte. Lie, however, was quite a bit off on his calculation: his representative would be gone nearly a year. The return to Palestine, though unwelcome, would prove to be a major turning point in Ralph Bunche's life.

ARRIVING IN PARIS, BUNCHE, WHO HAD not met the Swedish count previously, headed over to his hotel. He found Folke Bernadotte straightforward and ready to get to work. "The Count is affable, speaks good English, is fairly tall and slender, deep lined face but nice looking," Bunche wrote in his diary.[55] Paris was chilly and rainy, and Bunche's leg—soon to be longstanding problem for him—was hurting.

After brief and friendly meetings in Paris, in which the count made clear he did not favor the November General Assembly resolution calling for partition, the pair began a journey that would prove fateful, in different ways, for both. In a UN-chartered plane, along with Bernadotte's American wife and a small retinue, they departed Paris for the Middle East. Bernadotte had asked for the private plane, which the press dubbed "a mechanized dove of peace," to be painted white, the default color for UN vehicles of all kinds ever since; it also had "United Nations" written on the fuselage in large black letters in both English and French. (Bunche deemed the plane "very impressive.")[56]

The affable and down-to-earth Bunche, who had grown up in a modest house in South Los Angeles and was often slightly rumpled, with cigarette ashes on his lapels, was a contrast to the aristocratic and reserved count, who for their initial meeting in Paris wore his fitted Red Cross uniform and service medals and had slicked-back, silver hair and a personal doctor and a valet at his side. Yet the two became fast friends and indispensable colleagues. Bernadotte's wife later recalled her relief that Bunche was helping her husband, who neither knew much of the Middle East nor was an especially fluent English speaker. Bernadotte, in his diary,[‡] expressed the great value Bunche brought in his knowledge of the politics of Palestine. "On one occasion I thought I had found a solution that was both simple and acceptable," Bernadotte wrote, "When I placed it before Dr. Bunche, he laughed and informed me it was identical from beginning to end with a plan that had been discussed more than a year before, but for various reasons did not stand a chance."[57] Bunche would go on to call Bernadotte a man of great urbanity and indefatigable energy; a "treasured friend" who was "utterly honest and fearless."[58]

The Security Council had called for a truce in the fighting in Palestine and authorized Bernadotte to negotiate the terms and set the date for a ceasefire. This was a tall first order. Yet it would be necessary if a more meaningful peace was to be achieved. For their opening stop in this effort, Bernadotte and Bunche headed to Cairo. Their decision to visit Egypt first caused consternation among Israeli leaders but was not without logic. Before their departure, Bunche cabled Trygve Lie to discuss their approach. "Count considers it inadvisable for political, psychological reasons to proceed directly to Tel Aviv," Bunche wrote. "I agree. . . . Realize consultations in capitals of Arab states not strictly within paragraph 1A Assembly Resolution."[59] He was referring to the General Assembly's instructions. But, he continued, Bernadotte had persuasively pointed out the mediators had no clear set of Arab interlocuters. Beginning with Egypt would help establish a conversation. Moreover, as Bernadotte argued, neighboring Arab states had taken the offensive against Israel, and so any plausible attempt at a ceasefire ought to begin with them.

Flying in their UN plane, the mediators crossed the eastern Mediterranean to Egypt. In Cairo Bunche, overwhelmed by the heat and

---

[‡] Bernadotte kept a regular diary of his Palestine mediation, which was transcribed and put into narrative form by his secretary. This diary was published after his death as *To Jerusalem*.

the incessant noise, barely slept and often complained of feeling ill. Bunche and Bernadotte met with the prime minister of Egypt, who told them Arabs would never tolerate a Jewish state in the Middle East. Moreover, he stressed, lest the idea gather strength that a neighboring state such as Transjordan or Egypt could absorb the Arab population in Palestine, Palestine itself must be an independent state, not part of any existing Arab state.[60] The two mediators also met with the secretary of the Arab League, a courtly Egyptian known as Azzam Pasha, who assured them that Arabs and Jews were innately friendly. "The difficulty," he explained, "is not with the Jews in Palestine, but with the ideas and tactics of the Western Jews," who were now seeking to implant a Jewish state on Arab land.[61] Bunche found the meeting somewhat encouraging, but he was perhaps grasping to find grounds for optimism.

Bunche and Bernadotte changed into black tie and headed to dinner at the British Embassy. As befitted a great power that long controlled much of the region, the embassy was set on a prime vista on the edge of the Nile River. British officials, long experienced in the Arab world, apprised the mediators of the situation on the ground. So, too, did the local military attaches of the US, France, and Britain. The British officer characterized the current situation as a "phony war."[62] It did not seem phony to Bunche, who had seen the violence and its aftermath on his previous tour of duty. To Bunche's surprise, the American attache then bluntly denounced American policy in support of Israel, saying the Arabs were right to reject Israel and recounting how he told an Egyptian colleague that he wouldn't wish New York City to become a Jewish state. The situation was confusing, though politically the deck seemed to be stacked against Israel.

On May 31 Bunche and Bernadotte left Egypt and headed to Palestine itself, carrying new ID cards that read "Mission of the United Nations Mediator on Palestine" and featured explanatory text in English, Arabic, and Hebrew.[63] As they crossed the Suez Canal, separating Egypt proper from the Sinai Peninsula, an escort of British fighter jets swerved in and safely led the UN plane to Haifa, on the Israeli coast.[64] Bunche, gazing down at the huge Suez Canal, was blissfully unaware of how much time and effort he would later spend on it.

Photo 9.2 Bunche and Bernadotte

Arriving in Israel, Bunche knew right away the mediation would not be easy. "Palestine was a battleground," he later wrote of his arrival in May 1948, and indeed the team was occasionally fired upon.[65] Prior experience had taught him that levels of distrust were high and common ground elusive, if not wholly fantastical. To be sure, the mediation team had some leverage behind it. The newly independent Israel owed much to the UN, and the Arab states, too, understood that the great powers that controlled the Security Council could not be lightly ignored. While they faced daunting obstacles, the mediators were not without hope. Still, things took an inauspicious turn when on the drive into Tel Aviv their escort struck a boy on a bicycle.[66]

The mediators' first meeting with Israel's prime minister, David Ben-Gurion, did not go smoothly. Neither Bernadotte nor Bunche found Ben-Gurion easy. To some degree it was a clash of styles. "Bernadotte represented everything the Israelis were not," Bunche's assistant later recalled. Count

Bernadotte was "regal, he had wealth, and he had security . . . and he was slightly detached, not like an American who tries to fit into every situation."[67] In his diary, Bernadotte described the white-haired Ben-Gurion as possessing "a very bitter spirit."[68]

Bernadotte's immediate dislike of Ben-Gurion set a pattern. Indeed, the count clearly preferred the Arab leaders to the Israelis. Often aristocrats themselves, the Arabs tended to be elitist and to treat him cordially and with elaborate respect. After meeting with Azzam Pasha, for example, Bernadotte remarked that it was a "most interesting" experience. "The Secretary of the Arab League attracted me strongly; I felt an instinctive liking for him." Of King Abdullah of Jordan, Bernadotte wrote that "in his black, cassock-like cloak over the white linen robes and with a white turban on his greying hair, he gave me the impression of being a decidedly fascinating personality."[69] The Arab leaders, who clearly seemed exotic to the Nordic Bernadotte, courted and flattered him, at times invoking their shared noble lineages.[§] By contrast, "the Israelis clearly liked Bunche . . . Bunche was an egalitarian. Bernadotte was an aristocrat."[70]

Bunche and Bernadotte endeavored to consult with as wide an array of actors as possible. They were particularly concerned about the Arabs, who were the most resistant to a UN-led process. The mediators' initial goal was a truce that would allow time to negotiate a more stable and sustainable peace arrangement. The path to a truce, however, was not easy to discern. Neither side seemed willing to budge. Bunche was told by a seasoned former British official in Jordan that "both sides love to haggle and bargain. They should be told to take it or leave it." Bernadotte and Bunche took this advice. (Bunche would later say that King Abdullah also told him "you must force us" to accept a ceasefire.)[71] Presenting the opposing forces with a firm plan for a truce and a deadline of June 9, 1948, they waited for answers. The acceptances ultimately arrived on the very last day—with Israel's arriving forty minutes late.

---

§ A partial exception was King Farouk of Egypt, who demanded to know whether it was true that King Gustav of Sweden, Count Bernadotte's uncle, was indeed pro-Jewish and a Freemason.

Bunche hoped the truce was a sign he was nearly done: the day before it was finalized, he called New York, reminding another colleague that the secretary general had promised him a short tenure of "perhaps ten days or two weeks."[72] But behind the scenes, both Arabs and Jews sought to evade restrictions on weapons and materiel, and they jockeyed for advantage in anticipation of the time when the real fighting, inevitably, would resume. UN staff began to trickle into the region to assist in supervising the truce. The UN "Truce Supervision Organization" was created, an important precursor to the practice of UN peacekeeping that would be so central in later international crises. The New York Police Department donated fifty guns, but Bernadotte refused the shipment, believing that introducing weapons would only create more danger. While later UN peacekeeping missions would involve far more aggressive interventions by armed UN soldiers, basic principles of impartiality and a light footprint were being established.

The truce only papered over the Arab-Israeli conflict, of course. The generally zero-sum nature of land division heightened the stakes. After responding to an early allegation of a truce violation, one of the UN staffers recounted challenging an Arab colonel whose troops were shooting. "Do you really think it's worthwhile, I asked him, to fight over these few yards between you? In a very excited voice, the colonel said, 'Every inch matters!' And that's how both sides felt—they were talking about inches."[73] To Bunche and many of the others, this seemed troubling and hard to fathom, but a deep and unyielding attachment to the land was one of the few things both Arabs and Jews shared.

The truce did, however, give the mediators some breathing room to get negotiations going. The pace of the mediators' travel was fast, and the weather brutal: on June 15 it hit 113 degrees in Cairo, where the two mediators stayed in a non-airconditioned hotel. But they never stayed in any place long. In a letter home to Ruth, Bunche wrote: "we keep hopping from one to another like mad in our plane and often on just a few moments notice. As soon as we land anywhere we begin to confer and leave for someplace else immediately after the conference is over." This was to prove a theme of Bunche's career at the UN—he routinely traveled too much and worked too hard, as a result of which both his health and his relationship with his family suffered. "I get practically no sleep and miss many meals."[74]

Meeting with Israel's foreign minister, Moshe Shertok, in Tel Aviv, Bunche discussed the precarious situation. Shertok insisted that Israel's continued existence was non-negotiable. He urged that the Israelis had accepted the UN's plan of fragmentation and partition on the understanding that there would be economic union in Palestine. If these arrangements were not carried out, he said somewhat ominously, "the Jews are not bound."[75] Shertok also believed that the Arab assault on the new state was as much about consolidating Arab domination over other minorities throughout the Middle East as about Israel's existence per se. The emergence of a Jewish state, he explained to Bunche, "breaks that uniformity," encouraging other minorities to hope for something better. Shertok, perhaps playing to what he imagined was Bunche's proclivities, declared that the new Jewish state was a "bid for inter-racial, inter-religious, and inter-cultural understanding" in the region.[76]

A few days after the onset of the truce Bunche and Bernadotte decided to establish a headquarters outside of Palestine. By taking the talks out of the immediate territory, the mediators hoped the parties would gain perspective and find it easier to compromise. The mediators would of course have more control as well. The Greek island of Rhodes, a few hours by plane from Palestine and just off the Turkish coast, was chosen as the site. A relatively new and large hotel, the Hotel des Roses, became the meeting site. Situated on the beach, there were sea breezes and vistas, but not much else to distract the warring parties.

The truce they had negotiated was precarious, but it held. Bunche felt that "Bernadotte was the only one who could have done it."[77] (Later events would suggest that Bunche was in fact the better negotiator.) Their next steps were more controversial. In June 1948, the mediators drew up a plan and a proposed map that was, in several key respects, at odds with the General Assembly's partition resolution of seven months earlier. While it was a stretch to call the original UN resolution well liked, any change introduced volatility.

And changes there were. In his diaries, Bernadotte wrote, "the creation of a unitary state in Palestine with far-reaching rights for the Jews" would have been preferable. But, he noted, fourteen countries had by this time recognized the state of Israel, and Israel had shown substantial success on the battlefield, something he called "an extraordinary achievement." The challenges to an Arab-dominated single state solution were deep. Bernadotte continued:

> When my staff and I considered these questions now, we agreed on the following plan: the Jewish state should exist in some form, it should have its own diplomatic representation and its own representative at the United Nations. But in the long-range interests of both the Arab and the Jewish communities of Palestine it should be associated in some sort of loose union with the Arab part of Palestine and possibly also with Transjordan. Some frontier modification is also, in my opinion, necessary.[78]

Bernadotte proposed that Jerusalem be placed within Arab territory and under Arab control, with special provisions for the Jewish community there to ensure cultural and religious autonomy.

Brian Urquhart, Bunche's longtime colleague at the UN, has suggested that in addressing Jerusalem in this way the mediators were surely influenced by the contemporaneous crisis unfolding in Berlin. In the wake of the Second World War, Berlin had been divided among Britain, France, the US, and the USSR. In June 1948, just as Bunche and Bernadotte were considering the question of Jerusalem, the Soviet Union commenced a dramatic blockade of the city. Berlin was effectively surrounded by Soviet-occupied territory in what was soon to be East Germany, and in response the Western powers began a complex and expensive airlift to bring in food and supplies to the city.

The Berlin crisis gripped the world in the summer of 1948. Bunche and Bernadotte were certainly well aware of it. Bernadotte later wrote that under the original plan passed by the General Assembly, "Jerusalem would be surrounded by territory completely controlled by the Arabs. It is undesirable—or so I felt at the time—to set up an international zone . . . inside any given state."[79] Berlin certainly suggested the dangers of such an approach. But the mediators' proposed solution seemed to make things worse. Both sides in Palestine were now unhappy. Indeed, many within Israel now viewed Bernadotte as an imminent danger; he was perhaps "the most hated in man in Israel" and, over Israeli radio, extremists even began calling for his death.[80] The Arab side was no less happy about the continuing UN efforts to legitimate and embed the unwelcome state of Israel in Palestine. Fighting soon broke out, and Israel gained back substantial territory.

In desperation, Bunche flew to New York to push the Security Council to take further action. He spent five frantic days meeting with ambassadors and attempting to discern, and shift, the political winds. As a veto-bearing permanent member, the Soviet Union could stop any resolution it chose to, and Bunche feared they might do so. But after substantial debate the Council successfully passed another resolution. By July 19, 1948, a second ceasefire was in place.

DESPITE THE INTERNATIONAL CONSENSUS OVER THE ceasefire and the desirability of a negotiated solution, the UN mediation was nonetheless increasingly seen as a threat to the viability of the new nation of Israel. Israeli officials, whose views are much more abundantly documented than their Arab counterparts, thought Bernadotte was dangerously out of touch with the realities of the Middle East. One high-level Israeli later suggested that Bernadotte had

> absolutely no understanding or familiarity with the existential problem, you know, the real psychological problem that existed and unfortunately still exists between the Arabs and ourselves. He came to this problem the way you might approach any legal or territorial dispute . . . looking at the situation very factually. Whereas it was such a complicated situation, emotionally and psychologically.[81]

For their part, Bunche and Bernadotte were not so keen on the Israelis either—or their Arab opponents. Although his initial impressions of the often-blunt Israelis were not that favorable, over time Bunche grew to find

Photo 9.3 Bernadotte and Bunche at the UN

his Arab interlocutors even more irritating.** "My patience with Arabs wearing thin," he wrote in his diary. "They refuse to face realities and peddle myths ... even though intelligent they speak like children." The Israelis, he continued, were "much more intelligent and sensible."[82] Bernadotte continued to find the Israeli leaders obstreperous, and he felt, at times personally hostile to his mission. "I could not understand," he wrote in his diary in August 1948, "why the Jewish Government should adopt an attitude of such arrogance and hostility toward the United Nations representatives."[83]

In a letter home to Ruth, who had grown increasingly frustrated by his ever-lengthening absence, Ralph wrote: "this may be the most hazardous

---

** Bunche would later complain about Israelis as well. When in 1958 Dag Hammarskjold, the UN secretary general, scrawled a note to Bunche about the Israeli delegation mentioning the "brash self-righteousness ... of a certain people," Bunche replied, "they were at their emotional and arrogant worst on this, deliberately thumbing their noses at everyone."

trip of all . . . we are all being attacked in both the Arab and the Jewish press." Presciently, he said, "It is really a marvel that neither the Count or anyone of his party has ever been sniped at out here." Then, in a gesture Ruth could not have been pleased by, he added: "Just in case, I'm enclosing the will I told you about."[84]

Already the topic of Palestinian refugees was on their minds, and it would remain a great concern for Bunche for decades. Meeting with Israel's foreign minister in Haifa in late July, Shertok conceded to Bunche that the refugees were central to the question of a future peace and the "main victims" of the war, which was really between Israel and Arab states rather than Palestians per se. But, he emphasized, it was unthinkable that Israel would permit thousands of Arabs to return to Haifa and Jaffa now, with fighting underway.[85]

Though the situation was looking dire, the rest of the summer and into September the mediators kept at it, shuttling among capitals and meeting endlessly with the warring parties. Bunche saw Bernadotte off on a flight to Amman on August 1, noting that they were both waiting with frustration for a reply from Israel on the "Arab refugee proposal." Shortly after Bunche left for New York.[86] Back in the US, he met with Dean Rusk and Philip Jessup of the State Department to discuss the situation. The State Department expressed concern that, just a few months after the birth of Israel, the conflict in Palestine was getting out of control. Israel, the US believed, was beginning to feel it could achieve more without the mediation process, and, despite its paeans to the UN in its declaration of independence, it was increasingly emboldened to buck the organization. In a top-secret memo, Secretary of State George Marshall alerted President Truman to the gravity of the situation. The Israelis were growing ever more hostile toward the UN's military observers, Marshall argued. Moreover, "the refusal of the Israeli military governor in Jerusalem to cooperate" with Bunche and Bernadotte, as well as the existence of the hundreds of thousands of Arab refugees, were troubling portents for the future.[87]

Indeed, the refugee situation would prove tragic and vexing for decades to come. A little over a year after Marshall alerted Truman to the problem of refugees, in December 1949, the General Assembly would create the UN

Relief and Works Agency (UNRWA) to aid the refugees of Palestine, which then numbered some 750,000. Still operating today, many generations later, the UNRWA provides support and assistance to nearly 6 million refugees and their descendants, many of whom subsist in dozens of crowded refugee camps across the region.[88]

In August, Bunche met directly with George Marshall. What was to have been a fifteen-minute meeting grew to over an hour as the two men discussed the situation. Marshall offered unarmed American military observers, a proposal that was not taken up.[89] As fall closed in, the mediators worked furiously to prepare their recommendations to the UN. Largely written by Bunche, the report amended some of the earlier, more incendiary territorial suggestions, and now proposed that Jerusalem be internationalized, as indeed the original UNSCOP report had done. On September 16, the nearly 150-page report was sent back to New York. In a cover letter to Trygve Lie, Bernadotte wrote that "two matters require the most prompt action, namely certain decisions relating vitally to the peaceful settlement of the Palestine question, and humanitarian measures to relieve the desperate conditions of more than three hundred thousand Arab refugees."[90]

The next day, a sunny morning, Bernadotte climbed into a car near Jerusalem to head to Ramallah. After meeting with Arab Legion commanders there, he and his team returned to Jerusalem proper. Driving along a dusty road, a bullet struck the rear fender of Bernadotte's large Chrysler. The UN Chief of Staff in Palestine, a jovial fellow Swede named Aage Lundstrom, was riding with the count. Alarmed, he suggested they immediately detour. No, replied Bernadotte. "I have to take the same risks as my observers. Besides, I must show them that no one has the right to prevent me from crossing the lines." Arriving in Jerusalem, on the Jewish side of the city, the meditator's party took on an Israeli Army liaison, Captain Hillman, for the remaining part of the journey. Pointing to Hillman's gun, Bernadotte told him he would have to leave it behind. "None of our men are armed," he said. "The UN flag is our only protection."[91] The bullet hole, a manifestation of the continuing danger in Palestine, was visible in the car's fender.

Bernadotte's vehicle then headed back into the demilitarized zone of Jerusalem to the YMCA for lunch. The tall YMCA tower sat to the west of the Old City. It was directly across the street from the King David Hotel, which only two years before had been the site of a deadly bombing that killed over ninety people. The lunch completed, Bernadotte's party, now a small convoy, drove to the former headquarters of the British High Commissioner. After various stops, they then began to journey back to the YMCA, where Bernadotte intended to spend the night.

Normally, Bunche would be right beside Bernadotte on a day like this; the two rarely were seen apart in the field. But on this day Bunche was delayed and was not there. Bernadotte waited for Bunche to join them. When it seemed he would not arrive in time, his convoy headed out, a large blue and white UN flag fluttering off the lead car.[92] Bunche later told *The Today Show*, in 1969,

> We were to rendezvous in Jerusalem. . . . I was flying from Rhodes in a small plane and his big plane would pick me up in Beirut and it did. And I'd been out there with him for 5 months and had never once been late for a rendezvous . . . well, this particular day when I was to fly in his plane from Beirut to Jerusalem to meet him, the plane had for the first time some mechanical difficulty and [was] delayed 45 minutes.[93]

Bunche eventually arrived in Haifa, but while there he stopped to help his assistant, Doreen Mashler, with a passport issue. Because she had a British passport, the Israeli officials would not let her in. Eventually resolving the issue, Bunche took off from Haifa an hour late, landed in Jerusalem, and, as he later wrote in his diary, "proceeded across no-man's-land to the Mandelbaum Gate." But it was now late on Friday afternoon, and the only Israeli officer still on duty did not speak English. He refused to let Bunche's party pass. "I became very angry, finally furious, and virtually apoplectic," Bunche later wrote, at the thought of being late for the meeting with Bernadotte.[94]

Meanwhile, Bernadotte had moved on. Sitting in the back seat of his large Chrysler, Bernadotte watched as they climbed up a narrow road, now

HaPalmach Street, near the Rehavia district of Jerusalem. Beside him was a French officer, Colonel Serot, who was part of the UN observer team. Serot had asked to sit next to the count in order to personally thank him; during the war, Serot's wife had been among the many prisoners saved from the Nazis by one of Bernadotte's Red Cross missions. Suddenly, an Israeli Army jeep blocked the road. It was still daylight. Aage Lundstrom, who was sitting in the second UN car, later described the scene:

> The driver appeared to be trying to turn it, nervously and fumblingly, and in the end it stopped in the middle of the road. The four men in it were dressed in the khaki uniform of the Jewish Army with shorts and a peaked cap. Three of them jumped out [and] came toward our cars, two on the right-hand side of the cars and one on the left. . . . Captain Hillman called out something in Hebrew.

One of the soldiers, "clean-shaven, thin and very dark," went straight to the final vehicle, Bernadotte's. Approaching the car, he pointed his machine gun directly into the open window. In rapid succession he shot six bullets into Bernadotte, and another eighteen into Serot.[95]

> After firing a few more shots at our radiator, the man ran back towards the jeep . . . the two other men had opened fire at the same time on the wheels of the first car, evidently to prevent its following them. Then they jumped into the jeep, which set off at top speed and disappeared down a side road. The man who had committed the murder, however, did not have time to get into the jeep, but ran off into the surrounding countryside.[96]

Bernadotte's convoy was barely a mile from the Jerusalem YMCA. The UN team rushed to the nearest hospital in another vehicle, but the victims had been instantly killed in the barrage of bullets. The shooters, later identified not as Jewish Army soldiers but as members of the radical Lehi group, were simply posing as regular soldiers.

Lehi was deeply opposed to the proposed partition of Palestine and indeed to the entire UN process. Yitzhak Shamir, who would later become prime minister of Israel, was a leader of Lehi at the time. Many believe he was among those who ordered the killing of Bernadotte. The actual perpetrators, in particular the "clean-shaven, thin, and very dark" man who pulled the trigger, were never brought to justice. Years later, however, a man named Yehoshua Cohen would confess to being the murderer.[97]

On the *Today Show* two decades later, Bunche continued to describe how he narrowly missed the attack due to the plane's mechanical issues and a recalcitrant Israeli guard:

> so he held us there, but after almost an hour a car drove up furiously and an Israeli officer jumped out, barked something in Hebrew to this corporal—said to me in English, "Get in the car" and when I got in the car and he dashed off he told me that Count Bernadotte has just been shot.[98]

In his diary Bunche wrote that "when I saw the bodies, I saw a hole the size of a half dollar in Colonel Serot's left temple." Bunche could not help but think of the implications: "except for this guardian angel . . . I would have been in Serot's seat."[99]

In the wake of the ambush, Bunche declared the assassination an outrage against the international community. He later noted that leaflets distributed in Jerusalem in the days prior had read (in Hebrew) that "'No. 1' and 'No. 2' must be gotten rid of." The assassins, he wrote, "clearly supposed that Serot was me, as I was 'No. 2.'"[100] In an interview decades later, a Lehi member stated that the group knew that Bernadotte, "with his magnetic personality and all his influence," would lead the UN to endorse his hated plan for Jerusalem. "So we had to kill him on this day."[101]

Years after the attack, the assassin, Yehoshua Cohen, admitted that perhaps Lehi had made a mistake in the ambush on HaPalmach Street. "I know we killed the wrong man," Cohen said. "The black man was the right man. He was the man with the ideas."[102]

CHAPTER 10

THE PATH TO THE PRIZE

OUNT FOLKE BERNADOTTE'S murder shocked the world. Done in broad daylight on a Jerusalem street, it was brazen and an assault on the very notion of impartial mediation by the United Nations. Henry Morganthau Jr., the chairman of the United Jewish Appeal, declared the assassination "outrageous." Governor Thomas Dewey of New York, Harry Truman's rival in the presidential election that fall, was "shocked beyond measure." Ernest Bevin, the British foreign minister, called it "a dastardly crime."[1] Similar sentiments poured forth across the world.

Bernadotte's murder was also widely condemned in Israel, at least publicly. The Israeli government called the assassination an "insane attempt by gunmen to wreck Israel's relations with the United Nations."[2] Prime Minister David Ben-Gurion declared Lehi, the radical group behind the killing, "a gang of rogues, cowards and low schemers."[3] He used the aftermath of the assassination to crack down on the group; some 200 Lehi members were rounded up. But Israeli officials seemingly did little to find and punish the perpetrators. Moreover, many believed that they had done little to prevent the attack. Still, the Associated Press reported that "silent Israelis" respectfully lined the route of the car carrying Bernadotte's body from Jerusalem to Haifa.[4]

A few weeks later, the issue of the young Israeli state's complicity in the attack arose as Ralph Bunche appeared before the UN Security Council. "I find the conclusion inescapable," he said in October 1948, "that there was in this instance negligence on the part of the local Jewish authorities in Jerusalem. With minimal precautions this crime could not have been committed."[5] Several Security Council members expressed substantial skepticism about Israel's explanations for what had transpired that day on HaPalmach Street. The British representative, Alexander Cadogan, spoke of "the carefully organized murder" of Count Bernadotte and declared: "I would have expected the vigorous pursuit of the criminals." It was not merely a question of isolated truce violations, Cadogan stated, "but rather a threat to the foundations of the truce and to the authority of the Security Council."[6] On October 19, by unanimous vote, the Security Council passed a resolution noting "with concern" that Israel had not submitted a report on the progress of the investigation into the assassination. Bunche himself told Israeli foreign minister Moshe Shertok that "the Jewish state now faced its worst crisis with regard to international opinion and support."[7]

The General Assembly asked the International Court of Justice for an advisory opinion on whether the UN could seek damages for Bernadotte's murder; the World Court ruled that it could. Trygve Lie then submitted the claim to Israel. Israel argued that the murder, though "tragic," took place "barely four months after Israel emerged as an independent State from the chaos which prevailed in Palestine." "Beset by enemies on every side," Israel claimed it had not yet been able to restore order. It rejected any suggestion that it had not pursued a vigorous investigation into the crime. Nonetheless, Israel issued a check for $54,628 to the UN, as reparations for the "damage borne by the United Nations."[8]

Sweden launched its own official inquiry into the assassination; it charged that Israel's investigation had been so negligent that "doubt must exist as to whether the Israeli authorities really tried to bring the inquiry to a positive result."[9] The criminal investigation was delayed more than twenty-four hours, allegedly due to confusion over whether Israeli military or civilian police had jurisdiction. As a result, no effort was made to cordon off the crime scene or preserve evidence. Sweden ultimately recognized the state of Israel in 1950, but relations between the two nations remained frosty. In the early 1980s, when Israel's ambassador asked Olaf Palme, Sweden's prime minister, if he would respond favorably to an invitation to visit Israel, Palme replied, "tell them the first thing I will bring up is the murder of Folke Bernadotte."[10] Israel did not follow up on the invitation. A few decades later, Sweden became the first European Union member to recognize a new state in the region: Palestine.

Within the UN, the killing of Bernadotte was a stunning event. Unfortunately, it also proved pathbreaking: in the subsequent decades, many UN officials and peacekeepers have been killed—often deliberately— while in the field. Today, a small memorial to Bernadotte sits in the UN headquarters in New York, next to a ground floor meditation room facing First Avenue.

The assassination did not, however, halt the UN's mediation effort; Ralph Bunche was immediately appointed as Bernadotte's replacement. He was already seen by many in the region as the real mover behind the major decisions that had already been taken. As someone with substantial experience in Palestine and a deep knowledge of Bernadotte's thinking—indeed, he was the source of much of that thinking—he was the only logical choice to step into the role of mediator.

All the same, Bunche was surprised at the appointment. In a letter home to Ruth, he expressed concern, calling it a "thankless, hazardous task" and confessing, "now, I'm trapped."[11]

RALPH BUNCHE'S RAPID ELEVATION TO THE role of chief mediator meant that Bernadotte's death had less of an effect on the ultimate outcome of the mediation process than perhaps was anticipated. Bunche proved a very able mediator. Bernadotte was less attentive to the local situation and tended to try to impose solutions; Bunche was more pragmatic and focused on near-term armistices rather than sweeping and lasting change. His success

Photo 10.1 Bunche as Acting Mediator

nonetheless had deep repercussions. Indeed, nearly two decades later, Bunche would marvel, at the end of yet another Security Council meeting on the Middle East, that a Syrian official would speak of the armistice accords as if they "were a charter or a constitution or basis for a way of life. At Rhodes those long years ago, I saw them as only a temporary stepping stone between the indefinite cease-fire and an indispensable peace. I could never have dreamed that they would still exist in 1966."[12]

While Bernadotte was confident and experienced, and had strong views on how to proceed, he was a newcomer to Middle Eastern politics who arguably suffered from "exaggerated self-confidence" and "naivete" about the region.[13] Bunche, by contrast, had steeped himself in the situation for some time, often to his regret. James McDonald, the US special representative in Israel, thought Bunche was "widely informed [and] cogent in his arguments," and it did not hurt that he was "extremely charming."[14] Bernadotte himself shared that positive view: his widow later told Dag

Hammarskjold that Bernadotte regarded Bunche "as a god" and a man of exceptional ability and integrity.[15]

Bunche's appointment as mediator elicited relatively positive reactions from both sides. His "scathing protests to the Israeli government after Bernadotte's death earned him much credit in the Arab world and showed that he was fearless and unbiased."[16] At the same time, many Israelis saw him as a positive force, and local newspapers noted his status as a minority in America as a sign that he would likely be sympathetic to the Jewish position.[17] Abba Eban, who later became Israel's ambassador to the UN and foreign minister, declared in the wake of the assassination that "here of course Dr. Bunche comes to the rescue, a much more resourceful person than the Count himself."[18] Still, Bunche's task as mediator (in deference to Bernadotte's memory, he refused to use the title and was officially known as Acting Mediator) was daunting. Over and above anything else, the parties were currently warring. Time proved they were destined to stay warring.

Bunche faced other obstacles. One was his own safety. In June 1950, when the mediation was successfully behind him, Robert Lovett, a former US under secretary of state, told Bunche that the US government had been quite concerned about his well-being in Palestine during the mediation and that US security agents had been promptly sent to the region after Bernadotte's killing. These agents, Bunche recounted in his diary, had uncovered (and apparently foiled) a plot "aimed at Gen. Marshall and me. Four would-be assassins."[19]

Another obstacle was the former mandatory power in Palestine. Britain, a permanent member of the Security Council and consequently quite influential, had, in the Israeli view, "unconcealed hostility" to the establishment of a Jewish state.[20] Conversely, the US, the most powerful player of all, was generally supportive of Israel and its claims. Yet as the unexpected speech of the American ambassador to the UN a few months earlier calling for UN trusteeship over Palestine showed, behind the scenes the American position seemed to be contested. The Soviets, too, were highly interested in the outcome in the Middle East, but how they would play their hand was unclear. The Berlin blockade had effectively started the Cold War; now everything that ran through the UN, and especially the Security Council, would be assessed for its impact on this most deadly serious of conflicts. It was in this context that the General Assembly passed a new resolution on the Palestine situation on December 11, 1948, almost three months after Bernadotte's assassination. The resolution called for the creation of yet another official UN body, a three-member high-level Conciliation Commission.

Originally a part of Bernadotte's plan from the previous summer, the Conciliation Commission seemed to undercut Bunche's role as mediator. Indeed, the resolution specifically called for the new commission to take over the mediation if the Security Council so chose. It was in some sense an attempt to wrest control of the process from the Secretariat in favor of the member states. The three Conciliation Commission members were France, Turkey, and the US. For Bunche, the creation of the commission seemed both a marker that the politics of Palestine were becoming central to the international community and a welcome signal that the end of his role in Palestine was drawing near. He called Bernadotte's recommendations for a peace plan a "sacred legacy," but in reality, he was eager to get out and let others take over.[21] Now he perhaps had an opening. But how he would interact with the new commission remained uncertain. To Lie he sent a cable conceding that the procedures "governing my relations with Conciliation Commission [are] not entirely clear to me."[22]

The creation of the Conciliation Commission also marked a "historical turning point at which the Americans replaced the British in the Middle East."[23] To some degree this was the inevitable result of the tremendous power the US wielded in this era. In 1948, the US accounted for nearly 50 percent of the world's GDP. Its military had fought and won on two fronts, defeating—and, at that time, still occupying—two previously great powers. The US was the only nuclear power until 1949, when the Soviets secretly tested a successful bomb. Britain was in dire financial shape; Germany was flattened; France was slowly recovering from a humiliating occupation; China, vast and very poor, was in conflict and soon to undergo a communist revolution; and the Soviets, while militarily powerful, were economically backward and had suffered enormous casualties. In short, in 1948 the US was a superpower largely untouched by the destruction of the war and with a vast lead over nearly every competitor. It was now, in Henry Luce's famous words, clearly the American Century.[24] Ralph Bunche, as an American and a former State Department official, would often be seen as channeling the American view, even if he was now a UN official.

Meanwhile, further fighting had broken out in Palestine. Israel was proving surprisingly strong on the battlefield and had seized most of the Negev Desert. Some 750,000 Arabs fled or were expelled from areas now controlled by Israel in the process; this huge flow of refugees would prove a humanitarian and political nightmare for decades.[25] UN staffers on the ground warned Bunche that Israel would likely continue to push back the largely disorganized and ineffective Arab forces.[26] (Years later, Bunche would write in his journal, "Arabs took a severe defeat in the GA yesterday. They are as inept on the diplomatic field as on the battlefield.")[27]

The Security Council continued to put pressure on the combatants in a series of resolutions issued throughout the fall of 1948. By late November, with Bunche's encouragement, the Security Council had used its powers to force an end to the fighting. Appearing before the Council, now meeting in Paris, Bunche made the case for an armistice-based approach. "As I see it," he told the members, "the indispensable step at this moment is to move decisively toward a condition of secure peace in Palestine."[28] To do so, Bunche argued, it was essential to move out of the framework of the existing truce and into a new and sturdier framework. He acknowledged that "there is no magic in the word 'armistice' as against the word 'truce.'" But an armistice would be different in that it would "firmly" separate the opposing forces. The opposing troops were close together—"much too close together," Bunche said—and the resulting tension combustible. With agreed-upon lines of demarcation, he thought, a more lasting peace might be forged.

The members of the Security Council concurred; the Council decided that an armistice "shall be established in all sectors of Palestine." The parties in Palestine were to seek agreement via direct negotiations among themselves or through the mediator.[29] By enlisting the Security Council in this way, Bunche was able to ramp up the pressure on the Arabs and Israelis to come to some kind of agreement. That said, *what* the agreement would look like, and how it would be achieved, were impossible to say.

As 1948 wound down, Bunche, who later called himself "an incurable optimist," was somewhat pessimistic.[30] "I am not at all happy to find myself in this very hot seat," he wrote a friend. "I am doing the best I can, but I fear that is not enough. There are so many complications, interferences, pressures." Yet, he went on, he was consoled by the fact that he was "just a fill-in."[31] He believed, wrongly as it turned out, that his time as mediator was almost over. The Conciliation Commission, he thought, would any moment take over and relieve him of his duties—a prospect he viewed with relief.

In the meantime, he was indeed in a very hot seat. Both in Palestine and in New York, Bunche was attacked by various factions. Indeed, just after Thanksgiving in Madison Square Garden, Bunche received a very public and unusual attack on his efforts from W. E. B. Du Bois, who was speaking in New York City before the American Jewish Congress.

Du Bois first attacked the British. This censure was straightforward and even unexceptional, for many Jews deeply resented the British for their role in mandatory Palestine. But there was more. "What particularly touches me and induces me to make this brief statement to you," Du Bois announced to the crowd, is the "singular way" in which Black people have "unwittingly been made party to this betrayal of democracy."

> I need hardly recall the curious way in which African and Jewish history have been entwined for 3000 years . . . nor need I recall that the philanthropy of Jews has often helped the sons of the American Freedman in their still desperate struggle for manhood; rather, I wish to apologize in the name of the American Negro for the apparent apostasy of Ralph Bunche, the acting mediator of the United Nations in Palestine, to the clear ideals of freedom and fair play, which should have guided the descendent of an American slave.

Du Bois declared that he perhaps understood why Count Bernadotte, an aristocrat and a European, had been so mistaken about Palestine. But Ralph Bunche should have known better. "I wish he had stood firm against vacillation, compromise, and betrayal by our Department of State," Du Bois shouted to the crowd. "Since he did not, whatever the pressures and motives were, I ask forgiveness from you for him, in the name of fifteen million American Negroes."[32]

Du Bois's frontal attack deeply upset Bunche. "Du Bois made a vigorous and totally unjustified personal attack upon me in a mass meeting at Madison Square," he later vented to a colleague. "It was an attack upon my integrity, and my objectivity."[33] Yet Du Bois's critique, while intemperate and overly personal, not to mention largely at odds with the facts, reflected the avid support of many Black Americans in the 1940s for a Jewish homeland in the Middle East. As the historian Robin D. G. Kelley has described, at Israel's founding Black leaders and the Black press, "for the most part, were jubilant" about the new Jewish state. "There was virtually no mention of Arab dispossession.... Instead, they identified with the founding of Israel because they recognized European Jewry as an oppressed and homeless people determined to build a nation."[34]

Du Bois reflected this perspective. Throughout his life, Du Bois, like Bunche, had shown a strong interest in the global dimensions of race relations. He traveled widely, touring revolutionary Russia for months, corresponding with Nehru in India, and meeting Mao in China.[35] Du Bois was exceptional in his focus on international matters but hardly unique. And for those who were paying attention to foreign affairs, extraordinary changes were taking place. India and Pakistan had become independent from Britain in 1947, in the wake of a partition between largely Hindu India and Muslim Pakistan that was bloody and disruptive—and surely on many minds as they contemplated partition in Palestine. African independence movements were also becoming more active in the late 1940s. Many Black intellectuals in America had a great interest in the connections emerging among human rights, self-determination, and international law. Du Bois certainly perceived a deep tie between the treatment of Black people at home and their subjugation abroad. Given the many ways Du Bois and Bunche were in sync about the racialized patterns of domination in world politics, and the overriding importance—moral and political—of decolonization, Du Bois's critique of Bunche's mediation effort was especially painful. Three years later, at the height of his fame, Bunche was asked to be a sponsor for a tribute birthday dinner for

Du Bois. Bunche refused, saying it would be hypocritical to pretend he had forgotten the insult.

As this incident demonstrated, even in New York he could not escape the sharp emotions engendered by the conflict. Indeed, shopping on Fifth Avenue, just before he departed again for the Middle East, Bunche suffered a rebuke from a totally unexpected source: a shopkeeper: "I see you are leaving tomorrow. I suppose you are still trying to take the Negev from us."[36] Pressed to explain what was happening in the region, Bunche gave a radio interview in which he offered the "bold opinion" that the chances of large-scale fighting breaking out in the region were slim.[37] Then, a few days before the end of 1948, fighting did break out. The Israeli military again took the initiative, surrounding Egyptian forces in Falluja. (Among the Egyptian soldiers trapped was a young officer named Gamal Abdel Nasser, who would later become president of Egypt.) Despite the renewed hostilities, Bunche believed that the Israelis, "who did not start this war, desire peace."[38] The Arab states were losing ground and momentum.

Israel's continuing battlefield success, combined with increasing Security Council pressure, finally forced Egypt to agree to Bunche's proposed armistice negotiations. As the largest Arab state, Egypt's acquiescence to the proposed talks was very significant.[39] Movement was on the horizon.

The parley would begin in January 1949 on the Mediterranean island of Rhodes. Bunche had first visited the island earlier in the summer with Bernadotte, as they established headquarters. Rhodes, he had written to Ruth on his first visit, "is a beautiful island. . . . I can look out my window and see the Turkish coast not far away."[40] Bernadotte had chosen Rhodes in part because he found it an "idyllic and peaceful island" where it was "possible to shake one's mind free of the thousand-and-one details that had piled up around us."[41] Now, sequestered with the Middle Eastern adversaries in the Hotel des Roses, Bunche would hunker down and try to succeed where Bernadotte had not.

IN RHODES, THE WARRING PARTIES WERE hours away from the actual fighting. Part of Bunche's strategy in using the island was to make exit difficult; the delegations, he later wrote, "were trapped" because once there the negotiations would continue until one or both of the delegations "would take the responsibility for breaking them off." It was also seen as neutral territory, far from prying eyes and local pressures. Bunche, who hoped they would also be more reasonable in this distant and secluded setting, found the opening day of the mediation inauspicious. The delegates arrived on January 12, 1949, and were immediately hostile and wary. The Egyptians even refused to shake hands with the Israelis.[42]

Bunche tackled this daunting situation with substantial drive and an engaging approach. In his opening speech, he struck a pragmatic tone. He stressed that "we are not holding a peace conference here," but only seeking an armistice. It was a "deadly serious mission" they all were on.[43] He treated each side equally and even ensured they had the same kinds of rooms in the hotel and ate the same food. Still, he found that the parties had arrived with distinctive attitudes: The Israelis were "very confident about the future," whereas the Egyptians were "pitifully trusting and lean heavily on me."[44]

As is often the case in successful high-stakes diplomatic negotiations, a swirling and improvisational brew of coercion and charm was essential. Eventually, the delegates began to relax and talk and, after a while, even socialize a little. Bunche was adept at using the natural human desire to be social to get the delegates to let down their guards and listen to new ideas and approaches. This was no substitute for serious talks, of which there were many. But it helped to open the parties up to novel approaches and, perhaps, to see some as-yet hidden scope for compromise.

The central site of these ice-breaking efforts was the snooker table at the Hotel des Roses. Shabtai Rosenne, one of the Israeli delegates in Rhodes, later recalled Bunche's approach:

> My most vivid recollection of this physically huge man[*]—handsome and attractive in his own way, a soupcon of a smile on his lips, a bubbling sense of humor that never seemed to leave him, a healthy touch of cynicism—is with a half-smoked cigarette dangling from his lips, after dinner bent over the billiard table in the games

---

[*] According to Bunche's UCLA yearbook, he was only 5'9". But perhaps his presence was quite a bit larger.

room of the Hotel des Roses, vigorously playing a form of three-sided snooker with teams from the UN, Egypt, and Israel (possibly carefully choosing the winner for that night, or at least ensuring that it would not be the UN). There were drinks around the table and the atmosphere became relaxed and human. At around 10PM he would call a halt and summon members of one delegation or both to meeting in his room, where he would patiently, firmly and sometimes roughly give his analysis or reports from the delegations, probe reactions to this or that suggestion, first from one side and then from the other. These meetings would sometimes last until morning, such was Bunche's physical and mental stamina.[45]

And when Bunche would hit a dazzling shot on the snooker table, he would sometimes say, "Now you know how I spent my youth."[46]

At the Hotel des Roses, he could to some degree control and cajole the delegates. He held many cards: he was the representative of the UN, which all parties had reasons to care about; he was an American closely associated with the State Department; he was engaging, socially adept, and smart; and he was skilled at holding their feet to the fire when need be. That said, the parties lived in the region and would have to live with any outcome, whereas Bunche—and the UN—did not, and these were, for the most part, hardened men who had seen conflict and were not easily cowed or rushed into decisions.

The talks were held in winter, and the beachfront hotel was often cold and windblown. The delegates had little else to do other than stay inside and talk. As would prove true some fifty years later when the American diplomat Richard Holbrooke famously forced warring sides in post–Cold War Yugoslavia to hole up in an Air Force base in far-away Dayton, Ohio, isolation can be helpful for breaking logjams.[47] But the resulting agreements have to be accepted back home. They have to be implementable, and implemented. The balance between the spirit of creative cooperation that a skilled negotiator can engender in the room and the hard realities back home on the ground is always a difficult one to strike.

This was especially true for the situation in Palestine. Some in the region were already seeing the newly formed UN as weak and feckless; Ben-Gurion colorfully referred to it as "UNO, schmuno."[48] Bunche proved resourceful, as Abba Eban had predicted. But was that enough? Would the parties comply with their commitments? What if they did not? At any moment, things seemed likely to fall apart. When at one point an Israeli delegate angrily threw a pencil, it bounced off the table and hit one of the Arab delegates. That alone almost blew up the negotiations. But Bunche convinced the Israeli to apologize, and the talks were soon back on track. At times the insistence on shunning the other side was shown to be mostly performative. After a frosty initial meeting between two opposing delegates, Bunche convinced the two men to meet secretly. "This time," he later said, "they acted like long-lost brothers. Pretty soon they started to speak Arabic—and then apologized to me because they knew I didn't speak the language. I said, 'Hell, speak your Arabic—don't bother about me!' "[49]

Bunche's approach had two dimensions. One was to negotiate bilaterally with each Arab state. This tactic was broadly favorable to Israel, in that all talks were one on one, and it simplified the negotiations themselves, as the Arab states were rarely aligned and a multiparty process would have meant substantial time spent on coordination.[†] The second was to have a three-stage process of negotiation. He would first meet separately with each side. Then, he would have joint discussions with a representative of each side. Finally, he would at times hold more formal talks with all the players, including other UN officials. Along the way, informal talks occurred between the Arabs and the Israelis, without Bunche present. (An Egyptian on Bunche's staff sometimes acted as a secret intermediary between the parties, calling himself the "Black Market Mediator.")[50] Bunche sought flexibility and compromise throughout. In his opening remarks, he urged that there be "no tendency to be rigidly legalistic, picayunish about details or recriminations."[51] By placing himself in the middle of the parties much of the time, in what later become known as the Rhodes Formula, Bunche was able to maintain momentum while allowing the two sides to claim, or at least pretend, they were not really talking to their hated enemy.

[†] Arab unity was often ephemeral; Saadia Touval, in his 1982 book *The Peace Brokers*, relates a story told by Moshe Dayan, describing a 1949 meeting with King Abdullah of Jordan, in which the king urged the Israelis not to give the Gaza Strip to Egypt: "Take it yourselves, give it to the devil, but don't let Egypt have it!"

While time-consuming—Bunche stayed up until 2 or 3 a.m. nearly every morning in Rhodes—his approach proved successful. It helped that he had, as Bernadotte had once said, "incredible skill" in drafting text.[52] Israel's chief negotiator in Rhodes, Walter Eytan, later remarked that Bunche was so good that "sooner or later he was able to contrive a formula to defeat almost any problem."[53] Bunche also effectively deployed a mix of formal and informal elements: on the one hand, extensive use of the snooker table as an icebreaker; on the other, resort to formalities when necessary to drive the process home. For instance, when it became clear that the main conference room did not have a chairman's gavel, he eventually hired a local carpenter to make one. The delegates were often formally dressed in suits and ties, arrayed around an open square table, making the process all seem quite formal despite the seaside location.

Bunche began the mediation with a clever gambit. He first met with each side separately, to determine an agenda. Then, he called the Egyptians and Israelis together to the same room and moved to approve the agenda. There was a double purpose in this arrangement, he later explained. "Primarily, it was to get both sides to meet—but also, I wanted them both to get accustomed to taking formal action, and to signing something." What mattered most was that they jointly sign a document: anything that looked official.[54] Now, the seal was broken, and they had agreed to something.

The issues involved in the Rhodes talks were layered. At the most basic level was the fact that Arab states did not want to accept Israel's existence, and they had done little to prepare Arab peoples for the notion that the Jewish state now in their midst might be there permanently. The strategy of refusing to engage with the prior UN processes had, unsurprisingly in retrospect, failed to stop UNSCOP, the General Assembly vote, or Israel's declaration of independence. Moreover, Israel had proven quite powerful on the battlefield and had taken control of key areas, such as the Negev Desert. The Arab states were off balance but nonetheless unwilling to concede that they had lost control of a valued territory.

Still, when one stepped back, it remained the case that Israel was tiny; that there were several Arab states, not just one; and that some Arab nations, such as Egypt, were actually quite large. Ultimately, the Arabs could wield considerable power if they organized effectively. Moreover, both sides wanted the international community's support and feared what might occur if the great powers became more deeply involved in the region. Bunche saw his talks as focused on achieving a military peace, whereas the UN Conciliation Commission, once launched, would have a broader and more political ambit. This was his vision at least. Yet there was no easy way to disentangle the military from the political implications and therefore no way to avoid the deep divisions that so vexed the Palestine question.

This context made the process of even talking about solutions difficult. "Neither side anxious to meet the other, but both want me to persuade the other. What a life!"[55] Bunche wrote these words in late January 1949, as the prospects for success seemed dim. While he relished a challenge and seemed to find the mediation by turns fascinating and frustrating, he never gave up even as events headed in a bad direction. At this point, both sides were intransigent on certain issues and appeared, to varying degrees, unwilling to recognize reality. Still, he remained sanguine; though the Egyptians were in "no hurry," "as long as I can keep them meeting there is still hope."[56]

To jolt things forward, Bunche tried to present some hard truths. "Miracles seldom happen," he told the Egyptians, who were still seeking to oust the Israelis from the Negev Desert.[57]

AS JANUARY 1949 CAME TO A close, Ralph Bunche needed to find a way to spur the proceedings forward. Perhaps recalling how he and Bernadotte had succeeded the previous summer with an initial truce proposal that the parties could only accept or reject, he decided to present the Egyptians and the Israelis with a set of written proposals that were, as best he could judge, evenly balanced. It was a take-it-or-leave-it proposal, a gamble that he calculated just might work. His hope was that with the world watching, neither side would want to be seen as wrecking the negotiations.

In a letter to Ruth he wrote,

There is a cat and mouse game going on here between them and me—they would be happy if I would terminate the negotiations and thus relieve them of any responsibility. But I am not going to take that rap. . . . It's like having a bear by the tail and being afraid to let go. God knows I would like to let go, as I am dying to come home and be with you and Ralph[‡] and get some rest.[58]

At first his gambit seemed to work. Many details remained, but the parties inched closer. Trygve Lie cabled with encouragement, telling him to "keep going and smiling."[59] The outside world watched with great interest. Dean Acheson, the American secretary of state, even sent a note to David Ben-Gurion encouraging Israel to accede to Bunche's proposals.

Finally, on January 24, 1949, an agreement between Israel and Egypt was reached. Bunche "is a very remarkable man," Walter Eytan, the Israeli negotiator, wrote back to Tel Aviv.[60] The ceasefire between the two states was a big step forward, but many substantive issues remained to be hashed out. Indeed, just a few days later, Bunche would cable Lie that prospects for an actual armistice "are virtually nil."[61]

The UN Conciliation Commission was now formed, however, and, thinking they might work best together, Bunche invited the commission members to come to the Hotel des Roses and participate in the armistice mediation and, he added with some desperation, "assume full responsibility for all Palestine functions and thereby relieve me of all my present duties"[62] The commission declined. Bunche was frustrated by this refusal, which seemed to squelch his rising hope for an exit. He later believed the negative response reflected jealousy—that "the negotiations here—and I—are hogging the limelight." And, he added for good measure, "they envy my plane."[63] But whatever the reason, it seemed there was not going to be significant coordination between the two UN efforts.

To have two peace processes in the region working simultaneously was, to be sure, a little odd. Yet for the moment it was working. In part, this was because the American government served as the link between the two. Bunche was at this point only two years out from his old job at the State Department. He had many contacts in Washington and was trusted. The Truman administration in turn knew that he was the indispensable player at the UN and that any ultimate success in the Arab-Israeli conflict would

---

[‡] Ralph Jr., his son, who was then five.

flow through him. "We feel that no one but yourself should shepherd these delicate negotiations at this time," Dean Rusk wrote to him, foreshadowing a view Rusk would later hold, even more strongly, with regard to Bunche and Vietnam.[64] Bunche, who would spend much of his career as the primary interlocutor between Washington and New York, was seen as the key to a successful process.

Bunche tried to keep the Conciliation Commission apprised of progress, which also meant the US government was well aware of what was transpiring at the Hotel des Roses. For example, after proposing another compromise, which Egypt ultimately accepted but Israel criticized, he let Mark Ethridge, the American member of the commission, know the state of play.[65] The very next day, the Israeli government received a message from President Truman encouraging them to accept Bunche's plan.

Truman had in fact become quite focused on the Middle East. Years later, Ethridge recounted how Truman picked him to be the American delegate on the commission:

I kept demurring saying, no, I didn't want to go, I didn't feel any call to go; and finally Acheson picked up his white telephone to call Truman and said, "Ethridge is bucking, I'd like to bring him over."
Truman said, "Bring him over."
I went over and Truman began to put on the heat, as only he could, and I kept telling him my objections . . . and he said, "If you're so damn smart why don't you go over there and recommend a settlement?"
I said, "No, it's too late, you're stuck with this. . . ."
He said, "We're not stuck with anything."
I kept demurring and finally Truman lost his temper and he said, "Listen, I can get a million sons of bitches to make war tomorrow, can't I get one son of a bitch to help me make peace?"
I said, "When do I go Mr. President?"
He said, "Tonight."[66]

Truman's personal involvement in the Palestine process reflected both the US investment in the early UN and the growing strategic significance of the Middle East. Israel had also captured the imagination of many American

Jews, creating additional political pressures on Truman. Truman had been irritated by the intense lobbying around the UN General Assembly resolution on Palestine in 1947, but he continued to be supportive of the new Jewish state. (Still, he once complained in a cabinet meeting that "Jesus Christ couldn't satisfy the Jews while on earth, how the hell am I supposed to?")[67]

The British believed the growing American tilt toward Israel was clear. "As long as America is a major power... anyone taking on the Jews will be indirectly taking on America," opined Hector McNeil, the British deputy foreign minister.[68] This view was not unique to Britain. Even Truman's under secretary of state, James Webb, declared in 1949 that experience "suggests that Israel has had more influence with the US than the US with Israel."[69]

Over the coming decades the Middle East would consume substantial—many would argue inordinate—attention from American presidents. While lasting peace in the region continued to remain out of reach, American leaders continued to try to broker it. Within the UN, the strong support for Israel that marked these early years gradually eroded and then reversed. As many former European colonies gained their independence and joined the UN in the coming decades they strongly opposed what they saw as continuing imperialism. For many of these countries, Israel was akin to the "settler colonial" states, such as the US itself, where Europeans had violently displaced local populations and seized land and political control.[70] The Palestinian cause became a way to assert the rising values of anticolonialism and self-determination while also attacking the West and especially Israel's primary patron, the US. From the 1950s onward, in fact, the UN became the key site of the global struggle over Palestine. Israel's continuing occupation and encroachment in the West Bank after 1967 also drew extensive censure. Soon the entire concept of a Jewish state came under sustained attack.

By 1975, the General Assembly easily passed a resolution declaring Zionism itself to be a form of racism.§ Most of the West voted against the resolution, but the Soviet-aligned states, the Arab world, and many newly independent African states voted in favor. Israel, which began its history

---

§ The Israeli ambassador to the UN at the time, Chaim Herzog, famously tore the resolution in half at the end of his impassioned speech opposing the vote. The resolution was effectively revoked in 1991 by another General Assembly resolution.

stirringly invoking the UN in its declaration of independence, was soon dismissing the organization as endemically hostile. By 2016, the situation was so fraught that then-Prime Minister Benjamin Netanyahu could declare he was going to "reevaluate all our contacts with the UN" and possibly cease funding the organization.[71]

In 1949, however, this was all far in the future. The UN was still a friendly place for Israel, and to some degree the organization, or at least the Secretariat, saw the new state's success as part of its success. In fact, Trygve Lie strongly supported Israel and seemed to go out of his way to assist it in its struggle against the Arabs. Bunche, though sometimes viewed as pro-Israel himself, did not approve of this overt favoritism. The secretary general, he later mused, "was anything but objective on major issues such as Palestine."[72] Lie even passed secret information directly to Abba Eban, the Israeli representative at the UN. And at one point, Lie "went so far as to advise the Israelis to face off" with Bernadotte in the mediation and not appear accommodating.[73]

Israel was not the first state to gain independence in the UN era; in the decades to come many dozens more would follow. But it was the first for which the UN had such a direct hand in the process. In later years the UN, and Bunche himself, would act as a sort of doula of self-determination, guiding new states through the process of independence, advising them on matters of governance, economics, and administration, and providing an imprimatur of sovereign status to the newly born states. To be sure, Israel posed a unique set of challenges due to the geopolitical setting of the Middle East and the intense conflict its independence engendered. But even in this regard the birth of Israel was in a way a marker of things to come: many new states in the postwar era would suffer from violence in the wake of independence. UN peace efforts—including peacekeeping itself, a central innovation to come—would often prove essential to achieve some modicum of stability as decolonization gathered steam.

The UN in 1949 was new and untested as an arena and agent for problem solving. Indeed, in many respects the Palestine conflict was the first major challenge for the organization. For these reasons, the pressures on Ralph Bunche to succeed in Rhodes were intense.

CHAPTER 11

TRIUMPH

I N THE WINTER of 1949, at the Hotel des Roses in Rhodes, Ralph Bunche was growing increasingly frustrated. The pace of the armistice talks was slow and at times even seemed to be headed in the wrong direction. He did not feel he truly understood the complex emotions of his interlocutors, and he found the endless intrigue and grandstanding frustrating. The region had struck him as immensely complex and frustrating from his first days as part of the UN Special Commission on Palestine, and nothing he had learned since had changed his view. In his diary he wrote that he was "weary of Rhodes, Jews, and Egyptians, and very homesick."[1] His room was often like an icebox and the mood in some of the meetings no warmer. In a letter home that February, he vented to Ruth:

> I talk, argue, coax and threaten these stubborn people day and night, in the effort to reach agreement. I make a bit of progress here and another bit there, but it is so slow and so arduous. Sometimes I feel that I should just tell them to go home and forget about an armistice. I really don't care whether they agree or not.[2]

In an indication of where his mind was, he added: "Did you hear the prediction in the *N.Y. Post* that I would be the next Ambassador to Russia. Everyone's talking about it out here, but it is utterly ridiculous, of course."

Progress had surely been made in Rhodes, but his frustration illustrated how Bunche increasingly found both sides difficult and often dramatic. Each took (or feigned) offense easily, and it seemed any one issue might tank the negotiations. The entire thing felt like a highwire act. Still, he told reporters in early February that events had picked up: we might get an agreement, he explained, in "a day or two or a couple of weeks—or not at all."[3] Other sources—perhaps Bunche himself?—planted the story that he was set to leave in frustration at the Israeli unwillingness to accept "the Bunche Line."[4] His carefully crafted statements to the press leveraged the fact that the world was closely watching the situation in Palestine, and that helped him keep the pressure on the negotiating teams.

A key sticking point in February was the Negev city of Beersheba, which the Israelis had recently captured. The Egyptians continued to press for it, insisting it was essential to them, but Bunche knew there was no chance the Israelis would yield. He tried repeatedly to convince Egypt to move forward anyway. Bunche felt that they had more to gain overall in a deal, and standing firm on this issue would ultimately fail, leaving Egypt worse off. (To Trygve Lie, he cabled: "this is a thoroughly honorable agreement for the Egyptians . . . they will lose very much if they refuse to sign.")[5] The Israelis agreed to some more minor withdrawals, sweetening the deal. Both sides continued to parry for days. Amid this minuet Jordan agreed to enter into talks as well.* Bunche took this opportunity to ratchet up the pressure still further, suggesting that if agreement between Israel and Egypt was not reached, he would bring the Jordanians and Egyptians into joint talks with Israel, something the Israelis strongly opposed.

One morning, feeling desperate to shake things up, he sent a messenger to the Israeli team. Mr. Bunche would like to see you in his suite, the messenger told them. Somewhat surprised, the Israelis headed upstairs. He had the same message sent to the Egyptian team, who walked into the bedroom

---

* Then known as Transjordan.

suite as well. There, he greeted the two delegations. He then opened a large chest of drawers and withdrew a heavy round dinner plate, hand-painted in green and blue flowery swirls. The plate read "Armistice Negotiations" across the top and "Rhodes-1949" across the bottom. "Now look, look at these lovely plates which I prepared specially for you," he told the delegates. "When you sign the agreement, each of you is going to get one of these plates as a souvenir. . . . But if you don't reach agreement I personally will break these plates over your heads!"

Everyone burst out laughing, but soon the impasse seemed to be over. Walter Eytan of the Israeli delegation called it "a typical Ralph Bunche maneuver."[6]

ON FEBRUARY 18, 1949, THE SITUATION was finally looking up. The Egyptians provisionally agreed to the proposed arrangements and took a draft back to Cairo for final approval. Bunche reached out to Trygve Lie for help in closing the deal. Egypt, he explained, had to understand that the bargain on the table was their best option. Lie met with the Egyptian foreign minister three times in three days, putting the pressure on. Harry Truman even sent a personal note to King Farouk of Egypt, urging him to accept. The next day Bunche worked through the night, trying to massage the language into an accord both sides could accept. To reporters, he made clear he was open to almost anything that worked. There are "not three parties in these negotiations," Bunche said. "Anything sensible or ridiculous that the two delegations agree to put into the document would be all right with me."[7]

Finally, on February 23, agreement between Egypt and Israel came. Bunche was thrilled—not only at the success, but also at the prospect that he was one step closer to home. The first leg of the armistice accords was complete. To be sure, the agreement was not highly detailed, and deliberately so. For example, at Egypt's request there was no map—Bunche would later say, "there was no map because if there had been a map there would not have been an Armistice Agreement"—but the deal had enough detail to stick.[8] The first part of the multipart effort was complete.

The two sides immediately had an impromptu celebration. It was an improbable scene. A mixed doubles at ping-pong pitted Bunche's British secretary, Doreen Daughton, and Sam Souki, an Egyptian reporter, against an Israeli-Egyptian pair. " 'Some combination for the Near East!" Bunche noted.[9] The negotiators celebrated until 4:30 a.m. The next morning they formally signed the accord in a brief, twenty-two minute ceremony; Bunche in a suit and tie, cigarette dangling from his lips, perused the documents. The Associated Press reported President Truman was "immensely gratified" at the result and had congratulated Bunche for his fine work and "untiring efforts." Dean Acheson and Dean Rusk in a top-secret cable sent their congratulations and desire to see him personally as soon as possible to "talk over many matters [of] mutual interest."[10] Bunche himself called the mediation "important history" that, while quite difficult, had paid handsome dividends. For the first time in the long history of the Palestine dispute, he said, Arab and Jewish leaders had met, negotiated, and signed a formal agreement.[11]

Success was sweet. Yet he really had no time to rest. The Jordanian talks would soon commence on Rhodes, and they were likely to prove just as taxing as the Egyptian ones had been. On the other hand, success often breeds success, and he had proven that it was possible to find some common ground. That alone was a major card in his hands going forward. Bunche was beginning to acquire the special halo that would later make him seem like a master peacemaker. The *Christian Science Monitor* ran a long feature with the heady title "Triumph of a Mediator."[12] Bunche, the story noted, was now rumored to be the next US ambassador to the Soviet Union. The press often speculated about possible US government positions for Bunche, but this one did not come to fruition. Other agencies and universities began to take a closer look at him as well, and over the next weeks he received teaching offers from Berkeley, Columbia, and Stanford. These were very impressive options. Years earlier, Bunche had told the president of Howard that he was only leaving the university for a brief period and that he intended to return to academia. Yet despite many plum offers, he never returned to academic life.

The second round of talks in Rhodes began at the end of February 1949. The Jordanians sent their delegation—Bunche found them "unimpressive, timid, and not very bright"[13]—and the Israelis sent a new team, which

Photo 11.1 Bunche signing the First Armistice in Rhodes

included a Palestine-born colonel named Moshe Dayan, who would later become Israel's minister of defense and foreign affairs. ("Nice guy," wrote Bunche in his diary. "Too bad he has that black patch over his left eye.")[14] The Israelis, happy with the initial outcome with Egypt, had asked the Truman administration to keep Bunche going on this round. Although they sometimes criticized him publicly, the Israelis recognized Bunche's skill and the advantages of his approach for the young state, and they were convinced he was the only person who could see things through to victory. In private they were always very positive. "How friendly to me are Jews these days!" he wrote in his diary in early March.[15]

Jordan had already been talking to Israel at a high level, and so, as Bunche understood, this set of negotiations started in a very different place than the ones involving Egypt. In the "Yellow Room" of the Hotel des Roses, he addressed the two groups on the first day, noting that Egypt and Israel had just signed an armistice accord and encouraging a spirit of "reciprocal respect."[16] Yet it quickly became apparent that this spirit was absent. When the Israeli delegation entered the room on the first day of joint meetings, the Jordanian leader, already seated, refused to stand, even after Bunche asked him to. The Israelis, offended, refused to engage and returned to Tel Aviv. The situation righted itself eventually, but Bunche was losing patience ("I am disgusted") with the petty and symbolic games endemic to this conflict.[17] Still, he continued his approach, pushing the parties, reading cables even while in the bath, and, as always, beating everyone at billiards.

In an effort to speed up the process, a parallel but less protracted set of talks began between Israel and Lebanon. Bunche sent his deputy, Henry Vigier, to lead these efforts at a site near the Israeli-Lebanese border. The Lebanon discussions were at times bumpy. Trust remained very low; each side maneuvered shamelessly. Bunche in particular complained that the Israelis were "utterly outrageous" in these negotiations. At one point, one of the Israeli negotiators, Reuven Shiloah, casually and without asking, took some pistachio candy Bunche had sitting near him on a table. He then wrapped up some more to take home. One of Bunche's colleagues later quipped that Shiloah must have "thought it was the Negev."[18†]

The complex issue of Palestinian refugees continued to crop up. While no one anticipated the scale or duration of the refugee situation that would come in later decades, it was apparent even in 1949 that a grave humanitarian crisis was looming. In March, Dean Acheson cabled Bunche that a State Department official would be flying in to discuss the problem. The US proposal was, as Bunche described it, "to press Jews to take back Arabs in areas under their control" and to "pay compensation for land, property to all who cannot come back." Those who could not come back would be, under the American notion, "settled elsewhere," such as Jordan and Syria, with the US "playing (and paying) a prominent but not exclusive role" in fostering execution of the plans.[19] Had this proposal been implemented, the future of the Middle East may have been quite different. But it was not, and some six months later the UN create the UN Relief and Works Agency

---

† Shiloah later became the first director of the Mossad, the Israeli intelligence bureau.

to assist the huge and desperate refugee population. Despite its meliorative efforts, the conditions for refugees remained bleak and many were essentially trapped.

Meanwhile, the Lebanese talks revolved around the Israeli troops still on Lebanese territory. Bunche, frustrated, at one point cabled Lie that the Israelis were "deliberately blocking" agreement in an effort to put pressure on Syria, and he threatened to go to the Security Council with his charge.[20] In the Negev Desert, Israeli forces continued to advance on the ground; they had even reached the Red Sea, at what is now Eilat. Bunche finally persuaded Jordan and Israel to sign a ceasefire. With the ceasefire in place, the focus of the Israeli-Jordan talks shifted to Jerusalem—perhaps the most difficult and emotional issue for both sides; the issue that had ultimately led to the death of Folke Bernadotte.

The matter of Jerusalem was especially tricky because it was the home of several distinct religious sites and communities. Bunche proposed a plan that built on the concept of internationalizing Jerusalem, which had long been part of the international community's thinking about the complex and divided city. The Jordanians were open to the idea. Yet as he wrote with some exasperation in his diary, the Israelis "rejected [it] on the grounds of 'too much internationalization, which is premature.' "[21] Frustrated, he knew enough by now to simply continue and not let apparent walls foreclose a path forward. He was increasingly exhausted by the effort, however. New crises seemed to pop up constantly, and, as he cabled Lie, "we are all just hanging by our teeth." Perhaps it was no surprise that in interviews with reporters he spoke, as if it were inevitable, of his return to Howard and his agenda for further research into colonial rule.[22]

By late March, Henry Vigier had achieved initial success with Lebanon and Israel. Bunche was pleased and was beginning to feel his freedom approach. "I can see the end of my work in sight," he wrote in his diary. "It shouldn't be long now."[23] He was yearning to return home and leave the byzantine politics of the Middle East behind. In a letter to Ruth, as he saw what he hoped was the end on the horizon, his frustration with the process spilled over:

You can't imagine what it takes to hold these monkeys together long enough to squeeze agreement out of them. And such trickery, deceit, and downright dishonesty you have never seen. I swear by all that's Holy, I will never come anywhere near the Palestine problem once I liberate myself from this trap.[24]

With Bunche urging them toward conciliation, the parties continued to joust as winter turned to spring. The talks inched forward, sometimes turning into reverse. But the momentum to bring finality to the situation proved more powerful. On April 1, Moshe Dayan and his team returned from Israel with positive news: another deal was at hand. The armistice lines were becoming clear.

Bunche was relieved to see he was one step closer to escape. Yet he was somewhat conflicted. He felt that the outcomes were less than fair, especially to the refugees, even if the result ultimately achieved peace. He had success, but at what price? As he put it, it was "another deal, and as usual the Palestine Arabs lose. Abdullah of course, is mainly interested in extending his rule over Arab Palestine and getting the Jews to accept it."[25] He was receiving a master class in the complex and layered politics of the region. Still, on April 3, 1949, the two sides signed the armistice accord. Bunche told reporters that he was pleased; he called it a "virtual non-aggression pact" between Israel and Jordan.[26]

The final player, Syria, was now on deck. All seemed to be going well. Then, Syria suddenly suffered a coup on March 30. Bunche cabled Lie that the talks had been set to begin April 1; the coup pushed back the start of the mediation but thankfully did not derail the process.[27] Exhausted and wanting to return to New York and his family, he again delegated the talks to Vigier. The Israelis, who believed Bunche was the only one who could pull the negotiations off successfully, wanted him to continue to handle all talks; they even pressured Lie to force him to stay. Bunche objected firmly. "I am completely worn out physically and mentally after three months of uninterrupted negotiations," he told the secretary general.[28] Having been trapped on Rhodes in what seemed to be an endless and airless squabble, he could take no more. He also thought he could be more useful in New York, applying pressure via the UN and US, than laboring over more conflict between the parties. It was perhaps a self-serving rationale, but with his stature and experience now at a peak, it was not an unreasonable stance.

On his way back to the states, Bunche first stopped over in Beirut to meet with the UN Conciliation Commission. There he discussed the refugee problem with Mark Ethridge, the American member of the commission. Ethridge suggested that the US should adopt a "tough policy" on Palestinian refugees with Israel. Bunche next headed to Geneva and then to Sweden to lay a wreath on Bernadotte's grave.[29] After months sequestered in Rhodes, he realized he had become truly famous. Even the crown prince of Sweden paid him a visit. Once in Paris, reporters followed him everywhere, pressing him for quotes on what was happening. He was recognized all over town. Two men, he wrote in his diary, even "cornered me in the john and asked for autographs."[30] Boarding the *Queen Mary* to cross the Atlantic, he felt a twinge of anticipation about what to expect as he returned home. More than almost anywhere in the world, New York, as both the home of the UN and the largest Jewish city in the world, had followed the progress in Rhodes closely. Disembarking in Manhattan, he was swarmed by photographers and well-wishers. Greeted by New York City Mayor William O'Dwyer, he was given a police escort back home to Queens. In brief remarks at the harborside landing, he stressed what he saw as the primary lesson of Rhodes: the ability of the UN to mediate a serious conflict. Asked the secret of his success, he said "Keep on pitching, and then pitch some more."[31]

While the process was not yet over, Bunche was correct that the mediation had provided proof of concept for an important aspect of the new UN. As a generally neutral body, it offered a more easily legitimated way for the international community to shape outcomes. Some (such as the Soviets) would see this as simply a flimsy cloak for Western, or perhaps American, power. But it was more than that, and in the years to come the practice of mediation through the UN would prove attractive to many. Meanwhile, his skill and success caught the notice of the Truman administration. Seeking to bring him back to Washington, Dean Acheson offered him the post of assistant secretary of state. He declined, but State continued to push the idea. Visiting the White House to see Truman in May, he found the president "very congenial and [he] complimented my work highly." Bunche told Truman he appreciated the offer but preferred to stay at the UN. He added, "I couldn't afford the job in any case." (UN salaries were tax-free and comparatively generous.) Truman said he understood, and as the two men discussed the Palestine situation, the president complained that in the past "'they' had 'tricked him'—referring to Jews."[32]

Meanwhile, in Syria, the final set of talks were still muddling along. Even with the successes of the past few months the prospects constantly seemed on the edge of failure. That summer Ben-Gurion told the Israeli Knesset that "the conflict is not over" and may well "end only with force."[33] Yet Israel was in fact wary of much more conflict. It was seeking admission to the UN, which the Israeli leadership coveted as an important mark of independence and legitimacy. The first attempt at membership, in 1948, had been blocked in the Security Council. After the armistice with Egypt, a second attempt succeeded; the membership proposal now went to the General Assembly for approval.[‡] The lesson was plain: if Israel could make peace in the region, it would have a higher likelihood of acceptance by the broader international community.

Finally, on July 20, in a large tent in which the mediation talks had taken place, Syria and Israel signed the final accord. The agreement created a set of demilitarized zones—a Bunche innovation—along the border region between the two states. This approach seemed a smart one and was a substantial success at the time. Over time, however, the demilitarized zones proved to be a never-ending source of disagreement. Moshe Dayan later described how he challenged Bunche on the purpose of the zones. "I asked Bunche 'why are you taking this route? Why are you writing such things?' Bunche replied: 'There are topics on which we cannot reach an agreement. Afterwards, no one will go to war over such an issue.' "[34] Bunche was perhaps demonstrating his typical optimism, a quality that was in short supply in the Middle East. Or perhaps he was simply pragmatic—and tired. At this moment in time, he told Dayan, our job is to end the war.

SHORTLY AFTER HIS TRIUMPHANT RETURN TO New York, Bunche addressed the UN Security Council. In hindsight, his words from 1949

‡ Israel became a full UN member in May 1949.

underscore the sad and seemingly intractable nature of the Middle East conflict. The armistice agreements are not the final peace settlement, he conceded to the eleven ambassadors on the Council. But, he said—with what in time would prove to be undue confidence—they signaled "the end of the military phase of the Palestine conflict."

> The disputing parties have made very great strides toward peace. The armistice agreements, all but one of which have now been in effect for several months, are proving very effective. . . . [The current situation] gives support to my belief that all outstanding obstacles to permanent peace in Palestine, including the problem of the Arab refugees, who now suffer most from this unfortunate conflict, can and will be overcome by a mutual spirit of conciliation and by reciprocal concessions.[35]

Bunche's optimism about the Middle East was not unique to him; the mediation was widely seen as a major success. The desire to achieve peace was strong, and for some, including Bunche himself, desire may have trumped reality. He told reporters that he believed that the negotiations proved that the UN can "successfully stop a war" and, via mediation, "take the disputing parties by the hand and lead them along the road to peaceful and amicable settlement."[36]

Meanwhile, there was much excitement about his accomplishments. Speaking at a black-tie event soon after his return, with Eleanor Roosevelt sitting at his side, he declared to the crowd that "full peace" will soon be restored to the Holy Land. How could it be otherwise? he asked rhetorically; "Peace, I am sure, will reign in Palestine."[37]

Unfortunately, seven decades later peace in the Middle East remains elusive. The question of the UN's role in either alleviating or exacerbating the conflict is not easy to answer, in part because the UN has played so many roles and in part because there are in fact many UNs. The Human Rights Council; the Security Council; the General Assembly; the Secretariat itself—all have taken different stances on different aspects of the Arab-Israeli conflict. What is undeniable is that the marathon negotiations on the island of Rhodes were an early success that, in many ways, outlasted anyone's expectations about their impact—including Ralph Bunche's. Judgment of the Rhodes talks has continued in the decades since.§ While observers vary as to how skillful he really was and how successful his solutions proved (and some have questioned the aura that surrounds him), many participants believed him to be a superb mediator. Even the prickly David Ben-Gurion believed that Bunche handled the process "with great skill."[38] This skill involved in part his oft-noted ability to draft compromise texts that captured elusive common ground; in part his political realism; and in part even his gregarious charm that allowed him to push and push without blowing up the process.

Yet Bunche had another, very important, arrow in his quiver. In 1949, he was just a few years out of government service. Throughout his career he took pains to stress that he was an international civil servant at the UN and not an agent or lackey of the US. Yet he was also a former State Department and OSS official with close ties to key figures in Washington. In Palestine, of course, he did not yet have the prestige and position that would later make him a sort of shadow secretary general. But the Israelis and Arabs alike knew that Bunche had a direct pipeline to the Truman administration. They may have even wondered if he was following or implementing American preferences. This may at times have been true, but less because Bunche was deliberately doing so and more because Trygve Lie was so favorable toward both the US and the young state of Israel. In any event, Bunche's proximity to American leadership gave him a certain power on the ground, even if, in reality, his discussions with American officials were limited.

What is perhaps more consequential is how the Palestine effort marked the emergence of conflict management as a core task of the UN. Shortly after Rhodes, Bunche spoke of the settlement of disputes as "one of the most vital roles" of the young UN.[39] Conflict mediation had also been a goal of the League of Nations, but unfortunately the League largely proved impotent, being more a place for talk than for action. In Rhodes, Bunche had shown that a standing international organization could do more than

---

§ Decades later, Bunche's armistice accords became the unlikely basis of a major gang truce in Los Angeles, brokered not far from where he grew up. Modeled on Bunche's accomplishment, which the gang leaders saw as highly symbolic for their version of armed, territorial conflict, the so-called Watts Gang Treaty was negotiated in 1992.

simply provide a new forum for squabbling. This was a significant step in the building of the new postwar order, which was predicated on the notion that war would be checked by the great powers acting in concert via the Security Council. As the Cold War swiftly dampened that collaborative vision, mediation by the UN, though not especially focused on in San Francisco, grew in importance. To be sure, dispute resolution was not new; a half century before Bunche won the Nobel Peace Prize, Teddy Roosevelt had won the prize for mediating the Russo-Japanese War. Even earlier, the Permanent Court of Arbitration was created by the 1899 Hague Convention for the Pacific Settlement of International Disputes. What had changed was that there was now a standing, largely neutral, and generally trusted multilateral body that provided a focal point for such efforts. In Palestine, the UN added an additional feature: a small group of observers known as the UN Truce Supervision Organization. Bunche would later call this early precursor to peacekeeping the UN's "Peace Army in Palestine."[40]

In the years to come, conflict resolution became a core activity of the organization. Bunche's mediation was authorized by the Security Council, but much of the subsequent mediation has been far more informal. Over the ensuing years the annual fall meetings of the General Assembly, in which heads of state and government from around the world gather in New York, became a key site of speed-dating style diplomacy. Because the UN buildings are a neutral site, it is easy to have informal, unscripted discussions in the blur of activities that do not carry enormous political baggage back home—and may even remain secret. Stories abound of meetings happening surreptitiously in the building; perhaps even with one ambassador sitting in one chair, their back to another ambassador from some purported enemy state, but nonetheless carrying on a conversation that was wholly deniable if discovered. In short, the UN itself became central to the process of managing conflict. In the decades to follow, the UN's more formal "good offices" role would also grow.

Effective diplomacy is nonetheless often personal, and some are simply better at it—or better suited to the particularities of the diplomatic challenge they find themselves in—and Bunche seemed to fit well with the challenges in Rhodes. As one Israeli participant later wrote,

Bunche was tough; he could be harsh; he cajoled, he threatened; he charmed. If he twisted your arm, it hurt, and was meant to. But he was fair and open to argument and persuasion and to me was the incarnation of belief in the UN—not the United Nations as viewed through rose-tinted spectacles of a wishy-washy ideology but the UN as a necessity for the preservation of mankind in the nuclear age.[41]

Bunche certainly leaned in and used all his powers—analytic as well as charismatic—to achieve success. When later reflecting on the accomplishment, he spoke of the qualities he believed a good international mediator needed to have. The mediator should be "biased against war and for peace," he urged. They should be biased in favor of the "essential goodness of their fellow man" and believe that "no problem of human relations is insoluble."[42] These words were arguably feel-good exhortations, but Bunche seemed to truly believe them. Throughout his long career, he found plenty to dislike in his various interlocutors, but he retained a fundamental optimism and a belief that peace, if pursued vigorously and in good faith, was always possible. He later added one other unorthodox lesson he had learned: "Sometimes poisoning helps." To an audience in New York, he recounted that at one point in Rhodes all the participants came down with food poisoning, except a member of the Israeli delegation who kept kosher.[43] He found the two-day break to recover served as an effective cooling-off period. (And from then on, Bunche himself, who often suffered from stomach ailments while on the road, only ate kosher at the Hotel des Rhodes.)

For Bunche personally, the mediation was a milestone. His fame was already on the rise; now he was beginning to be seen as a sort of diplomatic superhero for the postwar age. The *Pittsburgh Courier's* headline in March 1949, as the negotiations were looking good, was indicative: "Bunche Acclaimed World's No 1 Diplomat."[44] That it was a Black man who had received this accolade was not lost on the many reporters (and readers) who were eagerly learning about his accomplishments. Years later he explained how his personal experience of discrimination gave him insight and even habits of mind that proved useful during the mediation:

I've often been asked the secret of our methods in mediating one of the most bitter and complicated disputes in modern times. The answer is difficult, but in terms of my personal approach one point may deserve emphasis. Like every Negro in America, I've been buffeted about a great deal. . . . I've always cultivated a coolness of temper, an attitude of objectivity when dealing with human sensitivities and irrationalities, which has always proved invaluable—never more so than in the Palestine negotiations. Success there was dependent upon maintaining complete objectivity.[45]

As this statement suggests, Bunche believed in the importance of a cool, analytic approach. He would often express distaste with emotion when it intersected with politics. He himself had not shied away from strong views in the past, such as when he referred to the "rape" of Africa in his short book, *A World View of Race*. But that was over a decade ago, and he was far more pragmatic and guarded now. It is not clear how much Bunche even believed in his Marxist arguments of the 1930s. And when engaged in the realm of politics rather than scholarship, he seemed to firmly believe that emotion often got in the way of solutions. He saw "irrationalities" as perhaps endemic to human nature but something to be suppressed, squelched, and sidelined as much as possible. As decolonization accelerated over the next decade, Bunche would sometimes find himself at odds with liberation leaders such as Patrice Lumumba and Kwame Nkrumah, who favored a hotter form of politics and would often seek to inflame rather than cool political passions. He considered this approach to be demagoguery and dangerous, and he denounced it—especially when racially or ethnically based, and especially when there was little national identity or sentiment to rein it in.

As the Palestine mediation wrapped up, Eleanor Roosevelt invited him on her weekly radio show. Asked what the most difficult aspect of the process was, he somewhat diplomatically replied, "first getting the parties to sit down together and then keeping them together until they reached agreement—they were often pretty sensitive people and ready to pull out."[46] Roosevelt next inquired about what aspect of his training was most valuable in Rhodes. Bunche interestingly cited not his race and the experiences of discrimination he endured, as he would later do, but instead his academic background and grounding in political science. Still, he ended up more and less in the same place: it was emotion that was the hindrance, and partisan and group thinking that blocked peace. As a social scientist and scholar, he explained to Eleanor Roosevelt with a surprising lack of doubt, "I know the value of complete objectivity." He stressed the importance of weighing both sides of a question. Leavening the conversation a bit, he noted that "as a father of three children I've had to do a lot of mediating" in his own house.

Prefiguring a later discussion the two of them would have over decolonization, Roosevelt pivoted to the future of Africa. "What can we expect, Dr. Bunche, from this great continent of Africa in the near future?" Very much, he replied. Africa is a continent great in resources and in human potential, and it must "continue along the road to self-determination." The issue of decolonization was becoming more heated in 1949. Palestine was a special case, but others were clearly looming, and the UN's increasing interest in and attention to colonies was troubling to the traditional imperial powers. The British, charging that the UN was engaged in a "full-scale assault" on colonialism, were threatening to boycott some of the UN processes. They even announced that they would not fly the UN flag in their trust territories, despite a General Assembly resolution requesting that all trust powers do so.[47]

The UN flag was not in and of itself very meaningful. Yet it symbolized the heart of a struggle Bunche had long been interested in: who really "owned" the formerly colonized trust territories, the trustees or the international community? Had the UN Charter ushered in a new age, or had it simply given cover to the continuing oppression of the nonwhite world by the nations of Europe? Two decades earlier, Bunche's Howard colleague, Alain Locke, had characterized the League of Nations mandate system as "A New Code of Empire." Bunche firmly believed the UN trusteeship system was no such thing, but that still remained to be proven.

While his time in Rhodes had made Bunche famous, he never lost his fixation on the necessity of a more just world, one free of race-based governance. Indeed, in a speech delivered just weeks after his conversation with Eleanor Roosevelt, he discussed the core role of the UN. The UN's voice was important in solving international conflicts. But, he stressed, it was not only on behalf of world peace that the UN's voice had been raised. That voice would also be increasingly heard for a just world. A just world, he explained, is a world in which "racial and religious bigotry are universally outlawed; a world in which all peoples, irrespective of race or creed are accepted as equals in a bond of human kinship; a world in which discrimination, segregation, underprivilege, imperialism, and colonialism will have become the unsavory relics of a dark age fortunately past."[48]

———

BUNCHE WAS IN THE DINING ROOM of the United Nations on September 22, 1950, finishing a late lunch, when his secretary tracked him down. The Nobel Committee had sent a telegram to let him know he had been awarded the Peace Prize. Bunche excitedly celebrated his good fortune with a rare and impromptu daytime champagne cocktail. He could not have been completely shocked at the announcement—his name had been bandied about since the end of the mediation—but he was at first unsure about whether he should or could accept the award. Always one to do the right thing and never to seek the spotlight, he thought the Prize might be too much. He went so far as to draft a letter about why he could not accept, as an individual, an award for what he felt was an institutional effort of the entire UN. Nonetheless, Trygve Lie disagreed, telling him it was fine to accept.[**]

That afternoon, he announced that he received the news "with great humility for I more than anyone recognize the extent to which my peace efforts in the Near East flowed from the strength of the United Nations." Speaking in gratitude to Bernadotte and the ten other members of the UN team who were killed in action in Palestine, he spoke of the UN as "man's sole hope for peace."[49]

The next days and months were transformative. President Truman personally called him with warm wishes. Years later, Bunche recalled that the conversation was "one of my most pleasant memories. . . . Harry Truman himself was on the phone congratulating me. I could hardly believe it."[50] Bunche told the New York Times that he was "a little flabbergasted" at the award. In the weeks to come, he toured Europe, prepared his acceptance speech, and even met Pope Pius XII. (The pope congratulated him, blessed his family, presented him with a silver medallion, and gave Ruth two

---

[**] Years later, Bunche told the story to Dag Hammarskjold, Lie's Swedish successor. Hammarskjold was clear: he would have agreed with Bunche.

rosaries.)[51] Dean Acheson stated that he could think of no individual more deserving of the prize. Moshe Sharett, Israel's foreign minister, praised Bunche for his herculean efforts and "inexhaustible patience, resource, and ingenuity."[52] Years later, in 1955, Edward R. Murrow interviewed him for his popular TV newsmagazine, *See it Now*. As Murrow and his crew visited his home in Queens one Friday afternoon, Murrow asked where he kept his Nobel Prize. Oh, it's around someplace, Bunche replied. "You mean it's not framed and hanging on the wall?" Murrow responded quizzically. No, said Bunche: "the only trophy on the wall is [a] little note scribbled by my son the day my Nobel prize was announced. I found it on a table when I got home that evening from the United Nations. It said 'Dear Daddy, I'm happy you got the Nobel Prize. Love, Ralph.'"[53]

In late November 1950, just before he left for the Nobel ceremony in Oslo, Bunche was invited to a dinner for the crown prince and princess of Norway. He was seated next to a Mrs. Lundbeck, the wife of a Swedish shipping executive. Mrs. Lundbeck, perhaps getting too familiar with the aquavit over the meal, proceeded to disparage Harry Truman when Trygve Lie offered a toast in his honor. "I hope he chokes," she whispered to Bunche. Perplexed and amazed, he at first thought she meant the secretary general. Truman, she continued, was "nothing but a haberdasher"; his presidency was "taking democracy too far."[54] He raised his eyebrows at this statement but, given the presence of the crown prince across the table, struggled to maintain his diplomatic sangfroid. A little later there was another toast, and Mrs. Lundbeck noted to Bunche that while toasting, she had looked him directly in the eye. "Is there anything amiss in that?" he asked, unsure where this was headed. Yes, she replied tipsily, in Norway a man who toasts looks the lady in the eye, and if she returns the look, "that can be taken as an invitation" and he can call her the next morning. Well, he quickly replied, this was "just a practice toast." But in any case, he swiftly added for good measure, "I don't know your number."

As the evening wore on, Mrs. Lundbeck switched from politics and flirting to race relations, though she still seemed to have sex on her mind. "Would you let your daughters marry colored men?" she asked him at one point. "My daughters happen to be colored," he replied with surprising calm to this affront. But he decided to clear the air, fully. "They are because I am. In fact, not only am I colored but I am an American Negro." Lundbeck, startled, quickly said, "Maybe so, but you are different." He ignored the insulting reply—one his grandmother would surely have deeply resented—and the dinner continued on around them. Trying to recover her composure, Lundbeck rapidly sought what she believed was safer ground. "Have you ever been to Norway?" she asked. "No," he responded, sensing a chance for polite retaliation, "but I will be going soon." After she inquired why, he explained it was for the Nobel Peace Prize. "Who is getting it?" she asked. No doubt with a hint of a smile, he answered, "Well, this is a little embarrassing. But this year, I am."

RALPH BUNCHE'S NOBEL LECTURE, DELIVERED IN December, focused on the UN at a time of great peril for the organization and for the world. The Korean War had begun in the summer of 1950, and by the time he arrived in Oslo the fighting was intense. The UN forces, under the command of the American General Douglas MacArthur, had engineered a dramatic and dangerous amphibious invasion at Incheon. By October the troops, largely American, had advanced into North Korean territory and were now being met by Chinese forces coming from the other direction. China at this point was just one year past Mao Zedong's stunning victory and was still desperately poor and weakened from years of conflict. All the same, the prospect of great powers at war was unnerving. Indeed, less than a week after Bunche's Nobel acceptance speech President Truman declared a national emergency, stating that "world conquest by communist imperialism is the goal of the forces of aggression that have been loosed upon the world."[55]

A few months before he left to receive the prize, and alarmed by the situation but cognizant that the UN was now facing its first real test as a peace organization, Bunche had called the Korean conflict "a turning point in modern history." It was also, he said, a major step forward for the UN, which had previously addressed only "little wars" in Indonesia, Kashmir, Greece, and Palestine.[56] In this tense geopolitical climate, in which he was increasingly hailed as a potential mediator for Korea, Bunche focused in Oslo on the necessity of the UN in a dangerous world. Reflecting his initial uncertainty about whether to even accept the prize, he was quick to down-play his own role in the peacemaking process in the Middle East: "If today we speak of peace, we also speak of the United Nations, for in this era, peace and the United Nations have become inseparable." If the UN cannot ensure peace, he declared emphatically, "there will be none."

From this point forward Ralph Bunche was lauded as a nonpareil peace-maker. Yet peace and security, despite occasionally cropping up in early term papers at UCLA, had never previously been his primary topics of interest or study, and as a scholar he had devoted little attention to the causes of war and peace. But he understood that while colonialism, his true passion, was primarily a question of justice, it strongly intersected with peace. And so he did not miss a chance to emphasize the importance of rolling back colonialism to the cause of peace. Here, at the Nobel ceremony, was an opportunity to make a peace and security case for the self-determination of Africa and Asia. The UN, he announced to the audience, was opposed to imperialism of any kind. It stood for the freedom and equality of all peoples and was engaged "in an historic effort to underwrite the rights of man. It is also attempting to give reassurance to the colonial peoples that their aspirations for freedom can be realized, if only gradually, by peaceful processes."[57] The UN was the linchpin in this process: through it, as the representative of the world community, self-determination could be achieved in a peaceful and expeditious manner.

The Nobel ceremony was a thrill and a great success. He received his medal, a cash prize of $31,674.08, and "thunderous applause from the audience."[58][††] He was now a star of the new postwar order—a man who embodied the global orientation of the midcentury, but also the aspirations for world peace through world law that animated so many in the wake of the horrors of the Second World War. A Black American journalist, covering the award ceremony, reported being "besieged by admirers" on the streets of Oslo as he was mistaken for their "hero."[59]

[††] At a party back in Washington, Bunche proudly showed friends a photocopy of the check—about $400,000 in 2022 dollars. With this money he bought a large Tudor-style home, replete with half-timbers, in the leafy neighborhood of Forest Hills, Queens.

Bunche returned from Norway to a new life. Parades ensued; the public clamored for his time; invitations to speak poured in; Harvard, where he had been a graduate student two decades earlier, even announced it was making him a professor, the first Black professor in the faculty of arts and sciences in the university's 300-year history. His daughter, Jane, then a freshman at Radcliffe, told the *Harvard Crimson* she knew nothing of the appointment.[60] (He never took up the post.) His life changed forever as he became a household name. His celebrity made him an enduring emblem of dispute settlement and familiar to all Americans as a peacemaker. Even as late as 2002, echoes of Bunche's celebrity continued: an episode of HBO's *The Sopranos* filmed many years after Bunche had died featured a brutal attack by one of the Mafia members on a Black construction worker attempting to mediate a worksite dispute: "Who the fuck are you, Ralph Bunche over here?"

Six months after receiving the Nobel Prize, Bunche was driving down Queens Boulevard not far from his home. He was suddenly rear-ended by another car. The two vehicles stopped, and the woman driving the car behind stepped out and walked up to Bunche, who had also stepped out of his car to inspect the damage. A group of men in the next lane rolled down their windows and one called out.[61] "Lady, of all the guys you could hit, why did you have to hit Dr. Bunche?"

The woman, flustered, did not answer right away. Bunche immediately assured her that the situation was OK. There was no real damage done; she could go on her way. The same man in the nearby car then yelled again: "Lucky it was Dr. Bunche you hit, lady!"

CHAPTER 12

BUNCHE FEVER

Since Dr Ralph J. Bunche arrived, the 420,000 inhabitants of this great Norwegian city have been stricken by a strange and unique fever. It has spread out over the city and mountains like an epidemic. But its reaction has been like an injection of a new type of serum, leaving its victims full of enthusiasm, hope, and confidence.

—"European Press Hails Bunche at Oslo Interview,"
The Chicago Defender, December 23, 1950

Issue #79 of *True Comics* featured an unusual figure on the cover. Under a depiction of the "World's Greatest Athlete" and next to a panel about a treasure hunt for "Sunken Millions" was written "Hero of Peace," across a drawing of a young-looking Black man in a suit and tie. The comic, released in October 1949, introduced readers to the incredible life of Ralph Bunche, world diplomat.[1] Bunche is first depicted as a young man in Detroit, the "grandson of a slave" later orphaned at the age of sixteen and raised by his "tiny" but fierce grandmother in 1920s Los Angeles. At UCLA, Bunche is shown in a classroom, a white professor lecturing that "students who are majoring in international relations must know that a basic understanding of racial relations comes first"—an interesting statement given the way the postwar discipline of international relations would largely erase race as a category of interest in the study of geopolitics.[2]

True Comics next depicted a dynamic young Ralph Bunche working his way through college ("carpet layer!," "janitor!," "waiter!") and then, after attending Harvard, bravely traveling to Africa to study colonialism: "The only way I can do my thesis is to do research, not from books, but on the spot!" Back in the US, he is shown traveling with Gunnar Myrdal in the South in the 1930s; at the OSS at the start of the war; and heading to the State Department as a racial pioneer. Eventually, the *True Comics* story worked its way to the main event: his work at the United Nations and on the vexing problem of Palestine. Secretary General Trygve Lie tells him, "We need you here at the United Nations, Dr. Bunche." In Palestine, he is shown as the effective originator of the plan for partition and "the man who more than any other one person was responsible for peace in Palestine." (The comic made no mention of Folke Bernadotte or his assassination in Jerusalem.) The final panels show another side of Bunche. After his success in the Holy Land, Bunche, a "father of three," is portrayed relaxing at home, in a suit and tie, with his wife Ruth nearby. He complains: "Look at me . . . one hundred and ninety pounds . . . I'm slowed down so that about the toughest exercise I can stand is billiards." Ruth replies, "You do have one other outlet. . . . Letting off steam when Jackie Robinson handles second base for the Dodgers!"

True Comics was just one of many periodicals, organizations, and individuals to come down with "Bunche Fever" in the postwar years.[3] In fact, the comic's publication preceded the award of the Nobel Peace Prize to Bunche in 1950 by a year. In many ways he was already a new kind of celebrity before the Nobel committee anointed him. The Peace Prize simply catapulted him into another, very rarified, realm of stardom.

As the first Black person to be awarded any Nobel Prize and the youngest to ever win the Peace Prize, Bunche quickly became a hero to many Americans. His arrival back to New York City was closely watched and celebrated. The *New York Times* showed him dressed in a heavy coat and homburg, smiling with Ruth by a Scandinavian Airlines plane at Idlewild Airport in New York.[4] NAACP Executive Secretary Walter White immediately announced a dinner in Bunche's honor. The invitations poured into Bunche's mailbox—speaking engagements, dinner parties, galas. He received more than 1000 invitations to speak in a three-month period. Streets and schools were soon named in his honor, including one near his childhood home in Los Angeles. He was offered the presidency of the City College of New York and over seventy honorary degrees in these years. Ernest Hemingway wrote that he would be "highly honored" if Bunche could meet with him in Paris.[5] A 1951 Gallup poll placed him ninth in the list of "Most Admired Men in the World," just behind the Pope.[6] He gave out the Best Picture award at the 1951 Oscars. Ralph Bunche, who once said, "I like to win," had just won one of the biggest prizes in the world.[7]

His everyday life changed rapidly. He began to have lunch at Toots Shor's, the legendary celebrity hangout on East 51st Street, not far from the UN. He attended Passover seders at the home of prominent *New York Post* gossip columnist Leonard Lyons.[8] He frequented the Dodgers—still in Brooklyn's Ebbetts Field at this point—and proudly caught a foul ball in one of their frequent midcentury World Series matchups. He sat ringside at heavyweight bouts in Madison Square Garden. He enjoyed the best seats at the Metropolitan Opera, often in general manager Rudolph Bing's personal box. He attended Broadway premiers and chatted with the likes of Humphrey Bogart and Lauren Bacall at the afterparties.[9] His name was bandied in the press as a possible candidate for mayor of New York City, the first of many times in his life he would be floated as a political candidate. And he received an endless stream of fan and hate mail—from job seekers to autograph seekers to those castigating the UN to, in more unusual examples, tape recordings of songs and pleas to assist in fights with landlords, as if his vaunted mediation skills could be swiftly deployed to solve any sundry dispute.[10] Ever polite, Bunche (and his secretaries) seemingly replied to all these entreaties, no matter how off the wall.

America caught Bunche Fever in the 1950s in part because Ralph Bunche was undeniably impressive; in part because he represented the success of something new and significant in the postwar era—the UN and multilateral peacebuilding—and in part because the nation, at least some

Photo 12.1 With Eleanor Roosevelt at the Waldorf-Astoria

of it, was hungry for an uplifting and uncontroversial symbol of Black accomplishment. The early 1950s were a time of rampant racial discrimination. Segregation was legally permitted and widely practiced. Few Black Americans were accepted by white society as leaders or models outside a very select set of endeavors. Bunche's fellow UCLA graduate Jackie Robinson had dramatically broken the color line in baseball in 1947, and two Black actresses had won Academy Awards by 1950. Black musicians dominated jazz, the central musical style of midcentury America. Politics were a different matter, however. Paul Robeson, Bunche's controversial acquaintance from London in the late 1930s, may have gained fame for his prowess in football, singing, and acting, but as he ventured into politics he was blacklisted as a communist and stripped of his passport. There were only two Black members in the entire US Congress when Bunche won his Nobel Prize.

In short, outside of entertainment, few Black professionals were known to white Americans in this era, let alone famous for succeeding in a traditionally white—and quite upper-class—endeavor such as diplomacy.* Bunche had broken though a new color line in 1950. His legend, as increasingly burnished in venues ranging from the *New York Times* to *True Comics*, was of a man of uncompromising principles, endless capacity for work, sharp intellect, and a magic touch in the now-crucial postwar arena of international diplomacy.

BUNCHE LIVED A SORT OF DOUBLE life in the immediate wake of the Peace Prize. He triumphantly returned from Oslo to a nation eager to learn more about him. Yet his primary role at the UN was the trusteeship process, then a largely obscure area just getting started. (Indeed, when in 1952 the General Assembly tried to appoint Bunche to a commission on the problem of apartheid in South Africa, his boss at the Trusteeship Division, Victor Hoo, said Bunche was too busy to be released from his regular duties to participate.)[11] Decolonization was just arriving on the political radar in 1950. A few Asian states had achieved independence since the UN's founding, but some of those that had become independent, like India, Pakistan, and the Philippines, had already been treated as quasi-independent for some time. India and the Philippines had even signed the Charter in 1945, before their formal independence. In this period, the US and Soviet Union painstakingly negotiated the entry of states into the UN, typically pairing them so that the balance of power between the two superpowers would not be significantly altered by the addition of new members. The trusteeship system itself was new and still largely untested. Bunche was now a big and famous fish returning to what was, at least for the moment, a relatively small part of the UN pond.

Bunche was nonetheless characteristically optimistic about trusteeship. In an essay published in late 1949, he had argued that there were "heartening signs" that the trusteeship system was already making a difference.

---

* Diplomats in this period were sometimes referred to as "Pale, Male, and Yale"—a reflection of the WASP dominance in foreign affairs that arguably still persists, in vestigial form, today.

In particular, he noted that 120 petitions had been submitted regarding trusteeship.[12] He gave the example of the Ewe people of West Africa, who had petitioned to be incorporated into a single political entity, rather than divided, as they were at the time, between British and French territories. (The Ewe's presentation to the Trusteeship Council in 1947 had characterized their request as a "simple one": the request "of a tribe of one million people to be allowed to live together under one roof.")[13] The first visit of the Trusteeship Council to these territories would as a result include special attention to the Ewe's plight. Bunche conceded that "miraculous results" from trusteeship were not realistic. But he had a substantial feeling of ownership over trusteeship, and he seemed to believe it could and would work well. While a world with no colonies was a much better world, he suggested in his essay, the UN was working to create a "new basis of hope" for the dependent peoples of the world.

Bunche was not wrong to suggest that the early work around trusteeship would prove important, and promoting independence around the world remained his primary mission at the UN even after the prize. His official position was not especially high-ranking, however, and it did not give him much autonomy. Still, the trusteeship system gave him a certain influence in this period on a process that would, over time, prove quite significant. Indeed, years later one of his UN colleagues would argue that Bunche and his team were critical to the rapid and largely unexpected disintegration of colonial empires that was about to unfold. Referring to the "Year of Africa," 1960, in which seventeen states gained their independence, the colleague argued that the table had really been set years earlier, during the early 1950s:

> When in 1960 the whole thing came to an end, it came to an end because of the efforts that Ralph Bunche exerted through his activities behind the scenes. For example, you take people like Sylvanus Olympio who was later to become prime minister of Togo, or Julius Nyerere [of Tanzania]. We helped them write their speeches. We advised them as to what they should do. This is not all very well documented because it couldn't be documented. And I think it was done because there was a Ralph Bunche who had the conviction that the system [of colonialism] had to be liquidated and we were going to do it, like it or not.[14]

At the same time, Bunche's work on self-determination was not what he was known for to the public in 1950. He was now a global diplomatic phenomenon, and his success at peacemaking shined a positive light on the new UN more broadly. As one journalist wrote, it was "remarkable enough that a poor Negro orphan has become one of the most eminent Americans of his time. But Bunche is less important as a man than as a symbol. As a man he has become the most famous figure in the United Nations, but as a symbol he represents the whole meaning of the United Nations."[15]

This fame gave him a new role: that of messenger, explainer, and at times even cheerleader for multilateral cooperation. Besieged with demands on his time, he gave numerous public talks. He used his fame to speak about the set of issues he cared the most about: the UN, colonialism, democracy, and civil rights. His most common theme was the importance of the UN as an organization of peace. Several speeches were literally titled "The Case for the United Nations."† He would often meditate on the specter of nuclear war in these remarks, and the concomitant need for new approaches to peace in a world where war was becoming unthinkable. At the Williams College commencement in 1951, for instance, in an evocative line, he declared that "the UN believes, and rightly so, in victory for humanity."[16]

While the UN dominated his many public speeches, Bunche also frequently raised the need for America to live up to its promised ideals. In doing so, he skillfully used the international context he was famous for, and the intensifying Cold War, to make the case for change at home as well as abroad. In an address at Columbia University in 1951, for instance, he declared that "we cannot have two brands of democracy—a pure or first-quality democracy for export, and an imperfect, factory-second quality for home consumption."[17] Bunche's warning reflected the very real discrimination and denial of full citizenship that Black Americans faced in midcentury America. But it also strategically deployed the Cold War conflict that was rapidly obsessing the nation and dividing the globe. His "two brands" trope,

---

† Interestingly, Bunche once wrote in his diary that he was "not a professional lecturer" and did "not like to make public speeches at all." Nevertheless, he somehow made hundreds, perhaps thousands, of speeches over the course of his career.

which he used many times in this era, leveraged the fact that the Cold War and the dramatic expansion of America's global reach put a new and quite serious spin on the quality of American democracy. To fight the Soviets for world leadership, the US sought to distinguish itself on the basis of its political, social, and economic character. Democracy and freedom were among the most important distinctions the US drew with the USSR. Yet time would show, as Bunche already sensed, that America's persistent forms of racial oppression would undermine its desire to outshine the Soviet Union in the eyes of the new states of Asia and Africa.

This weakness stemmed in part from the Manichean nature of the Cold War and the way it pushed each superpower to expand its reach, or at least contain the other's reach. Stalin famously said of the Second World War that this war "is not as in the past." The leader who occupies a territory "imposes his own social system on it. Everyone imposes his own system as far as his army can reach. It cannot be otherwise."[18] In a sense, Stalin was speaking of a new kind of empire, one that was not so much based on territorial control but rather on political and economic hegemony. The unraveling of the traditional European empires in turn gave each superpower a new set of states to attempt to pull into its orbit and deny to the other. Decolonization arguably even accelerated the Cold War: by freeing up a huge set of territories from other great powers, it drew the two superpowers into frequent confrontation as they sought to manage the processes of independence and win over the new states that resulted.

That many of these new states were African and Asian gave America's Jim Crow laws and practices a special salience. For years the Soviets had pointed to the entrenched nature of discrimination to skewer American righteousness over democracy. As early as 1946, *Pravda* was arguing that the US was a fundamentally racist society.[19] Even friends such as the UK had called out the hypocrisy in American support for self-determination for colonized peoples while engaging in the relentless, and legally sanctioned, suppression of the civil rights of parts of its own domestic population. Bunche identified this dynamic early on. Indeed, in 1943 he had written a memo for the Roosevelt administration regarding the president of Liberia's planned visit to the US. In the memo, he argued that the visit could be "mobilized . . . to impress Africans throughout the continent" while counteracting Japanese "racial propaganda" and highlighting "America's non-imperial relationship."[20]

Bunche was perhaps uniquely positioned to discuss, debate, and even deflect this line of attack. And because throughout his life he strongly opposed racial separatism, Bunche took umbrage at the comparisons to colonialism and self-determination. Part of it was his general patriotism: he saw himself and his community as the most American of Americans. But he also had no interest in—and in fact substantial antipathy toward—those who sought to either go back to Africa, as Marcus Garvey had counseled in earlier decades, or to hive off a self-sufficient Black nation of some kind. Still, even he could see that the US had a major vulnerability in the Cold War, and it happened to be one that he knew only too much about. And it was not just the Soviets who pressed this point; China would later take a similar approach. In 1963, for instance, just before the March on Washington, Mao Zedong decried the state of American race relations, declaring that Blacks in America "are enslaved, oppressed and discriminated against. . . . The overwhelming majority are deprived of their right to vote . . . the discrimination and persecution they suffer are especially shocking."‡

This dynamic made the quality of American democracy at home not only a central domestic issue but also a critical geopolitical issue. The American public was increasingly viewing the Cold War as an existential crisis that simply had to be won. Racism at home was hobbling that effort. The fictional words of his UCLA professor in *True Comics*—that "students who are majoring in international relations must know that a basic understanding of racial relations comes first"—were turning out to be quite prophetic.

Bunche ran with this tension and used it strategically to argue for greater racial justice abroad *and* at home. He characterized racism as a "crack in our democratic armor" that needed to be fixed.[21] Fortuitously, important parts of the foreign policy establishment increasingly agreed. As early as 1946,

---

‡ China today continues to press the US on race. In 2020, in the wake of George Floyd's murder, a Foreign Ministry spokesperson remarked that "racism against ethnic minorities is a chronic disease of American society."

Dean Acheson had pointed to racial discrimination as having "an adverse effect" on American foreign relations.[22] As the new "Third World" grew in importance, this belief only intensified and provided a powerful incentive for national security hawks in Washington to push back at Southern politicians.

To counter the rising criticism from abroad, the US scrambled to tell, or at least construct, a story of progress in race relations. The national security establishment sought to impart to the rest of the world the lesson that American democracy "made the achievement of social justice possible."[23] Consequently, the trajectory of race in the US became an important narrative in the Cold War, and the ability of the nation to advance racial equality became a source of what would later be dubbed "soft power."

Of course, for this strategy to work, racial justice in America had to actually improve. That was not always clear, though the courts in this era helped. In 1954, for example, the landmark case of *Brown v. Board of Education* provided an opportunity to make a Cold War case for civil rights. In its brief to the Supreme Court in *Brown*, the Eisenhower administration argued that racial discrimination had adverse effects in foreign affairs. Segregation "furnishes grist for the Communist propaganda mills, and it raises doubts even among friendly nations as to the intensity of our devotion to the democratic faith." Dean Acheson crisply stated that racial segregation in America's schools, which many at the time saw as a quintessentially local issue, "jeopardizes the effective maintenance of our moral leadership of the free and democratic nations of the world." Many overseas observers watched the case closely and saw the result, which overturned the legality of segregation in schools, as a sign of a changing nation. "At Last! Whites and Blacks in the United States on the same school benches," ran a perhaps overly sunny headline in the French West African newspaper *Afrique Nouvelle*. The *Hindustan Times* of India declared that "American democracy stands to gain in strength and prestige from the unanimous ruling."[24]

Bunche himself was cashing a check at a bank as the ruling in *Brown* came over the wires. He was so excited by the outcome that he left all his money on the counter. Later that summer, at the NAACP annual convention in Dallas, Texas, Bunche and Walter White both "taunted" and denounced the Soviet Union over its dismissal of the case as a "cold war gesture of propaganda."[25] The two men's faith in the significance of the ruling was, in retrospect, overly generous; *Brown* would prove difficult to implement, and many American schools are no less segregated some seven decades later. But in their remarks that day in Dallas, in their open attacks on the Soviet Union, Bunche and White also showed how strongly the Cold War was impacting every corner of American society. Bunche, having moved far from his radical scholarship of the 1930s, was now espousing a core message of the Cold War liberal consensus.

A few months after *Brown* was handed down, Chief Justice Earl Warren gave a speech to dedicate the new American Bar Center building. Echoing arguments Bunche had also made, Warren declared that the nation was in the midst of "a world war of ideas."

> Everywhere there is a contest for the hearts and minds of people. Every political concept is under scrutiny. Our American system, like all others, is on trial both at home and abroad.... The extent to which we maintain the spirit of our Constitution with its Bill of Rights will in the long run do more to make it secure and the object of adulation than the number of hydrogen bombs we stockpile.[26]

The effort to win this "world war of ideas" had many fronts. The US Information Agency, for example, distributed documentaries around the world that aimed to impart a favorable impression of America. These messages were sometimes seen as hypocritical in light of the many images of racial violence pouring out of the US. As a result, in 1954 a USIA study concluded that the agency had to work harder to "dispel the notion that the U.S. was undemocratic or abusive of racial minorities."[27] In response, the State Department, encouraged by Congressman Adam Clayton Powell of Harlem, sought to export the best examples it could muster, sending jazz greats such Dizzy Gillespie and Duke Ellington on tours of the world. Jazz was not just popular in the 1950s; its focus on improvisation and personal expression within a loose arrangement was, in the words of Voice of America host Willis Conover, "structurally parallel to the American political system."[28] Jazz seemed to represent the best of America—its creativity, freedom, and sense of freshness and excitement—and it was popular, pulling in great crowds around the world. America's secret weapon, wrote a *New York Times* reporter, "is a blue note in a minor key."[29]

The jazz friendship tours put a spotlight on the nation but not always in the ways the US government intended. When the State Department asked Dizzy Gillespie to come in for a pre-tour briefing, he curtly responded that "I've had 300 years of briefing." I know what they've done to us, Gillespie continued; "I sort've liked the idea of representing America, but I wasn't going over there to apologise for the racist policies of America."[30] Later, in 1957, Louis Armstrong, who did so much touring on behalf of America that he even recorded an album titled "Ambassador Satch," refused to tour the Soviet Union as the Little Rock segregation crisis played out, saying he would not defend the Constitution if it was not going to be enforced at home. (Bunche himself agreed, arguing that "incidents like Little Rock ... shatter the image of the US abroad that so many of us have worked so hard to build.")[31] These stark messages undermined the choreographed effort to present a rosy depiction of American race relations. Yet they also showed an openness to dissent and a willingness to challenge orthodoxy that were never possible in the Soviet Union.

In the same vein, the USIA produced films that presented a glossy, often sanitized vision of what Black people could achieve in midcentury America. Ralph Bunche's life story proved irresistible for this effort. His success had already been widely trumpeted as "evidence of the 'progress of the American Negro,' proof that American democracy was superior to Soviet communism."[32] Now that message could extend overseas. Indeed, when ABC in October 1955 aired a biopic called *Toward Tomorrow: The Ralph Bunche-Lucy Johnson Story*, the USIA decided to distribute it widely around the globe. The thirty-minute film was not a documentary featuring Bunche himself but rather a reenactment of key moments in his life. Part of a long-running ABC television series called *Cavalcade of America*, the adult Bunche was portrayed by an actor. The focus on his grandmother Lucy, who raised him through his teenage years and, by his own account, instilled in him a strong sense of accomplishment, was critical to the underlying narrative of minority accomplishment through hard work in the face of adversity. This Horatio Alger gloss on his life was a perfect vehicle to attempt to portray race as no barrier to accomplishment in midcentury America.§

⸻

IN HIS 1957 BOOK *BLACK BOURGEOSIE*, sociologist Franklin Frazier argued that "the few Negroes who have gained recognition consist chiefly of entertainers and leaders of organizations who have contacts with whites." Ralph Bunche, Frazier argued, had a unique position in this respect, "since not a week passes that the Negro press fails to carry news about him and his achievements."[33] Indeed, a wide variety of outlets in the 1950s fixated on Bunche as a salutary example of racial progress. A 1955 profile in the California Teachers' Association journal was emblematic; he was depicted as a "living illustration" that with the right skills and character anyone could "level the disharmonies of race prejudice."[34] To Frazier, successful strivers like Bunche were "exaggerated Americans" for whom "struggles against inequality and racial discrimination have no meaning beyond affirming the normative values and identities of the national community."[35]

While Bunche himself quickly became a member of the American establishment, as comfortable in the White House as at the Rockefeller Foundation, he nonetheless often bridled at this (mis)use of his accomplishments and life story. As he told one interviewer in 1963 about his alleged symbolic power as an example of racial progress in the 1950s, "that was all humbug. I couldn't get a hotel room in Birmingham or Atlanta or in Jackson—they would provide a motorcycle escort for me as a visitor and speaker, but no hotel or restaurant would accept me." In fact, not much had changed, he suggested: "today if I wanted to join the New York Athletic Club I couldn't."[36]

Bunche's professional success and popular fame were nonetheless undeniable. And his was not just an inspiring story that Americans gravitated to because it cast a positive light on democracy. At the end of the Second

⸻

§ In 1952, Bunche actually won the Horatio Alger Award of the Horatio Alger Association of Distinguished Americans, an organization established in 1947 to "dispel the mounting belief among our nation's youth that the American Dream was no longer possible."

World War, W. E. B. Du Bois had pithily, if acidly, noted that the nation had defeated Germany but not Germany's ideas. Bunche was an important and respected Cold War voice arguing that American ideas—if truly lived up to—were in fact the nation's most powerful weapon against Soviet totalitarianism.

Even in speeches that ostensibly focused on the UN, Bunche would weigh in on what he believed the American creed demanded of the nation. In a 1951 speech in New York City, for instance, he addressed racial and religious discrimination. He first noted that he was there to "speak as a partisan—a partisan of peace." The UN was essential in the postwar world, he argued, because there is "no security except in collective security." But he soon pivoted to the challenge of racial and religious discrimination, arguing that they harmed national unity.[37] He often stressed these points in the 1950s. At the same time, he was careful to resist being pigeonholed as a Black voice; he believed he was an American voice. Indeed, when in 1951 Bunche was feted at the NAACP's annual conference in Atlanta, he made a point (as he did many times later) of declaring to the delegates "I am not a Negro leader."[38]

Bunche Fever meant that he had the opportunity to elaborate his views on the American creed in mainstream publications, at a time when magazines had huge circulations. In one striking case, *The American* magazine ran a long piece by Bunche just before his Nobel award. He used the occasion to tell a tale aimed squarely at the heart of midcentury America. Titled "What America Means to Me," the essay burnished the Horatio Alger–like reputation that defined him for many Americans of the era.

"I was a stowaway once—a youthful adventure, which turned out to be a stroke of good fortune," he began.[39] In an effort to save money on train fare returning to Los Angeles from an ROTC camp in the Pacific Northwest, he decided to sneak aboard a freighter leaving Seattle's harbor. Quickly collared by the ship's captain, he was put to work in the kitchen as a "pea-sheller." The young Bunche proved so adept and industrious that "by the time we reached Los Angeles I was offered a job." That turned into three summers' work, which helped defray the costs of attending UCLA. After this plucky opening, he quickly pivoted to note that "a Negro in America must often make and fight for his own opportunities." There were two Americas for men and women like him. There was the America of ideals, and the one of reality. The US, he argued, had not afforded even minimum citizenship to Black Americans. Nonetheless, the beginning of progress toward racial equality had been made, and he was convinced that the American system was one that permitted and even encouraged advancement. "Serious social evils obviously exist in America," he continued. "But the virtue of the system is that its defects can be attacked and eliminated."

Toggling back and forth between paeans to American mobility and the reality that the Constitution's ideals remained deeply unrealized was signature Bunche. In a sense, he was presaging President Bill Clinton's memorable line from his first inaugural address that there is nothing wrong with America that cannot be cured by what is right with America. Ralph Bunche was convinced that American society was the best on offer—even for a Black man like himself. He forthrightly called out racism, but he did not believe that overtly castigating white society in the name of racial justice was ultimately effective. Bunche was unabashedly patriotic. At the same time, he saw no contradiction in delivering unvarnished truths about the fact that American society was not, in fact, in any way equal. His goal was not to denigrate America. On the contrary, he wanted *more* America, not less.

Bunche's tremendous popular stature in the early 1950s helped mainstream society absorb this message. Later, as the civil rights movement swelled in the face of Southern intransigence and Black activism grew more radical, he would sometimes be tarred as an "international Uncle Tom," an establishment figure who was dismissed by more outspoken figures such as Malcolm X and Muhammad Ali.[40] While Bunche did traffic in a form of respectability politics that was common to the Black middle class in the early 20th century, he arguably had a more persuasive impact because of it.* By skillfully weaving together his Horatio Alger–like qualities with his critique of racial injustice, Bunche made it harder for mainstream America to

---

* It is perhaps noteworthy that in a popular series of children's books in the 1970s which used various famous Americans to illustrate virtues—Thomas Edison for creativity, Ben Franklin for saving—Ralph Bunche was chosen for "responsibility."

reject his message. He broadly defended the basic status quo of midcentury American life, but he wanted it extended to all. Still, as the 1950s gave way to the 1960s, Bunche seemed to engender more criticism from Black activists. His uplifting personal story, critics believed, allowed the white majority to gloss over the grim reality and dire prospects of nearly all those in the minority. It was not enough to have a few token Blacks at the table, many argued. Black Americans need real opportunity. In Stokely Carmichael's famous quip, "you can't have Bunche for lunch!"[41]

However fair these later critiques were, Ralph Bunche was a man of his time, as reflected in his unwillingness to attack America more harshly. His formative years encompassed the rise of fascism, Russia's turn from revolutionary idealism to hardened totalitarianism, and the apocalyptic twenty years of crisis from 1919–1939.[42] From that vantage point, and with his pragmatic temperament, American democracy looked pretty good. On this central point, he rarely wavered. He was, to be sure, a man who had once published Marxist analyses of imperialism. But his commitment to these views was ultimately thin and perhaps reflected his relatively tenuous ties to the world of ideas. He was happy to leave his scholarly work behind when the call to join the Roosevelt administration came, and his prior Marxist ideas were, by and large, never heard from again. By the early 1950s at least, he seemed to believe that radicalism was counterproductive and that societal advancement through civil and democratic processes were the best, really the only lasting, path forward. Given these beliefs, improving America, not revolutionizing it, was the only viable course.

ON THE ROAD SPEAKING TO RAPT audiences, onstage greeting Fred Astaire at the Oscars, or even writing for mass audiences were no doubt memorable and heady experiences. Meanwhile, back in the UN, Bunche was still technically a midlevel official in the hitherto minor Trusteeship Division. As the 1950s dawned, trusteeship and its close cousin, decolonization, began to gain more momentum. As this development occurred, Bunche continued to stay in close contact with the US government. In 1950, for example, he acted as an informal consultant for the State Department. In a confidential background paper, he noted a number of developments concerning colonial Africa.[43] He began by arguing that colonial issues were becoming a more important subject at the UN than many had anticipated. The British, French, and Belgians were in fact expressing alarm at how active the UN now was on colonial affairs. Bunche argued that those three states "tended to isolate themselves by their rigid opposition" to many of the resolutions proposed, while the US, joined by three other powers with lesser colonial responsibilities—Australia, New Zealand, and Denmark—typically voted yes. But there was another important factor as well, one that was rising in importance in 1950. Bunche counseled that the US need to consider "the consequences which our policy [toward colonialism] will have on the outcome of the 'cold war' with the Soviet Union."

As the quotes around cold war suggest, in 1950 the term was still coming into common use. Walter Lippmann, the influential journalist, had used the phrase for the first time in late 1947.[44] Lippmann had allegedly picked it up from Bernard Baruch, the financier and advisor to Harry Truman. As the notion of existential, looming conflict with the Soviet Union became very real to ordinary Americans, the phrase caught on.

Bunche's confidential report for the State Department was pointing out a dynamic that would prove critical in the coming decades. The Soviets and the Americans were in a full spectrum conflict. A key domain was now the currying of relationships—and alliances—with new states. Neither superpower wanted to see the other's "social system," in Stalin's phrase, spread into what would soon be called the Third World. Colonial policy in the UN was a central piece of that process. The US had to balance its desire to assist its key European allies, some of whom were fixated on retaining their empires, against the political imperative to court, or at least not alienate, the newly liberated states now joining the UN. This issue would come to a head in a few years when the Suez Crisis unfolded in Egypt, but at this juncture it was not yet at full throttle.

Bunche's State Department report also noted that the General Assembly had just created a new committee to receive information from states with trusteeship responsibilities. This was a seemingly minor, bureaucratic step. Yet this new committee was not clearly contemplated in the UN Charter and it involved the General Assembly, not the Trusteeship Council. It would prove an important move in the General Assembly's growing activism around decolonization.

The backdrop was the seemingly innocuous provision of the UN Charter that required trust powers to report to the UN Secretariat information on their trust territories. Bunche himself had been a key source of that provision in San Francisco. To the State Department, he noted that the UK, France, and Belgium believed that the General Assembly had overstepped its powers and that the committee was illegal. Indeed, in the first meeting of the committee, the delegate from Belgium openly argued that it "exceeds the limits of the competence conferred by the Charter."[45] The opposition to a minor UN committee's asserted authority over dry reports was emblematic of the colonial powers' strong objection to the very notion of outside scrutiny.

The UN's growing deliberations over colonial governance also foreshadowed coming tensions elsewhere. One such tension was the relationship between sovereignty and human rights. On the one hand, self-determination and sovereignty were central goals of the UN Charter. The very purpose of trusteeship was to shepherd formerly colonized territories toward sovereignty and independence. On the other hand, the development of human rights agreements in the postwar era was, at its core, a challenge to traditional sovereignty. They superseded, or perhaps circumvented, the authority of the sovereign state. Constitutions might provide rights at the national level, but those rights could also be changed at the national level—or ignored. The postwar human rights movement was aimed at ensuring that all individuals, by dint of being human, had certain fundamental rights that had to be protected regardless of national law. That was a central lesson of the horrors of Nazi Germany. The international community had an important interest in how those rights were protected or vindicated.

The human rights movement developed slowly in the early years of the UN, but in the years to come human rights would sometimes be characterized by newly independent states as a Western imposition. These debates over "cultural relativism" waxed and waned, but the central issue—who determined the content of these rights, and how did they vary, if at all, around the globe—persisted. To states that only recently had escaped the yoke of foreign rule, the notion that the independence they craved was now hemmed in by new ideas about universal rights that sat above the sovereign state and limited its freedom was, at times, frustratingly akin to older colonial ideas about *missions civilisatrices*.

Even in its early years, the UN exhibited this fundamental tension. While the overarching goal of trusteeship was self-governance, the Trusteeship Council also had the aim of encouraging the protection of human rights. In practice, this meant that the UN sought to ensure that traditional practices that violated certain norms were stamped out. In late 1949, for example, the General Assembly expressed satisfaction with the recommendations of the Trusteeship Council concerning "the absolute prohibition of such practices as child marriage in trust territories." It went on to recommend the end of "whipping in Ruanda-Urundi" and decreed that corporal punishment "should be abolished immediately in the Cameroons and Togoland."[46] To some observers, the UN seemed to be engaging in the same sort of scrutiny and condemnation of local behavior that the colonial powers had.

To be sure, the British, French, and Belgian complaints about the UN's increasing scrutiny of colonial governance did not focus on local cultural autonomy. Indeed, the idea that the native populations in their overseas territories needed to learn supposedly modern behavior had long been central to their self-conceptions as enlightened colonialists. Rather, the Europeans were increasingly troubled by the very idea that the international community was now monitoring—and purporting to supervise—*their* behavior in overseas territories, and doing so with a rising attitude of distate for the very notion of colonial rule. In the coming years, attitudes toward empire would shift still further. By the end of the 1950s, empire in its traditional form, which had dominated world politics for centuries, would be in a rapid freefall.

BUNCHE SPENT THE BULK OF HIS time in the early 1950s on trusteeship issues. Yet the UN staff was small in those days, and given his record of success, he was already rubbing up against many decisions that went beyond his assigned role. The biggest issue for the UN in this era—the Korean War—was a prominent example.

The Korean War was complex in its origins, but it was not unconnected to colonialism. Japan had annexed Korea in 1910 and ruled it as a colony. After Japan's defeat in 1945, the Soviet Union and the US agreed to divide the Korean peninsula in two. The division was expedient and not intended to be permanent. Yet as the Cold War took hold, the two halves of Korea were quickly drawn into the respective orbits of the superpowers. With the Security Council stalemated by the prospect of a veto, the action moved to the General Assembly. In 1948, when the General Assembly voted to create a commission on the future of the peninsula and called for elections, the North refused to participate. Tensions grew sharper. By late 1949, the General Assembly was already noting with concern the prospect of "open military conflict in Korea."[47] In June 1950, shortly before Bunche's Nobel Prize was awarded, the North invaded the South.

When the fighting broke out, the Soviets were boycotting the Security Council over its unwillingness to seat the new People's Republic of China in the "China seat," rather than the now vanquished Nationalists of Chiang Kai-Shek. (Dean Rusk later told Bunche that the Soviet ambassador himself stated the boycott was at the direct order of Stalin.)[48] The Truman administration, stunned and dismayed by Mao Zedong's victory in 1949, had continued to support the Nationalists, who had fled to the offshore island of Formosa (now Taiwan). Without US support, the new People's Republic could not take control of the UN seat.** The Soviet absence from the Security Council allowed the Americans to rally a vote in favor of intervention.

The day of the Security Council resolution authorizing the Korean intervention Bunche was at a lunch event with Trygve Lie. They met in the "Stockholm Restaurant" on Long Island; the UN was still temporarily quartered in Lake Success, just past the New York City border. Participants at the lunch rushed back to the UN buildings to participate in the landmark vote. "This was a crucial day for the UN," Bunche wrote on a notepad on

---

** In early 1951, Bunche was floated in the *Washington Post* as a potential intermediary to "talk to the Chinese Reds about a peaceful negotiated settlement of the Korean and Far Eastern problems."

June 27, 1950. Invoking still-fresh Second World War parallels, he continued: "It was either decisive action or the certainty of starting a new chain of Manchukuo, Ethiopia, and Munich episodes." He saw the Security Council's action as critical; a sign that the organization, hobbled nearly from the beginning by superpower conflict, was finally working. "The UN is saved, and so is the world."[49]

This assessment was overly rosy. Bunche would continue to be quite optimistic regarding Korea: a few months later, as a guest on Eleanor Roosevelt's new radio show, he said the UN "has met its greatest test in Korea with colors flying."[50] Yet it was in many respects a difficult era for the UN and thus unsurprising that he and others in the young organization might seek small signs of hope. The US still dominated the UN—indeed, it would not use its veto until 1970, some twenty-five years into the organization's life—but the Soviets, unsurprisingly, felt the UN had quickly turned against them. Frequent veto wielders, they were generally unhappy with the direction of the organization almost from the start. By 1950, after the Soviet development of an atomic bomb the year before, many around the world feared the implications of a nuclear Armageddon. The UN at least offered a safe space for argument, but the arguments between East and West grew ever more vociferous, and the Soviets seemed to have lost any interest in the notion of the UN as an allied group. Stalin went so far as to argue in 1951 that the UN had been turned into an instrument of war; it was no longer "so much a world organization as an organization for the Americans, an organization acting on behalf of American aggressors."[51]

The US struggled with how to react to the rising tensions of the Cold War, but Truman generally hewed to a hard line. That same year he nominated George Kennan, the father of the doctrine of containment and the author of the Long Telegram, to be ambassador to the Soviet Union. Bunche, in a letter to Ruth, noted that this meant he was out of the running for that post. "The Kennan going to Moscow," he told his wife, "used to be in the State Department and I understand he is top-notch. One rumor concerning me is now settled, anyway."[52]

Meanwhile, it was not such a bad thing to remain in New York. There he continued to enjoy the abundant fruits of Bunche Fever: he attended

Broadway premieres and prize fights, saw Harry Belafonte play the Village Vanguard, and, perhaps the most exciting to him, eventually became a friend of the legendary Jackie Robinson. The two UCLA graduates were many years apart, but both had broken barriers and now were in the pantheon of famous Black Americans in the 1950s. A lifelong sports fanatic, Bunche was completely enamored of Robinson. Bunche's heavy workload, however, meant he was not always in the shape he thought he was. One day in the early 1950s he ran into an acquaintance who noticed he was in some pain. Bunche, nearing fifty, said he had a broken rib. How did it happen, the man asked. "Automobile wreck?" No, he replied. "I was out playing football with my young boy [Ralph Jr., then nine] and he broke my rib. Old athletes never learn, do they?"[53]

CHAPTER 13

LOYALTY

I have some shocking news. The House Un-American Activities Committee is going to investigate Dr. Ralph Bunche.

—Congressman Adam Clayton Powell, Jr., June 6, 1953

In May 1952, recovered from his football mishap with Ralph Jr., Ralph Bunche flew to Los Angeles. The State Department had hatched a plan to create a film about Nobel Prize winners apparently designed, he wrote in his diary, "to show that all such have come from free countries."[1] The film effort, like the contemporaneous jazz tours of Dizzy Gillespie and Louis Armstrong, was part of the growing American Cold War soft power offensive. The aim was to illustrate to the broader world the advantages of democracy—of freedom itself—and to highlight the distinction between life in America and life in the Soviet Union. A believer in American exceptionalism, Bunche was happy to participate.

Shortly after arriving in his hometown, he was taken to a film studio where a mockup of the Old City of Jerusalem had been built on a Hollywood sound stage. The State Department had arranged for a series of actors to play supporting roles as Bunche replayed key moments from his Palestine mediation. He had limited theater experience, but even he could see that some of the actors on this set were not from the A-list. As they reenacted the scene in which he was told that Folke Bernadotte had been assassinated in an ambush—a moment in which Bunche himself realized he had narrowly escaped death—the actor portraying the Israeli military liaison "overplayed and acted like he had a rump full of buckshot each time." On the other hand, he thought a "handsome Mexican" depicted one of the Israeli leaders well.[2] On this particular trip his leg pains, which would plague him for years, were beginning to worsen and they hampered him on set. In Beverly Hills, while giving a speech one evening of the trip, he even needed to sit down for part of the address. It was a sign of things to come. Though he was not quite fifty, in the decade to come age would swiftly settle upon him.

Later that summer, back in New York City for a Dodgers game at Ebbets Field, Bunche ran into General Douglas MacArthur, the famed hero of the Korean and Second World wars. President Truman, in a storm of controversy, had recently fired him for insubordination.[*] Bunche had not met MacArthur before. The two famous men politely discussed politics as the Dodgers came on to the field. To his surprise, MacArthur told Bunche that the real problem with the United Nations was that it was "too much a captive" of the US,[3] an assessment that was certainly shared by the Soviet Union. Back across the East River at the UN compound, Trygve Lie continued to find mostly frustration as the Soviets, viewing him as an American pawn, increasingly ignored and sidelined him. By the fall of 1952, Lie gave up and announced his resignation as secretary general. Bunche was curious about who would succeed Lie, though he was not especially sad about the change in leadership. Lie had always struck him as out of his depth and overly personalized in his politics. In particular, his strong pro-Israel bias had bothered Bunche during the Rhodes mediation.

Finding a successor that the permanent members of the Security Council could live with proved difficult, however. Bunche's continuing presence at the UN was also not assured. In the Republican presidential primary that

---

[*] Truman famously said of MacArthur: "I fired him because he wouldn't respect the authority of the President. I didn't fire him because he was a dumb son-of-a-bitch, although he was."

previous spring, Harold Stassen, a challenger who ultimately lost the nomination to Dwight Eisenhower, pledged to name a "qualified Negro" to his cabinet if elected. With Bunche Fever still raging, Stassen had singled him out as one promising option. Stassen and Bunche had worked together fruitfully in San Francisco in 1945. Calling him one the "most outstanding, upright, courageous, brilliant young diplomats in America today," Stassen added, his syntax a bit garbled but the message clear, that "it is men like Dr. Bunche which makes our country leaders in almost every field."[4]

As the wrangling over Trygve Lie's replacement continued, Eisenhower, just elected president, visited the new UN campus in Manhattan in November 1952. Walking through the soaring General Assembly chamber to applause, Eisenhower ran into Bunche. As the two shook hands, Eisenhower cryptically asked, "Who are you working for, the United States or the UN?" "I'm with the UN," Bunche replied. With a big smile, Eisenhower countered, "How in hell can the United States afford not to have you working for us?"[5] Ike offered him a position back in the State Department, but as always with these offers, Bunche demurred.

Meanwhile, the search for Lie's successor dragged into the new year. Eventually, after almost six months of internal debate, a candidate was selected. Dag Hammarskjold of Sweden was little known and, even after he arrived in New York, in April 1953, a bit mysterious to many in the organization. The patrician Henry Cabot Lodge Jr., the US ambassador to the UN, told Secretary of State John Foster Dulles that while his information was sketchy, "I am inclined to think that he would be satisfactory and that he may be as good as we can get."[6] In fact, the Swedish diplomat proved to be perhaps the most visionary of the men to hold the secretary general post. For Bunche, after a somewhat stiff and distant beginning to the relationship, Hammarskjold proved a leader, a partner, and even a friend.

DAG HAMMARSKJOLD WAS THE SON OF a former prime minister of Sweden. Trained as an economist, in a strange twist, Hammarskjold's PhD supervisor was Gunnar Myrdal, Bunche's colleague on the *An American Dilemma* book project in the late 1930s. Hammarskjold eventually became part of Sweden's foreign affairs ministry, and in 1951 (and onward) he was a member of the delegation to the United Nations General Assembly. It is not clear whether Hammarskjold and Bunche ever met at those early UN meetings, but they certainly could have: the organization was quite a bit smaller in those days. Hammarskjold's selection was largely the result of the Soviets' preference for someone from a neutral nation. The USSR had vetoed an earlier candidate, Lester Pearson of Canada, on the grounds that Pearson would inevitably be too close to the Americans. To break the stalemate, both sides, knowing little about Hammarskjold but liking the idea of a Scandinavian, went along with his candidacy. The position of secretary general, still ill defined in the early 1950s, would grow substantially during Hammarskjold's tenure.

Dag Hammarskjold was a unique figure in diplomacy. A solitary man who wrote a spiritual classic—his posthumously published book/diary *Markings*,[†] found by his bedside in his New York City apartment after his untimely death, was described by the *New York Times* as "perhaps the greatest testament of personal devotion published in this century"— Hammarksjold was also a savvy political animal. At the UN, he effectively navigated the treacherous waters of the Cold War time and again.[7] He garnered significant attention for his deft statesmanship and relentless focus, and appeared three times on the cover of *Time*, a powerful postwar arbiter of fame and significance.

Bunche and Hammarskjold had an awkward first encounter. At that time Bunche was still working in the Trusteeship Division. In that role he had continued to push for greater speed and focus on self-determination, often to the dismay of European states. As he noted in his diary during this era, "the colonial powers were not at all happy with me."[8] Whether European complaints influenced Hammarskjold's subsequent decision to reorganize the UN Secretariat and move Bunche into his executive office is unclear. But Hammarskjold seemed to quickly recognize both Bunche's innate

---

[†] Bunche would later slyly write in his diary of U Thant, Hammarskjold's successor: "Dag Hammarskjold wrote 'Markings'—U Thant will be known for his 'Droppings'—the often indiscreet replies he gives casually to reporters who buttonhole him in the corridors." The great W. H. Auden, relying on *Markings*, later dubbed Hammarskjold a "religious contemplative" and a "good minor poet."

talent and the political value of having a prominent, respected American close by. The two men first discussed his proper role in the organization in late November 1953. At a dinner held for Freedom House at a New York hotel, Hammarskjold penned a brief note on the back of his place card and passed it to Bunche: "What you said, Ralph, while we were waiting for the dinner makes me feel it more urgent than before to have a word with you about a few of my plans. Have you two minutes after this programme?"[9] As the event came to a close, they found a quiet place to talk. Hammarskjold told Bunche that he was his preferred candidate for one of the two new under secretary general without portfolio posts he was intending to create. Bunche had in fact recently been told by India's ambassador to the UN that Hammarskjold "had in mind to make me his 'number 2 man' in the reorganization" of the UN, so this discussion, while welcome, was not a bolt from the blue.[10]

Bunche immediately asked about his trusteeship work: would it continue? Hammarksjold replied that the trusteeship position would likely go to a Latin American. With regard to the new post, Bunche later wrote, Hammarskjold "repeated that he wanted me to know that 'you are my candidate,' but the impression I got was that [I] would be subject to approval in Washington."[11] On this instinct he was likely right: as one of the permanent five members of the Security Council and the single biggest donor to the UN budget, the US had substantial sway in hiring its nationals as well as filling top posts. Bunche of course had long been a favorite of the White House, and his vetting was undoubtedly bound to go well. Still, he was unsure at first of what it all meant. "My general impression," he wrote in his diary,

> was that he took advantage of my casual statement before the dinner to give me a hint, or possibly more than that, that he might not be in a position to continue my services under the reorganization plan, since official Washington might veto me . . . he said not one word concerning my service to the organization or of regret that I could not continue in Trusteeship, which he knows is my field of special interest and knowledge. He seemed to me to be cold, if a bit shamefaced about it all. When I told him I was devoted to the UN and was at his disposal, he half laughed

and half shrugged it off. I have the feeling that for some reason he is not very happy about my presence here.[12]

Whether Bunche was right that Hammarskjold was "not very happy about my presence" or whether the new secretary general was just socially awkward (or merely Nordic) was ultimately of no consequence, for after this initial bumpy start the two would become very close colleagues. In the meantime, Bunche was happy to remain focused on colonial issues. He was also open to a chance to work more intensively with someone whose policy views would almost surely be more compatible with his than was the case with Trygve Lie. Just the year before, Lie had asked him to "go easy" on colonial affairs. Hammarskjold, Bunche thought, "may have been testing my reaction, but in any case, without further discussion, he later designated me under secretary."[13] Bunche, who always had a strongly ambitious streak, readily accepted. The two soon became inseparable.

Brian Urquhart, who worked closely with both men, later wrote that, of all his senior UN colleagues, Hammarskjold probably regarded Bunche alone as his intellectual equal.[14] Bunche had had a surprising amount of familiarity with Swedes from his days with Gunnar Myrdal in the American South and with Folke Bernadotte in Palestine. Perhaps those experiences helped make the adjustment to Hammarskjold's reserved style and demeanor easier. Whatever the reason, the two soon forged a strong working relationship undergirded by genuine affection.

Hammarskjold, a notorious workaholic who never married, was a good match for Bunche's intense work ethic. Bunche would often have a working dinner at Hammarskjold's apartment, with the secretary general's pet monkey "Greenback" running around on a long leash.[‡] The two men could be found laboring into the night at Hammarskjold's dining room table, resolving some new crisis that had arisen.[15] Bunche shared his knowledge of

---

[‡] The new UN headquarters also had a "secret" apartment in the Secretariat Building for the secretary general, which was really just a small kitchen, bedroom, and living area tucked away near his office. Hammarskjold actually lived in a larger apartment on 73rd and Park Avenue. Eventually, the UN acquired a much closer townhouse for the secretary general on Sutton Place that is still used today.

how the UN worked on the 38th floor; the UN's iconic East River head-quarters had been opened for business shortly before Hammarskjold's arrival, and the secretary general's suite of offices were on that floor. Hammarskjold also utilized Bunche's acute political skills and broad Rolodex of contacts in a wide range of crises and initiatives. Bunche would later say that Hammarskjold was perhaps "the most unusual man that ever existed," one who had an uncanny sense of politics but who was, at heart, a somewhat reserved and ethereal intellectual. Austere and demanding, yet at times prone to anger—Bunche would later say "he could and at times did erupt"—the new secretary general seemed able to elicit great work from those around him, not least from Bunche.[16] Bunche was at times mystified, usually happily, by how well Hammarskjold could navigate the powerful currents around Turtle Bay.

Hammarskjold's boldness was exciting after the sometimes small-mindedness of Trygve Lie. Like Bunche, he thought that the UN needed to do more—much more. As Bunche expressed it, at times the UN had to "project itself into the very arena of conflict."[17] The UN has been likened to both an actor and a stage. It is a *stage* upon which states meet, debate, and posture; at times they even agree. But the UN can also be an *actor*, a side of the organization that was less obvious in the early postwar years. In time and in part due to the work of these two men, the UN became far more of an actor. To be sure, the UN was and remains a creature of the member states that fund it and control it. Yet, in a process of staccato evolution driven by varied crises, the UN became more independent in the 1950s and 1960s and was sometimes granted a fairly long leash. Palestine had provided proof of the concept that the UN was a useful tool for the international commu-nity. But the utility of the UN would prove quite varied during the postwar era. For Bunche, being at the heart of this process of change and adaptation was exciting and rewarding, and it was in many respects the arrival of Dag Hammarskjold that catapulted the UN into this new role.

The years with Hammarskjold were among the most significant in Bunche's career, though for both men the UN was at times intensely frus-trating. As their relationship deepened, Bunche and Hammarskjold would often pass private notes back and forth in meetings, critiquing the ongoing diplomatic combat and, on occasion, the combatants themselves. During a 1958 meeting over the difficult question of Cyprus, for instance, the two men scrawled acerbic asides that reflected their increasingly jaded view of international law and diplomacy:

Hammarskjold: Slim [Mongi Slim, of Tunisia] is a good lawyer—but I begin to wish all lawyers to go to hell.

Bunche: The lawyers—or the lawyer-minded—members are making a farce out of this. What is it in the legal approach that induces men to abandon common sense and even morality—in pursuit of a legal point?

Hammarskjold: Sometimes I believe—as a lawyer and a diplomat—that law is even more demoralizing than diplomacy.[18]

IN JANUARY 1953, BUNCHE, NOW ONE of the UN's most esteemed staffers, headed across the globe on a five-week tour. The trip was part of a role he would play much more in years to come: meeting with heads of state and government and massaging crises and difficult diplomatic relationships. He visited India, Pakistan, Egypt, and Israel. A key area of focus was Kashmir, a high Himalayan region on the border between India and Pakistan, which had become the locus of substantial enmity between the two South Asian states since the painful process of partition in 1947.

The United Nations was concerned that conflict over Kashmir might spark a wider war. Bunche's trip to the region was in part to assess the situation and get a direct read of the protagonists. During Bunche's visit Indian Prime Minister Nehru gave a speech arguing that one must "fight with all your might but always be ready for reconciliation." Quick to seize an opening, Bunche wryly suggested that Nehru "might apply that argument more fully to Kashmir." Bunche had little experience in India but had sometimes found the South Asian nation's representatives at the UN to be difficult; India was aggressive about decolonization (a view he shared) but did not always want to play by the UN rules. Still, he was fascinated by India and soaked up both its rich history and its bustling, crowded, impoverished present. He was struck by how English had become the lingua franca, and he was somewhat surprised that the Indians he interacted with seemed to harbor no great resentment toward the British. It was quite a contrast with his experience in Palestine a few years earlier.

While in New Delhi, he participated in an array of events, including a seminar about the legacy of Mohandas Gandhi, who, in a disturbing foreshadowing of the fate of his fellow apostle of nonviolence, Martin Luther King Jr., had been assassinated five years earlier. At a lunch with Nehru and Krishna Menon, India's long-serving UN ambassador, Bunche and the two Indian officials had a wide-ranging conversation. Among the topics were colonialism; Kenya, which had a large Indian heritage population and was then in the midst of the so-called Mau-Mau rebellion; and the Arab-Israeli relationship. They even debated New York's housing segregation problem. Menon, whom Bunche knew well from the UN, often frustrated him. (He would later say of the legendary long-winded diplomat that "he has a genius for stating a good case and in the same breath negating it by a wrong word or loose handling of fact.")[19] The lunch ended on an unusual note. Nehru kept a pet panda from China in the yard, and as the meeting wound down, they walked over to its enclosure and fed it bamboo leaves. Bunche found Nehru's panda to be "not at all friendly" and "very strong"— perhaps an apt metaphor for India's relations with China, with which it also shared a sometimes-contested border.[20]

The Indian government had put him up in Hyderabad House, a vast structure built in the 1920s and now used for official meetings. The palace reflected India's great wealth as well as its great privation. He was struck by the huge number of servants in the building. One, he wrote in his diary, "takes my shoes off and puts them on . . . buttons my suspenders, puts on my belt." He "would even clean my teeth if I let him."[21] He found the excessive service uncomfortable but thought it a vestige of British rule combined with India's rampant poverty. In his conversations with Indian officials he remained greatly concerned about Kashmir, a key reason he took the trip. The situation, he believed, was a powder keg, perhaps the most dangerous single spot on earth. Bunche feared that the religious divide between largely Hindu India and largely Muslim Pakistan made the potential for conflict there far more than a local issue.

On his way back from South Asia, Bunche stopped in the Middle East at the invitation of the Israeli government. There, too, religion threatened to amplify political conflict. On his visit to Jerusalem, he signed the airport guestbook—not entirely convincingly—with "It's wonderful to be back here." ("With no work to do," he added.)[22] His visit was allegedly unofficial, but at this point he was such an influential figure in the region that there was really no such thing. He made a point of visiting Cairo as well and claimed to have been mostly out of the mix of the Middle East in the last few years. He remarked to reporters that the region seemed in bad shape. "I saw refugees living in unbelievable conditions. . . . In 1948 everyone was willing to deal with the question of war. But now there is less willingness to deal with the residue of human suffering."[23] The observation perhaps unwittingly encapsulated the coming challenges of the UN in the 1950s and 1960s: immediate armed conflict would always receive more of the world's attention than the aftermath, and the lasting human suffering.

While in Israel, Bunche spoke with reporters about the larger global climate. He suggested that colonialism and trusteeship continued to be central issues at the UN. New states such as India and Israel, he explained, had a special role and responsibility in guiding the inevitable process of decolonization. He seemed eager to make the case that political liberation did not require violence. In his Nobel Prize lecture a few years earlier, he had argued that the UN was not merely a peace organization in the sense of preserving the peace or containing war. The UN was also there to make change—"even radical change"—possible without violence.[24] New states were beginning to enter the international system, such as Vietnam, Cambodia, and Laos. Africa was looming as the next major site of decolonization, and Bunche believed it offered a chance for the international community to show that it was possible to move peacefully toward a more just world. The atmosphere surrounding colonialism was rapidly changing, he suggested. Whereas debate in the early years of the UN was often on the relative merits of colonial rule and the need, supposedly, for continued foreign governance, now, in 1953, "there was no debate on this as all agreed that system must go." The only issue now, he declared, "was the pace at which it should be liquidated."[25]

MEANWHILE, BACK IN THE US A different form of conflict was arising. The increasing prominence of Senator Joseph McCarthy in American politics was troubling to Bunche. The nation was entering an era of perfervid anti-communism as the Cold War reached an early peak. In June 1953, as the Vassar College commencement speaker, Bunche decided to speak out about what he saw as a new form of radicalism on the right. To the graduates and parents—he and Ruth among them, as their daughter Jane was graduating that day—he declared that America was in the midst of a dangerous trend:

> There are some who are recklessly prone to brand as subversive anything which does not fit into their narrow pattern of thought, who inflate and exploit every incident by claiming to see behind it the Red hand of conspiracy. This tendency, if unchecked, will fatally undermine the solid foundation of confidence, trust, and freedom of thought and conscience upon which our society rests and from which it derives its unity and great strength.[26]

McCarthy's witch hunts were indeed extreme and would grow more so in the coming year. Yet McCarthy's ability to whip up an anticommunist frenzy reflected a broader obsession with communist subversion in the federal government. While the State Department and, eventually, the Army would become McCarthy's chief targets, the United Nations also engendered extensive scrutiny. Truman, just before yielding the presidency to Eisenhower in the January 1953, had issued an executive order that all Americans working in international organizations be the subject of loyalty investigations. There was no real basis for the notion that such Americans *were* disloyal, and the very premise of testing their loyalty ran against the principle of international civil service that the UN had strived to create. In fact, the Truman administration had initially insisted that it wanted no voice in selecting Americans working at the UN. (However, it was later alleged that in 1949 Trygve Lie had entered into a secret accord with the State Department to allow the US to screen all American personnel and applicants.)[27] One of the first things Henry Cabot Lodge did after Eisenhower appointed him ambassador to the UN in January 1953 was to request that J. Edgar Hoover "investigate American personnel at the UN."[28] Soon the FBI was visiting the UN campus to fingerprint Americans working there.§

This shift in attitude reflected the ascendency of right-wing suspicions about the new postwar wave of international organizations. Conservatives increasingly believed that the UN in particular was riddled with communist spies or their helpers. In the fall of 1951, the *Saturday Evening Post,* then one of the most widely read periodicals in America, even ran a long piece entitled "The Sinister Doings at the UN" that argued there was "strong evidence that a group of communist wreckers have penetrated the UN staff."[29] This view gradually spread throughout the nation. In Los Angeles, Bunche's home-town, the local district even directed high school teachers not to participate in the annual essay contest on the UN on the basis that the organization was full of communists. Visiting home in 1952, Bunche expressed puzzle-ment, calling the criticisms of the UN "unfounded" and "ridiculous": "Here is an American school system that bans something that the nation is for."[30] Bunche found the entire notion overblown and anti-American. Still, the UN's official neutrality and the presence of numerous Russian officials made charges of communist activity plausible to many Americans. As part of the turn toward suspicion, in early 1953 Warren Austin, the outgoing ambassador to the UN, requested that Trygve Lie halt the appointments of any new Americans to the Secretariat while the US searched for possible malfeasors. Lie, who was generally quite friendly to his host government, agreed in practice to this request and created a small advisory board to ad-dress any charges of subversive activity. Assuming Ralph Bunche was above reproach, Lie promptly appointed him a member.[31]

Bunche was certainly not a communist nor a Soviet agent. He found the loyalty obsession running through Washington disturbing and believed that it adversely impacted the morale and spirit of many of the Americans working at the UN. Nonetheless, to his great surprise and consternation he soon found himself subjected to charges of conspiracy

---

§ Some forty Americans were taken off the UN payroll over the course of the 1950s loy-alty investigations.

and disloyalty. A few months before his pointed remarks at the Vassar College commencement—and perhaps part of the reason he found the new paranoia in Washington so troubling—Bunche had been summoned to the federal courthouse in New York City. There he quietly met with members of the Senate Internal Security Subcommittee, which was investigating supposedly disloyal Americans working at the UN. He was interviewed by two Republican senators, Herman Welker of Idaho and William Jenner of Indiana. They quizzed him about his past, which did indeed contain some radical writings and associates, and they asked specifically whether he had ever been a member of the Communist Party.

Bunche had known many communists in the 1930s, and during those years he had also trafficked in what plausibly could be considered radical ideas. His 1936 book *A World View of Race* had certainly offered a Marxist-tinged analysis. Even earlier, in 1929, he wrote an unpublished essay directly titled "Marxism and the Negro Question."[32] There was of course nothing unusual or pernicious about academics exploring or even espousing quasi-Marxist positions in the prewar era. Communism had been taken seriously by many intellectuals in the prewar era, and the communist movement had long tried to make common cause with those seeking racial justice in America. As a result, Bunche had brushed up against both avowed communists and communist sympathizers. But he was never actually drawn to communism per se, and he had always found enthusiastic support for the Soviet Union, such as that of his friend Paul Robeson, perplexing. At times he was even quite harsh in his attitude toward communism: in some private notes, he referred to Black communists as "just plain opportunists." A "few are clever," he conceded, but "most are sheer nincompoops and misfits—debris."[33] Moreover, by the 1950s, he had moved on from his earlier radicalism, which had clearly been more in the realm of ideas than political movements. Moreover, his associations with Marxist thought and communist sympathizers during his Howard years had been noted and explored as early as 1942, when the FBI first ran background checks on him after he joined the Roosevelt administration's early intelligence apparatus.[34] In the years since, he had served ably at the State Department and the UN. Yet his academic past and dalliances with radicalism now seemed to be haunting him.

The interview was unsettling. And perhaps unsurprisingly, Bunche, now an American hero and Nobel laureate who had recently participated in State Department agitprop in the filming of his Palestine story in Los Angeles and had given innumerable speeches extolling American democracy, was a bit indignant at the treatment from his own government. He wrote to Senator Jenner after the meeting to express his dismay: "I would have taken it for granted that my long record of service to my country, and my public utterances, written and oral, throughout my adult career, were more than adequate testimonial to my unqualified loyalty to my country and my un-wavering devotion to the American way of life."[35] Here he was surely cor-rect: in the hundreds of public speeches he gave in this period, he routinely invoked his respect for the American system and lauded the US as a model for a multicultural future. He was certainly a very patriotic American. Moreover, he was at this point an international civil servant, meant in his professional work to be loyal not to the US but to the ideal of internation-alism represented by the UN. He took that idea seriously, even if he at times seemed overly inclined to view, as certainly others did, too, the interests of the UN and the interests of the US as largely aligned.

In his letter to Jenner, Bunche did not gloss over his more radical past, even if he conceded that some things looked different in retrospect:

> At some point in our discussions, Senator Welker, I believe it was, suggested that perhaps it would have been wiser not to have done some of the things I did in the thirties. Seen from today's perspective that may be true. But in the thirties the common and urgent enemy of peace and freedom was Hitler and his Nazi creed. Today it is communism alone. The lines now are much more sharply drawn, and the perspective of each of us is much simpler and clearer.[36]

Bunche's explanation was truthful; he was opposed to authoritarianism in any form, he believed in American democracy, and he saw communism as a grave threat. Still, the suspicions of the political right did not abate. He was called before the Senate Committee on the Judiciary in March 1953.

Under oath, he denied any affiliation with the Communist Party.[37] The issue should have ended there, but it did not.

A few months later, Bunche was working in Geneva on UN business. While there he inadvertently accepted an invitation to visit the Soviet Union. With the recent federal courthouse visit on his mind and concerned that he had misstepped and would be misunderstood if he actually went on the journey, Bunche wrote to Dag Hammarskjold. (He addressed the telegram "Dear Mr. Hammarskjold"—a far cry from his numerous later notes to "Dag.") As he recounted, while in Geneva a Soviet diplomat had casually offered to bring him to see Russia. He politely expressed interest but also concern about his busy schedule. Unbeknownst to him, the diplomat quickly ran the idea of a trip by Andrei Vishinsky, the long-serving Soviet ambassador to the UN. His Soviet counterpart soon told Bunche, to his alarm, that the powerful Vishinsky had approved the idea, and arrangements were now being made for him to visit Moscow "in two to three weeks." As Bunche told Hammarskjold, "I report this to you because of the unusual manner in which it has happened, the apparently unusual attention accorded it by officials in Moscow, and my own embarrassment in the circumstances."[38]

Bunche never went to Moscow as a guest of the Soviet Union in the summer of 1953. And he was quick to tell Hammarskjold of the awkward offer and, in light of the McCarthyite fervor sweeping Washington, to present it as a problem to be avoided. It is not clear that it made any difference, however. Bunche soon learned that in 1954 he would have to appear before the federal "loyalty board" that Truman had created, known officially as the International Organizations Employees Loyalty Board. The vast majority of Americans employed at the UN were subject only to minor paper investigations; Bunche, in part due to unfounded accusations of communist activity from two individuals he had known in the 1930s, was among the select few required to appear in person. In his diary, he noted with some bitterness the irony that as he found out about his loyalty investigation, "I had just returned from Haiti . . . where I was selling US democracy."[39]**

** Bunche had visited the Caribbean island for its 150th anniversary of independence from France.

A few days later Bunche appeared on Edward R. Murrow's evening broadcast, *Person to Person*. Visiting his home in Queens for the interview, Murrow asked if he missed life in Washington, DC. Bunche, who had lived in New York City for many years, responded that New York was "a very warm city." He was not pining for life in the nation's capital, he explained, even though he agreed that segregation there had been reduced and there was "nothing as inspiring as democracy at work." Murrow's broadcast illustrated how, now some three years after his Peace Prize award, Bunche continued to be presented to the nation as an inspiring story of accomplishment, even as behind the scenes the wheels of the national security investigation continued. In his introduction that evening, Murrow described Bunche as a man who liked to work and indeed could not "remember when he didn't have to work."[40] Murrow's timing was good for Bunche, and it reminded the millions of Americans tuning in of why he was an icon. But it did not change the forward momentum of the loyalty investigation. Perhaps unrelated, but perhaps not, in the *New York Herald Tribune*'s gossip column in February 1954 Bunche was said to be Mordecai Johnson's likely successor as the president of Howard University.[41]

The loyalty hearings finally began in May 1954. The hearings were allocated three days, though only two actually were used. The first day went on for a long twelve hours as Bunche fielded questions accompanied by his lawyer, a former State Department and UN official named Ernest Gross. The second day was adjourned for a quite unusual reason: Bunche was having dinner at the White House with the president. The occasion was the state visit of Emperor of Ethiopia Haile Selassie; also present at the dinner was a who's who of Washington, including Harold Stassen, Bunche's former boss at the State Department and Eisenhower's rival for the Republican nomination. As his presence at the White House evening suggested, Bunche's celebrity and proximity to power were not dimmed by the loyalty charges he was facing by day. Indeed, to many in Washington it seemed absurd that he was under scrutiny at all. The NAACP's Walter White called the notion that Bunche was disloyal to the nation "shocking" and labeled the hearing an "unseemly farce."[42] (White personally testified in Bunche's defense.) The efforts to question his loyalty seemed out of line even to some Republicans.

Eisenhower said in private that he would not permit a man like Ralph Bunche "to be chopped to pieces because of McCarthy." Indeed, a White House aide had told Bunche three months earlier that they regarded the process as "unnecessary and nonsense and had full faith in me."[43] Eleanor Roosevelt, still an icon herself, told a UN colleague that she was appalled to see the House Un-American Activities Committee was going to investigate Bunche. "Will you tell him if there is anything whatever I can do, I will gladly do it?"[44]

Bunche's celebrity, and almost surely his race, brought special attention to the accusations. The gossip columnist Walter Winchell, who was notoriously close to McCarthy, called him "a card carrying Communist." McCarthy, too, had singled out Bunche in his conversations with State Department officials, labeling him a "well-known Communist."[45] In the loyalty hearings that May Bunche was questioned extensively about his past connections to radical organizations and especially about his role in the National Negro Congress. Though a founder of the organization, he had left the NNC some time ago and indeed had come to view it as "a puppet" of the Communist Party.[46] Yet the NNC's embrace of communism continued to haunt him. Some former Black communists even accused him of participation in past party meetings.[††] Others supported him, denying he had any true connection to the Communist Party. Stressed and upset, Bunche went through the process with trepidation despite its evident absurdity.

Then, on the third day, it was over. To his immense relief, on May 28, 1954, he finally received, in the words of the *New York Times*, a "public and unanimous loyalty clearance" from the board. Henry Cabot Lodge called the clearance by the loyalty board "a fine thing and expected."[47]

Indeed, virtually the entire national security apparatus of the federal government had anticipated this outcome. A few months before his formal exoneration, during a meeting at the UN, Hammarskjold and Bunche casually exchanged notes in which Hammarskjold asked, "Have you heard anything more from the loyalty board?" Bunche replied that everything was going fine and that he hoped it would all be resolved soon. He then wrote: "the

---

[††] The Justice Department would later investigate his accusers for perjury.

whole system is fantastic." Recently, he scribbled, "a man came to see me from the CIA to ask my personal advice on one of their undertakings." Bunche was surprised in light of the ongoing investigation. "I explained that I was not 'cleared' as yet and before I could finish he said 'you are cleared with us or I couldn't speak to you!' "[48]

BOTH BUNCHE AND A SOVIET DIPLOMAT named Ilya Tschernychev had for some time had the title of "Assistant Secretary General for Special Political Affairs." The positions allowed Hammarskjold to deploy the two—in

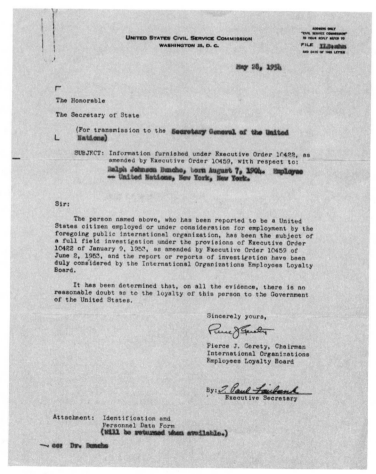

Photo 13.1 Letter of clearance from the Loyalty Board

reality, mainly Bunche—to whatever difficult task was most urgent. The pairing reflected the ongoing, usually fruitless, effort to convince the Soviets that the UN was even-handed when dealing with the superpowers. In the wake of Bunche's exoneration, Hammarskjold announced a plan to promote both men to higher posts. On January 1, 1955, the two were officially placed in the position of under secretary general. In advance of the move, the *Washington Post* editorialized that the "chief significance" of the reorganization was that "it will shift Dr. Ralph J. Bunche into a position where his talent as a trouble shooter can be more fully utilized."[49] He was now the highest-ranking American at the UN, and reportedly was paid a tax-free salary of $25,000.

Troubleshooting indeed became his primary role during this period. He had spent an enormous amount of time away from home and family during the long and involved Palestine effort. After the Nobel he had still traveled, though less. Now, he again seemed to be away almost incessantly. In early 1955, he spent three weeks in Latin America, a region he had little experience in, and then after a brief return was off for another three weeks in Paris, Geneva, and London, his more familiar diplomatic haunts. His fame continued to follow him as he traveled. In Paris that spring, with a bit of free time, Bunche went looking for a place known as Rose Rouge, where he had been told African dancers performed. In front of his hotel he saw a Black man he thought might have been African. "And in French I began to ask him if he knew it," he recounted. The man looked up quizzically and laughed, saying "man, I don't understand no French." Bunche began to walk away, but the man suddenly ran up and asked if he was Ralph Bunche. After he replied "yes," the man quickly waived his two companions over, and "they explained to me they were with Lionel Hampton's band in town for the night."[50]

In 1954, the American Political Science Association, the professional society of the academic community of political scientists, elevated him as its president. He had enjoyed a successful career as a political scientist while at Howard and, at least for the first few years of his federal service, seemed to expect to return to academia. Eventually, however, that notion—which was likely more talk or aspiration than anything else—faded, and he stopped discussing a possible resumption of scholarship and teaching. Yet he remained active in the discipline even as he made his decision to stick to diplomacy. 1954 was the 50th anniversary of the organization, and his selection meant he would give the annual presidential address.

Befitting a 50th anniversary speech, Bunche looked back at the early years of the discipline. Quoting from Woodrow Wilson and other prominent political scientists of the past, he surveyed the evolution of scholarship and, of particular interest to him, the waxing and waning connections to policymakers and statesmen. Interestingly, he did not discuss the work of the UN or the broader, and dramatic, change in the international order that was then underway as a result of the galaxy of international institutions established in the wake of the war. The discipline of international relations was also undergoing great empirical and theoretical change, but he did not give these shifts much consideration either. Toward the end of his address, he noted that there were topics that merited greater attention from the profession than they had thus far received. Two of his three examples were drawn directly from his own career. Bunche had scrawled in the margins of the speech "colonialism has been my major preoccupation," and indeed he began with colonialism.[51]

Calling empire one of the most difficult problems in politics, he argued that the postwar experience had "painfully demonstrated how much of the trouble and conflict in the contemporary world flows directly or indirectly from this faucet."[52] Despite this, he noted, American universities had been "regrettably slow" in grasping the significance of the imperial legacy in world politics. He next suggested that there was much to be learned about the "historical and entirely respectable" role of negotiation, conciliation, and "honorable compromise" in the settlement of disputes—another topic he had firsthand experience with, and one whose scope would grow with the rising number of new states in the postwar order.

Bunche closed his speech with some stirring, and—by his own admission—not especially scientific sentiments. Nonetheless, they arguably befitted a man with a bird's-eye view of the Cold War. Civilization, he declared in 1954, was in the grip of a "moral crisis":

the clear and present danger derives from the fact that our scientific knowledge far exceeds our knowledge of man; to such an extent, indeed, that man now has at his disposition a power of self-destruction never before approached.... It is my conviction that it is toward the fundamental unity of man that we must look for the only means whereby civilization and mankind may survive on this earth.[53]

Speaking later with reporters, he continued this theme. Yes, the UN had made mistakes. But if it did not exist, he argued, "we almost certainly would have been in an atomic World War III long ago."[54]

CHAPTER 14

SHOWDOWN AT SUEZ

Wherever, whenever, and how ever it appears, colonialism is an evil thing, and one which must be eradicated from the earth.
—President Sukarno, at Bandung, Indonesia, April 18, 1955

Wearing a suit and tie, Gamal Abdel Nasser walked up to a podium in the dark of night in the Mediterranean port city of Alexandria. The president of Egypt, Nasser had risen to power only a month before, in June 1956. Yet he already faced a major crisis. The United States had just told Egypt it would cancel funding for a new and improved dam of the Nile River at Aswan. For Nasser, who saw the "High Dam" as an essential economic, agricultural, and political objective for the poor nation, this was a major blow.

Egypt was at the pivot point of two major political issues of the 1950s. The first was the Cold War struggle between East and West. An avowed "neutralist," Nasser had played a key role in the conference of developing and newly independent states a year earlier in Bandung, Indonesia. This assembly, known as the Afro-Asia Conference, had given birth to what became the Non-Aligned Movement. The associated states sought to blaze their own path, free of the baleful influence of the superpower rivalry. Still, Egypt, like nearly all similar states, could not escape becoming a contested site in the Cold War, and indeed sometimes used that status to its advantage, actively playing one superpower off the other.

The second political issue involved the struggle between the forces of empire and the growing drive for self-determination and independence throughout the globe. Like many in the Non-Aligned Movement, Egypt had experienced Western colonialism and continued to seek greater autonomy from European powers. The colonial powers, in the view of Egypt, may have ceded it independence, but they continued to meddle in Egypt's domestic affairs and dictate to it economically. The Aswan Dam was a corrective that would provide stability and growth, enabling greater self-sufficiency. As Nasser explained to the Egyptian people, "we are struggling now to create a giant." Soon, however, "the giant shall stand on its feet empowered by the electricity from the great dam in Aswan . . . we shall redeem ourselves from unemployment and shame."[1] To get there, however, Egypt required resources to build the great dam, resources that it simply did not have.

Nasser was a powerful and charismatic orator, famous for continuing a speech in 1954 unabated after a would-be assassin fired eight bullets at him, shattering the glass lamp above him but leaving Nasser miraculously unharmed. After the shots had broken out, Nasser had continued to speak to thunderous applause, shouting that nothing would stop him or the progress of Egypt's revolution because "you are all Gamal Abdel Nassers."[2] In Alexandria in July 1956, there were no shots fired. But with perhaps equal drama, that night Nasser set in motion an international crisis that would consume the United Nations, severely diminish the power and prestige of Britain and France, and lead Ralph Bunche to put together the first armed UN peacekeepers.

Speaking from the dark stage in Manshiya Square, with a lamp lighting the desk next to him, Nasser's speech was "long, unscripted, not a little rambling, spoken no longer in the stiff formal manner that he had formerly used but in the Arabic of the streets, addressed directly, with a flavor of complicity, to the people."[3] Nasser, whom Bunche would later describe as possessing "weird eyes," "massive shoulders and a big head," and "a wild and rather furtive look," spoke that night of the need for Arab and national unity,

of the humiliating impositions of Western powers and—of central importance to his speech—of the history and future of the Suez Canal.[4]

The Suez Canal was a marvel of 19th-century engineering and an absolutely critical economic resource, one that permitted huge economies on
shipping from Asia and the Persian Gulf to Europe. Carved straight through
the desert at sea level and completed in 1869, the Canal, sometimes dubbed
"the highway to India," was especially important to Britain. Throughout
most of the Canal's history Britain was both the leading maritime power
and a huge empire with a far-flung array of distant Eastern possessions. The
Canal had never really been Egypt's—it was built and operated by a consortium of investors, led by a Frenchman named Ferdinand de Lesseps—
and thanks to an agreement with the then-ruler of Egypt, the Khedive Said
Pasha, the Suez Canal Company, of which Britain was a major shareholder,
had a ninety-nine-year lease. In his speech Nasser regaled his audience with
the history of the Canal, well known to all Egyptians listening, as well as
the newer, much desired project of the Aswan High Dam. The Canal, he
dramatically told the crowd, was supposed to have been built for Egypt, but
instead Egypt "became the property of the Canal." The West was now again
conspiring against Egypt, only this time by demanding that Egypt bend to
its political wishes in exchange for essential financing. America was pun-
ishing Egypt, and America's handmaiden, the World Bank, was doing the
same. Nasser continued on, telling a story of sitting with the president of the
World Bank, Eugene Black. "I started to look at Mr. Black, who was sitting
on a chair, and I saw him in my imagination as Ferdinand de Lesseps."[5]

Hearing the name "Ferdinand de Lesseps" spoken, Egyptian troops
throughout the nation immediately fanned out and, following a prearranged
plan, seized control of the offices of the Suez Canal Company. Nasser was no
longer waiting for the West's help; he was now taking matters into his own
hands. He continued speaking, long into the night, repeatedly discussing
the Canal's history and importance and speaking de Lesseps's name thirteen
more times, just in case his military forces had not heard the first invocation.
Nasser eventually explained to his nighttime audience, who were undoubtedly tiring by this point, the momentous events that were transpiring. The
Suez Canal was right now being taken over by forces of the government of

Egypt, he told the crowd, and as a result it had finally, as it rightfully should always have been, become the property of the people of Egypt:

> At this very moment, as I talk to you, some Egyptian brethren . . . are starting to take over the Canal Company and its property and to control shipping in the Canal, the Canal which is situated in Egyptian territory, which is part of Egypt and which is owned by Egypt.[6]

ABDEL GAMAL NASSER'S DRAMATIC NIGHTTIME NATIONALIZATION of the Suez Canal shocked the world. Nationalizing a major industry was not new. Just a few years earlier, India had nationalized Air India, taking a majority stake of the formerly private airline. More dramatically, in the same period Iran nationalized the Anglo-Iranian Oil Company, an ultimately ineffective but striking move that led to a successful counterattack in the form of an embargo by the British. But the British saw the connection between Iran's oil fields and Suez right away. If Iran were "allowed to get away with it," Emanuel Shinwell, the British defense minister, warned at the time, "other clients would nationalize their way to financial freedom. The next thing might be an attempt to nationalise the Suez Canal."[7] Soon enough, Shinwell was proved right.

Nationalizing foreign assets was always contentious. In this case, the Suez Canal was an iconic symbol of European engineering that was both foreign owned and foreign used. Essential to shipping from the Middle East to Europe at a time when oil was becoming an absolutely critical factor in the global economy, the Canal was a chokepoint that could be used to impose great costs on the West.* In 1955, the year preceding Nasser's nationalization, some 14,000 ships passed through the Canal—nearly forty every day.[8]

The desire to nationalize vital industries reflected the fact that states such as Egypt often lacked ownership over the most valuable resources within

---

* Something still true today, as the fate of the *Ever Given*, a massive container ship that became stuck and blocked traffic in the Suez Canal for nearly a week, dramatically illustrated in 2021.

their borders. The former colonial powers may have granted political independence, but they usually retained control over the most valuable economic resources, hobbling the ability of the postcolonial government to raise much-needed revenues and underscoring their continuing economic subservience. A few years later, in 1960, Ralph Bunche would witness the impacts of this dynamic quite dramatically when Congo, newly and abruptly liberated from Belgium, found itself at the mercy of powerful economic forces based in the West. Over time, the larger struggle between developing and developed states over their economic sovereignty would give rise to the OPEC oil cartel and its attendant global economic crisis, calls within the UN for what was dubbed a "New International Economic Order,"[9] and, ultimately, substantial disappointment on the part of many formerly colonized states, which found that taking back the cow did not always guarantee a steady flow of milk—or a market for it either. In this sense nationalization was closely linked to decolonization. As decolonization gathered steam in the years after the UN's creation, nationalization, an attempt to make independence economic as well as political, grew alongside it.

For Nasser, the Suez Canal was a thorn in Egypt's side, a constant reminder of foreign power over the nation. It was also a potentially potent source of revenue. With his Aswan dream in jeopardy, Nasser saw the seizure of the Canal as his only option. By controlling the Canal, Nasser could bring in new revenues to the Egyptian treasury and show the West that he did not, in fact, need their help. At the same time, he would strike a blow for Egyptian sovereignty, especially against the much-hated British. He would also strike a blow more generally for the small and weak states of the world. As he declared in a speech in September 1956, "We believe in international law. But we will never submit. We shall show the world how a small country can stand in the face of great powers threatening with armed might."[10] In the street, in the wake of the dramatic nighttime seizure, Nasser was hailed as "the Hero of the Canal."[11]

Nasser's sudden move against the Suez Company caused panic in London. The British immediately began strategizing about how to seize it back. Ultimately, the Suez Crisis would lead to a showdown that would sow disaster for the government of Prime Minister Anthony Eden and come to symbolize, in dramatic fashion, the crumbling of British power in the postwar era. It would also give rise to the first true peacekeeping mission of the UN, a mission, and ultimately an entire enterprise, in which Ralph Bunche would play a central role.

Given its international importance, the Suez Canal had been the subject of discussion in the UN well before the crisis of 1956. The Security Council had first discussed it in 1951. The issue then was Egypt's restrictions on Israel's use of the canal. Israel had brought the issue before the UN, claiming that Egypt's actions constituted an act of war and invoking "Mr. Ralph J. Bunche's declaration that the Egyptian restrictions on shipping were contrary to the Armistice Agreement."[12] (That Bunche's opinion was used by Israel as an argument from authority was a sign of how greatly his global stature had grown by 1951.) In an 8–0 vote, with the Soviets, China, and India abstaining, the Security Council agreed and called upon Egypt to end the restrictions and comply with the armistice agreement Bunche had forged in Rhodes.[13] The Canal's international dimensions were not limited to the Armistice Agreement, however. Under the terms of an 1888 treaty known as the Constantinople Convention, it was to remain open to free passage in times of war as well as peace.[14] In addition, the British still maintained army bases in the Canal Zone. These bases were highly unpopular with Egyptians, and in 1954 Nasser successfully pressured the British to begin to withdraw the 70,000 troops stationed there.[15]

Perhaps even more unpopular in Egypt than the British was the new neighboring state of Israel. While Bunche's mediation had provided stability and a measure of peace in the Middle East, tensions remained high, and Egypt, along with other Arab states, continued to view Israel with hostility. The feeling was mutual. In 1955 Israeli forces killed several Egyptians; attacks on Israel frequently emanated from the Egyptian controlled Gaza Strip.[16] The broader Suez Canal area was rife with geopolitical tensions and destined to entrain multiple states and interests if conflict were to break out.

In 1956, however, when Nasser seized the Canal, Bunche's Middle East days seemed largely behind him. His portfolio had grown to be very broad under Dag Hammarskjold's leadership and his elevation to the role of under secretary general. Soon, however, he would be dragged back into the region he had once bitterly called "this trap."

THE SUEZ CRISIS UNFOLDED IN THE wake of a bumpy first decade for the United Nations. There had certainly been some successes for the organization in the ten years since Ralph Bunche, along with Eleanor Roosevelt and Edward Stettinius, had sailed to London for the opening meetings. A slow accretion of new members had also been drawn in part from the rising ranks of newly independent states, such as Indonesia. In addition, there was the construction of the beautiful midcentury headquarters overlooking the East River, which had opened for business a few years earlier. Yet on the big issues—the peace and security of the world—the Cold War had largely wrung out whatever hope and optimism about the UN that had existed in San Francisco in 1945.

That the unity, such as it was, of the original Big Three powers would not last past the end of the war was hardly shocking to many at the time. Yet the speed and severity with which the Cold War stymied the collaborative pretensions of the UN was disappointing. Moscow had many complaints about the UN almost from the beginning and seemed ready to use its veto powers with stunning alacrity. The US, too, was questioning what role the UN would play in the new postwar order, now that it was abundantly clear that its dominant feature was not Allied cooperation but superpower rivalry.

Indeed, in 1954 a major conference on America's stake in the UN took place, a conference series that Dwight Eisenhower had begun as president of Columbia University but that continued after he became the US president. (Bunche was, of course, a key participant.) John Foster Dulles, Eisenhower's secretary of state, had already raised the idea of revising the UN Charter in light of changing circumstances. The Senate Foreign Relations Committee likewise held hearings on that notion. The Charter was never revised in a major way, though some amendments were later made; most significantly, the Security Council was expanded from eleven to fifteen members in 1965, in recognition of the much larger size of the UN membership. But the 1954 conference indicated that even the US, which had essentially created the

UN, served as host and home, and certainly dominated it in the early years, was, less than a decade in, having doubts about its ongoing utility.

Perspectives on the UN were about to change, however. Dag Hammarskjold's arrival ushered in a new era in Turtle Bay, one in which the UN would play a much more active role in many global crises. Some welcomed this change; others did not. But the change was undeniable.

Bunche had been active on a diverse array of issues in the period preceding the Canal seizure. In particular, Hammarksjold asked him to chair a committee to consider whether the UN should create a new agency to address the peaceful uses of atomic energy.[17] President Eisenhower had delivered a significant speech—Bunche later called the address, no pun apparently intended, "electrifying"—known as the "Atoms for Peace" proposal.[18] The speech, delivered to the General Assembly in late 1953, was based on the notion of finding peaceful uses of atomic energy. The US deployed it as a way to highlight the more positive side of a largely dark development in human history. By this point, both the Soviets and the British had obtained the bomb, and the fear of greater proliferation—and a nuclear Armageddon—was on the rise. Yet the prospect of a new and perhaps limitless form of energy, one that might be "too cheap to meter," was also very attractive. The UN embraced the idea of a role in supervising and shepherding such peaceful uses. The key was that the new UN agency would focus on helping states use nuclear technology peacefully. Henry Cabot Lodge, asked by reporters if the UN would ever have an atomic agency with "inspection" powers, replied: "That will be the day, all right!"[19†]

Bunche, who had no real background in science or technology, dove into the UN's foray into the atomic age with alacrity and his usual, often overly generous, optimism. In October 1954, the new UN committee on peaceful uses of the atom began its work, with Bunche as chairman. Leading another meeting in 1955, he announced to the delegates that they were "taking a great and perhaps the decisive step toward securing peace on earth."[20] And when the new International Atomic Energy Agency was launched two years

---

† Inspection of nuclear facilities may have seemed fanciful at the time, but it occurred in Iraq starting in 1991.

later in Vienna, Austria, he was the one to deliver the opening message. Sixty-five nations met in a Viennese concert hall for the assembly, dubbed the Atoms for Peace Conference. Bunche characteristically called the conference "an event of untold significance to the world."[21]

During the mid-1950s the UN, even as it seemed to many to have been stymied by the Cold War, became more popular with the American public. Polling showed that approval of the UN's progress rose from 50 percent in 1953 to 74 percent in 1955.[22] Bunche, too, remained quite popular. In late 1955 alone, *Ebony* magazine featured him on the cover for the 10th anniversary issue, ABC aired the "Ralph Bunche-Lucy Johnson Story" in prime time, and Edward R. Murrow interviewed him on his popular *See It Now* program.[23] Still, or perhaps because, of all this activity and attention, the complaints from the right about both the UN and Bunche did not abate. Indeed, in the fall of 1954 Bunche, alongside poet Robert Frost, received the Distinguished Service Award from the Theodore Roosevelt Association. Roosevelt's only surviving son, Archibald, protested the selection. Bunche, he said, mimicking the charges of Republican critics in recent years, had "a past record of close affiliation with Communism." Archibald Roosevelt boycotted the banquet. Bunche nonetheless accepted the award, pointedly noting in his address to the society that in his time, Teddy Roosevelt, "although basically conservative in outlook," had also been attacked "by shameless detractors" as a "radical." TR, Bunche declared, "would find himself in familiar surroundings today."[24]

BY THE TIME OF THE SUEZ Crisis in 1956, Dag Hammarskjold had become the face of the United Nations—the "secular Pope," as the role came to later be known—but Ralph Bunche was almost always right by his side, working behind the scenes to shape and implement the plans the secretary general proposed. Hammarskjold had been chosen because he seemed innocuous, but he gradually became comfortable with a more overt, active role within the organization. Bunche would later say of Hammarskjold that "his interest and immersion in political problems soon began to leave him less and less time" for policy; yet, he believed, Hammarskjold never displayed any reluctance about being carried in this direction. Bunche found that

Hammarskjold at times relished the political combat and did not want to be simply a bureaucrat: "he never seemed to be sorry about becoming more and more exclusively a political man."[25] Suez put the UN and its politics to the test in a new manner.

In the wake of Nasser's surprise nationalization tensions rose rapidly in London, Paris, Washington, and Tel Aviv. At the suggestion of John Foster Dulles, an international conference was organized, to be held in London, to try to find a resolution.[26] Though Nasser refused to participate, the Western allies, along with some others, nonetheless plowed ahead in an effort to sort out a peaceful path forward. The Soviet Union, seeing an opening, began to pay more attention to Egypt.

The US interest in Suez was indirect. It had much less economic exposure to the Suez Canal than did Europe. As British Prime Minister Anthony Eden prophetically said at the time, "we must never forget . . . that the Canal is in no sense vital to the United States."[27] Yet the Eisenhower administration still had important geopolitical interests in the outcome of the crisis. First, Suez was essential to America's allies; second, the crisis was threatening to bring the Cold War into a new battlespace; and third, whatever happened with Suez might create precedent, political or otherwise, for America's much more significant interest in Panama, where the US controlled the Panama Canal entirely and indeed claimed sovereignty over the land on both sides of the Canal, known as the Canal Zone.[†] Moreover, the US was in the midst of a presidential election, with Eisenhower, the incumbent, vying against Adlai Stevenson, then governor of Illinois and future UN ambassador. The postwar years had also dramatically changed how Washington saw the wider world; competition with the Soviet Union meant that Americans now had "strong views on countries and territories that had, only a few years earlier, meant little."[28]

The US had long wanted to balance support for its Western allies with its desire to cultivate strong relations with the many emerging independent

---

[†] The Canal Zone remained under US control until President Jimmy Carter agreed to hand over the Canal to Panama in 1977, an event that finally occurred much more peacefully in 1999, with Carter present and dramatically stating to the Panamanians, "It is yours."

states in Africa and Asia. The tensions between these two aims were acute and growing in 1956. As a result, the US was increasingly focused on how colonialism and its legacy was reshaping geopolitics. Indeed, just before Nasser seized the Canal, Dulles had met with Dean Rusk, the future secretary of state under President John F. Kennedy and long-time government official, who was then in the private sector. Dulles asked Rusk to create a high-level study group on colonialism and American interests under the aegis of the New York–based Council on Foreign Relations. The group's findings could then inform American policy on what seemed to be a coming flood of decolonization. Rusk invited Bunche, as one of the most knowledgeable Americans on colonial matters, to be a part of the effort, but he could not attend the first meeting and did not participate afterward.[29] Yet Bunche had already spoken on the record of his overall concerns about decolonization. He of course supported the move to bring self-determination to the peoples of Africa and Asia. But, as he had said at least as far back as 1954, there was a "very grave danger" that the drive for independence would bring new international crises.[30]

It was this fear—and the particular role the US might play in such crises—that led to the Council on Foreign Relations study. The study began from the premise that the coming breakup of European empires and the concomitant rise of anticolonialism in the UN were creating challenges for the Western alliance, a position the Suez Crisis would soon make abundantly clear. In the off-the-record meetings in New York, Rusk

> noted that there has existed for some time a large anti-colonial bloc of nations. . . .
> Until recently, the strength of numbers and opinion of these former colonial countries has not been a deciding factor [in the UN General Assembly] . . . but now their anti-colonialism is spreading to other issues and their number has been strengthened by new additions.[31]

The participants in the study group debated various aspects of colonialism, including how, increasingly, the rhetoric of decolonization included economic and not just political independence. Rusk then offered a tripartite framework for American policy toward the emerging postcolonial world.

First, he stated, the US did not need to be involved in every colonial dispute. Second, the US would "align itself with aspirations for independence in those cases in which force is used by the colonial power to maintain its domination." Third, the US would work toward developing viable economies in territories moving toward independence. Later, Rusk would arguably ignore much of his own counsel with regard to Vietnam.

The views of Rusk's study group closely anticipated, or perhaps guided, American policy with regard to the Suez Crisis. As tensions grew over the seizure of the Canal, the US made clear to its allies that any use of force was unwelcome. In a letter to Eden at the end of July 1956, Eisenhower wrote that he had given Eden his "personal conviction" as to the "unwisdom even of contemplating the use of military force at this time."[32] In a National Security Council meeting on August 30, Dulles emphasized "his own anxiety to avoid resort to military force against Egypt at least until such time as world public opinion had been mobilized and tested."[33] The Eisenhower administration saw itself as an honest broker of the thorny Suez situation, but events were quickly getting sticky as the Soviets became more deeply involved.[34]

Meanwhile, Britain, France, and Israel, each of whom had strong antipathy to Nasser and his actions, were concocting a dramatic and secret plan of their own. Unbeknownst to the US, they had decided that Israel would invade Egypt through the Sinai Desert, precipitating a conflict that would allow France and Britain to send forces into Egypt to quell. France, like Britain, saw the Canal as a vital conduit for Persian Gulf oil that could not be left in capricious foreign hands. France also believed that Nasser, as a standard bearer for the growing bloc of newly independent states and a strong voice against European empire, was fomenting and fueling the painful rebellion now underway in Algeria, a French colony in North Africa that was treated as an overseas French province. France had granted independence to Tunisia and Morocco shortly before the Suez Crisis began. But Algeria was different, and France was in the midst of a brutal but ultimately futile war to retain it. When the Anglo-French assault in Egypt began, leaflets dropped over Cairo called on the Egyptians to rid themselves of

Nasser.[35] (The *New York Times* would refer to this entire effort as the " 'Get Nasser' program of Britain and France.")[36]

France was not wholly wrong to see a connection between Nasser and its problems in Algeria. Both reflected a rising antipathy to Western dominance and colonial rule. As the Rusk study group had feared, the Suez Crisis brought to a head the increasing tension between the traditional colonial powers and the many states, often newly independent, that now sought to carve out a separate path in the Cold War world. The Bandung Conference the year before, at which Nasser had been a bit of a star, was a warning sign for anyone who was paying attention that the politics of empire were rapidly changing.

IN 1955, IN BANDUNG, INDONESIA, GAMEL Abdel Nasser had joined China's Zhou Enlai, India's Jawaharlal Nehru, and other leaders of the nascent Third World for a major global conference—one Indonesia's president, Sukarno, called the first "intercontinental conference of colored peoples in the history of mankind."[37] The goal, in part, was to forge an alliance of postcolonial states and navigate a third way between East and West: a neutral, nonaligned position that denounced colonialism and rejected the Cold War as the only political alignment that mattered.[§] In Washington, the conference was nonetheless largely seen through a Cold War prism. A National Security Council memo rejected the notion that the Bandung Conference represented a new, genuinely anticolonial movement, referring to the conclave as a "grimly amusing" spectacle of "world Communism holding itself up as the protagonist of local nationalist movements and anticolonialism."[38]

Others saw the Bandung Conference as less about communism than a much older force in world politics. Bandung was "the assertion of race," wrote George Sokolsky in the *Washington Post*.

[§] Not all the states at Bandung were former colonies. Some, such as the Gold Coast, were still colonies. Others, such as Japan, were former colonial powers. But they were all non-Western powers.

It represents first the assertion of racial equality of the Asiatic and African peoples. In time will come the assertion of racial superiority. Race is the most emotional, the most dynamic factor in human history. . . . [White people] are newcomers on the world scene who managed to turn ancient races into natives who live in colonies . . . these races learned to hate the white man, to hate him as a racial inferior, a racial parvenu who had come into possession of their world.[39]

Sokolsky, an outspoken anticommunist who had spent substantial time in China, was a sort of journalistic Asia hand favored by the right. His assessment of the Bandung Conference was hyperbolic and defensive, and a throwback to the race-war-focused geopolitical views of the 1920s and 1930s. Still, in some ways, Sokolsky was prescient: Bandung invoked neutrality and a new, separate path, but soon the Third World, as the nations assembled there were more generally known, was more vigorously opposing the West and, by the 1970s, was using their numerical advantages to try to reshape the world order in their favor. The principles articulated in the Final Communique at Bandung—colonialism is evil; domination and exploitation are contrary to the UN Charter; intervention is wrong—were not necessarily new, but they were posed in a far starker and more forthright manner than ever before.[40]

Bunche would not live to see the fruition of these efforts by the nascent Third World, which often foundered on the realities that power was still concentrated in the hands of the traditional great powers. Had he done so, he may well have been somewhat torn by his commitment to global racial justice coming into tension with his strong allegiance to America and its place in the world. The nations of the former colonial world also unsurprisingly proved to not be monolithic in their preferences, posing challenges for efforts at solidarity. Indeed, Nasser himself decidedly did not see sub-Saharan Africa as ancient Egypt's equal. Writing in his 1954 book *The Philosophy of the Revolution*, he declared: "we will never in any circumstances be able to relinquish our responsibility to support, with all our might, the spread of enlightenment and civilization to the remotest depths of the jungle"—words that just as easily could have come from the lips of Lord Lugard of Britain.[41]

The Bandung Conference occurred at a time when Bunche was some-what less engaged with decolonization. As his portfolio at the UN had expanded in the mid-1950s to include more varied and urgent tasks such as peaceful uses of the atom, and he was so frequently on the road speaking before varied audiences, Bunche had spent less time on trusteeship and decolonization. But the field was not especially lively in the early 1950s. From 1950 to 1955, only one new state joined the UN—Indonesia in 1950. This was not necessarily unexpected; few envisioned a huge wave of independence in the early postwar era, though soon enough that would happen.

Bandung itself received only modest attention at the UN. Bunche did not attend, though Congressman Adam Clayton Powell of Harlem did, against the strong advice of the State Department. (The State Department at first asked Powell to refrain from visiting the American Embassy while there, though it quickly reversed course, fearing that it would be seen as ostracizing a Black American at a conference devoted to racial divides.)[42] There is little evidence of what Bunche thought or said about Bandung at the time. In a 1955 op-ed in the *St. Louis Post-Dispatch*, written a few weeks after the conference, he glancingly mentioned Bandung as an example of "co-operation in peace efforts" developing among varied states, but nothing more.[43] At the UN's tenth anniversary ceremony that June, Dag Hammarskjold, in his keynote speech, focused on the supposed waning of the Cold War and mentioned the conference only to suggest that Bandung, alongside other recent multilateral developments, was a salutary example of the sort of peaceful cooperation the UN was intended to foster.[44] In short, neither Bunche nor Hammarskjold seemed to perceive Bandung as a major event at the time.

But Bandung proved quite significant, arguably auguring what was about to happen in Suez. It showed that a new consciousness was emerging, a new identity that in time would dramatically shift the terms of world politics and introduce a novel fault line: not East–West but North–South. This would only come to fruition in the future, but Bandung, later called the "most symbolic event" of the "revolt against the West," was a sign that it was coming.[45]

Only some observers picked up on this signal early. To Richard Wright, famed author of *Native Son*, the conference, which he attended and wrote a book about, was a meeting of "the despised, the insulted, the hurt, the dispossessed." What had these nations in common? Wright asked. "Nothing, it seemed to me, but what their past relationship to the Western world had made them feel."[46]** American officials may not have agreed—they remained fixed on the threat of communism—but privately some sensed the anger and knew the US had to get ahead of the decolonization process. The US needed to be, and most importantly needed to be *seen* to be, on the right side of history. The problem was that America's allies were not ready to give up their colonies. Navigating that path would not prove easy. Dulles even improbably proposed an "Anglo-American Bandung" that could help map out a path to decolonization and, most importantly, put the US "on the right side of the anti-colonial issue worldwide."[47] The event never happened.

In his opening speech to the assembly at Bandung, the leader of Indonesia, Sukarno, challenged the idea that colonialism's days were numbered. Sukarno declared that "[w]e are often told that 'colonialism is dead.'" Let us not be deceived or even soothed by that, he continued. "I say to you, colonialism is not yet dead. How can we say it is dead, so long as vast areas of Asia and Africa are unfree?"[48] Bandung was a call to arms to bring to a close the long era of European dominance over Africa and Asia.

Bunche, speaking with the prominent *New York Times* reporter James Reston a year after Bandung, described colonialism as a festering wound that continued to cause problems for the global body politic. Bunche called continued colonialism a fundamental security problem for the world. He presciently predicted that the UN would become "even more embroiled" in the issue in the coming years.[49] Indeed, almost two years earlier, in May 1954, well before Bandung, Bunche had spoken about the risks to peace he saw in the burgeoning drive for independence from European rule. He argued that it was likely that "Africa, in the coming years, will prove an even greater threat to the peace of the world than Asia."

Bunche was of course a strong supporter of African and Asian liberation. But he argued that the UN now found itself in a paradoxical situation. Promoting independence for new nations was consistent with its commitment to self-determination and racial equality. Indeed, it had been a central

---

** Wright's visit to Bandung was ironically funded, in part, by the CIA through the Congress for Cultural Freedom, a Cold War anticommunist organization.

part of his UN work for years. Yet the process of liberation was creating new nationalisms, a known and familiar driver of conflict. He wanted to see the new nations embrace internationalism—and to some degree they often did, eager to join the UN as soon as possible—but peace did not always follow.

"So much of the trouble and conflict in the world today has its roots in colonialism," Bunche had declared in 1954.[50] Suez soon proved the point.

IN THE RUNUP TO THEIR SECRETLY planned invasion in the fall of 1956, France, Britain, Israel, and Egypt traded claims and counterclaims about the Suez crisis in the Security Council.[††] Britain and France declared that Egypt's actions endangered free and open passage in the Canal, so vital to many states. Egypt replied that the nationalization had been undertaken in the "full exercise of its sovereign rights" and reaffirmed its guarantee of freedom of passage in conformity with the 1888 Convention, which did not in any way deprive Egypt of its right to administer the Canal.[51]

The 1888 Convention did seem to provide a legal framework for Suez. But as Bunche had discovered in Palestine, the complex imperial history of the Middle East created contemporary challenges that frustrated peaceful resolution. The treaty was signed at a time when Egypt was under the rule of the Khedive, a sort of loose vassal of the Ottoman Empire. More importantly, Britain had invaded Egypt in 1882 and had continued to treat it as a protectorate, in one form or another, until 1952, when a coup, led by Nasser, had finally freed Egypt from external rule. While legally Egypt was still bound by the Treaty of Constantinople, politically and morally many Egyptians felt these agreements were no longer valid; the Canal, which cut right through the nation's territory, was a vestige of the colonial past, and therefore it was theirs to do with as they saw fit.

For Nasser, the Canal and the associated British bases were irritants, constant reminders of Egypt's subservience to the West. By seizing the Canal, Nasser was proving that Egypt not only owned the Canal, but also could operate it effectively—contra the Europeans' frequent claim that it was too

---

[††] Bunche, meanwhile, had an alliance-forming of his own in the fall of 1956: his daughter Joan married Burton Pierce, a ceremony covered in the *New York Amsterdam News* with the headline "Bunche-Pierce Nuptials United Two Distinguished Families."

technically complex for the Egyptians to manage. Moreover, he was going to pay back all the European shareholders, so that it was less a "seizure" and more of a forced buyout. Nasser's legal and political positions were stronger than the British and French were admitting.

The European imperial powers nonetheless brought the matter of Suez up repeatedly at the UN, couching the problem as one of a wayward government reneging on a major treaty obligation, with important implications for the global economy and security. We are asking the UN, said Selwyn Lloyd, the UK's foreign minister, to uphold justice and respect for international obligations and to "redress a situation which endangered the economic and political life of many nations."[52] The Canal, the British argued, was not a domestic Egyptian issue but an international matter of the utmost importance. Egypt's counterarguments were also couched in internationalism but of a much different sort. Sounding the rhetoric of Bandung and noting the sharpening worldwide struggle between colonialism and liberation, Foreign Minister Mahmoud Fawzi declared to the Security Council that the choice his nation faced was a simple one: between "domination and freedom."[53]

The debates in the UN that fall remained at a stalemate. Then, without warning, on October 29, 1956, Israel, France, and Britain triggered their secret plan. Israel suddenly invaded the Sinai Peninsula. Two days later, France and Britain, faking indignation, demanded both sides withdraw their forces from the Canal area and threatened to invade to restore order. Soon the joint European invasion began, with air assaults leading the way. The Eisenhower administration was taken aback by this aggressive move against Egyptian sovereignty. Nonetheless, US intelligence had determined that there was an unusually high number of messages pinging back and forth between Tel Aviv and Paris in the days before the Israeli invasion, creating suspicion almost from the outset that the Europeans were "playing a double game."[54‡‡]

The Eisenhower administration was decidedly unhappy with this turn of events. As the US ambassador to the UK later described it, the British

---

‡‡ This perhaps was an early sign of the Americans' deep lead on the Europeans in signals intelligence—culminating in the Snowden affair decades later and German Prime Minister Angela Merkel's indignation that the NSA may have tapped her cell phone.

had been told over and over again at the highest levels not to use force. Their use of force without any warning came as "a profound shock" to the Americans.[55] The British continued to pretend that they had no warning of, and had no role in, Israel's invasion. To Eisenhower, Eden said "we would not wish to support or even condone the action of Israel."[56] Even this somewhat lawerly locution would turn out not to be true.

Within Egypt, Nasser's forces struggled against the invading troops. The Israelis swiftly conquered the Sinai Peninsula to the east of the Canal. Egypt in return sunk various ships and bridges in the Canal, blocking traffic. This created immediate problems, for the Canal brought in two-thirds of Europe's oil supply. British and French troops advanced on the Canal, purportedly with the goal of separating the combatants and "protecting" the Canal. It was now a full-blown international crisis.

The Security Council, with two permanent members involved, was of little use. Hammarskjold spoke before the Council about the stakes, a statement Bunche, in a personal note to the secretary general, called "clean and decent in stark contrast to the crude cynicism of the hour."[57] Still, Britain and France could veto any attempt to address the situation they did not like. That had been the point of the veto from the very earliest days at Yalta. Indeed, at one point, as condemnation rained down on the three collaborators, the French ambassador leaned over to Abba Eban, his Israeli counterpart, and whispered, "don't worry, there will be a veto."[58]

With the world unclear about what came next, into the breach rode the UN General Assembly. Normally by far the weaker body of the organization, the General Assembly had a new and untested weapon in its quiver. A few years earlier, guided by American Secretary of State Dean Acheson, the General Assembly had passed what became known as the Uniting for Peace resolution. The context at the time had been the Korean War. The US and its allies, frustrated by the Soviets' liberal use of the veto in the preceding years, had introduced a resolution aimed at circumventing the Council and empowering the General Assembly to be more engaged in security matters when the Council was blocked.[§§] In doing so, the US noted that "the

---

§§ Reflecting the rising frustration with the Security Council, the Council met only about 50 times a year on average in the 1950s; in the 1940s the average was closer to 130 times.

experience of the United Nations in the five years since the Charter came into force has demonstrated the value of the Assembly's role."[59] Specifically, the Uniting for Peace resolution of 1950 stated that

> if the Security Council, because of lack of unanimity of the permanent members, fails to exercise its primary responsibility for the maintenance of international peace and security in any case where there appears to be a threat to the peace, breach of the peace, or act of aggression, the General Assembly shall consider the matter immediately with a view to making appropriate recommendations to Members for collective measures, including in the case of a breach of the peace or act of aggression the use of armed force when necessary, to maintain or restore international peace and security.[60]

In short, when the Security Council is stymied by a veto or threat of a veto, the General Assembly can call an emergency special session and try to assert responsibility to direct the international response. (This exact approach was used in early 2022 in the wake of Russia's invasion of Ukraine.) Acheson, in putting this notion forward, was seeking a way to provide legitimacy and a formalized process to General Assembly action in the face of Security Council inaction.

Now, six years later, Uniting for Peace provided a new path forward. On November 2, 1956, at the first-ever emergency session called under the resolution,*** the General Assembly passed Resolution 997, which urged a ceasefire and called for reopening the Canal.[61] Egypt's representative denounced the aggression of the invaders and invoked the sanctity of the UN Charter. We thought the Charter "had put an end to the reign of force," he declared, and that "the era of the ultimatum and the ditkat, of bitter memory, had vanished."[62]

But it was not just Egypt attacking the Suez intervention. John Foster Dulles took to the green marble-backed podium of the General Assembly

---

*** Within days, the second emergency session would be called—for a totally different matter. Discussed further below, the Soviets, on November 4, invaded Hungary to stamp out a rebellion based in Budapest. The juxtaposition of the two crises, both involving permanent members of the Security Council, was highly unusual.

Photo 14.1 Secretary of State John Foster Dulles in the General Assembly

to directly criticize Britain, France, and Israel. In the days preceding the debate Dulles, meeting with the National Security Council, had shared Eisenhower's grave concerns about how the crisis would impact the greater Cold War. Dulles had told Eisenhower that unless the US acted appropriately, "all of these newly independent countries will turn from us to the USSR."[63] In New York, Dulles sought to dramatically demonstrate the American position by publicly breaking with its closest allies. "With a heavy heart," he said to the chamber, the US was "unable to agree with three nations with which it has ties of deep friendship."[64] The British, who challenged the General Assembly vote as illegal, were surprised and even shocked that the US was so hostile.

Yet the British should have foreseen the split. As Dulles put it in an emergency meeting of the National Security Council, the US had been "walking a tightrope" between the effort to maintain "our old and valued relations" in Europe and the need to cultivate new relations with the "numerous states which have escaped from colonialism."[65] In an off-the-record discussion with reporters, Dulles drew out the connections. The West, he told the reporters, was now on the edge of winning an "immense and long-hoped-for victory over Soviet colonialism in Eastern Europe." (This assessment would prove overly optimistic.) Yet, Dulles, clearly irritated with the Europeans and their delusions of imperial grandeur, declared that this was the "very moment chosen by Britain and France to make the United States declare herself for or against Western colonialism."[66]

Forced to choose by the Suez Crisis, the US chose "against." President Eisenhower asked, "How can we possibly support Britain and France if in doing so we lose the whole Arab world?"[67]

That night, after the historic vote in the General Assembly, Bunche met with Canadian Foreign Minister Lester Pearson. Pearson, widely known as Mike, had played an important role in passage of the ceasefire resolution. But Pearson believed that much more was needed. He suggested that a new and "truly international peace and police force" was required to return the situation in Egypt to some equilibrium.[68] As Hammarskjold would later write, however, Pearson "still had no clear idea at all about what kind of arrangements might be possible."[69] Ralph Bunche and Mike Pearson were tasked with figuring this out, and they debated how this bold idea might be put into practice.

Interestingly, the idea for a multinational UN force was arguably Anthony Eden's as much as Pearson's. In the House of Commons the day before the General Assembly vote, Eden was aggressively challenged on the unfolding events in Suez. Members of the opposition shouted in an uproar; the chaotic session was actually suspended for thirty minutes due to the disorder. Upon resuming, Eden sought to calm the chamber. He stated that Britain did not seek to impose by force a solution to the dispute. Rather, the "first and urgent task" was to separate the combatants. "If the UN were then willing to take over the physical task of maintaining peace in that area, no one would be better pleased than we."[70] Eden's wish, perhaps thrown out in a moment of inspiration—or desperation—would soon come true.

―――――――――――

ON NOVEMBER 4, THE GENERAL ASSEMBLY took up the idea of a "truly international peace and police" force. In a second resolution, passed in another emergency session, it asked Dag Hammarskjold to submit "within 48 hours a plan for the setting up, with the consent of the nations concerned, of an emergency international United Nations Force to secure and supervise the cessation of hostilities."[71] Hammarskjold, who firmly believed that his office at times needed to lead and not just follow, and that his unique role at the center of the organization gave him some running room to do so, welcomed the opportunity, and he quickly called on Ralph Bunche to spearhead the effort to devise such a force. Bunche was at this time the most knowledgeable member of Hammarskjold's inner circle with regard to the Middle East. He had rare firsthand experience with both the Israelis and the Egyptians, and he knew, from hard labor, the difficulties of negotiations between the parties. Bunche also knew that Hammarskjold, perhaps reflecting the antipathy many Swedes felt after Bernadotte's assassination, was no great fan of the Israelis and probably wisely sought to keep himself out of the direct talks. He was, Bunche had written in his diary early after the two men met, "vitriolic" about Israeli Ambassador Abba Eban, bordering on the "vindicative." Hammarskjold, he wrote, "unquestionably feels very strongly against the Jews."[72]

Hammarskjold asked Bunche to draft cables to London, Paris, and Tel Aviv requesting an immediate ceasefire. Perhaps realizing how badly they had blundered, all parties accepted. The secretary general then appointed a three-man group to monitor the fragile ceasefire. The members were Bunche; Bunche's Soviet counterpart, Ilya Tchernychev, and Constantin Stavropoulos, the UN legal counsel. In the press, Bunche was now being called "Mr. Peace."[73] To Hammarskjold, he was instead the "Minister of Defense" or, occasionally Corporal Bunche. Indeed, after the General Assembly resolution on an emergency UN force to keep the peace had been adopted, Hammarskjold turned to him and said, "Now, Corporal, get me a force."[74]

As Bunche did so, the modern practice of UN peacekeeping was born. To be sure, the idea of collective military intervention to police a volatile international situation was not entirely new. Great powers had interceded in other territories before, often claiming their motivation was to create or enforce peace. They had even internationalized territory, such as the Moroccan city of Tangier in the 1920s, to manage multinational disputes over sovereignty and control. Closer in spirit to the General Assembly's notion for the Suez Crisis, the League of Nations had considered a multinational force to deal with the Polish-Lithuanian dispute over Vilna in 1923, "with contingents promised by eight member states."[75] In more recent history, the UN Truce Supervision Organization, stood up in Palestine in 1949, was still operational at the time of Suez and, indeed, remained operational as of 2022. But the Truce Supervision Organization was an unarmed force. Similarly, in 1949, the UN had placed a "Military Observer Group in India and Pakistan" as a way to keep a lid on the simmering conflict between the two South Asian nations over the mountainous regions of Jammu and Kashmir. Here, too, the multinational forces were unarmed and merely intended to observe and investigate violations of a ceasefire. (Like the UN's Palestine Truce Supervision Organization, the UN's Kashmir observer mission was also still operational as of 2022.)

The planned UN force in Egypt would be different from these predecessors. Its soldiers would be armed and entering a zone involving not just conflict between small powers but one also involving two great powers. This was a novel and meaningful step. It was also a "leap into the unknown."[76] This model of peacekeeping would over the coming decades become one of the most important endeavors of the UN. Peacekeeping would grow to huge proportions, often dwarfing, in budgetary terms, everything else the UN did. Indeed, by the early 1990s, over 75,000 UN peacekeepers were deployed in more than twenty distinct missions.[77]

Peacekeeping would prove to be one of the UN's most high-profile—and successful—activities. One recent review concluded that "the data overwhelmingly reveal that peacekeeping, especially UN peacekeeping, is surprisingly effective."[78] One study found that peacekeeping missions that deploy at least 1000 military personnel (the force in Egypt ultimately had 6000, and some later missions many more) can also limit the spread of conflict geographically.[79]

Of course, none of this was known at the time Bunche met a number of other neutral ambassadors in the early days of November 1956 to discuss how to provide troops expeditiously. Canada, Colombia, India, and Norway all agreed to contribute forces. Joining them were Sweden, Finland,

Pakistan, Romania, and a few others. To put it all together, Bunche worked around the clock. As one of his secretaries, Lydia Fayon, recalled: "he would keep nine or ten secretaries going full speed, full time. When one wore out, he'd have a fresh replacement sent in. But there was no replacement for Bunche. He'd come in at 9:30 in the morning. And he'd be at his desk until 3 or 4."[80] Yet there was one respect in which he had it easy: in a marked contrast to peacekeeping missions today, where the secretary general's team often has to cajole states to contribute soldiers and material, the world was eager to participate in this new peacekeeping concept. Bunche soon declared that "[t]his is the most popular army in history." It was, he said, "an army that everyone fights to get into."[81]

Called UNEF (the UN Emergency Force), by its high point in March 1957, Bunche's army was composed of soldiers from a diverse array of nations. Because UNEF would operate within Egyptian territory and was not authorized by a binding Security Council resolution, it required the consent of the Egyptian government to deploy. Ultimately, Egypt and the UN agreed to a wide-ranging set of rules governing criminal jurisdiction over the troops, their movements, and the use of the UN flag. These questions were largely new for the UN and required extensive negotiation. Done in a rush, some of the details, it would later become clear, would pose serious challenges.

AS ALL THE EVENTS WITH REGARD to Suez were ongoing, a parallel crisis was emerging hundreds of miles to the north. On November 4, in Hungary, an uprising of political resistance elicited a massive invasion by the Soviet Union. Hungary had been under the Soviet thumb since the end of the Second World War. Josef Stalin's death in 1953 had emboldened resistance throughout the Soviet sphere; the rebellion in Hungary was aimed at pushing out the Soviet-backed regime and restoring Hungarian political independence.

On November 1, the new premier of Hungary, Imre Nagy, declared Hungary to be a neutral state. The Soviets, acting swiftly to ensure that no member of the Warsaw Pact deviated from Moscow's orbit, demonstrated their power. The Red Army poured in; the BBC reported that at least 1000 tanks entered the capital, Budapest.[82] Thousands were killed in the ensuing fighting. Hammarskjold, in a private note to Henry Cabot Lodge, Jr., wrote: "this is one of the darkest days in postwar times."[83] By November 11, as the UN mission in Suez was being planned, Hungary's nascent rebellion was over.

The crushing of the rebellion in Hungary by Soviet tanks and the Anglo-French-Israeli invasion of Egypt were distinct events with distinct causes. But to many observers the two interventions, juxtaposed in an intense few days in the fall of 1956, "were basically the same—aggressions by big powers against smaller ones."[84] Even within the US government, comparisons of the two crises were immediately invoked. As Soviet troops massed on Hungary's border, national security officials met in Washington to consider a response. The Suez parallel was immediately raised. "How is this situation different from Egypt?" asked one Defense Department official. "There are many fundamental similarities," replied a State Department colleague. "We should certainly do no less to the communists than we have done to our allies," replied his colleague. "It would be very dramatic to put up a resolution to the Security Council this afternoon."[85]

The American officials debated the value of a UN resolution condemning the Soviets, and whether the General Assembly or the Security Council would prove a more useful a venue. In the end, neither chamber much mattered for the plight of the Hungarians. Stymied by the fear of a nuclear conflagration, the US could do nothing to stop the USSR from rolling into its Eastern European satellite. The real difference between Suez and Hungary was that an angry US, seeking to avoid alienating Egypt and the Arab world generally, could and did easily stop Britain and France from intervening in the region.

In some ways, the contemporaneous invasion of Hungary only encouraged a tougher stance vis-à-vis America's allies and their empires. And with the creation of the UN Emergency Force, the British and the French now had a face-saving way to exit. This UN-centric approach to defusing the crisis strongly appealed to the US. The Eisenhower administration was very concerned about the possibility that the Soviets would step in to assist Nasser.[86] Consequently, the US insisted Britain and France accept a UN ceasefire on November 6. (To add to the political mix, Eisenhower was also up for reelection that week.) In a phone call the next day, the president told Anthony Eden that he was committed to the UN plan—"and very definitely."[87]

The twin crises of 1956 showed the world—if it was not already clear—something important about the new postwar order. The superpowers really did control their respective spheres of influence, albeit in different ways.

Eisenhower took to American television to address the gathering storms half a world away. He criticized the Soviets for their brutal repression of the Hungarians. Yet he saved his strongest words for his erstwhile allies. The US "was not consulted in any way" about the invasion of Egypt, he said, and "we do not accept the use of force as a wise or proper instrument for the settlement of disputes." After endorsing the UN's role in the crisis, he noted that there "could be no peace without law."[88] Eisenhower's speech made clear that only one path was possible for Britain, France, and Israel. The UN Emergency Force that Bunche and his team were furiously constructing was the only option to clean up the mess.

Indeed, Suez became a defining moment not only for Bunche, but for the entire UN. Seeing the writing on the wall, even British Prime Minister Anthony Eden now professed his belief in the importance of the organization, declaring himself to be "a United Nations man."[89]

CHAPTER 15

CORPORAL BUNCHE

You are soldiers of peace in the first international force of its kind. You have come
from distant homelands, not to fight a war but to serve peace and justice and
order under the authority of the United Nations.

—Dag Hammarskjold, to the UN Emergency Force

in Egypt, December 1956[1]

Ralph Bunche observed the events of 1956 from a unique vantage point.
What made the United Nations a true break with the past in world politics
was that it was a standing global body that incorporated all the major powers
of the world. In one room—or at least one building—all the protagonists
could meet, even if only to posture and berate. With regard to Suez, of
course, much more would happen. The chastened French and British were
now pulling out their troops; the new UNEF was moving in. (It would take
until December to make the exchange complete.) From the vantage point
of Turtle Bay, this was, as Dag Hammarskjold told reporters at the time, "a
precedent which the United Nations needs."[2] The trickiest part of the tripartite intervention in Egypt, however—that of Israel—continued in the
Sinai Desert and Gaza Strip and would soon be a central item on Bunche's
desk.

As the planning for UNEF was underway in early November, delegates from many member states filed into Bunche's 38th floor office to lend assistance. Egypt had not yet consented to UNEF's deployment. "But since we've got a number of offers, some of them with troops standing by, why don't we move them as near to Egypt as possible?" Bunche suggested to Hammarskjold. "Perhaps somewhere in Southern Italy?"[3] The secretary general agreed with the idea, and soon the airlift to the Naples airport— paid for by the US—began.

To sort out the myriad details, the UN team worked around the clock, often till 4 or 5 a.m. Bunche, Hammarskjold, and Andrew Cordier, Hammarskjold's executive assistant, would sometimes head to an all-night diner on Lexington Avenue at the end of a very long work day. Eating hamburgers in the pre-dawn hours in suit and tie, surrounded by taxi drivers and night shift workers, they would occasionally sign autographs for those surprised to find the men who dominated the front pages of New York's newspapers in their midst.[4] As the multinational force assembled across the Mediterranean, the pressure on Egypt to accept the UNEF plan grew.

With Nasser's consent finally in hand, the first wave of UNEF troops, composed of Colombians, Danes, and Norwegians, arrived in Egypt on November 15. Bunche said at the time that he moved troops into Egypt fast because "we wanted to demonstrate as quickly as possible that there was going to be a United Nations force."[5] The UN had created joint observer forces before, including one in Palestine that Bunche was intimately familiar with. UNEF was different, however; it was more of a fighting force, or at least it looked like one. Hammarskjöld, for his part, described UNEF as "paramilitary in character and much more than an observers' corps," while at the same time stressing, with Egyptian sensitivities in mind, that it was to be "in no way a military force temporarily controlling the territory" in which it was stationed.[6]

THE QUESTION OF HOW AGGRESSIVE OR interventionist peacekeepers ought to be—in essence, how much fighting would or could be done if things went badly—would prove a complex and difficult issue for UN peacekeeping in the decades to come. Bunche and his team watched the rollout of UNEF with anticipation. The fundamental premise, as one observer put it, was that "nobody will shoot at the world."[7]

Still, UNEF's conceptual and legal basis remained murky, even behind closed doors. In a meeting of the newly formed Advisory Committee on UNEF, Hammarskjold, Bunche, Lester Pearson of Canada, and other UN ambassadors debated the nature of Egypt's agreement to UNEF. "Colloquially, I think you can say it is an agreement," Hammarksjold suggested. But "legally, Mr. Pearson is right that it is not." We are "drifting into metaphysics," Hammarksjold continued—a zone he often liked—but "it is necessary to be careful about words."[8] Pearson then made an even more metaphysical statement:

> This is not a United Nations force in the sense that we are setting up something agreed by the United Nations with an indefinite tenure and principles that have been accepted. That is quite right. This is something of an emergency nature for an ad hoc purpose. [Still] I feel that the composition of the force, even for this purpose, is the responsibility and power of the United Nations itself.[9]

There were also practicalities. The Americans insisted that no permanent members of the Security Council participate in UNEF. That was meant to keep out Britain and France, of course, but also the Soviets. Eisenhower told Eden specifically to stay out lest the USSR try to come in. "What I want to do is this," Eisenhower explained in a transatlantic call. "I would like to see none of the great nations in it. I am afraid that Red Boy is going to demand the lion's share. I would rather make it no troops from the Big Five."[10]

Bunche had actually met with Eisenhower at the White House a few days before, on Halloween 1956, as the British and French had just begun their attack. His White House visit was on an unrelated matter: the creation of the International Atomic Energy Agency (IAEA), which had just been voted on at the UN. The idea of the IAEA was largely Eisenhower's, so this was to be a moment of congratulation before the presidential election of 1956. At the White House, Bunche, with an eye toward the election, commented to the press that one of the sacrifices made when working at an international organization is to give up voting in elections. "This becomes a little painful every four years," he joked.[11] Whether Bunche and the president discussed the rapidly unfolding crisis in Suez is unclear. But soon enough the new UN atomic energy agency was old news, and now, just a couple of weeks later, Bunche was consumed by the process of establishing the new peacekeeping force. Eisenhower, with the election safely behind him and furious at his Western allies, was busy directing American policy and showing the Europeans who really was the boss.

Bunche and his team worked feverishly in November, "unaware of what peacekeeping would involve, improvising as they went along, making mistakes."[12] Logistical obstacles had to be overcome, some prosaic, some not. Many states were happy to contribute troops to the mission, but they simply lacked the ability to get them to Egypt. As would prove true with many future peacekeeping deployments, major powers, in this case the US military with its massive logistical abilities, proved essential for the airlift. The UNEF forces needed to be transported, fed, housed, and trained for their unusual mission. To Bunche's surprise, many units insisted on bringing their jeeps and trucks. As he explained at the time, it is one thing to arrange for troop transport; it was "another thing to transport their vehicles.... they would leave their wives but they would never want to leave their jeeps."[13]

On November 14, Hammarskjold spoke to reporters at Idlewild Airport as he was departing for the region. This new force "is the first experience of its kind," he said. As the first truly international force, "let us hope it will succeed."[14] Political sensitivities about the participation of specific states were endemic. A number of NATO nations were involved, and to effect some balance, Yugoslavia and Indonesia were added. Hammarskjold and Bunche had to carefully manage the expectations and egos of disparate nations. As soon as Bunche had secured a military band from Pakistan, for instance (he was a fan of military bands), the Pakistani prime minister criticized Egypt publicly. In response, Nasser refused to let any Pakistanis participate in UNEF, but also dinged Brazil's forces to make it seem less obvious. "The less said about this the better," said Bunche to a colleague.[15]

Bunche was a blur of activity that fall. By November 21, he had nearly 800 peacekeepers in Egypt and almost 400 more in Naples readying to deploy. The choice of who to bring in was as important as where to situate them, and, in some cases, the specific deployments (Port Said; Port Fuad) were agreed to by the British and French.[16] "Provisionally," Hammarskjold told the press in late November, "our target is two combat brigades."[17]

What was important and proved rare in the future of peacekeeping was that—perhaps because of the novelty of the new peacekeeping force, or perhaps because of the general enthusiasm many states had for the UN in the early years—so many nations were excited to participate. "We couldn't even use half" of what had been offered, Bunche would later say.[18] As a result, he had to explain to disappointed nations why their troops were not going to participate. Egypt let Bunche know that it was being pressed by Czechoslovakia about why their troops were not selected for deployment.[19] To Czechoslovakia, however, Egypt claimed it had no control over the composition of UNEF, only that it was advised of proposals as a "matter of courtesy."

Bunche also coordinated operational matters, such as whether the UNEF forces should fly their national flags or the UN flag. Foreign flags had great resonance in a formerly colonized nation like Egypt, which was highly attuned to signs of outside interference. These decisions on insignia proved influential in the years to come. Bunche felt only the UN flag should be flown at UNEF installations.[20] At a meeting in Hammarskjold's office in early December, he explained his view. "I see no reason for the display of national flags," he said, because the troops were in Egypt only as part of the UN effort.[21] At a later meeting, he hammered more strongly on the flag point, after the Indian ambassador suggested that national flags be permitted on occasion. To Bunche this was a grave mistake. Egypt had consented not to national contingents, he explained, but to a multilateral UN force. "I, frankly, cannot understand why there should be any need for any national contingent to fly its national flag rather than the UN flag in Egypt."[22]

In a similar vein, he also believed UN berets and helmets were essential and that all UNEF vehicles needed to be white with UN markings. General E. L. M. Burns, a Canadian who had been appointed UNEF force commander, pushed back on this last idea. Is there any special reason, Burns inquired of Bunche, why ordinary UNEF vehicles should be painted all white, which is going to mean a "good deal of expense and delay?"[23] Burns

Photo 15.1 UNEF troops at airfield

had a point: it was faster, easier, and cheaper to just leave the jeeps as is and simply place a UN badge on the side door. Bunche's view, perhaps forged in Palestine while flying around in Folke Bernadotte's white plane, was that the UNEF troops had be *seen* as something new, neutral, different, and distinctive, not just a congeries of different national armies. To do that, they had to look cohesive and non-national.

Uniforms posed unique problems. Many national militaries had British-style uniforms. These were immediately seen as a problem because, as Bunche quipped at the time, the British "lack some popularity in that particular area."[24] While armbands and other UN insignia helped, it was not clear they were visible at a distance. After extensive efforts to obtain UN blue berets, his team finally decided to use plastic helmet liners.* These liners were not really meant to provide protection; but once they were obtained from a US supply depot in Italy, and sprayed light blue, they did the trick. The uniforms, jeeps, and flag issues could appear minor, but they were also major: they went to the heart of *what* exactly UNEF was.

An especially thorny challenge was how to navigate the long-standing conflict between Egypt and Israel. As the designated hitter of the UN Secretariat in Middle East matters, Bunche was tasked with meeting with Egyptian and Israeli leaders. Abba Eban, the Israeli ambassador to the UN, had known Bunche for years. Israel was a critical player not only because its invasion was the ostensible trigger for the Suez Crisis, but also because it had been in an almost constant state of conflict and tension with Egypt since its birth some eight years before. Egypt had attacked Israel in the wake of Israel's declaration of independence in 1948, and the enmity between the two had not abated. The Suez Crisis continued the pattern of struggle. Bunche told Eban that "the real importance of UNEF is that it does buy valuable time. It is not in itself a political instrument, but it does purchase time in which political developments can take place" in the broader conflict.[25]

When viewed from the vantage point of today, Israel's involvement in the Suez Crisis, though significant at the time, was simply one of many stages in the long struggle with Egypt and its other Arab neighbors. It would take until 1979 for Israel and Egypt to ultimately sign a peace treaty, after President Jimmy Carter brokered the Camp David Accords.

The historical implications for Britain and France were far more significant. The Suez Crisis in many ways dramatically accelerated the end of the imperial age. The Europeans' attempt to flex their muscle against Nasser had backfired, making them look weak and antagonizing the Americans and much of the rest of the world. Suez demonstrated that Britain and France cast just a shadow of their past might and influence. It was particularly

---

* Bunche was later pressed on whether berets should be worn at all times. As one cable from the field argued, "if the full symbolic value of UN berets and helmets is to be gained," the UNEF commanders had to determine the military dress of all contingents. The practice of mission armbands and the like dated back to the League of Nations, but Bunche took it significantly further.

humiliating for Britain. The crisis not only put great strain on the previously strong US-UK political relationship; it also set off a disastrous run on the British pound, with grave implications for the British economy. As the historians of empire William Roger Louis and Ronald Robinson describe, Suez was meant to be a show of British power. Instead, it exposed its fundamental weakness. Soon the sterling reserves were running low, and, as Louis and Robinson argued, Britain was facing a new and unpleasant reality: "either to float the pound—a 'catastrophe affecting not merely the cost of living but also ... all our external economic relations'; or to ask for massive American aid."[26] Only after Eden had agreed to leave Egypt did Eisenhower come to the rescue, authorizing aid from the International Monetary Fund. Suez has been called "Britain's last fling of the imperial dice"—and Britain crapped out.[27] Indeed, in less than a decade Lord Henderson, assessing the impact of Suez, declared that, in an astonishing turnabout from its peak a half-century earlier, "the British Empire now belongs to history."[28]

With British and French troops withdrawing as UNEF forces flowed in during the fall of 1956, the immediate dimensions of the crisis abated. (Domestically, it continued to reverberate a little longer: the debacle brought down Anthony Eden, who resigned in January 1957.) As of December 18, about 4000 UNEF troops had been deployed and, as Bunche reported to Hammarskjold, happily there were no casualties at all.[29] The UN's peacekeeping effort was generally applauded, though some European observers doubted it would work. But Europe's importance to the resolution of the crisis in Suez was rapidly diminishing.

THE THORNIEST REMAINING ISSUES CONCERNED THE Gaza Strip and Sinai. While Egypt permitted UNEF troops to move into the Sinai peninsula, Israel did not want UNEF to be stationed in Gaza—a thin strip of contested land along the sea, running up to the Egyptian border, and still today a site of often-intense conflict.

Even before the United Nations forces arrived in the region, David Ben-Gurion, the Israeli prime minister, had told the Israeli Knesset that the armistice lines between Israel and Egypt that Bunche had negotiated years earlier in Rhodes had no continuing validity. Moreover, Ben-Gurion declared, on no condition would Israel agree to the stationing of a foreign force, "no matter how called, in her territory, or in any of the areas occupied by her."[30] Israel's repudiation of the armistice accords was upsetting for Bunche but not shocking—he had seen the boldness the Israelis had shown before. Indeed, Israel opposed aspects of UNEF from the beginning.

In a meeting on November 28, Bunche, Dag Hammarskjold, and the UN's legal advisor, Constantine Stavropoulos, met with Abba Eban, Israel's representative. Together they discussed how the withdrawal of Israeli troops would proceed. Eban also wanted to discuss Israeli access to the sea, in particular via the Gulf of Aqaba and the Straits of Tiran. With the Canal still impassable, this passage was a lifeline for Israel. Could the UNEF forces secure the key islands around the strait, Eban asked? Bunche replied that they could.[31] Eban then asked a critical question: how long would UNEF be there? Hammarskjold was careful. He could not be definite, he told Eban. But he felt with a winter and a summer ahead, a "military balance of power" of some form could be worked out. One of Eban's assistants pushed: did that mean six months? Hammarskjold demurred and said there was—had to be—some "deliberate vagueness." He added that Nasser had asked him the same question. The conversation continued, at times a bit tense, around the various contingencies and scenarios that could ensue. Bunche, with some prescience—and perhaps with the experience of Count Bernadotte's assassination in mind—expressed concern that the UN insignia was coming to be regarded in Israel "as an enemy symbol."[32]

The ground troop movements were tricky to coordinate. To try to sort out a solution, as 1956 drew to a close, the UNEF commander E. L. M. Burns met with his Israeli counterpart, the eye-patch-wearing Moshe Dayan. Bunche had negotiated with Dayan at Rhodes and knew he was tough. In the wake of the meeting, Dayan and Israel agreed to retreat from the Sinai and Gaza, but they did so in stages, slowly, and only under intensifying pressure. Burns complained to Bunche that there was a "gulf between what Eban promises and what Dayan does."[33] Bunche agreed. The General Assembly chastised Israel over its foot-dragging behavior, passing a resolution in early February 1957 deploring Israel's failure to withdraw behind the Armistice lines.

Even the US began to bring its weight to bear on Israel. President Eisenhower, in a televised address that same month, pointedly asked whether "a nation which attacks and occupies foreign territory in the face of United Nations disapproval [should] be allowed to impose conditions on its own withdrawal."[34] In New York, Henry Cabot Lodge, Jr., the American ambassador to the UN, met with Bunche to discuss the situation. In a cable to the State Department, Lodge recommended that a high-level effort be made to persuade the Israelis that "they are going against their own best interests." The Israeli attitude, Lodge argued, was "dangerous to world peace, to the UN and to the US."[35] Under increasing American censure, the Israelis eventually relented and began to withdraw from Gaza faster.

A key question still remained. Who would actually govern the narrow seaside territory once the Israelis left? In the General Assembly Pearson, who later received much of the praise for the initial concept of UNEF (in the form of a Nobel Peace Prize), suggested that the UN should take over Gaza. The UN should accept responsibility, he argued, "to the maximum possible extent for establishing and maintaining effective civil administration; in fostering economic development and social welfare; in maintaining law and order."[36] This had not been the original vision for UNEF. Yet it arguably followed from the need to secure peace in a complex situation. The result was a significant evolution: not only was UNEF pioneering a new form of peacekeeping; it was also veering toward peace-building and even governing—something the UN would take on in earnest in later decades, as in East Timor in the 1990s. But in the 1950s this function was wholly new.

The proposal to internationalize Gaza was highly unpopular in Egypt. UN officials on the ground told Bunche that Egypt would never allow UNEF to become an "occupation force" on soil Egypt considered its own. If UNEF "cannot compel the Israelis to withdraw it might well be asked to leave and Arabs should take matters into their own hands."[37] These threats underscored a fundamental weakness of UNEF: absent the consent of the state whose territory the troops were on, the mission could not, as a matter of international law, continue. This would become glaringly clear a decade later when Nasser would withdraw his consent to some of the UNEF troops, helping to trigger, or at least make way for, the 1967 Six-Day War.

On March 1, 1957, Prime Minister Golda Meier announced Israel would fully withdraw from Gaza. As the Israeli forces retreated, UNEF troops moved in. The UNEF commander declared a few days later that, until further notice, "UNEF had assumed responsibility for civil affairs" in Gaza.[38] UNEF would act as the governing body, and the UN Relief and Works Agency, which had been created in 1949 to address the problem of Palestinian refugees in the region, would continue to provide food and other humanitarian goods. At the UN building, the UNEF advisory committee debated what it all meant. Pearson argued that UN rule in Gaza was not a problem. "Since when have the people of Gaza governed themselves?" he asked. Moreover, he argued to Arthur Lall, India's representative on the committee, the UN "is not an imperialist power." I know, replied Lall, but it "musn't become one."[39]

Hammarskjold and Bunche were apprehensive. UNEF itself was brand new and untested. And now the problem of Gaza had forced UNEF to expand its ambit into new tasks. Could it handle them? UNEF's governing role was a new twist, but all of the operation was at this point largely improvisation. To make it all work, Hammarskjold decided he had to have a trusted man on the ground. Ralph Bunche booked a plane for Egypt.

———

BUNCHE HAD HAPPILY LEFT THE MIDDLE EAST behind after his successful mediation. Palestine was a trap, he had felt, a place that had quicksand-like qualities and only grew more perplexing and frustrating the more time he spent there. In the intervening years, he was busy with other agendas, especially trusteeship, and while the Middle East consumed the young United Nations from the very beginning, it was not yet the endless source of strife that it would later become for the international community. The process of "liquidating African colonialism" was a critical one for the UN, he had told reporters at the start of 1956, and the job of the UN was "to show these people that their aspirations can be realized in a reasonable amount of time without resort to violence."[40] Now, with the Suez Crisis underway and violence looming, Bunche's hard-earned Middle East experience was essential to making that point stick.

Bunche's experience was especially important because Hammarskjold had spent little time in the region. To be sure, the secretary general had already proven himself to be a very skilled diplomat. Just a few months before Bunche left for Gaza, John Foster Dulles had conveyed to Bunche his great admiration for Hammarskjold's handling of Suez. As Bunche wrote in a letter to Hammarskjold, Dulles

> wished your attention drawn to the statement concerning you which Mr. Dulles made in his press conference yesterday (Tuesday); he referred to this three times ... he and many others in Washington are amazed at the persistence, stamina and dedication you have demonstrated, especially in the past few months. Dulles added that he knows something about "hard work" but that you break all records.[41]

Despite these accolades, Hammarskjold was in unfamiliar terrain with the Suez Crisis, and he leaned heavily on Bunche. Bunche felt confident in advance of the trip. As he packed his suitcase at their home in Queens, he soothingly told Ruth that "there's no need to worry this time. The war's over."[42]

Events on the ground seemed to be supporting this view. UNEF's entry into Gaza had occurred on March 6, as the Israelis finally withdrew. Things went smoothly at first; there was, as one analyst later wrote, "no vacuum of authority and hence no murdering or looting." The rioting "came later."[43]

En route to Egypt, Bunche stopped off in Accra, Ghana, for a more joyful event. The former British colony of the Gold Coast was celebrating its independence. The stop was ceremonial but significant. Ghana was one of the first African states to attain autonomy from its European rulers—Sudan had achieved independence the year before—but soon a flood of newly independent nations would join the international community. Indeed, in 1960, which Bunche would later dub "the year of Africa," seventeen new African states gained independence in a single stunning year.

Bunche's 1957 trip to Ghana and Gaza occurred at a pivotal point in the history of colonialism. The intervention in Suez would be widely seen as the last gasp of the imperial age: a disaster for the traditional European powers and their colonial agenda. Ultimately, the only real winners from the crisis were Nasser and perhaps the UN itself, which gained credibility for its creative problem solving. The year 1957 also ushered in the first of many transitions to independence for African colonies, a process that would soon yield over fifty new states across the continent and many more outside it. Some of the new states, however, proved to be troubled and conflict-prone, sometimes right from the outset. Governed along territorial lines drawn up in European capitals, they often comprised disparate ethnic and religious groups and had only a weak national identity. European rulers sometimes repressed what little cohesive identity there was. The combination practically invited conflict over the reins of power. Bunche would discover this up close in Congo in just a few years. Yet the independence process, while at times chaotic, was also inspirational, liberatory, and often joyous. Bunche would later say that, as with America itself, nations are never really prepared for independence.[44]

At Ghana's independence ceremonies, he saw many old friends from his former academic life in London and elsewhere. Prime Minister Kwame Nkrumah had invited several prominent American Black leaders to attend the ceremonies, including Dr. Martin Luther King Jr. and Congressman Adam Clayton Powell of Harlem. (Indeed, many of them shared the same Pan-Am flight to Africa with Bunche.) Even Bunche's old boss and nemesis from Howard, Mordecai Johnson, was there. Vice President Nixon, seated well behind Bunche at the ceremony, as if to underscore the repudiation of the West, officially represented the US government.

Bunche found the independence ceremonies remarkable and the new Ghanaian government impressive. "British democratic tradition at its very best here," he wrote in a note.[45] The parliament chamber was packed; delegates were literally sitting in each other's laps. The atmosphere was festive, and as midnight approached—the official moment of independence—"everyone, including the Prime Minister, had his attention riveted on the time." Nkrumah announced his attention to apply immediately for membership in the UN. Soon Nkrumah was hoisted over the heads of the members of the new parliament and carried out and across the street to the old polo grounds, where a throng—Bunche estimated 100,000—was "festive, gay, but not in the least unruly."[46] It was exactly the sort of independence he wanted to see: orderly, peaceful, and positive.

Bunche's PhD research on colonial governance had taken place not far from where he now stood, in what was then called Togoland and Dahomey. At the time, he had wondered what would become of the region and its people. The countryside was beautiful and bounteous, but the populace was poor, not well educated, and to Bunche in the 1930s, seemed perhaps not quite prepared for the strictures and competition of the modern world. Now, some two decades later, much had changed. Ghana was the pacesetter in a dramatic shift that would take virtually an entire continent from under the yoke of Europe and liberate it. Bunche's career at the UN had been forged around building a path to freedom for those societies suffering under foreign rule. It was with great excitement that he witnessed the flourishing of a widely held dream that day in Ghana in 1957.

Being among so many Black luminaries to mark the occasion of an African colony's freedom was also a very special experience. Bunche had only one year before sent what was probably the first correspondence between Martin Luther King and himself. In a telegram to King sent in February 1956, Bunche wrote: "I greet you as a fellow American and a fellow Negro." He applauded King and his work in the Deep South, saying he was acting in "the spirit of the finest American tradition and in the best interests of our country." He concluded by telling King that right was on his side and that "all the world knows it."[47] He and King met in person a few months later, when Bunche glowingly introduced the rising civil rights leader at an NAACP conference. He clearly admired King's bold new approach and the youthful energy he brought to the civil rights movement, contrasting it favorably with the older, church-based model of the South.[48]

Bunche and King continued to communicate that year; shortly after King's Montgomery bus boycott was upheld in the US Supreme Court in November 1956, during the very heart of the Suez Crisis, Bunche found a few minutes to again write to King. King, who saw Gandhi and his campaign of satyagraha as an inspiration, had earlier in the year asked Bunche for assistance in encouraging India's ambassador to the UN, Krishna Menon, to participate in King's Institute on Nonviolence and Social Change. Menon was a vociferous voice against colonialism and an outspoken critic of the West; Dwight Eisenhower called him "a menace" and a "master international manipulator."[49][†] Bunche told King that he had twice spoken to Menon and urged him to attend King's institute. He then added a more personal postscript: "What a *victory* you have had in the Supreme Court's full vindication of your fight for dignity! R——." Krishna Menon never attended King's institute, though perhaps because, like Bunche, he was totally consumed with Suez. As part of the emerging bloc of decolonized states, India saw itself as sharing common ground with Egypt, and Menon had sought to devise a plan, never implemented, to solve the crisis.

Now, King and Bunche were united in Accra. King later gave a famous sermon at the Dexter Avenue Baptist Church based on his trip to Ghana. In the sermon, he described the joyful scene he witnessed:

> And oh, it was a beautiful experience to see some of the leading persons on the scene of civil rights in America on hand to say, "Greetings to you," as this new nation was born. Look over, to my right is Adam Powell, to my left is Charles Diggs, to my right again is Ralph Bunche.

In his sermon, King related the event to his congregation, noting how Nkrumah and the other new leaders of Ghana, instead of wearing ceremonial robes to mark the day of independence, wore their prison caps to starkly symbolize how far they had traveled. (Nkrumah had in fact won the election from jail.) Whether King knew Bunche was en route to Egypt when they met in Ghana is unclear. Yet King in his sermon connected the independence celebration to Egypt—only in biblical terms:

> After Nkrumah had made that final speech, it was about twelve-thirty now. And we walked away. And we could hear little children six years old and old people

[†] Menon was a legendary and indefatigable speaker who once collapsed while speaking at the Security Council table, only to be revived later and to go on to speak for another hour. Menon holds the record for the longest speech at the UN—eight hours over multiple meetings.

eighty and ninety years old walking the streets of Accra crying: "Freedom! Freedom! . . . And everywhere we turned, we could hear it ringing out from the housetops. We could hear it from every corner, every nook and crook of the community. "Freedom! Freedom!" This was the birth of a new nation. This was the breaking loose from Egypt.[50]

The ties between the civil rights movement in America and the fight to end empire may have frayed from the heady years of the 1930s and 1940s. Yet the independence ceremonies in Ghana in 1957 illustrated that the connections were still there. Bunche had left much of his domestic focus behind when he entered the federal government at the dawn of the Second World War. But he continued to be an active participant in and frequent speaker to civil rights organizations and, as King's prominence grew and the centennial of the Emancipation Proclamation approached, Bunche gradually became more engaged in the rising protest movement King led. Eventually, he would appear with King in the March on Washington and in Selma, where they walked arm in arm to Montgomery.

Bunche and King represented different generations in Accra that day in 1957: King was in his twenties, Bunche in his fifties. They came out of different traditions: one a preacher, one a professor. Yet each saw much to admire in the other, and King sought Bunche's imprimatur just as Bunche sought King's. Bunche had a unique position and prestige in midcentury America. Indeed, when Nkrumah visited Harlem two years later, it was Bunche who gave the welcome, referring to the people of Ghana as "brothers of the skin and beneath the skin." (He was booed by some members of the audience, who in turn earned a rebuke from Thurgood Marshall, castigating their "racial chauvinism." "Nationalists Rapped for Booing Bunche" ran the headline in the New York Amsterdam News.)[51] By the mid-1960s, King was the tribune of an entire generation, some of whom only dimly knew who Bunche was and what he had accomplished. Though Bunche and King would occasionally disagree in the coming years, they had significant common interests and goals.

For both Ralph Bunche and Martin Luther King Jr. the prospect of a liberated Africa was a source of racial pride, but also one of inspiration for America itself. In Accra, at a reception following the independence ceremonies, King spoke with Vice President Richard Nixon. Forcing the Vice President to see the parallels—and feel how the wind was blowing—King pointedly told him, "I want you to come visit us down in Alabama where we are seeking the same kind of freedom the Gold Coast is celebrating."[52]

CHAPTER 16

TO GAZA

Ralph Bunche left the festive and positive air of Ghana's independence ceremonies and headed northeast across the African continent. His destination was a far more fraught and tense place: Gaza. As Bunche flew toward the vortex of the Suez Crisis in March 1957, Secretary General Dag Hammarskjold cabled with instructions for his delicate mission. The United Nations Emergency Force (UNEF) was established and, thanks to Bunche's hard work, was growing. Yet the peacekeeping force, a creative solution to a difficult situation, had an uncertain legal basis. Peacekeeping was nowhere mentioned in the UN Charter, and it had an unusual political genesis. The secretary general counseled Bunche that, as a result, the two UN leaders had to risk taking responsibility for "solutions and arrangements with undefined background and for that reason open to challenge although, of course, tacitly so developed as to be consistent with our basic stand."[1]

Hammarskjold was not always the clearest writer, but he was making a significant point here. UNEF was novel and, as he suggested, arguably at the outer edges of legality and political legitimacy for the UN. As a result, it had to be handled flexibly and carefully. There were risks. Still, the alternatives seemed far worse, and with the Eisenhower administration forcefully arguing that a UN solution was the only solution, Hammarskjold and Bunche had substantial political backing for the concept of a major multinational peacekeeping force.

Meanwhile, the British and the French seemed to have acquiesced to the inevitable. Having been beaten—even humiliated—by their own ally, they accepted fate and sought to exit the scene of the crime. The problem now was keeping the Israelis and the Egyptians from renewing battle.

After stops first in Italy and then in Cairo, on March 11 Bunche landed in Gaza. A narrow strip of land with a long west-facing coast, Gaza was shaping up to be the most complex and contested piece of land in the region. Stepping off his UN plane nattily dressed in a double-breasted suit and fedora, Bunche was greeted by UNEF military police in uniform. Protests in Gaza had just erupted before his arrival. An unruly crowd had tried to take down the UN flag and replace it with the Egyptian flag. UNEF's commander, in a cable to New York, described the gathering as "between two and three hundred." The "theme," the UNEF officer opined, "was cheering [Gamal Abdel] Nasser and demanding return of Egyptians to Gaza Strip."[2] The protestors rushed the gates of the UNEF headquarters, which were guarded by a small number of military police. Uncertain of their authority, the UNEF guards had lobbed tear gas to disperse the restive crowd. When that failed, they fired warning shots in the air—one of which, ricocheting, struck and killed a bystander. UNEF was at first unaware of this casualty, reporting that the situation was "well in hand" by Bunche's arrival.

The killing of a local Gazan threatened to explode an already precarious situation. Concerned by what he was hearing, Bunche hurried to tell Nasser personally of the death, assuring him that the incident was wholly accidental and that "every possible precaution" would be taken in the future to avoid similar tragedies. The situation in Gaza remained volatile, however, and Bunche worried about igniting further violence. Back in New York, Dag Hammarskjold was meeting with US Ambassador Henry Cabot

Lodge when Bunche sent a message, saying, as Lodge later cabled the State Department with some understatement, that "he believed [the] Gaza situation required reappraisal."[3]

Bunche in fact was quite uneasy, and he offered Hammarskjold a number of factors to consider with regard to Gaza. He feared the Arab population there could "easily get out of control."[4] The uncertainty as to who ultimately would govern the narrow strip was feeding the unrest. More troubling to Bunche, he saw the "beginning of anti-UN, anti-UNEF" feeling, "born of suspicion of UN intentions in Gaza." UNEF would likely need to use force in self-defense again, he told Hammarskjold, with "certain emotional reaction and outcry against UNEF." Bunche's political judgment was that some Egyptian governing authority was required to calm the situation. He knew that symbols carried great weight in the region, so some form of symbolic control might be as important as actual control. But whatever path was taken, a more precise delineation of the respective roles of the UN and Egypt in Gaza was essential. In the meantime he suggested that the local mayor, who had been imprisoned by the Israelis, be restored to authority as soon as possible.

Bunche then returned to Cairo to meet again with Nasser. He thought Nasser, despite his success seizing Suez, exuded insecurity in their talks. The Egyptian leader was suspicious and focused on politics throughout the parley. Speaking to reporters after the ninety-minute meeting, Bunche declared that the UN had "no intention to internationalize the Gaza Strip."[5] He was trying to say the right things—perhaps recalling how the proposal to internationalize Jerusalem had led to Folke Bernadotte's assassination a decade earlier—but in fact Bunche did not and could not know how the volatile situation would unfold.

In an effort to reassert authority over the territory, Nasser appointed Egyptian General Abdel Latif as governor of Gaza. Bunche agreed to this appointment, thinking it would help lower the political temperature. Yet it may have done the opposite. To make sure no one missed his arrival, General Latif entered Gaza accompanied by 150 military police in red hats and "armed with tommy guns."[6] While Gazans witnessed this overt display of power, Israeli Prime Minister Golda Meir was in Washington, complaining to John Foster Dulles about the Egyptians'—and the UN's—malfeasance. As the official State Department records from March 1957 report,

> The Israelis were perturbed because it was a question of hours between the Israel withdrawal and Egypt's practically taking over. Not only had an Egyptian General come in as Governor of Gaza, but he had brought a staff with him. On whose authority had he come into Gaza?[7]

Bunche was irritated by Israeli insinuations that he was somehow favoring Egypt. Meanwhile at the UN, the Israeli ambassador complained of "marauders" and "infiltrators" entering Israel from Gaza.[8]

The situation was cartoonish but familiar. Bunche was back in the maelstrom of the Middle East, in turn denounced by the Israelis for enabling the Egyptians and by the Egyptians for reviving colonialism via the UNEF troops. It was, he said, "like a bad dream returning to haunt one."[9]

THANKFULLY, GAZA GREW CALMER IN THE following weeks. The world seemed to take notice of the success; the March 23, 1957 cover of the *New Yorker* magazine featured a large image of the United Nations emblem surrounded by pairs of hand-drawn individuals in stylized outfits from all over the world. UNEF's focus began to shift to the more prosaic day-to-day issues of governing the territory. UN officials were soon forced to act like ordinary political leaders. They announced, for example, that UNEF had "come to the aid of Gaza citrus growers" by purchasing two tons a day of first-grade grapefruit and double that of oranges.[10] Bunche, raised in Southern California in its orange-growing heyday, likely enjoyed some of this citrus bounty, yet the mission creep it entailed was troubling.

Bunche's tasks gradually shifted from political damage control to inspecting the now-large UNEF forces and managing the myriad minor governance problems plaguing the area. His tireless efforts in Egypt were widely covered even as the tasks grew more mundane; "Bunche Still in Gaza" ran one unexciting *New York Times* headline.[11] He cabled Hammarskjold that their efforts were having some effect, though with some prescience he noted that ultimately, the Egyptians could readily assert more power and he—and UNEF—could do nothing about it. Still, things seemed headed in a good direction. In Gaza, he reported, people thronged the streets celebrating the Egyptian return, but were "not boisterously demonstrative." When some chanted "UNEF must go," the Egyptian leaders speaking told the crowd that UNEF was present "as our guests."[12]

Growing Egyptian support for UNEF in the spring of 1957 was in a sense not surprising. Egypt benefited immensely from UNEF since, as Bunche well knew, they could not in fact defend Gaza against the more powerful Israeli forces on the other side of the line. UNEF nicely provided an uncrossable buffer. It froze the conflict rather than ended it. But for the moment the conflict between the two antagonists was more political than military. Arab shepherds occasionally followed their flocks across the line of demarcation, and Israelis occasionally shot at them, but no casualties had yet been recorded. By March 19, Bunche could tell Hammarskjold that "Gaza is completely peaceful. . . . There are no demonstrations, no Egyptian troops, no inciting against Israel of which UNEF is aware."[13]

Meanwhile, to the south, the Egyptians continued to refuse Israeli ships access to the Suez Canal. The point was largely moot for the time being—the Canal still was being cleared of submerged and wrecked vessels which had been scuttled in response to the British, Israeli, and French invasion—but the basic issue was indicative of the bitter enmity between the two nations.

By early April 1957, Bunche was back in New York. Reflecting on his trip to the Middle East, he naturally thought of what progress had been made since his time on the island of Rhodes. He wrote in his diary that he sadly saw little change on a critical fundamental: "there can be no peace or real progress toward peace in the Near East until the problem of the Arab refugees is solved. The world evades that one."[14] The vexing challenge of Palestinian refugees had consumed Bernadotte when he was mediator; unfortunately, the problem would continue, in one form or another, to consume the region for decades. Back on the 38th floor, Bunche reported his observations to Hammarskjold. Gaza remained quiet and the UNEF troops, whom the locals, referring to their helmets, now called "Bluebells," were "very popular."[15] He described often seeing Indian or Swedish soldiers surrounded by

Photo 16.1 Bunche and Hammarskjold tour the Suez Canal

children asking questions about their homeland and seeking treats. Goats and sheep were occasionally detonating mines, but the damage was minimal. Bedouins had learned to deactivate them, and Bunche reported that there was now a traffic in plastic tops taken off the mines, sold as souvenirs for ash trays.

In May 1957, he again returned to the Middle East. The Suez Crisis as a great power crisis was effectively over; Britain and France may have been stung by defeat, but soon Britain at least was moving on and accepting the new reality, having made nice with Eisenhower in a Bermuda summit that spring aimed at restoring the "special relationship."[16] But not surprisingly, the Middle East dimensions of the crisis were more resilient. Before Hammarskjold joined him in the region, Bunche gave a warning. "Your road here will not be inviting. Though I believe much of the road is still open though most suspiciously and grudgingly so."[17]

The two men soon flew to Israel. Bunche had come to enjoy the austere beauty and ancient sense of place in the Middle East, even as the politics endlessly bedeviled him. Jerusalem in particular remained a sort of time portal to an ancient past, and one early morning with Hammarskjold, a religious and spiritual man, the two gazed over the walls and spires of the Old City. The Bible, they both agreed, gave an inaccurate impression of the Holy Land's geography.

Meeting with Israeli leader David Ben-Gurion, they debated the wisdom of UNEF, the legacy of Bunche's now nine-year-old armistice process, and especially the future of Gaza. Ben-Gurion sought to put a Cold War spin on the recent events, arguing that Israel's recent actions in the Sinai were responsible for "saving the Near East from Soviet domination."[18] To Bunche, who found this a stretch, Ben-Gurion seemed to have aged greatly and to be losing his grip. "The old man," he wrote in his diary, "has deteriorated to an unbelievable degree. . . . I fear he actually believes the false version of history he recites."[19] To his surprise, Bunche found the Israelis now even more prone to self-delusion than their Egyptian counterparts. The Israelis continued to be angry that Egypt was nominally governing Gaza. Hammarskjold reminded them that Bunche's negotiations had guaranteed that; the Armistice accords set up the lines of control and Gaza was Egypt's right under the agreement.

The Israelis had always trusted and liked Bunche, a feeling that the occasionally tense discussions that May in Jerusalem did not change. At one point Ben-Gurion put his hand on Bunche's shoulder and told him that he still thought he was "a good person." Later, at a reception at Ben-Gurion's house, his wife jokingly asked Bunche why he had "once been so nice and then changed." He replied that he had not changed at all. Israeli Foreign Minister Golda Meir, overhearing the exchange, piped up: "that's putting it bluntly, isnt it?"[20] Ben-Gurion then shocked Bunche by suggesting that Folke Bernadotte had been in some way responsible for his own death. Ben-Gurion at first simply expressed regret about Bernadotte's death. But then his face hardened, and, in a stern voice, he said: "but remember what Count Bernadotte did to us." Bunche, incredulous, asked Ben-Gurion to repeat what he just said. Asking if Ben-Gurion meant Bernadotte's report and proposals for Jerusalem, Ben-Gurion simply said, "Yes."[21]

Bunche was stunned by this exchange. Nonetheless, the atmosphere, despite this very tense moment, was generally "very friendly" with surprisingly little argument or recrimination. "Even Golda," he remarked, whom he and Hammarskjold sometimes referred to as "Old Gold," seemed relaxed and cordial.[22] The conversations were more restrained than their talks in Cairo with the Egyptians, but he feared more conflict was on the horizon. Thinking about the situation in the Middle East, he inevitably compared it to his first forays a decade earlier. "This is a 'jubilee year' for the UN on the Palestine question—it was ten years ago that the UN first became embroiled in this hot issue."[23] While the UN's initial foray into Palestine was an early and crucial test for the organization, and a laboratory for the very notion of multilateral mediation and peace-building, the UN was now unequivocally a major player in the region and a preferred tool of many states in dealing with the complexity of the Arab-Israeli conflict. Yet the situation was in some respects more difficult than ever before.

Back in the field, among the diverse array of UNEF troops, Bunche found the impression of order and discipline combined with joint, international purpose exciting; the UN, he believed, had accomplished something real with the formation of UNEF. Inevitably, however, his mind continued to slip back to the past. Of Jerusalem, he wrote, "What a mess of barbed wire and sandbag emplacements Jerusalem was in 1947 when in June UNSCOP arrived," referring to the UN Special Committee on Palestine.[24] Yet just as Jerusalem had changed, so, too, was Gaza changing. Peace now seemed to be settling in. The tensions of the early months after the Suez Crisis were abating. A first set of entertainers, the Golden Gate Quartet, even headed over in April to perform for the UNEF troops.

Soon the UN was trumpeting the success of peacekeeping in the Middle East. A press release in May 1957 declared that "a few months ago this was a land of ambush and sudden death. The quiet is broken now only by a few minor incidents. This change is due to the presence of UNEF."[25] By fall, it was alleged, newborn girls in Gaza were even being given the name "Unefa."[26] A Gallup poll in 1957 showed the impact of UNEF's apparent success back home. Asked if they favored the UN having "its own permanent armed forces"—including troops from the US—"to enforce UN decisions," the American respondents said yes by more than a 2–1 margin.[27] (This idea was never implemented.) By June, Hammarskjold opened a meeting of the advisory committee on UNEF by noting that the group had not met for a long time, and "the reason is quite simple. It has been an exceedingly undramatic period, which is, of course, all to the good."[28]

Bunche would later say that "nobody dreamed" UNEF would be needed for more than three or four months.[29] Yet the UNEF troops remained through the hot summer and into the fall of 1957—and then for another ten years, indeed, right up to the 1967 Six-Day War. In August 1957, Hammarskjold penned a confidential aide-memoire about his negotiations with Nasser over the peacekeepers. Because UNEF had been authorized by the General Assembly under the Uniting for Peace procedure, Egypt's consent to the foreign troop deployments on its territory was necessary.* Hammarskjold's document, which remained secret for almost a decade, would prove significant as recriminations flew in the wake of the Six-Day War and the precipitous withdrawal of UNEF troops just as fighting commenced. But in 1957 no one outside a small circle of UN advisors knew of the document or its agreed procedure, nonbinding to be sure, that UNEF troops would remain in place until both Egypt and the General Assembly concurred that their "task" had been completed.[30]

Soon the main issues Bunche contended with were a rash of vehicle accidents and a minor and perhaps groundless scandal over financial mismanagement and disarray. Occasionally, flocks of animals would wander from Gaza into Israel; Israeli troops would hold them for several days and, after returning them, "submit a bill for grazing charges."[31]† These were frustrating and petty disagreements but in a sense a sign of success: UNEF was no longer contending with possibly violent clashes between Israel and Egypt but instead with far more mundane matters.

As the days grew shorter and Christmas approached, the hard-fought normalcy seemed secure. Bunche and Hammarskjold decided to return

---

* Chapter VII of the UN Charter grants the Security Council extraordinary powers, including the power to override ordinary rules of international law that limit the use of force by one state on the territory of another.

† Even this stopped; Hammarskjold joked, after one of Bunche's periodic reports on incidents in the field, that "even our old friends, the straying camels, have stopped their subversive activities."

to Gaza—or rather Hammarskjold did and persuaded Bunche to join. Visiting from tent to tent, some decorated with ersatz Christmas trees and cotton snow, the two UN officials assessed the mood and tried to bring holiday cheer to the lonely, and by this point, largely bored soldiers of the world. The various national forces celebrated the high-level visit by cooking national meals (feijoada for the Brazilians; curry for the Indians; a Swedish Christmas feast), and Hammarskjold and Bunche chatted and snacked with them all. The Finnish regiment even built a sauna; Bunche declined their invitation to test it out. The Christmas trip was relatively easy for Hammarskjold, a lifelong bachelor, but Bunche, with three children and a wife at home, was conflicted on whether to join. Pressed by his boss and friend to go, he later agreed when Hammarskjold told him that "it was a Christmas experience I would not have missed for anything."[32]

WITH UNEF BUNCHE AND HAMMARSKJOLD ACCOMPLISHED an important advance for both the United Nations and the postwar international order. UNEF quickly became "an advertisement for successful peacekeeping."[33] Bunche was personally very pleased. In a note in 1957, he wrote that

> [s]eeing UNEF in operation out here and its remarkable success, I do feel a sense of quiet pride in the knowledge, known only to a few out here, that I was primarily responsible for the organization of the force, the getting off the ground, and have been directing it from the beginning. It is, perhaps, my finest achievement, exceeding the armistice negotiations.[34]

Later, visiting Rafah in 1966, he would tell the troops that "I think of all the UN peacekeeping efforts, none has been as successful as this one."[35] By proving the concept could work on a larger scale and under tougher conditions than the previous UN efforts involving military observers, such as in the disputed Himalayan region of Kashmir, UNEF helped to tee up the next major step in UN peacekeeping three years later: Congo, which would become one of the most controversial peacekeeping efforts of the postwar era.

Bunche was proud of peacekeeping perhaps because it was in many respects the flipside of decolonization. By the late 1950s, decolonization seemed to be moving forward with more speed than ever. While many states would gain independence in the years to come, especially in the early 1960s, enough had already done so—and seemed on the edge of doing so—that the process seemed to have unstoppable momentum. This very success, however, added to the UN's ledger of challenges, since so many of the new states created were poor, unstable, or riven by political pressures that unfortunately derailed the peaceful independence many hoped for. To Bunche this seemed to be a price well worth paying, if only because he saw no real alternative. Morally, self-determination was the only choice.

Photo 16.2 Bunche pins medal on UNEF soldier

White rule over Black Africa was unacceptable. Politically, his pragmatism counseled that the genie of independence could never be put back in the bottle. The trick, then, was for the UN to foster and assist the process of decolonization; broker agreement among differing factions when possible; encourage the new state to become a member in good standing of the international community; and, if it all went off the rails, police the situation as best it could, using a multilateral, diverse force, with the hope of inducing a lasting peace. Peacekeeping, in sum, could serve as a backstop to decolonization, but ideally, the UN would play a critical role of assistance that would obviate the need for external intervention at all.

The Suez Crisis was in many ways the fountainhead of this approach. Indeed, Bunche would later be called the "father of peacekeeping" because of this work.[36] Yet the crisis also strengthened the UN more generally. The resolution of Suez was the UN's; the architects were Bunche, Hammarskjold, and Pearson, the Canadian diplomat who first broached the idea of UNEF. Bunche had proven in Palestine that the UN could be a useful mediator; now, the UN was testing out a new role, that of peacekeeper and possibly—as the future missions would show—even peace builder.

While the UN's role in this complex process proved important, so, too, was the larger geopolitical context. Without US support, the UN would not have been able to enter such a fraught arena as Suez. With two permanent members of the Security Council directly implicated, this was a crisis that could have ended much like the parallel one in Hungary—left to unfold with nothing more than censure from the General Assembly and vetoed resolutions in the Council. Instead, President Eisenhower demonstrated the great depths of postwar American power, whipped his allies into line, and essentially delegated the roles of crisis management and peacekeeping to the UN. This was not so much a result of Eisenhower's abiding belief in the UN (though he was the person who famously called the UN "man's best organized hope to substitute the conference table for the battlefield") as it was fear that the Soviet Union would embroil itself in the conflict. In a surprising way, the Cold War had fostered greater multilateralism.

UNEF remained in place in Gaza and Sinai for another decade. There were minor squabbles over map points, "delaying tactics," and the like, but by 1958 the multinational force was largely operating without incident.[37] Nasser, now effectively crowned the king of the Arabs thanks to the way he had vanquished the British and the French, continued to bedevil the West. After a coup in Syria, Nasser merged the two nations in 1958 into the United Arab Republic, and threatened to do the same with Iraq. In Lebanon, the president amended the constitution to allow a second term, triggering rebellions throughout the country by largely pro-Nasser groups. Eisenhower intervened in response, and in return, criticism of the US rained down from the newly independent nations of the world. Eisenhower was advised in a National Security Council meeting that the US "must adjust to the tide of Arab nationalism," arguably a lesson the US has never quite learned.[38] The Aswan High Dam, which in a sense precipitated the Suez Crisis after the US withdrew its support for funding it, finally began construction in 1960—financed, in the end, by the Soviet Union.

IN THE SPRING OF 1958, DAG Hammarskjold, in an effort to rejigger his leadership team, gave Ralph Bunche the title of under secretary for special political affairs. Among other tasks, Hammarskjold put him in charge of the new UN atomic energy initiative to be based in Vienna. Meeting before his departure in the fall of 1957, Hammarskjold told Bunche he should judge how long to stay, since it was not clear how important the meeting would be.[39]

The International Atomic Energy Agency would spend much of its life as a UN backwater, infrequently on the front pages until its heyday of weapons inspections in Iraq decades later. Bunche attended the first conference of the new agency in October 1957, guiding the proceedings and spending several weeks in Vienna. The conference was important but not riveting—and Bunche questioned why it was being held in Vienna at all, though the city, a neutral spot between East and West, made some sense politically. With Ruth along for part of the trip, he took advantage of the posting to soak up the wonderful old cafes, visit the newly restored Staatsoper (for *Aida*), and even see the famed Lippazaner horses. On the way over they stopped off in Italy, visiting Capri and getting in some late summer sun.

One morning at their hotel, Bunche received a message that he was to call the US embassy in Vienna. Soon an American diplomat arrived and told him that the White House was inviting Bunche to become a member of President Eisenhower's new Civil Rights Commission. Bunche did not take long to consider the offer. He appreciated this show of "confidence" by the president, he told the State Department, and he generally supported Eisenhower's policy on civil rights. But, as with every overture from the American government since he had left the State Department, he answered that he could best serve his country by staying where he was.[40] Hammarskjold, learning of the offer, said he was very glad Bunche had turned Eisenhower down. "You belong here," he told Bunche; the UN would change "quite a lot" with your absence.[41]

Still, America's internal racial conflicts vied for Bunche's attention, and the post must have held considerable appeal. The White House overture came in the wake of the Little Rock desegregation crisis in the fall of 1957, when Governor Orval Faubus deployed the Arkansas National Guard to stop Black students from attending their local school. Eisenhower, in a dramatic show of federal power, in turn sent the 101st Airborne Division to escort the children, and he federalized the Arkansas National Guard. Bunche's comments on the crisis were quoted around the world. Violence surrounding school integration, he stated, was bound to have "a harmful effect on international opinion." "Photographs of jeering crowds and armed National Guardsmen stopping young boys and girls from entering schools are hardly good public relations."[42]

Bunche's growing ties with Martin Luther King Jr., together with disturbing incidents like Little Rock, began to draw him more and more into commenting on American race relations. And as more colonies around the world began to seek and claim independence, he naturally tied the developments together. Two years after Little Rock, in 1959, Bunche would speak in Birmingham, Alabama, and declare that the "world of 1959 is no longer a white man's world." Alabamans were not alone in their quest for racial justice, he told the crowd. New voices command attention around the globe, "the voices of yellow, brown, and black men."[43] It was, in a sense, a version of what King had told Richard Nixon that night in Accra, celebrating the transition to independent Ghana: "I want you to come visit us down in Alabama where we are seeking the same kind of freedom the Gold Coast is celebrating."[44]

Bunche's global prominence and domestic respect increasingly made him an attractive potential political figure. In 1958, the Liberal Party of New York even tried to draft him as their Senate candidate.[45] The idea was heralded in the Black press as one that would have "world-wide implications" at a time when the US was "suffering alarming propaganda reversals" due to racial oppression—and would bring "dignity and restraint" to the Senate.[46] He offered no comment to reporters and never ran. Indeed, he never ran for any elected office.[†] A few years later, Michigan State polled prospective Democratic candidates, including Bunche, against Republican Senator Jacob Javits of New York; Bunche was still seen as a potent political figure if he chose to enter the arena, but once again he demurred.[47]

As this suggested, Bunche's fame had not abated. In 1958, he flew to Los Angeles to dedicate the new Ralph Bunche Junior High in Compton, California, not far from his childhood home. He often toured celebrities around the UN. When Marlene Dietrich came to the East River campus, it was Bunche who showed her around the Security Council chamber. (Dietrich, noticing the horseshoe-shaped table, mused "if only we could put a secret love potion around all the seats.")[48] Even the biggest star of the era, Frank Sinatra, sought him out; Bunche gave Sinatra a personal tour of the UN headquarters in the summer of 1959.[49]

As the 1950s drew to a close, Bunche's health, never great, was beginning to suffer. Long a smoker, he was not especially attentive to his health; he simply worked too hard and slept too little. As his Middle East peregrinations illustrated, he was also on the road for very long stretches. Indeed, one writer referred to him as a "man of the world, but never at

---

† Had he run and won, he would have been the first Black senator in the nation since Reconstruction.

home."[50] He was still in his fifties, but his diminishing health would soon become a major challenge.

In the summer of 1959, with Gaza long gone quiet, he was again thrust into the headlines when Ralph Jr., then in high school, sought to join the West Side Tennis Club near their home in Forest Hills, Queens, but was barred because he was Black. The story quickly reached the New York papers when Ralph Sr. spoke out. Careful to stress that this incident was minor in comparison to what many Black Americans were suffering, especially in the South, Bunche nonetheless told reporters the discrimination his son faced "flows from the same wells of racial and religious bigotry." Indeed, he claimed he was glad this had occurred, so that the reality of racial bigotry—its pervasive nature, both major and minor—was "made real in this way for my son."[51] This was an implicit acknowledgment that his son had led an easier and more privileged life than he had. The tennis club story reverberated around the world, and for many it became an emblem of the perhaps less overt but still very persistent racism experienced in Northern cities. Bunche's prominence of course fed the contretemps, but the basic principle—could a private business discriminate?—was one that would prove nettlesome for years.

In the meantime, local political figures jumped to action. Within days, West Side Tennis Club officials were called in to testify before New York City's Commission on Intergroup Relations. Senator Jacob Javits of New York even called for the US Open and Davis Cup to be moved from the club.[52] Bunche was encouraged by the strong reaction across the nation, though he knew a large portion of it was due to his unique stature. Still, the incident spurred the New York Times to run an investigation of local private clubs, which revealed that none of the clubs in their sample had any Black members and "a few said they had 'some' Jewish" ones.[53] Facing an onslaught of bad publicity, the head of the tennis club resigned, and the club personally invited Ralph Sr. and Jr. to apply. (They declined—Bunche later told Jackie Robinson that he never sought membership as his "tennis playing days are far behind me.")[54]§

---

§ Bunche later claimed he received more mail over the tennis club incident than his Nobel Prize.

The Tennis Club incident was a reminder that, however diverse the UN might be, America remained deeply trapped in discrimination in 1959. Bunche had left Washington a decade earlier, and indeed he refused to return even when President Truman personally implored him because of the injustices of the segregation he had experienced there. New York was different, but clearly not quite different enough.

<hr/>

IN THE LATE 1950S, RALPH BUNCHE was often asked to assess UNEF's broader impact. The mission has worked extremely well, he opined in April 1958, "but it doesn't bring peace. It brings quiet."[55] A certain regularity had set in, even in Gaza. Fields, hardly distinguishable from one another, were being farmed on each side of the demarcation line as UNEF soldiers, no doubt bored to tears, observed. To Bunche's eye, it was "quite an amazing operation."[56]

Still, the refugee problem in Palestine—which he had viewed as the most serious challenge for a decade now—persisted. On one visit to Gaza he spoke to some farmers. As he recounted on the 38th floor after his return, a farmer there told him, "I take my children as close to the line as UNEF will permit in order to look across the line and see where my land used to be." These children, Bunche explained with some consternation, have never set foot on this land:

> There is a bitterness about this. Remove UNEF and the bitterness takes the form of violence. Until the basic problems are settled—and the most basic, in my view, is the refugee problem—I do not see anything that the two governments can do, and I think the problem of refugees is something which is bigger than just two governments. It covers the whole area.[57]

While he could not have predicted the terrible conditions and frequent violence that would later characterize Gaza, nor the rise of groups such as Hamas, he foresaw that the situation was, from a humanitarian perspective, untenable. Indeed, just five years after Bunche's conversation with the local farmer, the Norwegian sociologist Johan Galtung was likening the refugees housed in Gaza to the population in a prison, condemned to a "penalty of unknown minimum and unknown maximum duration."[58] That parallel—Gaza as an open-air prison camp—would gain substantial currency in the decades to follow.

A few weeks later, in April 1959, Bunche was in Washington attending the funeral of former Secretary of State John Foster Dulles. Dulles had been essential to the response in Suez and was a towering figure in American diplomacy. Among the many world leaders in attendance that day was the young King Baudouin of Belgium, who just a few months before had announced that Belgium would reverse course and begin the process of granting its vast Congo colony independence.

The following year, 1960, John F. Kennedy was elected president in a watershed election. The youthful Kennedy transfixed the world, and it appeared that he had a firmer grasp of the changes afoot around the world than his predecessor. As a reporter when he was a much younger man, JFK had covered the negotiations of the UN Charter. He had continued to keep a close eye on foreign affairs during his tenure as senator from Massachusetts. Appointing a group of wise men to guide him in foreign affairs—the so-called best and brightest, a term made famous by David Halberstam years later in his arresting chronicle of the American foreign policy establishment and the Vietnam War—Kennedy, like presidents before him, considered Ralph Bunche for a prominent appointment in his administration.

The politics of race in America were rapidly changing during this period, and Bunche remained one of the most famous and most respected Black men in the nation—especially by powerful whites. As one account notes,

> If Bunche had lost such admirers as Abner Berry and W.E.B. Du Bois in the fifties, he gained such notables as Averill Harriman, John D. Rockefeller III, and David Rockefeller—all of whom believed Bunche a loyal American capable of performing any important assignment. In fact, Harriman asserted that he suggested Truman appoint Bunche undersecretary of state.[59]

Prominent, powerful, respected, and white supporters like these easily trumped the baseless charges of communist activity that had dogged Bunche in the mid-1950s, let alone the more prosaic indignities such as the Westside Tennis Club. Still, Bunche made clear to Kennedy's team that he would prefer to remain under secretary general of the UN. Ironically, in light of the many earlier efforts to tar him as a communist, the position Kennedy was considering was American ambassador to the Soviet Union.

Meanwhile, Bunche's political prospects continued to be bandied about. The *New York Amsterdam News*, in the occasional *You Said It* column, asked a cross section of Black New Yorkers "What Negro man would you like to see become President of the United States?"[60] (The "poll" was taken in February 1960 during the presidential primaries.) Of the six answers featured, one respondent suggested Martin Luther King Jr; one Adam Clayton Powell Jr.; one Thurgood Marshall—and three named Ralph Johnson Bunche.

CHAPTER 17

THE YEAR OF AFRICA

Lumumba of the Congo has got a hunch
He's tired of using Mr. Ralph Bunche
His policy is very bold
His new office boy is Hammarskjold

—Song written on a menu of *The Equator Club*, Nairobi,

August 21, 1960

In July 1960, Ralph Bunche sent a telegram to Dag Hammarskjold. "Had good talk with Lumumba afternoon 4th . . . very encouraging and also we had a quite favorable impression of the man. He was businesslike, intelligent, informed, quick and smart. He is favorable to multilateral aid and hopes for prompt action."[1] The independence of Congo, one of the largest colonial possessions in Africa, had just occurred, and there was substantial apprehension about how the new nation would fare. Tiny Belgium had brutally ruled Congo for nearly a century; now it had done almost nothing to prepare the vast country for self-government. There were fewer than twenty college graduates among a population of nearly fifteen million, in a territory larger than Western Europe itself.

Patrice Lumumba, a charismatic thirty-five-year-old former postal clerk and brewery salesman, was the newly elected prime minister of

Congo. (Bunche would later describe Lumumba in more detail as "tall and sharp-eyed and rather raffish looking in his mustache and beard—and long hair. Whether the latter is an affectation or due to lack of time for a haircut I do not yet know." Later still, as Congo disintegrated, he would simply call him "a madman.")[2] Bunche sent the cable to New York in the wake of the independence ceremonies in the capital of Congo, then known as Leopoldville after King Leopold of Belgium, who in 1885 "founded" Congo.[3]

The year 1960 was a momentous one for Africans. Seventeen African nations achieved independence, over a dozen from France alone. Three were former UN trust territories, emerging from the trusteeship process that Bunche had put so much effort into during the 1940s. In a speech in Massachusetts a few months before his trip to Congo, he had declared 1960 "The Year of Africa"—a moniker that sticks to this day.

Belgian rule in Congo dated from the late-19th century Scramble for Africa. European states, wielding lethal new weaponry that overwhelmed their victims, had rushed to conquer and exploit as much of the continent as they could. To impose some order on this process of territorial aggrandizement, Otto von Bismarck, the powerful German chancellor, invited leaders from throughout Europe to meet in Berlin in 1885. The assembled delegates met in Bismarck's yellow brick mansion at 77 Wilhelmstrasse. Dressed in formal red court attire, and addressing the group in French, Bismarck told them the goal of the meeting was to coordinate a common approach and set of rules for dividing up Africa. Now usually referred to as the "Berlin Conference," the conclave was known in German as the "Kongokonferenz," after the crown jewel of African colonies: the Congo.

Through a series of complicated maneuvers, and with the assistance of famed explorer Henry Stanley, King Leopold had begun to obtain control over the Congo river basin in the years before the Berlin Conference. A neighboring smaller territory became a French colony, sometimes known as Congo-Brazzaville, after its capital. It was at Bismarck's palace in Berlin that King Leopold secured his claim in central Africa, what he once referred to as his slice of "ce magnifique gateau africain."[4] And for nearly forty years,

Congo would be brutally ruled as essentially Leopold's personal property.*
For another half century, until June 29, 1960, Congo would be Belgium's
imperial possession.

In late May 1960, with independence rapidly approaching, Hammarskjold
called Bunche into his 38th floor office. He asked him to travel to Congo to
represent the UN and advise the young government about to take charge.
The birth of what was now being called the Third World was fully underway.
Liberation movements were blossoming throughout Asia and Africa, and
while resistance by European elites persisted in some places, the dam had
effectively broken. By the Year of Africa, the UN was a focal point for many
of the liberation efforts. Decolonization occurred through or with the assistance of UN processes but also more broadly, as part of a general postwar
struggle over the self-determination of all peoples. The year 1960 was in
many respects the dramatic culmination of this struggle. Still, there were
challenges. Hammarskjold told Bunche he would probably need to remain
in the Congo "for some time after independence" because there "might well
be trouble" there.[5]

Hammarskjold's instincts were accurate. Congo's independence quickly
became one of the great political cataclysms of the Cold War. The remarkable political events in Congo severely tested the organization. But the
UN—and Ralph Bunche—survived the experience, and the process of decolonization ultimately continued, its momentum now unstoppable.

Bunche stood at the center of the postwar dismantling of empire, just
as he sat at the center of the festivities in Leopoldville, Congo, in that momentous summer of 1960. Nearby was Patrice Lumumba and also King
Leopold's descendant, the young King Baudouin of Belgium, resplendent
in a white military dress uniform and hat, accessorized with dark glasses
and a sword. Independence Day in 1960 was full of hope and promise, even
though darker notes redolent of the chaos to come could be heard in the
speeches given later that day. Soon Congo would begin to break apart, and
Bunche would be ordered out of his Leopoldville hotel at gunpoint, with

---

* King Leopold would in never set foot in his domain, though he profited immensely
from it.

barely enough time to hide confidential documents behind his bathroom toilet. The resulting struggle for power became the first major Cold War conflict in Africa, led to the attempted secession of the fabulously mineral-rich province of Katanga, and, ultimately, resulted in the abduction and assassination of Patrice Lumumba—as well as the death of Dag Hammarskjold in a mysterious plane crash in the jungle near the border with Rhodesia.

The Congo crisis would consume Bunche's life for months, even years, but it was in many respects the culmination of his life's work. The liberation of African and other peoples from European rule was not merely a political issue for him. It was personal and also moral. The central question, he had said a few years earlier in a speech at Fisk University, a historically Black college in Tennessee, was simple: "Can white people ever accept darker peoples as equal?"

AS UNDER SECRETARY GENERAL FOR SPECIAL political affairs, Bunche was a frequent emissary of the United Nations. An important part of his duties was to travel the world to witness, and in essence to midwife, the birth of new states. This particular task was rapidly accelerating in importance in 1960. When the UN's headquarters in New York City fully opened for business in 1952, there were sixty member states. By the Year of Africa, the building, which had been designed for about seventy state delegations, would hold ninety-nine.[6] Decolonization was occurring much faster than many had imagined even just a decade before. As one analysis at the time pointed out, in Africa in particular the movement toward independence proceeded much more quickly during 1960 "than even the most informed observers would have anticipated in 1959, let alone in 1958 or earlier." This was certainly true of Congo. The large influx of new members "came as something of a surprise to the United Nations as an institution and, in many ways, as something of a surprise to the new members themselves."[7]

As decolonization unfolded, Hammarskjold would occasionally attend independence ceremonies himself. Yet his broader responsibilities more often kept him in New York.[†] Bunche would then stand in for

---

[†] After independence during the Year of Africa the Somali government improbably gave Hammarskjold a pet monkey. Hammarskjold named it "Greenback" and had it

Photo 17.1 Congo Independence Day invitation

Hammarskjold, representing the organization at independence events, overseeing the process of dissolution with former colonial powers, assisting new leaders in becoming UN members, and providing political guidance as new governments took power.

The UN's imprimatur was important in this process. Alongside the acquisition of a flag, a currency, and often a national airline, becoming a UN member was one of the more visible manifestations of sovereignty newly independent states could claim. As one Congolese official noted, "in the minds of colonized peoples" admission to the UN was "a kind of seal set on their independence."[8] As a result, applying for UN membership was often one of their first acts. Indeed, Prime Minister Lumumba was so eager that he sent a telegram requesting Congo be admitted to the UN several days *before* the handover of power. Hammarskjold cabled Bunche, then

brought back to New York, where it lived in his UN apartment. Bunche later recalled that the normally austere Swede had "poignant affection for Greenback," who was "an irrepressible show off, a born 'ham.'"

in Leopoldville, to let him know of the mishap. "From our point of view," Hammarskjold said, this was "somewhat embarrassing as Congo not yet independent."[9]

A top State Department official of the era referred to Bunche as a kind of nursemaid to these new governments.[10] Former colonies had begun joining the UN as early as 1948 (Burma) and 1950 (Indonesia). The UN grew quite slowly in the early 1950s, with 1955 a particularly big year for new members. Many of these were European states: Austria, Finland, and Portugal, for example. But quite a few had just achieved independence from foreign rule, such as Cambodia and Ceylon (now Sri Lanka.) The process was comparatively measured, however, because the US and the Soviets had quickly become concerned about maintaining a balance of power within the UN. But soon the powerful pressures of self-determination became overwhelming. Progress accelerated in the late 1950s with Ghana, Tunisia, Malaya, and Morocco all liberated from colonialism. The most significant year for newly independent states, however, was clearly 1960.

The growing rollback of European empire, along with the creation of the UN Emergency Force in the Middle East, were bright spots for the UN by 1960. The Security Council had struggled to maintain relevance in the zero-sum conflict of the Cold War. The vetoes—and their threat—cascaded forth. In 1959, the year before Congo's independence, the Council met just five times in total. In this context, the retreat of European rule from Africa and Asia was one of the few goals of the organization that were successfully met.

The Trusteeship Council had been envisaged as a centerpiece of the independence effort. But it was the General Assembly, which had gained newfound power and prestige in the wake of the UN's successful intervention in the Suez Crisis, that became an even more significant site of anticolonial politics. By the Year of Africa, the General Assembly had established a "dominant position" in the UN with regard to decolonization.[11] Newly independent states increasingly used the chamber in the late 1950s and early 1960s to lambast their former European masters. As their numbers grew, the attacks grew in volume and vitriol. The world was spinning faster, and soon the colonial powers were puzzling over the seemingly widespread view that "the possession of colonies is in itself something reprehensible."[12]

RALPH BUNCHE TRAVELED WIDELY IN THE historic Year of Africa, meeting with liberation movements, newly elected presidents and prime ministers, and traditional tribal chiefs alike. In a poignant letter written just as the year was dawning, Ruth Bunche, who had already suffered through so many years of his overseas travel, wrote to Ralph, already in Africa, that "I do hope this year will be filled with peace, harmony, and love for us, Ralph . . . I yearn also for loving companionship and I hope I'll get it in 1960. Keep well and come home soon."[13] He would unfortunately be away for very long stretches in 1960. It was a period of tumultuous and exciting change across the continent, yet dark clouds could already be discerned. Visiting Ghana, Bunche found Kwame Nkrumah surrounded by large and "vicious-looking" dogs—said to be a gift from Gamel Abdel Nasser of Egypt—and already exhibiting the traits that would lead him, a few years later, to become de facto dictator and "president for life."[‡][14] Nonetheless, in 1960 there was still substantial optimism about African independence. These new states had young and often charismatic leaders who were eager to build their societies and join the international community. Bunche, in turn, saw the UN as a crucial institution in this process, one that could smooth the transition to independence while inculcating important postwar values of internationalism and multilateralism.

Bunche set out for Congo on June 23, 1960, exactly one week before power was to be handed over. Patrice Lumumba had triumphed in the elections held in May and was now set to become prime minister. The president, something of a figurehead, would be a more stolid rival named Joseph Kasavubu, known as "King Kasa" to his followers. (Carl von Horn, the Swedish general later put in charge of peacekeeping in Congo,

---

‡ Nkrumah was not alone in attempting to stay in office permanently. Postcolonial Africa faced considerable problems with political succession in the decades to come. Indeed, so few African leaders left office voluntarily that, in 2007, Sudanese billionaire Mo Ibrahim established a $5 million prize to go to an African leader who was both democratically elected and left office at the end of their constitutionally mandated term.

described Kasavubu as "inordinately conscious of status and occasion"—a trait that would create difficulties with the popular and far more vibrant Lumumba.)[15] Lumumba, a self-taught beer distributor, had shown an aptitude for politics after his earlier career as a postal worker was cut short by his conviction and imprisonment on embezzlement charges. King Baudouin, whom Lumumba had met and spoken with on Baudouin's first visit to Congo in 1955, had granted Lumumba a royal pardon—an ironic development in light of what was to transpire between the two men on Independence Day.[16]

Congo had moved toward independence with surprising speed. In a message that Bunche conveyed on his behalf, Hammarskjold dryly noted to the nation's leaders that "the political evolution in your country has been distinguished by an exceptionally rapid pace."[17] A petition from local elites demanding a timetable for decolonization had first been sent to Belgian leaders only two years earlier. Lumumba, one of the authors, was as usual forthright: independence "is not a gift," he had declared, but "a fundamental right of the Congolese."[18] At the time Congo, which had been ruled with stunning repression and violence for much of its history, seemed to many to be decades from self-rule. Indeed, right up until the first days of 1960, most Belgians and many observers worldwide assumed that Congo would become independent "only twenty or thirty years" after French and British colonies gained independence; that is, something around 1990.[19] Now, in the summer of 1960, it was suddenly happening.

Congo's rush to independence shocked many in the West, even human rights advocates such as Eleanor Roosevelt. Roosevelt, who led the drafting of the UN's Universal Declaration of Human Rights, dedicated an episode of her highbrow PBS talk show *Prospects of Mankind* to the Year of Africa. Joining her for the discussion in the spring of 1960 were Julius Nyerere, the soon-to-be prime minister of independent Tanganyika (now Tanzania), and, representing the UN's perspective, Ralph Bunche. Tellingly titling the episode "Africa: Revolution in Haste," Roosevelt set the stage. On the first program of this series, she said in her distinctive mid-Atlantic accent, which made her sound like a long-lost cousin of the Queen, "I mentioned that nationalism seemed to be moving too rapidly in Africa. At that time, of course, independence for the Belgian Congo was in the distant future." Roosevelt let out a small laugh, as if the whole notion was head-spinning. Today, she continued, we know that the Congo will become free on June 30th, after a "headlong rush toward independence."[20] Roosevelt was voicing an increasingly common concern in the Year of Africa: that some nations, in particular Congo, were simply moving too fast; they did not appear ready for independence, and trouble surely awaited.

Roosevelt and her guests sat with an unmarked black map of Africa on the wall behind them, its very lack of lines seeming to symbolize the still-undetermined contours of postcolonial Africa. She turned to Nyerere for comment. After Nyerere noted that one did not typically need time to be "ready" to retrieve one's stolen property, Bunche, sitting across from Roosevelt and Nyerere on a midcentury chair, jumped in to address the critical question of whether African independence was happening "too fast." Bunche, who knew Roosevelt well from the UN's early days, seemed to want to politely challenge the entire premise. "When people are seeking freedom, they're always impatient," he interjected. "And I think that's good."[21]

Three months after this exchange, Bunche was on his way to Congo for the independence festivities. It was a trip that would test his belief in the benevolent power of impatience. Stopping off en route in Brussels, he was taken aback by how openly scornful Belgian officials were of the new Congolese leaders. Belgian rule had long been rapacious and disdainful, and Belgium had shown little interest in cultivating a local elite. But the level of Belgian contempt for the Congolese jolted Bunche. Once on the ground in Leopoldville, he met with Belgians who seemed more sympathetic to the challenges the Congolese faced in their rapid journey to self-rule. Both groups, moreover, seemed very interested in a UN presence and had a desire, as one of his colleagues remarked to him, to "internationalize" the problem in a way that was "a little pathetic."[22]

Writing to Hammarskjold a few days later, Bunche noted that

[t]he attitude of sincere striving to pull this situation out of the fire which seems to characterize the high echelon of Belgian officialdom here appears to me to be in marked contrast with something close to derisive contempt most thinly veiled,

for all Congolese leaders, which I encountered on Friday in Brussels . . . the banter back and forth across the table between the Belgian officials in the presence of several Congolese, in the most outmoded paternalistic and condescending tone, was downright embarrassing.[23]

Paternalism and condescension, let alone unfiltered racism, were unfortunately easy to find in this era. The open obsession with racial hierarchy that had characterized the early 20th century had faded after the Nazis brought overtly racialist politics into disrepute. But many of the underlying attitudes clearly persisted.

Emblematic was the concept of *évolués*. Belgians had long referred to Black men like Lumumba and Kasavubu, who had some education perhaps, but mainly dressed in Western fashion, spoke good French, and renounced traditional practices and folkways, as *évolués*: "evolved ones." Belgium even instituted a system of identity cards that *évolués* could obtain, granting them—after very careful inspection of their homes and families of course—select privileges normally enjoyed only by the European settlers in Congo.[24] To many European minds, central Africa was still a thoroughly primitive place: in need of outside assistance and unprepared for self-governance. These overtly racist attitudes were especially prevalent for Congo. Immortalized in Joseph Conrad's *Heart of Darkness*, Congo had always been central to the Western imagination of exotic, primitive, and dangerous Africa. To many Westerners in 1960, the notion that it would now join the ranks of Sweden, France, and Argentina in the UN was fascinating, if not almost incomprehensible.

A *New York Times* headline from the period declaring that "Congo Rises from Stone Age to Statehood in Few Decades" was representative of this mindset. The story went on to say that "fifty-five years ago, in the heartland of darkest Africa . . . the wheel was not used, language was not written, cannibalism and witchcraft were common, and the site of the capital, Leopoldville, was still a dense jungle." Independence was "introducing the twentieth century overnight to a primitive people divided into many warring tribes." Was the Congo truly "ready?" the Paper of Record seemed to be asking. And in Bunche's files, dated 1960 and inexplicably labeled "Top

Secret," was a sheet of paper titled *The Song of the Congo*.[25] The opening verses are something out of Kipling:

> This is the song of that incredible land,
> Where the jungles spread and the mountains stand,
> And the deep brown river rolls on to the sea,
> Hey Ho for the Congo, the land that's for me!
> There the Cannibals stalk in search of their prey,
> The dance round their pot while the traveler stray,
> Steam boils and bubbles to make a thick soup,
> While the warriors scream, they yell and they whoop.

In short, the European attitudes of white supremacy Bunche had attacked some two decades before were still very much in evidence. Indeed, they seemed hardly disguised at all. Yet by 1960, the political momentum of anti-imperialism had become unstoppable. Belgium, caught in the middle as a tiny state with a huge colony far away in central Africa, had decided to accept fate and suddenly move, with what some saw as reckless speed, toward decolonization.

The Congolese leaders were also of course eager to move quickly, even if crucial basic issues—such as the name of the new state—had yet to be finalized. (Bunche reported that "Kongo" was a leading candidate, but in the end, the more French "Congo" was chosen.) Almost no Congolese had any real experience in governance. In fact, Belgium's underlying intention in moving with alacrity toward independence seemed to be to remain effectively in charge of Congo, with just a superficial layer of pliable local leaders on top. As one Congolese leader recounted of the immediate aftermath of independence:

> All of us were happy, or at least cheerful and satisfied, at being ministers. . . .we argued about offices . . . and how they should be shared among us . . . and though we sat so comfortably in our sumptuous official cars, driven by uniformed military chauffeurs, and looked as though we were ruling this large and beautiful country, we were in fact ruling nothing and a prey to whatever might happen.[26]

Supporting this interpretation was the fact that even after the handover Belgians still controlled the military, known as the *Force Publique*, as well as some 70 percent of the Congolese economy. Lumumba and Kasavubu were meant to be puppets easily manipulated by a Belgian bureaucracy left intact, with independence functioning essentially as a veneer over continuing Belgian power. The Congolese might reign, but the Belgians would rule.

Bunche saw a glimmer of this cynicism in the disparaging way the Belgians he met in Brussels spoke to the Congolese leaders there. As UN emissary, he could do little about it, though he found the Belgian attitudes repellent. And he was, of course, deeply interested in what role the UN would play in the life of the new state. Now in Leopoldville, the Belgian-developed capital of Congo, Bunche checked into the Hotel Stanley, named after the famous British explorer. Built in a postwar style, it would serve as the headquarters of the UN in Congo for several weeks, until, as the situation in the new nation deteriorated, he moved the operation into a nearby apartment building known as Le Royal.

His first task in Leopoldville was to assess the new leadership and the political currents. One challenge was language. Although he could toss out a sentence or phrase here and there, Bunche did not in fact speak French very well. (To a colleague he characterized his command of the language as "lousy.")[27] As a result, he relied on an interpreter, a Chinese UN official who traveled with him. Bunche was nonetheless warmly welcomed in Congo. As Thomas Kanza, later Congo's ambassador to the UN, recounted, from the moment of his arrival he "had been received by the Congolese with the greatest sympathy and the most profound respect." Kanza believed that this warm reaction reflected Bunche's African heritage: "The fraternity of race," he suggested, "played a part that must not be underestimated."[28]

After an early meeting with Patrice Lumumba, Bunche turned to one of his UN colleagues, Sture Linner. "What is your impression? How do you sum him up?" he asked. "There is something in his eyes that worries me," replied Linner. Linner suggested he might be "on drugs." Still, he went on, "I think you have there the potential for a great leader." Bunche concurred. "I agree with you completely. There is something I cannot put my finger on, maybe drugs, maybe something else."[29] Bunche sent an assessment to

Hammarskjold from Leopoldville. Congo's leaders are very friendly to the UN, he explained, but know "little or nothing about us." However, he continued, our most enthusiastic supporters here are the Belgian officials who see the UN as the "saving factor" in their future relations with the Congolese and "who tell me repeatedly that the Congolese will 'listen' to us and will follow our advice."[30]

This was an important point. For Bunche and Hammarskjold, Congo, and indeed the entire Year of Africa, presented a significant opportunity: a chance to help create new states in a critical and emerging part of the world and embed the UN and its ethos of sovereign respect and international rule of law in their politics. Bunche in particular had long seen decolonization as a moral and political imperative and empire as the logical and political epitome of white supremacy. The UN, he believed, was intended to fundamentally recast the international order: to further the process of dismantling the old world of empires and to welcome new states into the fold of a more just and equal postwar international community. Africa provided the largest canvas on which this could be achieved. The important thing, he thought, was to learn from the past. Bunche had also long seen Africa as a sort of blank political slate on which the best of the modern world could be written. In what was one of the only publications to emerge from his PhD research in the 1930s on African colonial governance, he had written that Africa was "one place in this troubled world where mistakes previously committed may be corrected; where, indeed, a new and better civilization may be cultivated."[31] Now, some twenty-five years later, he was in a position to test and implement this principle.

The UN was the crucial transmission belt in this updated version of the trustee concept that had animated colonial policy since the late 19th century. The key difference was twofold. First, and hugely important, former colonies would in fact gain independence. Second, rather than a single colonial power, it was the UN, as the agent of the international community writ large, that would act as the stabilizer, tutor, and consigliere as new governments took power for the first time.

Bunche no doubt felt some trepidation about this process; he was pragmatic and unromantic about the challenges of self-government, and would in fact soon grow quite critical of Congo's missteps. But he believed it was the moral destiny of Africa to be free, and he was excited to be a witness and assistant to the process. Whatever misgivings he had about Lumumba, Bunche thought he was ready and able to do this. As he later explained in a speech at Columbia University, Lumumba, "it must be said, was one of the few Congolese who seemed to grasp the vital necessity of national unity in a new nation, and he strove against all the divisive forces of tribalism and special interest to promote this unity."[32] The unhappy fact, he continued, was that there was not a "true national spirit" in Congo; "divisive factors of tribalism and sectional, even personal, interests" were too strong. Bunche, and the UN generally, could guide the process of building a state. But as he discovered, they had no ability to help craft a nation.

Bunche's initial meetings in Brussels also highlighted another important angle to the liberation of Congo: the role of the Cold War. In 1960, the Soviets were eager to be seen as a leader in the burgeoning decolonization movement. Pushing the issue was a savvy way to put the West in the spotlight, divide it, and, ideally, weaken it. Later that year, at the fall opening of the General Assembly, the USSR even proposed a declaration on the granting of independence to colonial peoples. The initial Soviet draft pulled no punches. It strikingly referred to the "swish of the overseer's lash" and the colonial rulers' "executioner's axe."[33] The draft called for immediate independence for all colonies—and also, in direct aim at the American Cold War practice, the elimination of all foreign bases. The Soviet draft was a bit too much, however, for some of the non-aligned states. A declaration was eventually passed, but it was one written by the newly independent states in different, more diplomatic language and with no mention of foreign bases. In a sign of the rapidly changing mores around colonialism, however, the resolution passed without a single negative vote.*

Now, a few months before the General Assembly meetings, the question was how the Soviets would see the situation in Congo. Belgian officials stressed to Bunche that the Soviet Union had designs on the new nation, and perhaps vice versa. As he recounted to Hammarskjold, the Belgians

---

* Many of the colonial powers, and the US, abstained.

implied "that we alone stand in the way of the Congolese being taken in by Moscow."[34] Indeed, some eventually saw the UN's efforts in Congo as simply the hidden hand of the West, with Hammarskjold and Bunche doing Brussels' and Washington's bidding. Congo was already being teed up as the next battleground in the Cold War; a future domino that might lead others to fall eastward.

INDEPENDENCE DAY IN CONGO DAWNED ON June 30, 1960.[§] The ceremonies in Leopoldville began that day and continued on July 1, with a "Fete de l'Independence" ironically set for *Stade Roi Baudoin*—King Baudouin Stadium—an arresting emblem of how entangled the new state of Congo and the old state of Belgium continued to be. The young Belgian monarch had flown in for the occasion, arguably a misreading of the political situation on the ground. On the drive in from the airport, riding in a slow-moving open Lincoln Continental, the King's ceremonial sword was snatched by a souvenir-hunter (neatly dressed in a dark jacket and tie) who, in a moment of triumph, clutched it above his head in celebration. It was a sign, perhaps, that the situation in Congo was teetering on the edge of shambolic and a potent symbol of the shifting political order in Africa. "Very symbolic! Like he was snatching the King's power," noted one observer, who many years later became the foreign minister of Congo. Armed police soon surrounded the interloper as the spectators lining the broad tropical avenue looked on in amazement.[35]

Watching the independence parade that day, Bunche was troubled. Congolese troops marched down Leopoldville's broad tropical avenues in formation, and fighter jets flew overhead. But the troops were led by Belgian officers, white men. At previous independence celebrations, such as that of Ghana in 1957, national troops were commanded by national officers drawn from the local populace. Here, the former colonial power seemed to

---

§ In a sign of how rapid the pace of change was in 1960, the very next day saw the birth of the Republic of Somalia, amalgamated from the Italian-controlled Trust Territory of Somaliland and State of Somalia, which a mere five days earlier had declared independence from Britain.

be hedging and not quite taking its hands off the steering wheel. Bunche no doubt thought of his meetings in Brussels the week before. Turning to his aide, he said, "Something is wrong."[36]

The formal independence ceremonies began in the grand circular hall of the National Palace. Built to be the residence of the Belgian governor-general, the Palace was a colonnaded, modern building situated on the grassy banks of the Congo River facing French Brazzaville on the other side. The room was filled with members of the new Congolese government, Belgian officials, and foreign dignitaries such as Prince Hassan of Morocco and King Kigeri of Rwanda. Participants had come from all over; even tiny Israel sent a delegation.[**] Most in attendance, including the new Congolese leaders, wore dark Western suits and ties, but here and there traditional African headdresses with seashells, feathers, and animal skins could be spotted.[37]

Bemedaled and wearing a striking white military uniform, King Baudouin addressed the dignitaries and new Congolese leadership gathered in the Chamber of Deputies. Standing at a microphone and holding his notes in is hands, the king fully channeled the prewar creed of the White Man's Burden. Baudouin's tone-deaf and bombastic speech stressed the importance of Belgium's role in the history and development of Congo. He even praised the "genius" of his great grand uncle, King Leopold II, who for decades had ruled Congo and presided over some of the most horrific atrocities ever perpetrated in Africa. As if to underscore his hauteur, he declaimed that "it is up to you, gentlemen, to demonstrate that we were right to have confidence in you." King Baudouin's remarks were punctuated with ceremonial gunfire. Bunche, writing later, called Baudouin's speech a "grave error."[38]

The new president of Congo, Joseph Kasavubu, followed the king in the chamber but offered only a mild and diplomatic, even obsequious, response. Then Patrice Lumumba, who was sitting next to Belgian Premier

---

[**] In a long report to Hammarskjold a few days later, Bunche, who had substantial experience with the Israelis, noted with some surprise that they were "very active here with an offer of 100 scholarships and much behind the scenes talk."

Gaston Eyskens, stood to speak. Lumumba was a late addition; he had not originally been scheduled to speak at this ceremony. Film of the event shows Lumumba furiously scribbling as King Baudouin spoke, perhaps revising his remarks on the fly. Malcolm X would later call it the "greatest speech" by the "greatest black man who ever walked the African continent."[39]

Speaking in French and wearing a dark suit, narrow bowtie, and maroon sash—signifying Belgium's highest honor, the Order of the Crown, which he had just received the night before—Lumumba began by welcoming the "victorious independence fighters." He then proclaimed the "glorious history of our struggle for liberty."[40] That struggle, he said, put an end to the "humiliating slavery which had been imposed on us by force." Lumumba spoke in a calm voice and cadence, but his words were sharp and uncompromising, and they rapidly deflated the false bonhomie of the event. He reminded the assembled Congolese of

[t]he ironies, the insults, the blows that we had to submit to morning, noon and night because we were Negroes...

We have seen our lands seized in the name of allegedly legal laws which in fact recognized only that might is right.

We have seen that the law was not the same for a white and for a black, accommodating for the first, cruel and inhuman for the other.

We have witnessed atrocious sufferings of those condemned for their political opinions or religious beliefs, exiled in their own country, their fate truly worse than death itself...

All that, my brothers, we have endured.

Then, in an arresting phrase, very likely apocryphal but oft-quoted, Lumumba declared to the king and the other Belgian leaders in the room, "as from today, we are no longer your monkeys."[41]

Patrice Lumumba's electrifying speech upended the ceremonies. Congolese gave him a standing ovation. Belgian leaders "had tears in their eyes" in the aftermath.[42] The proceeding paused for an hour while the king, whose veins on his forehead had "stood out as an indication of the violence of his feelings" during the speech, threatened to leave.[43] The *Guardian* called the speech "pugnacious" and "offensive."[44] The *New York Times* reported that Lumumba's speech "produced comments of surprise and disappointment among Belgian and other Western representatives." The Soviet diplomats present, however, "seemed to be enjoying the occasion."[45] In six months Lumumba, who to many Congolese was now the face of resistance to Belgian domination, would be dead.

Reporting back to Hammarskjold, Bunche was a bit unnerved. He told the secretary general that "the operation of handing over powers here was quite ragged."[46] The independence ceremony became a crisis "and nearly a disaster" because of Lumumba's "acid, hard hitting anti-colonial speech." But he placed his finger on the cause: "The King's speech, which was the first, boasting of Belgian contributions . . . was maladroit and ill-advised to say the least." Leopold's rapacious rule was one of unremitting horror for many Congolese, and the paternalistic rule by the Belgian government which followed, while improved, was hardly much better.[††] Lumumba, Bunche told the secretary general, could not resist the provocation; the opportunity was too great to attack the king and "make big political capital by lambasting the departing masters" while also "implicitly whacking" his rival, Kasavubu.

Bunche, long an experienced diplomat, seemed a bit startled by Lumumba's blunt and intense address in such an august and formal setting. Unlike most of the foreign press covering the event, however, he understood that the real misstep had been King Baudouin's. Still, even some in Congo were unnerved by the remarks. One political ally of Lumumba's said: "I was in the audience and I was struck dumb. Lumumba acted like a demagogue . . . he's committing political suicide, I thought."[47] Recounting the events to Hammarskjold in copious detail, Bunche described being in a car soon after the event with Thomas Kanza. The vehicle was attacked by a group of political opponents, including a "burly, half-drunk rogue," who

---

[††] Indeed, Belgian rule was so bad that a doctoral dissertation by a historian named Newton Gingrich—who went on to become speaker of the House of Representatives and later famously deemed Barack Obama "anticolonial"—described Belgian education policies in Congo as "appalling" and "dismal."

began to beat on the car. "It was Kanza's car, but I ordered the driver to get away quickly," he wrote. "These people take their politics . . . very emotionally." (Coming from Bunche, this was not a compliment.) He then made an important prediction: unless there is strong leadership and strong government, "there can be a disintegration approaching calamity."[48]

Bunche's unease about the handover of power was prophetic. The entire Independence Day affair was an augury of what was to come. A couple of days later, at a sporting event meant to mark the celebration, Lumumba snatched the trophy from Kasavubu and awarded it to the winners. Then, in less than a week, the real chaos began.

The first steps involved the army. Congolese soldiers in the Force Publique mutinied against their white Belgian officers. The Belgian commander, Lieutenant General Emile Janssens, had written on a blackboard at a large meeting of officers, "Before Independence = After Independence."[49] Often pointed to as a key spark of the mutiny, Janssens's open acknowledgment of Belgium's intentions simply slipped the mask off of elite attitudes toward postcolonial Congo. Soon the military uprising, which easily overpowered the few Belgian officers left, spread throughout the country. Europeans, who were already on edge, began to flee.

Disorder ensued quickly in part because so much of it had been anticipated. Eleanor Roosevelt was not the only one who feared Congo was not ready to assume self-rule. Just days before the independence ceremonies, one of Bunche's UN colleagues argued that "even if all goes well" the system in Congo would be highly lopsided. Unless the Belgians continue to play a major role, he predicted, "there may be prolonged chaos."[50] In the weeks before Independence Day, news outlets also portrayed rising racial anxiety among Europeans. Reports in the West often seemed to stoke fears as much as describe them. Tension is rising to "near-panic" among whites, the Associated Press reported, in the wake of "anti-white threats" in local newspapers. A chief concern, the AP claimed, "is for the white women. African propagandists are boasting they will be 'ours' after independence. The newspaper of one native nationalist movement said soon it would no longer be a crime for Africans to rape white women."

These and other alarmist stories spread substantial fear in the West of what was to come. One reporter suggested that only deft political maneuvering could save the situation: "A broadly based coalition government wide enough to include extreme Congolese nationalists is being urged as the sole hope of saving the Belgian Congo from anarchy and revolution when this enormous colony achieves independence June 30." This particular story was prescient about other events as well: "'Lumumba will be premier or he will be assassinated or will become a terrorist," gloomily predicted one observer.[51]

As disorder spread rapidly in the wake of the July 5 mutiny, many European residents were terrified. Belgian men even disguised themselves as women to get priority on transportation out of the country.[52] Foreign delegations in the country, also fearful of the repercussions of rising violence, quickly appealed to the Belgians to restore calm. In response, armed Belgian soldiers were dispatched, ostensibly to protect their citizens, but without the approval of the now sovereign Congolese government. This was a critical turning point in the crisis and a violation of the new nation's sovereignty. Rather than a celebration of African liberation, Congo's independence was quickly becoming a demonstration of continuing European power and control. The *Force Publique* was seemingly ungoverned, Europeans were bolting across the Congo River to the French colonial city of Brazzaville in panic, and Belgian troops were rolling in. Order was breaking down.

Bunche was in his Leopoldville hotel on July 8 when he saw vehicles outside filled with Congolese soldiers brandishing weapons and shouting. No one seemed to be in control. Eyeing the scene from his balcony, he saw the troops point their guns at the ambassador of Israel. Soon, gun-toting soldiers were banging at his door, ordering him downstairs. He quickly hid some confidential documents behind the toilet and followed them to the lobby, where other guests, ordered to remain in place, cowered as the soldiers milled about. Eventually, the armed men left. Bunche would later tell reporters that a "mutinous army" had gained control of Leopoldville. There was, he said, nothing to oppose it. "The city was completely at their mercy. They were strongly armed and they came into buildings, hotels, houses and apartment houses, and I am frank to say that I have never been so frightened in my life as I was at that time."[53] From this point forward, only eight days into Congo's independence, he would remain in nearly constant contact with Dag Hammarskjold as the two attempted to chart a path out of the careening chaos.

Bunche also wrote to his son, Ralph Jr, later that day:

Dear Ralph,

The way things have been here all day today and are going tonight, I cannot be sure when I can mail this letter to you. In truth, I cannot be positive at this moment if I ever will be able to mail it. For there are some heavily armed Congolese soldiers down in the lobby right now ordering people around pretty roughly at gun point. It is touch and go when one of them may erupt and start banging away with one of those automatic rifles they carry . . .

It is quite dangerous to go out in the daytime and forbidden to go out at all after 6 p.m. The streets are completely deserted now and this is like a dead city.

I have five people with me—four men and a woman—and they all hold up extremely well under this strain. You can never be sure what is happening when a shot is heard, or a knock on the door or the telephone rings. . . . One couldn't run away if one wanted to, as there are no planes operating. But you can't run away from duty in any case.

Well, if things work out all right in the end this predicament we are all in now will later seem quite amusing. Wouldn't it be ironic, though, if I should now get knocked around here in the very heart of Africa because of anti-white feeling—the reason being that I am not dark enough and might be mistaken for a "blanc"! Well, life is full of ironies.

The menace he experienced as soldiers rampaged through the city could soon be observed throughout Leopoldville and the provinces. In response, Belgian airborne troops dispatched more widely around the vast country; fighting broke out and some Belgian soldiers killed Congolese troops and civilians. The Congo crisis was quickly becoming an international crisis.

Then, just as events in the capital were intensifying, Moise Tshombe, the Congolese leader of the mineral-rich province of Katanga, met with Bunche.

He told him of his intention to secede from the new Congo state. Bunche had first met Tshombe a few days after independence, when Tshombe came to meet with him at his suite at the Stanley Hotel. Tshombe expressed what Bunche called "great dissatisfaction" with the concept of a centralized government. Tshombe, wielding a "surprising" knowledge of the US Articles of Confederation period, informed him that he preferred a looser federation in Congo, one that would give much more autonomy to Katanga.[54]

A large southern province near the Rhodesian, now Zambian, border, Katanga was the home of the largest and most valuable mines in Congo. The mines had long been the primary source of wealth in the colony. Congo was in fact incredibly mineral-rich. It produced 85 percent of the cobalt, 65 percent of the industrial diamonds, and 35 percent of the copper in Africa, as well as abundant high-grade uranium, which had become increasingly important for nuclear power and weapons.[55] Indeed, after Albert Einstein alerted FDR to Katanga's huge supply of high-grade uranium, it became the source used in the Manhattan Project—and in the atomic bomb dropped on Hiroshima. During the Second World War, the OSS, Bunche's first employer in the US government, even sent operatives to the area to ensure the uranium mines did not fall into German hands.[56] (There is no direct evidence that Bunche was part of that effort, though he was one of the only Africa experts at the OSS at the time and likely the only one who had actually visited Congo.) Tshombe, with foreign mining company support, was using the widening unrest across the nation to break Katanga and its riches away.

The move sent Congo careening toward dissolution. Katanga's secession would cripple the nation's finances and potentially lead other provinces in the huge nation to seek their own autonomy. Bunche described the situation as a "powder keg."[57] It is perhaps not surprising that in his classic *The Wretched of the Earth*, written as the Congo Crisis was unfolding, Frantz Fanon declared that "decolonization, which sets out to change the order of the world, is, obviously, a program of complete disorder."[58]

CHAPTER 18

KATANGA

T HE ATTEMPTED SECESSION of the province of Katanga was a body blow to the young government of Congo. Prime Minister Patrice Lumumba feared that his new nation was coming apart almost as soon as it was born. Increasingly concerned that the West was conspiring to destroy the young nation, Lumumba argued that Moishe Tshombe was simply an "agent of the Belgian imperialists," doing their bidding to keep control of Katanga's vast wealth.[1] Feeling desperate, he immediately requested a meeting with Ralph Bunche to discuss assistance from the United Nations. Bunche was, of course, prepared to render advice to the new leader; that was the core part of his purpose in flying around the world to handmaiden the handover of power. But he found Lumumba's request—to bring armed UN peacekeepers to the Congo to stem the secession and quell the growing disorder—a "complete surprise."[2] Congo was all of ten days old.

In a cable to Dag Hammarskjold on July 10, 1960, Bunche relayed his dismay: "I made it perfectly clear that UN could not repeat could not participate in actual policing internally or in providing fighting men."[3] On this point he was stating conventional UN policy on the new art of peacekeeping: peacekeepers were limited in their mandates and were supposed to use arms only in self-defense. Intervening in civil wars was not part of their portfolio. Yet Bunche was ultimately proven wrong: the UN did eventually provide "fighting men," and they would become deeply involved in policing throughout Congo.

Congo's request for peacekeepers had in fact been spurred by the United States. In Leopoldville, American ambassador Clare Timberlake had concluded that given Belgium's intervention of troops, a UN force was the best way to tamp down the coming anarchy and, perhaps more important to the US, keep the Soviets out of the new state. In a cable marked "Secret-Eyes Only," Timberlake wrote to Secretary of State Christian Herter that his idea "should keep bears out of the Congo caviar."[4] Timberlake ran his idea by Bunche as well. As he thought further, Bunche, too, began to see the logic of UN intervention. The situation was rapidly spinning out of control; perhaps a show of foreign troops under UN auspices could halt the violence and allow a reset. The Suez Crisis just three years earlier provided a template; he knew how to stand up a force. He told Timberlake that it could be done but that it would require an official request from Lumumba. Timberlake in turn explained the situation to Lumumba, and, soon enough, Bunche had his official request.

Three days after his meeting with Lumumba, Bunche was warming to the idea even more. Cabling back to UN headquarters, he opined that "I believe UN may be able to save this situation." Would it be possible, he asked Hammarskjold, to "undertake any of the following actions, assuming Secco gives [the] green light?"[5] ("Secco" was an early, now rarely used, portmanteau for the Security Council.) Bunche suggested various options, including French-speaking armed observers, helicopters, light planes, military police, even a military band: it "may sound, may even be silly . . . but it would trumpet the international presence."

The following day, claiming it was threatened by a communist insurgency, Tshombe formally announced the secession of Katanga. He sought to rest the secession on principle, but his move was clearly a power play backed by

Belgian and other foreign mining interests. Tshombe had been sidelined by Lumumba in the runup to Congo's independence, and he sought to portray Lumumba, and the Leopoldville central government generally, as a foreign force seeking to control Katanga.[6] Soon the self-proclaimed Katangan state was appealing to outside powers for legal recognition as a sovereign entity. Foreign mining interests, by paying taxes to Katanga and not the central government, began financing the breakaway province and starving Lumumba's government. Belgian forces and foreign mercenaries streamed in to defend the secession.[7] With abundant resources at his disposal and the tacit backing of important forces in the West, Tshombe could mount a formidable challenge to the weak central government in Leopoldville. Lumumba's rule was crumbling.

Unsure and threatened, Lumumba and Joseph Kasavubu, the president of Congo, stepped up their requests for UN intervention while also appealing to friendly African states such as Ghana to send troops immediately. Bunche was rapidly growing concerned. Unless the UN acted quickly, he urged in a blizzard of cables to Hammarskjold, the outcome would be further Belgian intervention and the "probable involvement before long of French forces across river"—a reference to neighboring Congo-Brazzaville, at that time still a French colony. Although France had embraced independence for many of its African colonies in 1960, it was still an active colonial power with long historical and cultural ties to Belgium. The unilateral military intervention of a great power like France would dramatically change the calculus. Time was of the essence, Bunche thought: "there must be a quick and impressive manifestation of 'moving in' by the UN," he told the secretary general, if the effort was to be effective.[8]

Convinced by Bunche that rapid action was needed, and with a plea on hand from Lumumba, on July 13 Hammarskjold did something no secretary general had ever done before: he requested an emergency meeting of the Security Council. Activating the Security Council brought the leading powers, who had their own interests in the outcome, more directly into the Congo crisis. The threat of communism was, of course, predominant for many Western powers. The Cold War was growing hotter in the summer of

1960.[*] Just weeks before, an American U2 spy plane had been shot down over the Soviet Union; the pilot, Gary Powers, was captured. Later that fall, Soviet Premier Nikita Khrushchev would famously bang his shoe in anger at a General Assembly meeting in New York. In this context, any crisis, indeed the birth of any new state itself, was inevitably assessed through the Manichean lens of the superpower struggle that had divided the world.

In the face of this tense standoff, many of the newly independent states sought to chart a separate course. This effort had crystallized in the international conference in Bandung, Indonesia, five years earlier. The Bandung states aimed to find a third way between Moscow and Washington. Patrice Lumumba's ruling party in Congo was generally aligned with the Bandung approach, as were many new African leaders: Nkrumah in Ghana, but also Sekou Toure in Guinea and Gamel Abdel Nasser in Egypt.[9] Yet as the recent Suez Crisis had amply illustrated, the emerging Third World was nonetheless becoming an increasingly important site of proxy conflict, and Africa therefore a natural Cold War battlefield. The Soviets were more overtly anti-imperialist and enthusiastic about the rapid decolonization of European empires; the US, especially under Eisenhower, supported the more measured approach favored by its NATO allies, even as it blocked them in Suez. (The US also had its own doubts; the late secretary of state John Foster Dulles, just a few years earlier, had remarked that he believed none of the African colonies were capable of governing themselves anytime soon.)[10]

Neither superpower had paid much attention to Africa by this point. The State Department did not create a Bureau of African Affairs until 1958. Nonetheless, American leaders had begun to see Africa as an important new front in the Cold War. Richard Nixon and his wife even toured the continent in 1957 (his appearance at Ghana's independence celebrations was a keystone of the trip). In language that perhaps Ralph Bunche could have

---

[*] Tensions between the superpowers waxed and waned in this era. Just the year before, the Harlem Globetrotters had visited Moscow, charming (and confusing) Russian audiences and meeting—and even hugging—Nikita Khrushchev. Two years later in 1962, the Cuban Missile Crisis would bring the world to the brink of nuclear Armageddon.

used, Nixon warned that the treatment of Black Americans at home was hindering the nation's success in the Cold War battle for hearts and minds. "We cannot talk equality to the peoples of Africa and Asia," he proclaimed, "and practice inequality at home."[11] More to the point, the vice president declared, the emergence of new free nations in Africa could be "decisive in the struggle" between communism and freedom.[12]

Nixon was, of course, not alone in connecting the Cold War and civil rights. Bunche, who dealt daily with the Soviets, certainly was familiar with how they liked to point to American racism at home as a way to turn Africans and Asians away from the US. He thought Nixon was right: by moving more rapidly toward justice at home for its own racial minorities the US could better combat the Soviets abroad in the newly emerging Third World—especially, of course, in Africa.

IT WAS AGAINST THIS COMPLEX COLD War backdrop that the Security Council took up the distant Congo situation in the summer of 1960. The Council provided a new forum for debate on the coming tide of African independence. But the superpowers would also find their own individual methods of intervention.

The resolution approved on July 14 was simple and even terse. The Security Council "call[ed] upon the government of Belgium to remove its troops from the territory of the Republic of the Congo." It then authorized Dag Hammarskjold, in consultation with Congo's government, to coordinate and provide military assistance. The resolution passed 8–0, with three abstentions: Britain, France, and China.[13†] The Council worked through the night—until almost 3:30 a.m.—to complete its task. The succinct language of the resolution seemed decisive in some respects, yet would prove troublesome in the years to come.

As a legal matter, the most significant aspect was the call for Belgium to remove its troops from Congo. In ratifying the UN Charter, all member states pledged to comply with resolutions of the Security Council. This was

---

† In this era, the Security Council had only eleven members; five, as now, were permanent.

one of the major advances of the UN; the Council possessed sweeping law-making powers that bound member states to its commands. Belgium had defended itself by claiming that their intervention was humanitarian in nature and necessary under the circumstances. Once the Security Council acted, however, these justifications were no longer germane, whatever their strength: Belgium was now obligated to withdraw. The Security Council's call for peacekeeping troops, on the other hand, exemplified the UN's newly muscular organizational role. Nations could always individually send troops if the government of Congo requested; what the resolution did was provide a method to coordinate these contributions, place them under international command, and add a dollop of legitimacy to the process.

From the perspective of the superpowers, the Security Council foray into the Congo Crisis had several advantages. For the Soviets, it had the effect of ousting a NATO member (Belgium) and substituting international troops in their former colony. And it allowed them to be seen to support Lumumba and the decolonization of Africa more broadly without intervening directly. The US also found much to like in this approach. Eisenhower, like Khrushchev, preferred to use the UN, which would not be seen as overt great power meddling. While the US increasingly worried that Congo was moving into the Soviet orbit—Soviet advisors were already arriving in Leopoldville—it resisted Lumumba's entreaties for direct assistance in favor of a UN approach that cloaked its hands. A UN-led intervention could help forestall a Soviet-Congo alliance without leading to a direct superpower confrontation. As a State Department official later put it, the UN presence "sort of buffaloed the Soviets . . . they knew how to have a confrontation with us, but they didn't know how to have a confrontation with the UN."[14]

The US also had one ace up its sleeve: Ralph Bunche and Dag Hammarskjold broadly agreed with the Eisenhower administration on the threat posed by Soviet interference. When the UN peacekeeping forces in Congo were finally stood up later that summer, Bunche briefed the incoming general in charge, Carl von Horn of Sweden. Bunche spelled out the tasks facing the UN force. After listing the official duties—replacing the Belgian troops, restoring order, training the Congolese troops—he added a point that did not appear in any of Hammarskjold's instructions. Since Lumumba's "known Communist sympathies had already resulted in appeals for Soviet help," Bunche continued, "we must be ready to prevent any unilateral interference from outside."[15]

The US was quickly coming to the conclusion that it had to intervene in less obvious ways, however. Patrice Lumumba's fiery anticolonial speech on Independence Day had unnerved many in Washington. He appeared to be increasingly unpredictable, and perhaps was cozying up closer and closer to communism. Seeing a threat to core American interests, a flurry of diplomatic activity in support of unseating the Prime Minister ensued.[16] By August, the director of the CIA, Allen Dulles, had come to a shocking conclusion: he cabled the CIA station chief in Leopoldsville that Lumumba's "removal must be an urgent and prime objective and that under existing conditions this should be a high priority of our covert action."[17]

The first UN peacekeepers arrived just days after the Security Council resolution passed, but the influx was slow. As the troops fanned out across the huge territory, it became clear that the UN was still little known to the people of Congo. Brian Urquhart, Bunche's long-time colleague, later recounted that he was asked at one point, "The UNO? What tribe is that?"[18] Congo remained precarious and tense. On July 19, Bunche, normally an optimist, told Hammarskjold he thought the situation was "virtually hopeless."[19]

A week after its first Congo resolution, the Security Council was set to meet again, with Belgium and Congo both given an opportunity to speak. Hammarskjold cabled Bunche before the meeting. The Africans here were worried by stories that the Belgians were introducing new troops, the secretary general explained. "What can you say about this matter which will certainly be raised in [the] next Secco meeting?"[20] Belgium was increasingly seen as the motive force behind Katanga's secession, making Western colonial domination a centerpiece of the growing debate in New York. The discussion that ensued in the Security Council chamber was heated and unearthed the deepening political fissures among the foreign powers. The Soviet ambassador repeatedly characterized Belgium's actions in Congo as "aggression." Henry Cabot Lodge, the US ambassador, said little, simply reiterating the American position that no foreign troops enter Congo unless they were part of the authorized UN force—a stance that implicitly was aimed at the Soviets as much as Belgium. By contrast, France and Britain strongly supported Belgium, while acknowledging that the foreign troops ultimately needed to leave. France called the charges of aggression "ridiculous" and stressed that Congo's government was in part to blame for the situation: "We cannot forget that the UN is responsible for defending human rights and that the Congolese Government, by its first acts, has allowed these inviolable rights to be trampled underfoot."

In making this statement, France was voicing an argument that would continue to echo for decades to come: human rights violations could and should be grounds for forcible intervention by foreign powers. Indeed, Belgium was making precisely this claim. First arguing that Congo was in a state of utter disorder in which Europeans were being raped and killed, Belgium declared that action had to be taken "to avoid more serious bloodshed" and to "put an end to the acts of violence."

> The intervention of Belgian metropolitan troops is thus justified . . . by the total inability of the Congolese national authorities to ensure respect for fundamental rules which must be observed in any civilized community and by the Belgian Government's sacred duty to take the measures required by morality and by public international law.[21]

While the controversial doctrine of humanitarian intervention was not new—it dates at least to the 19th century—it received new energy as many former colonies gained independence and often fell prey to civil conflict and disorder. Part of the controversy over humanitarian intervention was whether the basic principles of sovereignty enshrined in international law permitted it at all. But part was also whether it was simply a renewed and cloaked form of European domination.[‡]

[‡] In 2000, the Group of 77, the organization of developing states, many of which were former colonial states, (and which numbered far more than seventy-seven) declared at its summit in Havana that "we reject the so-called 'right' of humanitarian intervention, which has no legal basis in the United Nations Charter or in general international law."

Europeans had long couched their control of nonwhite peoples in terms of principles, not merely power. The so-called standard of civilization of the 19th century, as a matter of international law, had justified the unequal treatment of—and even the outright conquest of—many foreign societies. King Leopold himself used humanitarian aims to justify his initial claims over Congo; likewise, Ferdinand de Lesseps, who built the Suez Canal through Egypt, declared the opening up of Central Africa by Europeans to be "the greatest humanitarian work of this time."[22] The League of Nations mandates system embodied this race-based humanitarian mindset as well, expressly requiring imperial powers such as France to "guarantee freedom of conscience and religion, subject only to the maintenance of public order and morals, the prohibition of abuses such as the slave trade, the arms traffic and the liquor traffic."[23] When Italy invaded Ethiopia in 1935, it argued before the League that the abolition of slavery in the African state was an important motive and justification for its aggression.

While the explicit use of "civilization" as a measure to judge nations had largely died out after the Second World War, for some in the West the protection of human rights became a new and more appealing rationale for intervention in the affairs of less powerful nations. As Makau wa Mutua has argued, human rights "fall within the historical continuum of the European colonial project in which whites pose as the saviors of a benighted and savage non-European world."[24] In their invocation of the importance of protecting human rights in Congo, France and Belgium were echoing this view.

To be sure, the postwar approach to foreign intervention had marked differences with its predecessors. Postwar interventions tended to eschew political control and looked, for support, to human rights principles agreed upon by the international community. Yet the postwar doctrine of humanitarian intervention could drift, as some observers have argued, "distressingly close to doctrines that inspired European colonialism" in the past.[25] Claims of humanitarian intervention were not limited to the West, of course; Vietnam intervened in Cambodia in the 1970s, citing humanitarian imperatives; so, too, India in what is now Bangladesh. And the *absence* of intervention in the face of a brutal genocide would be a source of shame for many with regard to Rwanda in 1994.

In short, humanitarian intervention had an uncertain legal and philosophical foundation and was at best selectively applied. For newly independent states such as Congo, it often seemed merely to be a wolf in sheep's clothing; a basis for continued control by the colonial powers in a new and racially neutral guise.

Despite the differences voiced by the various great powers over Belgium's intervention in Congo that summer, the Security Council was, in the end, unanimous in its demand that Belgium "speedily" withdraw its troops.[26] Congo's ambassador to the UN, Thomas Kanza, gave an impassioned plea for Congolese territorial and political unity. He underscored the gravity of the situation: by intervening in a serious way, "the UN will have prevented . . . Congo from becoming a battlefield and the cause of a third world war." Along the way, Kanza specifically praised the efforts of Ralph Bunche.

The Belgian foreign minister retorted that his nation had been "outrageously slandered." He then declaimed, in words that echoed King Baudouin's antagonistic speech just weeks before: "Where Congolese unity is concerned, may I recall that this unity is Belgium's doing. Before we came to Africa there was no Congo."[27]

This claim—that nationhood was not organic but instead grew directly out of colonization—was not unique to Belgium. Winston Churchill said the same thing about India. But whatever the origin of Congo's national unity, the secession of Katanga threatened it. Katanga also posed a deep challenge for the United Nations. The organization, at this point less than fifteen years old, was premised on respect for national sovereignty. Nations came together at the UN to cooperate and address shared global challenges, but they had pledged to stay out of each other's internal politics. That Congo was only three weeks old did not matter; it was still a sovereign state. The UN Charter made clear that the organization could not intervene in the domestic affairs of a state. Katanga's attempted secession was, formally, an internal matter, a civil war, for which the UN ought to play no role. Bunche, back in Congo, patiently explained to Patrice Lumumba that the Charter forbade the UN to intervene in the Katanga crisis. Lumumba called this interpretation "a bad one."[28]

Photo 18.1 Patrice Lumumba

In reality, of course, Katanga's secession was not truly or solely a do-mestic matter; it was heavily supported by Western mining interests.§ Many Belgians wanted to retain control over the most economically significant parts of their former colony. Katanga's secession was an acknowledgment that events were not turning out as planned, and now the mining firms were taking more direct action. Bunche knew as much, privately calling Tshombe, the putative leader of the secession, "a puppet and nothing more."[29]

---

§ Minerals would curse Congo for decades to come. By the 2000s, the mining of coltan, a critical material for electronics such as cellphones, proved a continuing source of conflict among various warlords in eastern Congo.

Bunche, who had placed so much hope on Congo's independence and understood its importance to the wave of liberation sweeping Africa, was desperate to try to keep the situation from boiling over. The disorder and violence in Congo, however, seemed more than he could countenance, and he was above all pragmatic. While Lumumba's request was the impetus for bringing in UN peacekeepers, by this point Bunche agreed that peacekeepers were needed. He had lost faith in the volatile prime minister and knew that without immediate help the new nation could splinter rapidly. The question was how best to mount an effective multinational military force.

With escalating racial tensions in mind, Bunche believed it was essential to have a mix of white and Black troops in the UN peacekeeping contingent. Two days later he cabled Hammarskjold: in view of the "mounting fear of Europeans here I regard it as indispensable to announce quickly and *seen* soonest [the] inclusion of a non-African contingent."[30] Having white soldiers backing Lumumba's government would help tamp down the growing racial dynamic of the conflict, he thought, and perhaps calm European flight out of Congo. Suggesting two of the whitest nations on earth (and throwing in a Latin region to mix it up), Bunche continued: "would Austria, Iceland or South America afford any prospect?" Despite this effort, the first set of UN peacekeepers to enter Congo was entirely African: from Ethiopia, Ghana, Guinea, Mali, and Tunisia. Many were poorly trained and arguably unprepared for the violence to come. Troops from Morocco showed up with a marching band and two goats for mascots.[31] Soon others joined, including a small contingent of Dutch medical officers. Bunche had his white soldiers.

The UN had sent troops into conflict situations before, as in the Suez Crisis three years earlier. But it had never done so on this scale and never in such a tumultuous situation. Dubbed the *UN Operation in Congo*, and generally known by its French acronym ONUC, it was at the time the largest peacekeeping operation ever launched by the UN. The influential American columnist Walter Lippmann called it the most advanced and sophisticated experiment in international cooperation ever attempted. Dag Hammarskjold called it "the craziest operation in history. God only knows where it is going to end."[32] As ONUC's initial commander, Hammarskjold chose Ralph Bunche.

ON JULY 16, 1960, IN LEOPOLDVILLE, Bunche's voice came over radios throughout the city. The troops of the peacekeeping force, approved just days before by the UN Security Council, had begun arriving in the vast and only two-week-old nation. Bunche was now the face of the international intervention.

The foreign peacekeepers, he announced into the humid tropical air, "will do everything they can to help restore calm, harmony, and safety for all, whites as well as blacks, in this troubled land. . . . This alone can save your marvelous country from disaster."[33] He sought to explain the rapidly evolving situation in Congo—and the role of the still mostly unknown UN—to whomever was listening. In particular, he tried to tamp down the rising racial tensions and assure listeners throughout the country that ONUC was there to stop the violence and protect civilians, not support a particular political position, party, or race.

Still, race *was* a growing division in Congo in the summer of 1960. Katanga's secession lent an unstable element of civil war to the rapidly devolving situation. But in some respects a racial war was unfolding. Bunche, who had long believed race to be a critical fault line in world politics, feared the consequences of such a conflict—especially there, where the Belgians had ruled with such brutality that some scholars later referred to it as a holocaust.[34] "Active hostility to Belgians now developing rapidly," Bunche warned Hammarskjold by cable. "African clerks at Post Office Saturday morning would serve only Africans and locked several European women in rooms."[35] Later, as the ONUC troops flowed in from various nations, he would write that the Guinean troops were "dismaying." Their commanding general, he continued, "informed [my] chief of staff that Guineans are here to fight Belgians, and he wishes to go straight to Katanga." The UN's forces, the Guinean leader declared, should drive the white settlers "into the sea."[36]

Even before independence, Western news reports had portrayed rising racial fears among Europeans in Congo. Before the handover, the Associated

Press reported that tensions were "rising to near-panic among whites."[37] These and other stories did much to spread fear among Europeans of what was to come. During the first weeks of June 1960, Sabena, the Belgian airline, had to organize seventy extra outbound flights from Congo to accommodate the flood of Europeans seeking to get out before the handover of power.[38]

Years later, in 1969, Bunche spoke in Hawaii of the risks of a world race war. Race, he declared to the crowd, was all pervasive in world politics and presented a formidable obstacle "to that harmony amongst peoples that is essential to a world at peace." By this point, race relations were mainly a domestic issue in the American mind, not a global one. Yet the most challenging issues at the UN, Bunche noted, were in fact racial—a reflection of enduring global discrimination but also of the rising number of newly independent states, especially from Asia and Africa. These new states were often not content to simply *be* independent; they wanted both an accounting for the past horrors of colonialism and a more just recasting of the international order in the future. The injustice they fought had been founded and perpetuated on racial lines. If the white world did not listen, Bunche feared, it might set up a coming clash that could turn apocalyptic: White people, he said, must find a way to "purge themselves completely of racism, or face an ultimate fateful confrontation of the races which will shake the very foundations of civilization, and indeed threaten its continued existence and that of most of mankind as well."[39]

The prominent Nazi Herman Goering had once called the Second World War the great racial war. Bunche seemed to be suggesting that unless the growing racial conflict around the globe was addressed urgently, the next great war would truly be a war of race against race. Perhaps he had seen glimpses of that ominous fate in Congo in the summer of 1960.

The challenge in Congo was not just the careening disorder and violence. It was also that the expectations of whites and Blacks about postindependence life had differed so drastically. Independence had come with astonishing speed, and as a result, there had been little time to adjust or align political presumptions. Indeed, they were fundamentally at odds. Though a fervent believer in decolonization, Bunche did not sugarcoat his view that the people of Congo were underprepared and overly optimistic, as if independence would suddenly turn the economic and political tables and bestow upon them the life they had seen the Belgians enjoy. The Belgians, by contrast, were mired in the past and somehow expected to retain their long-held economic power and political privilege in a superficially Black-led society. Bunche caustically summarized the situation to Hammarskjold: "Europeans scared and bitter and expecting worst. Africans scared and bitter and expecting miracles. Such as instant withdrawal of Belgian troops, food immediately in their outstretched hands, and quick tangible boons from independence."[40] These hopes were bound to be dashed, and the resulting frustration would, unsurprisingly, soon enable a strongman to seize power.

Meanwhile, the world was watching Congo with growing alarm. Bunche and ONUC seemed to the last line of defense against growing chaos. Even the conservative *New York Daily News* wrote: "Let the record show that on July 23, 1960, the *Daily News*, lifelong enemy of the UN and all it stands for, publicly acknowledged humanity's debt to 'UN troubleshooters Dag Hammarskjold and Ralph Bunche' for the strenuous efforts they are making to avert disaster in the Congo."[41]

Yet on the ground, Bunche was not so sure disaster was going to be averted. "Sizing up situation here on basis of all info available," he cabled Hammarskjold the next day, "I can conclude only that it is virtually hopeless for the present." Patrice Lumumba's government was hardly in control in Leopoldville, let alone the countryside. The military, now free of their Belgian officers but without a new command structure in place, was a looming threat. Alarmed, Bunche reported that the armed troops were roaming dangerously, "drinking openly and heavily" in the streets.[42]

Bunche and Hammarskjold had placed much hope on Congo's independence and understood its importance to the wave of political liberation sweeping Africa. A few months earlier, in a speech in Tokyo titled "The New Concept of a United Nations 'Presence,'" Bunche had discussed with pride the power of the UN to calm postwar conflict and stem the cycle of violence. "The mere arrival of a United Nations 'presence,'" he had said in Japan, can have a "quieting effect" on the local situation; in fact, he argued, thus far this has "always been the result."[43] He hoped the same would prove true in Congo—though the stresses there were already far larger than those in any previous crisis the UN had entered in its short fifteen-year history.

As ONUC troops dispersed throughout the enormous country, Bunche struggled to create a cohesive peacekeeping mission. By the end of July, there were over 11,000 peacekeepers from around the world. His experience with peacekeeping during the Suez Crisis three years earlier had been politically momentous but operationally simpler. Multilateral peacekeeping was innately complex, and the scale and scope of ONUC made the challenges far harder. Each national contingent had its own weaponry, rules, and equipment—not to mention language. As one officer commented, "troops arrived, officers arrived, commanders arrived, and nobody quite knew what they were supposed to do."[44]

Eventually, the UN sent a Swedish general, Carl van Horn, who had been in charge in Suez, to run the military side. Bunche had established the Suez operation and knew van Horn well. His arrival freed Bunche, who had no real military experience, to focus on the fraught and fragile matter of politics. The world, one of his UN colleagues wrote at the time, was now "reaping the whirlwind of Belgian misrule."[45]

TRAPPED IN CONGO IN THE YEAR of Africa, Bunche veered between optimism and fear. ONUC was off the ground, he wrote in his diary; "rather bumpy flying but I think the worst is over and this greatest of all UN efforts will succeed." He and his team in Leopoldville met frequently with Congolese leaders that July in an attempt to broker a pathway to stability.

As prime minister, Patrice Lumumba was the key player and the most popular politician in Congo. A mesmerizing orator and autodidact, he had impressed Bunche at the start. But even before Congo had achieved independence, Bunche had prophetically written Hammarksjold that "time and events will quickly put Lumumba to the test."[46] By late July, the tests were flying in fast and furious, and Bunche would turn to describing him as "a madman" and a "frightened but utterly maniacal child,"[47] threatening outsiders when he did not get his way. Bunche later described a typical, if largely calm, meeting with Lumumba in the summer of 1960. We from the

UN are here, he would tell Lumumba, to help you get your government set up, your courts opened, your schools running, "but we won't interfere in your internal differences." Lumumba listened diffidently. His only concern seemed to be the breakaway province of Katanga and its putative leader, Moishe Tshombe. Lumumba's reply was simply "When are you and your UN soldiers going to go and get Tshombe?"[48]

Bunche was not about to get Tshombe, but he had at least convinced Belgium to agree to withdraw its forces from Leopoldsville and return to their bases.[49] This was a major step forward—though the fact that it required his hand was hardly a ringing endorsement of Congo's sovereignty. Hammarskjold reported the result of Bunche's negotiations with the Belgians to the Security Council, stating that ONUC was now restoring order. Yet, while positive news, Belgium's military retreat could be interpreted as a feint; Belgium's real agenda was protecting its people and its economic assets, and while the former could now be protected by UN troops (with Belgian forces nearby if needed), the latter could rely on a different protector: Lumumba's nemesis, Tshombe, who was now using Belgians, foreign mercenaries, and his own men to consolidate power and strengthen his claim to independence.

Lumumba, increasingly frustrated with his loss of power and authority, was walling himself off and seeking assistance mainly from fellow Africans. "Almost every time I go to see him," Bunche cabled Hammarskjold on July 20, "the Ghana Ambassador, who is a fool but dangerous, is just leaving with his bizarre entourage of Ghana police with tommy guns, soldiers, and fellows bare shouldered in Kente cloth togas."[50] To Lumumba, the West had now revealed itself as the true enemy of Congo. We know the objects of the West, Lumumba declared in a speech that summer. "Yesterday they divided us on the level of tribe, clan and village. Today, with Africa liberating herself, they seek to divide us on the level of states." The Cold War, Lumumba argued, forced everyone into antagonist blocs. The West's goal, even in the Year of Africa, was to "deepen the division in order to perpetuate their rule."[51]

Later events would prove Lumumba's fears were not without justification. Desperate for outside help, Lumumba flew to New York in late July to meet directly with Hammarskjold. He then continued on to Washington, where, unaware of growing American alarm about him, he implored US Secretary of State Christian Herter for assistance. The *New York Times* reported that at the State Department the Congolese leader issued a "plea for men and money" to keep his now twenty-seven-day-old nation alive.[52] Herter, who found Lumumba "irrational" and "almost psychotic," refused.[53] Shortly after this meeting, the Eisenhower administration, which had given Lumumba the code name "Stinky" (the Belgians, tellingly, used "Satan"), began to consider the possibility of assassinating him.[54]

Meanwhile, Bunche worked around the clock to ensure ONUC was operating effectively. He prepared a briefing document for senior officers that stressed some key limiting principles of the new practice of peacekeeping. Many of these principles built on his experience in Suez. First, ONUC had "no fighting function." (This principle would be tested, and altered, in the months to come.) Second, ONUC "must *never* intervene in domestic disputes." This clearly reflected the Security Council's position; as one resolution of the period declared, the UN force could not be a party to or "in any way intervene in or be used to influence the outcome of any internal conflict, constitutional or otherwise."[55] Bunche listed a few other principles and then added a cautionary word: mindful of Lumumba's speech on Independence Day, he instructed the ONUC officers not to use the "tu" form of French, as "the Congolese are a sensitive and proud people."[56]

Some began to speculate that Katanga's secession had always been the plan. Thomas Kanza, Congo's UN ambassador at the time, later claimed, plausibly, that Moishe Tshombe had discussed Katanga's secession even before Congo itself was independent.[57] Katanga was vexing in another way. It was perhaps narrowly correct to say that the province was attempting to secede. Yet if one stepped back, what did it mean for a distant province to break away from a vast and thinly populated nation that was only three weeks old and contained a diverse set of peoples speaking some 200 different languages and dialects and representing nearly 500 ethnic groups? Was that really secession, or was it simply an outgrowth—or acknowledgment—that Congo's existing borders were European constructs, that Congo in 1960 lacked a robust national identity, and that perhaps, given Africa's sordid history of colonial domination, the borders drawn by the colonists should not necessarily be respected?

These questions were thorny ones. As Bunche once argued, independence along European-chosen borders was probably the most tragic legacy of colonialism. Congo itself, he believed, lacked a "true national spirit" and also lacked leaders who saw the value in national loyalty and governance for all within their territory.[58] Africa's borders were "distinctly artificial." The resulting "ahistorical units" now had to make their way as weak states in a pitiless world.[59]** Luckily—for the most part—respect for borders became a powerful norm in the postwar world. Rather than dispute borders, most postcolonial states simply accepted them. (As Kenya's ambassador to the UN described it much later, in the immediate aftermath of Russia's invasion of Ukraine in 2022, most African states, despite having arbitrary borders set by distant Europeans, "agreed that we would settle for the borders we inherited . . . not because our borders satisfied us but because we wanted something greater forged in peace.")[60] This norm was largely salutary—territorial wars were a key cause of war in the 18th and 19th centuries—but it had some negative effects. Perhaps one of the more serious but often unrecognized effects is that the wide acceptance of even so-called artificial borders meant that unscrupulous leaders could focus their limited power inward, on rivals or even the populace at large. This proved highly relevant for the trajectory of Congo. As one analyst notes, Joseph Mobutu, in the years to come, "was able to focus his efforts on extracting resources for personal gain in part because he did not need a strong military to defend his country's borders."[61]

For the UN, however, these questions were largely immaterial: Hammarskjold, a lawyer who did not always like lawyerly thinking, was nonetheless a Charter purist who believed that the sovereignty of a state must always be respected. That meant the UN must maintain territorial integrity no matter how "artificial" a state's border might appear and must

---

** Key exceptions included Ethiopia, which had recognized a sovereign power by Europeans since the 19th century, and Liberia, whose unique history of founding by Americans gave it a special status.

remain above the fray with regard to domestic affairs. Hammarskjold and Bunche also firmly believed the independence of Africa was both morally right and important for the UN, which would guide and gain from the process of expanding the international community. If that process grew too violent and chaotic, not only Africa but the UN would suffer.

Katanga's secession, of course, challenged these certainties. In the eyes of many, Belgium's failure to offer any preparation to the new Congolese government was largely to blame for the perilous situation. On July 21, King Baudouin, no doubt glad to be able to skewer Lumumba after his humiliation at the independence ceremonies, expressed his support for Belgian troops in Katanga. In a radio broadcast, the thirty-year-old king declared that like all revolts Katanga's was carried out by a minority. "Whole tribes led by sober and honest men" have asked us to stay and help them build a new nation in Katanga, said the king.[62] Belgium, he declared, was there merely to assist the process. The king's true feelings were underscored when, a few months later, Tshombe was flown to Brussels to receive the Grand Cordon of the Order of the Crown.

Given this complex mix of developments, it was not going to be easy to reunite Congo. Despite what he had told Lumumba, Bunche believed ONUC troops might eventually have to be deployed in Katanga, if only to keep the situation from fracturing in a manner that could spill over throughout central Africa. Either way, Congo seemed headed for disaster. An analysis in the *Washington Post* evocatively likened the nation to a new *Marie Celeste*—the famed ghost ship—"afloat, equipped, going nowhere, crewless, lost, a mystery and a prize on the high seas of power politics."[63]

ON JULY 25, 1960, THE REPUBLICAN National Convention opened in Chicago. Richard Nixon would be chosen as the presidential candidate to compete against Democratic candidate John F. Kennedy. As his vice president, Nixon selected Henry Cabot Lodge, the patrician American ambassador to the UN. Lodge, who had been an active participant in the Security Council debates that summer, spoke directly in his acceptance speech about the issues at stake in Congo. With American leadership, he declared, the UN had been able to play a decisive part in "snuffing out the potential wars which menaced the world in Suez in 1956, in Lebanon in 1958, in Laos last September, 1959." Pivoting to the current moment, Lodge said the same was true in Congo, where, "within the last two weeks . . . that great American Ralph Bunche has given such brilliant leadership."[64]

On the very same day as Lodge's speech, Hammarskjold flew to Leopoldville. Perhaps not coincidently, Patrice Lumumba was at that moment in Washington, DC. Hammarskjold nonetheless heard a mouthful from Lumumba's vice prime minister, Antoine Gizenga, about the UN's unwillingness to be more aggressive. Meeting with Lumumba's cabinet a few days later, Hammarskjold announced that to better assess the situation, and specifically to negotiate what role ONUC could or would play, Bunche would travel to meet Tshombe. Bunche would, he said, be followed on the next day by the first UN military units, and the withdrawal of Belgian troops would then commence "immediately." The plans, Hammarskjold stated with surprising confidence, "are fixed." The UN forces would gain control of the security of a "united Congo."[65]

Hammarskjold's official instructions to Bunche in preparation for his departure for Katanga laid out a Sisyphean assignment: your task, he said, was to discuss with the Belgians the "modalities for the withdrawal of Belgian troops" and their replacement by UN forces.[66] Bunche would also have to judge the risks of widespread violence if ONUC forces were to enter Katanga. "Were you to arrive at the conclusion that resistance by force represents a serious risk," Hammarskjold continued, and for that reason advise against the entry of UN troops, "I shall, upon receipt of your report, ask for the immediate convening of the Security Council."[67] The next move on the Congo chessboard rested on Bunche's assessment.

Katanga, deep in the interior and near the border with white-ruled Northern Rhodesia, was a five-hour flight from Leopoldville. En route on August 4, Bunche wondered what to expect. There may be hostility, of course, he wrote to Ruth, before noting that he was "dreadfully tired" "as I got less than three hours sleep last night and even that was more than the night before." Venting, he declared: "I cannot begin to tell you how complicated and maddeningly frustrating our operation out here is."[68]

Photo 18.2 Bunche in Katanga

Once on the ground, he found Tshombe and his Belgian team of advisors friendly. But they were unyielding. As he weighed the options, Bunche tried to foresee the volatile political future of a nation that was less than six weeks old. The signals were not good. He witnessed armed men marching in the streets of the provincial capital and other signs of preparation for conflict. On August 5, in the midst of a final meeting with Tshombe, he was suddenly told that there was a problem with the arrival of the UN plane coming to pick him up. Rushing to the local airport, he found an unnerving situation: Katangan soldiers, as well as Belgians with grenades dangling from their belts, were in position near the runway as if to attack the incoming plane. A Katangan leader, "wild with excitement and rage," told him they would fire on the plane if it attempted to land.[69] Bunche, alarmed, convinced the agitated man to follow him into the airport control tower, where the two radioed the UN pilot together. After agreeing that the plane would be inspected upon landing and then immediately take off for Leopoldville with Bunche on it, the Katangan forces put down their weapons.

This hair-raising encounter suggested that conflict was easily triggered. Bunche had to decide what advice to give the secretary general. As he later put it, "I advised Mr. Hammarskjold not to send the force to Katanga for the time being. I greatly doubt that a UN peace force could be stationed for very long in any country if, even in self-defense, it would have to turn its guns on civilians rather than military forces."[70] He feared that a Katanga uprising led by Belgians but comprising mercenaries and locals would inevitably be bloody and hard to contain. He told Hammarskjold that Tshombe's opposition was "unqualified and unyielding" and that he, Bunche, had been warned repeatedly that all force possible would be used against UN troops in the province.[71] Hammarskjold, trusting his deputy, agreed. ONUC would not—at this point—try to take back Katanga.

Still, Hammarskjold thought he needed to meet with Tshombe himself. He flew to Congo and then into Katanga with four aircraft carrying two Swedish battalions. (Lumumba, incensed, later declared that "Swedes are only Belgians in disguise.")[72] Little changed, but the meeting was at least peaceful. Sensing a chance to strengthen their claim as the anti-imperialist superpower, the Soviets attacked the decision not to move ONUC into Katanga. *Pravda*, the Soviet house newspaper, dramatically asked:

> What functions is Mr. Hammarskjold fulfilling? Whose interests is he defending in the Congo? . . . The prestige of the UN is being trampled in the mud. Imperialist intervention in the Congo is only [the] first act of a drama being planned by NATO colonialist powers to bring peoples and states of Africa to their knees.[73]

Some later argued that Bunche, in what was still a largely American-dominated organization, simply "consciously or unconsciously" acted to advance US policy in Africa, which naturally incorporated the views of its NATO ally Belgium and feared any leader, like Lumumba, who seemed antagonistic to Western interests and perhaps even to capitalism itself.[74] Bunche, a patriotic American who saw the Soviet Union as a repressive and threatening nation, may well have implicitly followed US attitudes toward Congo. But there is no evidence he was pro-Belgian with regard to Congo, and he was, of course, a lifelong opponent of colonialism.

Indeed, Bunche's private correspondence amply demonstrates that he was deeply frustrated by Belgium. The Belgians "simply cannot face the fact that they have lost out here.... Brussels will require some very straight talking to get rid of illusions," he cabled Hammarskjold at one point. "The UN should have some special punishment for fools."[75] Bunche's advice more likely reflected that he was simply by nature careful and cautious. He was committed to the emerging principles of neutrality in UN peacekeeping, but he also genuinely seemed to fear what might happen if UN troops would have to do battle against the forces protecting Katanga. Lumumba continued to harangue him about ONUC and the UN's unwillingness to take sides. At one point, facing another long series of complaints from Lumumba and close to losing his temper, Bunche in desperation pulled out a cable he had just received. He thrust the text, which was of Hammarskjold's firm rejection of Katanga's bid for membership in the UN, in Lumumba's hands. The prime minister's face "lit up in near ecstasy when he read the message."[76]

Bunche continued to feel under immense pressure. Shortly after his August journey to Katanga, he reached out to a UN colleague. There has never been a UN mission, he vented, where the "emotional tension has been so intense and sustained over so long a period." The pace, he complained, was relentless: "there has been no let-up, ever. Crises occur, hour by hour." Time for Bunche seemed to slow down. "It has been more than two months since we arrived out here and, *vraiment*, it seems like two years."[77] Despite his controversial recommendation that ONUC should not enter Katanga, he knew the breakaway province was a powder keg likely to ignite eventually. The future of postcolonial Africa seemed to be implicated in this struggle: at stake was who would control the vast natural resources of the continent—Blacks or whites—but also whether the emerging new nations would inherit their preexisting colonial borders or immediately be subjected to challenge and, perhaps, fracture along various fault lines. Indeed, one of the primary tasks of many of the new governments gaining independence in the Year of Africa was to forge and develop a national consciousness from often disparate peoples. If Katanga showed that the borders inherited at liberation were not sacrosanct, civil war might break out in many other places.

Bunche thought only an immediate withdrawal by Belgium could save the situation. "I cannot believe that in light of brink of disaster to which Congo has led entire world, it will be impossible to muster sufficient international pressure to compel Belgians to do the one and only thing that can offer hope," he told Hammarskjold.[78] International pressure was indeed growing; soon more than thirty UN members deployed troops to Congo, in what ultimately became a force of nearly 20,000 soldiers. Still, Lumumba, growing more vitriolic, started to demand that the white peacekeepers be removed. On two occasions, soldiers of the Congolese army even attacked ONUC staff.[79] Writing to Ruth, Bunche complained that

> that madman Lumumba is recklessly on the attack now—and most viciously—against Dag and the UN—and we will probably be in for a rough time. . . . It is a tragedy, but it looks as though this greatest of international efforts will be destroyed by the insane fulminations of one reckless man. We may be washed up here in a few days.[80]

Bunche's rare moment of pessimism was not borne out. Even as Lumumba increasingly became more strongly anti-Western in his rhetoric, Kwame Nkrumah of Ghana advised him to not go too far. While the UN troops' unwillingness to enter Katanga might be frustrating, the alternative, in light of the Cold War, was possibly worse. If the Congo became a battlefield between East and West, Nkrumah warned, it would be "a disaster for all of us in Africa."[81]

Yet Congo *was* becoming a battlefield between East and West. Lumumba, frustrated by his reception in both New York and Washington, began to look more assiduously for help from the Soviet Union. At the UN, Congo's representative declared that if the Security Council's resolutions continued to be "badly interpreted," the UN's efforts would not lead to the liberation of the Congo but to the effective reconquest of the country.[82] Moreover, a new problem had arisen. Yet another resource-rich province, South Kasai, was also attempting to secede. Feeling desperate, on August 15, Lumumba asked Soviet Premier Nikita Khrushchev for military equipment.

Bunche did not necessarily see a problem with this request. There is no bar against using equipment from the big powers, he noted in a press conference; "we use a lot of American equipment."[83] The US, however, saw things differently. Convinced Lumumba was now fully embracing communism, American officials took to referring to him as "Lumumbavitch." In a mid-August National Security Council meeting, Eisenhower snapped that Lumumba was "forcing us out of the Congo."[84] Katanga, Ike suggested, might even be recognized as an independent nation. In the subsequent days, the US government continued to debate the problem. A head-to-head conflict with the Soviets in Africa was not desirable. But something had to be done to ensure that Congo was not the first African domino.

The CIA station chief in Congo, Lawrence Devlin, cabled Washington:

> Embassy and station believe Congo experiencing classic Communist effort to take over government. . . . Whether or not Lumumba actually Commie or just playing Commie game to assist his solidifying power, anti-West forces rapidly increasing power Congo and there may be little time left in which take action avoid another Cuba.[85]

Allen Dulles, the director of the CIA and the brother of the late John Foster Dulles, shared this assessment. It was his conclusion, Dulles wrote to Devlin, that if Lumumba continues to rule Congo, the inevitable result will "at best be chaos and at worse pave the way to communist takeover of the Congo with disastrous consequences for the prestige of the UN and for the interests of the free world generally."[86] To forestall this outcome, the CIA would now try to remove Lumumba from power, and indeed assassinate him if necessary.

This was a pivot for the Eisenhower administration but not an entirely unsurprising one. The CIA had been paying attention to Lumumba since well before independence. Its early assessments of him were cautious. An April 1960 memo characterized the political situation in Congo as "fluid" and declared that "we are opposed to any 'stop Lumumba' campaign." While he was unscrupulous, the CIA argued, Lumumba was one of the few, if not only, Congolese leaders with "a Congo-wide appeal and standing."[87]

Any attempt to derail his rise to power might backfire, the CIA counseled. It took only a few months—and just a few weeks of Lumumba's actual rule—for the agency to reverse course and begin planning to kill him.

Perhaps not coincidentally, at about the same time the CIA was debating whether to assassinate Lumumba, the American ambassador to Congo, Clare Timberlake, phoned Ralph Bunche. Referring to the ferry across the Congo river to French colonial territory, Timberlake implored: "Why don't you do something to end the goddamn blockage of the ferry?" The ferry was an important source of mail into Leopoldville. Of perhaps greater interest to Timberlake, the ferry was also the means by which the diplomatic pouch, the legal term for embassy packages that under international law could not be opened by the host government—that is, by Lumumba's government— traveled. The laws of diplomacy do not specify the size of the "pouch," nor its contents, and indeed, examples abound in history of misuse of the concept—including a foiled attempt to kidnap a former Nigerian govern- ment minister using a diplomatic pouch. Bunche's notes, long stored in his files, detail the ensuing conversation with Timberlake:

Bunche: *Perhaps the embassies might protest.*
Amb. Timberlake: *What good would it do? You will just* have *to take over the* Force Publique.
Bunche: *On what authority?*
Amb: *Just* take it *because you have to.*
Bunche: *I haven't heard (US Ambassador to the UN Henry Cabot) Lodge say anything like that in the Secco.*
Amb. Timberlake: *No, of course not.*[88]

As Timberlake was pressing Bunche to have ONUC take more decisive— and probably illegal—action in Congo, back in Washington the CIA was busy weighing various options to assassinate Lumumba. One idea was a special sniper sent to Leopoldsville. "Hunting good here when the light is right," a CIA officer crassly wrote.[89] Eventually, Dulles chose a more clan- destine path. He ordered Sidney Gottlieb, the CIA's top scientist, to fly to Congo armed with a deadly substance made of cobra venom.[90]

Devlin, the CIA station chief, met Gottlieb in a Leopoldsville café near the American Embassy. Gottlieb, under cover, identified himself as "Joe from Paris." Retreating to Devlin's living room, Gottlieb explained his purpose and his special package. "Jesus H. Christ!" Devlin exclaimed. "Who authorized this mission?" President Eisenhower himself, Gottlieb explained, as he handed over the kit of poison and suggested Devlin's men somehow smear it on Lumumba's toothbrush.[91] This Bondesque cloak-and-dagger mission epitomized the 1960s CIA but ultimately proved impossible to carry out. In the end, Lawrence Devlin rightly surmised that Lumumba's Congolese rivals, perhaps with some assistance, would do the dirty work for the US.

CHAPTER 19

THE CONGO AND THE COLD WAR

UN HQ is seat of murder!

—Placard outside the United Nations, 1961[1]

Patrice Lumumba, losing his grip domestically and arousing ire internationally, was increasingly isolated as the violent summer of 1960 drew to a close. In his corner stood Ghana, as well as the Soviet Union, now increasingly shedding any pretense of nonintervention and overtly seeking to assist him against the West. In opposition to Lumumba was a more formidable lineup. The US wanted Lumumba out; indeed, it preferred him dead. Moishe Tshombe and his Belgian forces and mercenaries were engaging in a ruthless battle for Katangan independence. The UN, in the person of Ralph Bunche, was unwilling to deploy ONUC forces as Lumumba wished. (Bunche was now referring to Lumumba in his diary as "the Congolese Ogre" and the "Jungle Demogogue.")[2] Even many Congolese had turned on Lumumba. When a crowd outside protested a speech he was giving, he had troops fire over their heads, declaring that the crowd was not "true Congolese" and simply "representatives of white imperialism."[3]

And now a new source of discord had emerged: Congo's president, Joseph Kasavubu. The rivalry between the two leaders had been growing since the initial preindependence elections in May, in which the fiery, charismatic Lumumba had defeated the dour Kasavubu. As early as Independence Day, Bunche had observed that relations between the two were strained, even hostile. The two men, whenever together at meetings with Bunche, would "studiously ignore" each other, exchange no words beyond those absolutely necessary, and at times openly squabble.[4] Finally, as if Congo did not have enough problems, they turned on each other.

On the night of September 5th, Kasavubu came on the radio. He announced that he was exercising his constitutional powers as president and head of state of Congo to dismiss Lumumba and his government. In his haste and nervousness, he referred to Lumumba as the "Prime Mayor."[5] A new prime minister, Joseph Ileo, would now assume power. Soon after Kasavubu signed off, another voice, "sharp and strident," came over the radio.[6] It was Lumumba. He denied that his power had been revoked by Kasavubu. He declared that he, Lumumba, would remain in authority, and it was in fact Kasavubu who was being dismissed. Two more times that night Lumumba came back on the radio to assert his authority.

The situation was utterly confusing. UN official Andrew Cordier* shut down the Leopoldville radio station to ensure there were no further broadcasts, a decision that may have favored Kasavubu, who had access to the radio across the river in Brazzaville, where the government was hostile to Lumumba. Before the dueling radio broadcasts, Kasavubu had asked the UN for protection as he planned his putsch. As with the secession of Katanga, here, too, the UN was in a bind: a battle between two leaders for control, one head of state and one head of government, was a clearly internal matter and unprecedented in the short history of UN peacekeeping. (To many, however, it seemed the UN was perceptibly favoring Kasavubu.)[7] Nor was there much clarity in the political climate or legal structure of Congo. Given the speed of the power transfer in 1960, the Congolese constitution had been hastily written; there were few if any norms in place to act

---

* Bunche had just returned to New York days before, as explained further below.

as guardrails as the political process skidded off the road. Now, with both men attempting to oust the other from power, the situation in Congo had grown even more dangerous. On top of a civil war, Congo now faced a constitutional crisis.

As sometimes occurs in such crises, an extraconstitutional solution appeared. On September 14, the chief of staff of the army, Joseph-Desire Mobutu, only twenty-nine years old and an avid reader of Winston Churchill, suddenly stepped into the fray. Mobutu was a familiar figure in the Congolese leadership and someone especially close to Lumumba. In fact, Lumumba and Mobutu had been friends in the frantic years before independence, part of the small circle of Congolese *evolués* active in the liberation movement. They would often dine together, comparing notes on politics, and once, some eighteen months before, even went to a political rally together, riding on Mobutu's scooter—Lumumba sitting on the back and Mobutu, prophetically, driving.[8] Those days of friendship, however, were long past. Announcing he was "neutralizing" both the prime minister and the president, Mobutu seized control and relieved both men of their political positions. But in fact it was Kasavubu who would retain some semblance of power, and Lumumba who would be politically exiled and, eventually, hunted down and executed. Mobutu may have once been close to Lumumba. But Kasavubu, more pliable and amenable to the West, made a better partner for Mobutu, who had larger ambitions.

Mobutu returned to the world's headlines four years later, when he staged a more decisive coup that installed him directly in power, a position he would retain nearly until his death in 1997. Soon to become notorious for his extremely cruel and rapacious dictatorial rule, Mobutu later renamed the nation "Zaire." With his signature thick dark glasses, leopard skin hat, and eagle-topped carved wooden scepter, Mobutu would brutally dominate Congo with an intense cult of personality for decades. All the while he plundered Congo's wealth, impoverishing the nation while he traveled the world on a chartered Concorde. To commemorate the tenth anniversary of his assumption of power and to thrust his nation—and himself—once more into the global spotlight, Mobutu staged the 1974 "Rumble in Jungle," the Muhammad Ali-George Foreman heavyweight fight in Kinshasa, the renamed capital. (In a sign of his growing kleptocracy, Mobutu secured the fight with a guarantee of an unheard-of $10 million purse.) But between Mobutu's first seizure of power in the late summer of 1960 and his peak of global fame in the wake of Ali's stunning upset in the sweltering Kinshasa night, Congo would undergo many more, often deadly, twists and turns.

RALPH BUNCHE HAD RETURNED TO NEW York just days before Mobutu's surprising move. Back at the UN headquarters on First Avenue, colleagues thought he looked "very tired . . . and much older."[9] His health was deteriorating. The trip to Congo had gone on far longer than he had envisioned; a three-week visit to the tropics had stretched to three months, each month exhausting and at times unnerving. Congo in the summer of 1960, Bunche later wrote in his diary, "was a nightmare." Despite his intense efforts, Congo, which should have been a shining example of the New Africa emerging from European colonialism, was looking like a disaster.

Bunche felt he could do little more good there. "I'm a patient man," he said at the time, "but my patience has worn thin."[10] In a press conference in early September in New York, he stated that he had returned from "the toughest mission I ever had" and also "the most challenging and inspiring." A BBC reporter named Kee asked him if the fighting between Lumumba's troops and Tshombe in Katanga developed further, would it be the role of the UN peacekeepers to "come between them?" Bunche replied that this was not the basis on which the UN operates. "We do not participate in what would be civil strife."

Kee: How then do you reconcile the UN's duty not to interfere in civil strife with its duty to maintain law and order?
Bunche: As I said earlier, there are subtle and sophisticated distinctions in these matters, and this would certainly be one of them.
Kee: Would you refer back to the Security Council for further instruction?
Bunche: Yes, that's right. Let me say this. . . . If one thinks of conditions in many states throughout the world, one can readily conclude how dangerous, in my view, how fatally dangerous, it would be if the UN should go into the business of participating in civil wars.[11]

While this all sounded good in theory, in practice maintaining any sort of neutrality would prove very difficult in the years to come.

Shortly after this exchange, the annual diplomatic Olympics known as the opening of the UN General Assembly began. Each September thousands of ambassadors, heads of state and government, and interested observers descend on the UN headquarters to begin a new year. Even in 1960, with a much smaller UN than the one today, the General Assembly opening was a major event. Indeed, that fall an unprecedented number of world leaders streamed in from all corners of the globe.

The year 1960 was a pivotal one for the UN, not only because it was the Year of Africa, but also, and relatedly, because so much change was afoot in the global system. The Cold War and its superpower rivalry had long dominated the UN. Now new states and new leaders, many adherents to the Bandung movement's belief in nonalignment, were scrambling the traditional political divisions in Turtle Bay. Newspapers were calling the 1960 General Assembly "one of the most important international meetings in history" and a potentially "decisive battle" in the Cold War.[12] Outsize personalities such as Kwame Nkrumah of Ghana, Gamel Abdel Nasser of Egypt, and a revolutionary new Cuban leader named Fidel Castro, who in his beard and battle fatigues—for a grueling four and half hours—addressed the delegates in the soaring General Assembly hall, were creating a more electric, if unpredictable, atmosphere. It was perhaps unsurprising that in this already remarkable session Nikita Khrushchev famously banged his shoe on his desk.[13]

For Bunche and Hammarskjold, Congo was the single biggest issue at the General Assembly. Both men were true believers in the rapidly unfolding process of decolonization, but the resulting politics sometimes left them dismayed. Already commentators were calling on the UN to do more for Congo; one column in the *Washington Post* called for a "new kind of 'colonialism'" in which the UN itself, with its "unparalled availability of technicians and funds" and its "scrupulous fairness," would take over governance of the new state.[14] (Although this idea was not picked up at the time, decades later, in East Timor, the UN did in fact run a state for a period.) Kwame Nkrumah, in his address to the General Assembly, argued that the UN should lead the fight against imperialism by protecting the right of self-determination for all peoples and excluding any recalcitrant colonial powers from the UN itself.[15] Hammarskjold and Bunche's insistence on neutrality in the civil conflict was wrongheaded, Nkrumah argued; Tshombe's government in Katanga was an active lawbreaker.

"Nkrumah's performance was nauseating," Hammarskjold told Bunche. Bunche, who had personal experience with Nkrumah, replied that Ghana's leader "is after all an out and out racialist and an unprincipled demagogue with an insatiable lust for prestige and power in Africa—his dream." To realize this dream, "he will stop at nothing."[16] To Bunche, "racialists" and demagogues of any stripe were to be deplored; this was one reason he had revised his estimation of Lumumba so drastically over the course of the summer of 1960. A few years later, as the American civil rights movement developed more radical branches, Bunche would declare in a speech at Howard University that "I vigorously opposed Hitler's brand of racism...similarly I find contemptible a racialist approach by any Negro."[17] He would pointedly single out the Nation of Islam for criticism, but he could easily have said the same of Nkrumah or, perhaps, Lumumba. He saw plenty of fault elsewhere as well, however. When he publicly rebuked the Belgians at the General Assembly for failing to adequately prepare Congo for independence, he drew an official protest from the Belgian delegation.

Bunche also did some scolding of the Soviets. Without naming names, but seemingly looking at Khrushchev and channeling the White House, he told reporters as the General Assembly got underway that the "ferocity of the attacks" on the UN of late may be traced to the fact that the UN "moved too fast and too well in the Congo and got in someone's way. Something was thwarted there."[18] Eisenhower agreed, praising the UN's efforts in Congo and noting that the organization had been "flagrantly attacked by a few nations for their own selfish purposes."[19]

Congo and the unraveling of European empire dominated the fall of 1960. Khrushchev dramatically called for the independence of all colonies by the next year. An extreme and unworkable demand, it nonetheless was emblematic of the growing conviction that European colonialism had to end—and swiftly. In response, by early December the General Assembly passed a more measured, but nonetheless striking and influential, resolution on the decolonization process. The resistance that France, Britain, and the other colonial powers had long exhibited to the UN's "meddling" in their affairs had not disappeared. But by the Year of Africa the momentum of liberation was, as the General Assembly put it, "irresistible and irreversible."[20]

In part, this was because the strength, if not always the solidarity, among newly independent states that had been first forged at Bandung five years earlier was growing stronger, and indeed was accelerating. With greater numbers, the members of the new Third World could now use the General Assembly, where each sovereign state, large or small, was equal and wielded the same vote as any other, to pronounce and push forward a striking agenda of anti-imperialism. In Resolution 1514, passed in December 1960, the General Assembly famously declared that "the subjection of peoples to alien subjugation, domination and exploitation constitutes a denial of fundamental human rights, is contrary to the Charter of the United Nations, and is an impediment to the promotion of world peace and co-operation."[21] Colonialism must come to a "speedy and unconditional end." The resolution became a landmark in postwar history: the "bible of the anti-colonial religion."[22] Notably relevant for Congo, the resolution declared that any attempt aimed at the "partial or total disruption of the national unity and the territorial integrity of a country is incompatible" with the UN Charter. In other words, Katanga's attempt at secession was contrary to international law. To make the point even sharper, the next day the General Assembly voted up another resolution, on economic matters, that called for the sovereign right of every state to "dispose of its wealth and its natural resources."[23] Resolution 1514 passed overwhelmingly. Indeed, such was the felt moral case for decolonization in late 1960 that no state dared vote against it, though several abstained. One liberation fighter, leading a conflict against Portuguese rule in Africa, declared that this showed that colonialism was now an "international crime."[24]

The General Assembly's newfound assertiveness was a harbinger of things to come in Turtle Bay. Bunche would not live to see the ambitious efforts to establish a "new international economic order" in the 1970s or the many ensuing condemnations of South Africa (and Israel). But the rapid pace of decolonization meant that the UN itself was undergoing a transformation. Great powers still ruled the Security Council, but elsewhere the developing nations wielded their majority powers, and they reshaped the organization accordingly. By the 1990s, a leading scholar could write, almost as an aside, that while the UN was ostensibly a global organization it was in fact now "dedicated to Third World and North-South issues."[25] Meanwhile the Cold War context continued to lend the Congo Crisis a heightened sense of tension. Bunche reported to American officials that the growing Third World bloc in the UN was eager to assist Congo in reclaiming Katanga. "Algeria, Indonesia, and possibly Morocco, Guinea, Ghana, the UAR [Egypt], and Sudan" were offering troops to help reintegrate Katanga, he explained.[26] The USSR, in turn, was offering the logistical airlift to get them all into position. That fall in New York the Soviets attacked Hammarskjold as a lackey of the West and the colonialist forces. In taking this position, they were attempting to play to the rising tide of newly independent states. The US was in turn supportive of the UN leadership, even as Khrushchev explicitly called for the allegedly colonialist Hammarskjold to resign.

As these political currents swirled in New York, Bunche was again being discussed for a post in Washington. The 1960 campaign between Nixon and Kennedy was in full swing as the fall General Assembly took place. Nixon's vice presidential candidate, Henry Cabot Lodge, knew Bunche well from his long tenure as UN ambassador. Nixon, too, had met Bunche in Ghana and thought well of him. In fact, it was Nixon who suggested the idea of Bunche in Lodge's old role. Both Nixon and Lodge saw Bunche, a highly respected and well-known Black man, as very capable and potentially a useful symbol of Republican progress on race. Nixon said he would "certainly be given very serious consideration" for the role of ambassador.[27] The *Los Angeles Sentinel*, in an editorial in October, quoted Lodge describing Bunche as "one of the three or four greatest living Americans" and proposed that he be appointed secretary of state.[28]

American politics was growing increasingly conscious of race relations in the early 1960s. The civil rights movement was gathering steam; just days after election day in 1960, six-year-old Ruby Bridges was escorted to elementary school in New Orleans, accompanied by four federal marshals. In this context, Bunche, whose fame still ran deep with the public, and who was well known and respected in white America, presented a very appealing choice for a prominent role in a Republic administration.

Nixon's rival, John F. Kennedy, likewise had reached out to Bunche via his brother, Robert F. Kennedy. Bobby Kennedy and Ralph Bunche knew each other already. The younger Kennedy had invited Bunche to speak at the University of Virginia Law School back in 1951, when Kennedy was a student. The invitation to Bunche, who refused to speak to segregated audiences, caused a contretemps at the Southern university, but the Law School, after pressure from Kennedy and other students, had acquiesced. (Bunche delivered his "two brands of democracy" speech—a pointed but apt choice for the South, in which he declared that "we cannot convert the masses of Asia and Africa to a democracy qualified by color.")[29] Now, with the 1960 presidential campaign running hot, Bobby Kennedy told Bunche that his brother wanted an advisor on foreign affairs who was "practicing" rather than just a theorist.[30] Bunche, who had often been approached by presidents before, was flattered but insisted he could not leave the UN.[†]

In the end, the younger and more dynamic Kennedy prevailed over Nixon in an exceedingly close race. JFK could not lure Bunche to Washington, but he would keep an eye on him nonetheless, including studying his poll numbers in a hypothetical primary campaign for the Senate in 1962. Over the next few years, President Kennedy would also call Bunche personally, seeking, as presidents sometimes do, advice and outside perspectives from those not in his White House bubble.[31]

Back in Congo, Joseph Mobutu was now claiming control, to the degree there was control. But larger forces were taking an ever greater interest in the situation. Mobutu, for example, had visited Lawrence Devlin the night before his coup, seeking support from the US. The meeting, according to Devlin, "was full of suspense."[32] Devlin attempted to avoid directly

---

[†] Shortly after Kennedy's win, *Jet* Magazine speculated that Bunche would be named secretary of state; Murray Kempton of the *New York Post* endorsed the idea, writing a column in early December 1960 titled "Why Not Bunche?"

answering Mobutu's requests for American affirmation, knowing he could not get a quick answer from Washington. Mobutu, insistent, pressed Devlin, who ultimately (it appears) gave Mobutu the signal he desired. In the wake of Mobutu's takeover Patrice Lumumba fled to the officer's mess hall of the Ghanaian forces in Congo, where he sought sanctuary. Raj Dayal, the Indian diplomat who had replaced Bunche as head of ONUC, arrived at the mess hall that night to find a "mass of angry humanity, many with lighted bramble torches," menacing the building.[33] (In a September 15 letter to Bunche, Brian Urquhart vividly described Lumumba's situation: "Patsy is holed up in the laundry of the Ghana Brigade's officer's mess," with 200 men "hollering for his blood outside.")[34] UN forces stood around the building with bayonets fixed, guarding Lumumba. The eerie scene portended the accelerating conflict between Congolese factions and the UN troops, who, soon enough, would fire on each other.

There was now effectively a political vacuum in Congo. No legitimate, widely recognized governmental leader really existed. The UN itself refused to recognize the Mobutu-Kasavubu government. A struggle played out over who controlled Congo's seat at the UN. Questions of which governmental claimant was the true representative of a state were not new in Turtle Bay. In 1960, China's seat continued to be held by the tiny nationalist government that had fled to Taiwan after Mao's victory in 1949. Congo's seat, which did not involve the Security Council, was less contentious. But there was still substantial disagreement over who spoke for the huge nation. After extensive maneuvering, in late November the Kasavubu-Mobutu forces eventually prevailed and took the seat at the UN.

Lumumba returned to his Leopoldville residence, subject to virtual house arrest. He was surrounded by both UN forces keeping others out and Mobutu's forces keeping Lumumba in. At one point, Congolese troops even tried to execute a clearly invalid arrest warrant against Lumumba; ONUC soldiers refused to comply.[35] Lumumba's paranoia was proving prescient. Fearing for his life, he engineered a daring escape into the countryside as November drew to a close. Mobutu accused ONUC forces of assisting Lumumba to flee. Whether ONUC was sufficiently remaining above the fray or inserting itself in the Congolese political drama was soon a question in New York as well. Hammarskjold cabled Dayal: "In corridors here there is a lot of speculation as to the UN's participation in the escape of Mr. Lumumba."[36]

For its part, Belgium continued to consider Lumumba a serious threat. His devastating speech on Independence Day had infuriated King Baudouin and the Belgian officials in attendance. There were, to be sure, strong economic interests that drove Belgium to support Katanga and to fear the young prime minister and his growing closeness with the Soviet Union. But the vendetta against Patrice Lumumba was more personal, and his speech attacking Belgian rule, as Congo's security chief later testified in Brussels, was "the detonator."[37]

ON DECEMBER 2, 1960, JUST FIVE MONTHS after assuming power as prime minister and only days after escaping Leopoldville, Patrice Lumumba was tracked down and arrested by Mobutu's forces. A group of UN peacekeepers witnessed the arrest but did nothing.[38] Lumumba was at first flown to Camp Hardy, the base where the Army mutiny had began some five months before. When he arrived, without glasses and his hands tied, "someone stuffed a piece of paper in his mouth: the text of his famous speech."[39]

Lumumba was then taken to Elisabethville, the provincial capital of Katanga. Held in captivity and tortured, he was shot to death in the dark of night by a firing squad on January 17, 1961—allegedly with Moishe Tshombe watching.[40] The body of Patrice Lumumba was never recovered.

While the documentary evidence is fragmentary and, on certain key points, inconclusive, the complicity of the Belgian government in Lumumba's abduction and killing is relatively clear. A Belgian parliamentary commission of inquiry in 2001 concluded that "certain members of the Belgian government and other Belgian figures have a moral responsibility in the circumstances which led to the death of Lumumba." While some four decades later no document or witness could prove any government official "gave the order to physically eliminate Lumumba," the commission declared that it was nonetheless "manifestly clear that the government was unconcerned with Mr. Lumumba's physical integrity."[41] (One could perhaps say the same of the US: the CIA, already plotting to kill him, was informed of

Lumumba's abduction and did nothing. President John F. Kennedy, just inaugurated, stated he was "deeply shocked" by the murder.)[42] Other accounts place the responsibility for Lumumba's fate squarely on the highest levels of the Belgian government, in particular Prime Minister Gaston Eyskens, who sat beside Lumumba and Ralph Bunche at that fateful Independence Day celebration.[43]

Lumumba's meteoric rise to fame and shocking death roiled the world. When the news of his death reached the West, protests erupted. In Egypt the Belgian Embassy was burned, and Belgians were assaulted around the world.[44] Riots broke out at the UN when the news broke. Protestors poured down the gallery of the Security Council chamber. US ambassador to the UN Adlai Stevenson, who was speaking as the protestors burst in, paused and removed his glasses, peering up at the melee in confusion.[45] The protestors, who included poet Amiri Baraka, decried the West's involvement in Lumumba's murder. But they also attacked Dag Hammarskjold's supposed personal role in the Congo fiasco—a favorite claim of the Soviet Union. Within the Security Council, the Soviets called the situation in Congo a "criminal farce." The crimes committed by the colonialists against the colonial peoples have been many, the Soviet representative thundered. But "this new crime is exceptional in that it was perpetrated from first to last under cover of the blue flag of the United Nations."[46]

On First Avenue more protestors had gathered, holding signs denouncing the UN. Walking out to the street, Bunche saw a Black man carrying a sign that read "Kill Bunche." When he asked him who this Bunche character was, he was told, "I guess he's some joker in the UN."[47]

Like many charismatic leaders killed at a young age, Lumumba left a legend that became a potent symbol of what could have been. He became a "martyr of decolonization, a hero to all the world's repressed, a saint of godless communism."[48] Countless books and films depicted Lumumba's brief, sharp political life. The Soviets, seizing the opportunity, promptly renamed their new Moscow-based university for students from the growing Third World "Patrice Lumumba University" (only to strip Lumumba's name after the fall of the Soviet Union in 1991).[49] Not surprisingly, many in the West saw the intense reaction to Lumumba's assassination as simply communist disinformation and manipulation at work.

Yet Lumumba had undoubtedly become a *cause celebre* well before his murder. Writing in the *New York Times Magazine*, James Baldwin underscored the connections between Lumumba's killing, the dramatic liberation of Africa taking place, and the growing civil rights movement in America:

> The fact that American Negros rioted in the UN while Adlai Stevenson was addressing the Assembly shocked and baffled most white Americans....According, then, to what I take to be the prevailing view, these rioters were merely a handful of irresponsible, Kremlin-corrupted provocateurs. I find this view amazing. It is a view which even a minimal effort at observation would immediately contradict....
> One of these facts is that the American Negro can no longer, nor will he ever again, be controlled by white America's image of him. This fact has everything to do with the rise of Africa in world affairs.[50]

Baldwin was certainly right in pointing out that Lumumba, for all his failings, had electrified the African diaspora throughout the world.

Yet Ralph Bunche did not see things this way. Unlike many in the West, he had extensive personal experience with Lumumba. Bunche had long left his radical mindset behind; Lumumba's manic style and politics were not his. It would certainly be surprising if Bunche's stature and age at this point did not feed an appreciation of quiet diplomacy and measured, consensual progress. Yet even in his private writings he was highly critical of Lumumba. As he would scrawl in his office notepad in the late 1960s, "In the '30s I was in the front ranks of civil rights militants and was regarded by many as 'radical' and by some as 'subversive' but I never made wild or reckless statements, never stooped to demagoguery."[51] Bunche was almost personally offended by those who were in his view brash and reckless and attention-seeking.

This was especially true with regard to matters of race. He felt strongly that colorblindness was essential to peace and racial separatism both unjust and, even if Black-led, ultimately a recipe for political disaster. This was one source of Bunche's distaste for Nkrumah and the Pan-Africanism he tried to push to prominence. Lumumba's increasingly race-based appeals troubled him. Indeed, separatism of any form seemed to dismay and even alarm him. In his diary, near the end of his life, he mused:

> I don't care too much for white people, because most of them are so very aware of their whiteness. I don't care too much for black people either, because today especially they are trying so hard to be aware of their blackness and to establish that only black is good, right, and beautiful. Just give me people.[52]

Still, as James Baldwin wrote in his *New York Times* essay, by the Year of Africa something had begun to change for many Black Americans. Bunche was growing out of step with this new mood. Detailing the many ways Black people had been forced to repress their identity in the past, Baldwin declared, "None of this is so for those who are young now." The power of the "white world to control their identities was crumbling as these young Negros were born; and by the time they were able to react to the world, Africa was on the stage of history."[53]

For those who saw African liberation from colonial rule as a critical, long-overdue turning of the historical wheel, Patrice Lumumba was justly regarded as a martyr killed by the reactionary forces of the West. For Ralph Bunche, Lumumba's death was a tragedy. But it was mostly so for the Congolese people, who were denied any real elected government and now, on top of all the ills of colonialism that Lumumba powerfully catalogued in his electrifying retort to the king on Independence Day, had to endure a tragic and violent start to their liberation from colonial rule.

IN MARCH 1961, BUNCHE TRAVELED TO Ohio to speak at Oberlin College. His speech was titled "Africa Tests the UN." Bunche declared to the crowd that the title was "almost a ridiculous understatement." Africa, or "more precisely the Congo," he explained, "threatens the very existence of the UN."[54] Bunche was being hyperbolic, but only a little. Although he had left the conflict-ridden Congo months before, Congo had not left him. Congo, he told a friend shortly after his Oberlin trip, was the sort of problem "that does stay in one's blood, once there has been exposure."[55]

Patrice Lumumba's killing by firing squad in the dark of night just weeks before Bunche's Oberlin speech was a violent punctuation mark in a conflict that had gripped the international community. Lumumba's death had done little to stop the struggle for power in Congo. Powerful forces, including those from neighboring, white-ruled states such as Northern Rhodesia, continued to support separatist claims. From New York Bunche tried to direct the UN peacekeeping forces, now almost 20,000 troops strong, in the vast nine-month-old nation.

For Bunche, the Congo Crisis had been a harrowing experience when he was there; in fact, it was "a nightmare." Yet while the intensity was somewhat lowered now that he was back in New York, Congo continued to consume a huge share of his attention. In part, this was because Congo was emblematic of a much wider issue. Africa, which had only previously been the focus of this much energy and interest from the West during the late 19th-century Scramble, was now the center of an accelerating movement of decolonization. African liberation was happening much faster than many expected. Yet it was also clear that the process was going to be bumpy at times. The situation in Katanga raised difficult questions about the meaning of self-determination at a time when that concept was increasingly viewed as sacrosanct. The General Assembly's landmark resolution on colonialism in December 1960 had declared that territorial dismemberment was bad, but so, too, was "alien subjugation." Which was the situation in Katanga?

Equally apparent was that the Congo Crisis pitted the Soviets against the Americans at a time of great tension in the Cold War. Soviet attacks on the UN leadership were also growing. Concerned that his status as an American was jeopardizing the UN Secretariat's appearance of impartiality, and with an attractive offer from the Rockefeller Foundation in hand, Ralph Bunche submitted a letter of resignation to Secretary General Dag Hammarskjold in June 1961.[56] Hammarskjold wisely refused it.

Soviet dissatisfaction over the UN operation in Congo extended to a key practical issue: how to pay for it. Peacekeeping had not been envisioned in the UN Charter, and there were few established rules about who would pay for it. The mission in Congo was proving very expensive not only because of its huge scale, but also the great distance most troops and equipment had to travel for deployment. The enormous expense foreshadowed a key challenge, one that Bunche would later refer to as the problem of "the tin cup."[57] In 1960, however, there was no template for handling the unexpected costs. The UN had agreed to cover the direct costs of travel, "billeting and rations" for the troops, various supplies, and a daily overseas allowance of 86 cents.[58] The budget committee of the UN ruled that these costs would be assessed on the member states on a percentage basis. This was the normal method for UN members to pay their dues; the idea was to treat the costs of the intervention like any ordinary expense. The Soviets refused to pay, arguing that the assessment decision should have been put before the Security Council—and, hence, was subject to a veto. France similarly refused.

As a result of the conflict over payments, the Kennedy administration periodically made voluntary contributions to keep the UN solvent.[59] By the end of 1961, the UN's deficit was well over $100 million, nearly $1 billion in 2022 dollars.[60] The dispute eventually went all the way to the International Court of Justice. In 1962, the Court declared that the Congo expenses were legally binding on all UN members. The Soviet and French positions were without merit, in part because ONUC's activities were not against a state and therefore were not enforcement measures of the sort delegated strictly to the Security Council.[61‡] France and the USSR ignored the ruling. The Soviet ambassador announced the USSR would pay "not one kopek" for the "illegal" peacekeeping operation in Congo.[62] U Thant, Hammarskjold's successor, would later say that as a result the organization was "on the verge of financial bankruptcy."[63]

Meanwhile, the Congo Crisis continued. Thomas Kanza, Congo's UN ambassador, called Lumumba's murder part of a process of neocolonialism.[64] Many agreed, and saw Katanga as the same. Bunche would later say that Tshombe was thoroughly dependent on European support; the majority in Katanga was opposed to secession, and he was not "as the myth has it, a popular leader."[65] International conferences were held to attempt

---

‡ The vote was 9–5. The Soviet and French judges dissented.

to address the situation diplomatically. After these efforts failed to gain Tshombe's support, the diplomatic approach seemed to be at a dead end.

With few options left, the next step was a dramatic one: the UN peacekeepers would abandon their more neutral posture and begin an offensive to attempt to stitch the country back together. The Security Council essentially directed ONUC to "round up the foreign mercenaries, use military force to stop violence of any sort, and end the Katangese effort at independence."[66] The aggressive resolution, adopted 9–0, with the Soviet Union and France abstaining, was passed on February 21, 1961. The decision effectively reversed the stance Bunche had taken after he flew to Katanga the previous August. He had feared the result if peacekeepers engaged in warfighting on what was, in a sense, enemy-held territory. Now, that fear would be tested. More troops were added to ONUC in preparation, which now comprised soldiers from eighteen different nations. In addition, the Security Council resolution, for the first time, spoke of "systematic violations of human rights and fundamental freedoms and the general absence of the rule of law in Congo."[67] The resolution was seen in Congo as an unjustifiable intervention in its internal affairs, a violation of sovereignty. Kasavubu, in a turn of phrase that must have gotten under Bunche's skin, even called it an attempt at "trusteeship."[68]

In the subsequent months, UN forces launched several large offensives against mercenaries and foreign soldiers in Katanga, replete with colorful code names such as Operations Morthor and Rumpunch. For UN peacekeeping this would be a high—or low—point in its history. The UN had not hitherto done anything on this scale, nor nearly as aggressively. The UN Emergency Force in the Middle East, Bunche's original peacekeeping force, was different: it was interposed between hostile nations, keeping the peace. Here, the peacekeepers were inside a single nation and were actively fighting in an attempt to create peace. Even airpower became part of the battle for Katanga.[69] It would be many decades before such a forward-leaning UN mission would be again pursued.

Later events would lead to intense controversy over the merits of this bellicose approach. But even in the spring of 1961 some saw the UN's actions as worrisome and urgent. Others preferred to focus on ending what they saw as the true source of the problem: Belgium's neocolonial support of Katanga, and the white world's refusal to exit Africa. Kwame Nkrumah called Congo "the heart of the world's trouble" and accused some in the international community of trampling the law under foot "in order to achieve their objective of perpetuating colonialism."[70]

The rhetoric and the stakes were growing higher. The UN itself seemed to hang in the balance. Indian Prime Minister Jawaharlal Nehru, whose troops were part of the peacekeeping forces, stated that spring that the mission "must succeed." Otherwise, Nehru declared—echoing Bunche's words at Oberlin College—"the Congo would blow up and with it, Africa and the UN."[71]

DESPITE NEHRU'S EXHORTATIONS, SUCCESS IN CONGO was not immediately apparent. A year had passed since Ralph Bunche had first flown to Belgium to discuss the impending independence of the new nation. So much had occurred since those heady and optimistic days. Bunche had initially puzzled over the personalities in the new government and the

Photo 19.1 ONUC soldiers on patrol in Congo

attitudes of the exiting Belgians. Now Lumumba was dead, Mobutu and Kasavubu were in power, and the standoff in Katanga continued unabated. To some the country seemed to be inexorably heading for a full-scale civil war. Bunche was dejected and deeply concerned.

In New York, unlike in Leopoldville the previous summer, he was at least able to occasionally enjoy a break from the stress of managing the crisis. In June 1961 he attended an event at the private Lambs' Club, where the National Cartoonist Society was somewhat unusually feting one of the security officers down the hall from Bunche's office on the UN's 38th floor. The guard, a Norwegian named Arne Rhode, received the "Amateur Cartoonist Extraordinaire" award. But even at this unusual and lighthearted event the intense geopolitics of the day intruded. Bob Hope joked that the UN was Nikita Khrushchev's "rumpus room" and that the Soviet leader strangely "wears his shoe on his right hand," referencing the infamous shoe-banging incident of the previous fall at the General Assembly.[72]

A few weeks later Dag Hammarskjold accepted an invitation to return to Leopoldville to try to revitalize the diplomatic process. He planned to speak directly with Tshombe. President Kennedy was increasingly pressuring the UN to ensure that Congolese politicians the US deemed too cozy with communist forces not take control. Bunche, not eager for more ground time in Congo, fatefully decided to stay back in New York.

The Katangan secession merited Hammarskjold's personal intervention because it attracted intense interest from those hoping for a continuation of white rule in Africa. Mercenaries—including former elite French soldiers who had experience in combat in the colonial world—were flooding into Katanga, lured by high wages and the chance to fight the UN, which they resented for its role in humiliating Britain and France a few years earlier in the Suez Crisis. As Bunche's deputy Brian Urquhart later said, the "ordinary" mercenaries in Katanga

> were a bunch of clapped-out British, South Africans . . . who were mostly adventurers; this lot were, in the first place, professional soldiers and, in the second, had huge battle experience. They had been in Dien Bien Phu, Algeria, and god

knows where else, were very, very good officers and were fanatical, all-white, anti-black, right-wing officers.[73]

These sorts of dangerous mercenaries, plus the connections to white-ruled Rhodesia next-door, added to the impression that the conflict in Congo was much larger than just one province attempting to secede from one new nation. The "Year of Africa" had begun full of light and hope. Now, substantial darkness was encroaching.

In September, shortly before Hammarskjold flew to Congo, Tshombe bombed UN forces in Katanga. Katangan ground forces then dramatically surrounded and captured many of the UN peacekeepers in a town known as Jadotville. The peacekeepers eventually surrendered and were taken as prisoners of war. Kennedy, concerned that the UN might "get licked" in Congo, asked Secretary of State Dean Rusk to call Bunche in New York. Rusk told Bunche that if the UN failed to prevent a communist takeover in Congo, Congress would have Rusk's head. To make his position clear, Kennedy refused to assist with further troop transport to Africa.[74]

Rusk and Bunche had a long-standing relationship, and early on in the Kennedy administration Rusk told him to call him "any time" to provide his views on what Washington was doing.[75] Rusk had long been a UN supporter within the American foreign policy elite; as early as the Truman administration, he had sought to make the case that the UN was a "useful vehicle for American goals."[76] Bunche also spoke frequently with other American officials, including JFK himself. This tight tie between Bunche and American officials had been true for a long time. A couple of years later, in response to a challenge regarding his independence at the UN, he stated in a press conference that

> I am more proud of one fact than anything else in my sixteen years of service with the United Nations, and that is that my government at no time has ever attempted to give me any instructions or advice on anything I have had to do in the United Nations. . . . am a servant of the United Nations.[77]

Bunche's umbrage at the suggestion that he might be biased or subject to American pressure was undoubtedly genuine. He had an excellent reputation, and he took that reputation seriously. Others shared his view: U Thant later said he could not think of anyone in the upper echelons of the organization who was less nationalistic in his approach to his work.[78] Yet Bunche's statement to the press corps was not entirely accurate: certainly Clare Timberlake, the first American ambassador to Congo, had attempted to explicitly give him instructions regarding the ferry from Brazzaville to Leopoldville at a time when the US was seeking to assassinate Lumumba. (There is no evidence, however, that he followed Timberlake's "advice.") Bunche's papers also contain many memos from US officials, often marked confidential and with instructions that they were "for your eyes only." These memos step right up to the line of instruction, or at least active collaboration between Bunche and American officials.[79] As the most important American in the UN, Bunche throughout his career was a crucial connector and go-between for official Washington and the 38th floor of the UN.

To be sure, it is not surprising that one of the most senior and influential officials at the UN would have had frequent contact with officials in the most powerful nation on the planet. All secretaries general have had to delicately accommodate American—and other—political interests, especially of permanent Security Council members. Indeed, high-ranking UN officials frequently receive such "instructions" from powerful states. Bunche's special role as interlocutor between the US and the UN would only grow during the remaining years of the 1960s, when the US, frustrated by U Thant and fixated on the Vietnam War, sought to deploy Bunche as their backchannel to the UN. The US was particularly influential in Turtle Bay in the early 1960s. American logistical reach meant that the UN often relied on the US for critical tasks. Troop transport for peacekeeping typically entailed American planes. The same could be true for communications. During the early days of the Congo Crisis, the most reliable means of communication with New York was the American Embassy in Leopoldville. Bunche and his colleagues used it often—which meant the US government knew before anyone else what was happening in Congo.[80]

Ralph and Ruth Bunche were in Maine in September 1961, dropping Ralph Jr. off at Colby College, when the secretary general's office tracked him down. Hammarskjold told him that he had decided to personally visit Congo and wanted him to go with him. As Bunche hurried back to New York, Hammarskjold began to have doubts about the wisdom of the plan. It was probably better, he now suggested, for Bunche to hang back to deal with the inevitable questions that would arise from the trip. Hammarskjold instead said he would bring Heinz Wieschhoff, a more junior UN staffer who had expertise on Rhodesia. Bunche agreed. Then, at Idlewild Airport to see the delegation off, Wieschhoff's wife pulled Bunche aside. Her husband was quite sick, she said; she implored Bunche to tell the secretary general that Wieschhoff should not go. Seeing her distress, he agreed and began to walk over to Hammarskjold. Wieschhoff, observing the conversation, "guessed what it was about and swiftly intercepted me and begged me not to speak with Dag about his illness," Bunche later wrote. Bunche, torn, agreed not to say anything, but he knew that had Hammarskjold been aware, he would have ordered Bunche to travel with him to Congo instead.

The incident at Idlewild Airport gnawed at him later. "Had I not listened to Heinz . . . I would have been on that fatal trip."[81]

CHAPTER 20

THE DEATH OF HAMMARSKJOLD

Dial K for Murder
— Signs outside the United Nations buildings, September 19, 1961

Dag Hammarskjold arrived in Congo in September 1961. He quickly cabled Ralph Bunche to discuss the increasing American pressure he was facing. As a matter of principle, Hammarskjold did not want to bend too much to the most powerful state in the world. "It is better," the secretary general argued, "for the UN to lose the support of the US because it is faithful to law and principles" than to "survive as an agent whose activities are geared to political purposes."[1]

This point was debatable: given the vast American resources, the UN almost always had to consider its support for difficult actions. And, to some observers—certainly the Soviets—it was too late to be proclaiming the UN's independence: they believed Hammarskjold, like his fellow Scandinavian Trygve Lie before him, had already shown himself to be a puppet of the West. Bunche's closeness to the secretary general was just icing on the cake; as far as the Soviets were concerned, Bunche had never really left the State Department and was essentially a conduit for American interests.

Hammarskjold in fact had shown great skill in blunting the excesses of the powerful permanent members of the Security Council without losing their support. Yet like all secretaries general since, he had to carefully balance fidelity to the wider international community with the basic fact that the US supplied a huge fraction of the UN budget, held a permanent seat on the Security Council, and was the leader of the West in the midst of the Cold War. Hammarskjold's popularity and high level of respect gave him more latitude in that regard than many of his successors, but the limits were real. And while the Soviets were right to see him as generally leaning more toward the US than the USSR, that was in large part because the Soviet agenda at the UN was so often intransigence and disruption.

Two days after arriving in Leopoldville, Hammarskjold, accompanied by his entourage, flew to Katanga. Wearing a light-colored suit and sunglasses, he boarded a chartered DC-6 flight at 4:51 p.m. on September 17, 1961. Hammarskjold was headed to Ndola, a town in northern Rhodesia near the Katanga border, where he would meet privately with Moishe Tshombe. Northern Rhodesia was at the time ruled by a white minority government that was deeply invested in Katanga's secession and hoped to ally with Belgian settlers there in a sort of white alliance. Hammarskjold's aim was to convince Tshombe, face to face, to finally end the secession. The flight across Congo was long and, to avoid Katangan jet fighters, circuitous. Congo's vast expanse unfurled beneath Hammarskjold as the plane flew in radio silence. Approaching the airport around midnight local time, suddenly the plane disappeared from radar.

Back in New York, Bunche received word that the plane was missing. He immediately feared the worst. He sought additional information but communication was limited and at first none was forthcoming. Bunche fretted and paced. In the middle of the night he called Brian Urquhart, his deputy. "You've got to come into the office immediately," he said. "I just know something terrible has happened."[2] The wait, dragging on, was painful as they tried to maintain hope. A few hours later Bunche was told that a US Air Force plane had spotted the wreckage of a plane about 10 miles from the airport in Rhodesia.[3] It soon became clear that the UN plane had crashed in the surrounding forest for reasons unknown. Trees were knocked down and the aircraft was found smashed into a giant termite mound.

Nearly all on board were burned beyond recognition; the sole survivor, a UN security officer named Harold Julien, died a few days later. Among the dead was Heinz Wieschhoff. Bizarrely, one body at the crash site was found almost untouched: Dag Hammarskjold's. Stuck mysteriously in his white shirt collar, his tie splayed over his shoulder, was an ace of spades, widely known as the Death Card.[4]

THE DEATH OF DAG HAMMARSKJOLD WAS a shocking blow for the international community. Speculation ensued immediately, much of it centered on the idea that the French-made jet fighter in Tshombe's possession may have accidentally, or even deliberately, shot down the UN plane. For Bunche, the incident recalled the death of Folke Bernadotte in Jerusalem a decade earlier: a peace-seeking Swedish boss, tragically killed in the line of duty. In a strange twist, both men were killed on the identical day, September 17. And

PHOTO 20.1 Dag Hammarskjold at Leopoldville Airport

in both cases, Bunche ordinarily would have been sitting in the next seat—and would almost surely now be dead.

In this case, however, the loss to Bunche was even graver. He certainly had liked and respected Folke Bernadotte. But he and Dag Hammarskjold had forged a unique partnership in the preceding eight years. He would work by day with Hammarskjold on the 38th floor of the UN building but also often dine at home with him in his Manhattan apartment as the secretary general's pet monkey, Greenback, cavorted on the staircase. Hammarskjold and Bunche had lived very different lives, but they shared a true sense of mission about the UN. Hammarskjold's death also boded ill for the UN itself. Bernadotte's murder was an early signal that not all would see the peace organization as a welcome and legitimate actor. Hammarskjold's death was murkier, as the cause was unclear. Yet the impact was far greater, for the secretary general was not only the leader of the organization but had been leading at a time of great change and grave peril in global affairs. Indeed, in the wake of the crash, the *Economist* pessimistically asked if the UN was now destined to die as well.[5]

Still in shock, Bunche traveled to Sweden for Hammarskjold's funeral. Held in Uppsala, where Hammarskjold had grown up, it brought out a diverse array of dignitaries as well as ordinary Swedes. One hundred thousand individuals first gathered in Stockholm for a memorial service, which included a speech delivered by Sture Linnér, the Swedish chief of ONUC.[6] A long torchlight procession paraded through the streets of Stockholm, the city covered in darkness as most storefronts and homes had turned off their lights out of respect. At the official service in Uppsala, Vice President Lyndon Johnson, Trygve Lie, and other notables from around the world were in attendance. The service was followed by a funeral procession to the Hammarskjöld family grave, where he was laid to rest. As the casket was lowered, Bunche was standing next to his colleague Sture Linnér, both men observing silently.[7] He could not help but think of how he could have, perhaps should have, been on the plane with Hammarskjold.

After the funeral, Bunche visited Bernadotte's grave in Stockholm. Back in New York, he organized a memorial concert at the UN for Hammarskjold. American oil entrepreneur and occasional diplomat Jacob

Blaustein donated a large sculpture in Hammarskjold's honor.[*] In another strange link to Bernadotte's death twelve years earlier, local authorities made only a surprisingly tepid attempt to uncover the cause of death. In the immediate aftermath, no search party was sent out; the plane's wreckage was only discovered the following afternoon. Some witnesses claimed that they were denied access to the crash site in the morning and that police—or someone—had already been there.[8] Certainly, the bizarre ace of spades found on Hammarskjold's body suggested something more than a straight-forward aeronautical mishap.

The suspicious nature of the crash added to the sense of tragedy. Three days after the incident, Harry Truman was quoted in the *New York Times* as saying "Dag Hammarskjold was on the point of getting some-thing done when they killed him. Notice that I said 'when they killed him.'"[9] Anticommunist European exiles, blaming the Soviets and Nikita Khrushchev, whose antipathy for Hammarskjold was well known, marched outside the UN carrying signs that read "Dial K for Murder."

In the *New York Times'* first story in wake of the plane wreck—written by a twenty-seven-year-old foreign correspondent named David Halberstam—the paper noted that "much concerning the crash remains inexplicable."[10] Some sixty years later, little has changed. The enigma of Hammarskjold's death has received renewed attention in recent years as declassified documents have allowed new evidence to come to light. A documen-tary film in 2019 ("Cold Case Hammarskjold") and a book on the topic, published in 2011, entitled *Who Killed Hammarskjold?* have popularized the incident and raised more questions than answers. In 2016, Secretary General Ban Ki-moon recommended that the case be reopened to explore the evidence unearthed in recent years. The Tanzanian judge chosen to lead the effort uncovered "an array of new witnesses, sensitive archives, infor-mation about previously unknown Western mercenaries, the presence of

---

[*] The sculpture, an oblong, abstract shape with a perfectly circular hole through it, now sits in the large pool in front of the main UN entrance. The pool, which was already in place before Hammarskjold's death, is lined with rocks brought from the island of Rhodes.

rogue aircraft in Katangese and Rhodesian skies, and a plot by elite French officers to assassinate UN leaders in the Congo."[11]

The official UN report, however, also noted that several key nations did not fully cooperate with the investigation in the crash. As a result, the report stated, the "attack hypothesis"—that Hammarskjold's plane was deliberately targeted and perhaps shot down by forces unknown—could not be dismissed.[12]

AS RALPH BUNCHE SCRAMBLED TO KEEP the Congo mission operating in the fall of 1961, the great powers debated Dag Hammarskjold's successor. The second European—and second Scandinavian—to serve as leader of the UN, Hammarskjold had predicted that the "Secretary-General who comes after me will be one of the Afro-Asians."[13]

The Soviets had other ideas. As unhappy with Hammarskjold as they had been with Trygve Lie, they suggested a wholly different approach: a "troika" of three leaders who would share the role of secretary general, one each from the East, West, and Third Worlds. It was a clever ploy to enlist the growing ranks of newly independent states to their putative reform. Bunche himself was suggested for the post by various people. "In Dag's Death Crisis, Will the UN Turn to Bunche?" ran one headline that fall.[14] Bunche's candidacy went nowhere—no great power has ever had its national named as secretary general—nor did the Soviets' troika concept capture the imagination of the other member states, who rightly saw it as a way to weaken the effective leadership of the organization, the inevitable result being more power for the Security Council and its permanent members. The UN members stuck to the Charter and sought to find a single candidate around whom they could coalesce.

The eventual choice, as Hammarskjold had predicted, was a candidate from a formerly colonized nation. The little-known Burmese diplomat U Thant took office on November 30, 1961.

U Thant was a very different leader than Hammarskjold.[†] As Brian Urquhart, who worked closely with both men, later wrote, Thant

---

[†] Thant, solo, was his full name; U is an honorific. Hammarskjold by contrast had five names.

was in almost every way the opposite of Hammarskjold. He was simple and direct where Hammarskjold was complicated and nuanced; a man of few words where Hammarskjold was immensely articulate; a devout conventional Buddhist where Hammarskjold was inclined to a personal brand of mysticism; a man of imperturbable calm where Hammarskjold could be highly emotional about his work.[15]

Thant was perhaps also more open and interested in what subordinates had to say; Hammarskjold, by contrast, could be somewhat imperious. In Bunche's opinion, Thant often chose to give way and "seek cover" rather than fight, whereas Hammarskjold did the opposite and could be testy and even "vindictive." Bunche later suggested that Thant's outward appearance "of being Buddha-like in his composure and calm" was deceptive; he was actually prone to be nervous and tended to pace around the office, chain-smoking cigars.[16] Perhaps unexpectedly, Thant was also, in Bunche's view, more likely to consult with the major powers whereas "Dag depended more on the small states" and considered them the best defenders of the UN.[17]

While Bunche never had the sort of close relationship with U Thant he enjoyed with Dag Hammarskjold, he came to respect and like Thant, though he was often bemused and even puzzled by him. He was especially surprised by how deeply Thant believed in astrology. Thant often had a former secretary come to visit him on the 38th floor of the UN building, supposedly to inform him about developments in the Burmese press. "But this is a cover, for they discuss astrology," Bunche wrote in his diary, even though "this seems incredible and like cheap fiction." He found the astrologer morose and prone to predict disaster; yet, despite his evident disdain, "she tries to convert me to the stars."[18] Thant's astrological fervor was an open secret in the upper reaches of the Secretariat. When the son of one of the 38th floor officials was born in 1967, Thant spent an evening making a detailed astrological chart. He also believed in UFOs and wanted the UN to study them—a suggestion Bunche gently talked him out of.

Prior to his elevation, Thant had served as Burma's ambassador to the UN, including one year as vice president of the General Assembly. He was consequently well versed in the UN's working methods, and as a citizen of a former British colony—Burma became independent in 1948, when Thant was thirty-nine—he fully understood the sources and implications of the decolonization movement that was rapidly reshaping world politics. This experience would prove significant not only for Congo, but also for another highly vexing issue looming on the UN's horizon: Vietnam.

Colonialism's dramatic evolution in the postwar order was made abundantly clear in U Thant's first days on the job. India, after some preliminary saber-rattling, suddenly sent 30,000 troops across the border into the Portuguese colony of Goa.[‡] For nearly five centuries, Portugal had ruled the small territory on the western coast of India. Since the UN's founding Portugal had resisted the notion that Goa was part of its empire. Indeed, it had refused to report to the UN on Goa as it was required to do under the Charter's provisions regarding "non-self-governing" territories. Instead, Portugal had claimed that Goa was simply a quite distant but integral part of Portugal. In making this conceptual sleight of hand—that an erstwhile colony was actually part of the motherland—Portugal was not alone; France, for example, had been making the same claim about Algeria for many years, though its proximity across the Mediterranean made that argument perhaps easier to accept.

Viewing Goa as stolen, in late 1961 India annexed it by force. Surprisingly, there was little real pushback in the UN itself—despite a warning from President Kennedy not to attack. The Security Council immediately called a meeting over India's action. Most Western states supported the view that the annexation had clearly violated the UN Charter's cardinal rules against territorial aggression. But the Soviet Union, joined by Liberia and the United Arab Republic (the name then used for Egypt), voted against a resolution condemning India. The Soviet veto was, of course, decisive. India's ambassador used the moment to clearly lay out his country's views on colonialism. The idea that Goa was an integral part of Portugal, he declared, was "a remarkable myth." India's invasion had not violated any international prohibition because Portugal's title was never sound, and so there could be "no question of aggression against one's own frontier, against one's own

---

[‡] "Goa" generally included Goa itself as well as the neighboring Portuguese colonial territories of Damao and Diu. Portugal did not accept the annexation until 1974.

people."[19] India even asserted that its move was in self-defense—a permissible ground for the use of force under international law—and added that Portugal had long had the opportunity to return Goa to its rightful owner.

These were clever arguments that could not be dismissed out of hand. Still, the fact remained that India had used force to regain territory. The seizure of Goa, as a result, struck some as a blatant violation of the Charter. Indeed, US ambassador to the UN Adlai Stevenson proclaimed that

> [t]onight we are witnessing the first act in a drama which would end with the death of the Organization. The League of Nations died, I remind you, when its members no longer resisted the use of aggressive force.... We have witnessed tonight an effort to rewrite the Charter, to sanction the use of force in international relations when it suits one's own purposes. This approach can only lead to chaos and to the disintegration of the United Nations.[20]

With stalemate in the Security Council, however, there were no lasting repercussions for India. A large slice of the world community viewed India's action as a wholly acceptable response to Portugal's refusal to decolonize and was perhaps an unwritten codicil to the Charter's strict rules on territorial aggression. Yes, the Charter had been written to forestall aggressive war, but neither Roosevelt, Churchill, nor Stalin likely anticipated the aggression stemming from an attempt to recapture territory under colonial rule. Goa seemed to be an argument that article 2 (4) of the Charter, which rendered the threat or use of force illegal, had a carveout for colonialism.

In so doing, Goa posed an early version of an even deeper question that would arise again, perhaps most notably in the 1999 Kosovo intervention by NATO: could a use of force be illegal but legitimate? The text of the Charter rules on force was fairly clear, but India had a strong case—especially by 1961—that Goa should be in its possession and not be ruled by distant, tiny Portugal. If the legal text was violated but the cause was just, what happened? Which was more important, peace or justice? While the US took the side of peace, the General Assembly chose justice, passing a resolution in the immediate wake of the annexation chastising not India but Portugal for its failure to comply with the UN Charter. Colonialism's moral stature was rapidly declining, and with it, even otherwise illegal actions seemed to many governments to be legitimate, if not legal and even salutary. Justice, in short, appeared ascendant. Colonial rule was increasingly cast as a moral and human rights issue of the first order. Yet also, increasingly, it was portrayed as a crucial security issue. Perhaps peace and justice were not alternatives but complements. By the 1960s, the conviction was spreading that "the continued existence of any dependency by itself created a threat to peace and security."[21] Colonialism—and not the use of force to end it—was said to be the real threat. This was a new twist but one that had important ramifications for European powers.

Goa, in short, provided a punctuation mark to a more profound change underway in the world, one that Bunche supported and encouraged, even if from his high perch on the 38th floor he could rarely speak overtly about it. In an elaboration of the 1960 Declaration on the Granting of Independence, which had denounced alien subjugation and self-determination, in November of 1961 the General Assembly created a new committee. The Special Committee on Decolonization, sometimes known as the "Committee of 24," was intended to provide more vigorous oversight of the process of decolonization. It would do so from the vantage point not of the great powers but of the growing mass of smaller developing powers. In the committee's own words, it was intended to "finish the job" of decolonization.[22] More than twenty-five newly independent states had joined the UN in just the past five years; the pressure to move the final colonies to independence was growing. As one prominent account at the time noted, the UN was now "a very different body" from the one its creators fashioned in 1945: "Few could have believed at that time that the tidal wave of anticolonialism would sweep so drastically over the domains of the imperial powers and leave behind in its wake an organization so largely populated by the new Asian and African states which emerged from the deluge."[23] The new special committee represented the institutionalization of this movement. It was this change, as much as changes in ideas, that allowed India to swallow Goa with minimal indigestion.

In the West, the recapture of Goa in 1961 was inevitably linked to the continuing conflict in Congo, but largely as a shared examples of the breakdown of global order and the putative weakness of the UN. Days after India's invasion, a *Wall Street Journal* headline read "The US and the UN: Administration Grows More Skeptical of UN as a Keeper of Peace," with subheads noting recent events in both Goa and Congo ("Is Peace in Congo Durable?")[24] Increasingly, many saw the UN as a body now under the sway of the new Third World. As one UN official put it at the time, "the Afro-Asian people have taken over and are running the United Nations, even running away with it."[25]

Yet in many ways Congo—and even Goa—were the exceptions, not the rule. Decolonization more often occurred peacefully, with surprising swiftness and widening support. Even France and the UK were increasingly unwilling to vote no in the General Assembly on matters of decolonization, preferring to abstain rather than stand against the tide.[26] The resistance to this sea change was concentrated in the right wings of the traditional colonial powers, and Lumumba and Congo were sometimes used as the emblem of what was wrong with increasingly swift pace of decolonization. Speaking before the UN Association in December 1961, for example, Alec Douglas-Home, the British foreign secretary, declared that "everyone has seen the chaos in Congo" and knows that it "derives from a premature grant of independence to a country who[se] people were totally unprepared for their new responsibilities."[27] Similar views, couched in terms of governing capacity but redolent of racism, if not outwardly so, could be heard on the US right. Writing in the *National Review* in 1962, prominent conservative William F. Buckley castigated the "tyrannous parliamentary majority" in the General Assembly and complained that its influence on the West was "disastrous." Buckley went even further, claiming, as the Belgians and French and others had for decades, that it was in the interest of the colonized themselves to remain colonized. It was, Buckley suggested, not the European powers but the UN and its decolonization agenda that was "the true enemy of the native populations of Africa."[28]

These arguments had been commonplace a generation earlier. As 1962 approached, they were a last gasp, and soon essentially never heard again.

AS THE CONGO CONFLICT CONTINUED, THE United Nations itself became a target. At one point, Brian Urquhart, Bunche's longtime deputy, was even beaten and kidnapped by Katangan paramilitaries. Amazingly, the abduction occurred within earshot of a US senator from Connecticut, Thomas Dodd, who was visiting to assess America's role in the conflict.[29] Urquhart was released at Moishe Tshombe's instruction, but in the coming months more UN vehicles were hijacked and more hostages were taken by Katangan forces. These attacks, not unlike Bernadotte's assassination in Jerusalem, augured a future in which the UN would often be seen not as a neutral peacemaker but as an outside intervenor with no special rights or privileges.

To many Americans, including the national security establishment, U Thant was relatively unknown and untested. Could he handle this new, more difficult phase in Congo? As the *Wall Street Journal* noted at the time, whatever effectiveness Thant possessed in US eyes was "traced to the fact that an American, Ralph Bunche, has been playing perhaps the key role in fashioning Congo policy."[30]

Meanwhile, the increasingly intense fighting meant the US was more and more embroiled in ONUC. President Kennedy was occasionally calling Bunche directly, checking in to get out of his bubble and discuss a range of issues. Shortly after Hammarskjold's death, Bunche had raised the idea that the UN forces needed more air cover. Kennedy was supportive and authorized American fighter jets to Congo to assist UN forces if necessary.[31] (Ultimately, fighter jets were loaned by the Swedish, Indian, and Ethiopian air forces.) The UN was escalating the battle and bombing ground targets. Bunche would coyly refer to ONUC's actions as "a bit bolder than usual."[32] Yet peacekeeping was rapidly coming to resemble war making. The focus remained on Katanga, but it was unclear how much independence or strength Tshombe actually enjoyed. Tshombe talked a good game of fighting, but he did not seem to be much of a warrior himself. At a dinner organized to meet with the Katangan leader, an officer of a Ghurka regiment lept to his feet and proposed a blood oath of peace, slashing his hand. As the blood spurted out, Tshombe fainted.[33]

At his first press conference as secretary general on December 1, 1961, U Thant had called Tshombe a "very unstable man." Later, he would call Tshombe's coterie "a bunch of clowns."§[34] Defying his popular image as a

---

§ Bunche, meeting Thant soon after, was shocked and immediately asked if the reports that he called Tshombe a clown were true. Thant confirmed.

Buddhist peacemaker, Thant was soon seeking to exert more force, urging the British that "we need those bombs" (referring to twenty-four 1000-pound bombs.)[35]

Despite Tshombe's attempts to solidify his secession, no outside power had yet accepted Katanga as an independent state. This was critical; without it, Katanga could not reap the benefits of statehood, which included the protections of the UN Charter against attack, the ability to receive aid from the World Bank and other international institutions, and the legitimacy that went with sovereign status. When Tshombe sought a visa to come to the US, Kennedy refused.[36] Yet the domestic American politics of the Congo Crisis were complex. Kennedy, like other American leaders before him, was trying to thread the needle between support for the newly strengthening decolonization movement and loyalty to traditional American allies, who generally saw the strident anticolonialism of Lumumba and his followers as a worrying sign. Kennedy wanted to ensure the US was on the right side of decolonization. Yet anticommunists such as Senator Dodd, who sat on the Senate Foreign Relations Committee, viewed Congo's central government as dangerously close to the Soviets. Tshombe appealed to their world vision. (Dodd was also alleged to receive a monthly "stipend" from Tshombe.)[37] Many American newspapers, fixated on what they considered a burgeoning communist threat in Africa, often spoke out in favor of Katanga's bid for independence.

Bunche remained in New York as 1962 dawned, with occasional brief trips back to Africa. Thant, despite his taunts of Tshombe, was not nearly as focused on Congo as Dag Hammarskjold had been. Indeed, American officials felt "the best thing about Thant's Congo policy was that he left it almost entirely in the hands of Ralph Bunche."[38]

When twenty-one UN soldiers were killed in battle, Bunche took action, traveling to Leopoldville where he met with Cyrille Adoula, then Congo's prime minister, and the American ambassador, Edmund Gullion. At Kennedy's instigation, Bunche and Gullion brokered a meeting between Tshombe and Adoula; the president had asked Thant to appoint Bunche as mediator. At first the mediation appeared successful; Tshombe surprisingly renounced Katanga's secession and agreed to recognize the central

Photo 20.2 Bunche en route to talks in Katanga

government. Bunche still seemed to have a magic touch. But soon the secession was back on.

The process eluded any stable resolution. The Soviets continued to decry the role of the West, calling the Congo tragedy the result of "blatant interference in the domestic affairs of a young state."[39] Meanwhile, the Soviets and the Americans were finding new chessboards for doing battle. The space race was on: John Glenn had orbited the earth in February 1962, the first American to do so. (Bunche met the astronaut when Glenn visited the UN a few weeks after his historic feat, posing for photos with Bunche and Adlai Stevenson.) On the literal chessboards, a young American named Bobby Fischer won a major chess championship, becoming the first non-Soviet in history to do so. And at the Security Council, the two superpowers argued that spring over the Caribbean island of Cuba and whether the US was, in the words of the Soviet ambassador, posing a threat to Cuba, which was "fraught with the danger of serious complications."[40]

Bunche was steeped in other conflicts that year as well: the persistent struggle between India and Pakistan over the Himalayan region of Kashmir, the subject of ten Security Council meetings alone in 1962; a new conflict in the Southeast Asian territory of West Irian that pitted Indonesia against its former colonial rulers in the Netherlands; and the familiar problem of Palestine, where Israel had attacked Syrian forces that spring, drawing an admonition from the Security Council that both sides obey the armistice accord Bunche had negotiated over a decade earlier. Writing to a colleague, he sounded a jaded note about the biggest challenge of all: "The Congo goes on in the manner you know all too well, up and down, senseless and mad."[41]

Bunche was back in Congo in October 1962 when the Caribbean threat "fraught with the danger of serious complications" that the Soviets had warned about took shape. But the problem turned out to be somewhat different than what they had meant in March. The Soviets had secretly brought nuclear weapons to Cuba. When the US exposed the Soviets' dangerously aggressive move, the Cuban Missile Crisis broke out, immediately bringing the Cold War to one of its hottest moments and the world to the terrifying brink of Armageddon. The standoff starkly illustrated the stakes of superpower interference in smaller states. Adlai Stevenson went before the Security Council and dramatically confronted the Soviets over the missiles, wheeling in surveillance photos as the Soviet ambassador refused to admit their deployment. The UN proved an important arena in the crisis, but beyond that it could do little else. The superpowers were fated to bluff and joust with each other until, finally and fatefully, one blinked. The world breathed a great sigh of relief after the October crisis over Cuba abated.

Then, on November 7, 1962, former First Lady Eleanor Roosevelt died. Bunche had spent substantial time with Roosevelt in the years since their first meeting over lunch at the White House in 1941. They remained friendly. When her grandson sought a summer job at the UN, he had to politely let her know that while there was no such work opportunity at the UN itself, he would refer the inquiry "to Adlai, who, I am sure, will do whatever he can."[42] Roosevelt, he told the New York Times after her death, was "one of the noblest persons of our time."[43] She was a beacon of hope, he said, for the underprivileged, discriminated against, oppressed, and victimized of the world.

Held at St James Church in Hyde Park, near the Roosevelt estate in upstate New York, her funeral brought together every living American president. At the lunch before the service, Bunche chatted with Joseph Lash, who had recently published a biography of Dag Hammarskjold. Harry Truman came over to Bunche, "put one hand on my shoulder and the other on Joe Lash's and said, "You're talking to one of the greatest public servants we have."[44] Over lunch, Bunche spoke with President Kennedy privately out on the verandah. At the service to follow, he sat directly behind Kennedy and First Lady Jacqueline Kennedy in the church. As the attendees were led in a hymn, Bunche, while singing along to "Rock of Ages," observed JFK and Jackie in front of him. Writing in his diary later, he noted that Jackie was singing "without looking at the hymnal; the President was singing too— but he was looking."**[45]

With Eleanor Roosevelt's passing there were fewer and fewer links to the birth of the UN.

At a press conference in early January 1963, Bunche expressed confidence that national unification would finally be achieved in Congo. Referring to Moishe Tshombe, he stated that "I cannot believe that one man can thwart the will of the Congolese people and government and indeed the will of the entire world."[46] Bunche was certainly frustrated by the now years-long conflict. Yet in this case, his optimism, long tested, proved well founded. Tshombe's resolve to fight increasingly seemed to be wavering, and his forces were in retreat. On January 21, ONUC troops entered the town of Kolwezi, the last real holdout in Katanga. A significant and hard-fought moment, it finally brought the Congo Crisis to an end— though substantial work remained to be done to truly stitch the nation together again.

With relief at the outcome, Bunche penned a brief note in his diary. "Big day for the Congo operation. Peaceful entry into Kolwezi. . . . That about winds up the military phase and takes us over the big hump—after two and a half years! We ought to breathe a bit easier now." His mind went

---

** Shortly after the funeral, President Kennedy named Bunche to a committee focused on human rights and Eleanor Roosevelt's other major interests.

Photo 20.3 UN troops patrol outside Elisabethville

immediately to his friend and colleague, now tragically fallen. "I feel I've done something for Dag now."[47]

AS THE CONGO CRISIS WAS WINDING down in early 1963, a new and potent postcolonial crisis was brewing. Formerly part of French Indochina, Vietnam had become independent in 1954. Ho Chi Minh's Viet Minh forces had been active since 1941 and had fought French rule for almost a decade until their decisive victory at Dien Bien Phu. The battle was the catalyst for Eisenhower's fateful statement that Vietnam could become a "domino" leading to the fall of other Asian states to communism. In the wake of the 1954 Geneva Accords, aimed at negotiating a reconciliation in Vietnam, the long, sinuous coastal nation was divided into two, with communist rule in the north and a Western-backed government in the south. By 1963, American forces were increasingly active in Vietnam, though still in small numbers. Vietnam was just beginning to register in the headlines, but it would soon consume American foreign policy, world opinion, the presidency of Lyndon Baines Johnson, and much of Ralph Bunche's final years at the United Nations.

Just a month after the end of the Katanga rebellion, in February 1963, Bunche was in Stockholm for a meeting of the Hammarskjold Foundation. U Thant tracked him down and told him to head immediately to the Middle Eastern nation of Yemen, then in the midst of growing civil conflict in the wake of a coup. Thant wanted Bunche on the ground to help assess and, ideally, calm the situation. Arriving after the long journey, he was greeted by the Yemeni ambassador to the UN and ushered into a black car with a military escort. Heading off on a dirt road into town, Bunche immediately could see that there was little order and much volatility. His car was quickly surrounded by shouting onlookers. Some even clambered onto the moving vehicle. Noticing people drawing pictures in the dirt with a stick and then throwing stones at the image, Bunche, inquiring, was told those were pictures of the kings of Saudi Arabia and Jordan. The crowd denounced not only the Arab royals but also the British, next door in Aden: Yemeni and British forces had already clashed in minor border disputes.

As the crowd gathered on the road out of the airport grew more restive, they began to swarm the car, shaking their fists at the Yemeni ambassador and the military attache ostensibly guarding them from the front seat. Soon the situation grew more grave. The mob, some of whom had guns and many who had the traditional curved knives of the region, began to rock the vehicle from side to side. The Yemeni ambassador unconvincingly tried to blame the violence on khat, the commonly chewed narcotic leaf of the region. Bunche grew fearful as the situation intensified. Should they leave the car? he asked. As he later wrote, "the young colonel said if we got out of the car we would be immediately stoned to death. . . . For the first time in my life I felt that this was it."[48] The protesting Yemenis closed in further and seemed ready to smash the windows. Finally, in desperation, the driver gunned the engine and sharply turned, heading off into the open desert. Bouncing across the rocky landscape as the car threatened to overheat, they barely escaped the mob.

Finally arriving safely in the capital of Yemen, Sanaa, Bunche walked up the ancient stone steps in the old city. Wearing a dark suit, colorful tie, and sunglasses and holding his hat, he was now surrounded by a large contingent of soldiers. A huge crowd formed in the rear, much more peaceful this time, as he headed to meet with President Abdullah Sallal. His Yemeni mission was one of the less celebrated, but still significant, crises in his long UN career. Civil war had been raging in the Arab nation since the coup had deposed the previous royalist government. The royalists were backed by the conservative Kingdom of Saudi Arabia; the rebels, now in power, were backed by Nasser's Egypt.[††] The Kennedy administration recognized the new rebel-led government in Sanaa but took a generally neutral stance, unsure of where American interests ultimately lay. The Soviet Union had also recognized the new Yemeni government as early as October 1962, and it was actively assisting Egypt in supplying troops and equipment to it. With the world's attention riveted by the Cuban Missile Crisis, Nasser operated with little scrutiny in Yemen, at least initially.

Yemen was a tragic example of the costs of the Cold War. The preferences of the two superpowers in the Yemeni conflict did not grow out of any real attention to or interest in the country, for Yemen offered little strategic advantage to either. British Prime Minister Harold Macmillan later claimed that in November 1962, just after the coup, Kennedy admitted to him that he did not even know where Yemen was.[49] But the fact that the Soviets were involved in the dusty territory was reason enough for America to pay attention. By the time of Bunche's urgent flight to Yemen, McGeorge Bundy, Kennedy's national security advisor, summarized the White House view this way: "Our immediate concern is less with what transpires inside Yemen than the prospect that our failure to recognize the new regime will lead to escalation of the conflict endangering the stability of the whole Arabian Peninsula."[50] While Bundy did not say the word "domino," he may as well have.

For their part, the Soviets were barely less uninformed than Kennedy was. Khrushchev, after reading a cable from his ambassador to Yemen, reportedly said, "Monarchy is by nature a reactionary regime. [The Yemenis] have toppled it and established a Republican regime, which is naturally more progressive. Therefore, we should support the Republicans and offer them aid."[51] In short, neither superpower seemed to have any real interest in

[††] At this time known as the United Arab Republic.

Yemen aside from what it potentially meant for the global chess game and the triumph of their ideology.

On the one hand, this sort of toying with smaller nations—simply viewing them as pawns in a grand game—led to enormous suffering in the Cold War years. Vietnam, and even its neighbors Cambodia and Laos, became Exhibit A of this phenomenon. On the other hand, the lack of any deep superpower interest opened the door to a greater role for the UN and in theory permitted a less inflammatory approach to solving the putative international crisis. As Suez and Congo suggested, however, it was often the case in the postcolonial world that the "crisis" was to a large degree an international crisis *because* of great power interest.

Shortly after the Yemeni situation came to his attention, Kennedy considered sending a special American representative. He soon shelved the idea in favor of deploying the UN and sending Ralph Bunche. The uncertain implications of face-to-face conflict made Bunche and the UN attractive, for most of the world perceived them to be largely neutral players. The Soviets were far more skeptical on this point. They still viewed Bunche, who was at least the second most powerful man in the organization, as fundamentally an American operative. Still, the UN was often the preferred choice in the postwar era to mediate the internal disputes that were increasingly cropping up, and so the Soviets acquiesced. Speaking again to tribal leaders in Yemen in the winter of 1963, Bunche assured the crowd that the "United Nations is your friend." The crowd seemed receptive; some had placards reading "Down with British Imperialism," but others said "Long Live UN."[52] Describing the recent Congo Crisis, Bunche tried to assure the crowd that there was a "worse situation" in Congo and that the UN "sent a police force there ... [and] brought peace." Bunche's efforts seemed to calm things. An Egyptian general gratefully presented him with oranges, cake, and, surprisingly, two bottles of whiskey.[53] By April, Yemen and its protector, Nasser, had agreed in principle to the deployment of UN observers.

Bunche feared Yemen could easily become another Cuba. Still, he did not see another peacekeeping operation as the right response, or even feasible given the politics in Turtle Bay. He certainly did not want to get placed in charge of it. Instead, he proposed to Thant that he attempt to bring the main players together for mediation and install an observer mission in the country. In the end, Thant followed Bunche's plan. In July 1963, the observer mission began its work. The mission was deliberately limited. Bunche cabled the military head that summer that the mission "has no mediation, investigation, inspection functions not directly related to the observation responsibilities." He added pointedly: "Limit contact with Royalists."[54] Chary from his experience in Congo, he wanted to ensure that the UN did not appear to be supporting any government other than the central government in Sanaa.

CONFLICTS CONTINUED TO BOIL OVER AROUND the world, but in 1963 conflict was also close to home. As the civil rights movement gained steam in the centennial year of the Emancipation Proclamation, Bunche was increasingly pondering the future of racial justice in America. In the summer of 1963, in the wake of scenes of snarling police dogs terrorizing peaceful Black marchers in Alabama, the Associated Press sought him out for a long interview on the view from the UN. Asked first whether the African and Asian states criticized the US for its racial failures or applauded the steps recently taken forward, he was forthright that both praise and critique had occurred. But he stressed that the shocking images of brutality—including one, an eerie foreshadowing of the murder of George Floyd nearly six decades later—were at the moment overwhelming any real sense of progress. "Those pictures of the police dog slashing at the Negro man, of the policeman with his knee on the neck of the prostrate Negro woman," he replied, "they've had wide circulation and they've inspired some very bad reactions."[55]

After briefly establishing the basic point that racial injustice at home was harmful to America's image abroad—a point he'd made many times since the late 1940s—Bunche pivoted to specifics about the burgeoning civil rights movement. Asked if the presence of children in the Birmingham, Alabama, marches was dangerous—a suggestion recently made by Attorney General Robert F. Kennedy—he quickly rejected the notion. What were the children really doing? he asked. They were marching to a park they were "not permitted to play in." They were, in short, simply doing what children *should* be doing. Moreover, he argued, the children had the most at stake in this movement.

Bunche rejected the idea that any further patience on the part of the Black community was necessary. The "young American Negro today," he declared, "insists on having all that is his due as an American and having it NOW." Lest there was any doubt he was rejecting RFK's position, he declared that he would have been proud to have had his own children participate in the marches through Birmingham. His criticism of the Kennedys was tempered, however. He was an admirer and confidant of JFK and felt that the young president understood the new world of the 1960s far better than Eisenhower had. Asked now if President Kennedy was "doing enough" for civil rights, Bunche was diplomatic: no one ever does enough, he replied. Yet, he continued, Kennedy had done more than anyone since Abraham Lincoln to further the cause of racial justice. The interview closed with a pivot to the more radical approaches looming on the horizon. Bunche stated a familiar position: those who favored Black separatism, such as Elijah Muhammad's Nation of Islam, were "pitifully wrong and misguided" and were merely echoing the essentialist positions of white supremacists.

The interview was vintage Bunche. His strong and confident sense of right and wrong; his unerring aim for the respectable, centrist, common-sense approach; and his rejection of separate but equal, whatever the source, were all themes he had struck again and again. In the coming years, he would become more active in the civil rights movement, joining Martin Luther King not only in the 1965 March from Selma to Montgomery, where he appeared on the cover of *Ebony* Magazine arm-in-arm with King, but also on stage at the Lincoln Memorial in August 1963, just weeks after his interview about Birmingham, as King lyrically and arrestingly rang out his iconic "I Have a Dream" speech.

The March on Washington both captivated and polarized America, and it also made news around the world. Tass, the Soviets' official news agency, referred to the "repulsive picture of racial oppression and exploitation" the March highlighted. Other foreign observers offered more charitable interpretations. The British *Herald* wrote that "Today, without question, the clock jumped and history changed." The London-based Arab newspaper *Al*

Hayat even suggested a link between the rising power of the American civil rights movement and the UN itself: "It is natural that the American black loses all restraint when he sees the representatives of thirty black countries in the United Nations walking like masters in New York while his own freedom is restricted."[56] In fact, the connection between the UN's home in the US and the civil rights struggle went in several directions. UN diplomats had long complained about discrimination, especially in and on the way to Washington. In 1961, the ambassador of newly independent Chad, Adam Malick Sow, was en route to Washington when he stopped for coffee at the Bonnie Brae diner in Maryland. Refused service, he complained directly to President Kennedy. The governor of Maryland was forced to issue an apology in response. (Kennedy, to an aide, complained, "Can't you just tell the Africans not to drive Route 40?")[57] Bunche saw these connections on a daily basis and knew that America's continuing racial injustice was not only a grave social and political disaster; it was also doing real harm to the nation's global image.

IN 1989, THE HISTORIAN EVAN LUARD declared that the Congo operation was "immeasurably the largest, most complex, and most controversial the United Nations has ever undertaken."[58] The military phase, as Bunche had put it, had ended already, but substantial political repair remained to be done. By the summer of 1963, the true end of the crisis seemed finally close at hand. With a set of leaders now holding what he termed a "broader vision of political development," Bunche felt Congo's national unity had been adequately restored.[59] Eighteen months after the end of the Katanga secession ONUC officially shut down operations.

Unfortunately, however, Congo's larger woes were far from over. A Lumumba-inspired government in the Eastern Congo had now declared itself to be independent. Tshombe returned to power in 1964, only, in a miraculous turnabout, this time as prime minister. Congo's constitution was rewritten in an attempt to bolster stability, but the power struggles continued. After the government ground to halt, in 1965 Joseph Mobutu once again seized power. This time he would not relinquish it for three decades.

Looking back, many have dissected the UN's involvement in the decolonization of Congo and in particular the roles and culpability of the main individuals involved. Each often made momentous decisions on the fly under trying circumstances. Dag Hammarskjold, Ralph Bunche, and others in what was known internally as the UN's "Congo Club" all faced enormous challenges. Bunche and Lumumba in particular have been viewed by some analysts as a political mismatch, their urgent meetings in the summer of 1960 a "fatal encounter" that yielded a tragic outcome.[60] Lumumba, of course, managed to create a wide variety of enemies in his brief political career; his fate was probably overdetermined, and there was little Bunche could do to save him. ONUC's intervention was critical to Congo's future but, particularly when it turned more aggressive, quite controversial. Peacekeeping had little direct authority from the UN Charter. Often referred to as stemming from "Chapter VI and a half," it was a legal hybrid, developed in the heat of the moment and, in an evolutionary process, accepted over time by the international community. ONUC tested the bounds of what was acceptable in peacekeeping. It also presaged a problem that would arise repeatedly in future missions: alleged crimes by peacekeepers.[61] Often poorly paid, lightly supervised, and far from home, peacekeepers on other missions have been credibly accused of more serious forms of malfeasance, including sexual abuse of locals, smuggling, and assault.

Congo itself suffered immensely in the decades that followed Mobutu's second coup in 1965. Propped up by the West as a bulwark in the Cold War (a few months before his assassination, President Kennedy hosted Mobutu at the White House), Mobutu proved disastrous to the people of Congo. His increasingly bizarre and all-encompassing cult of personality brooked no challengers: he jailed and repressed ordinary Congolese, and four former cabinet ministers who displeased him were publicly hanged before 50,000 spectators in a stadium. Even as he raided the nation's wealth for European shopping trips, Mobutu pursued a policy of *authenticite*, which sought to purge Congolese society of outside influences and even clothing and, in a Maoist style, reshape the nation from the ground up. In addition to renaming the nation Zaire, he grandiosely renamed himself Mobuto Sese

Seko, short for "the all-conquering warrior who, because of his endurance and inflexible will to win, will go from conquest to conquest leaving fire in his wake."[62] Less than a year before his death in 1971, Bunche would awkwardly stand with Mobutu at the UN as U Thant handed the Congolese autocrat a UN 25th anniversary medal.

Mobutu's policies ultimately wreaked havoc on the nation. As Zaire crumbled economically and its infrastructure fell apart, by the early 1990s the nation ran up one of the highest rates of inflation in world history, an astounding 24,000 percent per year. Mobutu was forced to flee by 1997 and died that same year. His $400 million palace carved out of the bush north of the capital, once known as the African Versailles, lays in ruins, trees growing through the collapsed roof and empty swimming pools. After Mobuto's ouster, war soon broke out throughout the eastern part of the country, bleeding from and into neighboring states. Yet another dictator, Laurent Kabila, assumed power. By 1999, almost four decades after the creation of ONUC, the UN once again had peacekeepers in Congo. The mission, dubbed MONUSCO, for UN Stabilization Mission in Congo, was still deployed in 2022. Congo today remains conflict-prone and desperately poor, with crumbling colonial-era roads barely knitting the huge nation together.

Ralph Bunche did not live to see the full scope of Mobutu's reign of terror in Congo. He did not know what continuing horrors would befall the people of Congo. Yet he was by nature an optimist, and while Congo in the aftermath of the Year of Africa was a low point in the path to African independence, he was undeterred. A political scientist by training, he nonetheless knew that politics was not something to be understood through causal laws or easily manipulated through precise action. Politics was unpredictable, and the achievement of lasting peace required tenacity, and often improvisation, to succeed.

A few months before the festivities of Congo's Independence Day in 1960, Bunche had given a speech in Tokyo. Japan was just fifteen years removed from the horror and inhumanity of the Second World War. After widespread destruction and occupation by the US, it had, improbably, become one of America's closest allies. His topic that day was peace. "Whatever peace-making may be," he declared to the assembled crowd in Tokyo, many of whom had fought and lost loved ones in the war, "it is not a science; while only on occasion does it resemble an art. It is largely a gamble."[63]

CHAPTER 21

KENNEDY AND JOHNSON

The single most important test of American foreign policy today is how we meet the challenge of imperialism; what we do to further man's desire to be free.
                                             —John F. Kennedy, United States Senate, 1957[1]

On September 13, 1963, an unusual visitor came to the United Nations building. Frank Sinatra, at that point one of the most famous performers in the world, had agreed to give a concert in the General Assembly chamber for the annual UN Staff Day. Joining Sinatra in the crowded hall was Richard Rodgers, the famed creator of Broadway classics such as *Oklahoma!*, *The Sound of Music*, and *South Pacific*, and stage star Martha Wright. That evening Secretary General U Thant hosted a reception and dinner for Sinatra and his guest, actress Jill St. John (who would later famously and improbably date Henry Kissinger). For the special occasion, Ralph Bunche, who was a big fan of Broadway theater, brought along Ruth Bunche.

Sinatra had previously visited the UN at least once, in 1959 for a private tour. Bunche had met with Sinatra then and had personally guided him around the UN campus. Much earlier, both men had also shared a place on the *Honor Roll of Race Relations* from the New York Public Library. Today, however, it was U Thant who introduced the Chairman of the Board.

Calling Sinatra a "great uplifter of spirits," Thant welcomed the singer and the crowd. First, Martha Wright joined Richard Rodgers to perform some musical numbers, including *South Pacific*'s "I'm in Love with a Wonderful Guy." Sinatra then took the stage and sang a few classics from the George Gershwin and Cole Porter songbook as the Bunches listened attentively in the soaring, beautiful, midcentury General Assembly hall.

At one point during the performance Sinatra paused to engage the audience. "Do you mind if I smoke? Am I allowed to smoke in here?" The crowd chuckled a bit. After Sinatra joked about the newfangled filtered cigarettes he was smoking, he turned reflective. "I thought I would just have a few puffs and chat with you for a minute. . . . It's essential that we relax, particularly in the kind of work that all of you people are involved, with the stress of the world and the hotspots around the world: the Congo, Vietnam, Lake Tahoe—everything's hot today."

Some of the staff in the General Assembly chamber laughed at Sinatra's joke ("Anybody want to buy a used casino?" he asked), which referred to his recent, highly publicized troubles with the Nevada gaming license authorities. Sinatra was in hot water because an infamous and blacklisted Mafia kingpin, Sam Giancana, had recently been spotted on the premises of Sinatra's Cal-Neva resort in Lake Tahoe.[2]

Congo, of course, was fresh in the minds of the UN audience that day; the multinational peacekeeping force in the troubled country was still deployed throughout the vast territory on the day Sinatra sang. Vietnam— and in Sinatra's mind, perhaps Tahoe—was the newer hot item on the global agenda. Vietnam had been the site of a protracted and bloody colonial struggle with France, and now, in 1963, was rapidly displacing Congo as the most important front in the Cold War. A couple of months after Sinatra visited the UN, South Vietnamese leader Ngo Dinh Diem was assassinated in a coup that had the tacit support of the American government. At this point, US forces in Vietnam numbered less than 20,000. Within a few years those levels would rise dramatically, culminating, in 1969, in over half a million American troops deployed.

A week after his performance, a friend of Sinatra's (and some later alleged, of mobster Sam Giancana, too) would speak in the same chamber, only this time with less banter and irreverence. At the opening of the annual General Assembly, President John F. Kennedy declared in momentous tones that "the world has not escaped from the darkness." The long shadows of conflict and crisis envelop us still, Kennedy said, implicitly referencing the Cuban Missile Crisis that had terrified the world just eleven months earlier. "Rising to its responsibility, the United Nations helped reduce the tensions and helped to hold back the darkness." Today, he continued, the clouds have lifted a little so that "new rays of hope can break through." It was a bright and sunny, almost summer-like day in New York City, 80 degrees in fact, but in the room there were no windows to highlight the metaphor. Kennedy then declared his faith in the organization. "My presence here today is not a sign of crisis, but of confidence. . . . I have come to salute the United Nations and to show the support of the American people for your daily deliberations."[3]

Listening to President Kennedy's address, Ralph Bunche was transfixed. "His speech was magnificent—in my view the best ever given in the General Assembly," he wrote.[4] He had met the charismatic Kennedy before, and Kennedy had toyed with the idea of appointing Bunche to a prominent ambassadorship. The two had continued to stay in touch, Kennedy occasionally calling Bunche to seek advice.

On this day, Bunche and U Thant welcomed the president inside the delegate's entrance lobby, just off First Avenue. Beaming and surrounded by a sea of men in dark suits, Bunche leaned in to shake Kennedy's hand. Adlai Stevenson, the American ambassador to the UN, accompanied the president. Kennedy, who suffered from recurring back pain, seemed to be in severe discomfort as he walked through the UN building. Soon a doctor was called; "probably to give him an injection," Bunche later surmised.[5] (Kennedy requested a Bloody Mary to top it off.) Thant, Bunche, Stevenson, and Kennedy discussed the ongoing Congo mission, as well as the smaller crisis in Yemen. Kennedy then left with the amiable Bunche, chosen as the best person to chaperone the president, to meet and greet some of the staff.

The world was entering a period of great transition in 1963. The Year of Africa had only been declared three years earlier. Within the last decade, dozens of newly independent nations had streamed into the global order.

Photo 21.1 Bunche welcomes JFK to the UN

Substantial progress in the fight to end empire had been made; the few colonies still left seemed doomed, though the struggle in places like Angola and Djibouti would extend into the 1970s. Depending on how one counted, over forty formerly colonized states had recently gained their independence. In short, the goal that Ralph Bunche had long held—to bring self-determination, political independence, and moral equality to the peoples of Africa and Asia—was coming to fruition. And it was happening much faster than he had ever imagined possible back in the 1930s, when he first proposed to the Harvard Government Department that he study colonial administration in Africa for his PhD.

It was a striking change in the international order and one that had lasting repercussions. As one prominent political scientist put it at the time, "One of the world's great revolutions has been accomplished with a minimum of revolutionary action and sacrifice."[6] Bunche, born at the peak of European empire, and who now nearing sixty, was watching it come to an end.

And where colonialism had not ended—and where racism continued to define political rule—the General Assembly remained relentlessly focused. South Africa in particular became the subject of great attention. White rule there posed a different problem from that of traditional colonialism. South Africa was a sovereign state with a state-sanctioned regime of white rule and apartheid. Yet the UN members increasingly scrutinized and pressured it, even calling, in 1962, for UN members to break off diplomatic relations with and boycott South Africa.[7] In the fall of 1963, Oliver Tambo, the vice president of the African National Congress, the leading liberation organization, was invited to the UN to testify before the Special Political Committee of the General Assembly. Bunche was certainly no fan of South Africa or its policies, but he had some concern about the implications of Tambo's appearance, which he flagged to U Thant. The testimony by a citizen of a member state without that state's consent set a precedent that had "far-reaching implications for future UN deliberations," he wrote. The feelings over apartheid, he explained, were "so strong that no member (other than South Africa in a letter) raised any questions about the precedent being established. Only a few years ago this would have provoked heated and prolonged debate."[8]

There was also change at home in 1963. The civil rights movement was reaching a hopeful step in the centennial year of the Emancipation Proclamation. Just two weeks before Sinatra serenaded the UN staff, gospel legend Mahalia Jackson had sung at the Lincoln Memorial as part of Martin Luther King Jr.'s iconic March on Washington. Ralph Bunche had stood on the stage with King that late August day, listening to A. Philip Randolph, John Lewis, and other luminaries speak to the vast crowd from the podium. Bunche had first spent time with King in 1957 at Ghana's independence ceremonies and had corresponded often with him in the years since—as he did, for example, in May 1963, congratulating King on his efforts in Birmingham "in the face of brutal provocation."[9]

As his presence onstage at the Lincoln Memorial suggested, 1963 marked a reemergence of sorts for Bunche in the American civil rights movement. He had never stopped caring about the struggle for racial justice. Yet for him, racial oppression was a worldwide concern, and he did not necessarily see his absence from the frontlines of the American civil rights movement as any sign he had abandoned either that movement or the problems it attacked. Decolonization, he believed, was fundamentally a project of global racial injustice. Yet while Patrice Lumumba and other African leaders still stirred and inspired some at home, for the most part attention in America to Africa was waning, and more importantly, the sense that the struggle for racial justice at home could be fought on the global plane, using global tools, had faded. The "bold black strategies of the postwar era were rebuffed" during the 1950s, never really to return.[10] Now, a more narrow, domestic strategy of civil rights, grounded not in UN instruments or principles but in the US Constitution's Bill of Rights, held sway. Yet this strategy seemed to be working, however slowly and unevenly, and King and his acolytes were, in Bunche's view, making progress.

As he assessed both of these trends, Bunche certainly had reason to savor a sense of accomplishment. Yet he seemed more concerned about the future than ever before. He had also begun to think more about his retirement from the UN and life beyond the 38th floor.

Bunche wanted to reengage with many of the ideas and efforts that he had left behind when, in 1941, he entered the Roosevelt administration as war loomed. In the spring of 1963 he spoke on civil rights in Virginia and was picketed with signs reading "Bunche for Communism."[11] At the funeral of Medgar Evers in June, he declared that Evers's murder was a "national disgrace" and that he viewed his trip as a pilgrimage. "The Negro of today," Bunche announced, "can be infuriated, but no longer can he be intimidated."[12] That Bunche was now more outspoken on America's race problems, even as he was ever more important within the diplomatic universe, did not mean he always agreed with the tactics or positions of the new generation of civil rights leaders. He did not mince words when he perceived strategic missteps in the movement. Indeed, later he would even criticize King when King began to overtly link the war in Vietnam to the civil rights struggle.

For example, speaking in April 1963 at Vassar College, Bunche declared that he was "sickened by bigoted racists." Then, in a move that perhaps surprised the young audience, he made clear what he meant: he lumped in

Harlem Congressman Adam Clayton Powell, who had recently criticized Bunche as too quiet on civil rights, with the notorious white supremacist Senator James Eastland of Mississippi.[13] Powell, he announced, was "anti-white and anti-Jewish; as vile, despicable, and dangerous as Eastland's typical anti-Negro utterances." Bunche then circled back to a point he had frequently made over the past fifteen years of the Cold War: that segregation and racial oppression were not only a domestic cancer; they harmed the US abroad at a time of great peril. Bringing it all home, tying together the strands of his life's work, he returned to the mission of the UN itself. "Whether man is going to survive depends on man's relation to man. The UN defends this; it opposes bigotry, discrimination, segregation."

RALPH BUNCHE'S IMPORTANCE WITHIN THE UNITED Nations had never been higher than in 1963. With Dag Hammarskjold sadly killed two years earlier, and a new and less dynamic secretary general in the quiet, unassuming U Thant, Bunche was widely seen as the most experienced and tested leader in the building. Indeed, when in late 1962 Thant had come to the end of Hammarskjold's original term in office and would need to be reappointed for a new term of his own, he saw his future at the UN directly tied to Bunche's. One day Thant told Adlai Stevenson that his decision to run for election would be much influenced by "Ralph's intentions." If Bunche will "stay with me," Thant continued, he, too, would stay on.[14] Thant was perhaps stating his true feelings, that he needed Bunche's wise counsel to navigate the treacherous waters of the Cold War UN. But he was also likely signaling that he, Thant, knew how essential Bunche was and, more importantly, how essential the *Americans* believed Bunche was. With Bunche's agreement to stay on, Thant was reappointed secretary general the following month.

Meanwhile, Bunche's increasing prominence on civil rights matters attracted the ire of some of the more radical leaders. Adam Clayton Powell, for instance, claimed that he had not heard from him "since we helped fight to get his son into the Forest Hills Tennis Club." The dig, coming on the heels of Bunche's comparison of Powell to white supremacists, surely reflected the growing antagonism between the two New Yorkers. Yet it landed in part because it had a grain of truth (though Bunche was actually far more active in civil rights than Powell gave him credit for) and in part because it played on the increasingly common image of Bunche as the white man's favorite Black man; a person removed from the common struggle of the Black masses, able to live—and play tennis—in tony Forest Hills. Affronted, Bunche took solace in his older allies. Jackie Robinson, writing to Bunche in November 1963, had said, "as far as I am concerned, there are not many who have made the kind of contribution that you have made." Robinson assured him that he did not intend to sit by and "allow anyone to attack you as Adam and Malcom [sic] did.[15] Bunche replied that Powell may not have heard from him because "Adam does not speak very often in the deep south as I do and seems to avoid NAACP meetings."[16] Nor, he noted, had Malcolm X been at the March on Washington two months earlier.

In an effort to hammer home his commitment to racial justice, in his letter to the influential Jackie Robinson (which Bunche pointedly cc'd to the editor of the *New York Amsterdam News*), he quoted at length from a recent address he had given in Mississippi:

> I reject racists and racism, whoever and wherever they are, and whatever their color, as poisonous and vicious, as evidenced by the infamous so-called white citizens councils. I deplore Negroes embracing, as the Black Muslims and Adam Powell have done, a black form of the racist virus. I take my stand firmly and unflinchingly as an American. This is my country; my ancestors and I helped build it . . . I am determined to fight for what is mine.

Back at the UN, Bunche continued to run the Congo peacekeeping operation from New York, even as it slowly wound down and Congo fell off the front pages. His mastery of the new art of peacekeeping would carry him that same year to the Mediterranean island of Cyprus, the India-Pakistan border, and back to the Middle East. As the conflict in Vietnam metastasized into a full-blown conflagration that would take the lives of hundreds of thousands of Vietnamese, kill countless neighboring Cambodians and Laotians and over 50,000 American soldiers, and damage the presidency of

Kennedy's successor, Lyndon Baines Johnson, Bunche would again serve as the most important interlocutor between Washington and Turtle Bay.

Things in Washington, of course, changed dramatically in the wake of President Kennedy's stirring speech at the opening of the UN General Assembly in September. Kennedy's shocking assassination two months later in Dallas, Texas, stunned the nation and the world. The first televised funeral of a slain American leader brought the country to a halt for days and engendered grief around the globe. Kennedy had been a strong supporter of the UN, and within the international community he offered an invigorating breath of change and youth after the stolid Eisenhower years.

Part of Kennedy's appeal internationally was his keen sense for changes in world politics, even as a senator. In 1957, in a speech that garnered wide notice—indeed one that garnered more attention than any he gave before being president—he had criticized France for its refusal to grant independence to Algeria, and in turn he criticized the Eisenhower administration for its support for France. At the time, Algeria was one of the most significant fronts in the battle over decolonization. Kennedy seemed to see what Eisenhower should have seen, especially after the Suez Crisis. "The most powerful single force in the world today," Kennedy declared,

> is neither communism nor capitalism, neither the H-bomb nor the guided missile—it is man's eternal desire to be free and independent. The great enemy of that tremendous force of freedom is called, for want of a more precise term, imperialism—and today that means Soviet imperialism and, whether we like it or not, and though they are not to be equated, Western imperialism.[17]*

Ralph Bunche stood 100 percent behind Kennedy's views on imperialism. (Algerian nationalists, the year before Kennedy's speech, had actually requested that Bunche mediate the dispute with France.) Kennedy's 1957 speech had reflected the rising tide of political strife over the rapid unwinding of European empire, and was one of many he gave on the topic in the mid-1950s.[18] By 1963, when Kennedy spoke at the UN of the "long

---

* Kennedy's speech was titled "Imperialism—The Enemy of Freedom."

shadows of conflict and crisis," the organization was increasingly consumed by the issue of colonialism and its aftermath. While the Cold War had dominated the early years of the organization, now the axis was becoming less East-West and more North-South.

The newly independent states used the UN more and more to press the argument that not only did the world need to finish the process of decolonization—which meant, at this point, places like South Africa, Rhodesia, Angola, and, to a degree, Vietnam—it also needed to revamp the entire international system on a more just, fair, and racially neutral basis. Decolonization was the first step; loosening the iron grip of the West on the economic and political resources of the Third World was next. The "right of peoples and nations to permanent sovereignty over their natural wealth and resources" and the need to rebalance and redress the injustices in the global order were proclaimed again and again by the General Assembly.[19]

And so it was no surprise that at the General Assembly that fall, while Bunche thrilled to Kennedy's words, many observers also took notice of the remarks of a different speaker, one who starkly highlighted these sharper issues of race and justice in world politics. Emperor Haile Selassie I of Ethiopia, wearing a suit and regally bearded, stood at the General Assembly chamber's lectern with the iconic green marble wall behind him and spoke to the assembled delegates. He first noted that, decades earlier, he had personally implored the League of Nations to recognize the looming rise of fascism and the dire plight of his own nation in the face of Italian aggression. The League ignored him then, he said. But things were better today. Approvingly citing Palestine, Suez, and Congo—all of which bore Bunche's hand—Selassie said the UN had "dared to act" to preserve peace and hence offered hope to a troubled world.

Haile Selassie then spoke the words that are most remembered today. Invoking a recent meeting in Addis Ababa, Ethiopia's capital, of African leaders to establish the new Organization of African Unity, Selassie argued that the cause of peace that so animated the UN's founders in 1945 required that the racial hierarchies that had defined world politics for centuries be banished once and for all. "On the question of racial discrimination," Selassie lyrically declared, the Addis conference taught several lessons:

That until the philosophy which holds one race superior and another inferior is finally and permanently discredited and abandoned;

that until there are no longer first class and second class citizens of any nation;

that until the color of a man's skin is of no more significance than the color of his eyes;

that until the basic human rights are equally guaranteed to all without regard to race;

that until that day, the dream of lasting peace and world citizenship and the rule of international morality will remain but a fleeting illusion, to be pursued but never attained.

And until the ignoble and unhappy regimes that hold our brothers in Angola, in Mozambique and in South Africa in subhuman bondage have been toppled and destroyed . . .

Until that day, the African continent will not know peace. We Africans will fight, if necessary, and we know that we shall win, as we are confident in the victory of good over evil.[*]

Haile Selassie's arresting speech underscored the urgency many around the world in 1963 felt about the continuing power of race in the international system. Bunche certainly shared that urgency. At the same time, it was clear that many traditional hierarchies of power were under great challenge. As a now-entrenched member of that hierarchy and one who believed deeply in playing, usually discreetly, within the bounds of the system at which he had excelled, Bunche had mixed feelings about how the increasingly vocal bloc of the Third World was flexing its muscle. He certainly disliked the approach and style of some African leaders, such as Kwame Nkrumah, especially when they castigated the UN, and in a sense Bunche himself, for an unwillingness to forthrightly support Lumumba in Congo. Bunche had followed Selassie's story since the 1930s, when he had tried to assist Selassie in a tour of America in the wake of Italy's invasion.[20] He knew Selassie represented a strong African resistance to European domination.

---

[*] If these words seem familiar, they became the unlikely basis of Bob Marley's 1976 song *War*. Marley, like many Jamaicans, was a Rastafarian who believed that Selassie, born Ras Tafari Makonnen, was a living god.

And he likely found his speech, with its ardent desire for a colorblind future echoing King's iconic address from the Lincoln Memorial just weeks before, much more congenial than what he was often hearing from the newer generation of postcolonial African leaders.

A MONTH BEFORE KENNEDY'S ASSASSINATION THE White House had informed Bunche that he would receive the Medal of Freedom. Kennedy had decided earlier that year to systematize the Medal of Freedom process and had appointed a new medal committee, which, in addition to his brother Bobby, the attorney general, included George Ball, the under secretary of state, and Henry Cabot Lodge, the former US ambassador to the UN. Lodge knew Bunche well and had been impressed by his herculean work in the Suez and the Congo crises.

The day before Bunche headed to the White House for the Medal of Freedom ceremony, he visited the Sands Point Country Day School on nearby Long Island. Bunche ended up spending two hours at the school, answering tough questions the young students posed on current events. He refused to criticize the late President Kennedy's handling of Vietnam and Cuba, and he emphasized that the time was coming when, if only for practical reasons, "Red China" would assume the Chinese seat at the UN.[21] For years, the US had strongly opposed a UN seat for the Peoples Republic of China, arguing that Taiwan properly represented the vast nation. Mao Zedong's government would not successfully wrest the Chinese seat, and its permanent veto on the Security Council, from the Nationalists until just a few weeks before Bunche's untimely death in 1971.

Bunche's experience with China was limited, although Mao, seeking to cement his role as a leader of the decolonized world, was increasingly interacting with both African leaders and prominent Black Americans. W. E. B. Du Bois had famously visited Mao in China a few years earlier, and later in the 1960s, radical leftist leaders such as Huey P. Newton of the Black Panthers would see Mao as a prophet of revolutionary change. Mao's aphorisms ("political power grows out of the barrel of a gun"; "a revolution is not a dinner party") seemed tailor-made for the intense, often violent political conflict of the era. Bunche, of course, was no revolutionary and no fan of Mao. Communist China's ascendancy was simply a political fact that had to be acknowledged. While China was still weak and poor in the early 1960s, he understood that the largest nation on earth could no longer be denied its rightful place at the tables of the UN based on a legal fiction. But the fact that such a huge and important state had experienced a communist revolution weighed heavily on American foreign policy.

Bunche arrived at the White House to receive the Medal of Freedom on December 6, 1963. He had returned there many times since his first meeting with Eleanor Roosevelt in 1940; indeed, his last visit had been just seven months before, where over dinner he and President Kennedy had discussed the ongoing strife in Birmingham, Alabama. The visit on this day was, of course, the most poignant. The events in Dallas had been as harrowing for Bunche as they had been for most Americans, and he, and the nation, were still in shock. Standing at a lectern in the East Room of the White House, the newly installed President Johnson spoke to the assembled guests with Bunche at his side, a wide blue ribbon bearing the Medal of Freedom crossing Bunche's chest. With the death of JFK still fresh, Johnson looked serious and Bunche subdued, almost solemn, staring slightly downward as Johnson spoke.

Two weeks later, Johnson visited the UN for the first time as president, his wife Lady Bird at his side. Greeting U Thant as he walked into the vestibule of the UN lobby—Bunche for some reason cheerfully clapping as the two shook hands—Johnson smiled and then reached out to Bunche, shaking his hand and pulling him in closer with a knowing smile as he spoke, using his physical presence and sheer size to control his interlocutors as Johnson was famous for doing. He was there to address the General Assembly for the first time; in his speech that day, he declared of Kennedy that "world peace has lost a great champion." Yet he urged the delegates to look forward and recognize continuity. "I have come here today," Johnson declared, "to make it unmistakably clear: that the assassin's bullet that took his life did not alter his nation's purpose." He then turned to the UN itself. "We have seen too much success to become obsessed with failure." The peacekeeping machinery of the UN, he argued, had worked in the Congo and the Middle East and elsewhere. The UN may not be the consortium of the Allied powers envisioned in San Francisco, LBJ seemed to be saying, but it still had accomplished a lot. Most importantly, "the great transition from colonial rule to independence has been largely accomplished."[22]

Of course, important aspects of this "great transition" had not quite been accomplished. In a meeting with his chief national security advisors a few days before his UN visit, Johnson had declared: "I am not going to lose Vietnam. I am not going to be the President who saw Southeast Asia go the way China went."[23]

Johnson had not started the Vietnam War; he had inherited it from Kennedy. (Charles de Gaulle, who had some familiarity with colonial wars, had presciently warned Kennedy as early as 1961 that Vietnam was "an endless entanglement.")[24] And by the time of his ascension to the presidency, Johnson had not yet initiated the tremendous increase in American forces in Vietnam that would cause so much death and destruction and imperil his presidency—and any hope of peace in Southeast Asia—in the process. There were still less than 20,000 Americans troops deployed at this point. But already it was clear to those who were looking carefully that the war was not going in a good direction.

———

FOR MANY AMERICANS IN 1964, RALPH BUNCHE personified the UN. His stature as a peacemaker and master of diplomacy was untouched. But as the domestic politics of race grew more intense and more radical, his role as a figure of respect and leadership among Black Americans began to be questioned more frequently.

In February 1964, a young Muhammad Ali, then still known as Cassius Clay, defeated Sonny Liston for the heavyweight championship of the world. Ali was now perhaps the most famous athlete in America. With reporters in New York a few days after his upset victory, the outspoken boxer, who would visit the UN the following month, discussed his growing links to the controversial Nation of Islam organization and, in particular, to his frequent companion, Malcolm X. Malcolm X could lead Black Americans to freedom, Ali told the reporters. But, he continued, "there are some other good men." Ali noted that different people liked different leaders. "Some people like Martin Luther King and some people like Adam

Photo 21.2 Bobby Kennedy, U Thant, and Ralph Bunche at the UN

Clayton Powell," he continued. "Some even like Ralph Bunche, who can go around the world and try to make peace for other people, but they don't do nothing here to make peace for their own people."[25]

Ali's criticism struck a chord: to some Black Americans, Bunche now seemed a distant figure, one who might regularly appear on the front page of major newspapers like the *Washington Post* or *New York Times* but always in connection to some faraway and perhaps little-known global crisis. Stokely Carmichael would famously say, to Bunche's example of minority success, "you can't have Bunche for lunch!"[26] (Malcolm X, despite his criticisms of Bunche, nonetheless reportedly displayed a drawing of Bunche, Du Bois, and King in his Harlem office.)[27] All the same, Bunche remained important to the civil rights movement more broadly. Martin Luther King Jr. certainly saw his value, though also Bunche's vulnerability as a symbol, perhaps even a token, of racial progress. "The Negro wanted to feel pride in his race?" King asked rhetorically in 1964. "With tokenism the solution was simple. If all twenty million Negroes would keep looking at Ralph Bunche, the one man in so exalted a post would generate such a volume of pride that it could be cut into portions and served to everyone."[28] We do not know what Bunche thought of King's statement. But it is clear that Bunche was increasingly troubled, returning to issues of race and equality in his thoughts and private writings in this era, clearly mulling over what had happened over the course of his lifetime and how the fate of Black America had in some ways improved, and in others not.

Much of the nation, however, still wanted to know what Bunche thought about world politics. In Austin, Texas, Governor John Connally of Texas declared him an honorary citizen of Texas. Delivering a Rotary Club speech, Bunche puckishly declared "Peace is dull." The UN, he told the audience, is merely a "struggling firefighter in the world's brush fires." He then told a few war stories for the crowd. He recounted his time in the Leopoldville hotel right after the Congolese Army mutiny began, seeing local soldiers milling about "cradling machine guns in one hand and Western beer in the other." "Here I had been a Negro all my life; fought for civil rights in the United States; and had worked for the suppression of strife in African countries ... and I was about to be bumped off as a Belgium paratrooper." It was, he said, "the greatest irony of my life." He finished his Austin speech with a birds-eye view of the civil rights struggle, invoking his now familiar claim that there were two extremes, white and Black, and that both needed to be rejected.[29]

Thousands showed up to see Bunche at his next stop in Houston, where the mayor gave him the key to the city. Then, en route to a TV interview, his motorcade was hit by a car. The driver, a Mrs. Charles White, happened to be the only Black member of the Board of Education of Houston. Mrs. White hit a police officer on a motorcycle with her large Lincoln Continental; the officer somersaulted in the air and came up with his nose gushing blood.[30] While the motorcade idled, the police ticketed her for negligence, though the mayor, perhaps eager to sweep the episode under the rug, personally told Bunche he would waive it. Bunche finished the day attending a 150-person dinner with "the whole power structure of the city." In his diary, he dubbed Texas "the most fantastic trip I have ever taken"—a bit of exaggeration that suggested he may have been tiring of his more dramatic trips abroad.

Bunche could not avoid these overseas trips altogether, however. In April 1964, he headed off to assess UN forces in several postcolonial hotspots around the world. The primary one, seemingly headed for a deadly blowup, was the conflict between Greeks and Turks on the Mediterranean island of Cyprus. Cyprus, not unlike nearby Palestine, had a complex history of colonial domination. British rule had ended in 1960, and Cyprus joined the UN as an independent state a few months later. At the time of Cyprus's independence, the population was mainly ethnically Greek, but there was a large Turkish minority and significant tensions between the two. Unstable from its inception, the ethnic and constitutional balance in independent Cyprus did not last long. (Bunche would later say that "the trouble with Cyprus is there are no Cypriots.")[31] Fighting broke out at various points in 1963 and 1964. In March 1964, the Security Council authorized a peacekeeping force for the island.[32] Bunche was sent out to the island in April, where he was to meet with the UN commanders and try to assess and tamp down the conflict.

Bunche first flew to Athens to meet with the Greek leadership and then to Cyprus itself. Upon arrival, he was met by the Indian officer in charge of the UN forces, General Prem Singh Gyani. Gyani, smiling broadly and wearing the now-standard blue UN beret, chatted briefly with Bunche as he got off the plane. Bunche quickly headed to the Cypriot capital, Nicosia. He told reporters he was there for a "three-day routine visit." Arriving at the presidential palace, he was escorted in to see the president, Archbishop Makarios, strikingly dressed in black robes and religious headgear, a huge chain and pendant hanging low around his neck. The two discussed the rising violence on the island for two hours.[33] He then met with Makarios's Turkish counterpart, Fazil Kutchuk, who, perhaps eager to outdo his Greek counterpart in all things, spoke for nearly three hours.

More violence broke out during his visit. In the Kyrenia Pass, an area on the northern part of the island, ethnic Greeks and Turks, a mere 400 yards apart, were shooting each other. A Turkish Cypriot, watering his garden with his teenage daughter, was killed by gunfire shortly before Bunche toured the location by Land Rovers. Seeing burnt-out and looted buildings, nearly all abandoned, he despaired for the future. The Greek officials spoke of "Turkish terrorists" and the need to contain them.[34] Perhaps flashing back to the tensions of Jerusalem in the late 1940s, Bunche was rattled by the depth and seeming senselessness of the ethnic hatred on display. "It is not possible to really get the feeling of what is going on by remote control from New York," he told reporters on the scene. "But after one sees what is going on, one cannot always believe what one sees." He found the situation confusing and perhaps pointless, calling it an "incoherent war."[35]

Bunche was troubled by the recurrence of outbreaks of violence such as these. It was not just Cyprus; Yemen, Congo, and Vietnam—all bore the same signature. Colonialism may have been well in retreat, but as John Foster Dulles had declared at the UN as early as 1947, it had borne some "very evil fruit." Self-determination on the basis of nationalism often seemed to require sorting, and too often that sorting was turning violent.

In a cable to headquarters, he told U Thant that the situation in the Mediterranean needed more than a military response; a more active UN political presence was necessary for any lasting peace to take hold. While Bunche could play that role, he told Thant that he thought his American nationality posed too much of a challenge: "It would put me under a hand-icap in the work in Cyprus and this factor would very much show up in local criticism." Moreover, he said, it would certainly expose Thant to political attack.[36] Whether Bunche really believed this or, entering his sixties, simply wanted to avoid another extended and trying overseas posting, Thant took the advice and appointed another official to the role of mediator. Bunche did make an important—if symbolic and typically Bunche-like—suggestion, however: he proposed placing thousands of UN flags around the island, dotting the various outposts of the peacekeepers and trumpeting the international presence.

As he departed from the Nicosia airport after this short visit, Bunche was asked by a local reporter if he was optimistic about the situation in Cyprus. "I am a professional optimist," he replied.

> If I were not a professional optimist through 21 years in the United Nations service, mainly in conflict areas—Palestine, Congo, here, and in Kashmir—I would be crazy. You have to be optimistic in this work or get out of it. . . . That is, optimistic in the sense of assuming that there is no problem—Cyprus or any other—which cannot be solved and that, therefore, you have to keep at it persistently and you have to have confidence that it can be solved. . . . And so, personally, I am always inclined to pessimism, but professionally I am inclined to optimism.[37]

Bunche's long answer was interesting and perhaps a bit cryptic. What did it mean to be "personally" inclined to pessimism but professionally an optimist? Did his personal pessimism perhaps reflect his concern that the problems of racial equality he had long believed could be solved, eventually, via hard work and the dismantling of overt barriers, were proving more resilient than he feared? By the mid-1960s, the twin animating concerns of his life and career—racism abroad in the form of empire, and racism at home in the form of segregation and discrimination—appeared to be moving on somewhat different tracks.

By 1964, the first concern was showing great success: decolonization was certainly not over, but it was occurring far faster than almost anyone imagined possible when Bunche labored in San Francisco in 1945 to work into the UN Charter provisions that he hoped would accelerate and stabilize that process. The second concern was arguably also moving forward but more fitfully and unevenly, and soon enough would blow up in the form of assassinations and riots—or uprisings—in places like Watts and Detroit.[†] While in Cyprus, Bunche did not elaborate on his distinction between

---

[†] The 1965 Watts riots (Bunche was clear he did not consider them uprisings), which took place not far from Bunche's former childhood home in Los Angeles, would particularly trouble him. As he became more convinced that ghettos were the problem, he would later say that the "one remedy" for something like Watts was "the dispersal of every black ghetto in this land."

"personal" pessimism and "professional" optimism, yet it was not unlikely that he was thinking about the complexities of racial justice and the very different paths he saw ahead.

The next stop on the peacekeeping tour was an uneventful visit to Gaza to check on what was perhaps Bunche's most successful creation, the UN Emergency Force. From Gaza he headed further east to the disputed territory of Kashmir in the high Himalayas, stopping in both Pakistan and India to meet with key leaders. In Kashmir, the UN Military Observer Group in India and Pakistan had been surveying the tense standoff between the two antagonistic South Asian nations since 1949. UNMOGIP, as the mission was known in the clunky UN style, was small but important: both India and Pakistan were populous states with substantial enmity. UNMOGIP was not a peacekeeping force per se but rather unarmed observers. Bunche told reporters in New Delhi that his visit had "no political significance" and was simply aimed at strengthening the "effectiveness" of the UN mission.[38]

In South Asia, he met with the president of Pakistan, Ayub Khan, who, while wearing pajamas due to a recent surgery, told him that the sole obstacle to peace between India and Pakistan was India's dream of an empire in Kashmir.[39] Bunche in turn met with Khan's counterpart, Prime Minister Jawaharlal Nehru of India in Delhi. Nehru and Bunche had first met many years earlier, during the Truman administration. Now, Bunche was seeking to understand the position of the more powerful India and determine whether there was not some way to tamp down the rising conflict between the two nations.

To get a better sense of the situation on the ground, Bunche set off for Kashmir itself. Reporting back to U Thant, he recounted that "I decided to follow the cease-fire line straight up the center of Kashmir, visiting our observer posts on both sides of the Line and talking with observers and senior military officers on each side." By "Line" he was referring to the so-called Line of Control, the high elevation de facto border between India and Pakistan. For three full days, in rocky terrain that must have pained him, he toured the Line by jeep. "The scenery...is beautiful but the terrain is rugged and often severely mountainous," he wrote.[40] Moreover, the weather was harsh and the roads were poor and in many places nearly impassable. Still, he enjoyed seeing the incredible vistas of the Himalayan range and praised the professionalism of the UN observers. Within a year, however, Pakistani troops in civilian disguise would pour over the Line of Control, and the problem of Kashmir would be back before the Security Council.

RALPH BUNCHE'S HOTSPOTS TOUR IN SPRING 1964 reinforced his prior belief in the power of peacekeeping. He was a strong proponent of the ability of UN forces to make a difference in contested territories. His conference room, referred to as the "UN War Room," was filled with maps of deployments and charts of the various peacekeeping missions he was supervising in the postcolonial world. He took satisfaction that through these efforts peace could be forged. But he also recognized that even the most basic function of the UN—talking—was often underrated as a tool of peace. "Perpetual talking in the United Nations is far better than shooting as a means of settling international disputes," he said at one point. The UN's "chief contributions have been averting world atomic war through checking dangerous world situations . . . and resisting aggression . . . while at the same time carrying on constructive efforts toward making economic and social advancement and greater freedom."[41] He was right: the UN was easy to criticize as a place of hot air, but in fact all that talking often served a purpose. The alternative, history proved, could be far worse.

Soon after returning from his peacekeeping tour, Bunche headed to speak at Howard University. He briefly reminisced about his earlier life at Howard and then began, as he usually did, with a discussion of the challenges facing the UN. After assessing UNEF, Congo, and the like, he pivoted to the issue of race. The UN, he told the Howard audience, took race seriously: "The problems of *race* in all their manifestations—prejudice, bigotry, discrimination and segregation—are a major source of UN concern." And he implied that as a result the entire world "is aware of what happens here," meaning America.

Bunche then recounted his own experiences as a Black man in the South in the 1930s during the research he conducted with Gunnar Myrdal and observed that conditions had improved over the years—but not nearly enough. He told the Howard audience how, with Ralph Jr., he had attended a Dodgers game a few years back during which a man behind them shouted the N-word at Hank Aaron. "I swung sternly around and growled, 'why the racial slur? Can't you leave your prejudice out of the ball park?' Silence. Later, I felt a timid tap on my shoulder: 'Sorry, Sir, but I feel that way about *all* the Braves.'" Picking up on his remarks back in Austin, Texas, however, Bunche, perhaps surprisingly to his young audience, again took pointed aim at what he saw as the rising radicalism within the civil rights movement. He opposed the increasingly common calls for Black separatism, especially the more frequent claims, made by men like Elijah Muhammad, that white people were "devils."[42]

He then shifted his attention to the ascendant Republican senator, Barry Goldwater of Arizona, criticizing him for his opposition to the civil rights movement—and his extreme and backward-looking conservatism. Goldwater, he said, was "also dubious about the UN and he has described it as 'premature'—and I suppose it is, when viewed from the 19th century." On a roll, he even managed to get in a swipe at Muhammad Ali, then still Cassius Clay. "I have never known a man to spout so much gibberish as Clay—in my eyes, he is a mediocre fighter, too." On this last point, Bunche's politics and finely honed sense of propriety seemed to have blinded his sportsman's eye: Ali had not only won a gold medal at the Rome Olympics in 1960; he had just months before defeated the formidable Sonny Liston for the heavyweight crown, in a fight widely considered one of the greatest of the 20th century. Some of the Howard students undoubtedly rolled their eyes at his attack on Ali. Bunche, a boxing fan who would sometimes sit ringside, as he did the following year for the Floyd Patterson–George Chavulo heavyweight fight at Madison Square Garden, surely knew better.[43‡]

Ali, who was catnip to reporters, represented a new model of Black celebrity, and one Bunche did not approve of. Indeed, Ali in many respects was the Anti-Bunche: brash, charismatic, spotlight-seeking, and contentious.

‡ Floyd Patterson had said of his 1963 bout against Sonny Liston that he felt intense pressure—including from Bunche himself—to defeat Liston, who was widely seen as an associate of criminals with an unsavory reputation. "Ralph Bunche said I had to win," Patterson told reporters.

Indeed, when Ali had visited the UN in March 1964, Bunche was no-where to be seen. Denied by the UN a formal press conference, Ali met with reporters crowded into the press office of reporter Charles Howard. Alongside Ali was Malcolm X, newly interested in the UN. His famed speech, "The Ballot or the Bullet," which he would give in just a few weeks, called for a human rights revolution in the struggle against white supremacy. "Expand the civil-rights struggle to the level of human rights, take it into the United Nations," he had declared, "where our African brothers can throw their weight on our side, where our Asian brothers can throw their weight on our side, where our Latin-American brothers can throw their weight on our side." Malcolm X would even begin to draft a petition to the UN, in the spirit of W. E. B. Du Bois's earlier UN petition.[44]

As the two charismatic men fielded questions, Ali made clear his interest in meeting the people of the world because, he said, "I'm the champion of the whole world."[45] Touring the UN campus, Ali met with ambassadors from Liberia and Mali, including Sori Coulibaly, chair of the General Assembly's special committee on decolonization. Ali's choice reflected the rising power of the General Assembly and the salience of the idea that there was now a large and clearly defined postcolonial Third World, standing apart from the Cold War blocs.

By 1964 the energy around decolonization was increasingly concen-trated in the General Assembly. By its nature, the General Assembly was more self-governing and less closely tied to the UN's leadership team, and, as a result, Bunche was less and less connected to the debates unfolding there. In the coming years, the General Assembly's centrality for the new Third World would only accelerate. And as decolonization approached completion, new issues emerged. Self-determination and independ-ence, for example, appeared to be less urgent by the mid-1960s, and the challenges of what was beginning to be called *neocolonialism* and *de-pendency* grew more urgent. In short, economic issues began to overtake political issues for the spotlight, though a key argument of many newly in-dependent states in this era was that economics *was* deeply political—and deeply unjust.

A concrete example was the growing controversy over nationalization or expropriation. The Suez Crisis of 1956 had been sparked by Egypt's sudden seizure of the Suez Canal. The challenge of one government taking the property of another government, or at least the property of another government's nationals, was not a new one. Yet it was occurring more frequently now, and it took on a new intensity in the postwar era. Many postcolonial states found that while they may have secured political independence, they lacked economic independence. As in Congo, foreign firms continued to own plantations, mines, and other valuable resources. Expropriation—that is, simply taking those plantations or mines and declaring them the property of the new nation—was a blunt but expedient response. Indeed, by 1962 the General Assembly passed a resolution on the ownership of national resources, declaring that expropriation "shall be based on grounds or reasons of public utility, security, or the national interest which are recognized as *overriding purely individual or private interests.*"[46]

These efforts to recast the rules of the global economy, challenge property rights, and redistribute assets and gains would persist past the 1960s and reached a crescendo in the 1970s in the form of the push for a New International Economic Order. Bunche, who died in 1971, missed much of the incendiary politics that surrounded the fight over neocolonialism. Yet his earlier Marxist instincts would undoubtedly have recognized the importance of taming global capital and the often racially skewed ways the global economy operated.

Still, Bunche did not express enormous concern about or sympathy with the notion of neocolonialism. To be sure, much of his focus throughout the 1960s was on peace and security rather than economics and development. Yet there were plenty of opportunities to say more about how the international system disfavored the postcolonial world economically, and he did not readily take them up. Self-determination surely had an economic component, but Bunche had by this point left his Marxist inclinations far behind. He now seemed to see independence as mainly a political and even a dignitary issue. Indeed, even in his address decades earlier to the Mont

Tremblant Conference during the Second World War—the speech that Bunche himself felt had launched him on a successful diplomatic career—he had chosen to emphasize these dimensions of respect. The real objective of plans for international organizations must be a good life for all people. Central among its features, he argued, was the right to "walk with dignity on the world's great boulevards."[47]

CHAPTER 22

FROM SAIGON TO SELMA

The conventional army loses if it does not win. The guerilla wins if he does not lose.

—Henry Kissinger, "The Vietnam Negotiations," *Foreign Affairs*, 1969

Arriving by helicopter on the South Lawn of the White House on the morning of August 6, 1964, Ralph Bunche and U Thant disembarked to the sounds of a Marine band. President Lyndon Johnson and his wife, Lady Bird, greeted the party as they walked down the short set of stairs to the grassy expanse. The delegation, which included UN Ambassador Adlai Stevenson, squinted in the bright summer sun as they posed for photos next to the helicopter, all clad in dark suits aside from Lady Bird, who wore a stylish turban and dress. Out of respect for the UN's mission of peace, the honor guard was unarmed and there was no twenty-one-gun salute. U Thant later called the White House visit in the summer of 1964 the "most unforgettable" experience of his time as secretary general.[1]

Meeting in the Oval Office with the president, Bunche and Thant discussed the metastasizing conflict in Vietnam. Still seeking some form of mediated solution, Thant suggested that the US agree to engage privately with the North Vietnamese. He told Johnson that the Americans were misreading the situation in Southeast Asia. He knew North Vietnamese leader Ho Chi Minh, the secretary general said; the two had met a decade before in Hanoi. Thant thought Ho was strongly influenced by France and French culture and, at least at first, was not especially interested in communism. Johnson, referring to the North Vietnamese, replied that the US was "ready to get out of there tomorrow if they will behave."[2]

After the meeting, Lady Bird took Thant and Bunche on a brief tour of the White House grounds, pointing out the flowers the Kennedys had planted and where various native Texas trees would be placed in the coming months. The UN team then headed to the State Department for a two-hour lunch, where they discussed Vietnam but also the volatile situation in Cyprus and the ongoing crisis at the UN over peacekeeping costs. That evening Johnson hosted a state dinner for Thant. It was the first time any president had ever hosted any secretary general in this manner. It was an interesting move by Johnson. The president did not appear, in fact, to want the UN to play a major role in Vietnam. But he did seem to want to be *seen* to be seeking peace. Hosting U Thant for a formal White House event, Ralph Bunche by his side, was an easy way to signal that interest and perhaps be perceived as inclined toward multilateral conciliation. Thant indeed was "deeply moved" by how gracious and welcoming Johnson was.[3]

As the state dinner began, the president took Thant and Bunche, along with Adlai Stevenson, Robert McNamara, the defense secretary, and Dean Rusk, the secretary of state, upstairs to the Yellow Room of the White House. Johnson gave Thant photos of the moon taken from the Ranger 7 spacecraft just days before, and Thant in turn gave Johnson a silver tea set from Burma, adorned (in an ironic twist for a Democratic president), with an image of an elephant.[4] The guest list for the dinner included the usual mix of powerful senators, representatives, and governors but also Walter Kronkite, David Brinkley, Gregory Peck, and Henry Cabot Lodge. Downstairs, over a meal of crab, chateaubriand, and coffee parfait, Johnson jovially declared that it had been "a good day." He made a point of noting the "growing respect for the peacekeeping and peacemaking purposes of the United Nations," which suggested without promising that there might be some way the UN was going to prove useful in the Southeast Asian crisis.[5]

Photo 22.1 Bunche and Thant arrive at the White House

The dinner eventually gave way to dancing. Perhaps to underscore a sense of hope and assuage fears, the 140 guests at the White House were led in an impromptu sing-along of "Puff the Magic Dragon" by the evening's musical entertainment, the young folk trio Peter, Paul, and Mary. Bunche, an avowed music lover but one who declared his fandom ended at jazz, listened as the trio also sang "Blowin' in the Wind," the song made famous the year before by Bob Dylan. The lyrics, ringing out right in the East Room of the White House as Lyndon Johnson listened, were strikingly prophetic: "How many deaths will it take till he knows that too many people have died?"[6]

THE SUMMER OF 1964 MARKED A turning point in the growing Vietnam conflict. The American naval vessels *Maddox* and *Turner Joy* had apparently been struck by North Vietnamese torpedoes within two days of each other, just before Lyndon Johnson hosted U Thant at the White House. Both ships were in the Gulf of Tonkin, an area of the South China Sea between the coast of Vietnam and Hainan Island, China. In response, Johnson submitted to Congress what became known as the Gulf of Tonkin Resolution, and Congress passed it overwhelmingly. The resolution provided the primary legal authorization for the war, accelerating American involvement in Vietnam.

The Vietnam War would soon vex Ralph Bunche more than any other conflict he had been involved in throughout his many years at the UN. Vietnam was becoming a major world conflict, yes, but it was also an American conflict, and Bunche, as a proud citizen, soon found himself very troubled by what he considered a misguided and even immoral war. Within a few years it would also become a personal war. In 1969, his only son, Ralph Jr., would head to Saigon, deployed as one of the tens of thousands of young American men sent to fight communism halfway around the world. That the Vietnam War had roots in the fight against European empire which had been Bunche's mission for so many decades only added to his sense that America was making a huge and costly mistake by following France into battle in the far-off Southeast Asian nation.

That summer and fall, Bunche diverted himself by paying frequent visits to the 1964 World's Fair, located in Flushing, Queens, near his home. Appointed a board member of the Fair in 1964, he dove into the process with gusto. As his colleague Brian Urquhart later wrote, Bunche seemed to see the World's Fair as a symbol of what international cooperation "could, and should, be."[7] The official theme of the fair, *Peace through Understanding*, certainly seemed tailor-made for his sensibilities. Built by the controversial Robert Moses, the New York World's Fair in the end proved an economic

disaster.* But to many visitors, it provided a window on the emerging nations that Bunche had long championed. Twenty-four African states
teamed up to create an Africa Pavilion. To officially dedicate the pavilion,
the king of Burundi even visited in May, surrounded by a dozen deputies
holding six-foot ceremonial spears and accompanied by drummers.[8] For
many Americans, the Africa Pavilion provided a window into a new postcolonial world, one they hitherto visualized as lands run by Europeans in pith
helmets and safari jackets, but that was now the home of some two dozen
newly sovereign nations.

The World's Fair provided an interesting alternative universe of the UN
itself. In October 1964, a group of diplomats even visited the fairgrounds
to celebrate "Peace Through Understanding Day." Anatoly Dobrynin, the
Soviet ambassador to the US, came along as well as a host of friendlier
diplomats. The spirit of cooperation was marred, however, when Indonesia
announced it was going to close its national pavilion. President Sukarno
of Indonesia said this move was retaliation for "the open support" the
US had given to "the neocolonialist project of Malaysia."[9] The new state
of Malaysia had been created the year before through the merger of an
already-independent Malaya with several other former British colonies
in Southeast Asia. The World's Fair Corporation seized the Indonesian
Pavilion in response, locking out workers who had come to tune the gam-
elan instruments.

Ralph Bunche could not have been happy about how the complex
postwar politics of decolonization were intruding on the ideals of his be-
loved Fair. Creating a world of peace and harmony among nations was
proving impossible, even if it was attempted on a dollhouse scale in a park in
Queens. But Indonesia's move showed something important about world
politics in 1964. Although there were occasional alliances among the newly
independent states of Africa and Asia, and they often worked together in
the General Assembly, the "spirit of Bandung"—the 1955 conference that
became a marker of the political emergence of what was being called the

---

* The imperious Moses did not adhere to the official international rules for such fairs,
and as a result many larger nations boycotted it.

Third World—was perhaps more illusory and fragile than many hoped. Indeed, Indonesia went so far as to briefly resign as a member of the UN in January 1965 over the issue of Malaysia.

Bunche enjoyed the Fair but was as usual on the road more than he wanted. That fall alone he visited Geneva, Prague, Budapest, Belgrade, Rome, Paris, London, Entebbe, Lusaka, Nairobi, Khartoum, and even Ndola, the site of Dag Hammarskjold's fatal crash a few years before.[10] It was an exhausting schedule for a man now in his sixties. As an active shopper, he often used these opportunities to bring back gifts for Ruth and his children. Not unrelatedly, he also enjoyed the honor in late 1964 of being chosen as the most stylish man in America—albeit in the somewhat less competitive "public service" category. He eked out a close victory over the patrician Henry Cabot Lodge, his former colleague at the UN and one-time candidate for vice president. Bunche was still a handsome man and a stylish dresser; even now he was still depicted in the Black press as a bit of a heartthrob. (As a child, he once reminisced, women would often exclaim about his "big, brown eyes.") Sitting next to Jackie Kennedy at a lunch for former French Prime Minister Edgar Faure a few months after his best dressed award, Mrs. Kennedy declared that "my sister will be envious when I tell her I have talked with you at lunch today, she has a crush on you!"[11]

But more serious issues were consuming his attention as 1965 began. There was Vietnam, of course—Adlai Stevenson was increasingly in Bunche's office, commiserating and complaining about the White House's increasingly hawkish positions—as well as the many other international matters, large and small, that constantly cropped up. Bunche was also perturbed by Indonesia's decision, albeit ultimately temporary, to leave the UN and what it might portend.[†] Until now, new nations had clamored to join the UN, seeking validation of their newly won sovereignty. In some cases, they tried to join even before they had secured it—as when Congo had awkwardly sought admission in the days before its independence. Indonesia's move suggested a possible and worrisome new countertrend. In a letter to

---

[†] After a coup later in 1965, Indonesia returned to the UN, and the incident was treated as a pause in cooperation rather than as a true withdrawal.

Photo 22.2 Thant and Bunche head to Geneva

his occasional penpal Valerie Betts,[‡] of Birmingham, UK, Bunche called Indonesia's move a very serious blow, though he wrote, perhaps trying to reassure himself, that the UN was "strong enough and indispensable enough to survive all shocks."[12]

Nonetheless, Bunche was concerned about the stability of the UN, especially the continuing debate over arrears in dues that had arisen from the very expensive Congo peacekeeping operation. While the mission had already wound down, the conflict over payment had not. Stalemate in the General Assembly had ensued as the parties debated whether the Soviets and the French would lose their votes. Fearful of what was at stake in the dues debate, Bunche contacted an old classmate from Howard, Hobart

---

[‡] Bunche never met Valerie Betts, it appears, but they corresponded for years after she wrote to him about a UN matter. "I greatly enjoy her letters and look forward to receiving them," he wrote in his journal. He imagined—but seemed not to know—that she was "middle-aged, a spinster, and an invalid . . . I have not told Ruth because I fear she would not understand why I do this and that it is all entirely innocent."

Taylor, now a special counsel to LBJ and one of the highest ranking Black men in the federal government.

Bunche first called Taylor to sound him out and then sent him a letter and a position paper he had drafted, which he took pains to explain was a "purely personal statement."[13] The UN, he wrote Taylor, was gravely threatened by the notion that members could withhold dues for operations they did not like. The US and the USSR had to work together if they were to save the organization. Bunche suggested that the US take the high road, with the goal of saving something that was ultimately in America's national interest. His missive to his friend was a salient example of how he sometimes put his many ties within the upper echelons of the US government to good use, despite his protestations that he was an international civil servant who did not serve the US or its interests. To be sure, the reverse was much more common: for example, Dean Rusk, Adlai Stevenson, or some other major figure seeking out Bunche in an attempt to shape the debate in Turtle Bay. As the letter to Hobart Taylor showed, however, at times Bunche himself attempted to reverse the flow of influence. After making the case that the US should bend to save the organization, he asked Taylor to extend his "warm greetings" to Lyndon Johnson—a small reminder that while he might be a UN official, and not working in the White House, he was nonetheless on a first-name basis with the president.

Bunche's letter did not seem to have much impact, however. The US at first argued that France and the USSR should lose their right to vote in the General Assembly because of their failure to pay, as the UN Charter seemed to demand. This great power struggle tied up the UN at a critical time. Indeed, in 1964 no votes were taken at all in the General Assembly; the members were frozen by the prospect of taking sides between such powerful players. Eventually, the US relented. In a meeting with Thant and Bunche, Secretary of State Dean Rusk raised the issue and took what Bunche presciently termed "a most ominous position."[14] The General Assembly could ignore the Charter's rules on dues, but only if that applied to all assessments, not just special ones. Bunche was concerned by the implications of this position, but this appeared to be the only way forward at a time of intense pressure. Declaring that a precedent had been set—and, as it turned out, a very significant one—the US allowed the French and Soviets to vote.[15] By the late 1990s, when it was the US that was much less happy with the UN, the American government was at one point well over a billion dollars in arrears. Yet, thanks to the earlier precedent over Congo, it never lost its vote.

The UN's financial woes were not high on Lyndon Johnson's agenda in early 1965. In addition to Vietnam, Johnson was increasingly focused on his domestic priorities, in particular getting a voting rights statute through Congress. The civil rights struggle was heating up, and race relations were growing more tense in northern cities, including Bunche's adopted home-town, New York City. Just days after Bunche interceded with Taylor, Malcolm X was assassinated in Washington Heights. Bunche was no great fan of the former Malcolm Little. His fiery style and oppositional poli-tics were the antithesis of what the respectable, establishment Bunche thought appropriate, but also what he believed was strategic and effective in a white-dominated world. But the assassination—one of many in the tur-bulent decade—was nonetheless deeply disturbing. Having helped found the National Negro Congress in the 1930s and as a board member of the NAACP for decades, Bunche still considered himself a civil rights cam-paigner. The rising violence and tension in the movement and within the larger society were troubling.

One result was that the elder Bunche was increasingly drawn to the younger Martin Luther King Jr. King certainly impressed Bunche. Indeed, when, in 1964, Bunche had been given the opportunity to introduce King at an NAACP conference, he readily accepted. After prefacing his remarks with references to the Universal Declaration on Human Rights and the linkages between the civil rights movement and efforts against apartheid in South Africa, Bunche continued to couch the fight for racial justice in global terms. He called King a "true evangelist of equality" and a "very courageous American."[16] He seemed to want to use whatever political and social stature he had to bolster King's approach, which he believed was the only way for-ward since it was based on nonviolence and claims grounded in dignity and morality and common human decency. And having grown up in a strict Baptist household, Bunche was familiar with and comfortable with King's religiously grounded style and approach.

As the civil rights movement placed increasing political and moral pressure on the nation and both Republicans and Democrats sought to burnish their credentials with minority groups, Bunche continued to be viewed as a viable political figure. His more frequent forays into domestic affairs may well have pushed this along. In May 1964, the *New York Times* mentioned him as one of several possible candidates for one of New York's Senate seats. Bunche himself had not publicly expressed interest, however.[17] He would later say that while he had often been asked to go into politics, he just felt it wasn't for him. To be a good politician "you've got to tolerate idiots as well as geniuses, and I'm a little impatient with idiocy. And I could never go out and ask anyone to vote for me, and eat pizza pie and bagels and lox, and all that."[18] Still, Bunche, a well-known and respected figure, seemed an attractive option to many. He was also discussed as a possible president of the NAACP, which, surprisingly at this point, still had a white president, Arthur Spingarn. Interviewed about the future of the organization in 1964, the eighty-six-year-old Spingarn noted that Ralph Bunche had been suggested as a possible successor but, he cautioned, "the young people say he has been brainwashed—anyone who gets along with white people is suspect."[19]

Bunche never pursued the NAACP post. While Spingarn was not wrong to say that Bunche got along with white people, there is no sign that had anything to do with Bunche's decision not to seek the NAACP presidency. Attending a largely white high school, UCLA, and then Harvard, and having worked for years at the State Department, he indeed had substantial experience—and had achieved substantial success—in white-dominated settings. As if to illustrate Spingarn's point, just days later, in early June, Bunche headed to Washington for yet another state dinner at the White House, this time in honor of Israeli Prime Minister Levi Eshkol. Bunche saw his stature among white Americans as earned and appropriate, having grown out of his basic drive and competitiveness and his hard work. White settings simply made the stakes higher and the win all the sweeter. When I think back on my school days, he later said, "when I was the only Negro in the class ... I was determined to show I was as good as the white kids."[20]

His prominence in American society in turn gave him a big megaphone, which he continued to use. In various commencement speeches that season, for example, he again lambasted Barry Goldwater, the Arizona arch-conservative, over his views on proposed civil rights legislation in Congress. Goldwater had called race relations a matter of the heart, and thus not amenable to legal fixes. Bunche strongly disagreed. "The American Negro is seeking only rights, not affection," he declared at the University of Maine.[21] Bunche had always discussed racial discrimination in his public speeches, but he was increasingly speaking out in more specific terms, taking on the issues that were increasingly roiling the nation.

That fall Martin Luther King Jr. became the second Black American to win the Nobel Peace Prize. Bunche immediately sent King a telegram, thrilled at the choice. On his way to Norway in December 1964, King visited Bunche at the UN, posing for photos, alongside his wife, Coretta

Photo 22.3 Bunche, MLK, and Coretta Scott King at the UN

Scott King, in front of a large world map. A few months later, in March 1965, Bunche joined King for the historic march from Selma, Alabama, to Montgomery, the state capital, 50 miles away. King invited him to join him, and Bunche declared that he was happy to do so. "I had thought of going on my own," he told reporters, but was afraid he might be seen as seeking the limelight.[22] In his reply to King's invitation, he mentioned that his declining health would inhibit his walking. His diabetes and other ailments had taken a marked turn for the worse in recent months. Indeed, at Christmas 1964, he dashed off a short note to himself remarking that he had been unusually generous because it began to "register with me that at my age with my ailments I cannot be very certain about how many more such opportunities will be permitted me."[23]

Having warned King of his limitations, Bunche departed for Alabama. Aside from his work on the Myrdal project in the 1930, he had spent little time in the South. But he had seen enough to know how deep the hatred and discrimination ran and how urgent, even three decades later, the work there remained.

Even as major newspapers carried news of Bunche's decision to join King's 1965 march, it was clear that many young people were far less attuned to his activities. Days before he flew to Selma, Bunche received a letter from two Howard students. "Recently, there was a heated discussion in our dormitory," the letter conveyed, "as to active participation by prominent Negroes in the Civil Rights Movement."

> Your name was mentioned in the course of the conversation and none of the participants could connect you with any of the activities of the Civil Rights Movement, such as The March on Washington or Dr. King's and related organizations activities. We would appreciate any information concerning this situation as soon as possible. Thank you very much for your cooperation.
>
> Yours truly,
>
> (Misses) Margaret Allen & Agnes Cross

Troubled by the fact that his efforts on behalf of the civil rights movement were apparently not filtering down to college students, even at Howard, he took the time to pen a somewhat testy reply. "Frankly, I do not get many letters such as yours," he wrote the two young students. "But invariably after my civil rights speeches,"

which, by the way, are always reported in the press, I get a number of denunciatory letters from irate whites. I am afraid I would have to say that the participants in the dormitory discussed were not very well informed. As to the March on Washington, Mrs. Bunche & I participated in it and I actually was one of the speakers that day at the Monument. For your information, I have been in civil rights struggle all my adult life, and I believe that there are only a few Negroes—and these were the leaders such as DuBois, James Weldon Johnson, Walter White, A. Philip Randolph, Martin Luther King and James Farmer—whose voices were heard on the issue more often or more forthrightly than mine . . .

I was participating in demonstrations, protest meetings & picket lines in Washington, D.C. as far back as the early 30's, when I was a faculty member at Howard when, indeed, one was sometimes investigated for such activities, as I was. I Joined Dr. King in support of the bus boycott in the midst of that struggle.[24]

Clearly piqued by this exchange, Bunche headed to join King in Alabama. The young Howard students would not have to look hard to see evidence of his role there; the cover of *Ebony* magazine in May 1965 was a vivid photo of the phalanx of marchers, Bunche in the front row, jacket off, tie carefully clipped, arm in arm with King.

Martin Luther King began the famous march from Selma to Montgomery preaching from the steps of the redbrick Brown's Chapel on a cool, sunny spring day. He praised President Johnson for his support for crucial voting rights legislation. Then, coming down the church steps, King took Ralph Bunche's hand and began to walk. With flowers hung around their necks, King, flanked by Bunche on one side and Baptist minister Ralph Abernathy on the other, led thousands of marchers down the road to Montgomery.[25] Guarding the marchers were federal troops as well as FBI agents, a sign of the growing tension and violence in the South. Wearing a hat and sunglasses, Bunche looked somewhat frail and unsteady as he walked alongside

King. But he was glad to be there at the center of the action, in a mode he felt comfortable in, fighting for a cause that was just and even righteous.

That same day, March 22, the *New York Times* reported, under the headline "Hope Is Renewed in Cyprus Talks," that Greece and Turkey appeared to be moving closer to a negotiated settlement over the strife-torn island. The story was just below the photo of Bunche and King marching on the road to Montgomery. The *Times'* frontpage that spring day summarized the public understanding of Bunche and his career in the mid-1960s. His visit to Cyprus the year before had begun a more focused process of conflict mediation, and he would continue to monitor Cyprus, as he monitored so many similar conflict zones around the world, from his "war room" on the 38th floor. Internally, however, he was increasingly looking toward retirement from the UN, and, perhaps feeling some angst about his almost three-decades-long hiatus from a serious focus on domestic issues, he was increasingly thinking about American race relations. King's Selma to Montgomery march embodied the sort of civil rights movement Bunche felt he could support, and he was happy to lend his gravitas when possible.

As the march continued for several days, Bunche, back at the UN, announced that he found the Alabama effort "thrilling and magnificent." He would return to it later in the week, as the much smaller column of marchers—only 300 were allowed to actually go the full distance, accompanied by armed federalized national guard troops—continued on into Montgomery. (Among the marchers could be seen the UN flag, held aloft alongside the American one.) Bunche was deeply impressed with King's effort in Selma. "Consciences were at work in Alabama," he told reporters: "the world is overwhelmingly with us in this struggle."[26] He eagerly returned to the South for the final stage of the march. Arriving in Montgomery with King and Andrew Young, he hopped out when their car was stopped by armed soldiers as they approached the State Capitol. "I'm Dr. Bunche, Undersecretary General of the United Nations, here for the march." Sorry sir, replied the soldier, this is not the United Nations. "My orders are no left turn." Finally, a Montgomery policeman noticed King in the back seat and told the soldier to let the car through: "This is the man!"[27]

At the Alabama statehouse, where Governor George Wallace, an avowed segregationist, refused to see the march leaders—calling them "outsiders and meddlers"—a crowd of 30,000 had assembled. Joan Baez; Peter, Paul, and Mary; and Harry Belafonte performed. The National Anthem was sung. Taking the stage as the opening speaker, Ralph Bunche called out the "superlative leadership" of King and proclaimed that "Governor Wallace should understand that no American can be an outsider anywhere he goes in America."[28]

JUNE 1965 WAS THE TWENTIETH ANNIVERSARY of the signing of the UN Charter. Lyndon Johnson, speaking in San Francisco for the commemoration, encouraged the members of the UN "individually and collectively, to bring to the table those determined to make war."[29] After his speech, the president spoke with U Thant about Vietnam. As Bunche approached the room for the meeting, he noted that Adlai Stevenson, red-faced, was leaving. Bunche asked what was going on. "He doesn't want me present," the agitated Stevenson said, referring to Johnson. Bunche, concerned, told Thant that he should probably also exit, leaving the two principals to hash things out. Stevenson, too dovish for Johnson, appeared to be on the outs.[30]

Johnson seemed to be digging in on Vietnam that summer, but so, too, was U Thant. The secretary general's interest in Vietnam was unwavering, at times to the great irritation of American officials. Bunche was often the one asked to explain Thant's thinking to the White House and maybe try to rein him in. A few weeks before the UN anniversary, Bunche had explained to the Americans that Thant was going to call for an immediate cessation of hostilities. (Johnson, by contrast, was moving in the opposite direction, initiating "Operation Rolling Thunder" that same month, a massive and brutal bombing campaign in the North.) As Stevenson reported to Dean Rusk, "Bunche informed me that the Secretary General would consider any appropriate language extending the 17th parallel to include infiltration through Laos. He will welcome any suggestions . . . with respect to policing requirements during the cease fire period."[31]* When U Thant next mentioned to reporters that he might travel to Beijing and Hanoi to explore a

---

* The 17th parallel was a key divide between North and South Vietnam.

possible peace agreement, the White House was intrigued. As the *Boston Globe* reported, the Johnson administration informed Thant that it would not object to a Peking-Hanoi visit in an effort to bring about a negotiated settlement. "Words to that effect were passed on by the US delegation to the UN earlier this week via Ralph Bunche."[32] As the *Globe*'s story explained, Bunche was a key intermediary and may have even been the source of the idea that Thant should take the trip in the first place. In the end, though, the trip did not take place: Hanoi refused to meet with Thant, terming any UN role in the war "inappropriate."[33]

Thant, who had lived under colonialism in Burma, was persistent in part because he saw the war as not just geopolitical but moral and also racial in nature. He had told Adlai Stevenson that American actions in Vietnam were alienating Asian public opinion. "The peoples of Southeast Asia," he explained, "see a racial angle in the United States intervention."[34] Bunche agreed with Thant that race was central to the conflict, but he also was cautious about drawing out the connection. Soon enough, however, he would make the same claim himself.

The UN's twentieth anniversary celebrations almost were postponed. When Bunche told Stevenson that Thant was considering delaying them, Stevenson resisted, suggesting that a postponement would be interpreted as a "sure sign of the complete failure of the UN."[35] Thant ultimately went forward, perhaps fearful of sending precisely this signal. The anniversary provided an opportune moment to reflect on where the world body had started and where it found itself now. Bunche, of course, had been a witness to the entire arc of UN history. He was in the room at the earliest discussions at Dumbarton Oaks while the Second World War was still being fought. And he was still there even as it had evolved into the large, diverse organization of 1965. Despite its impressive growth, many observers in 1965 saw the UN as a noble failure. Its primary mission—the preservation of peace and security—seemed to have been quickly derailed by the Cold War. The hoped-for close cooperation among the great power "policemen" never really happened. Indeed, that spring the Soviets were demanding that the Security Council condemn the American intervention in the Dominican Republic, which had allegedly been undertaken to protect American nationals and done as an inter-American force, though one that happened to be thoroughly dominated by the largest of the American states. (Bunche, who directed the UN's representatives in the Dominican Republic, called it "just about the messiest situation we have had to get involved in.")[36] Yet cooperation between the two superpowers was likely unrealistic from the start, as George Kennan and others had warned. The UN's structure of great power condominium may have made sense at Yalta, but it was premised on a foundation that eroded almost as soon as Japan signed the document of surrender onboard the USS *Missouri* in the fall of 1945.

Still, the UN had proven itself useful, even essential, in other, less obvious ways in the two decades it had been operating. As one prominent analysis at the time rightly argued, the UN's track record on mediation and peacekeeping—two of Bunche's signature accomplishments—was laudatory, and more attention ought to be given to them. "One must regretfully observe," wrote Benjamin Cohen in the *Washington Post*, "that most national statesmen, while paying lip service to the United Nations and tearfully lamenting its ineffectiveness and professing to wish to see it strengthened, have done precious little to develop and dramatize its great potentialities in the field of peacekeeping and pacific settlement."[37] This side of the UN was not exactly what the framers of the Charter had envisioned twenty years earlier in San Francisco, but it was nonetheless significant. Indeed, while great powers and their wars had been the focus of the deliberations in 1945, the UN was increasingly far more important to small powers. The great powers still controlled the Security Council and called the shots on the most important matters. But the rise of nuclear weapons had meant that actual great power conflict appeared to be almost extinct. Territorial aggression of the sort Germany and Japan engaged in in the runup to the Second World War was also much diminished, and when it did occur—say in Goa, in 1962—the international community sometimes viewed it as a righteous or at least respectable act, one that redressed the wrongs of the past.[38]

The process of decolonization, on the other hand, had proven to be far more momentous than anyone imagined at the UN's founding. It had certainly arrived far more swiftly than anyone imagined. Almost an afterthought at Dumbarton Oaks, decolonization had yielded many of the most important changes in the world of 1965: not only a new and more diverse system of states, but also an entire agenda of new issues for the UN. Some of these issues, such as "peacekeeping and pacific settlement," directly bore Bunche's handiwork. Others, such as human rights, the environment, and global health, would come to fruition only after his death. Not all of this was clear by the UN's 20th anniversary, but, for those who were looking, it was coming into focus. Asked the following year by a junior high school student why the UN was important, Bunche answered that the UN had two basic objectives: peace and "human advancement."[39] These goals, he explained to young Robert Davis of the Bronx, were closely related. The first had been the central purpose of the UN from the earliest days at Dumbarton Oaks. The second was more implicit in the early years but was rapidly coming to seem more and more central.

Within weeks of the anniversary celebrations, Bunche received a shock: Adlai Stevenson was dead of a sudden heart attack. Stevenson perhaps would not have lasted in his post much longer, given how LBJ had been freezing him out of discussions. But now there was an important position unexpectedly to be filled and many possible contenders. Bunche's name was among those bandied about, even as he flew to London to escort the body back.[40] As with previous overtures from the federal government to take a major position, however, he made clear he did not want to leave—or felt he could not leave—his UN post. In this case, he in particular believed that his views on the war in Vietnam made a position in the Johnson administration untenable. Indeed, when the foreign minister of Cyprus, during a meeting with Bunche and Thant, asked if the rumors that Bunche was going to be the new US ambassador were true, Thant laughed and said: "Ralph is international, much too international for that." Bunche repeated something he had said before, that he would not return to the US government save in times of war. And he wouldn't fit well if he did—"can you envisage me expounding US policy on Article 19 or Vietnam?" he asked the others.[41]§

Yet even as he was rejecting this idea out of hand, the Soviets continued to push the notion that he was a biased mouthpiece for the Johnson

---

§ Article 19 referred to the UN Charter's provisions on dues and financing.

administration. At a dinner organized for the UN's twentieth anniversary, a colleague pulled him aside to let him know of a recent closed-door attack by the Soviet ambassador, Nikolai Fedorenko, alleging that Bunche was advising Thant "on the basis of instructions from the Pentagon."[42] Dean Rusk, seeing Bunche, put his arm around his shoulders and said, laughingly, "Ralph, I know you are a good civil servant. I heard about Fedorenko's charge today and I also have had complaints about you!" At the dinner, Fedorenko caught Bunche's eye across the table and, to his amazement, gave him a silent toast.** A few weeks later, the Russian diplomat asked him about the situation in Kashmir. Bunche replied that he saw no reason for optimism. Fedorenko laughed and said, "Doesn't the Pentagon have some?"[43] Bunche, confused by the whiplashing signals but always concerned about propriety, whispered in Thant's ear that perhaps he should be pulled off the Kashmir issue so as to forestall any claims of bias.

After Stevenson's memorial in Washington, Bunche and Thant met yet again with Dean Rusk on Vietnam. The three spoke for ninety minutes. Thant and Rusk "disagreed on just about everything," including the very facts of the conflict. Rusk began to "doodle furiously" and Thant, in his one tell of stress, was shaking his legs. The meeting was not successful, and "the exchange produced no glimmer of hope," Bunche wrote in his diary. But Rusk soon after called Bunche at his home to sound him out about a different, confidential matter. What might happen at the UN, Rusk inquired, were the president to nominate a "nationally prominent Jew" to be the new American ambassador?

Bunche, of course, had long experience with Arabs and Jews in the UN, and that experience unfortunately did not suggest optimism. He replied that though he hated to say it, the move would have some negative repercussions. The Arab delegates at the UN would likely not accept him (Bunche, rightly, assumed it was a him), and, he believed, they might not deal with him. Rusk listened, concurring, and noted that he and Bunche both "dislike this sort of thing."[44]

** In January 1968, when Fedorenko retired, he told Bunche: "I hope you will not remember any unfriendly things I said about you. You know they were not meant even though at the time I had to say them."

The person Lyndon Johnson had in mind as ambassador was Supreme Court Justice Arthur Goldberg. Goldberg, a lawyer with little international experience, was an unusual choice. Yet whatever Bunche and Rusk's misgivings, he was the one LBJ wanted, and Rusk soon enough called Bunche to encourage him, "as a friend and an American," to talk up Goldberg for the UN post. The justice was brilliant and a dedicated public servant, Rusk insisted, and, of course, the US cannot discriminate in its officials on the basis of religion or race. When Bunche informed Thant about Rusk's request to gently lobby on Goldberg's behalf, he called it improper and contrary to the UN Charter. More importantly, the secretary general thought Goldberg's appointment would be a "disaster."[45]

IN JULY 1965, PRESIDENT JOHNSON ANNOUNCED an additional 50,000 men would be sent to Vietnam. That same month, Richard Nixon, now in private legal practice but still active in Republican politics, attacked the UN. Republicans had long viewed the UN as a hotbed of communism—Ralph Bunche's own loyalty hearings in the 1950s were a signal example of how far they pushed this concept—but now, they believed, the UN was becoming not just pro-communism but overtly anti-American. (While highly exaggerated, this was not a wholly outlandish assessment: the US would cast its first, ill-considered, Security Council veto just a few years later over white-ruled Rhodesia, in part due to perceived anti-Westernism in the organization.) Bunche, increasingly seen as the only UN official with reach and respect in the eyes of the American public, responded in a speech at the Ambassador Hotel in Los Angeles. Nixon's charge that the UN is controlled by "weak and neutral nations" is "sheer humbug," said Bunche. "My good friend Dick Nixon hasn't been around the UN for a long time . . . he should visit there more often to see how it works."[46] Bunche gave a spirited defense, but Nixon's antipathy was a sign of where things were going for the Republican Party and much of the nation.

Meanwhile, the arrival of Arthur Goldberg as the new ambassador to the UN in July 1965 provided a momentary hope that the dynamic between the US and U Thant could improve. Goldberg was not a typical diplomat. During the Second World War, he served in the Office of Strategic Services,

Bunche's first government home and the precursor to the CIA. He served as secretary of labor in the Kennedy administration, after which, in 1962, he was appointed to the Supreme Court. Goldberg's move to the UN was a rare example of a Supreme Court justice leaving the bench for another government position.[††]

Goldberg's ardent desire to bring peace to Vietnam was widely seen as undergirding his decision to try his hand at diplomacy. Yet—and he himself later said as much—he failed miserably in this goal and was out after three years. As he later described his decision to trade the Supreme Court for the Security Council, "Nobody can twist the arm of a Supreme Court justice [but] we were in a war in Vietnam. I had an exaggerated opinion of my own capacities. I thought I could persuade Johnson that we were fighting the wrong war in the wrong place."[47]

Bunche grew to like Goldberg, but his first impression of the new and unseasoned ambassador was mixed. He struck Bunche as perhaps overly impressed with himself, a bit stiff, and certainly enamored of deference. In presenting his credentials to the secretary general, a formality for all ambassadors, Goldberg was

> very formal—even a little pompous—at the beginning. He had a pile of typed pages before him from which he was reading while trying to appear not to be. It was as though he was addressing an audience and he spoke quite loudly. . . . he spoke frequently of his service on the Supreme Court and how difficult it was for him to leave it, and he seemed to have certain mannerisms of the bench, moving his head and shoulders with magisterial dignity and deliberateness and sitting very erect.[48]

Later on, Bunche bemusedly noted that even at the UN Goldberg still wanted to be called "Mr. Justice."[49]

Goldberg's relationship with Lyndon Johnson, never great, was irreparably harmed by both his dovish views and his occasional flashes of judicial imperiousness. At a meeting of the National Security Council with Johnson

---

[††] James Byrnes, who left the Supreme Court to become Truman's secretary of state, was another case familiar to Bunche: Byrnes had been the leader of the first US delegation to the UN meetings in London in 1946.

early in his tenure, Goldberg directly criticized a suggestion to increase the bombing of North Vietnamese targets. At one point Goldberg even said to Johnson "you can't do that." LBJ, clearly annoyed at the impertinence of his underling, snapped back, "I'm the President of the United States and of course I can do it." Goldberg quickly backed down, but the damage was done.[50]

IN AUGUST 1965, JUST WEEKS AFTER Bunche visited his hometown, the city's Watts neighborhood erupted in violence. Bunche, who had grown up near Watts, was deeply troubled by the violence—troubled enough to issue a personal statement to the press on a domestic matter, something he rarely did. "The ominous message of Watts for all America, I fear, is that it has produced, raw and ugly, the bitterest fruit of the Black ghetto."[51] He was increasingly concerned about the problem of ghettos, and while some saw hope in a positive Black separatism, he remained fervently opposed. For him, there was no choice but to seek a better, more just integration of the races.

That same month Bunche again met with Goldberg and Thant to discuss Vietnam. Thant was distressed at the intensifying American bombing campaign in the north and continued to press Goldberg on the need to avoid civilian targets such as irrigation dams.[52] Thant also expressed regret that he was struggling to get traction as a mediator among the various parties. Goldberg, switching topics, asked Bunche to discuss a rising dispute between Israel and Jordan and the existing dispute in Kashmir. In the vertiginous mountain region, the standoff between India and Pakistan was growing more grave. U Thant had recalled the general in charge of the UN observer team for consultations in New York, and in August he discussed sending Bunche back to South Asia to mediate. But just the day before, the Indian government had indicated that, despite the high regard with which it held Bunche personally, a visit "would serve no purpose" unless the UN acknowledged the "open aggression" of Pakistan.[53] Bowing to political reality, Bunche stayed in New York.

He may have also welcomed the chance to stay home. Bunche was increasingly feeling his age. A chain-smoker and never especially mindful of his health, he worked too many hours of the day and slept far too little at night. He traveled extensively in difficult places where diseases were rampant and health care was limited. In 1965, he was also diagnosed with a hemorrhage in his left eye. His vision, which had long been failing, had now grown so weak that he could no longer drive safely; the UN had now begun to send a security officer to his Queens home to pick him up each morning.

"He fought the idea like mad," Ruth Bunche later said of the UN's car and driver. "He hated the idea of being driven to work, and driven home again. But there was nothing he could do about it."[54] (Bunche would later give it a more positive spin, saying that being driven gave him more time to write down his thoughts and made the trip in from Queens "seem very quick.")[55] His handwriting became large and loopy as he tried to write in a way he could later read. Indeed, in a letter that fall to Ralph Jr, then in the UK, he asked Ralph to type rather than hand-write his letters home, since he could no longer read his handwriting. He also described his other, worsening, ailments, calling himself a "walking wounded" of the famous blackout that occurred on November 9, 1965, in New York City.[56] Trapped high on the 38th floor, he had tried to wait out the power outage, working by candle-light. Eventually growing too cold, he decided to join U Thant in the long trip down the stairs. He was fearful of the implications for his injured leg, but, seeing little choice, headed down—only to injure the other leg in the process. Bunche increasingly began to look for a way to exit the UN grace-fully and take the time with Ruth and his family he seemed to have never had in the last twenty-five years of breakneck work. But somehow it was never the right time.

Ten days after the blackout, as part of her famous American charm offen-sive, Princess Margaret of Great Britain came to the UN. She had just visited President Johnson at the White House. The royal visit brought a break from the dispiriting focus on Vietnam but was not without its own controversy. Bunche, who brought Ruth to the office for the occasion, met with the prin-cess and her husband, Anthony Armstrong-Jones. Standing out in a large cylindrical wool hat, pink dress, and long gloves, the princess mingled with various officials at a pre-lunch reception hosted by the UK's ambassador.

The reception, however, was boycotted by all the African states in an effort to underscore Britain's role in the controversial declaration of independence, just a week before, of white-dominated Rhodesia.[57] South Africa, both because of its apartheid system and its unyielding control over the former League of Nations mandate of South West Africa, was increasingly becoming a pariah at the UN. Rhodesia would soon join South Africa in the ranks of deeply ostracized states in the international community. Six months later, the Rhodesia issue would lead to what Bunche termed "just about the blackest day at the UN" he had ever experienced. When the British requested a meeting of the Security Council to address Rhodesian sanctions and proposed a resolution that was weaker than the Africa bloc wanted, the president of the Council, a Malian, hid in the building rather than hold a vote. Bunche found the admittedly childish maneuver surprisingly disturbing and thought it would "put the UN on the road to ruin" if it was replicated.[58] But it illustrated how heated the politics of decolonization and discrimination had become.

Meanwhile, the British royal couple left the somewhat fraught UN reception to attend a small lunch in the Dag Hammarskjold Library, at which Ralph and Ruth were guests. Bunche, seeing the Princess standing by the window, went up and chit-chatted with her. The Bunches had traveled to Jamaica in 1962 for the island's independence and had met Princess Margaret there in Kingston. (Bunche later somewhat cattily noted in his diary that "she is rather affected but genuinely blasé I think" and her husband is "runt-sized.")[59] Then the two had a conversation that illustrated the waning age of decolonization. Standing with the princess at the UN, he told her that the colony of British Guiana was soon to become independent, probably in the spring of 1966. Princess Margaret replied that it was so small and poor, to which Bunche noted, "not as small as the last member we welcomed into the UN, thanks to your government." What nation was that, Margaret asked. The Maldive Islands, he replied. "Where are they?" replied Margaret. "That's just it," answered Bunche, "we didn't even know."[60]

AS 1965 CAME TO AN END, US involvement in Vietnam grew dramatically. There were now almost 200,000 American troops deployed in Southeast Asia. Debate over the war was at a fever pitch in American politics and, increasingly, throughout the world. In November, Norman Morrison, a thirty-one-year-old Quaker, doused himself in kerosene in front of the Pentagon and, letting his eleven-month-old baby daughter go to the arms of a stranger, lit a match and immolated himself. One week later, a similar suicide took place at the gates of the UN. Sitting down in front of the Dag Hammarskjold Library at dawn, Roger LaPorte, a twenty-two-year-old former Catholic seminarian, struck a match to the gasoline he had poured over his body as daylight broke. Surviving only to the next day, he reportedly said he was protesting "war, all war."[61]

These shocking suicides followed many others in Vietnam by Buddhist monks that were arrestingly and disturbingly photographed for the world to see. Shortly after LaPorte lit himself aflame, Under Secretary of State George Ball accompanied Arthur Goldberg to another visit with U Thant in New York. The White House emissaries were trying to find some peaceful way forward in the war—or at least appear to do so. Bunche was the only other UN official present. Ball first attempted to butter up Thant by telling him he had "a solid group of admirers" in Washington and that he was "doing a difficult job admirably." Thant then launched into a very long description of his many efforts at conciliation in Southeast Asia, encouraging the US to do more. Ball politely insisted that the US saw no indication of a willingness from the other side to sit down "unconditionally."[62] The meeting was more formal than substantive, and the next steps were not clear. The US and the UN continued to want to dance, it seemed, but could not agree on the tune.

As New Year's Eve approached, Bunche was offered a job by New York City's Mayor-Elect John Lindsay. Lindsay called him a few days before the inauguration to offer him the post of head of housing—calling it the agency "with the most power in the city."[63] It must have been tempting. Yet as usual, Bunche demurred, saying he was still needed at the UN.

A few weeks later, in early 1966, Pope Paul VI suggested arbitration among the combatants in Southeast Asia under UN auspices. Pressure was mounting for the Johnson administration to take some conciliatory action. But the US was increasingly skeptical about Thant as a go-between. As early as 1964, McGeorge Bundy, the national security advisor, had told Johnson that Thant was a "neutralist Burmese" (neutralism being the original term for what became known as the Non-Aligned Movement) who was unlikely to see the larger—meaning Cold War—picture in Vietnam.[64] The many meetings between Thant, Bunche, and American officials, and between Bunche and his various interlocutors on the US side, whether Adlai Stevenson, Dean Rusk, or later Goldberg or Ball, only reinforced the lack of agreement, approach, and even trust between the US and the UN.

Speaking with Thant a few weeks into 1966, Bunche told him he would definitely not be available much longer at the UN; he was "tired and my health was not good."[65] Thant likewise did not seem interested in staying on as secretary general; he told Bunche that his mother in Burma was aging and that his wife wanted to return home. The two seemed to warily engage the question of their respective departures, knowing that at some level their fates at the organization were intertwined.

Seeking some respite from the relentless work, Bunche flew out to Hawaii for a conference, where he enjoyed a chance to swim in the warm Pacific, and then later he traveled to San Francisco and Portland to speak at a few colleges. He had always looked forward to these events, which usually meant engaged young crowds and a chance to connect with local notables. He was still typically treated as a star, and while he did not like to admit it, that sort of treatment was nice. In this case, the trip west meant some old friends were present, including an old girlfriend from his Los Angeles days, Eugenie Geherke. He even visited Ralph Bunche Elementary in Oakland, California. Yet his health was increasingly worrying him. In his journal Bunche wrote

> I enjoy these visits to college campuses, especially the small ones, but I don't know
> how much longer I can schedule them. I have trouble reading my notes, I lost my
> voice for awhile at both Reed and Whitman, and midway in my Reed talk I had
> a period of great fatigue and aching legs, but it passed. I don't yet know the full
> implications for my active life of the combination of being in the sixties and having
> diabetes. It is already abundantly clear that the adjustment for me will be extremely
> difficult.[66]

Bunche returned to life on the 38th floor, worried more than ever about the war. He saw no easy or clear way out. Negotiation, he told a friend at the time, "is the only answer," and he was working hard toward that goal but with little to show for it.[67] Perhaps it was unsurprising that in a quiet moment he penned a brief note in his journal that "the work on peace-keeping operations as I had found it in recent years was more interesting and in a quiet way more self-satisfying and rewarding than any I had done since becoming a member of the Secretariat."[68] Whereas Vietnam seemed to pit his strong moral compass, support for the UN, and belief in mediation against his professional duty and sense of patriotism, peacekeeping, for all its headaches, evidenced the positive side of the UN and a personal sense of accomplishment.

By the spring of 1966, Bunche, in a conversation with Arthur Goldberg, stated that Dean Rusk's negative attitude toward U Thant was one reason Thant was seriously considering not running for another term as secretary general. Goldberg replied that he thought the US would ultimately support Thant, if only because "it would be impossible to get agreement on anyone else."[69] At a Gridiron Club dinner in March, Bunche sat next to Dean Acheson, the legendary secretary of state of the Truman years. Acheson confided that he thought the late Adlai Stevenson hadn't done well as UN ambassador. Clearly in an expansive mood, Acheson added that the UN was wrong to have been in Congo; a somewhat strange position given how the Eisenhower administration had strongly encouraged the UN presence to keep the Soviets out of the area. The UN was also wrong to be in Cyprus, he stated. Acheson confided that he could have settled the Cyprus dispute "if only the President had let him." Acheson also thought the UN more broadly was not working out as an organization and now had too many new members from "immature emerging nations."[70]

Acheson's last comment hit at the heart of Bunche's life's work and his principled belief in decolonization. It also raised a broader question of the purpose and personality of the UN, now in its third decade. Was it a consortium of the great powers, with the Security Council their platform and legitimating force, or was it a universalist organization that took to heart the principle of international law that all states were juridically equal sovereigns? The rapid rise of the Third World had not radically altered the power of the Security Council nor changed the composition of the powerful Permanent Five members.[‡‡] But the rush of new states *had* radically revamped the General Assembly, which was increasingly vocal on a host of issues—sovereignty over natural resources, racist regimes in South Africa and Rhodesia, the importance of nonintervention—that did not always accord with the interests of the traditional great powers. This shift may well have led the great powers to seek to compromise more among themselves. Indeed, they began to do so in this era, successfully passing more resolutions and avoiding some of the intractable conflicts that had plagued the early Cold War years.[71]

A couple of months later, Bunche himself picked up on this theme of the UN's evolving purposes. Asked about peacekeeping as he arrived in Cyprus, he noted that opinions differed on its merits and its financing. But, he added, there also were basic political differences about whether the UN primarily should be "a place for exchanges of views by governments, an international marketplace of ideas, or whether it is to be this plus operations such as peacekeeping."[72] This was indeed a major difference. The UN was clearly a stage; was it also an actor? In the end, although he would not live to see it, the latter conception would prevail and peacekeeping, as well as many other operations humanitarian in nature, would become huge elements in the organization's portfolio. The UN's role as a stage or arena would never falter, but its actor tendencies would grow substantially.

In June 1966, still trying to prove his peaceful bona fides by elevating the UN, Lyndon Johnson hosted the first-ever reception for UN ambassadors at the White House. While many communist states boycotted the event, over 300 guests did attend, Bunche among them. The White House affair was glittering and flattering to the many ambassadors present. At the event, Bunche soon found himself in conversation with Arthur Goldberg. The two men discussed China, parsing the views of Dean Rusk, before being summoned upstairs to the residence to meet privately with Lyndon Johnson. Thant, who was approaching the end of his first term full as secretary general, was still weighing whether to run for a second term. As a

---

[‡‡] The rise in membership did yield an expansion of the Security Council, in 1965, from the original eleven members to fifteen. No new permanent members were added.

permanent member of the Security Council, the US had the ability to block that effort if it chose.

As the men arrived at the top of the stairs to meet the president, Goldberg, perhaps unaware of Bunche's many prior interactions with Johnson, announced that "Ralph is one of the two absolutely indispensable men at the UN"—quickly adding that Thant was the other. Downstairs, after the brief meeting with the president was over, Dean Rusk told Bunche the real deal: "You will just have to stay on whether U Thant does or not."[73]

CHAPTER 23

SEEKING AN END

Mankind must put an end to war or war will put an end to mankind.
—Martin Luther King Jr., March 31, 1968

On April 3, 1966, the Friars Club, a private club that catered to comedians, Broadway stars, and other celebrities, honored the hugely popular entertainer Sammy Davis Jr. with a gala dinner. Davis, who had once quipped, in response to a query about what his golf handicap was, "my handicap? I'm a one-eyed Black Jew!," was a charter member of the Sinatra Rat Pack, a frequent Las Vegas headliner, and a successful singer, dancer, and actor—but also one who had triggered controversy with his Swedish wife, May Britt, in the years before the Supreme Court struck down antimiscegenation laws in the wonderfully named 1967 case of *Loving v. Virginia*.

Some 1300 guests packed the ballroom at the Waldorf Astoria Hotel for the Davis gala, which raised funds for the Friars' charity fund. The event drew a who's who of New York City. Senator Jacob Javits, Mayor John Lindsay, Tony Bennett, Sidney Poitier, and Sammy Davis Jr.'s mother were all in attendance. So, too, was Robert F. Kennedy, a living link to his brother JFK and, somewhat surprisingly for a legendary Bostonian with a thick New

England accent, now a senator from New York. With Johnny Carson serving as the emcee, Ralph Bunche was among the several guests who spoke in Davis's honor. His remarks followed those by Javits and Kennedy, and he received a tremendous reception from the audience at the Waldorf. Indeed, as Bunche recounted later, to his surprise he received a "veritable ovation, far greater than that received by either Javits or Kennedy." As the audience cheered and cheered, Bunche stood up again and sat down quickly, but the applause kept coming and Buddy Hackett yelled at him to stand up again and take a bow; "I did and then had to get up again, that was the 3rd time."

At the end of the black-tie evening, Bunche headed out to return to his home in Queens. As he settled in the car, he heard a tap on the window. Looking out, he saw Bobby Kennedy and his wife Ethel standing there. Bunche quickly opened the door as Kennedy shouted to him, "that was one hell of a hand you got there, I am glad I don't have to run against you!"[1]

Bobby Kennedy, long and deeply immersed in national politics, was a shrewd judge of political appeal. He may well have been aware that his brother, as president, had read polls of Ralph Bunche's prospects as a possible New York senatorial candidate. The Friars Club dinner and the fulsome compliment from Kennedy—who perhaps was already contemplating a run for the presidency himself—were a welcome break for Bunche from the tension and frustration that surrounded the United Nations in 1966. The war in Vietnam was convulsing the nation and likewise was increasingly consuming Turtle Bay. Back in January Secretary of State Dean Rusk had told him to "call him anytime" and give his views about the war.[2] But in fact Bunche rarely felt he could give his true views to Rusk, someone he had known for decades. He took his role as a neutral international civil servant seriously; but even more so, he knew he was the person the Johnson administration relied on to understand, explain, and convey messages back and forth to the UN, and in particular to U Thant. Bunche did not completely hide his concern about the war—indeed, he often shared it with Ambassador Arthur Goldberg, who was one of the administration's chief doves—but he also adopted a studied neutrality when he was privy, as he often was, to debates at the highest levels.

This was especially true because his boss was a key figure, though an increasingly controversial one, in the debate over the Southeast Asian war. U Thant's desire to mediate the conflict was potentially helpful to the US, but by 1966 he was also, perhaps mainly, considered an irritant by the administration. Indeed, that same spring, at a Gridiron Club dinner in Washington, DC, Rusk pulled Bunche aside and asked, "Can't you keep Thant quiet?" In his diary, Bunche commented that "they are very sensitive and snippish in DC these days."[3]

In the wake of the Friars Club tribute, Bunche sent Sammy Davis Jr. a letter congratulating him on having become chairman of the Life Membership Committee of the NAACP.* Writing to a fellow Black man, he was perhaps a bit more forthright about racial prejudice than he often was in his public remarks. To Davis, he acknowledged that his "superb talent" had carried him "to the pinnacle despite the severe handicap of race." But, he continued (and Bunche just as easily could have been talking about himself), it was simply not good enough for a select few to "crash through the barriers of race and make it big." Channeling his long-held optimism in the American project, he insisted that America must—and he told Davis he believed it would—achieve a society in which every individual, without regard to his race, color, or religion, could "find his just level on the sole basis of his worth."[4]

IN WASHINGTON IN THE SPRING OF 1966, hawks were ascendant and doves were diminishing—or fleeing. Arthur Goldberg's star was clearly sinking. Like his predecessor, Adlai Stevenson, he was simply too dovish for the White House, and in addition, the former Justice Goldberg had the temerity to tell Lyndon Johnson within the confines of the White House what he could and could not do. U Thant was also weighing his own future and considering whether or not to run for another term as secretary general. Bunche, the confidante of both men, was critical to their success,

---

* Sammy Davis Jr had already sent a note of appreciation on his personal stationery—which featured a silhouette of Davis dancing with jazz hands—saying it was "a great thrill for me" to have had Bunche there.

but in his own way, he was also considering an exit from the stage. "If Thant Quits the UN, Expect Bunche to Follow" ran a headline in the *Los Angeles Times* that year.[5]

Bunche was increasingly vocal about retirement as he entered his sixties. His diabetes seemed to be worsening daily, his eyesight was almost gone, and he felt more tired than ever before. Vietnam weighed on him, and he felt stymied and unsure what he—or the UN—could realistically accomplish. Perhaps, he wondered more and more, it was time to retire and enjoy life with Ruth and the grandkids with the years he had left. His strong sense of duty and palpable commitment to the issues kept him on the fence, however. He certainly had options. Princeton offered him a post in which he could "write his own ticket"; yet, like Harvard's offer years earlier, he never took it up.[6] Attending the premier of *Russian Adventure*, a cinematic visit through the varied landscapes of the Soviet Union hosted by singer Bing Crosby, Goldberg and Bunche discussed the future. Bunche, per usual, was noncommittal about his preferences.[7]

Most of 1966 found Goldberg and Bunche working behind the scenes to shore up the relationship between President Johnson and U Thant. Goldberg had recently told the secretary general that the president, and indeed all of Washington, was "cold" on the UN these days.[8] Goldberg's goal was to show the world that the US still believed in the UN as a force for peace. As the *Los Angeles Times* reported, it was Goldberg who recently persuaded the president to open the White House for an unprecedented reception for UN ambassadors to honor Thant. The gala was "a graceful way of showing all concerned—particularly Thant—that the Johnson administration thinks highly of the UN."[9] Meanwhile, behind the scenes the White House continued to view Thant with suspicion. Sitting at a White House dinner for Indira Gandhi earlier that year, Bunche had chatted with special assistant to the president Jack Valenti and his wife, who told him that Thant "was against us in Vietnam" and, as an Asian, was naturally suspicious of the West.[10] Nonetheless, the charm offensive continued, and Thant and Bunche were flown down to DC on a private jet and then ferried in a limousine straight to the White House to meet Johnson.

It was well known by now that Bunche was the linchpin in this marriage of power and politics. "The key inside man on every UN peace operation," wrote the LA Times, "is Bunche, one of the most esteemed Americans in the world." That spring Goldberg had told Bunche he feared the organization might collapse if he and Thant both left. The "logical step," Goldberg continued, was to make Bunche secretary general. This was, of course, impossible, given the widespread norm that no permanent member of the Security Council could have its national as head of the organization.[11] But, had it not been for the strength of that practice, it was not a crazy idea. Bunche *was* the key man in the increasingly crowded and critical field of peace operations, and he had more experience than anyone with the UN's workings. But it was not to be. In the wake of the White House soiree he was back in the field, flying to Cyprus and Israel, meeting with political leaders on all sides, and trying to find, or maintain, peaceful paths forward. Bunche was on familiar ground, even if the various conflicts often seemed paused rather than resolved. There was, of course, no similar trip to Hanoi or Saigon.

Bunche traveled widely that spring and summer. In May 1966 he was in Bellagio, Italy, for high-level seminars. He also visited the UN Emergency Force in Egypt, providing a rare moment of excitement for the then-mostly bored foreign peacekeepers. He was even the subject of an enthusiastic multi-page photo spread in *The Sand Dune*, the official UNEF magazine. Bunche enjoyed watching a friendly national soccer game in the desert and, like a politician on the stump, toured a Punjabi battalion, sampling chapati for the first time and deeming it "delicious." Speaking to UNEF troops at Rafah, he declared that when "I think of all the UN peacekeeping efforts, none has been as successful as this one."[12] As if to remind him of what had been accomplished, just a few weeks before his visit his erstwhile negotiating adversary Moshe Dayan sent him a signed copy of his new book, *Diary of the Sinai Campaign*.[13]

From UNEF Bunche headed to Jerusalem, where he met with Abba Eban, the Israeli minister of foreign affairs. The two discussed the regional tensions, but Bunche also requested that Israel erect a monument to the slain Folke Bernadotte at the site of his assassination in Jerusalem. (The monument was never built.) His visit to Jerusalem sparked an early version of the ongoing debate over the legitimacy of Israel's claim to the city as its capital. Shortly after the meeting with Abba Eban, General Odd Bull, the Norwegian in charge of UNEF, wrote to Bunche that another Norwegian diplomat had told Bull that Norway was no longer looking for embassy space in Tel Aviv. The diplomat argued that Bunche's meeting with Eban showed that "even the UN accepted [the Israeli] position" on Jerusalem as the permanent capital.[14] Bunche was surprised and dismayed by this account; and as it turned out, Norway's embassy remained in Tel Aviv. Still, the incident illustrated the endless tensions over places and the easy missteps—or misunderstandings—that were possible in such a volatile region in which every move was analyzed for symbolism and slant. Departing Israel for Cyprus, Bunche escaped the Palestine morass, only to reenter a different policy maze. Cabling U Thant, he reported that even in Nicosia, over glasses of chilled watermelon juice with Cypriot leaders, the conversation veered to the grave situation in Vietnam.

Ralph and Ruth also took a European trip that summer that was a blend of work and play. It began with a four-day holiday in Ireland. Speaking to reporters at the Dublin airport, he took a moment to discuss the issue rising on minds around the world. For the first time in an international conflict, he said with some hyperbole (or perhaps historical amnesia), it had been "impossible to establish communications with some of the principals directly involved. I refer to North Vietnam, the Viet Cong, and mainland China. It is impossible to get a dialogue started."[15] Switching to Cyprus, Bunche was again uncharacteristically dour: "if you ask me if I see light I would have to say no." But, he noted, stalemate is not unusual in international peacekeeping, and sometimes conflicts persist until they don't. It was a very weak sort of optimism for Bunche. (Cyprus's conflict turned out to be the persistent kind; more than fifty-five years later, UN peacekeepers still remain on the island.)

A few days after arriving in Ireland, the Bunches moved on to the Mediterranean, where they were guests of Princess Grace in the glittering city-state of Monaco. The occasion was "American Week," which involved various celebrities and diplomats eating barbecue and playing baseball. Although his vision had deteriorated to the point that he could barely see,

Bunche, perhaps the highest profile baseball fan at the event, was somehow appointed umpire in the big ball game. He told each pitcher that he would call balls and strikes on the honor system: "you tell me what it is, and I'll call 'em that way." Hit in the arm by an errant pitch, he later took refuge in the spa as Prince Rainer declared baseball a "dangerous game."[16]

By the end of July 1966, Ralph and Ruth had returned to New York. A planned final leg of the vacation to Corsica and Sardinia was cut short by heightened tensions in the Security Council over the Middle East. The debate was at one level familiar: was Israel, as the Arab states charged, acting in an aggressive and illegal manner? But the touchstone for the debate was Bunche's set of accords from Rhodes a decade and a half earlier. He was, of course, dismayed that the conflict persisted, but he was also surprised at how central the accords still were in the Arab-Israeli conflict. Indeed, he wrote to a friend that, while in the Security Council chamber:

> I found it difficult to believe my ears when I kept hearing the Syrian Representative referring to the Armistice Agreements, which after all were entered into in the winter and spring of 1949, and by me as their architect, as though those Agreements were a charter or a constitution or basis for a way of life. At Rhodes those long years ago, I saw them as only a temporary stepping stone between the indefinite cease-fire and an indispensable peace. I could never have dreamed they would still exist in 1966.[17]

IN LATE JULY 1966, BUNCHE TOOK Ralph Jr., now twenty-three, out for a fishing trip off Long Island. The father and son team caught seven bluefish, a tasty summer catch. (Bunche offered two of the fish the next day to U Thant, who took them home to make a Burmese curry.)[18] The summer fishing, the time in green Ireland with Ruth, the Mediterranean baseball games—this all sounded—minus the baseball injuries—fairly idyllic. Within days, however, he would be hospitalized.

During his stay in the hospital that summer, brought on by a severe injury to his foot, he had many well-wishers. The great Duke Ellington sent him a large basket of fruit and nuts. Many dignitaries, ambassadors, and political leaders came to visit. They generally wanted to wish him well, but Bunche's centrality to the UN was such that they also wanted to seek counsel and do business. On August 16 Arthur Goldberg visited. As they often had in the past, the two men debated what fruitful role the UN might play in Vietnam. The topic turned again to U Thant and his possible mediation efforts, and Bunche advised Goldberg that it was probably better if Thant pulled back.[19] So busy was the traffic in his hospital room that, just two days after Goldberg's visit, the Israeli ambassador called upon Bunche and then, in the mist of their conversation, his Egyptian counterpart showed up as well. The Six-Day War between the two nations was not far away (it began less than ten months later), but the two rival ambassadors and Bunche, the architect of the UN Emergency Force in the region, swapped stories and talked of politics, Bedouin customs, and UN gossip. Soon yet another Middle Eastern ambassador arrived—this one from Yemen.[20]

Meanwhile, on Capitol Hill, Vietnam was not the only issue consuming Congress. Growing unrest in American cities in 1966 was spurring concern among the political class. At a Senate hearing in August, Bobby Kennedy spoke of the growing "crisis in the cities," declaring that "we give our money and go back [to] our homes and maybe swimming pools and wonder, Why don't they keep quiet? Why don't they go away?" Kennedy may have been a liberal, but his questions reflected the often crude and disparaging way racial oppression was viewed in the 1960s. One of the Senate witnesses, Claude Brown, the author of the bestselling gritty memoiristic novel *Manchild in the Promised Land*, declared that all the white community had done was "placate the Negro, keep the Negro cool." Twenty-five years ago, Brown told the Senate committee, white America "gave us Joe Louis to identify with, and then 18 years later gave us Ralph Bunche, but that didn't work out too well so they give us civil rights bills."[21] As this invocation illustrated, Bunche's image of aptitude and accomplishment was increasingly read not as a salutary Horatio Alger–like tale, but instead as the token exception that proved the unjust rule.

By summer's end, Bunche was out of the hospital. He had recovered enough from his injuries to visit the striking new Metropolitan Opera House, opened just days before for the fall 1966 season, to see Leontyne Price in *Antony and Cleopatra*. Bunche, who had loved music and theater all his life, often visited the Met as a guest of Rudolph Bing, the general manager. Bunche had grown up obsessed with vaudeville and described his musical taste as "catholic," but "drawing the line at rock and roll." (Still, he was underwhelmed by the performance that evening: it had the "spectacular quality of *Aida*, without the equivalent musical quality—I'll take Verdi.")[22]

As happy as he was to get out of the hospital, he increasingly felt frustrated by his ailments. He was now in his sixties, and he knew his sight was unlikely to improve. "Will I end up completely blind?" he wrote in his diary, noting that he was "in danger whenever I am on the stairs."[23] Rumors continued to swirl that Thant, Bunche, or both were leaving the UN. The *New York Times* reported that Bunche was under consideration as a candidate of the Liberal Party in the New York gubernatorial campaign then underway. Asked for comment, Bunche replied he had not yet been approached and that any comment would be "presumptuous."[24] Interestingly, Bunche did not say he was not interested. The Canadian foreign minister, Paul Martin, came to see him that fall to plead with him to stay at the UN. It would be a disaster if you left now, Martin implored.

As if to illustrate the dour views many now held about the UN, in October 1966 the British newspaper the *Observer* ran a long essay provocatively titled "Is the UN Finished?" Surveying the good (Congo, the Middle East) as well as the bad (Vietnam, the Cold War, the continued exclusion of the People's Republic of China) after two decades of the world organization, the essay described the rise of what was essentially a new form of politics in Turtle Bay, that of the "diplomat-politician." Breaking down the key players, the analysis turned to Bunche. Bunche, the *Observer* argued,

> is now rated by some a burned-out case. He does not look it. He is gentle and wise, devoid of illusions, but not perhaps of hope. He could retire honourably at any moment into a plum job with one of the great American foundations. Others see him as the best political brain of the UN outfit whose departure would hurt more than that of U Thant himself.[25]

The concern over his possible departure from the organization was arising everywhere now. It was increasingly clear that Bunche was indispensable to the UN, and as the well threatened to run dry, many suddenly grew very worried about the water supply.

Meanwhile, the Johnson administration kept up its charm offensive on U Thant in public, even as it often criticized him in private about what they considered his meddlesome efforts on Vietnam. Goldberg told Bunche that Johnson was personally concerned about reports that Cambodia, Algeria, and other postcolonial states were planning a declaration in the General Assembly on Vietnam. The US believed Thant was backing it and saw it as a betrayal. Thant defended himself, claiming that he had been approached about a declaration but had said he could not be involved. Still, Bunche saw the draft statement and thought the original text was suspiciously close to the secretary general's views. Indeed, he wrote in his diary that it "could have been drafted by U Thant himself."[26] (Perhaps Thant did not share all his views or actions with his American consigliere.) After the Soviets, allegedly encouraged by Hanoi, expressed doubts about the idea of the declaration, it was later shelved. But whatever the document's true source, it was clear the postcolonial world was increasingly fixated on Vietnam, and that tendency only accelerated the growing divide between the US and the UN.

Perhaps still concerned that the General Assembly was starting to gang up on the US, Johnson stopped in to see Thant in October 1966. It was an "unprecedented, first ever visit by a President to the UN just to talk with the Secretary-General."[27] The president had been speaking at a lunch event nearby and decided to pay an impromptu visit to the 38th floor. Arthur Goldberg called Thant's office moments before to warn him of the sudden visit, and as Johnson walked across First Avenue, shouts of "hey, hey, LBJ, how many kids did you kill today?" rang out. Bunche tried to supervise and smooth over the meeting between the two leaders. Afterward, Johnson declared that "I had a very delightful and stimulating meeting with the Secretary-General and Dr Bunche." That may have even been true. But nothing changed with regard to Vietnam.

Days later, the Bunche family suffered a terrible tragedy. At 2 a.m. Ralph was awakened by a phone call. On the line was his son-in-law, Burton, calling to tell him that the Bunches' daughter Jane was dead from a fall. The *New York Times* reported the next day that Jane's body had been found in the courtyard of the couple's Riverdale, Bronx apartment complex. Jane was only thirty-three.[28]

Ralph and Ruth were stunned and heartbroken over the sudden death of their daughter. Bunche told reporters that he was completely shocked; he knew Jane was "not ill or anything like that . . . all we know is she is gone."[29] When he finally returned to the office, he seemed lost and undeniably distraught. His secretary, Lydia Fayon, said that "we all loved him like a father. Now—we wanted to help. But we didn't know how."[30] In the days that followed, the New York press covered Jane's death as a mystery. The *New York Amsterdam News* noted that the police were treating the case as a live investigation. "Nothing we have uncovered thus far would indicate any foul play," Detective Roy Hayes of the New York Police Department told reporters. But what had occurred remained unclear. (The death certificate listed "fell or jumped from height" as the contributory cause of death.)[31] Jane's three young children all went to stay temporarily with Ralph and Ruth in the big Tudor house in Kew Gardens.

In the aftermath of Jane's tragic death, Bunche poured himself into his work and sought distractions. He traveled to Cape Kennedy to see the launch of Gemini XII. He found the blastoff awe-inspiring: at the end of the countdown, he vividly described, "there is a breathtaking pause before the vehicle slowly and majestically begins to rise, with a bright flame at its tail, trailing a brilliant white plume."[32] The dawn of the space age was exciting and impressive, but the weight of the troubles here on earth, and of the loss of his daughter, still weighed heavily. He felt more pessimistic than ever about Vietnam and less sure he wanted to remain involved in global affairs. Jane's death seemed to make him question his choices, and whether he ought to devote what time he had left to family. Many invitations continued to pour in, but Bunche, who had always maintained an active social schedule, was far less interested now.[†] He even tendered a letter of resignation to U Thant in January 1967, who immediately asked him to reconsider.

[†] Among them an invitation, apparently declined, to the "party of the century," Truman Capote's legendary Black and White Ball at the Plaza Hotel, held on November 28, 1966.

Even before the letter, Thant, alerted to the idea, pushed back. "Ralph, I wish you to stay," he told him. "In fact, my belief that you would stay was an important factor in my own decision to stay."[33]

As the two top UN leaders engaged in this wary dance over their futures, Arthur Goldberg, who had caught wind of the resignation attempt, told Bunche that he simply had to stay on: it would be "disastrous" otherwise. When Bunche noted that his eyes were failing, Goldberg countered that he wasn't needed there for his eyes, but for his "knowledge and judgment."[34] Bulgaria's ambassador buttonholed Bunche in the corridor to tell him "you are an American, but a very good American," and much needed.[35] The press continued to speculate about his future. Gossip columnist Leonard Lyons reported that recent claims that he "had changed his mind about retiring" were untrue.[36]

Shortly after, Bunche visited the White House for the signing of a treaty to limit military activities in space—an effort to keep the endemic problem of war out of at least one new domain of human affairs. President Johnson leaned in, as Bunche came through the receiving line, and said, "don't you leave the UN."[37]

U Thant also kept up the pressure in his unique way. He would sometimes ask Bunche to sit beside him in his 38th floor office. Thant sat in a large black easy chair, while Bunche sat nearby, as they chatted obliquely about the future. The secretary general "always resisted any real discussion of the subject from my point of view," Bunche complained; "sometimes we would just sit and say nothing."[38] In March 1967 Bunche finally announced that he would remain at the UN a little longer, but it was clear he was not happy about his decision. ("Bunche Relents," read the headline in the *New York Times*.) The decision, he announced to the press in a surprisingly pointed set of remarks, "came at the cost of the abandonment of plans and dreams" that he and Ruth had held for years.[39] The choice to stay on at the UN was, he said, driven by loyalty—to U Thant and to the organization and, though he did not say it, to the cause of peace itself. The president of the Rockefeller Foundation offered him a very attractive position, but he turned the offer down, a decision that he said (in private) was one of genuine disappointment and anguish. Ever the good soldier, he was remaining at the UN, he explained in a letter, because "I could not walk out in an unpleasant atmosphere with an intimation of 'desertion.' "[40]

Secretary of State Dean Rusk called to confirm the good news. Rusk told him he was "delighted" to see he was staying on, adding, "the President will be very happy to know this."[41]

RALPH BUNCHE HAD MADE HIS PEACE in remaining at the UN for a few more years, but he spoke out more on domestic affairs as 1967 unfolded. He even commented on the policy proposal of the governor of California, Ronald Reagan, to begin charging tuition at Bunche's alma mater, the University of California. Bunche pointed out that he probably could not have attended UCLA without its free-fee structure.[42] (He lost that battle, and tuition has been rising ever since.) Visiting UCLA later that winter, he took in a basketball game and dined with the campus leadership; among the guests at the Bel Air Hotel dinner was a new UC regent and fellow alumnus named H. R. Haldeman.

Bunche's more frequent forays into domestic affairs in the late 1960s raised some hackles back in Turtle Bay. For example, the Soviets attacked him over his efforts to defend embattled Harlem representative Adam Clayton Powell, Jr. Bunche was certainly no fan of Powell. The two had traded barbed attacks in recent years, and Bunche often considered the congressman a reckless demagogue. Following extensive allegations of corruption, Powell was barred by a vote of the House of Representatives from taking his seat in Congress. Yet even Bunche thought this punishment went too far, and spoke out against it. Soviet delegates at the UN, always eager to find a way to tar Bunche, complained that his speech in support of Powell had been circulated by the UN press office. Speeches of high-ranking UN officials were routinely circulated to the UN press corps though the Secretariat's press office; this speech was not treated differently. Yet in this case, the Soviets argued, the remarks were on a purely domestic issue of American politics, and so Bunche, they contended, had abused his position as an international civil servant. As this tempest illustrated, the Soviets continued to have a bullseye on Bunche and to view him as a threat to their efforts to remold the Secretariat into a more pliable bureaucracy. And it highlighted how tricky it was for him to reenter domestic affairs in a forth-right way.

Comments on California and Harlem politics notwithstanding, Vietnam still commanded Bunche's attention. In 1967, the prospects for peace seemed as remote as ever. In March of that year, the Senate Foreign Relations Committee flew to New York to discuss the war. Spending three hours at the UN, the senators met with Bunche and U Thant. Senator William Fulbright, the chairman of the committee, was "amazingly frank," Bunche thought. Fulbright was worried about Vietnam but also the war's possible creep into Thailand, and said it was impossible to communicate with Johnson, who did all the talking and "no listening."[43] Fulbright had early on supported the Gulf of Tonkin Resolution, but he had become rapidly disillusioned by the war effort. In 1966, he had begun televised hearings on the conflict in the Senate; these hearings proved so influential that Johnson, fearful of their growing impact, pressed the networks to air *I Love Lucy* reruns instead.[44] Speaking to reporters at the UN, Fulbright called the visit to New York an experiment but, laughing a bit, conceded that "in all honesty, the Secretary General," who in this regard was perhaps not so different than LBJ, "did most of the talking." Bunche remarked to reporters that Thant had never spoken more candidly about Vietnam, "not even to God."[45]

Protests around the nation were growing that spring as American troop levels rose still further and the brutal bombing of North Vietnam acceler-ated. Johnson was seemingly consumed by the war, almost unable to focus on anything else. In a meeting at the White House with the prime minister of Afghanistan, Johnson ignored the poor nation's pressing economic is-sues and launched into a tirade about Vietnam for over an hour. Telling the prime minister the US was only hitting the North "lightly"—and tapping his fingers on the man's thigh by way of illustration—Johnson declared, now shaking his fist angrily, that if he wanted, the US could "destroy them with our might."[46]

Then a new dimension of the Vietnam debate arose. At Riverside Church on April 4, 1967, Dr. Martin Luther King Jr. made headlines when, for the first time, he spoke directly about the foreign conflict. Internally, King and his circle had spent weeks debating whether he should address the war. As a young David Broder reported in the *Washington Post*, King went through a turbulent month of soul-searching before the Riverside speech that provoked a "long, secret struggle" within the civil rights coalition.[47] In the end, King decided to plunge ahead with an address, titled *Beyond Vietnam*, forthrightly laying out his critique of America's role.

A time comes, King declared that day at Riverside Church, when silence is betrayal. That time "has come for us in relation to Vietnam." In their quest for independence from colonial rule, Vietnam had sought to link its struggle to America's own. Yet the nation had refused this gesture. Even though they quoted from the Declaration of Independence in their own declaration, "we refused to recognize them." Instead, King explained,

> we decided to support France in its reconquest of her former colony. Our government felt then that the Vietnamese people were not ready for independence, and we again fell victim to the deadly Western arrogance that has poisoned the international atmosphere for so long.
>
> With that tragic decision we rejected a revolutionary government seeking self-determination and a government that had been established not by China—for whom the Vietnamese have no great love—but by clearly indigenous forces that included some communists.... Surely this madness must cease. We must stop now.[48]

King's speech hit many of the points that the postcolonial world had been making in the General Assembly and elsewhere. The struggle between Europe and Asia; between colony and colonizer; between self-determination and paternalistic rule—all were here in King's remarks. The speech was heartfelt and powerful, but it led to a storm of criticism from the American political establishment. The *Washington Post* editorialized that King had "diminished his usefulness to his cause, to his country, and to his people" by wading into the murky and treacherous waters of foreign policy. *Life* magazine called his remarks fit for "Radio Hanoi."[49] Perhaps surprisingly, Ralph Bunche was also critical of King. Speaking with reporters, Bunche declared that King's engagement with the war was a strategic mistake of the first order. King, he insisted with surprising determination, must "positively and publically give up one role or the other."

By 1967, the issue of how the civil rights and antiwar efforts underway in 1960s America might coalesce or commingle was, of course, on the minds of many people, not just Martin Luther King. The NAACP, of which Bunche remained a director, recently had voted unanimously to oppose efforts to link the two movements. Bunche himself supported this position; he believed the roiling and unpredictable politics around Vietnam would ultimately harm the civil rights movement and blunt its momentum. He, of course, had strong views on both civil rights and Vietnam, and perhaps more than any other single person in America he had a deep understanding of both issues. He was nonetheless dismayed by King's move. Arthur Goldberg agreed; he thought King's remarks in New York meant the "movement may well be hurt no matter how strongly King disavows."[50] But it was also true that keeping the civil rights movement and its moral authority out of the Vietnam debate was likely to help LBJ, who was increasingly struggling politically. Regardless of his motives, Bunche was unsparing in his assessment of King's pivot into geopolitics. "Like us all, of course," King makes mistakes, he declared to reporters. "Right now, I am convinced, he is making a very serious tactical error which will do much harm to the civil rights struggle."[51]

Stung by the widespread criticism, King appeared to retreat a bit. He denied that he had tried to "fuse" the two movements and called the claim that he did so a "myth." Still, in direct response to Bunche's charge, he declared: "I'm not going to quit, either publicly or positively."[52] Moreover, King announced in Los Angeles days later, "until we get rid of this war and get rid of our obsession with it as a nation," national problems of poverty and urban blight would not be fixed. King still saw the two issues as innately connected, not only because they both had a strong moral underpinning but also because improving civil rights simply cost money that the war was rapidly spending. (This last point Bunche agreed with, at least later: to the *New Yorker*, he said toward the end of his life, if the "thirty billion dollars annually spent by this country on the war in Vietnam were channeled into an all-out effort, at all levels, to mobilize the war on the ghettoes, we'd make a good start in the war on racism.")[53]

Seeking common ground, Bunche and King ceased sparring through the press and spoke by phone on April 13. Bunche came away convinced that King saw things his way—or at least was willing to say so in public. King was "much disturbed by my criticism," he thought.[54] "He was wrestling with his conscience . . . [and] said he had wanted to consult me" about his recent speeches but "never got to do so." Bunche accepted this explanation and told King the matter was behind them. "King's Statement Satisfies Bunche," ran the *Washington Post* headline.[55] Internally, however, King told a somewhat different story: he told his team that he felt sorry for Bunche, who King said had claimed on the call, unconvincingly, that he thought King was literally trying to fuse the two movements, rather than simply find common ground. "He wasn't telling the truth," King explained, "and he was trembling and all. So I just got off him."[56]

King and Bunche had an important reason to reach an accommodation quickly: on Sunday, April 16, 1967, over 100,000 people would march against the war in New York City, culminating in a huge rally outside the United Nations. The march, of which King would be a central member and leader, was the largest antiwar rally the nation's largest city had yet seen.

Photo 23.1 King in Bunche's UN office

The day of the march, King and a small entourage headed to Bunche's UN office as the crowd massed outside. Bunche and King greeted each other cordially, smiling as they entered the suite. King handed him a note that read: "We rally at the United Nations in order to affirm support of the principles of peace, universality, equal rights, and self-determination of peoples embodied in the Charter and acclaimed by mankind, but violated by the United States." Signed by King, it read: "Presented to Dr. Ralph J. Bunche, April 15, 1967."[57] Crowded on the office couch, the group listened as Bunche, sympathetic, told them of the UN's "great frustration and disappointment" over the conflict. Outside after the meeting, King read the petition he had just presented. Reporters immediately asked about his disagreement with Bunche. King said that was old news. "Dr. Bunche made it very clear that the UN...is very much concerned about the war in Vietnam," King emphasized. Asked if Bunche supported his views on Vietnam, King demurred, saying Bunche supported the views of U Thant on Vietnam.[58]

King's visit with Bunche at the UN symbolized the often symbiotic relationship the two men had in the mid-1960s. The two shared the honor of the Nobel Peace Prize and were the only Black Americans to have won the award. King was a dominant figure in American life. He was not yet the icon he would become but a charismatic leader to millions and a respected and influential voice on racial justice. Bunche in turn represented an older model of respectability; the many jabs taken at him by younger, more fiery figures from Muhammad Ali to Stokely Carmichael simultaneously made Bunche seem both past his prime and somehow still relevant to the conversation. For King, Bunche's enormous esteem in white America—especially in the highest echelons—was invaluable, and especially so as King pivoted to the problems posed by Vietnam.

King's moral fervor about the war was, in substance, close to Bunche's own views. Yet Bunche could not countenance King explicitly linking the challenges in such a public way at such a delicate time. Privately, he wrote that King did "neither the civil rights movement nor himself any good" by participating in the Spring Mobilization, and had to "disassociate himself from the extreme acts and statements" made by some of the marchers, by which Bunche meant burning draft cards and the like.[59] Still, the two men had much to gain from one another. Bunche's respect for King ran deep, as was his desire to be part of the new and vibrant movement for racial equality at home. From the March on Washington to Selma to their reconciliation in New York, the two saw that much work was to be done—and at least at times, they wanted to do that work together and to be seen to be doing it together. The swirling, heated politics around the twin movements against the war and for civil rights were complicating that effort, but for the moment, the two Nobel laureates appeared to be back in alignment.

IN MAY 1967 A CABLE ARRIVED at the United Nations from the commander of the UN Emergency Force in Gaza. Egypt[‡] was demanding that UNEF troops depart Gaza and Sharm al Sheik, the coastal city in the Sinai Peninsula that sat next to an important chokepoint to the Red Sea. The Egyptian letter to the head of UNEF had explained that Egypt's military was "ready for action against Israel" and that the UN should "withdraw all these troops immediately."[60]

UNEF forces, which had been in place since the Suez Crisis of 1956–1957, had been quietly patrolling for years, even as low-level conflict continued sporadically. Yet, after Israel retaliated against some cross-border attacks with its own assault on a village in Jordanian territory in November 1966, and later engaged in an aerial dogfight over Syria, the periodically volatile region seemed to be once again heading toward open and more intense conflict. The Soviets helped nudge the conflict by falsely reporting to Egypt and Syria that Israeli troops were massing on their borders.[61] Egypt's request for withdrawal came on the heels of many years of quiet in the region. When asked in April 1966 whether anyone wanted to take the peacekeepers out, Bunche confidently replied, "neither Egyptians nor Israelis want them out. No one wants the responsibility."[62] By the spring of 1967, however, the simmering conflict between Israel and its Arab neighbors was clearly taking a turn for the worst.

By its nature, UN peacekeeping depended for its success on the will of the states involved. UNEF had seemingly kept a lid on the Middle Eastern

---

[‡] At that time, known as the United Arab Republic.

tensions for a decade. But it really only worked if the parties wanted it to work. Egypt's demand to remove UNEF would allow those tensions to reach a climax. Bunche and Thant saw a huge danger in the request to withdraw. But they felt constrained by a demand coming from a sovereign state and felt they had no real alternative.

After the initial cable from Gaza arrived, Bunche and Thant met with the ambassadors of all the troop-contributing countries in UNEF. It was May 17. The group assembled in Thant's 38th floor office to consider the implications. Perhaps seeking a way to stall, the secretary general focused on the formalities. There is no request to me yet, Thant told the ambassadors, only to the UNEF commanding officer. "You do not consider that legitimate?" asked the Danish ambassador. "I do not consider it correct procedure," Thant replied, for the request to made from one military officer to another military officer.[63] It needed to come at a political level. The UN's legal counsel stressed that once Egypt withdrew its consent for the peacekeeping force, they had no choice but to remove the troops. Thanks to the threat of vetoes by Britain and France in the Suez Crisis, UNEF was a product of the General Assembly, acting under the "Uniting for Peace" procedure designed to allow the Assembly to step in when the Security Council was deadlocked. Had it been a Security Council mission, Egyptian consent may not have been legally necessary. But the existing posture meant that under international law the troops could only remain in Egypt with the agreement of the government. Egyptian troops were already moving into an area currently patrolled by UNEF; as Bunche noted in the meeting, the two forces were currently in the same area. "They are in joint occupation at the present time. That is the situation." It was a dangerous one, he thought.[64]

Bunche and Thant debated further how to react. Egyptian leader Gamal Abdel Nasser claimed that he did not actually want all UNEF troops withdrawn, but he did want to see troops removed from certain key areas. Bunche did not think this made any sense. Nasser wanted UNEF out only where Nasser wanted to fight. As Bunche wrote in a memo to the Egyptian government, the purpose of UNEF was to prevent a recurrence of fighting, "and it cannot be asked to stand aside in order to enable the two sides to resume fighting."[65] A guest attending Passover with gossip columnist Leonard

Lyons shortly before Egypt's demands were cabled to the 38th floor had noted that if the differences between the Jews and Arabs had been solved millennia ago, Bunche would never have had a Nobel Prize to win. Now and then, Bunche quipped in response, "I feel I ought to give it back."[66] His joke was looking more prophetic by the hour as war loomed. He knew from experience that Nasser was a risk-taker and that Israel would not take change lightly. (Indeed, some analysts have characterized the runup to the war as a risky game of chicken by Nasser in which, unfortunately for him, Israel did not back down: "a form of brinkmanship that went over the brink.")[67] Bunche's usual optimism was slipping away.

Egypt's formal request for withdrawal finally arrived on May 18. U Thant immediately convened another meeting of the relevant ambassadors and told them he now felt bound to withdraw. The Canadian ambassador, George Ignatieff, pushed back, maintaining that this was a grave and serious threat to the peace; could there not be more diplomacy?[68] Brazil's representative agreed. But many of the others agreed with Thant that the UN really had no choice but to withdraw. Bunche concurred. There were legal aspects, he acknowledged, but "there is the aspect of hard facts too." UNEF involved consent, he continued, and once Egypt withdrew that consent, "there was not a thing in the world that UNEF troops can do about it." He had noted in the meeting the day before that UNEF had only been deployed on the Egyptian side, and not the Israeli, because Israel had in fact never consented to troops on their territory. Bunche was also concerned about the safety of the UNEF troops if the UN insisted on keeping them deployed. Drawing on his unpleasant Congo experience, he recalled a "very wise statement" made to him by the late Patrice Lumumba. Lumumba, he explained, had said: "We do not need any governmental action to get rid of the UN force here. Anytime we become displeased with it, all I have to do is go on the radio and make a statement and the people will be turned against the force." Lumumba was quite right, he told the group.[69]

As they debated further, Ignatieff again suggested that they not act precipitously and instead bring the matter before the General Assembly or the Security Council for discussion. Bunche interjected. "May I say just a word? This point is extremely important. Here I would like to speak very,

very frankly." At this point, he said, "the most dangerous thing" from the perspective of the troops that could be done would be to suggest that Egypt's withdrawal of consent was insufficient, or subject to some debate in Turtle Bay. The actual movement of UNEF troops could take a bit of time, he thought, but the principle that Egypt decided was critical. "I happen to know that some of [the] things said here yesterday immediately got to them and caused very considerable indignation."[70] All in all, the options seemed quite limited: the UN troops were almost surely going to withdraw, and quickly. War seemed inevitable.

U Thant told Bunche that he thought UNEF's departure would be "disastrous" and that he would try one more time to convince Nasser to reconsider. The secretary general suggested to Egypt's ambassador that he and Bunche immediately head to Cairo to meet with Nasser. As Thant later recounted, the ambassador replied that although Ralph Bunche was held in very high esteem in his country, " 'from President Nasser to the man in the street,' he suggested that I should go to Cairo without Ralph."[71] As an American, Bunche was seen to be too close to the distrusted US government and, perhaps by extension, too close to the Israelis. Interestingly, Lyndon Johnson, eager to see the UN broker a resolution, offered Thant Air Force One for the trip to Cairo—an offer conveyed through Bunche, who did not think such visible American assistance was going to help.

As Thant arrived in Cairo, Bunche cabled an update of discussions in the Security Council. "The question on [the] lips of everyone here," he closed, "is when will [the] Secretary General be seeing President Nasser?"[72] The kindling in the Middle East had sparked further when Nasser closed the Straits of Tiran, which provided a route to the Red Sea and, as a result, vital access to the southern Israeli city of Eilat. Thant replied that the mood in Cairo was "very tense," but that he would have dinner with Nasser that night.[73] Bunche cabled back that there was much resentment in New York about Nasser's move on the Straits of Tiran. The fact that it was issued "on the eve of your arrival in Cairo" was being interpreted as an "affront" and "even a kick in the teeth."[74] Bunche seemed to be almost goading the famously even-tempered Thant to get angry at Nasser. (Years later he would say that he sometimes wanted Thant to "cuss somebody"; the comment, made at the White House in front of President Richard Nixon, a legendary curser, was ostensibly framed as praise but seemed to get at a nugget of Bunche's occasional frustration with the often imperturbable Thant.)[75]

Thant's visit to Egypt ultimately changed nothing. Forging an alliance with Jordan and Syria, Nasser seemed intent on conflict. Thant wrote to the prime minister of Israel, Levi Eshkol, pleading that he exercise restraint, and to Nasser, urging him to "avert the catastrophe of a new war."[76] The Johnson administration was growing concerned about the accelerating pace of events as well. When Syria's ambassador accused the US in the Security Council of being one-sided, Arthur Goldberg took umbrage, noting that the US had voted against Israel in the most recent instance before the Council. Moreover, he argued, during the Suez Crisis it was the US, "standing against old friends and allies," that brought the matter before the UN.[77] Most importantly, Goldberg stressed the importance of Bunche's armistice accords. In light of those accords, he declared, neither side had the right to engage in belligerency. Behind the scenes, LBJ urged Israeli restraint and implored the Soviets to intercede with Nasser. "Israel," Johnson told Israeli Foreign Minister Abba Eban, "will not be alone unless it decides to go it alone."[78]

As the arguments shot back and forth in the Security Council chamber downstairs, Bunche and Thant tried to slow the process of UNEF withdrawal, hoping that minds would change. They did not succeed. On June 5, 1967, the fighting began. Bunche, alerted by a cable officer on 24-hour duty, called U Thant at home at 3 a.m. "War has broken out!" he told the bleary-eyed secretary general. Bunche arrived at the office shortly afterward to begin to strategize. Later that morning, Thant reported that two Israeli aircraft had entered the airspace over Gaza.[79] A UNEF convoy had been strafed by aircraft fire and Egyptian planes had sortied over Israeli territory. Shots had been fired in Jerusalem and on the Syrian-Israeli border. The Israeli and Egyptian ambassadors offered conflicting accounts of battle; charges of "treacherous aggression" rang out across the horseshoe-shaped Security Council table. In an early version of an email exchange, Bunche traded messages back and forth with UN officials in the region over a "teletypewriting machine."[80] Yet there was really little that could be done. In less than a week, in a stunning victory, Israel trounced its enemies

Photo 23.2 Bunche and Arthur Goldberg in the Security Council

and conquered large swaths of territory—including the West Bank, Gaza, and Jerusalem. Over almost before it began, the conflict became known, due to its brevity, as the Six-Day War. Precipitously begun but decisively finished, the war would reshape the balance of power in the region for decades.

UNEF, struggling to get out of the way, lost more than a dozen peacekeepers in the onset of hostilities. The Security Council issued a tepid resolution on June 6 calling for a ceasefire among the "governments concerned" but not naming names.[81] Although it passed unanimously, it had little discernible impact. Israel's victory was overwhelming. Israeli deaths were less than 1000; Arab deaths, close to 20,000.

The war was a turning point in the politics not only of the Middle East but also of the UN. For the Israelis, the UN was rapidly becoming viewed as an unhelpful and even hostile organization. (Within a few years, the UN would become a hotbed of anti-Zionist rhetoric that would turn many in Israel strongly against the organization.) "The UN only complicated matters and delayed a solution," said one Israeli diplomat at the time. Israeli Foreign Minister Abba Eban, on his way out of a Security Council meeting, told a reporter that "sometimes I think if they would leave us alone we'd be better off."[82]

The UN could not, of course, leave the region alone. Indeed, the Middle East had been the most common topic of Security Council meetings by this point. Bunche was exhausted by the relentless pace that summer. Asked by a reporter how he managed to keep going, he replied that kept a drawer full of fruit and nuts—"that's how I stay alive." The 38th floor, he continued with a grin, "is my prison."[83] He was frustrated by Israel in this period but also found the volatile Arab states difficult. During a meeting of the Security Council to discuss the conflict, Saudi Ambassador Jamil Baroody spied Bunche whispering in Thant's ear during his long speech. "Do not disturb the secretary general, Dr. Bunche," Baroody interjected, as the proceedings were aired live on television. "I want him to hear every word I say, my dear Dr. Bunche . . . he should learn what we have suffered." Bunche, irritated at the grandiose Saudi, fired off a somewhat intemperate letter to the ambassador. The next day, as the refugee crisis was under discussion, Baroody walked around the Security Council table to the Council president's chair and took to the microphone to malign Bunche for his letter. Baroody, incensed, asked "Who does he think he is?" U Thant defended Bunche, calling him very able and loyal; still, Bunche felt compelled to apologize to Baroody, who, having saved face, then called him his "brother" and declared the two "had kissed and made up."[84]§

The incident epitomized to Bunche the frustrations and posturing of the Arabs. The recriminations over the war continued far beyond Baroody's petty complaints, however. Bunche and Thant, blamed by many for the precipitous withdrawal of UNEF troops, were irritated by what they saw as an unfair and unsophisticated understanding of the limitations of UN peacekeeping. In mid-June, Bunche sent off a long letter to the *New York Times*, taking issue with several claims made by the veteran reporter James Reston

---

§ Bunche's letter of apology to Baroody was not in fact all that apologetic; he began with a terse "I regard the incident as closed" and went on to say that he could not accept being "publicly demeaned by a delegate and admonished as might be directed at a child."

and making the case that the UN had no choice but to pull out entirely when Egypt so demanded.[85]

The debate over UNEF's withdrawal was inflamed in part by what became known as the "Hammarskjold Memorandum." The memo, disclosed in the *New York Times* on June 18 and allegedly written in August 1957, had been kept secret for a decade.[86] The memo conveyed the late Dag Hammarskjold's account of his private negotiations with Nasser and stated that the two agreed that Egypt could not order UNEF out of its territory unless both Egypt and the General Assembly concurred that UNEF forces had "completed their task." Hammarskjold had forced Nasser to acquiesce to this arrangement by threatening to withdraw the UNEF troops, which kept Israeli forces at bay, immediately in the summer of 1957. The arrangement was kept private, the *Times* reported, "apparently to spare Mr. Nasser's feelings on sovereignty and because Mr. Hammarskjold assumed that he himself would be dealing with any dispute about the issue."

The unveiling of the Hammarskjold Memo was itself the subject of debate. According to one account, on May 19, as tensions were growing, a former American official at the UN named Ernest Gross called Bunche and requested an urgent meeting.[87] Bunche and Gross knew each other; Gross had been a legal advisor at the UN during the 1950s and had even served as Bunche's attorney when he went before his loyalty board hearings in 1954. Gross now handed him a copy of the secret memo. The memo's validity was unclear; it was unsigned and was apparently not in official UN files. Indeed, as one contemporaneous report explained, "no hint of its existence could be found when senior UN officials searched the UNEF records last month."[88] When reporters called Andrew Cordier, Hammarskjold's former executive assistant, Cordier, now the dean of Columbia Law School, claimed to remember the memo. But Cordier said he had chosen not to raise it since U Thant had already announced UNEF's withdrawal and doing so might undermine the secretary general's authority at a sensitive moment. Other accounts have Gross handing the memo to Stephen Schewebel, who later became the American judge on the International Court of Justice, but at the time was the director of the private American Society of International

Law, in the expectation that the Society would publish it.[89] Eventually, the *New York Times* published the memo in full, after the Six Day War was over.

The Hammarskjold memo underscored several important points about the resolution of the Suez Crisis. First, the peacekeepers had been deployed with Egypt's consent. While the General Assembly jumped into the fray in 1956 in a creative fashion with UNEF, its powers were by design limited and local consent was essential. Second, Hammarskjold, knowing this, had tried to tie Nasser's hands, but this form of personalized diplomacy could not last beyond the personages involved—and only one was still alive in 1967. Nasser, having little interest in revealing any private agreements from the past, had no reason to raise the memo's existence. Third, whatever the arrangement for the UN forces in the region, a lasting peace between Israel and its Arab neighbors was probably never really possible. As later events highlighted, a host of American presidents would try desperately to achieve peace in the Middle East and would nearly always fail. The UN's failure to keep UNEF in place beyond a decade was, arguably, no failure at all: even a decade of relative peace in that part of the world was an accomplishment.

Bunche, reflecting on the war shortly after its outset, was troubled by the ramifications for the region and for the UN. The armistice agreements he labored over so many years earlier were, he thought, now shattered. The losers, he predicted, would be the Arabs, who found Israel "vastly superior" in the military confrontation and would, he predicted, be even more outgunned in the diplomatic confrontation to come. Yet it turned out that the professional optimist was too pessimistic in some respects. He believed that UNEF was "finished" and that the result of the conflict would be a "sharp curtailment if not a complete end of peacekeeping activities in that area."[90] Yet, in fact, UNEF was reborn six years after the Six-Day War, in what is now known as UNEF II. UNEF II only lasted a few years; formed in the wake of the 1973 Arab-Israeli War, by 1979 it was over. But it showed the continuing utility of UN peacekeeping in the region.

Knowing none of this, Bunche was disconcerted by the Six-Day War. He believed that UN peacekeeping, one of the premier innovations in geopolitics in the 20th century, was now at "a low tide." Moreover, the decline of peacekeeping, he jotted down to himself, "cannot fail to affect adversely the standing and prestige of the UN itself."[91]

ON VIRTUALLY THE SAME DAY THAT the Six-Day War began, another bombshell landed. This one was quite a bit smaller but more targeted at the 38th floor. General Carl von Horn of Sweden, who headed several key early peacekeeping efforts for the UN, published a memoir entitled *Soldiering for Peace*. The book had been published a few months earlier in Britain, but the American edition's release gave renewed attention to von Horn's critiques of the still-novel system of UN peacekeeping. Horn accused Israel of deploying "beautiful girls to seduce members of the UN truce supervision organization in Jerusalem so that secrets could be forced out of them under threat of blackmail."[92] He claimed that UN personnel engaged in smuggling goods in and out of the region. And he critiqued Bunche directly. With regard to Congo, von Horn claimed that Bunche actively worked to undermine his control of the peacekeeping mission and regularly circumvented normal channels of command. Unfortunately, von Horn wrote, "Ralph knew nothing about military matters and never seemed to grasp the fact that unless there is real unity of command no force can operate with any degree of success ... I found some of his methods insufferable."

The book was a harsh critique, but it did not do any lasting damage to Bunche's reputation or to the larger enterprise of multilateral peacekeeping. Nonetheless, it was an early harbinger of some of the recurring attacks on peacekeeping that would be leveled in the future: the commingling of political and military agendas; the difficulty in ensuring a cohesive approach among the myriad troop-contributing countries; and the occasional criminal activities that some UN peacekeepers would engage in when in the field.

Whatever the perils of peacekeeping, war making seemed worse. Whereas the Six-Day War was over in less than a week, the Vietnam War seemed to never end. Just weeks before the Arab-Israeli conflict broke out, U Thant had alarmingly stated that he feared a direct confrontation between the US and China over Vietnam was "inevitable" and, as a result, the "initial phase of World War III" was already taking place.[93] Arthur Goldberg quickly challenged Thant's remarks, but Thant was making clear that he saw the Vietnam War as the world's most urgent geopolitical issue. Others agreed. A group of former Nobel laureates announced a peace mission to Vietnam in July 1967. (Bunche was quick to disassociate himself from the effort and called it "presumptuous.")[94] That same month, fighting again began in the Middle East. Bunche spoke with the ambassadors of Egypt and Israel and found both receptive to a ceasefire. Bunche, sunny again, thought this was a good sign. It should be regarded as an "encouraging feature," he thought, that these nations, so eager to fight, are also "so ready to stop."[95] The ceasefire worked; he had done it again, he scrawled on a scrap of paper, "for the nth time."

Yet as the "nth time" comment suggested, he was increasingly wondering why he was still toiling away on issues such as this—and how long he could last. That summer he wrote:

> It is astonishing to me that elderliness has come upon me so suddenly. I have been going at full speed for many years with no thought of life coming to an end or even having to slow my pace. Now I find myself at the eminence of age 63 and all sorts of ailments, aches, and pains begin to assail me. All this disturbs me and even shocks me, for there are so many things I wish to do, things [I] have been putting off under the relenting pressure of a life thus far of always demanding work.[96]

A few weeks later, a reporter told him a joke: Do you know the difference between LBJ and LSD? he asked. "LSD is a drug. LBJ is a dope." Bunche, not surprisingly, deemed the joke "cruel and crude."[97] But the casual way the reporter told it was yet another sign that Johnson's authority was crumbling, and Vietnam was the cause. That fall, Goldberg told Bunche some unwelcome news: he was planning to step down. Goldberg confided that he was rarely receiving calls from Johnson anymore. As a dove on Vietnam as the US doubled down on its aggressive approach, Goldberg felt increasingly out of step. Indeed, the ambassador even revealed to Bunche that the reason he had never told U Thant that LBJ had written a letter to Ho Chi Minh seeking peace efforts was that he, Goldberg, was never told about it.[98] Bunche was not surprised that the ambassador was frozen out—Goldberg and Johnson were clearly not a match—but Bunche was disappointed, largely because he shared Goldberg's dour assessment of the war. "LBJ's policy of escalation in Vietnam has not paid off," he scrawled in his diary.[99] He did not see a peaceful path forward, though he continued to do what he could to find some areas of agreement and action between Turtle Bay and the White House.

Then, just before Thanksgiving, Goldberg phoned U Thant and said they had to meet immediately—with Bunche there. Sitting down in the quiet of the secretary general's office, Goldberg told the UN officials that Secretary of State Dean Rusk had instructed him to let them know the US had "hard intelligence" that Turkey would be "moving on Cyprus" the next day. Rusk and Goldberg felt the situation was very dangerous and that the UN had to step in somehow to avert armed conflict. The White House may have indeed been concerned about the ramifications of violence in Cyprus, but surely also welcomed a chance to shift the spotlight from Asia to the Mediterranean. Specifically, Goldberg suggested, the secretary general should send a special representative to Cyprus immediately.[100]

Bunche interjected that they already had a special representative for Cyprus. (Bibiano Osorio-Tafall, a Spanish diplomat, had been recently appointed.) Sending another emissary would likely not have much impact, he argued, and might offend the incumbent by suggesting he was not up to the job. Instead, he suggested, why not have U Thant issue an appeal for restraint to the parties and maybe send a personal representative to the capitals of Greece and Turkey? Goldberg seemed excited by this approach and immediately suggested that Bunche was the right man for this job, too. This was not the outcome Bunche wanted, and he countered that it would be "much wiser" to send a different high-level Secretariat representative, Jose Rolz-Bennett of Guatemala, who had recently visited Cyprus and knew the issues.

In the end, Thant, perhaps sensitive to his clear desire to stay out of the fray, decided that Bunche was needed back in New York to attend to issues percolating from the Six-Day War. Bunche had successfully dodged the assignment. But whether he liked it or not, it was clear that he continued to be viewed as the UN's indispensable troubleshooter by Washington.

CHAPTER 24

AN IDEALIST AND A REALIST

*Peace, like war, can only be won by bold and courageous initiatives and by taking
some deliberate risks.*

—Ralph Bunche, remarks at UCLA, May 1969

On March 31, 1968, a Sunday, people throughout the United States tuned
in to their favorite evening television shows only to find them preempted by
an unexpected presidential speech. Lyndon Johnson, sitting at his desk in
the Oval Office, spoke first of the escalating war in Vietnam and then spoke
some more—for forty full minutes. At the very end he dropped a bombshell. "With America's sons in the field far away," Johnson intoned,

> with America's future under challenge right here at home, with our hopes and
> the world's hopes for peace in the balance every day, I do not believe that I should
> devote an hour or a day of my time to any personal partisan causes or any duties
> other than the awesome duties of this office—the presidency of this country.
> Accordingly, I shall not seek, and will not accept, the nomination of my party for
> another term as your president.[1]

Johnson's announcement that he would not run for president that
November caught even the networks by surprise. For a man so focused on

and even obsessed with political power to relinquish it in one stroke was simply unimaginable to many Americans. Although Johnson had told almost no one of his intentions, U Thant nonetheless claimed to have seen the resignation coming. The next day, back in their offices on the 38th floor of the UN, the secretary general told Ralph Bunche that he had anticipated Johnson's withdrawal from the race as early as last November based on a "reading of the stars." The stars, the astrology-fixated Thant explained, had simply been "very bad for LBJ in 1968."[2]

Bunche had met with President Johnson just the month before at the White House and had noticed nothing unusual. Johnson had seemed in a good mood; he was cordial and friendly, Bunche recounted in his diary, "calling me Ralph, saying how much he valued the work I was doing and what a great service I was rendering." Bunche had feared LBJ might be a "little cooler than usual" because of some of Bunche's recent speeches on Vietnam and domestic race relations. Yet the president appeared unperturbed—or perhaps he saw Bunche as useful enough to his immediate agenda to overlook any contrary remarks.[3] Now, with Johnson publicly committed to leaving the White House at the end of his term, a new element of uncertainty was injected into the painstaking, and thus far quixotic, search for peace in Vietnam.

Just a few days later, another, far more tragic, shock struck the nation. Standing outside on the balcony of his room at the Loraine Motel in Memphis, Tennessee, the Reverend Martin Luther King Jr. was shot dead by James Earl Ray. King was only thirty-nine years old. Like many Americans, Bunche was stunned at the brutal murder and "sick at heart." He later described the trip to Atlanta for King's funeral as the saddest journey he had ever made. To King's widow, Coretta, Bunche sent a telegraph explaining that he mourned "Martin's death with mixed feelings of anger, dismay, and sorrow. The despicable racist assassination which took this great man . . . is a profound American tragedy."[4]

Lyndon Johnson's withdrawal from the election had added uncertainty to the already intractable situation in Vietnam; now Martin Luther King's assassination added fuel to Bunche's increasing concern with the state of American race relations. And, too, it perhaps encouraged his broader willingness to speak his mind about the world. In the aftermath of the violent Chicago Democratic Convention later that summer, in which police beat protestors in the streets, Bunche called Coretta Scott King. He told her he found the police brutality on display on the nation's television sets sickening. Yet, surprisingly, he said the violence was nonetheless welcome. Black Americans knew the tactics of the police only too well. But now, on the streets of Chicago, the harsh truth was "irrefutably revealed" for all Americans to see. Bunche predicted that the "Gestapo-like," "savage" practices of the police could no longer be denied, for they now were being exercised against white Americans as well. He believed the crackdown at the Democratic Convention provided "an indispensable object lesson"—an "education"—for the nation.[5]

Bunche's mind was continually drawn to global conflict as well. Fearful of the ongoing escalation of the war in Vietnam, he increasingly spoke in stark terms of the war's rising stakes. "Choose Negotiations or Holocaust, Bunche Says," ran one headline that winter.[6] In an address to the Los Angeles World Affairs Council in February 1968, a few weeks before President Johnson's announcement of his withdrawal from the race, he had pessimistically argued that failure to negotiate in Southeast Asia would lead inevitably to a nuclear exchange. Vietnam was the source of the greatest frustration at the UN since the organization's founding, he explained. This war was "the first and only war since the UN began that it cannot intervene in one way or the other," he told the crowd—a somewhat surprising reading of Cold War history that seemed to ignore the fact that a decade earlier in Hungary, under the cover of the Suez Crisis, Soviet tanks had rolled across the border to brutally put down the rebellion against communist control. (They would do the same in Prague a few months later.) Few in Los Angeles that day questioned Bunche's assertion, however, and he received a standing ovation before heading to the roof to board a helicopter to the airport. From there he jetted to New York en route to yet another White House meeting. The topic, of course, was Vietnam.

The year 1968 was a one of unrelenting and searing violence and sorrow. On June 6, Robert F. Kennedy, campaigning to take Lyndon Johnson's place in the White House, was gunned down in the kitchen of the Ambassador

Hotel in Los Angeles. The assassination, by a young Palestinian activist named Sirhan Sirhan, occurred shortly after Kennedy had won the
California Democratic primary. Upset that Kennedy had supported Israel
in the Six-Day War the year before, Sirhan shot him in retaliation.[7]

Meanwhile, the war in Southeast Asia was growing yet more intense and
brutal. Young American men were being called up to fight in a conflict that
for many caused fear and frustration—for some even moral disgust—and
sent others fleeing across the border into Canada. Vietnam was also becoming very personal for Ralph Bunche. "Ours is a very sad household
today," he wrote on June 10, 1968, a few days after Bobby Kennedy's death.
"Ralph Jr. reported for military service this morning."[8]

THAT RALPH BUNCHE'S ONLY SON HAD been drafted into a war he deeply
opposed provoked mixed and complicated feelings, but mostly he feared
for his son's safety. Bunche was not a pacifist. In fact, he had tried and failed
to enlist in the Second World War, but stymied by physical ailments, he instead had to settle for joining the Office of Strategic Services. But this war
was most unlike the Second World War. That was a worthy, even existential struggle against rising fascism that he fully supported. This conflict, he
believed, was both morally and politically wrongheaded. Yet unlike many
fathers with power and position, he did not attempt to secure a relatively
safe post at home for his son in a National Guard unit or, at the very least,
an assignment to a noncombat role far from the front lines. Bunche's strong
sense of integrity and duty did not allow it, even as Ralph Jr. seemed to want
him to get on the phone and make the problem go away.

But the decision weighed on him. A year later, in 1969, as his son was finally deploying to Vietnam, Bunche wrote about the morning Ralph Jr. left,
looking "natty" in his officer's uniform and trying to be casual and brave. Yet,
the older Bunche noted, the "little things hurt the most"; his son had closed
out his bank account as he prepared to fly out and asked that the money be
invested in his sister Joan's name. As Ralph Sr. began to dress for work, he
spotted on his tie rack three of Ralph Jr.'s best ties, all ones that the father
had admired on the son, and that the son was now giving to him—perhaps,
he feared, for a long time.

Ralph Sr. found himself increasingly angry that fall morning. They had already tragically lost their daughter Jane. Now,

> our son, the youngest of the three, was being taken off to an utterly senseless, use-less war, a war that could bring no good to anyone, that no one could possibly win, that our country had never intended to get into, but had got into simply by stages and accidents and now lacked the courage to get out of it.[9]

He had a strong urge to denounce the war publicly, openly, and fully, but he felt he was "really trapped": to do so, given his stature and the attention his condemnation would receive, would not only embarrass his son but also increase the risk for him "by making him a marked man." And so Bunche headed off to work on the 38th floor that day, wearing one of Ralph Jr.'s ties, never saying a word to Ruth about his anger and his frustration and intense bitterness.

When his son made a final phone call from San Francisco in November 1969 before flying out to Bien Hoa, Vietnam, Bunche told him to protect himself and think of himself because he would now be an unwilling partici-pant in a game of life and death. The phone call home was strained and sad, and eventually Ralph Jr. said he had to go, the plane was about to depart. I hope to see you in a year, he told his parents. It was, Bunche thought, "like a sledgehammer smashing at my heart."[10]

Bunche resisted pulling any strings for his son, but that did not mean that the US government was unaware of who would soon be among its armed forces many thousands of miles away in Long Binh, guarding routes into Saigon. A few days later, President Richard Nixon sent Bunche a personal letter. "I know the concern and anxiety you must feel about your son leaving for Vietnam," Nixon wrote, "and I just want to assure you that we are going to do everything humanly possible to bring this war to an early and just end. I hope you will be able to keep the pressure on some of the representatives of other countries to work toward a peace that will help to ensure there will be no further Vietnams."[11]

Bunche, in reply, offered his prayer that the president's efforts to end the war would be successful. Whether he believed that Nixon truly sought peace or that Nixon was unwilling to really try and was more likely in fact to escalate the war is unclear. He was indeed suspicious of the new president. Bunche replied that he would continue to do "what little I can" to end the conflict, with the goal of bringing about a world community free, "as you yourself say, of any further Vietnams."[12] Rising up the Billboard charts as Bunche replied to Nixon was Creedence Clearwater Revival's antiwar anthem "Fortunate Son," which directly invoked the unfairness in how some—such as "the senator's son"—claimed patriotism but avoided fighting in the war, while the many thousands of ordinary American boys were sent off to battle.

In the summer of 1968, however, Ralph Jr.'s deployment was still in the future. Lyndon Johnson was still president and the election that would usher a Republican back into the Oval Office was months in the future. LBJ continued to press the UN angle on Vietnam, hoping that somehow it would prove useful in solving his most vexing political and strategic problem. In a visit to the UN headquarters in June, he again discussed the conflict with U Thant and Bunche. Thant expressed some regret about Ambassador Arthur Goldberg's imminent departure. Johnson, in a bantering manner, acknowledged the loss but voiced his dissatisfaction with the former justice, saying "Arthur's alright, but he has to be kept straight now and then."[13] Goldberg had hoped to return to the bench after his UN tenure was over, but by this point, annoyed at his impertinence and dovishness, Johnson was not interested in reappointing him. Goldberg later expressed great disappointment to Bunche over this turn of events, undoubtedly regretting his hubris at having left the august and genteel perch of the Supreme Court to try his hand in the more rough and tumble world of international politics. Perhaps, as some speculated, the president had assured him the bench would still be there for him, but that promise—if it ever existed—proved worthless. Goldberg, embittered, predicted to Bunche that the Supreme Court was destined to go into decline.[14]

Goldberg's replacement was George Ball, a veteran State Department official. Ball was the eighth US ambassador to the UN Bunche had worked with. (He would work with three more ambassadors before his death—the last being George H. W. Bush.) At the White House for Ball's swearing-in,

Bunche saw Goldberg. In his remarks Johnson "did finally say a few complimentary things" about the former justice, though Bunche thought the president was far from effusive.[15] Used to very close relationships with American representatives, Bunche did not click with Ball and found him arrogant and inaccessible; "Ball has not caught on here at all" was his terse assessment of the new man shortly after his arrival on the job.[16] Indeed, Ball seemed to agree: he left the post after just a few months, replaced briefly by James Wiggins, and then, after Richard Nixon's victory over Hubert Humphrey in the November 1968 presidential election, by Charles Yost. By this point, Bunche was the American with the most UN experience by far; the rapid turnover of US ambassadors was making his expertise and longevity even more significant.

Nixon visited the UN shortly after his victory at the ballot box. It was his first trip to the UN headquarters since 1956, when he was vice president. The president-elect brought along Henry Kissinger, his future national security advisor, and William Rogers, soon to be his secretary of state, for a meeting with Thant and Bunche. Nixon had actually encountered both men before—Bunche at Ghana's independence ceremonies in 1957 and Thant in Burma, in 1953, when Thant improbably was his guide. The secretary general helpfully fished out of his pocket a yellowing clipping of a news photo of the two men together in Southeast Asia, Thant dressed in robes.

As they stood in front of the UN buildings, Thant at first attempted to introduce Nixon to Bunche. Nixon, who had grown up near Los Angeles and attended nearby Whittier College, quickly interceded to say "we're old UCLA friends" and told Bunche "you always do win in basketball," as the two talked of sports and Southern California. (When Bunche slyly noted that UCLA also trounced Whittier in football, Nixon's obsession, he jokingly replied, "low blow.") As they walked to the 38th floor, Nixon turned to the more voluble Bunche and said, "It must be very discouraging at times for you to work here." Never discouraging, but often frustrating, Bunche replied. Nixon, the phrase catching his ear, looked at Bunche knowingly and, as if pondering the concept, repeated "Never discouraging, but often frustrating."[17]

Photo 24.1 Nixon, with Thant and Bunche, at the UN

In the press briefing that followed, Nixon gave a surprisingly positive take on the UN visit. His remarks also offered an insightful perspective on how the UN was rapidly evolving as the 1970s approached. In some respects Nixon, more than the many UN critics who simply saw failure in the ineffective struggles over Vietnam, the Middle East, and the like, was remarkably perceptive about the organization's future. He told the assembled reporters that he had discussed a number of issues with the UN leadership that were not in the headlines:

> Not the political activities, but the economic and other activities that are tremendously exciting and in which there is general agreement among the members of the United Nations—in the field of education, in the field of health, and others. It is this side of the United Nations story that needs to be better known in America and around the world.[18]

Nixon was right. These issues, which rarely dominated the news, were growing increasingly important to the UN. There was another area to note as well, one Nixon would make a signature one before his legacy was irreparably destroyed by Watergate and would prove fertile for the UN for decades to come. The president, his spokesman reported at the time, was "keenly interested" in the talks then ongoing at the UN on the "problems of the human environment," such as "pollution of the air, earth, seas, and rivers." The environment was a very new topic, still nascent on the global agenda. Yet it would come to life a few years later at the landmark 1972 Stockholm Conference on the Human Environment.

Ralph Bunche was cautiously optimistic about his fellow Californian as president. To be sure, he had publicly criticized Nixon before, and he privately used his well-known nickname "Tricky Dick." Indeed, in the runup to the election, Bunche wrote in his diary that Nixon was dangerous; "an utter hypocrite, without conviction or principle."[19] Still, he thought Nixon's visit to the UN was very helpful, and the president-elect, despite his earlier harsh rhetoric, appeared cordial to everyone in the building. Nixon also seemed surprisingly focused on the UN's actual work. Nixon's advance team had told Bunche that this was a courtesy visit with no substance that needed discussion; yet the moment Nixon got to the 38th floor offices he began asking serious questions, evidencing that he had done a substantial amount of homework.[20] This was a good sign to Bunche, who, like many who followed the vicissitudes of the US-UN relationship, could see the growing fractures and feared what American antipathy, or at least indifference, could do to the organization.* Nixon, as someone who was on record as a UN critic, was especially one to watch. His remarks at the UN building, and the care he clearly had given to his preparation for the visit, were encouraging.

The defeated Democratic candidate, Hubert Humphrey, himself a devotee of the UN and its mission, also visited the UN's headquarters shortly after the election. Calling the UN the "last best hope," Humphrey promised to be a constructive companion to the new president and not a "carping

---

* The Republican Party's drift from the UN would accelerate after Nixon. By the 1980s and 1990s, there was open hostility to the organization and the dues arrears increased. Senator Jesse Helms, visiting the UN in 2000, even threatened that the US might pull out of the organization. The dues were eventually paid—Helms was even induced to wear a UN hat by the late, legendary diplomat Richard Holbrooke—but many members of the GOP continued to hold very negative views of the UN.

critic."[21] Humphrey's voice of support was welcome, but it was a difficult time for the organization. Not only Vietnam was testing the UN's relevance; the recent Soviet intervention in Prague, the Six-Day War—the examples of UN impotence seemed to be multiplying.

Indeed, the brutal crushing of Prague's reform movement just months before Nixon's victory had been another sad instance not only of the costs of the Cold War but also of the special rules for great powers which the UN Charter, for all its strengths, had deliberately and permanently entrenched in its provisions. Bunche had never liked this aspect of the Charter, and he liked it even less now. The Soviet veto in the Security Council meant the UN could do nothing about the USSR's violent crackdown, aside from chastising the Eastern Bloc in a special meeting called just hours after the first tanks crossed the Czech border. Just as was the case with Hungary in 1956, the Soviet Union put down a rebellion with little consequence.

In the wake of the Soviet invasion, over a lunch at the Finnish Mission to the UN, Bunche and Gunnar Jarring, a Swedish diplomat, were chatting with some others. Jarring mentioned recently seeing the 1966 comedy *The Russians Are Coming*, adding that he found it quite funny. "It isn't so funny in my country," a Romanian diplomat whispered.[22]

IN FEBRUARY 1969, *TODAY SHOW* VIEWERS awoke to coverage of Ralph Bunche's interview with NBC reporter Pauline Frederick. Bunche recounted the dramatic and now twenty-one-year-old story of the murder of Count Folke Bernadotte, ambushed in Jerusalem in 1948. Delayed by a plane and various officious Israelis, Bunche had been late to meet Bernadotte and was frustrated. "I had never known a man who was more of a stickler for punctuality than Folke Bernadotte.... I had never been one minute late" for any appointment with him, he told NBC viewers.[23]

Nonetheless he *had* been late, and on that sunny September day, Bunche explained, Bernadotte did not wait for him to arrive. Then, sitting in the back of his chauffeured car as it drove outside the Old City, Bernadotte was gunned down—as was the man sitting next to him, where Bunche would normally have been sitting himself. "When I saw the bodies I saw a hole the size of a half dollar in Colonel Serot's left temple. He had taken the first slug,"

Bunche continued to tell the *Today Show*. "We'll never know, of course, whether he had reached over to grapple with the assassin or whether he was hit and fell forward."

Pauline Frederick switched gears a bit. "I understand you're not necessarily a devotee of the principle of the brotherhood of man," she asked. "Why is that?" I used to use those terms, Bunche replied. Calling them nice terms, valid and fine, he nonetheless suggested that brotherhood was often asked to do "too much." It was not really practical. Most importantly, he said, it was not necessary to have brotherhood to have "coexistence." Mutual respect was what mattered, he argued. Dignity. These were the keys; anything else was superfluous to achieving global harmony and cooperation.

Bunche appears never to have called himself a realist, at least not in the sense that political scientists use the term. Yet he was veering closer than ever before to a broad version of realist thinking about international affairs. (U Thant, who certainly knew a thing or two about Bunche's mind, would say at his funeral that Bunche was both an "idealist and a realist.")[24] Often derided for its heartless, amoral qualities, realism—perhaps personified in its extreme form by Henry Kissinger, who just weeks before Bunche's interview had been appointed Nixon's national security advisor—did have a thin moral core, in that it saw peace and "coexistence" among the great powers as the highest values. In Kissinger and Nixon's hands, a realist foreign policy would go much further, and soon it meant supporting brutal dictators on the right, eschewing human rights, and even ignoring—and arguably aiding—a genocide in what is now Bangladesh, all sacrificed in the name of the allegedly larger aims of the Cold War and America's national interest.[25] When Bunche's old interlocutor Golda Meir came to the White House a few years later seeking American support to allow Jews from the Soviet Union to escape persecution, Kissinger, himself Jewish, told Nixon that the issue simply was "not an objective of American foreign policy." And "if they put Jews into gas chambers in the Soviet Union, it is not an American concern. Maybe a humanitarian concern." "I know," Nixon responded. "We can't blow up the world because of it."[26]

Bunche did not live to see much of the Nixon administration, and he would never have countenanced the brutality and coldness—and often untrammeled racism—that marked so much of Nixon's allegedly realist foreign policy in the 1970s. His thinking about coexistence shared little with the approach that was about to emerge from the White House. And with regard to Vietnam, the most controversial and significant issue on the global agenda in 1969, he differed deeply with the two men now in charge of American foreign policy. Yet in his disavowal of brotherhood as a goal, even as a meaningful aspiration, the chastened Bunche was drifting closer than he ever had before to a central theme of realism, one in which the need for global balance and stability, for simple "coexistence," was the only sustainable lodestar in geopolitics.

Bunche had long declared himself a professional optimist, and in some ways he still was. Yet increasingly, as he entered his final years, he was unsettled by the death and destruction that had consumed so much of the postwar world since the triumph of the Allies in 1945. Now, the war in Vietnam was only growing larger and more destructive; in 1968 the US troop presence peaked at over 500,000—and, of course, among the multitude of young American soldiers fighting and often dying in the jungles of Southeast Asia was Ralph Bunche Jr.

As Bunche looked back over his long career, he still found particular solace in the one area that perhaps was emblematic of the search for "coexistence": peacekeeping. Peacekeeping as he conceptualized it did not take sides in a conflict. Rather, it interposed impartial forces between combatants in an effort to foster the conditions for peace and create space for diplomacy and negotiation. In Congo, the largest peacekeeping mission to date, these principles had arguably broken down; the Katanga crisis had effectively forced the UN to take sides in a civil war, though he had resisted doing so for some time. Still, the basic notion of peacekeeping was neutral, even indifferent, between the claims of the two sides. And this approach was often effective. In an interview in 1969, he noted that his Nobel Peace Prize had "attracted all the attention."[27] But, he continued, citing his role in charge of peacekeeping operations in the Congo, the Middle East, Kashmir, and elsewhere, he felt "more satisfaction in the work I've done since."

The proudest effort of his career, he opined, was the creation of the UN Emergency Force during the Suez Crisis. Peacekeeping inverted the traditional understanding of armed forces. For the first time, he explained proudly, we had "found a way to use military men for peace instead of war."

———————

THE YEAR 1969 BEGAN WITH A funeral. The United Nations' first secretary general, the Norwegian Trygve Lie, died just before New Year's Eve and now, a few days later, Ralph Bunche was at the memorial service in Oslo. At the service, where he gave the eulogy, he sat next to Vice President Hubert Humphrey, the son of a Norwegian immigrant. Police were in abundance after Norwegians had thrown rocks at the American Embassy in Oslo in protest of Humphrey's role in the Vietnam War.[28] (Humphrey would soon be out in any event; Richard Nixon's inauguration was just days away.) The Soviet Union, still holding a grudge against the pro-Western Lie, did not send a representative.

On the flight home, the man in the seat next to Bunche struck up a conversation. Perpetually overworked and jetlagged, Bunche liked to be left alone on flights; he never relished the opportunity for "another seminar on the conduct of the UN, the Middle East, or Vietnam—or worse still, the race problem." In this case the man was starstruck, immediately praising him as an inspiring example for all Black Americans. Bunche "cut him off right there." I am no such symbol, he insisted to the hapless seatmate; the only example I might be, he continued, was of the advantages of having a grandmother "as fine as mine."[29] Such familial luck was no basis for a just society, he emphasized. More than ever he seemed unhappy with aspects of his exalted status among white Americans, and was quick to underscore that his success, while he believed it well deserved, was no substitute for true social change.

Back home in Queens, he composed a letter to his son in Vietnam. He complained that his eyes were worse than ever, and now he had a pinched spinal nerve to boot. He conceded that while these conditions had probably delayed his writing, "the truth of the matter is I just don't know what to say that could be helpful to you." Perhaps he was trying to explain his unwillingness to use his clout to keep Ralph Jr. far from actual harm. War, he continued, is "a senseless and dirty business. I am sorry you are anywhere near it."[30]

Later that spring, along with Ruth, Bunche headed to UCLA for the dedication of Bunche Hall. The building, a modern-looking, thin, brown tower with large windows on the north side facing the tony hills of Bel Air, was not dissimilar in shape to the UN Secretariat building Bunche had spent so many years working in. Bunche Hall was only eleven stories tall, not the thirty-nine of the UN building, but it towered over the verdant, low-rise UCLA campus. In the front, outside near the bank of elevators, was placed a large plaque and a not-especially reminiscent bust of Bunche. He appeared very pleased at the honor and happy as always to be back at his alma mater. He seemed perhaps most excited to have a chance to meet with UCLA basketball great Kareem Abdul-Jabbar, who at that time was generally known as Lew Alcindor. Posing in a suit and tie in front of the building with Abdul-Jabbar, who wore a colorful African-style print shirt and cap, Bunche smiled for the cameras. The two UCLA basketball players were standing close together but separated by more than four decades, at least two generations, and some seventeen inches of height.

To the students and faculty assembled at UCLA Bunche declared: "One does not anticipate or even dream of an occasion of this kind. At least, I never have." He seemed genuinely touched by the dedication from his alma mater. "I can say confidently only that I am immodestly happy, that I am at once proud, humble, and a little concerned about having to live up to something like this." Noting that the building had already acquired a nickname—"the Waffle"—he offered hope that it would someday be known as "Bunche's Waffle." (A dream that did not come true.) Any way he looked at it, he quipped, "Bunche Hall is beautiful—may I be permitted to add— even though it isn't black."[31]

The UCLA visit was a pleasant respite and a chance to hark back to more carefree days. The weight of responsibility and his many brushes with the full breadth of human hatred had taken their toll on Bunche. He was now reputed to be a bit cautious, even old-fashioned, certainly very respected and respectable—a great man in the conventional understanding—but perhaps somewhat out of touch with America in 1969. Not that a man in his sixties could avoid this fate in the 1960s (or probably ever): it was part of the nature of social change, and especially so at a time with the youthquake of the postwar baby boom rumbling forcefully through America. The contrast of the diplomat Bunche's sober suit and the young Abdul-Jabbar's embrace of stylish African-style prints is at one level fully to be expected; on another, it was an interesting contrast because it was Bunche who actually had spent substantial time in Africa, who really knew something about Africa, and who interacted—virtually every single day—with actual Africans.[†]

Indeed, a few months before he visited UCLA, Bunche jotted down his thoughts on the new embrace of African style. A good many Americans, he noted, were giving expression to "a newly found pride in race" via African hairstyles, dress, and jewelry, and were "paying lip service to Africa."[32] But he cast a slightly critical eye on this shift. These manifestations, he wrote, would be more meaningful and impressive "if they were accompanied by an active concern about the tragic plight of millions of black people" in South Africa, Angola, Rhodesia, and Mozambique. "Why is there no black power pressure of any significance applied to the US government to take a much stronger stand against racism and colonialism?" he asked. In posing this question, he was channeling a view he had long held—indeed, a view that even appeared in his PhD proposal in the early 1930s—that a more global perspective was urgently needed.

By 1969, Africa as a symbol had taken on new meaning in Black political thought. James Baldwin had already noticed this new meaning in the wake of Patrice Lumumba's murder, writing in 1961 that "the American Negro can no longer, nor will he ever again, be controlled by white America's image of him." This fact, Baldwin argued, had "everything to do with the rise of Africa in world affairs."[33] And while it ebbed and flowed, the embrace of all things African was still going strong eight years later as Bunche toured UCLA. He was intrigued but also a bit confused by this renewed linkage and the larger connections to the civil rights struggle. He wanted to understand more about what was happening in America and he increasingly wrote down, both on scraps of paper but in longer passages, his musings on

---

[†] Abdul-Jabbar, after a stellar career in the NBA, went on to become a distinguished author of Black history and, in an interesting tangent with Bunche, one of the State Department's cultural ambassadors.

race relations and racial justice, distilled from decades of life and thought and observation. Clearly trying to make sense of the turbulence and violence of the decade, Bunche was returning to the domestic issues that consumed his earlier life but had fallen largely by the wayside during his three decades as a diplomat and policymaker.

Bunche's writings from this period evince an introspective and sometimes troubled mood. One short entry was devoted to the phenomenon of Black power. Black power was not a new concept, he argued. The National Negro Congress, of which he was a founder, was, "in a sense, a 'black power' movement."[34] He conceded, however, that the new incarnation was stronger, more insistent, and likely more visible and powerful. Of himself, he jotted down elsewhere that "I am not bitter, nor am I angry. I rely only on reason, candor, and truth" in the fight for racial justice. He acknowledged that he enjoyed a certain status and station in life. His fame and position meant he did not any longer "*feel* the color bar, personally, in a tangible sense." As the West Side Tennis Club incident a few years earlier had demonstrated, he could bring huge resources to bear in a battle against personal discrimination and sometimes win. Yet there was a decisive difference, Bunche explained, between being accepted genuinely, as an equal, and "being tolerated for some reason." Many whites wholly misunderstand the extent of pain and even animosity in the Black community, he continued. They misjudged the depth of Black America's despair and resentment, the "increasing bitterness," even, perhaps, feelings of "hostility."[35]

In another essay, also never published, Bunche seemed to struggle with how strongly to identify with this new, more forthright mood. He began with typical modesty, noting that he made no claim to expertise on the problem of race in America. But, he said, "I have 64 years of living in this society as a Negro and today I identify with my people, with black people." Was "today" implying that he had not always done so? "I am," he then declared in a surprising turn of phrase, "a partisan in the black revolution."[36] "Revolution" was not a word Bunche commonly endorsed. Seeming almost chastened by this embrace of revolutionary fervor, he immediately repeated his usual rejection of "racial chauvinism." He announced that he preferred to live in an integrated society, but he added an important caveat, not usually one made in the past: "if that is possible." His oft-proclaimed optimism seemed to be fading.

Indeed, Bunche did seem to warm to the idea—or at least the rhetoric—of revolution as the 1960s drew to a close. On a scrap of paper in this era he jotted down, "Nothing could be more American than the black revolution . . . the revolution, in short, is for the fulfillment of the promise of the US Constitution for black as well as white Americans." And on ABC News, asked about the Black Panthers and their avowed willingness to use violence, Bunche again endorsed nonviolence as the only path forward. But he quickly qualified his remarks, in a somewhat surprising manner for those who did not understand his deep-seated pragmatism. He was not against violence in principle, he explained, "because I think we're in a revolutionary situation here." The struggle for Black equality, he continued, "is a revolution and means a revolutionary change in the mores of society . . . and in the course of revolution any means are justifiable in my view." His only true difference with the Black Panthers, he seemed to say, was one of tactics: "I think violence for the Negro is not a practical step forward."[37]

Bunche was increasingly concerned about enduring, even intensifying, segregation. The violence and despair he saw in communities around the nation, even in his own childhood community of South Central Los Angeles, disturbed him greatly. Yet another unpublished essay was titled "Upheaval in the Ghettos."[38‡] Many Black Americans, he argued, had experienced little change in their status, despite the important legislative and moral victories of the civil rights movement. They are, he wrote, still "segregated tightly in their housing, their schools, their hospitals, their churches." Ghettos seemed to consume Bunche's attention because they embodied—and entrenched—the racial division he had long fought against. The violence in Watts and elsewhere was a sign of the deep dissatisfaction "burning painfully inside every Negro in the country today," whether they lived inside or outside the ghetto. "I am no exception," he wrote. With reference

---

‡ In a cover note Bunche wrote that the sole purpose of the essay was to record his reactions to "the recent racial disturbances in our cities." There was, he said, "no thought of publication."

to South Africa and even to Cyprus, he dissected the rage and frustration around him. He diagnosed the cause of urban violence in a very Bunchian fashion: in an abiding refusal by white America to accept "the Negro as a person."

During the negotiations over the UN in San Francisco, W. E. B. Du Bois had arrestingly written that "colonies are the slums of the world."[39] Bunche had fought for decades to end colonialism, and while the work was far from over, by 1969 considerable, even substantial, progress had been made. The crowded corridors of the UN buildings he strode down every working day, filled with a diverse array of diplomats from dozens of newly independent states, were a living testament to this success. Yet, even as the global "slums" Du Bois and Bunche decried had been largely cleared and sometimes beautifully rebuilt, it seemed to Bunche—and it greatly concerned him, even despaired him—that the slums at home tenaciously clung to existence.

RALPH BUNCHE'S GROWING FRAILTY PERHAPS LENT a special urgency to his desire to speak his mind. In an address at the University of Hawaii in 1969, he took direct aim at the notion, integral to Henry Kissinger and Richard Nixon's thinking, that national interests overwhelmingly drove foreign policy decision making. As developed in the postwar discipline of international relations, the theory of realism tended to scrub away the messy, prewar elements of race and empire in world politics. In this new conception only states, sometimes aridly defined as "units," engaged in the pursuit of power and survival in an anarchic international system.[40] Domestic politics, social divisions, ideologies, emotion—these were not central factors. Bunche by contrast saw racism as driving, even distorting, the pursuit of power among nations. Race, he argued, was in fact at the root of many problems and conflicts in world politics. And race was certainly at the core of the most pressing foreign policy challenge of the day: the Vietnam War. "Would the United States be engaged in that war if the North Vietnamese and the National Liberation front were white?," he forthrightly asked.[41]

The war itself was an outgrowth of colonialism. Division along racial lines was the "very essence" of colonialism as an institution. Colonialism may be deep in retreat, Bunche insisted, but its "evil legacies" would bedevil the world for years to come. It was the direct source of a host of intractable conflicts: Vietnam to be sure, but also the Middle East, Nigeria, Southern Rhodesia, and Kashmir. Even where armed conflict did not take place, he urged, racism infected world politics. Many had queried, Bunche told his audience (and he did not disagree), whether the People's Republic of China would not already have been admitted to the United Nations if "the Chinese were not 'yellow' people—and so many of them."

His speech that day, he acknowledged, was "gloomy." So he tried to close his remarks with a small dose of good news, news that he took some degree of personal pride in. Colonialism was in its twilight, he told the audience; since the UN had come into existence, more than 800 million individuals had gained their political independence. Indeed, there were nearly sixty new states in the world that not long before had been ruled by Britain, France, the Netherlands, or other European powers. If the world continued in this salutary direction, he suggested, it just might pull back "from the brink of self-extinction."§

FEELING THAT TIME WAS SLIPPING AWAY, Bunche more and more took the opportunity to travel for pleasure. After the speech in Hawaii, Ruth joined him for a thirty-eight-day journey around the world, along with their daughter, Joan. The family watched the Apollo 11 launch from Tokyo, saw the lunar walk from Manila, met with the prime minister of Thailand in Bangkok, and celebrated his birthday in Istanbul.[42] The trip was extensive but taxing; in Bangkok he suffered a retinal hemorrhage and, as he poignantly wrote in his journal, was now "almost sightless."[43]

By September, Bunche was back at his desk. Despite his advancing age and rapidly declining health (a diary entry bemoaned shoelaces as an "abomination" but lauded escalators as "among mankind's greatest boons"), he was still handling some of the trickier challenges at the UN.[44] A striking

---

§ His speech occasioned a flurry of questions at a UN press conference shortly afterward, in which reporters pressed a UN spokesperson to clarify if U Thant had known of and "authorized" Bunche's striking remarks. The secretary general had known, was the answer, but had not authorized it.

example was the growing conflict in Northern Ireland. Bunche was given the task of greeting and meeting the controversial Protestant leader Ian Paisley, who was then visiting New York City, a major center of the Irish diaspora.

In 1969 Northern Ireland was just entering the three violent decades now known as "The Troubles." In August there had been riots and violent clashes in the region, and British troops had deployed to Belfast and other towns. Soon bombings and battles would range from Belfast to London. Northern Ireland was a distinctive example of colonial conflict. It was in Europe; all the sides were white; and the history and geography made it easier to contest who was the oppressed and who was the oppressor. At bottom, however, it was not without ties to the liberation movements in Africa and elsewhere Bunche knew well: here again were British troops fighting to maintain their rule and local actors—at least some of them—fighting to oust them.

The growing conflict was now moving out of the islands of northern Europe and over to New York City. The city's mayor, John Lindsay, refused to meet with Ian Paisley; in heavily Catholic New York City there was no political upside. But Bunche had little choice: Northern Ireland was becoming ever more tense and violent, and, a few weeks earlier, when the foreign minister of Ireland had met with U Thant in New York, he had even suggested UN intervention to stem the rising tide of violence. Paisley told Bunche he was staunchly opposed to any UN role in Northern Ireland.[45] So, too, he claimed, were most people in the small territory. Bunche found Paisley forbidding; a "burly man" with a "mask-like countenance" who was "somewhat frightening in his intensity and in the cold glint in his eye."[46] As he listened to the "fanatically" anti-Catholic Paisley recount the grievances and growing violence in Northern Ireland, Bunche thought depressingly— and prophetically—of Cyprus and its endless group-based strife.

After their meeting, Paisley talked with the press, stressing the complaints of Northern Ireland's Protestants and insisting that the situation in the small territory was an internal matter about which Ireland should "keep its nose out."[47] U Thant, faced with a new and difficult issue, again saw Bunche as a possible solution. Thant had previously told the Irish foreign minister that it was unrealistic to seek a UN peacekeeping force in Northern Ireland; the

British would never accept it. Now Thant had a new idea. Would Bunche be willing to act as a UN special representative to Northern Ireland? Bunche doubted London would accept this idea either, but either way he felt his American nationality would be a disadvantage. This was an argument he was increasingly deploying to fend off proposals that he troubleshoot this or that world crisis; whether or not he really believed his citizenship was a hindrance, it was certainly a departure from his earlier days when, despite some minor protests to Ruth, he readily jumped on a plane to almost anywhere. He instead proposed former Supreme Court justice Earl Warren, who had just stepped down from the Court a couple of months before.[48] The secretary general listened, but the position never came to fruition.

As Northern Ireland loomed on the UN agenda, other topics remained well ensconced. Shortly after Paisley's visit, as the General Assembly met for its annual fall meeting, it again took up the Middle East. The UN body resolved that Israel withdraw from the "occupied Arab territory" and that there be guaranteed frontiers for all countries in the area.[49] Bunche, undoubtedly tired of the issue, told the *ABC News* that the conflict that had consumed so much of his professional life was "not insoluble, but of course is highly emotional." (U Thant took a more pessimistic view, warning that the world may be witnessing the beginning of "another one hundred years war" in the region.)[50] Then, in November 1969, Ralph Jr. finally deployed to Vietnam, leaving Bunche deeply fearful of the coming months.

As the year drew to a close, Bunche, against his doctor's orders, flew to Geneva for one day of meetings regarding the future of the contested Persian Gulf territory of Bahrain. The dispute turned on whether Britain, which had controlled Bahrain for nearly a century, or Iran, which had even longer ties, properly had or should have control of the small territory. A third alternative was independence; Bahrain was one of the few colonial outposts still left in the world by late 1969. The UK and Iran sought to have U Thant mediate a way forward, but the Soviets, always eager to rein in the UN Secretariat, complained that Thant's team should not be taking such "good offices" initiatives without prior consultation with the Security Council. As they had often done in the past, the Soviets sought to place the

Photo 24.2 Bunche at the Security Council

Security Council at the center of almost everything, thereby enhancing their own power.

Bunche, the most experienced member of the Secretariat, argued that by this point UN mediation had become customary and accepted.[51] The Soviets countered that past practice could not justify these actions; mediation was an "illegal practice [which] was forced upon the United Nations in the past by certain Powers contrary to and in violation of the Charter."[52] A few months later, however, things in Turtle Bay calmed down. The Security Council endorsed the results of Bunche's mediation effort in a vote. The USSR had backed down and supported the effort to devise a peaceful transition in Bahrain. With Vietnam almost totally dominating the news, few noticed the accomplishment. The UN's director of Public Information wrote a letter to a junior editor at the *New York Times* chastising them for failing to even mention how a "difficult and potentially dangerous" situation in the Middle East had been ably solved by the UN.[53] (Bunche, operating at higher levels, forwarded the complaint directly to Abe Rosenthal, who ran the paper.) The world's attention, unfortunately, was mostly elsewhere.

After a successful UN-sponsored referendum, eventually Bahrain declared independence in 1971 and joined the UN as a member state. As New Year's Day 1970 approached, only a few European colonial possessions remained. Many of those that did—such as Portugal's southwest African territory of Angola—were in the crosshairs of the decolonization movement. Bunche's early interest in colonialism was, as he had long hoped and dreamed, rapidly becoming moot.

THE *LOS ANGELES TIMES*, WRITING IN 1970 about the United Nations, noted that age was "creeping up on top officials."[54] One ambassador, quoted off the record, referred to the senior Secretariat staff as a "gerontocracy." The average age of the top staff was almost sixty, and Ralph Bunche, now sixty-six, was said to be "nearly blind" and suffering from bursitis and other ailments.

These descriptions were largely accurate. Bunche's vision had deteriorated greatly and his handwriting by this point was huge and looping, scrawling across page after page in an effort to transcribe words he could

Photo 24.3 Mobutu, Thant, and Bunche

later read. On a trip to the Soviet Union, his hosts had a special pair of glasses made that resembled opera glasses, but they were too ungainly to really be useful. Papers and reports had to be read to him. Colleagues found his mind to be as sharp as ever, but the process slowed things down. He had still not retired, and as the year progressed it was becoming clear that he would have to retire very soon. He was, unsurprisingly, feeling uncertain about his future. The "prospect of death comes more often to my mind these days," he jotted down one day while in the General Assembly chamber.[55] His ailments were "more aggravated and aggravating" and he was in ever more pain. Though he remained active on certain issues, the Middle East especially, he was unable to work at nearly the pace he was used to.

He was still a respected voice, however. Interviewed on ABC's "Issues and Answers," he surprisingly spoke as much about domestic matters as global politics. Black leaders in America had little faith in President Richard Nixon's administration or his policies, he explained. Racism was the nation's chief problem, and Nixon had to "wage war" against it "on the same scale as the Vietnam War."[56] The next day the interview led to a storm of questions at the UN. Carl Rowan, a Black former Kennedy administration official and now a syndicated columnist, devoted a column to the interview, accurately noting that it was "too late to label Bunche a 'hothead' or 'rabble-rouser.' "[57] Yet it was precisely Bunche's reputation as a measured, mainstream voice that made his critique of Nixon impactful. As the interview was dissected in the days that followed, Bunche sought to temper interpretations of his remarks, arguing that he had denounced Nixon's officials but not the president himself—and, in typical Bunche fashion, clarified that he himself was "not in the category of Black leaders."[58]

Bunche had now mostly given up writing letters by hand, and in a missive dictated to Ralph Jr., stationed in Long Binh, Vietnam, he told his son how, while watching Bob Hope's Christmas Show, Ruth had carefully scanned their TV screen for a glimpse of him. At one point Ruth believed she saw him, "wearing a floppy fatigue hat and laughing." "Was it possible this was you?," he asked plaintively.[59]

The year 1970 also marked the twenty-fifth anniversary of the UN, bringing a flurry of commemorative activity. The UN's silver birthday promoted introspection among many diplomats. As one of the few officials still at the organization who was present at the creation, Bunche was his usual blend of optimism and realism—though perhaps realism was gaining on optimism. He explained to his pen pal Valerie Betts that he was not attending the San Francisco celebration because "I could not bring myself to feel there was much to celebrate about at this time."[60] Publicly, he was more in character, but only barely. One must believe man can be saved—or salvaged, he said in the runup to the anniversary. Otherwise "one's work, all diplomacy, the United Nations itself, become a fateful travesty and all mankind would be utterly doomed."[61] This was not a ringing endorsement of the prospects for world peace. Britain's Lord Caradon gave a pithier and perhaps more insightful take: "I do not weary of repeating that there is nothing wrong with the United Nations except the members."

Many observers, even insiders, indeed were pessimistic about the UN's prospects as the 1970s began. The *Jerusalem Post's* headline—"The UN: 25 Years of Failure"—was an overwrought but not uncommon view.[62] Others found more prospects for hope. The influential international lawyer Philip Jessup, for example, argued that it was a mistake to see the UN only as a talking shop or meeting place in which actions were generally ineffectual and time more often was wasted by diplomats pontificating. It was also wrong to see the UN entirely in terms of conflict. Instead, Jessup suggested, in words that Bunche himself could have written, the UN is one "of the most convenient channels for serious international negotiations and 'quiet diplomacy.' "[63] His Bahrain mediation the year before was a signal example of this practice.

Jessup was perceptive about the UN's actual contributions. Still, he did not discuss what Richard Nixon had mentioned when he visited the UN as the president-elect: the UN's rising engagement with issues of health, welfare, economic development, and environment. These issues had not been uppermost in San Francisco and at Dumbarton Oaks. Rather, they were of interest largely to the developing world. Yet developing states now represented the bulk of the organization's membership, and the UN's traditional focus on war and peace was beginning to give way to a broader set of concerns—such as education, vaccination, and food security—that arguably were of greater consequence to the average child born in the 1960s than any Security Council resolution or peacekeeping mission. This evolution made assessments of the organization tricky. To those who still saw it as a straightforward peace and security body, the failures were many, even if overemphasized. But to those who saw its purpose as more encompassing—as an organization that worked to improve the life, health, and welfare of vulnerable individuals around the globe—the UN was far more impressive.

To honor the UN's 25th anniversary, President Nixon hosted a dinner at the White House in July 1970. The Vietnam War was reaching a morbid crescendo that summer. Henry Kissinger had begun his secret negotiations with the North Vietnamese in Paris earlier in 1970; Nixon had also begun secret bombings—secret to the West, at least—of suspected North Vietnamese sanctuaries across the border in Cambodia. At home, protests against the war were growing larger and stronger. In May, at Kent State University in Ohio, the struggle over America's Vietnam policy crossed a Rubicon as four students were killed and nine wounded when National Guard troops opened fire on protestors.

At the White House dinner, Nixon declared the world a better place because the UN was there. Over a table of salmon and chateaubriand, the president called on Bunche to give some remarks about the Middle East. Bunche demurred, limiting his words to ambiguous praise of U Thant and his steady equanimity. "I'd like to see him angry now and then," Bunche told the assembled guests in the State Dining Room, nearly all of whom were familiar with the secretary general's imperturbable style and demeanor. "I tell him he ought to cuss somebody," he continued, but Thant would not take the advice. Nixon quietly interjected that Thant "can't do it."[64]

Thant, speaking before Congress earlier that day, had nonetheless summoned the courage to call Vietnam the "worst horror story of modern times."[65]

Meanwhile, as summer turned to fall, Bunche's health went from bad to worse. At home in Queens he fell and broke a rib, ending up in New York Hospital. He struggled to return to work. He had delegated much of the Middle East mediator role he had played for decades to Gunnar Jarring, a taciturn Swede.** This move opened some space for other issues, though Bunche was increasingly out of the office and unable to engage. In September, multiple jetliners were hijacked and held in Jordan; in response, the Security Council held an emergency session, one of many to come that would find the body addressing the growing threat of transnational terrorism. Bunche was present, advising Thant, but more and more he was behind the scenes while Jarring garnered attention as the world's newest hope for peaceful mediation. There was some good news that fall, however: Ralph Jr. returned from Vietnam safely in October.

As 1971 began, Bunche was hospitalized with bronchitis for nearly eleven weeks. While in the hospital he was paid a visit by the newest American ambassador to the UN, George H. W. Bush. Growing concerned that the end was near, Bunche began to make preparations for his retirement and his papers. That month he signed a memo, countersigned by U Thant, that accorded control of his personal papers to Ruth, to his daughter Joan, and to Brian Urquhart, his long-time deputy, in the event of his death or incapacitation.[66] In March he was again struck ill. He came into the office that spring only occasionally. In May he met with Bush, Secretary of State William Rogers, and others at the UN to discuss the prospects for peace in the Middle East under the new Egyptian president Anwar Sadat. Ill yet again, he even slipped briefly into a coma in June.

This proved the final straw for his UN career. U Thant, seeking to ensure that Ruth had adequate support in the future, arranged for Ralph's retirement to guarantee that some pension funds would go to her if he died. When the decision was made public, President Nixon called Bunche an "inspiration" and said he would be "sorely missed" at the UN.[67] The *New York Times*, reporting on his retirement in September 1971, wrote an extensive front-page story recapping his career and the many crises he had managed over his long and illustrious diplomatic career; it was almost an obituary in form and detail.[68]

** Jarring at one point tersely answered reporters with a "no comment" about a recent Middle East mission. Bunche, usually loquacious and popular with reporters, was asked about it later and joked that Jarring "must have been misquoted."

The *New York Times* was unfortunately not far off in its estimation. Admitted to New York Hospital on November 30, on December 9, just after midnight, Ralph Bunche died peacefully. The next day and in the days afterward, tributes and assessments poured forth from politicians, diplomats, and newspapers around the world. President Nixon, who telephoned Ruth to express his personal condolences, called him one of the "greatest architects of peace in our time." The nation "is deeply proud of this distinguished son" and profoundly saddened by his death, he declared. "But we are also strengthened by the inexhaustible measure of dedication and creative action that spanned his splendid career."[69] U Thant, speaking before the UN General Assembly, called Bunche an "international institution in his own right" and someone who "transcended both race and nationality in a way that is achieved by very few."[70] Israeli Prime Minister Golda Meir noted that there was hardly anybody outside of Israel "who was so intimately connected" with the state from its very emergence.[71] The city of Los Angeles ordered flags flown at half-staff until after his funeral.

In its obituary, the *New York Times* wrote that Ralph Bunche

> could haggle, bicker, hairsplit, and browbeat, if necessary, and occasionally it was. But the art of his compromise lay in his seemingly boundless energy and the order and timing of his moves. His diplomatic skills—a masterwork in the practical application of psychology—became legendary at the United Nations . . . as such, he was the highest American figure in the world organization and, incidentally, the most prominent black man of his era whose stature did not derive chiefly from racial militance or endeavors specifically on behalf of his race.[72]

In an editorial, the *Times* called him the "personification of the United Nations." Yet the paper noted that it was sadly ironic that he died just as the UN stood "helplessly by at the outbreak of a new and savage war in Asia."[73] The *Los Angeles Times*, in a tribute to one of the city's most prominent sons, described him as simultaneously a symbol of Black achievement and a reminder of "the unfinished business of equality."[74] Above all, the newspaper wrote, Ralph Bunche "demonstrated and elevated the dignity of man."

His funeral, on a windy, bright, sunny winter day, was held at the Riverside Church on the Upper West Side of Manhattan. George H. W. Bush, Henry Kissinger, head of the NAACP Roy Wilkins, Governor of New York Nelson Rockefeller, Mayor of New York City John Lindsay, and a congeries of politicians, diplomats, and friends were in attendance. In a nod to his long-standing love of music, Leontyne Price sang a cappella. In his eulogy, U Thant called his long-time aide and consigliere a "practical optimist" whose life was devoted to the endless quest for peace.[75]

These paeans were expected for a man who had held enormous stature in American, indeed global, life for over two decades. None of the major obituaries, however, noted that just a year before his death, the General Assembly promulgated what would later be seen as a milestone in the evolution of the organization. In the fall of 1970, at the twenty-fifth anniversary session, it passed the Declaration on Friendly Relations and Co-Operation. The Declaration called out colonial rule as a violation of the foundational premises of the UN Charter. Specifically, it decried "the subjection of peoples to alien subjugation, domination and exploitation," opposed foreign intervention in the domestic affairs of independent states, and pronounced that the principles of equal rights and self-determination of peoples constituted a significant contribution to international law.[76]

The resolution, passed without any dissenting vote, was largely the product of the many new members of the UN who had recently escaped colonial rule. From an original fifty member states, the organization had nearly tripled in size by December 1971, straining the capacity of the campus built on the East River of New York. The presence of these numerous new and independent states at the United Nations, more than any of the eloquent expressions of admiration and respect from presidents and prime ministers pouring in from around the world, was perhaps the finest testament to the life and work of Ralph Johnson Bunche.

EPILOGUE

When in the course of human events it becomes necessary for one people to dis-
solve the political bands which connected them with another, and to assume
among the powers of the earth, the separate and equal station to which the Laws
of Nature and of Nature's God entitle them ...
> —American Declaration of Independence, July 4, 1776

In no more than two decades between the 1950s and 1970s, vast colonial em-
pires that had taken centuries to assemble almost totally disappeared.
> —Robert Aldrich and John Connell, *The Last Colonies* (1998)

In the fall of 1932, on board the *Foucauld*, Ralph Bunche looked out at the approaching coast of French West Africa. Stepping onto the dock upon arrival, for the first time he set foot in a European colony. The experience was bewildering, fascinating, and disturbing all at once. One thing was clear, however. Whites were on the top of the hierarchy and Blacks were subordinate. While much was new to him on his initial foray into the prewar colonial world, this feature was unfortunately all too familiar. Mordecai Johnson, the president of Howard University, had chastised him for "going all the way to Africa to find a problem."[1] Yet Bunche's study of colonial rule was simply shining a light on the same problem that interested many of his Howard colleagues. Racial subordination was a rampant feature of the prewar era, and in European empire he found both a subject and a cause that would animate his life's work while resonating with his own life story.

Bunche began his doctoral research on colonial governance as the late-19th-century Scramble for Africa was still in living memory. Born in 1903, he had come of age at the height of global white supremacy. Europeans had conquered nearly the entire continent of Africa, and few seriously expected political independence to come anytime soon. Colonialism's global expansion was rooted in power disparities and power rivalries. Yet it was still often viewed, or at least couched, as a mission of good works. As one French leader put it, colonial rule was "liberating the primitive societies from the great calamities which are ravaging them and which are called: disease, ignorance, superstition, tyranny."[2] It was also a form of racial domination, making it a twin to the Jim Crow laws ascendant throughout a large swath of America—though Bunche in the 1930s was firmly of the belief that economics, and not race, provided the true foundation for both phenomena. "Racialism," he wrote at the time, "is a myth, albeit a dangerous one, for it is a perfect stalking horse for selfish group politics and camouflage for brutal economic exploitation."[3]

The League of Nations system he sought to study in French West Africa was predicated on the notion that some peoples, "not yet able to stand by themselves," required continuing foreign rule.[4] The eurocentric "standard of civilization" in international law had long provided an answer to who would offer the necessary tutelage. To be sure, by the interwar period white world supremacy was increasingly questioned in intellectual circles. Even avowed racists such as Lothrop Stoddard, author of *The Rising Tide of Color: The Threat against White World-Supremacy*, shifted to writing books about finance and debating, rather than simply dismissing, leading Black thinkers such as W. E. B. Du Bois.[*] Soon bestsellers such as Wendell Willkie's *One World* would make the case for "equality of opportunity for every race and every nation."[5] Yet even for those observers, like Bunche, who believed colonial rule was morally wrong, the notion that African or Asian colonies were necessarily ready to govern their own affairs was far from widespread.

---

[*] Du Bois's writing was now regularly appearing in establishment journals such as *Foreign Affairs*, the influential house organ of the Council on Foreign Relations, on topics such as colonial rule, the future of Liberia, and the "inter-racial implications of the Ethiopian crisis" of 1935.

The unraveling of European empire nonetheless occurred with surprising speed in the wake of the Allied victory in the Second World War. The reasons for its fleet demise are manifold and often raise as many questions as they answer. Why was it that ideas of self-determination took root widely in the 1940s and 1950s when, just decades before, they had been largely dismissed outside the context of Eastern Europe? Why did racial equality become at least a *norm* that many Western nations subscribed to, after decades, even centuries, of white domination that was justified, and at times even valorized, as a form of natural hierarchy and civilizational altruism? Scholars have analyzed these questions, but as with nearly all such questions, the answers are often murky and intersecting. One thing can be said with certainty, however: Ralph Bunche's professional home, the new United Nations, became a critical arena in which these complex trends played out.

From the earliest days of the wartime planning for the UN, Bunche believed the organization could be an important force for good in the fight against the injustice of colonial rule. He believed this even as he himself saw some positive dimensions to colonialism. "It cannot be questioned," he claimed in the runup to the San Francisco conference, that colonization has brought "much progress" to dependent peoples.[6] But he was convinced empires nonetheless had to be rolled back. His first major task as part of the State Department wartime planning team was to develop a system of trusteeship to supplant the League of Nations mandates he had studied in French West Africa. The UN trusteeship system ultimately aided only a discrete set of colonial territories. Yet it helped to establish and entrench a set of norms and practices around what the UN Charter called non-self-governing territories that had an impact well beyond the confines of the limited number of trusteeships. That impact was then felt—and extended—in the UN General Assembly. Bunche did not foresee how significant the General Assembly would prove to be to the process of decolonization; in fact, almost no one did. Yet once the General Assembly began to address the issue of colonial rule, it became the political center of a rising effort to end empire.

Led by highly motivated actors such as India, the General Assembly showed both creativity and persistence in how it seized agenda-setting and oversight powers. The General Assembly had been intended to largely be a place of talk, not action: what Senator Arthur Vandenberg had once called "the world's townhall meeting place."[7] But it became something more with regard to decolonization. Creating a strong tailwind behind these efforts was the new power configuration of the postwar world, in which the United States and the Soviet Union thoroughly dominated the traditional European powers. Both superpowers, for varying reasons, saw traditional colonies—the so-called blue water or overseas territories—as generally inimical to their interests, even as they held onto their own conquered and adjacent lands. The Cold War had complex implications for decolonization. But the fact that great power status now depended more on nuclear capabilities than colonial assets, and that the chief protagonists often portrayed themselves as allies of the newly independent nations, fostered the spread of independence. The rise (or return) of free trade in the West, pushed along by American preferences, also rendered traditional colonies less valuable and, as a result, generally less worth fighting over. Struggling to right their own ships in these unfamiliar geopolitical waters, some European powers readily let go of their colonies, whereas others clung on bitterly, at least to particular territories, such as Algeria or Angola.[8]

As decolonization took root, it created a ratchet effect. Newly independent states eagerly joined the UN, seeking to bolster and cement their newfound sovereign status. Once there, they became part of the diverse but rapidly growing bloc of former colonies. As the "Third World" grew in size and power, it used the General Assembly, with its one-nation/one-vote structure, to critique the colonial powers. Here, too, the Cold War enabled change; by quashing Franklin Delano Roosevelt's vision of a great power police force, the superpower standoff in the Security Council naturally shifted more power and energy to the General Assembly, "the stronghold," in influential Egyptian international lawyer George Abi-Saab's words, "of the Small powers."[9]

Ralph Bunche viewed this more activist General Assembly favorably, in part because he felt the veto of the permanent five members of the Security Council was a "big defect" of the UN Charter.[10] He saw the General Assembly's rising importance and authority as a useful corrective. By insisting on taking the UN Charter's language seriously, and diligently using the tools at their disposal, the anticolonial faction pushed and pushed further as the dam broke. While there were notable holdouts, such as Portugal, by the end of Bunche's career European empire had essentially collapsed. Even by 1958, with much of the decolonization process still to unfold, the émigré American historian Hans Kohn could write that the future observer "may regard as the greatest 'revolution' of the twentieth century not Lenin's overthrow of the short-lived free regime in Russia in November 1917 but the less conspicuous . . . and yet more far-reaching process which brought Europe's four hundred years old dominion of the globe to an end."[11]

THE FIGHT TO END EMPIRE THREADS together many facets of Ralph Bunche's life: as a scholar, policymaker, diplomat, and even civil rights campaigner. As the process of decolonization accelerated in the late 1950s, Bunche, by now a major figure in the United Nations, was increasingly focused on ensuring that new or nascent states received the guidance they needed—and the aid they often required as political factions, within and without these new states, used or threatened violence to achieve their aims. Bunche certainly believed in self-determination. But he was hardly rosy-eyed about it; to work, he was sure, independence required internationalism. Yet his career was not defined simply by his effort to bring justice to governance in a peaceful and measured manner. He was by nature a pragmatist and a problem-solver. When in 1941, with war looming, he took a fateful step and joined the Roosevelt administration's early intelligence bureau, he entered a world of politics and policy. He did this because he saw Nazism as a grave danger and categorically rejected the view that, as he put it, "the war is a white man's war and a good thing for the Negro."[12]

Bunche's patriotism and affinity for American values drew him into foreign affairs. But they also made him a perfect vehicle for postwar liberals, eager to see in his success signs that gradualism and integration worked. Despite the oppression he and other Black people faced, he still thought America the best model there was and integration the only path forward. Indeed, this was a view he consistently espoused throughout his career. "I seek total integration," he wrote toward the end of his life, "which means to me the Negro taking his place in the very mainstream of American life."[13] In a 1963 speech, he declared that he stood "firmly and unflinchingly" as an American.[†] "This is my country; my ancestors and I helped build it . . . I am determined to fight for what is mine."[14] American democracy, he proclaimed as early as 1940, "is bad enough. But in the mad world of today I love it, and I will fight to preserve it."[15]

To do that, Bunche left academia and entered government. This turned out to be an arena in which he excelled and thrived. He had been a prodigious writer while at Harvard and Howard, yet his scholarship, while well regarded, never had the impact of his work outside academia. Indeed, while Bunche was a respected professor during the 1930s he seemed to write far more than he actually published, and some of his better-known publications, such as his short Marxist-inflected book *A World View of Race*, he later repudiated.

Perhaps this pattern revealed that he was ultimately more interested in practicalities than puzzles. Once in government he threw himself into the policy challenges he found there with the same "athleticism," to borrow his colleague Alain Locke's vaguely damning description of Bunche, that he had shown at Howard, Harvard, and even UCLA.[16] Ever the competitor, he sought to win, whether the opponent was a rival team or, more often, a thorny problem that appeared to resist any resolution. As one of his Harvard classmates noticed early on, he was indeed an optimist, but mainly because he had the confidence of the successful.

His gift for problem solving really became apparent once he joined the United Nations. He surely could have had a successful career in the State Department, or likely any number of other settings. But the UN offered an unusual perch in the 1940s. While by no means free of racial discrimination, the UN was a unique institution. It had no dominant national culture and, over time, it became a strikingly diverse workplace, especially in the context of midcentury America. That—and its location in New York—was

---

[†] Compare Malcolm X, who in his famous *The Ballot or the Bullet* speech in 1964, declared "No, I'm not an American. I'm one of the 22 million black people who are the victims of Americanism."

reason enough for Bunche and his family to seize the opportunity to move north from the segregation of Washington, DC. Immersed in a multicultural setting long before the word came into common usage—and one that was decidedly a mosaic, not a melting pot—Bunche could see, in very tangible ways, that diverse peoples could work together for common ends. Toward the end of his life he wavered in his belief in humankind's essential brotherhood, calling instead for simple "coexistence." Yet he did not change his basic view that peace was possible. As he told the *New Yorker*, "I've always had faith in the essential goodness of people. I think that basically man is good. He can be misled, but he's *good*."[17] These sentiments fed his commitment to UN peacemaking as readily as his belief in the vision of integration offered by Martin Luther King, Jr.

Bunche's move to the UN also reflected his appetite for challenge and change. The UN offered a novel set of situations in which negotiation, personal persuasion, and sound political instincts could make a real difference. His analytical skills had long been lauded by colleagues, as had his prodigious work ethic. Yet what really made him stand out was his ability to read people, create trust, find compromise, and craft solutions that all could live with. In the UN he was able to wield these skills to great effect. In doing so, he was present at the creation of a number of key practices that deeply shaped the impact of the organization on the postwar era and helped make the UN, as he believed, indispensable to our world. Two stand out, and in practice both relate to and often grew out of the process of decolonization he championed.‡

The first is conflict mediation. It was his skill at finding agreement that ultimately turned Ralph Bunche from a successful but largely anonymous diplomat into a national and even global star. Mediation by an outside party was not new to international politics when he sat down with Israelis and Arabs at the Hotel des Roses in Rhodes. Indeed, Teddy Roosevelt had won

‡ At the very end of this project, I came upon a scrap of paper in an old notebook of Bunche's that had *Autobiography* written across the top. The remainder read: *Chapters on: The Formative Years; On the Racial Front (Desegregation); Decolonization; On Behalf of Peace.* The book was never written, but this breakdown suggests he, too, saw decolonization and peacekeeping/peacemaking as the twin throughlines of his UN career.

the Nobel Peace Prize almost a half century earlier for negotiating the end of the war between Japan and Russia. Elihu Root, American secretary of state and international lawyer, similarly won the prize in 1912 for his work on conflict mediation and arbitration. Mediation and its sister, arbitration, were essential parts of the late-19th-century effort of international lawyers to use process and reason to resolve disputes between nations—an effort that rapidly ran into the rocky shoals of the 20th century and seemed, by midcentury, to strike many as utopian.

Yet what Bunche achieved in Rhodes revitalized international mediation. And it was significant not only for the warring peoples of the Middle East but also for the larger postwar project of international cooperation through multilateral institutions. By showing that the new United Nations could act impartially and facilitate peace even in the most difficult of conflicts, he provided proof of concept for an aspect of the organization that had received little attention at Dumbarton Oaks and San Francisco.§

Bunche's effort in the Middle East, born of a deliberate move by one great power to rid itself of a seemingly intractable colonial problem, was backed by the Security Council but ultimately implemented by the UN Secretariat itself. In the wake of his success, the UN became a more active global mediator, often with Bunche playing the central role. Cyprus, Bahrain, Yemen, even Congo were all examples in which he actively sought to defuse disputes and alleviate conflict. While some postcolonial conflicts, such as Vietnam, were simply too large—or too hot—for any mediation to work, the fact that mediation was ineffective in certain settings should not obscure its larger utility for postwar order. But it does suggest that there are real limits to its power. Indeed, while the Middle East may have been the source of Bunche's fame as a mediator, the UN's centrality to the region rapidly dropped in the decades after his death, especially with regard to Israel and the Palestinians.

---

§ To be sure, the UN Charter refers to "mediation, conciliation, arbitration," and other dispute settlement methods in Article 33. But these are contained in the passages on the Security Council, not the Secretariat. The heart of the Security Council's powers, as envisioned by Roosevelt, Churchill, and Stalin, had been the policing role of the permanent members. Mediation was a bit of an afterthought.

As one scholar has noted, neither at Camp David (1978) nor at Oslo (1993 and 1995) was the UN a presence: "Bunche would have been sorrowful."[18]

He may have been more pleased by a different and quite surprising legacy of his landmark mediation. In 1992, after years of increasingly deadly violence in Los Angeles, the leaders of various warring street gangs sought to negotiate a truce. When Anthony Perry, one of the gang members, began to explore models, he came across the Israeli-Egyptian Armistice Accord negotiated in Rhodes. Reading about it in the library of the University of Southern California, he immediately saw parallels: the two conflicts, though thousands of miles apart, were both "fights over land rights, turf, and grudges people just won't let go."[19] Perry thought that using an existing and famous international truce as a template would lend seriousness and attention to their effort. He grew even more convinced when, to his amazement, he discovered that the author of the Middle East armistice had grown up just a few miles from Watts, the location of the gangs in question. The *Los Angeles Times* covered the unusual connection to Bunche's earlier effort, as did *Jet* magazine. What was ultimately dubbed the Watts Gang Truce was lauded in the city and beyond and led to an "almost immediate" reduction in violence.[20] The gang truce held for several years, though, like its earlier Middle East counterpart, it eventually and unfortunately was overtaken by larger events.

Ralph Bunche's stature as the father of modern conflict mediation made him famous. Yet the second advance, that of peacekeeping, was clearly his proudest achievement. Peacekeeping grew from its origins in the early UN Trust Supervision Organization and the post–Suez Crisis UN Emergency Force to a robust practice that became central to the organization's mission. Multinational peacekeeping was also not wholly unprecedented. Yet it was also not clearly contemplated by the UN Charter or its creators. Many have argued that peace operations fit in neither Chapter VI or Chapter VII of the Charter's language about the Security Council and its powers. As Bunche himself remarked, peacekeeping falls "somewhere between" the two, and indeed is sometimes referred to as a "Chapter VI and a half" procedure.[21]

Born of necessity (Secretary General Boutros Boutros-Ghali later explained that it "had to be invented"), peacekeeping proved very useful in a Cold War world.[22] And it became even more useful after the Cold War ended. Peacekeeping became so common that the special budget for it typically dwarfs the regular budget for everything else the UN does. During Bunche's career, a total of ten missions were created.[23] By the 1990s, a peak period for UN peacekeeping, on average nearly four missions were established each and every year. In recent years, the pace has slowed somewhat—since 2000, the UN has averaged closer to one new mission a year—but peacekeeping's political importance has not waned, even as controversy has often ensued. Peacekeeping has been shown to have a large, positive, and statistically significant effect on reducing violence. Moreover, "the power of peacekeeping is all the more striking given that the UN tends to intervene in the toughest cases."[24] In his introduction to the 2015 report of the High-Level Independent Panel on Peace Operations, Secretary General Ban Ki-moon rightly called peacekeeping "the most visible face of the Organization."[25]

The birth of peacekeeping in the postwar era reflected significant changes in geopolitics. Newly independent states were proliferating; by definition they had new and untested ruling coalitions. The Cold War often intensified power struggles within these states, as the Congo Crisis tragically demonstrated. The UN Charter at first appeared ill equipped to address these problems; it was designed to outlaw aggressive war by one state against another, not police internecine conflicts. Yet outside of a few notable instances, such as the 1956 Suez intervention, the 1961 invasion of the Portuguese colony of Goa by India, or the 1990 invasion of Kuwait by Iraq, the actual invasion or seizure of territory by one state from another—a hallmark of previous centuries—became relatively rare after 1945.[26]

In its place arose a different form of conflict. What international lawyers call "non-international armed conflict" is warfare that occurs within a given state, not between states, though it may and often does involve outside forces and militias. Beginning in the 1960s, the number of civil wars and secessionist movements grew dramatically, peaking in 1991 with over fifty such internal conflicts ongoing.[27] The most recent data show closer to thirty such wars occurring today. Many of these conflicts took place in former colonial territories. And because the resulting fighting could and often did spill over into neighboring states, the international community took a strong interest. This could lead to an invitation from a challenged central government to external allies for help—perhaps, in the 1960s especially, to one of the Cold War antagonists—but increasingly it led to a UN peacekeeping mission. While this trend thrust the UN into a new set of challenges, it also illustrated the value of the organization for this purpose. (There is some evidence that the Security Council has been less likely to send troops to places where the permanent members have "strong ties," suggesting that the leading powers do not want peacekeepers to meddle in areas where their interests are directly affected—an implicit acknowledgment of peacekeeping's power.[28]) As Bunche explained in 1967, the UN "has had the courage the League of Nations lacked—to step in and tackle the buzz saw."[29]

While peacekeeping missions have been concentrated in the postcolonial world, they have also increasingly been staffed *by* the postcolonial world. The initial peacekeepers that Bunche gathered and deployed came from a wide array of states that nonetheless reflected the UN's early Western bias. From the 1990s onward, however, most peacekeepers have come from outside the West. Had he lived to see it, the late Brian Urquhart noted in the early 2000s, Bunche "would have been appalled at the current tendency of Western governments to allot peacekeeping duties more and more exclusively to third-world governments."[30] Still, major powers often play a role in peace-building referred to within the UN system as "friends": states with an interest in the outcome of a conflict. In a small group, and in coordination with the secretary general, they help backstop and nudge the process of peace forward. As former Assistant Secretary General Michael Doyle has written, through the mechanism of a friends group the UN's "scarce attention and even scarcer resources can be supplemented by the diplomacy, finances, and clout of powerful, interested actors."[31] The UN in turn lends legitimacy to their interventions, taking something that was in the past often unilateral and self-aggrandizing and checking its worst tendencies.

As one analysis argued in 1982, even before the huge uptick in peacekeeping of the 1990s:

The United Nations may have been shoved to the sidelines long ago when it came to the political ordering of the world. And in recent years, many Americans may have become disillusioned with the sterile debates and double standards of the General Assembly. Yet the United Nations has undeniably chalked up one proud success—peacekeeping in conflicts where the vital interests of the great powers were not directly involved.[32]

In short, the UN proved a very useful vehicle for managing the postwar politics of peace, even if it worked quite imperfectly at times. (Indeed, as Bunche presciently asked in 1964, "how can a successfully functioning United Nations peace force ever be withdrawn without disastrous consequences?")[33] In recent decades peacekeeping has been criticized for overly reflecting the desires of the Security Council and its permanent five members, for entrenching great power control over small states, for wreaking havoc on poor populations—such as the tragedy of Haiti and cholera in the 2000s—and for malfeasance by peacekeepers themselves, from petty smuggling to sexual abuse. Peacekeeping has even been accused of unduly and dangerously prolonging conflicts, allowing them to fester and recur.[34] Nonetheless, the political utility of peacekeeping in a crisis often renders it an attractive, even irresistible, option. This is one reason the Security Council, frequently depicted as stalemated in the postwar era, in fact turned again and again to authorize peacekeeping missions. This gave the organization a greater utility than many appreciated. As early as 1962, one analyst argued that the "traditional policy" of the US could be summed up in a single sentence: " 'If possible, do it through the UN.' "[35] The late former American ambassador to the UN and secretary of state Madeline Albright famously put it this way: if the UN "didn't exist, we would have to invent it."[36]

MEDIATION AND PEACEKEEPING HAVE NO NECESSARY connection to decolonization. Yet because the retreat of colonial rule was so often imbued with political strife, the United Nations was frequently forced to step in to try to manage, dampen, and even avert conflict where possible. It is not surprising that Africa, the most colonized continent, has also been the location of the largest number of peacekeeping missions. While the Western Hemisphere has had eight missions total and Europe and Asia each nine, Africa has had twenty-five.[37]

The fragility of many postcolonial states was apparent almost from the start. As decolonization gathered steam, Frantz Fanon, the influential theorist of colonialism, became "obsessed with the 'curse of independence': the possibility that nationhood in the Global South, though inevitable, could become an 'empty shell,' a receptacle for ethnic and tribal antagonisms, ultranationalism, chauvinism, and racism."[38] Fanon's fears were sadly often realized in the decades to come. Some postcolonial states transitioned well. But others became cauldrons of internal violence or—and—subject to rapacious rule by tyrannical regimes who, either through kleptocracy or simple mismanagement, impoverished their peoples. Congo was perhaps the most arresting example. Joseph Mobutu's three decades of brutal dictatorship and garish looting of the national wealth came on the heels of nearly a century of horrific Belgian rule and was almost immediately followed by a metastasizing conflict in the early 21st century that some have called Africa's Great War.[39]

Ralph Bunche shared some of Fanon's concerns about the postcolonial world, though it is not clear that the two ever met or that he read Fanon's masterpiece, *The Wretched of the Earth*.** Bunche began his academic career sharing the elite view that African independence was a long way off. On the ground in French West Africa in the 1930s, he puzzled over what would become of the peoples there, who he saw as whipsawed by the dazzling influx of European technology yet tied to traditional political and social structures.[40] Over time he nonetheless became a firm believer that calls for restraint until colonies were "ready" for independence were simply wrong, and in any event untenable. "When people are seeking freedom, they're always impatient," he told Eleanor Roosevelt in 1960 on her televised talk show. "And I think that's good."[41]

** Fanon died as the Congo Crisis was unfolding, just a few months after Dag Hammarskjold's deadly plane crash near Katanga.

Yet Bunche also believed that independence in many cases needed to be pursued deliberately and carefully. Most importantly, it should be sought with the assistance of the international community. It was the UN that could square the circle of the yearning for independence with the reality that some societies—for a host of reasons ranging from imposed and arbitrary borders to European intransigence to a lack of national capacity—were poorly equipped to take the reins of government right away. The Congo Crisis illustrated the sometimes acute need for UN assistance in state-building that Bunche championed. Belgium had done almost nothing to prepare Congo for self-rule and in fact had worked assiduously to ensure there were few educated Congolese trained to step in and administer the vast new state. Even as little as two years before the handover of power, many assumed independence was decades away. Bunche, like many observers, knew this lack of preparation and expertise was a potentially serious problem—it was one reason Eleanor Roosevelt had almost laughed on live television at the prospect of Congo's sudden independence.

Yet he also saw an opportunity. To Secretary General Dag Hammarskjold, in the days before independence, he wrote that the new Congolese leaders such as Patrice Lumumba were very friendly to the UN, though they "know little or nothing about us."[42] As he arrived in Leopoldville in the summer of 1960, in the midst of the great Year of Africa, Bunche saw his role as to educate the new leadership on what the UN could do and to ensure that the UN's technical, political, and, in the end, even military assistance could be brought to bear to help smooth out the bumps on the road to self-determination. This was a role the UN—and Bunche—would play often as dozens of new states struggled to find their footing in the postwar world.

This process continued long after his death. Years later, the UN would even assume the role of sovereign in some cases (a role that had been suggested in Congo in the aftermath of the summer of 1960, but never implemented). In East Timor in 1999, following decades of Indonesian occupation and centuries of Portuguese colonization, the UN took over the task of governing the territory, creating what some called "The United Nations Kingdom of East Timor."[43] Following popular referenda and the writing of a constitution, East Timor became independent—and a member of the UN—in 2002. The UN's assistance to postcolonial states varied widely; East Timor, while not the only example of direct UN governance, was the subject of a far more comprehensive program than most other cases of aid and advice. Were these efforts the *mission civilisatrice*, reborn? Perhaps, but certainly in a very different form.[44] These tangible forms of assistance were also typically flanked by more intangible boosts. In particular, UN membership provided an important symbol of sovereignty to states eager to shed their earlier subordinate status. Independence and statehood did not depend on joining the UN. But to many postcolonial leaders the organization offered validation, protection, and a chance—especially collectively—to have a voice in shaping the postwar world and its emerging set of rules.

To be sure, much of this was quite literally about voice. The advances were largely rhetorical in nature: the UN was deliberately designed to make sure small states had limited power. Yet the power of rhetoric—the ability to shape and develop new norms of international behavior—was a form of influence and authority that Roosevelt, Stalin, and Churchill, sitting in Yalta in 1945 and casting the contours of the new UN as their forces advanced upon Berlin and Tokyo, may not have fully appreciated. With the Security Council often stymied by the Cold War in its envisioned role of policeman of the world, the General Assembly's seemingly feeble rhetorical capabilities proved more potent than many expected. Some of this was exercised through relatively mundane processes aimed at revamping and codifying key aspects of international law. Yet through more ambitious efforts such as the landmark Resolution 1514 of 1960, the "Declaration on the Granting of Independence to Colonial Countries and Peoples," the new group of young states also sought to delineate right and wrong in the realm of governance.

Not all of these efforts worked, especially when they touched on economics rather than politics. Still, the colonial powers, many of whom found their own national power decisively weakened in the 1950s, no longer seemed to have much appetite for fighting back on the core issues. Indeed, they rarely dared to even vote against the resolutions that condemned colonialism itself, preferring instead the quiet approach of simply abstaining. The result was substantial space for the postcolonial states to begin, albeit imperfectly, to build "an anti-imperial world order," one in which "colonial domination was illegitimate for the first time in modern international society."[45]

That this accomplishment took root as the civil rights movement gathered steam in America only served to highlight the connections Bunche saw between racial injustice at home and abroad. The civil rights leader he most admired, and often joined forces with until his tragic murder, was Martin Luther King, Jr. King's approach of nonviolence and normative change deeply appealed to Bunche, even as it was increasingly challenged by those who thought, echoing Mao Zedong, that true political power grows out of the barrel of a gun.

FOR RALPH BUNCHE, AS PRAGMATIC AS he was, these projects of normative change were critical. The lines between legitimate and illegitimate, between respect and disdain, were always central to him. During the still-dark days of the Second World War, as the Allies began to think about a brighter future, he gave a speech about the ultimate purpose of a postwar peace organization. He argued that the plans for international organization then underway were "all means and not ends." The objective must be "the good life for all people." That good life, he argued, necessarily included peace, security, and education. But in an unusual turn of phrase that, while tapping into an important element of equality, perhaps unwittingly said as much about his own experiences and psyche as the needs and desires of most people, Bunche raised one end above all others: "the right to walk with dignity on the world's great boulevards."[46]

A few years later, in the wake of his successful effort at peacemaking in Rhodes, he gave a fuller take on what he believed was required in a truly just world:

A just world . . . is a world in which racial and religious bigotry are universally outlawed; a world in which all peoples, irrespective of race or creed are accepted as equals in a bond of human kinship; a world in which discrimination, segregation, under-privilege, imperialism and colonialism will have become the unsavory relics of a dark age fortunately past.[47]

In some ways Ralph Bunche found the aim at home, in America, easier to describe. "As a Negro," he explained in 1954, "my demand is very simple. I just want to be an American."[48]

NOTES

Preface

1. 22d Academy Awards, Best Picture presentation. https://www.youtube.com/watch?v=D1L-584xzMI
2. Ben Keppel, *The Work of Democracy* (Cambridge, MA: Harvard University Press, 1995), at 70.
3. "The Talk of the Town," *The New Yorker*, January 1, 1972, at 15.
4. Keppel, *The Work of Democracy*, at 13.
5. Robert Harris, "Ralph Bunche and Afro-American Participation in Decolonization," in Michael Krenn (ed.), *The African-American Voice in US Foreign Policy Since World War II* (New York: Routledge, 1999), at 172.
6. Ralph Bunche, speech at Fisk University, Nashville, Tennessee, May 5, 1956. Schomburg Center for the Study of Black Culture, Bunche Archives, Box 15/1 A-1.
7. Samantha Power, "United It Wobbles," *Washington Post*, January 7, 2007.
8. Keppel, *Work of Democracy*, at 89.
9. Bunche, speech at NAACP Freedom Fulfillment Conference, Washington, DC. March 10, 1954, Box 14B, Schomburg Center for Black Culture Archives.
10. Joan Liu, recollection, no date, UCLA Archives, Collection 364, Box 2, Folder 12.
11. Bunche, notes, no date (but likely 1968), UN Archives, Box 370/39/16.
12. Bunche, notes, June 14, 1966, UN Archives, Box 370/38/1.
13. "The Faith of Ralph Bunche," *New York Times*, December 10, 1971, at 42.
14. https://www.un.org/en/chronicle/article/preparing-next-generation-join-conference-table

Chapter 1

1. UCLA Ralph Bunche Archives Digital Collection, "The Ideal Scrapbook," https://digital.library.ucla.edu/catalog/ark:/21198/zz0009gvc3
2. "The Ideal Scrapbook."
3. Clipping, newspaper unknown, UCLA Bunche Archive, Box 457, Folder 1.
4. Ralph Bunche, dedication speech at UCLA for Bunche Hall, May 23, 1969, UN Archives, S-1078/50/12.

5. Bunche's name was initially Ralph Bunch; he added the "e" and the middle name Johnson later. Jane Johnson Taylor, *One American Family: A Personal Family History* (unpublished family chronicle), 1988, at 133 (Gift of Peter Taylor).

6. Taylor, *One American Family*, at 129, uses 1903 and is probably decisive. UCLA's plaque on Bunche Hall uses 1904.

7. Charles P. Henry, *Ralph Bunche: Model Negro or American Other?* (New York: New York University Press, 1999), at 11.

8. Bunche, note, no date, UCLA Archives, Collection 364, Box 3, Folder 7.

9. Taylor, *One American Family*, at 145.

10. Bunche was on the East Coast at the time. Bunche, notes, no date, UN Archives, Box 370/38/17.

11. Bunche, note, October 15, 1967, UN Archives, Box 370/38/5.

12. Bunche, "Nana," unpublished essay, no date, UN Archives, S-0852/1/11, at 1; Bunche, "My Most Unforgettable Character," *Reader's Digest*, September 1965, at 2.

13. Interview with Bunche, January 1, 1962, UN Radio Classics Series, UN Audiovisual Library C2036.

14. Bunche, "What America Means to Me," in Charles P. Henry (ed.), *Ralph J. Bunche: Selected Speeches and Writings* (Ann Arbor: University of Michigan Press, 1995), at 269.

15. Robert McFadden, "Dr Bunche of UN, Nobel Winner, Dies," *New York Times*, December 10, 1971, at 42.

16. Bunche, "Nana," at 8.

17. Bunche, "Nana," at 9.

18. Bunche, personal note, July 15, 1967, UN Archives, 370/38/5. Ben Keppel suggests that Bunche, like many of his generation, may have tended to scrub away the harsh edges of his early life, preferring a hazy nostalgia. Keppel, "Thinking Through a Life: Reconsidering the Origins of Ralph J. Bunche," *Journal of Negro Education*, 73, 2 (Spring 2004), at 118.

19. George Getze, "Bunche Takes Slap at Idea of UC Tuition," *Los Angeles Times*, February 11, 1967.

20. "Not Lonely for DC, Asserts Dr. Bunche," *Afro-American*, January 23, 1954.

21. Bunche, notes, no date (but after 1965); UCLA Bunche Archives, Box 20, Folder 3; "Nation Mourns Ralph Bunche," *New York Amsterdam News*, December 18, 1971.

22. Bunche, "Nana," at 3.

23. Bunche, "Memories," no date, UN Archives, Box 370/38/8; Bunche, "Nana," at 5. Bunche wrote that he had experienced relatively little racism as a child in Detroit and Albuquerque, where the discrimination, he claimed, was mainly aimed at Italians and Mexicans.

24. Cecilia Rasmussen, "Ralph Bunche Spent a Lifetime Battling Bias, Seeking Peace," *Los Angeles Times*, January 28, 2001.

25. The Talk of the Town, *The New Yorker*, January 1, 1972.

26. Brian Urquhart, *Ralph Bunche: An American Odyssey* (New York: Norton, 1993), at 441.

27. Bunche, dedication speech at UCLA for Bunche Hall, May 23, 1969, UN Archives, S-1078/50/12.

28. Bunche, "Nana," at 17; Talk of the Town, *The New Yorker*.

29. Keppel, "Reconsidering the Origins of Ralph J. Bunche," at 119.

30. Bunche to Ronald Hosie, *Daily Bruin*, April 21, 1966, UCLA Bunche Archives, Box 259, Folder 1; Bunche, notes, UN Archives S-1078, Box 50/12; Bunche, speech at the NAACP Freedom Fulfillment Conference, DC, March 10, 1954, Schomburg Center Bunche Archives, Box 14B.

31. Bunche, "The Young Negro," speech given in Los Angeles (location unknown), 1927, UCLA Bunche Archive, Box 339, Folder 4.

32. UCLA Academic Transcripts, UCLA Bunche Archive, Box 457, Folder 1.

33. Bunche, note, no date (but likely 1960s), UN Archives, 370/38/24.

34. William Levering Lewis, *W.E.B. Du Bois: The Fight for Equality and the American Century* (New York: Henry Holt, 2000), at 14.

35. Bunche, "That Man May Dwell in Peace," 1926, UCLA Bunche Archive, Box 339, Folder 3.

36. Benjamin Rivlin, "The Legacy of Ralph Bunche," in Benjamin Rivlin (ed.), *Ralph Bunche: The Man and His Times* (New York: Holmes and Meier, 1990), at 21.

37. Interview with Ralph Bunche, January 1, 1962, UN Radio Classics Series, UN Audiovisual Library, C2036.

38. Letter from Bunche to Du Bois, https://credo.library.umass.edu/cgi-bin/pdf.cgi?id=scua:mums312-b037-i302.

39. Urquhart, *Ralph Bunche*, at 43.

40. Urquhart, *Ralph Bunche*, at 373.

41. The Talk of the Town, *The New Yorker*.

42. Letter, Bunche to Rieber, October 26, 1927, UCLA Archives, Collection 364, Box 3, Folder 7.

43. Letter, Rieber to Bunche, December 13, 1927, UCLA Bunche Archives, Box 457, Folder 1.

44. Letter, Bunche to Hosie, *Daily Bruin*, April 21, 1966, UCLA Bunche Archives, Box 259, Folder 1.

45. Bunche, "Negro Political Philosophy," in Henry (ed.), *Selected Speeches and Writings*.

46. Bunche, "The Negro in Chicago Politics," *National Municipal Review*, May 1928. UCLA Bunche Archives, Box 393, Folder 5.

47. Henry, *Model Negro or American Other?*; see also Robert Vitalis, *White World Order, Black Power Politics* (Ithaca, NY: Cornell University Press, 2015) on the Howard school more generally.

48. "The Talk of the Town," *The New Yorker*.

49. Bunche, notes, no date, UN Archives, Box 370/38/24.

50. Jeffrey C. Stewart, *The New Negro: The Life of Alain Locke* (New York: Oxford University Press, 2018), at 669–670 (quoting Harold Lewis).

51. Bunche, "My Most Unforgettable Character," *Reader's Digest*, September 1965, at 6.

52. *Interview with Ralph Bunche*, UN Radio Classics Series.

53. Bunche to Vic Kelley, May 12, 1970, UCLA Archives, Collection 364, Box 3, Folder 7.

54. Phone interview, James Dandridge, Howard class of 1953, October 12, 2020. Dandridge later became a State Department official.

55. David Anthony, "Ralph Bunche and the Dawn of Africanist Scholarship," in Robert Hill and Edmond Keller (eds.), *Trustee for the Human Community: Ralph Bunche, the United Nations, and the Decolonization of Africa* (2010), at 19; Nathan Huggins, "Ralph Bunche the Africanist," in Rivlin, supra, at 72.

56. Bunche, PhD proposal draft, no date but likely 1932, UCLA Bunche Archives, Box 6, Folder 9.

57. Stewart, *The New Negro*, at 631.

58. Stewart, *The New Negro*, at 631, 645.

59. Raymond Buell, "The Destiny of East Africa," *Foreign Affairs*, 6, 3 (1928), at 408; Pearl T. Robinson, "Ralph Bunche the Africanist," in Robert Hill and Edmund Keller (eds.), *Trustee for the Human Community: Ralph J. Bunche, the United Nations, and the Decolonization of Africa* (Athens: Ohio University Press, 2010).

Chapter 2

1. Margaret Macmillan, *Peacemakers: The Paris Peace Conference of 1919 and Its Attempt to End War* (London: John Murray, 2001); Paul Kennedy, *The Parliament of Man: The Past, Present, and Future of the United Nations* (New York: Vintage Books, 2006).

2. Pitman Potter, "The Origins of the System of Mandates under the League of Nations," *American Political Science Review*, 16, 4 (1922).

3. Ted Widmer, "A Century Ago, the Modern Middle East Was Born," *New York Times*, December 25, 2019.

4. Susan Pedersen, *The Guardians: The League of Nations and the Crisis of Empire* (New York: Oxford University Press, 2015), at 1.

5. Gerrit Gong, *The Standard of Civilization in International Society* (New York: Oxford University Press, 1984); Nele Matz, "Civilization and the Mandate System under the League of Nations as Origin of Trusteeship," *Max Planck Yearbook of International Law* (Leyden, The Netherlands: Brill, 2005).

6. Anthony Pagden, *Peoples and Empires* (New York: Modern Library, 2003), at 109.

7. Pedersen, *Guardians*, at 24.

8. Alain Locke, "The Mandates System: A New Code of Empire," in Charles Moleworth (ed.), *The Works of Alain Locke* (New York: Oxford University Press, 2012).

9. Potter, "Origins," at 571.

10. Adom Getachew, *Worldmaking after Empire: The Rise and Fall of Self-Determination* (Princeton, NJ: Princeton University Press, 2019), at 22.

11. Benjamin Kidd, *The Control of the Tropics* (New York: Macmillan, 1898), at 56.

12. Frederick Lugard, "The White Man's Task in Tropical Africa," *Foreign Affairs* (October 1926).

13. Gail Gerhart, review of Lugard, "The Dual Mandate in Tropical Africa," *Foreign Affairs* (September/October 1997).

14. Partha Chatterjee, "The Legacy of Bandung," in *Bandung, Global History, and International Law* (Cambridge, UK: Cambridge University Press, 2017), at 668.

15. Herbert Gibbons, "The Place of the United States in a World Organization for the Maintenance of Peace," *Annals of the American Academia of Political and Social Science* (July 1921), at 85.

16. Makau Mutua, "Why Redraw the Map of Africa: A Legal and Moral Inquiry," *Michigan Journal of International Law*, 16 (1995), at 1120.

17. On the spread of the states system see, Hedley Bull and Adam Watson (eds.), *The Expansion of International Society* (London: Oxford University Press, 1984). This was an interactive and complex process, something Bull and Watson acknowledged (see Introduction, at 6). For differing accounts, see Antony Anghie, *Imperialism, Sovereignty, and the Making of International Law* (Cambridge, UK: Cambridge University Press, 2004); Getachew, *Worldmaking after Empire*.

18. Mutua, "Map of Africa," at 1114–1115.

19. Crawford Young, "The Heritage of Colonialism," in John Harbeson and Donald Rothschild (eds.), *Africa in World Politics* (Nashville, TN: Westview, 1991), at 19.

20. Bunche, prospectus draft, no date but likely 1932, UCLA Bunche Archives, Box 6, Folder 9, at 2.

21. Bunche, prospectus draft, supra.

22. Bunche to Rogers, June 11, 1932, UCLA Bunche Archives, Box 6, Folder 3.

23. Jeffrey C. Stewart, *The New Negro: The Life of Alain Locke* (New York: Oxford University Press, 2018), at 599.

24. Stewart, *New Negro*, at 645–647.

25. Evelyn Cunningham, "Race Leaders with Sex Appeal," *Pittsburgh Courier*, February 9, 1952.

26. Bunche, notes, July 1932, UCLA Bunche Archives, Box 281, Folder 2.

27. Bunche, notes, July 1932, UCLA Bunche Archives, Box 281, Folder 2.

28. Bunche, notes, July 1932, UCLA Bunche Archives, Box 281, Folder 2.

29. Brian Urquhart, *Ralph Bunche: An American Odyssey* (New York: Norton, 1993), at 52.

30. Bunche, Speech, Vermont Avenue Baptist Church, February 10, 1936, UCLA Bunche Archives, Box 339, Folder 17.

31. Edmund Keller and Robert Hill, "Introduction," in Robert Hill and Ed Keller (eds.), *Trustee for the Human Community: Ralph Bunche, The United Nations, and the Decolonization of Africa* (Athens: Ohio University Press, 2010), at xii.

32. Charles P. Henry, *Ralph Bunche: Model Negro or American Other?* (New York: New York University Press, 1999), at 67.

33. Martin Kilson, "Ralph Bunche: African American Intellectual," in Hill and Keller, *Trustee for the Human Community*, at 3.

34. Bunche to Ralph Jr., July 8, 1960, in UCLA Archives digital collection. https://oac.cdlib.org/ark:/13030/hb6n39p29w/?brand=oac4

35. Pedersen, *Guardians*, at 324.

36. Bunche, PhD dissertation, at 138.

37. Bunche, PhD dissertation, at 389.

38. Urquhart, *Ralph Bunche*, at 53.

39. Bunche, "Light on the Dark Continent," *The Southern Alumnus*, April 1935, UCLA, Bunche Archives, Box 393, Folder 9.

40. Bunche to C. A. Le Neuve, Director General of the Union Coloniale Francaise, June 13, 1933, UCLA Bunche Archives, Box 6, Folder 3.

41. Stewart, *New Negro*, at 361.

42. Pearl Robinson, "Ralph Bunche and African Studies," *African Studies Review*, 51, 1 (2008), at 4.

43. Robert Vitalis, *White World Order, Black Power Politics* (Ithaca, NY: Cornell University Press, 2015), at 14.

44. Wentworth Ofuatey-Kodjoe, professor of political science, City University of New York, interviewed in PBS, *Ralph Bunche: An American Odyssey* (Documentary, 2001).

45. Ralph Bunche, "French Educational Policy in Togoland and Dahomey" (1934), in Charles P. Henry, *Ralph Bunche: Selected Speeches and Writings* (Ann Arbor: University of Michigan Press, 1995), at 116.

46. Bunche, "French Educational Policy," at 117.

47. Bunche, "French Educational Policy," at 137.

48. Henry, *Model Negro or American Other?* at 73.

49. Bunche, "Light on the Dark Continent."

50. Bunche, "Triumph or Fiasco," *Race* (Summer 1936), at 93.

51. Letter to Lewis Hanke, in Robert Edgar (ed.), *An African-American in South Africa: The Travel Notes of Ralph J. Bunche* (Athens: Ohio University Press, 1992), at 36.

52. Woodson to Bunche, Letter, October 3, 1932, Bunche Archives, UCLA, Box 1.

53. Sue Donnelly, "An American in London: Ralph Bunche at LSE," 2017. https://blogs.lse.ac.uk/lsehistory/2017/10/09/an-american-in-london-ralph-bunche-at-lse

54. Urquhart, *Ralph Bunche*, at 63.

Chapter 3

1. Ralph Bunche, *A World View of Race* (Washington, DC: The Associates in Negro Folk Education, 1936), Bronze Booklet Series, at 38.

2. Charles P. Henry, *Ralph Bunche: Model Negro or American Other?* (New York: New York University Press, 1999), at 78.

3. Carlo Rosetti, "B. Malinowski, the Sociology of 'Modern Problems' in Africa and the 'Colonial Situation,'" *Cahiers d'Etudes Africaines*, 100 (1985), at 477.

4. Anthony Pagden, *Peoples and Empires* (New York: Modern Library, 2001), at 114.

5. Bunche to Herskovits, in Robert R. Edgar (ed.), *An African-American in South Africa: The Travel Notes of Ralph Bunche* (Athens: Ohio University Press, 1992).

6. Sue Donnelly, "An American in London: Ralph Bunche at LSE," 2017. https://blogs.lse.ac.uk/lsehistory/2017/10/09/an-american-in-london-ralph-bunche-at-lse

7. Brian Urquhart, *Ralph Bunche: An American Odyssey* (New York: Norton, 1993), at 67.

8. Henry, *Model Negro or American Other?*, at 78.

9. Ben Keppel, *The Work of Democracy* (Cambridge, MA: Harvard University Press, 1995), at 69.

10. Urquhart, *Ralph Bunche*, at 71.

11. Edgar (ed.), *An African-American in South Africa*, at 16.

12. Edgar (ed.), *An African-American in South Africa*, at 53.

13. Bunche, Remarks at Morgan College, March 22, 1939, UCLA Bunche Archives, Box 340, Folder 14.

14. Bunche, "An Analysis of the Political, Economic, and Social Status of the Non-European Peoples in South Africa" (no date, but 1941–1944), UCLA Bunche Archives, Box 57. Folder 3.

15. Edgar (ed.), *An African-American in South Africa*, at 14.

16. Edgar (ed.), *An African-American in South Africa*, at 22, 121.

17. Edgar (ed.), *An African-American in South Africa*, at 63, 54.

18. Bunche, Proposal to the Social Science Research Council, 1938, UCLA Archives, Box 17, Folder 3.

19. UCLA Archives, Bunche Diary, Box 279, Folder 2.

20. Ralph Bunche, "The Irua Ceremony among the Kikyu of Kiambu District, Kenya," *Journal of Negro History*, 26, 46 (1941).

21. Bunche, "The Irua Ceremony," at 52.

22. Urquhart, *Ralph Bunche*, at 80.

23. Letter to Dean Downing, in Souad Halila, *The Intellectual Development and Diplomatic Career of Ralph Bunche: The Afro-American, Africanist, and Internationalist*, PhD Dissertation, USC, 1988, at 64.

24. Henry, *Model Negro or American Other?*, at 86.

25. "The Talk of the Town," *The New Yorker*, January 1, 1972.

26. Robert A. Dentler, "The Political Situation and Power Prospects of African Americans in Gunnar Myrdal's Era and Today," in Obie Clayton (ed.), *An American Dilemma Revisited: Race Relations in a Changing World* (New York: Russell Sage, 1996).

27. Henry, *Model Negro or American Other?*, at 93.

28. Benjamin Rivlin, "The Legacy of Ralph Bunche," in Benjamin Rivlin (ed.), *Ralph Bunche: The Man and His Times* (New York: Holmes and Meier, 1990), at 21.

29. Henry, *Model Negro or American Other?*, at 94.

30. Henry, *Model Negro or American Other?*, at 107.

31. Ralph Bunche, "The Negro in the Political Life of the US," *Journal of Negro Education* (1941), reprinted in Henry, *Selected Writings*, at 95.

32. Bunche, "The Negro in Political Life," at 105.

33. Bunche, "The Negro in Political Life," at 110.

34. Locke, "A New Code of Empire," at 509.

35. Locke, "A New Code of Empire," at 509.

36. Daniel Immerwahr, "A New History of World War II," *The Atlantic*, April 4, 2022; see also Richard Overy, *Blood and Ruins: The Great Imperial War, 1931–1945* (Penguin, 2021), at 4; Oona Hathaway and Scott Shapiro, *The Internationalists: How a Radical Plan to Outlaw War Remade the World* (New York: Simon & Schuster, 2017), at 192.

37. Bunche, *A World View of Race*, at 2.

38. Bunche, *A World View of Race*, at 38.

39. Bunche, *A World View of Race*, at 40.

40. William Levering Lewis, *W.E.B. Du Bois: The Fight for Equality and the American Century* (Henry Holt, 2000), at 424.

41. Jeffrey C. Stewart, *The New Negro: The Life of Alain Locke* (Oxford University Press, 2018), at 743.

42. Hannah Arendt, "Imperialism: Road to Suicide: The Political Origins and Use of Racism," *Commentary*, December 1, 1945.

43. Bunche, *A World View of Race*, at 45.

44. Bunche, *A World View of Race*, at 96.

45. Robert Vitalis, *White World Order, Black Power Politics* (Ithaca, NY: Cornell University Press, 2015), at 149.

46. Ian Frazier, "When WEB Du Bois Made a Laughingstock of a White Supremacist," *New Yorker*, August 26, 2019. https://www.newyorker.com/magazine/2019/08/26/when-w-e-b-du-bois-made-a-laughingstock-of-a-white-supremacist

47. Pagden, *Peoples and Empires*, at 112.

48. Warren G. Harding, "Address of the President of the U.S. at the Celebration of the Semicentennial Founding of the City of Birmingham, Alabama," October 26, 1921. https://voicesofdemocracy.umd.edu/warren-g-harding-address-at-birmingham-speech-text/

49. Lewis, *W.E.B. Du Bois*, at 14–15.

50. Niall Ferguson, *The War of the World: 20th Century Conflict and the Descent of the West* (New York: Penguin Press, 2006), at xlii.

51. Mark Mazower, *No Enchanted Palace: The End of Empire and the Ideological Origins of the United Nations* (Princeton, NJ: Princeton University Press, 2009), at 54.

52. W. E. B. Du Bois, "The Realities in Africa," *Foreign Affairs*, July 1943.

53. Frank Hanighen, "No Colonies for Anybody," *The New Republic*, May 10, 1939.

54. Ralph Bunche, Presidential Address, *American Political Science Review*, December 1954, at 969.

55. Bunche, "Africa and the Current World Conflict," in Henry, *Selected Writings*, at 143.

56. Bunche, "Africa and the Current World Conflict," at 146.

57. Adom Getachew, *Worldmaking after Empire: The Rise and Fall of Self-Determination* (Princeton, NJ: Princeton University Press, 2020), at 42.

58. Bunche, "Africa and the Current World Conflict," at 146.

59. Bunche, "Africa and the Current World Conflict," at 143 (introductory note by Charles P. Henry).

60. Lewis, *W.E.B. Du Bois*, at 410.

61. Lewis, *W.E.B. Du Bois*, at 467.

62. Edgar (ed.), *An African-American in South Africa*, at 317.

Chapter 4

1. Bunche to Eleanor Roosevelt, May 3, 1940, UCLA Bunche Archives, Box 33, 2.

2. Bunche, "Memo on Interview with Mrs. Franklin D. Roosevelt," May 15, 1940, UCLA Bunche Archives, Box 33, Folder 2.

3. Bunche, "Memo on Interview with Mrs. Franklin D. Roosevelt," May 15, 1940, UCLA Bunche Archives, Box 33, Folder 2.

4. NAACP Freedom Fulfillment Conference, Washington, DC, March 10, 1954, Box 14B, Schomburg Center for Black Culture Archives.

5. Bunche, "The Negro's Stake in the World Crisis," December 6, 1940, UCLA Archives, Box 341, Folder 2.

6. Bunche, note, 1941, UCLA Archives, Box 281, Folder 5.

7. Bunche, note, 1941, UCLA Archives, Box 281, Folder 5.

8. Penny von Eschen, *Race against Empire: Black Americans and Anticolonialism, 1937–1957* (Ithaca, NY: Cornell University Press, 1997), at 41.

9. Bunche, "What America Means to Me," *The American Magazine* (1950), reprinted in Charles P. Henry (ed.), *Ralph Bunche: Selected Speeches and Writings* (Ann Arbor: University of Michigan Press, 1995), at 273.

10. Bunche to Willard Park, November 7, 1940, UCLA Bunche Archives, Box 1, Folder 2.

11. E.g., Ralph Bunche, Interview with William George, Vice-Consul, Liberia, September 15, 1941, UCLA Bunche Archives, Box 54, Folder 2. On Pan-Africanism, see Brenda Gayle Plummer, *Rising Wind: Black American and Foreign Affairs* (Chapel Hill: University of North Carolina Press, 1996), at 156.

12. Bunche to Read, February 6, 1942, UCLA Bunche Archives, Box 54, Folder 8.

13. Bunche, *Pocket Guide to North Africa* (rev., 1944), UCLA Bunche Archives, Box 56, Folder 7.

14. Plummer, *Rising Wind*, at 110; Souad Halila, *The Intellectual Development and Diplomatic Career of Ralph Bunche: The Afro-American, Africanist, and Internationalist*, PhD Dissertation, University of Southern California, 1988, at 114.

15. Bunche, "French Policy toward Arabs, Jews, and Italians in Tunisia (Secret)," 1943, UCLA Bunche Archives, Box 56, Folder 8.

16. Bunche, Remarks at Morgan College, March 22, 1939, UCLA Bunche Archives, Box 340, Folder 14.

17. Bunche, "What America Means to Me," at 273.

18. Bunche, "What America Means to Me," at 273.

19. Julius Adams, "Profile of a Peacemaker," *New York Amsterdam News*, May 21, 1949.

20. Stettinus to Bunche, March 27, 1943, UCLA Bunche Archive, Box 73.

21. Henry, *Model Negro or American Other?*, at 127.

22. "Still at It," *The New Yorker*, December 2, 1944, at 26.

23. Smith Simpson, "The Commission to Study the Organization of Peace," *American Political Science Review*, 35, 2 (April 1941).

24. Lawrence Finkelstein, "Bunche and the Colonial World: From Trusteeship to Decolonization," in Benjamin Rivlin (ed.), *Ralph Bunche: The Man and His Times* (New York: Holmes and Meier, 1990), supra at 109–110.

25. Bunche, *A World View of Race* (Port Washington, NY: Kennikat Press, 1936).

26. US State Department Office of the Historian, The Atlantic Conference and Charter. https://history.state.gov/milestones/1937-1945/atlantic-conf

27. Oona Hathaway and Scott Shapiro, *The Internationalists: How a Radical Plan to Outlaw War Remade the World* (New York: Simon and Schuster, 2017), at 191.

28. Atlantic Charter, August 14, 1941. https://www.nato.int/cps/en/natohq/offic ial_texts_16912.htm

29. Richard Toye, *Churchill's Empire: The World That Made Him and the World He Made* (New York: Henry Holt, 2010), at 222. 214.

30. Penny M. von Eschen, *Race against Empire: Black Americans and Anticolonialism, 1937–1957* (Ithaca, NY: Cornell University Press, 1997), at 27.

31. David Levering Lewis, *W.E.B. Du Bois: The Fight for Equality and the American Century, 1919–1963* (New York: Henry Holt, 2000), at 470.

32. *The Atlantic Charter and African from an American Standpoint: A Study by the Committee on Africa, the War, and Peace Aims* (New York: The Committee on Africa, the War, and Peace Aims, 1942); Robert Vitalis, *White World Order, Black Power Politics* (Ithaca, NY: Cornell University Press, 2015), at 110. Bunche was listed as a Howard faculty member, as much of the work occurred before his move into government.

33. *The Atlantic Charter and Africa*, at 32, 1.

34. Sam Moyn, *The Last Utopia: Human Rights in History* (Cambridge, MA: Harvard University Press, 2010), at 88.

35. The phrase "the Insular Cases" is used to refer to this line of decisions, the most famous of which is *Downes v. Bidwell*, 182 U.S. 244 (1901).

36. Kal Raustiala, *Does the Constitution Follow the Flag? The Evolution of Territoriality in American Law* (New York: Oxford University Press, 2009), at 78.

37. Michael Lind, "The Imperial Fallacy," *The American Prospect*, September 24, 2007.

38. Johan Hari, "The Two Churchills," *New York Times*, August 12, 2010.

39. Toye, *Churchill's Empire*, at 262.

40. Toye, *Churchill's Empire*, at xi.

41. Vitalis, *White World Order, Black Power Politics*, at 116.

42. Bunche, "Materials on Planning for Post-War Colonial Status," September 21, 1943, UCLA Bunche Archives, Box 54, Folder 4.

43. Bunche, "What America Means to Me," at 274.

44. Henry, *Model Negro or American Other?*, at 132.

45. Toye, *Churchill's Empire*, at 253.

46. Justin Morris, "Origins of the United Nations," in the *Oxford Handbook of the United Nations* (New York: Oxford University Press, 2018), at 4.

47. Raymond Betts, *France and Decolonization, 1900–1960* (New York: Macmillan, 1991), at 61.

48. Mark Mazower, *Governing the World: The History of an Idea, 1815 to the Present* (New York: Penguin, 2012), at 197.

49. *Declaration by United Nations*, 1942, text at https://avalon.law.yale.edu/20th_cent ury/decade03.asp

50. Winston Churchill, *The Second World War: Triumph and Tragedy* (New York: Penguin, 1948), at 537.

Chapter 5

1. W. E. B. Du Bois, *Color and Democracy: Colonies and Peace* (New York: Harcourt Brace, 1945), at 6.

2. Adom Getachew, *Worldmaking after Empire: The Rise and Fall of Self-Determination* (Princeton, NJ: Princeton University Press, 2019), at 1.

3. Brian Urquhart, *Ralph Bunche: An American Odyssey* (New York: Norton, 1993), at 115.

4. Peter Clarke, *The Last Thousand Days of the British Empire: Churchill, Roosevelt, and the Birth of the Pax Americana* (Bloomsbury, UK: Bloomsbury Press, 2008), at 7.

5. Penny von Eschen, *Race against Empire: Black Americans and Anticolonialism, 1937–1957* (Ithaca, NY: Cornell University Press, 1997), at 104.

6. Kenneth Rose, *The Great War and Americans in Europe* (Routledge, 2017), at 331.

7. Oona Hathaway and Scott Shapiro, *The Internationalists: How a Radical Plan to Outlaw War Remade the World* (Cambridge, UK: Cambridge University Press, 2017).

8. Justin Morris, "Origins of the United Nations," in Thomas G. Weiss and Sam Daws (eds.), *Oxford Handbook on the United Nations*, 2nd ed. (New York: Oxford University Press, 2018), at 1.

9. Hathaway and Shapiro, *The Internationalists*, at 198; George Schild, *Bretton Woods and Dumbarton Oaks: American Economic and Political Postwar Planning in the Summer of 1944* (New York: St. Martin's Press, 1995), at 61–62.

10. Cordell Hull, Opening Speech, reprinted in *New York Herald Tribune*, August 22, 1944, at 26.

11. Peggy Mann, *Ralph Bunche: UN Peacekeeper* (New York: Coward, McCann, and Geoghegan, 1975), at 104.

12. "Peace Delegates Admire Skyline, See Nightclub," *New York Herald Tribune*, August 27, 1944, at 13.

13. Mann, *UN Peacekeeper*, at 109.

14. "Progress at Dumbarton Oaks," *Los Angeles Times*, August 30, 1944, at A4.

15. Paul Gordon Lauren, "First Principles of Racial Equality: History and the Politics and Diplomacy of Human Rights Provisions in the United Nations Charter," *Human Rights Quarterly*, 5, 1 (February 1983), at 10.

16. "Dumbarton Oaks Conferees to Discuss Colonial Plan," *New York Amsterdam News*, September 2, 1944.

17. Mann, *UN Peacekeeper*, at 99.

18. On this transformation, see Steven Wertheim, *Tomorrow, the World: The Birth of US Global Supremacy* (Cambridge, MA: Harvard University Press, 2020). Daniel Immerwahr refers to this as a "pointillist empire." Immerwahr, *How to Hide an Empire* (MacMillan, 2019), at 20.

19. US State Department, *Foreign Relations of the United States*, The Conference at Malta and Yalta (1955), at 78–79.

20. von Eschen, *Race Against Empire*, at 70.

21. Charles P. Henry, *Ralph Bunche: Model Negro or American Other?* (New York: New York University Press, 1999), at 134.

22. Bunche, "Trusteeship and Non-Self-Governing Territories in the Charter of the United Nations," *Department of State Bulletin*, December 30, 1945.

23. Richard Toye, *Churchill's Empire: The World That Made Him and the World He Made* (Brownsville, TX: Griffin, 2011), at 253.

24. Halila, *Intellectual Development and Diplomatic Career of Ralph Bunche*, at 120.

25. Hathaway and Shapiro, *The Internationalists*, at 208.

26. Paul Kennedy, *Parliament of Man: The Past, Present, and Future of the United Nations* (New York: Random House, 2006), at 36.
27. Morris, "Origins," at 5.
28. Urquhart, *Ralph Bunche*, at 115.
29. Bunche, Speech at Fisk University, Nashville, TN, May 5, 1956. Schomburg Center for the Study of Black Culture, Bunche Archives, Box 15/1 A-1.
30. Bunche, "Upheaval in the Ghettoes" (unpublished essay), July 1967, at 21. UN Archives Box 52/1/13.
31. Adam Hochschild, *To End All Wars* (Boston: Mariner Books, 2011), at 362.
32. Bunche to Conyers Read, November 3, 1942, UCLA Bunche Archives, Box 54, Folder 4.
33. "Dr Bunche Lectures on Trusteeship at Wellesley," *New Journal and Guide*, October 19, 1946.
34. Lauren, "First Principles," at 17.
35. Samuel Zipp, *The Idealist: Wendell Willkie's Wartime Quest to Build One World* (Cambridge, MA: Harvard University Press, 2020).
36. Harry Truman, *1945: Year of Decisions* (New York: Doubleday, 1955).
37. Norman Angell, "Expansionism: Fact and Fiction," *The Spectator*, September 20, 1935.
38. Niall Ferguson, *The War of the World: Twentieth Century Conflict and the Descent of the West* (New York: Penguin Press, 2006), at 279.
39. Toye, *Churchill's Empire*, at 310.
40. Kennedy, *Parliament of Man*, at xi.
41. https://www.trumanlibrary.gov/library/public-papers/2/address-joint-session-congress
42. Stephen C. Schlesinger, *Act of Creation: The Founding of the United Nations* (New York: Basic Books, 2003), at 115.
43. For example, "Arrangements for International Trusteeship," draft, April 26, 1945, UCLA Bunche Archives, Box 69 Folder 2; see also Lawrence Finkelstein, "Bunche and the Colonial World," in Benjamin Rivlin (ed.), *Ralph Bunche: The Man and His Times* (New York: Holmes and Meier, 1990), at 118.
44. "Race Issue Raised at Frisco," *New York Amsterdam News*, May 5 1945, 1A.
45. Bunche to Ruth Bunche, May 13, 1945, UCLA Archives, UCLA Archives, Collection 364, Box 3, Folder 8.
46. On Pasvolsky and the early State Department effort, see G. Schild, *Bretton Woods and Dumbarton Oaks. American Economic and Political Postwar Planning in the Summer of 1944* (Basingstoke, UK: Macmillan, 1995), chapter 3; on Stettinius, see "Foreign Relations: The Optimist," *Time*, November 7, 1949. http://content.time.com/time/magazine/article/0,9171,801055,00.html
47. Sen. Arthur Vandenberg, "American Foreign Policy," January 10, 1945. https://www.senate.gov/artandhistory/history/resources/pdf/VandenbergSpeech.pdf
48. Stanley Meisler, *The United Nations: A History* (rev. ed.) (New York: Grove Press, 2011), at 13.
49. Bunche, "That Man May Dwell in Peace," 1926, UCLA Bunche Archive, Box 339, Folder 3.

Chapter 6

1. Stephen C. Schlesinger, *Act of Creation: The Founding of the United Nations* (New York: Basic Books, 2003), at 122.

2. Brian Urquhart, *Ralph Bunche: An American Odyssey* (New York: Norton, 1993), at 117.

3. Schlesinger, *Act of Creation*, at 154; 68.

4. Charles P. Henry, *Ralph Bunche: Model Negro or American Other?* (New York: New York University Press, 1999), at 136.

5. Oona Hathaway and Scott Shapiro, *The Internationalists: How a Radical Plan to Outlaw War Remade the World* (Cambridge, UK: Cambridge University Press, 2017), at 211.

6. Andre Visson, "Glimmers in San Francisco: United Nations Inside Front," *Washington Post*, May 5, 1945, B4; Roscoe Drummond, "San Francisco Woos Senate," *Christian Science Monitor*, May 10, 1945, at 1.

7. Bunche to Ruth Bunche, May 13, 1945 UCLA Archives, UCLA Archives, Collection 364, Box 3, Folder 8.

8. P. Bernard Young, "Dr Bunche Advanced in State Department on Rare Merit," *New Journal and Guide*, May 12, 1945, at 7.

9. Julius Adams, "Dr. Bunche Bares Secret OSS Job: Named to Foreign Affairs Inner-Circle," *New York Amsterdam News*, September 22, 1945; Michael Carter, "Stettinius Promises to Follow FD's Program," *Afro-American*, May 5, 1945.

10. Stephen Wertheim, *Tomorrow, the World: The Birth of US Global Supremacy* (Harvard University Press, 2020), at 15.

11. David Bosco, *Five to Rule Them All: The UN Security Council and the Making of the Modern World* (2009), at 259 (quoting Robert James, *Anthony Eden: A Biography* [New York: McGraw-Hill, 1987]).

12. Stanley Meisler, *The United Nations: A History* (New York: Grove Press, 2011), at 18–19. Senator Vandenberg wrote in his diary that the smaller nations "simply surrendered to the inevitable." Justin Morris, "Origins of the United Nations" in the *Oxford Handbook of the United Nations* (Oxford University Press, 2018) at 53.

13. Bunche, letter to Ruth Bunche, May 13, 1945 UCLA Archives, UCLA Archives, Collection 364, Box 3, Folder 8.

14. Harry Truman, *1945: Year of Decisions* (New York: Doubleday, 1955), at 192–193.

15. Letter to Ruth Bunche, quoted in Urquhart, *Ralph Bunche*, at 118.

16. Schlesinger, *Act of Creation*, at 100.

17. Schlesinger, *Act of Creation*, at 101.

18. Schlesinger, *Act of Creation*, at 97–99.

19. Penny von Eschen, *Race against Empire: Black Americans and Anticolonialism, 1937–1957* (Ithaca, NY: Cornell University Press, 1997, at 7–8; see also Brenda Gayle Plummer, *Rising Wind: Black American and Foreign Affairs* (Chapel Hill: University of North Carolina Press, 1996), chapter 4.

20. von Eschen, *Race against Empire*, at 42.

21. Carol Anderson, *Eyes Off the Prize: The UN and the African-American Struggle for Human Rights, 1944–1955* (Cambridge, UK: Cambridge University Press, 2003), at 52.

22. David Levering Lewis, *WEB Du Bois: The Fight for Equality and the American Century: 1919–1963* (New York: Henry Holt, 2000), at 509.

23. Mark Mazower, *No Enchanted Palace: The End of Empire and the Ideological Origins of the United Nations* (Princeton, NJ: Princeton University Press, 2009), at 17.

24. Meyer Weinberg, *The World of W.E.B Du Bois: A Quotation Sourcebook* (Westport, CT: Greenwood Press, 1992), at 209.

25. Anderson, *Eyes Off the Prize*, at 31.

26. See, for example, Bunche, "Comparison of the Trusteeship Proposals Submitted by the US, UK, and France," UCLA Bunche Archives, Box 69, Folder 5.

27. Peggy Mann, *Ralph Bunche, UN Peacemaker* (Coward, McGann, 1975), at 126.

28. Finkelstein, "Bunche and the Colonial World," at 120.

29. Mazower, *No Enchanted Palace*, at 62.

30. Neal Stafford, "State Department Analyzes How UNO Trusteeship Works," *Christian Science Monitor*, January 24, 1946.

31. Julius Adams, "Dr. Bunche Bares Secret OSS Job: Named to Foreign Affairs Inner-Circle," *New York Amsterdam News*, September 22, 1945.

32. Jessica Pearson, "Defending Empire at the United Nations," *Journal of Imperial and Commonwealth Studies*, 45, 3 (2017), at 528.

33. Henry, *Model Negro or American Other?*, at 138. Gerig referred to Ben Gerig, one of his colleagues at the State Department.

34. Ralph Bunche, "United States Responsibility Toward Colonial Peoples," Society of Ethical Culture, April 13, 1946, UCLA Bunche Archives, Box 341, Folder 19.

35. Mazower, *No Enchanted Palace*, at 63; Plummer, *Rising Wind*, at 149.

36. Sam Moyn, "Imperialism, Self-Determination, and the Rise of Human Rights," in Akira Iriye et al., *The Human Rights Revolution: An International History* (New York: Oxford University Press, 2012), at 161.

37. Daniel Gorman, "Britain, India, and the United States: Colonialism and the Development of International Governance, 1045–1960," *Journal of Global History* (2014), at 472.

38. Bunche, "The Colonial Issue and the UN," Fisk Hillman Lecture, Nashville, May 5, 1956, Schomburg Archives Box 15/1 A-1.

39. Crawford Young, "Ralph Bunche and Patrice Lumumba: The Fatal Encounter," in Robert Hill and Edmond Keller (eds.), *Trustee for the Human Community: Ralph Bunche, the United Nations, and the Decolonization of Africa* (Ohio University Press, 2010), at 130.

40. Universal Declaration of Human Rights, 1948, https://www.un.org/en/univer sal-declaration-human-rights. See also Samuel Moyn, *The Last Utopia: Human Rights in History* (Cambridge, MA: Harvard University Press, 2010); and Moyn, "Imperialism."

41. Bunche, "The Colonial Issue and the UN."

42. Richard Toye, *Churchill's Empire* (New York: Henry Holt, 2010), at 222.

43. *Foreign Relations of the United States*, 1945, Vol. VI, Statement by President Truman. https://history.state.gov/historicaldocuments/frus1945v06/d401

44. Urquhart, *Ralph Bunche*, at 123.

Chapter 7

1. Bunche, notes, no dates but likely late 1945, UCLA Archives, Box 281, Folder 4.
2. Bunche, notes, no dates but likely late 1945, UCLA Archives, Box 281, Folder 4.
3. Bunche, "That Man May Dwell in Peace," 1926, UCLA Bunche Archives, Box 339, Folder 3.
4. David Levering Lewis, *W.E.B. Du Bois: The Fight for Equality and the American Century: 1919–1963* (New York: Henry Holt, 2000), at 543. See also Brenda Gayle Plummer, *Rising Wind: Black American and Foreign Affairs: 1935–1960* (Chapel Hill: University of North Carolina Press, 1996).
5. Adom Getachew, *Worldmaking After Empire: The Rise and Fall of Self-Determination* (Princeton, NJ: Princeton University Press, 2019), at 10. See also Sam Moyn, "Imperialism, Self-Determination, and the Rise of Human Rights," in Akira Iriye et al. (eds.), *The Human Rights Revolution: An International History* (New York: Oxford University Press, 2012), at 161.
6. Michael Barnett, "The New United Nations Politics of Peace," *Global Governance* (Winter 1995), at 84.
7. NAACP, *An Appeal to the World: A Statement on the Denial of Human Rights to Minorities in the Case of Citizens of Negro Descent in the United States of America and an Appeal to the United Nations for Redress* (1947); Penny von Eschen, *Race against Empire: Black Americans and Anticolonialism, 1937–1957* (Ithaca, NY: Cornell University Press, 1997).
8. Carol Anderson, *Eyes Off the Prize: The United Nations and the African American Struggle for Human Rights, 1944–1955* (Cambridge, UK: Cambridge University Press, 2002).
9. Bunche, "Trusteeship and Non-Self-Governing Territories in the Charter of the United Nations," *Department of State Bulletin*, December 30, 1945, at 1037.
10. Harry Truman, Navy Day Address, October 27, 1945, https://millercenter.org/the-presidency/presidential-speeches/october-27-1945-navy-day-address#:~:text=We%20shall%20not%20let%20our,operate%20in%20an%20imperfect%20world.
11. "Bunche Airs Danger," *Christian Science Monitor*, January 28, 1956.
12. Bunche, "Nobel Lecture" (December 11, 1950) available at www.nobelprize.org (emphasis added).
13. Bunche, diary, December 30, 1945, UCLA Archives, Box 281/8.
14. Bunche, diary, January 8, 1945, UCLA Archives, Box 281/8; Brian Urquhart, *Ralph Bunche: An American Odyssey* (New York: Norton, 1993), at 130.
15. *The Papers of Eleanor Roosevelt: 1945–1962, Part I: United Nations Correspondence and Publications*, Introduction, at x; Joseph Lash, *Eleanor: The Years Alone* (New York: Norton, 1972), at 31.
16. Bunche, diary, January 4, 1946, UCLA Archives, Box 281/8; Peggy Mann, *Ralph Bunche: UN Peacemaker* (New York: Coward, McCann, and Geoghegan, 1975), at 136.
17. Urquhart, *Ralph Bunche*, at 125–126.
18. Urquhart, *Ralph Bunche*, at 128–129.

19. Clement Attlee, January 10 1946, UN Audiovisual Library, https://www.youtube.com/watch?v=XSjO0v2tcAg

20. Bunche, notebook, January–February 1946, UCLA Archives, Box 281, Folder 8.

21. Bunche, "Trusteeship and Colonies," *The New Republic*, October 28, 1946, at 542.

22. Neal Stanford, "State Department Analyzes How UNO Trusteeship Works," *Christian Science Monitor*, January 1946, at 3.

23. "Demand for All Colonies to Be Placed under Trusteeship," *South China Morning Post*, January 19, 1946.

24. Evan Luard, *A History of the United Nations, Volume 2: The Age of Decolonization* (New York: Macmillan, 1989), at 124.

25. Stanford, "State Department Analyzes How UNO Trusteeship Works."

26. Bunche, diary, January 23, 1946, UCLA Archives, Box 281/8.

27. United Nations Charter, Article 73.

28. UNESCO Constitution, Preamble (November 1945).

29. George Padmore, "Trusteeship Issue Rocks UN," *The Chicago Defender*, February 2, 1946, at 7. Padmore was an acquaintance of Bunche's from his London days and a well-known thinker on colonial issues and Pan-Africanism. On France's fixation with empire, see Tony Chafer, "Decolonization in French West Africa," in Thomas Spears et al. (eds.), *Oxford Research Encyclopedia, African History* (London: Oxford University Press, 2017), at 1.

30. Benjamin Rivlin, "The Legacy of Ralph Bunche," in Benjamin Rivlin (ed.), *Ralph Bunche: The Man and His Times* (New York: Holmes and Meier, 1990), at 12.

31. Bunche, diary, January 28, 1946, UCLA Archives, Box 281, Folder 8.

32. Dulles, "Statement Regarding Non-Self-Government Peoples Resolution," February 9, 1946, UCLA Archives, Box 69, Folder 8.

33. Bunche, diary, February 10, 1946, UCLA Archives, Box 281, Folder 8.

34. Shashi Tharoor, *India: From Midnight to the Millennium* (New York: Arcade, 2012), at 7.

35. Jessica Pearson, "Defending Empire at the United Nations," *Journal of Imperial and Commonwealth History* (May 2017), at 537.

36. Bunche, diary, January 29, 1946, UCLA Archives, Box 281, Folder 8.

37. Bunche, note, N.D., UN Archives, Box 370/39/2.

38. Brian Urquhart, *A Life in Peace and War* (New York: Harper and Row, 1987), at 100.

39. Mark Mazower, *Governing the World: The History of an Idea, 1815 to the Present* (New York: Penguin, 2012), at 153.

40. Bunche, diary, February 7, 1946, UCLA Bunche Archives, Box 281, Folder 8.

41. Locke to Bunche, December 1, 1945, UCLA Bunche Archives, Box 69, Folder 8.

42. Bunche, "Nana," unpublished essay, no date, UN Archives, S-0852/1/11 at 1.

43. Mann, *UN Peacemaker*, at 141.

44. Bunche, note, no date, UCLA Bunche Archives, Collection 364, Box 3.

45. Bunche to Johnson, September 17, 1946, UCLA Bunche Archives, Collection 364, Box 3.

46. The Talk of the Town, *The New Yorker*, January 1, 1972.

47. Robert Edgar (ed.), *An American in South Africa: The Travel Notes of Ralph J. Bunche* (Athens: Ohio University Press, 1992), at 6.

48. Urquhart, *Ralph Bunche*, at 109.

49. Urquhart, *Ralph Bunche*, at 109.
50. Souad Halila, *Intellectual Development and Diplomatic Career of Ralph Bunche*, PhD Dissertation, USC, 1988, at 136.
51. Urquhart, *Ralph Bunche*, at 126.

Chapter 8

1. George Kennan, "Telegram (Long Telegram)," February 22, 1946, at https://digital archive.wilsoncenter.org/document/116178.pdf.
2. Kennan, "Long Telegram."
3. UN Security Council Official Records, 23rd Meeting, February 16, 1946, S/PV/ 23. The Security Council had held twenty-three discrete meetings in London when Vishinsky cast his veto.
4. Peter Wallensteen and Patrik Johansson, "Security Council Decisions in Perspective," in David Malone (ed.), *The UN Security Council: From the Cold War to the 21st Century* (Boulder, CO: Lynne Rienner, 2004), at 18.
5. Brian Urquhart, *Ralph Bunche: An American Odyssey* (New York: Norton, 1993), at 126.
6. William Roger Louis and Ronald Robinson, "The Imperialism of Decolonization," *Journal of Imperial and Commonwealth History* (1994), at 465.
7. Bunche, Remarks at the Society for Ethical Culture, April 13, 1946, UCLA Bunche Archives, Box 341, Folder 19.
8. Evan Luard, *A History of the United Nations: Volume 2, the Age of Decolonization, 1955–1965* (MacMillan, 1989), at 75.
9. Bunche to Hoo, September 16, 1946, UCLA Bunche Archives, Box 83, Folder 2.
10. Louis Lautier, "United Nations May Decide on Colonies," *New Journal and Guide*, September 21, 1946.
11. Lautier, "United Nations May Decide on Colonies."
12. Bunche to Ruth, no date but summer 1946, UCLA Bunche Archives, Collection 364, Box 3, Folder 8.
13. United Nations, *The Legal Status of the West Bank and Gaza* (1982). https://www.un.org/unispal/document/auto-insert-203742
14. Bunche to Hoo, memorandum, September 16, 1946, UCLA Bunche Archives, Box 83, Folder 2.
15. Speech by Dulles, Fourth Committee, November 1946, Schomburg Center for the Study of Black Culture, Bunche Archives, Box 45/19.
16. UNGA Resolution 1514 (XV), December 14, 1960.
17. Rupert Emerson, "Colonialism, Political Development and the UN," *International Organization* (Winter 1965), at 486.
18. Daniel Immerwahr, "A New History of World War II," *The Atlantic* (May 2022).
19. Speech by Singh, Fourth Committee Working Papers, November 1946, Schomburg Center for the Study of Black Culture, Bunche Archives, Box 44/1.
20. Speech by Liu-Chieh, Fourth Committee Working Papers, November 1946, Schomburg Center for the Study of Black Culture, Bunche Archives, Box 44/1.

21. Speech by Bottomley, Fourth Committee Working Papers, November 1946, Schomburg Center for the Study of Black Culture, Bunche Archives, Box 44/1.
22. Speech by Pradenas, Fourth Committee Working Papers, November 1946, Schomburg Center for the Study of Black Culture, Bunche Archives, Box 46/1.
23. Walter Sullivan, "South Africa Bars Tribes UN Trip," *New York Times*, December 3, 1951.
24. Carol Anderson, *Eyes Off the Prize: The United Nations and the African American Struggle for Human Rights, 1944–1955* (Cambridge, UK: Cambridge University Press, 2003), at 87.
25. Louis Henkin, "US Ratification of Human Rights Treaties: The Ghost of Senator Bricker," *American Journal of International Law* (April 1995).
26. General Assembly Resolution 103(I), November 19, 1946.
27. Fourth Committee Working Papers, November 1946, Schomburg Center for the Study of Black Culture, Bunche Archives, Box 44/1.
28. C. Brooks Peters, "Trusteeship Body Due to Be Formed," *New York Times*, October 17, 1946, at 4.
29. Speech by K. Bailey, Fourth Committee Working Papers, November 1946, Schomburg Center for the Study of Black Culture, Bunche Archives, Box 44/1.
30. Debate, December 4, 1946, Fourth Committee, Schomburg Center for the Study of Black Culture, Bunche Archives, Box 45/8.
31. Bunche, "The Colonial Issue and the UN," Fisk Hillman Lecture, Nashville, May 5, 1956, Schomburg Archives Box 15/1 A-1.
32. Ollie Stewart, "UN Trustees Expect to Help Territories," *The Baltimore Afro-American*, April 5, 1947, at 1.
33. Lawrence Finkelstein, "Bunche and the Colonial World," in Benjamin Rivlin (ed.), *Ralph Bunche: The Man and His Times* (New York: Holmes and Meier, 1990), at 125.
34. UN General Assembly Resolution 289 (IV), "Question of the Disposal of the former Italian colonies." See also Ann Dearden, "Independence for Libya: The Political Problems," *Middle East Journal*, 4, 4 (October 1950).
35. Joseph Wechsberg, "Letter from Libya," *The New Yorker*, November 10, 1951.
36. Draft Statement by Trygve Lie to the Trusteeship Council [written by Bunche], March 26, 1947, UCLA Bunche Archives, Box 70, Folder 2.
37. Evan Luard, *A History of the United Nations* (New York: St. Martin's Press, 1982), at 126.
38. Kal Raustiala, *Reporting and Review Mechanisms in Ten Multilateral Environmental Agreements* (UN Environment Programme, 2001)..
39. Daniel Gorman, "Britain, India, and the United States: Colonialism and the Development of International Governance, 1945–1960," *Journal of Global History* (2014), at 481.
40. Peggy Mann, *Ralph Bunche: UN Peacekeeper* (New York: Coward, McCann, and Geoghegan, 1975), at 148.
41. Brooks Peters, "Trusteeship Body Due to be Formed," *New York Times*, October 17, 1946.
42. Luard, *A History of the United Nations*, at 126.

43. Bunche, "Trusteeship and Non-Self-Governing Territories in the Charter of the United Nations," *State Department Bulletin*, December 30, 1945, at 1041.

44. William Roger Louis and Ronald Robinson, "The Imperialism of Decolonization," *Journal of Imperial and Commonwealth History*, 22 (1994), at 46.

45. Finkelstein, "Bunche and the Colonial World," at 126.

46. Crystal Nix, "UN in Bronx: Recalling Exciting Early Days," *New York Times*, October 20, 1985, at 9.

47. "Work on UN Site Behind Schedule," *New York Times*, November 25, 1948.

48. *The United Nations at 70* (Rizzoli, 2015), at 48.

49. *Report to the General Assembly on the Permanent Headquarters of the United Nations*, Doc A/311, July 1947, at 18: "it is well to plan on a possible membership of at least seventy;" *The United Nations at 70*, at 134: "the compound was built to accommodate delegates from 70 to 80 countries"; George Dudley, *A Workshop for Peace* (Cambridge, MA: MIT Press, 1994), at 54, showing plans for a UN campus with seventy delegations; "Fact Sheet: History of UN Headquarters," https://visit.un.org/sites/visit.un.org/files/FS_UN_Headquarters_History_English_Feb_2013.pdf; Adam Bartos and Christopher Hitchens, *International Territory: The United Nations, 1945–95* (New York: Verso, 1994), at 4.

50. "Dr Bunche Lectures on Trusteeship at Wellesley," *New Journal and Guide*, October 19, 1946.

51. "A Peep behind the Scenes at the Work of Dr. Ralph Bunche," *Pittsburgh Courier*, April 20, 1946.

52. Bunche to Hastie, February 24, 1947, UCLA Bunche Archives digital collection. https://oac.cdlib.org/ark:/13030/hb2t1nb2pz/?brand=oac4

53. "Dr Bunche Urges Race to Pull Out of 'Mental Rut,'" *Atlanta Daily World*, March 6, 1947.

54. Anderson, *Eyes Off the Prize*, at 93.

55. Charles Martin, "Internationalizing 'The American Dilemma': The Civil Rights Congress and the 1951 Genocide Petition to the United Nations," *Journal of American Ethnic History*, 16, 4 (1997), at 39.

56. Virginia Clemer, "Negroes Appeal to UN on Bias in United States," *New York Herald Tribune*, October 24, 1947.

57. George Streator, "Negroes to Bring Cause before UN," *New York Times*, October 12, 1947, at 52.

58. "Bunche: World Facing Explosive Situations," *Boston Globe*, October 8, 1962, at 19.

59. Anderson, *Eyes Off the Prize*, at 81.

60. Letter, Robeson and Yergan to Bunche, October 24, 1946, UCLA Bunche Archives, Box 83, 1.

61. Urquhart, *Ralph Bunche*, at 67.

62. "At the Bar of Mankind," *The Daily Worker*, December 19, 1951.

63. Martin, "Internationalizing 'The American Dilemma,'" at 46–47.

64. "Charge of US Genocide Called Red Smoke Screen," *Washington Post*, December 16, 1951.

65. Anderson, *Eyes Off the Prize*, at 3.

66. David Levering Lewis, *W.E.B. Du Bois: A Biography* (New York: Henry Holt, 2009), at 531.

Chapter 9

1. Elad Ben-Dror, *Ralph Bunche and the Arab-Israeli Conflict: Mediation and the UN, 1947–1949* (London: Routledge, 2015), at 160.
2. Robin Wright, "How the Curse of Sykes-Picot Still Haunts the Middle East," *New Yorker* (April 30, 2016). https://www.newyorker.com/news/news-desk/how-the-curse-of-sykes-picot-still-haunts-the-middle-east
3. Wright, "Curse of Sykes-Picot."
4. Balfour Declaration. https://avalon.law.yale.edu/20th_century/balfour.asp
5. UN Special Committee on Palestine, Report to the G.A., Vol 1 (1947) GA A/364 (September 3, 1947), para 74.
6. Keith Kyle, *Suez* (London: Weidenfield and Nicolson, 1991), at 23.
7. William Roger Louis and Ronald Robinson, "The Imperialism of Decolonization," *Journal of Imperial and Commonwealth History* (1994), at 467.
8. UN Special Committee on Palestine, Report to the G.A., Vol 1 (1947) GA A/364 (September 3, 1947), para 116.
9. Palestine was one of two League mandates not placed under trusteeship; the other was the very contested territory of South West Africa. See Evan Luard, *A History of the United Nations, Volume 2: The Age of Decolonization* (New York: Macmillan, 1989), at 123–125.
10. Ben-Dror, *Ralph Bunche and the Arab-Israeli Conflict*, at 11.
11. Bunche, notes, June 11, 1947 (turning down the offer), UN Archives Box 370/50/1.
12. Bunche, "The Case for the UN," Speech at the Midwood Jewish Center, Brooklyn, February 19, 1951 Schomburg Archives, Box 14-A.
13. "A Symbol and an Answer," *The Christian Science Monitor*, December 5, 1947, at 24.
14. UN Special Committee on Palestine, Report to the G.A., Vol. 1 (1947). GA A/364 (September 3, 1947), Preface.
15. Bunche, "Tight Spots and Close Calls in the Service of the United Nations," no date, UN Archives, Box 30/40/20, at 1.
16. Kati Marton, *A Death in Jerusalem* (New York: Arcade Publishing, 1994), at 110.
17. UN Special Committee on Palestine, Report to the G.A., Vol. 1 (1947), GA A/364 (September 3, 1947), para 32.
18. Bunche to Ruth, June 29, 1947, UCLA Archives, Collection 364, Box 3, Folder 8.
19. Bunche, diary, July 6 and 11; August 22, UCLA Urquhart Archives, Box 5, Folder 4; Elad Ben-Dror, *The Road to Partition: UNSCOP and the Beginnings of United Nations Involvement in the Arab-Israel Conflict* (unpublished book manuscript, 2021), at 71.
20. UN Special Committee on Palestine, Confidential Report Series No. 1, "Religious Interests and Holy Places," UN Archives, S-0605, Box 4, Folder 12.
21. Bunche, diary, July 1, 1947, UCLA Urquhart Archives, Box 5, Folder 4.

22. Bunche, diary, June 23 and 24, 1947, UCLA Urquhart Archives, Box 5, Folder 4.
23. Ronen Bergman, "A State Is Born in Palestine," *New York Times Magazine*, October 7, 2011.
24. Bergman, "A State Is Born."
25. Bunche, diary entries, July 4, 1947, and June 27, 1947, UCLA Urquhart Archives, Box 5, Folder 4.
26. Ben-Dror, *Road to Partition*, Chapter 3.
27. Bunche, diary, July 7, 1947, UN Archives, Box 370/50/1.
28. Bunche, diary, July 24, 1947, UCLA Urquhart Archives, Box 5, Folder 4.
29. Bunche, diary, July 24, 1947, UCLA Urquhart Archives, Box 5, Folder 4.
30. Bunche, diary, July 24, 1947, UCLA Urquhart Archives, Box 5, Folder 4.
31. Bunche to Gerig, July 23 1947, UCLA Urquhart Archives, Box 5, Folder 1.
32. Bunche, diary, July 4, 1947, UCLA Urquhart Archives, Box 5, Folder 4.
33. Bunche, diary, August 16 1947, UCLA Urquhart Archives, Box 5, Folder 4.
34. Bunche, diary, July 28, 1947, UCLA Urquhart Archives, Box 5, Folder 4.
35. Bunche, diary, August 25 1947, UCLA Urquhart Archives, Box 5, Folder 4.
36. Bunche, diary, August 21, 1947, UCLA Urquhart Archives, Box 5, Folder 4.
37. Bunche, diary, September 1, 1947, UCLA Urquhart Archives, Box 5, Folder 4.
38. The earlier, 1937 UK Peel Report had suggested something similar, but this was the first international articulation of the concept.
39. Ben-Dror, *Road to Partition*, at 284; 324. Ben-Dror disputes Bunche's characterization of the majority's view, however.
40. Harry S. Truman, *1946–52 Years of Trial and Hope: Volume 2* (New York: New Word City, 1956).
41. Bunche, speech at Southern Methodist University, Dallas, TX, April 8, 1958, in Schomburg Archives, Box 15/4.
42. Quoted in Marton, *A Death in Jerusalem*, at 114.
43. Marton, *A Death in Jerusalem*, at 114.
44. Bunche, diary, March 19, 1948, UCLA Urquhart Archives, Box 5, Folder 5.
45. John G. Rogers, "Bunche Likely to Head U.N.'s Palestine Staff: Grandson of Negro Slave Is Favored as Chief of Secretariat for Partition," *New York Herald Tribune (1926–1962)*, December 3, 1947, at 16; "Bunche May Head U.N. Secretary Staff." *The Palestine Post (1933–1950)*, December 3, 1947, at 1.
46. Palestine Commission Advance Group, Progress Report, March 15, 1948, UCLA Urquhart Archives, Box 5, Folder 4.
47. https://mfa.gov.il/MFA/ForeignPolicy/MFADocuments/Yearbook1/Pages/4%20Establishment%20of%20a%20United%20Nations%20Truce%20Commissi.aspx
48. Bunche, diary, May 14, 1948, UCLA Urquhart Archives, Box 5, Folder 4.
49. Lie to Marshall, May 16, 1948, UCLA Archives, Urquhart Collection, Box 5, Folder 4.
50. Marton, *A Death in Jerusalem*, at 75.
51. Cary David Stanger, "A Haunting Legacy: The Assassination of Count Bernadotte," *Middle East Journal*, 42, 2 (Spring 1988), at 265.

52. Gunnar Jahn, "Presentation Speech," 1950 Nobel Prize. www.nobleprize.org/prizes/peace/1950/ceremony-speech

53. Lie to Bernadotte, May 21, 1948, UCLA Archives, Urquhart Collection, Box 5, Folder 4.

54. Bunche Diary, May 20, 1948, UCLA Archives, Urquhart Collection, Box 5, Folder 5; Ralph Bunche, "What America Means to Me," in Charles P. Henry (ed.), *The Selected Speeches and Writings of Ralph Bunche* (Ann Arbor: University of Michigan Press, 1996), at 274.

55. Bunche Diary, May 25, 1948, UCLA Archives, Urquhart Collection, Box 5, Folder 5.

56. Bunche Diary, May 27, 1948, UCLA Archives, Urquhart Collection, Box 5, Folder 5.

57. Folke Bernadotte, *To Jerusalem* (London: Hodder and Stoughton, 1951), at 36. Bernadotte's diaries and notes to his assistant were published posthumously.

58. Bunche, "United Nations Intervention in Palestine," Colgate University, May 20, 1949; Marton, *A Death in Jerusalem*, at 120.

59. Marton, *A Death in Jerusalem*, at 122.

60. Meeting Notes, May 29, 1948, UCLA Archives, Urquhart Collection, Box 5, Folder 4.

61. Meeting Notes, May 30, 1948, UCLA Archives, Urquhart Collection, Box 5, Folder 4.

62. Bunche, notes, May 31, 1948, UCLA Archives, Urquhart Collection, Box 5, Folder 4.

63. United Nations ID Card, UCLA Bunche Archives, Box 435, 1.

64. Bernadotte, *To Jerusalem*, at 36.

65. Bunche, "Tight Spots," at 2, UN Archives, Box 30/40/20.

66. Bunche notes, May 31, 1948, UCLA Archives, Urquhart Collection, Box 5, Folder 4.

67. Marton, *A Death in Jerusalem*, at 134.

68. Bernadotte, *To Jerusalem*, at 38.

69. Bernadotte, *To Jerusalem*, at 42.

70. Marton, *A Death in Jerusalem*, at 134.

71. Bunche, Speech at UCLA, April 21, 1965, Schomburg Center for the Study of Black Culture, Bunche Archives, Box 16/5.

72. Record of conversation between Bunche and Cordier, June 8, 1948, UN Archives, Box 370/50/7.

73. Marton, *A Death in Jerusalem*, at 142.

74. Urquhart, *Ralph Bunche*, at 160.

75. Bunche, notes, June 19, 1948, UN Archives, Box 370/26/15.

76. Bunche, notes, June 19, 1948, UN Archives, Box 370/26/15.

77. Ben-Dror, *Ralph Bunche and the Arab-Israeli Conflict*, at 58.

78. Bernadotte, *To Jerusalem*, 118; Stanger, "A Haunting Legacy," at 261.

79. Bernadotte, *To Jerusalem*, 152.

80. Donald Macintyre, "Israel's Forgotten Hero: The Assassination of Count Bernadotte—and the Death of Peace," *The Independent*, September 18, 2008; Urquhart, *Ralph Bunche*, at 165.

81. Walter Eytan, quoted in Marton, *A Death in Jerusalem*, at 147.

82. Urquhart, *Ralph Bunche*, at 164.
83. Bernadotte, *To Jerusalem*, at 209.
84. Urquhart, *Ralph Bunche*, at 171.
85. Bunche, notes, June 6 1948, UN Archives, Box 370/26/15.
86. Bunche, notes, August 1, 1948, UN Archives Box 370/50/2.
87. Marton, *A Death in Jerusalem*, at 199.
88. https://www.unrwa.org/palestine-refugees
89. Bunche Diary, August 9 1948, UCLA Archives, Urquhart Collection, Box 5, Folder 5.
90. Bernadotte, *To Jerusalem*, at 235.
91. Marton, *A Death in Jerusalem*, at 11.
92. Aage Lundstrom, "Epilogue: The 17th September," in Bernadotte, *To Jerusalem*, at 257. Lundstrom was part of the UN team and a witness to the assassination.
93. Bunche Interview, *The Today Show* (NBC), February 1969, Bunche Archives, Schomburg Center for the Study of Black Culture, Bunche Archives, Box 14/B.
94. Bunche, "Tight Spots," at 3.
95. Stanger, "A Haunting Legacy," at 262; Macintyre, "Israel's Forgotten Hero." Bunche offered a different count of the bullets, saying more were shot into Bernadotte. Bunche, "Tight Spots," at 4; UN Archives, Box 30/40/20.
96. Lundstrom, "Epilogue," at 260.
97. "Yehoshua Cohen, Obituary," *Los Angeles Times*, August 14, 1986 (noting that Cohen, who later became close with Ben-Gurion and shared the same kibbutz, had admitted to Ben-Gurion that he was the killer).
98. *The Today Show*, supra.
99. Bunche, "Tight Spots," at 4, UN Archives, Box 30/40/20.
100. Stanger, "A Haunting Legacy," at 263; Bunche, "Tight Spots," at 4.
101. Urquhart, *Ralph Bunche*, at 179.
102. Marton, *A Death in Jerusalem*, at 254.

Chapter 10

1. "Shock Voiced Here at News of Killing: Bernadotte Tributes by Jewish, Arab Leaders Are Emphatic—Dewey Issues Statement," *New York Times*, September 18, 1948, at 2; Cary David Stanger, "A Haunting Legacy: The Assassination of Count Bernadotte," *Middle East Journal*, 42, 2 (Spring 1988), at 263.
2. Stanger, "A Haunting Legacy," at 263.
3. Donald Macintyre, "Israel's Forgotten Hero: The Assassination of Count Bernadotte—and the Death of Peace," *The Independent*, September 18, 2008.
4. "Bernadotte's Body Taken to Haifa," Associated Press, September 19, 1949.
5. Camille Cianfarra, "Israel Is Assailed by British, Chinese on Count's Slaying," *New York Times*, October 14, 1948.
6. Cianfarra, "Israel Is Assailed."
7. UNSC Resolution 59, October 19, 1948; Bunche, diary, September 18, 1948, UN Archives, Box 370/50/10.

8. Letter from the Ministry of Foreign Affairs, Israel, to the Secretary General, June 14, 1950, https://www.un.org/unispal/document/auto-insert-178849/; *Reparation for Injuries Suffered in Service of the United Nations*, International Court of Justice, Advisory Opinion of April 11, 1949.

9. A. P., "Israel Silent on Report," *New York Times*, March 11, 1950. https://www.nyti mes.com/1950/03/11/archives/israel-silent-on-report-has-not-received-statem ent-of-sweden-on.html

10. LarsLinder,*GöranBurén:"MordetpåFolkeBernadotte,"*DagensNyheter,March28,2012, https://www.dn.se/kultur-noje/bokrecensioner/goran-buren-mordet-pa-folke-bernadotte/ (translation David Silverlid).

11. PBS, *Ralph Bunche: An American Odyssey* (2001), film by William Greaves.

12. Bunche to Betts, July 28, 1966, UCLA Bunche Archives, Box 20, Folder 2.

13. Saadia Touval, *The Peace Brokers: Mediators in the Arab-Israeli Conflict, 1948–1979* (Princeton, NJ: Princeton University Press, 1982), at 51.

14. James McDonald, *My Mission in Israel, 1948–1951* (New York: Simon & Schuster, 1951), at 60.

15. Bunche, note, May 1967, UN Archives, Box 370/23/12.

16. Elad Ben-Dror, *Ralph Bunche and the Arab-Israeli Conflict: Mediation and the UN, 1947–1949* (London: Routledge, 2015), at 100.

17. Ben-Dror, *Ralph Bunche and the Arab-Israeli Conflict*, at 100.

18. Hilde Henriksen Waage, "The Winner Takes All: The 1949 Island of Rhodes Armistice Negotiations Revisited," *Middle East Journal*, 65, 2 (2011), at 284.

19. Bunche, note, June 1950, UCLA Archives, Box 281, Folder 14.

20. Shabtai Rosenne, "Bunche at Rhodes: Diplomatic Negotiator," at 179, in Benjamin Rivlin (ed.), *Ralph Bunche: The Man and His Times* (New York: Holmes and Meier, 1990). Rosenne was a member of the Israeli delegation to Rhodes.

21. Touval, *The Peace Brokers*, at 55.

22. Bunche to Lie, March 1, 1949, UCLA Bunche Archives, Collection 364, Box 8, Folder 2.

23. Ben-Dror, *Ralph Bunche and the Arab-Israeli Conflict*, at 149.

24. Henry Luce, "The American Century," *Life*, February 17, 1941.

25. Benny Morris, *The Birth of the Palestinian Refugee Problem* (Cambridge, UK: Cambridge University Press, 1988), at 1.

26. Elad Ben-Dror, "Ralph Bunche and the 1949 Armistice Agreements Revisited," *Middle Eastern Studies*, November 2019, at 3.

27. Bunche, note, July 5, 1967, UN Archives, Box 370/39/1.

28. S/PV/381, Security Council Meeting Notes, November 15, 1948 (Bunche remarks).

29. UN Security Council Resolution, S/RES/62 (1948), November 16.

30. Bunche, "What America Means to Me," in Charles P Henry (ed.), *Ralph J Bunche: Selected Speeches and Writings* (Ann Arbor: University of Michigan Press, 1996), at 274.

31. Bunche to Lisicky, in Brian Urquhart, *Ralph Bunche: An American Odyssey* (New York: Norton, 1993), at 197.

32. W. E. B. Du Bois, speech before the American Jewish Congress, November 30, 1948, W. E. B. Du Bois Papers, University of Massachusetts, Amherst Library. https://credo. library.umass.edu/view/pageturn/mums312-b199-i035/#page/2/mode/1up

33. Souad Halila, *The Intellectual Development and Diplomatic Career of Ralph Bunche: The Afro-American, Africanist, and Internationalist*, PhD Dissertation, University of Southern California, 1988, at 95.

34. Robin D. G. Kelley, "Apartheid's Black Apologists," in Jon Soske and Sean Jacobs (eds.), *Apartheid Israel: The Politics of an Analogy* (Haymarket Books, 2015).

35. Bill Mullen, *Un-American: WEB DuBois and the Century of World Revolution* (Philadelphia: Temple University Press, 2015).; David Levering Lewis, *W.E.B. DuBois: The Fight for Equality and the American Century, 1919–1963* (New York: Henry Holt, 2000).

36. Bunche, diary, January 8, 1949, UN Archives, Box 370/50/11.

37. "Israelis Accused in Report to UN," *New York Times*, December 28, 1948.

38. "Israelis Accused in Report to UN," *New York Times*, December 28, 1948.

39. Bunche was already feeling out other counterparties; Bunche to Lie, January 17, 1949 ("Impression is strong that other Arab states about ready to follow Egyptian example"), UCLA Bunche Archives, Collection 364, Box 8, Folder 4.

40. Kati Marton, *A Death in Jerusalem* (New York: Pantheon, 1994), at 145.

41. Folke Bernadotte, *To Jerusalem* (New York: Hodder and Stoughton, 1951, published posthumously), at 92.

42. Ben-Dror, "Ralph Bunche and the 1949 Armistice Agreements Revisited," at 4. Urquhart, by contrast, reports "handshakes all around" and a congenial atmosphere. Urquhart, *Ralph Bunche*, at 201.

43. Sam Pope Brewer, "Egypt, Israel Open Rhodes Talks," *New York Times*, January 14, 1949; UN Department of Public Information, Bulletin, February 1, 1949, UCLA Archives, Collection 364, Box 8, Folder 4.

44. Bunche, notes, January 28, 1949, UCLA Archives, Collection 364, Box 8, Folder 1; Bunche, notes, January 23, 1949, UCLA Archives, Collection 364, Box 8, Folder 4.

45. Rosenne, "Bunche at Rhodes," at 177.

46. Robert McFadden, "Dr. Bunche of UN, Nobel Winner, Dies," *New York Times*, December 10, 1971.

47. George Packer, *Our Man: Richard Holbrooke and the End of the American Century* (New York: Penguin Random House, 2019).

48. Stanley Meisler, *The United Nations: The First 50 Years* (New York: Atlantic Monthly Press, 1995), at 182.

49. McFadden, "Dr. Bunche of UN."

50. Bunche, diary, February 8, 1949, UCLA Archives, Collection 364, Box 3, Folder 3.

51. Rosenne, "Bunche at Rhodes," at 181; for more detail, see F. P. Henderson, "How to Write an Armistice," *Marine Corps Gazette* (April 1984). Henderson was an aide to Bunche at Rhodes.

52. Bernadotte, *To Jerusalem*, at 144.

53. Meisler, *The United Nations*, Chapter 3.

54. McFadden, "Dr. Bunche of UN."

55. Bunche, notes, January 20, 1949, UCLA Archives, Collection 364, Box 8, Folder 4.

56. Bunche to Lie, January 20, 1949, UCLA Archives, Collection 364, Box 8, Folder 4; "Armistice Talks with Egyptians on Brink of Failure," *Washington Post*, January 24, 1949.

57. Ben-Dror, *Ralph Bunche and the Arab-Israeli Conflict*, at 164.

58. Urquhart, *Ralph Bunche*, at 206.

59. Bunche, diary, January 30, 1949, UCLA Archives, Collection 364, Box 8, Folder 2.

60. Ben-Dror, *Ralph Bunche and the Arab-Israeli Conflict*, at 166. Bunche viewed it as a means of "saving the conference." Bunche to Lie, Cable, January 24, 1949, UCLA Archives, Collection 364, Box 8, Folder 4.

61. Bunche to Lie, January 27, 1949, UCLA Archives, Collection 364, Box 8, Folder 4.

62. Bunche to Lie, January 28, 1949, UCLA Archives, Collection 364, Box 8, Folder 4.

63. Bunche, diary, February 8, 1949, UCLA Archives, Collection 364, Box 3, Folder 3.

64. Ben Dror, *Ralph Bunche and the Arab-Israeli Conflict*, at 167.

65. Bunche, diary, February 4, 1949, UCLA Archives, Collection 364, Box 3, Folder 3.

66. Oral History Interview with M. Ethridge, June 4, 1974, The Truman Library. https://www.trumanlibrary.gov/library/oral-histories/ethridge

67. https://www.haaretz.com/us-news/harry-truman-recognizing-the-new-state-of-israel-1.6073618

68. Waage, "The Winner Takes All," at 286.

69. *Foreign Relations of the US*, Vol. VI, 1949, at 1127.

70. For example, Rashid Khalidi, *The Hundred Year's War on Palestine: A History of Settler Colonialism and Resistance, 1917–2017* (New York: Henry Holt, 2020).

71. "Israel to Reassess Ties with UN, Says Benyamin Netanyahu." https://www.theguardian.com/world/2016/dec/24/israel-reassess-ties-united-nations-settlement-benjamin-netanyahu

72. Bunche, note, no date, UN Archives, Box 370/39/2.

73. Waage, "The Winner Takes All," at 289.

Chapter 11

1. Bunche, diary, February 2, 1949 UCLA Archives, Collection 364, Box 3, Folder 3.

2. Bunche to Ruth Bunche, February 8, 1949, UCLA Archives, Collection 364, Box 3, Folder 8.

3. Sam Pope Brewer, "Progress Positive in Rhodes Parley, Bunche Declares," *New York Times*, February 6, 1949.

4. "Jewish Refusal: Bunche's Latest Plan Rejected," *South China Morning Post*, February 3, 1949.

5. Bunche to Lie, February 20, 1949, UCLA Archives, Collection 364, Box 8, Folder 6.

6. PBS, *Ralph Bunche: An American Odyssey* (Documentary, 2001).

7. Sam Pope Brewer, "Bunche Optimistic on Rhodes Parley," *New York Times*, February 19, 1949.

8. Meeting of the Advisory Committee on UNEF, January 26, 1957, Transcript, UN Archives, Box 316/119, at 21.

9. Bunche, notes, February 23, 1949, UCLA Archives, Collection 364, Box 8, Folder 8.

10. State Department, Cable, Top Secret, February 25, 1949, UCLA Archives, Collection 364, Box 8, Folder 8.

11. "Egypt Signs Armistice with Israel," *Christian Science Monitor*, February 24, 1949; "Short Ceremony Laid Basis for Permanent Peace," *Palestine Post*, February 25, 1949.

12. Frances Ofner, "Triumph of a Mediator," *Christian Science Monitor*, March 1, 1949.

13. Bunche, diary, February 28, 1949, UN Archives, Box 370/50/12.

14. Bunche, diary, March 5, 1949, UCLA Archives, Collection 364, Box 8, Folder 2.

15. Bunche, diary, March 4, 1949, UCLA Archives, Collection 364, Box 8, Folder 2.

16. Bunche, Opening Statement, March 4, 1949, UCLA Archives, Collection 364, Box 8, Folder 2.

17. Bunche to Lie, Cable, March 4, 1949, UCLA Archives, Collection 364, Box 8, Folder 2.

18. Bunche, diary, March 18, 1949, UCLA Archives, Collection 364, Box 8, Folder 2.

19. Bunche, diary, March 25, 1949, UCLA Archives, Collection 364, Box 8, Folder 2.

20. Bunche to Lie, March 17, 1949, UCLA Archives, Collection 364, Box 8, Folder 2.

21. Bunche, diary, March 16, 1949, UCLA Archives, Collection 364, Box 8, Folder 2.

22. Bunche to Lie, Cable, March 23, 1949, UCLA Archives, Collection 364, Box 8, Folder 2; Ofner, "Triumph of a Mediator," 1949.

23. Bunche, diary, March 20, 1949, UCLA Archives, Collection 364, Box 8, Folder 2.

24. Elad Ben-Dror, *Ralph Bunche and the Arab-Israeli Conflict: Mediation and the UN, 1947–1949* (London: Routledge, 2015), at 207.

25. Brian Urquhart, *Ralph Bunche: An American Odyssey* (New York: Norton, 1993), at 217.

26. "Armistice Is Signed by Trans-Jordan and Israel," *Washington Post*, April 4, 1949.

27. Bunche to Lie, March 30, 1949, Collection 364, Box 8, Folder 2.

28. Ben-Dror, *Ralph Bunche and the Arab-Israeli Conflict*, at 220.

29. Bunche, diary, April 6, 1949, Collection 364, Box 8, Folder 1.

30. Bunche, diary, April 12, 1949, Collection 364, Box 8, Folder 1.

31. PBS, 2001; "UN at Work: Mr. Bevin in New York and Mr. Bunche at Rhodes," *The Sphere*, April 16, 1949.

32. Bunche, diary, May 25, 1949, UCLA Archives, Collection 364, Box 2, Folder 13.

33. Ben-Dror, *Ralph Bunche and the Arab-Israeli Conflict*, at 223.

34. Ben-Dror, *Ralph Bunche and the Arab-Israeli Conflict*, at 238.

35. Statement before the UNSC, August 4, 1949 in the UCLA digital collection. https://oac.cdlib.org/ark:/13030/hb4489p0xb/?brand=oac4

36. George Dugan, "UN Can Stop War, Bunche Declares," *New York Times*, May 23, 1949.

37. Bunche, "Excerpts upon Return from Palestine." https://video.alexanderstreet.com/watch/ralph-bunche-excerpts-upon-return-from-palestine-silent-and-spoken-footage?context=channel:ralph-bunche

38. David Ben-Gurion, *Israel: A Personal History* (American Israel Publishing, 1971), at 318.

39. Bunche, "UN Intervention in Palestine," speech in Philadelphia, June 6, 1949, UCLA Bunche Archives, Box 344, Folder 11.

40. Transcript, "The Eleanor Roosevelt Program," Episode 1, Part 2, October 11, 1950, The Eleanor Roosevelt Papers, https://www2.gwu.edu/~erpapers/radiotv/doc.cfm?_p=erprg&_f=erprg_001_pt02

41. Rosenne, "Bunche at Rhodes," at 185.

42. Bunche, speech at Colgate University, May 20, 1949, cited in Gunnar Jahn, "Presentation Speech," 1950 Nobel Prize. www.nobleprize.org/prizes/peace/1950/ceremony-speech

43. Leonard Lyons, "The Lyons Den," *Washington Post,* January 3, 1950.

44. "Bunche Acclaimed World's No 1 Diplomat: World Hails Bunche," *Pittsburgh Courier,* March 5, 1949, at 1.

45. Bunche, "What America Means to Me," in Charles P. Henry (ed.), *Ralph J. Bunche: Selected Speeches and Writings* (Ann Arbor: University of Michigan Press, 1996), at 274.

46. Bunche Interview Transcript, May 12, 1949, UCLA Bunche Archives, Box 344, Folder 2.

47. Leon Edel, "Britain Defies UN on Its Trusteeships," *Daily Compass,* November 23, 1949.

48. Bunche, "UN Intervention in Palestine," Speech in Philadelphia, June 6, 1949, UCLA Bunche Archives, Box 344, Folder 11.

49. UN Department of Public Information, Press Release, September 22, 1950, UCLA, Bunche Archives, Box 415, Folder 7.

50. Bunche, note, September 14, 1966, UN Archives, Box 370/38/5.

51. Bunche, note, December 3, 1950, UCLA Archives, Collection 364, Box 8, Folder 1.

52. "Bunche Surprised by News of Prize," *New York Times,* September 22, 1950.

53. "Edward R. Murrow Answers the Question: Are Celebrities Human?" *New York Herald Tribune,* November 6, 1955.

54. Bunche, note, September 14, 1966, UN Archives, Box 370/38/5.

55. Presidential Proclamation 2914, December 16, 1950.

56. "Bunche Calls UN Action in Korea 'Turning Point in Modern History,'" *New York Times,* September 25, 1950.

57. Bunche, "Some Reflections on Peace in Our Time," December 11, 1950, UCLA Archives, Box 415, Folder 5.

58. Bunche, note, December 10, 1950, UCLA Archives, Collection 364, Box 8, Folder 2; "Four Americans Get Their Nobel Prizes," *New York Times,* December 11, 1950.

59. Arnold Mille, "Peace Award Gives Norway Bunche Fever," *New Journal and Guide,* December 23, 1950, at 12.

60. "Bunche Asked That College Disclose Teaching Post," *Harvard Crimson,* October 26, 1950. https://www.thecrimson.com/article/1950/10/26/bunche-asked-that-college-not-disclose/

61. Bunche, note, June 1951, UN Archives, Box 370/38/5.

Chapter 12

1. *True Comics* #79, October 1949.

2. Robert Vitalis, *White World Order, Black Power Politics* (Ithaca, NY: Cornell University Press, 2015).

3. Arnold Mille, "Peace Award Gives Norway Bunche Fever," *New Journal and Guide*, December 23, 1950, at 12.

4. "One UN Official Leaves for Europe, Another Returns," *New York Times*, December 23, 1950, at 5.

5. Charles P. Henry, *Ralph Bunche: Model Negro or American Other?* (New York: New York University Press, 1999), at 157.

6. George Gallup "Eisenhower Leads List of 10 Most Admired Men in World," *Washington Post*, January 31, 1951.

7. "The Talk of the Town," *The New Yorker*, January 1, 1972.

8. Jeffrey Lyons, *What a Time It Was! Leonard Lyons and the Golden Age of New York Nightlife* (New York: Abbeville Press, 2015), 45, 468.

9. Bunche, note and ticket, UN Archives, Box 370/38/20.

10. See, for example, Bunche to Ivan Browning of Los Angeles, December 29, 1966 (thanking him for sending tapes of his singing) and the presumably unrelated Annie Browning of New York City, who wrote to Bunche the same year asking for help with her landlord. UCLA Bunche Archives, Box 259, Box 1 (Correspondence).

11. General Assembly Official Records, 7th Session, 417th Plenary Meeting, March 30, 1953, at 579.

12. Bunche, " International Trusteeship System," in Trygve Lie (ed.), *Peace on Earth* (New York: Hermitage House, 1949), at 116.

13. Sylvanus Olympio, Presentation to the Trusteeship Council, December 8, 1947, UCLA Bunche Archives, Box 70, Folder 10.

14. Notes, "Ralph Bunche Conference," May 6, 1986 (New York), UCLA Archives, Collection 364, Box 3, Folder 1.

15. Ben Keppel, *The Work of Democracy: Ralph Bunche, Kenneth B. Clark, Lorraine Hansberry, and the Cultural Politics of Race* (Cambridge, MA: Harvard University Press, 1995), at 62.

16. Bunche, Williams College Commencement Speech, June 17, 1951, Schomburg Center for the Study of Black Culture, Bunche Archives, Box 14-A.

17. Bunche, Speech at Columbia University, March 12, 1951, Schomburg Center for the Study of Black Culture, Bunche Archives, Box 14-A.

18. Robert Service, *A History of Modern Russia* (Cambridge, MA: Harvard University Press, 2003), at 305.

19. Charles Martin, "'The American Dilemma': The Civil Rights Congress and the 1951 Genocide Petition to the United Nations," *Journal of American Ethnic History*, 16, 4 (Summer 1997), at 40.

20. Bunche, "President Barclay's Visit in Relation to PW" (Secret), June 1, 1943, UCLA Bunche Archives, Box 57, Folder 15.

21. "US Policy Worries Europe, Bunche Says," *New York Times*, December 7, 1951.

22. Martin, " 'The American Dilemma,' " at 36.

23. Mary Dudziak, *Cold War Civil Rights: Race and the Image of American Democracy* (Princeton, NJ: Princeton University Press, 2000), at 13. See also Keppel, *The Work of Democracy*.

24. Dudziak, *Cold War Civil Rights* and Mary Dudziak, "Brown as a Cold War Case," *Journal of American History* (2004).

25. John Popham, "Loyalty of Negro Hailed by Bunche," *New York Times*, July 5, 1954.

26. Earl Warren, "The New Home of Our Profession: The American Bar Center Dedication Address," *American Bar Association Journal*, 40, 11 (1954), at 956.

27. Melinda Schwenk, "Negro Stars and the USIA's Portrait of Democracy," *Race, Gender and Class in Media* 8, 4 (2001), at 117.

28. Penny von Eschen, *Satchmo Blows Up the World: Jazz Ambassadors Play the Cold War* (Cambridge, MA: Harvard University Press, 2006), at 16. For a broader take on the Cold War and culture, see Louis Menand, *The Free World* (New York: Farrar, Straus, 2021).

29. Von Eschen, *Satchmo Blows Up the World*, at 10.

30. Hugo Berkeley, "When America's Hottest Jazz Stars Were Sent to Cool Cold-War Tensions," *The Guardian*, May 3, 2018.

31. Bunche, Interview with Woody Klein, *New York World-Telegram*, July 29, 1963, UCLA Bunche Archives, Box 233, Folder 5.

32. Nikhil Singh, *Black Is a Country* (Cambridge, MA: Harvard University Press, 2004), at 168.

33. Franklin Frazier, *Black Bourgeosie* (New York: Collier, 1962), at 158.

34. "Ralph Bunche: A Great Californian," *CTA Journal*, October 1955, at 5.

35. Singh, *Black Is a Country*, at 42.

36. Bunche, Interview with Woody Klein, *New York World-Telegram*, July 29, 1963, UCLA Bunche Archives, Box 233, Folder 5.

37. Bunche, "The Case for the UN," February 19, 1951, East Midwood Jewish Center, Brooklyn, NY, Bunche Archives, Schomburg Center for the Study of Black Culture, Box 14-A.

38. Bunche, "Address to the NAACP," July 1, 1951, Atlanta, GA, Schomburg Center for the Study of Black Culture, Bunche Archives, Box 14-A.

39. Bunche, "What America Means to Me," in Charles P. Henry (ed.), *Ralph J. Bunche: Selected Speeches and Writings* (Ann Arbor: University of Michigan Press, 1996), at 267.

40. The line was Malcolm X's. Bunche, Interview with Woody Klein, *New York World-Telegram*, July 29, 1963, UCLA Bunche Archives, Box 233, Folder 5.

41. Jonathan Holloway, "Ralph Bunche and the Responsibilities of the Public Intellectual," *Journal of Negro Education*, 73, 2 (2004), at 125.

42. E. H. Carr, *The Twenty Years Crisis: 1919–1939* (New York: Harper and Row, 1939).

43. The paper has no author or date, but it has many hallmarks of Bunche's writings and was kept by Bunche in his personal files. "Background Paper for Use at the East-West African Consular Conference, 1950," Labeled Confidential. UN Archives, Box 370 1, 1.

44. Andrew Glass, "Bernard Baruch Coins the Term Cold War," *Politico*, April 16, 2010. https://www.politico.com/story/2010/04/bernard-baruch-coins-term-cold-war-april-16-1947-035862#:~:text=On%20this%20day%20in%201947,States%20and%20the%20Soviet%20Union.

45. Report of the Special Committee, UNGA Official Records: Fifth Session, Supplement 17 (1951), at 2.

46. UN GA Resolution 323 (IV), November 15, 1949.

47. UN GA Resolution 293 (IV), October 21, 1949.
48. Bunche, notes, December 14, 1970, Schomburg Center Bunche Archives, Box 19, Folder 18.
49. Brian Urquhart, *Ralph Bunche: An American Odyssey* (New York: Norton, 1993), at 115.
50. Transcript, "The Eleanor Roosevelt Program," Episode 1, Part 2, October 11, 1950, The Eleanor Roosevelt Papers. https://www2.gwu.edu/~erpapers/radiotv/doc.cfm?_p=erprg&_f=erprg_001_pt02
51. Quoted in Mark Mazower, *Governing the World* (New York: Penguin, 2012), at 247.
52. Bunche to Ruth Bunche, November 25, 1951, UCLA Archives Collection 364, Box 3, Folder 8.
53. Ralph McGill, "Story of a Boomerang," *Atlanta Constitution*, February 21, 1952, at 1.

Chapter 13

1. Bunche, diary, UCLA Bunche Archives, Box 282, Folder 3.
2. Bunche, diary, UCLA Bunche Archives, Box 282, Folder 3.
3. Brian Urquhart, *Ralph Bunche: An American Odyssey* (New York: Norton, 1993), at 242.
4. Charles Hairgrow, "Stassen Would Put a Negro in His Cabinet," *Chicago Defender*, February 16, 1952, at 3.
5. "Ike Confers with Dr. Ralph Bunche during United Nations Tour," *Atlanta Daily World*, November 25, 1952.
6. Luke Nichter, *The Last Brahmin: Henry Cabot Lodge, Jr. and the Making of the Cold War* (New Haven, CT: Yale University Press, 2020), at 140.
7. Warren Hoge, "Swedes Dispute Translation of a UN Legend's Book," *New York Times*, May 22, 2005.
8. Bunche, note, no date, UN Archives, Box 370/38/10.
9. Place card, UCLA Bunche Archives, Box 282, Folder 5.
10. Bunche, diary, UCLA Bunche Archives, Box 282, Folder 5.
11. Bunche, diary, UCLA Bunche Archives, Box 282, Folder 5.
12. Bunche, note, no date, UCLA Bunche Archives, Box 282, Folder 5.
13. Bunche, note, no date, UN Archives, Box 370/38/10.
14. Urquhart, *Ralph Bunche*, at 257.
15. Roger Lipsey, *Hammarskjold: A Life* (University of Michigan Press, 2013), at 136.
16. Bunche, "The United Nations Operation in the Congo," in Andrew Cordier and Wilder Foote (eds.), *The Quest for Peace* (New York: Columbia University Press, 1965), at 120.
17. Bunche, *Operation in the Congo*, at 122.
18. Bunche and Hammarskjold, note, December 4, 1958, UN Archives, Box 370/38/10.
19. Bunche, notes, undated, UN Archives 370/38/11.
20. Bunche, diary, UCLA Bunche Archives, Box 282, Folder 4.
21. Bunche, diary, UCLA Bunche Archives, Box 282, Folder 4.

22. "Bunche, in Israel, Urges Refugee Aid," *New York Times*, February 8, 1953; "'It's Good to Be Back' Says Bunche as Guest of Government," *Jerusalem Post*, February 8, 1953.
23. "Bunche, In Israel, Urges Refugee Aid," *New York Times*, February 8, 1953.
24. Bunche, "Some Reflections on Peace in Our Time," Oslo, December 11, 1950. http://www.nobelprize.org/prizes/peace/1950/bunche
25. "It's Good to Be Back' Says Bunche as Guest of Government," *Jerusalem Post*, February 8, 1953.
26. "Bunche Blasts 'Smearing,' Born of Intolerance," *Washington Post*, June 9 1953.
27. Shirley Hazzard, "Breaking Faith," *The New Yorker*, September 25, 1989, at 63.
28. Nichter, *The Last Brahmin*, at 137.
29. Craig Thompson, "Sinister Doings at the UN," *Saturday Evening Post*, November 17, 1951, UN Archives S-0844-0002-07.
30. "Attacks on UN Upset Dr. Bunche," *Los Angeles Times*, May 13, 1952, at 2.
31. "Canadian Jurist to Head 3-Man UN Loyalty Panel," *St. Louis Post-Dispatch*, January 15, 1953; "Lie Lauds Check-Up on UN Americans," *New York Times*, January 17, 1953.
32. Charles P. Henry, "Civil Rights and National Security," in Benjamin Rivlin (ed.), *Ralph Bunche: The Man and His Times* (New York: Holmes and Meier, 1990), at 52.
33. Brenda Gayle Plummer, *A Rising Wind: Black Americans and Foreign Affairs* (Chapel Hill: University of North Carolina Press, 1996), at 173.
34. Henry, "Civil Rights and National Security," at 53.
35. Urquhart, *Ralph Bunche*, at 248.
36. Urquhart, *Ralph Bunche*, at 248.
37. Henry, "Civil Rights and National Security," at 54.
38. Bunche to Hammarskjold, July 13, 1953, Dag Hammarskjold Collection, Kungliga Biblioteket, Stockholm, Sweden.
39. Ben Keppel, *The Work of Democracy* (Harvard University Press, 1995), at 70.
40. "Not Lonely for DC, Asserts Dr. Bunche" *Afro-American*, January 23, 1954.
41. Hy Gardner, "Coast to Coast," *New York Herald Tribune*, February 1, 1954.
42. "Bunche Inquiry Called a Farce," *New York Times*, May 27, 1954.
43. Bunche, notes, UCLA Bunche Archives, Box 282, Folder 8.
44. Joseph Lash, *Eleanor: The Years Alone* (Norton, 1972), at 232.
45. PBS, *Ralph Bunche: An American Odyssey* (Documentary, 2001).
46. Jonathan Holloway, "Ralph Bunche and the Responsibilities of the Public Intellectual," *Journal of Negro Education*, 73 (2005), at 134.
47. A. M. Rosenthal, "Dr Bunche Cleared by Loyalty Board," *New York Times*, May 28, 1954, at 10.
48. Bunche and Hammarskjold, note, February 1, 1954, UN Archives, Box 370/38/10.
49. "UN Trouble Shooter," *Washington Post*, April 21, 1954.
50. Bunche, diary, April 10, 1955, UCLA Archives, Box 282, Folder 10.
51. APSA presidential address draft, Chicago, September 9, 1954 (written in his own hand as addendum), Bunche Archives, Schomburg Center, Box 14B.

52. Bunche, "Presidential Address," *American Political Science Review* (December 1954), at 969.
53. Bunche, "Presidential Address," at 971.
54. "Dr Bunche Holds UN Averted War," *New York Times*, September 13, 1953.

Chapter 14

1. Guy Laron, *Origins of the Suez Crisis* (Baltimore, MD: Johns Hopkins University Press, 2013), at 8.
2. Robert Doty, "Nasser Escapes Attempt on Life," *New York Times*, October 27, 1954.
3. Keith Kyle, *Suez* (London: I. B. Taurus, 1991), at 132.
4. Brian Urquhart, *Ralph Bunche: An American Odyssey* (New York: Norton, 1993), at 281.
5. Kyle, *Suez*, at 133.
6. Kyle, *Suez*, at 134.
7. William Roger Louis and Ronald Robinson, "The Imperialism of Decolonization," *Journal of Imperial and Commonwealth History* (1994), at 474; Reza Ghassemi, "Iran's Oil Nationalization and Mossadegh's Involvement with the World Bank," *Middle East Journal*, 65, 3 (2011).
8. UN Department of Information, "The Suez Canal Question," *Yearbook of the United Nations* (1956).
9. UN General Assembly Resolution 3201 (S-VI), 1974.
10. Charlotte Peevers, "Altering International Law: Bandung, Nasser, and the Suez Crisis," in *Bandung, Global History, and International Law* (Cambridge, UK: Cambridge University Press, 2017), at 574.
11. Laron, *Origins of the Suez Crisis*, at 152.
12. Report of the Security Council to the General Assembly, General Assembly Official Records, Seventh Session Supplement, No. 2 (A/2167) (New York, 1952), at 1.
13. UN Security Council Official Records, *S/PV 558* (September 1, 1951).
14. Constantinople Convention, signed October 29, 1888. https://www.suezcanal.gov.eg/English/About/CanalTreatiesAndDecrees/Pages/ConstantinopleConvention.aspx
15. "Suez Canal Zone," National Army Museum. https://www.nam.ac.uk/explore/suez-canal-zone
16. "Dwight Eisenhower and the Suez Canal Crisis of 1956," in Alex Roberto Hybel (ed.), *US Foreign Policy Decision-Making from Truman to Kennedy* (London: Palgrave Macmillan, 2014), at 102.
17. Benjamin Rivlin, "The Legacy of Ralph Bunche," in Benjamin Rivlin (ed.), *Ralph Bunche: The Man and His Times* (New York: Holmes and Meier, 1990), at 17.
18. "An Interview of Ralph J. Bunche by Arthur Rovine," April 13, 1966, UCLA Archives, Collection 364, Box 12, Folder 4.
19. Thomas Hamilton, "UN Starts Study of Its Atom Role," *New York Times*, October 2, 1954, at 1.

20. "Dr Bunche Envisions Wise Use of Atom," *New York Times*, November 25, 1955.
21. AP, "Atoms for Peace Conference," *Times of India*, October 2, 1957, at 7.
22. Luke Nichter, *The Last Brahmin: Henry Cabot Lodge, Jr and the Making of the Cold War* (New Haven, CT: Yale University Press, 2020), at 149.
23. "It Happened in New York," *Atlanta Daily World*, November 4, 1955, at 2.
24. "Theodore Roosevelt 'Radical Too,' Bunche Notes in Receiving Award," *New York Times*, October 28, 1954, at 37.
25. Roger Lipsey, *Hammarskjold: A Life* (Ann Arbor: University of Michigan Press, 2013), at 185.
26. Winthrop W. Aldridge, "The Suez Crisis: A Footnote to History," *Foreign Affairs*, 45, 3 (1967). Aldrich was the US ambassador to the UK during the Suez Crisis.
27. Kyle, *Suez*, at 277.
28. Odd Arne Wested, *The Cold War* (New York: Basic Books, 2017), at 133.
29. Study Group on Colonial Problems, Attendance List, in Archives of the Council on Foreign Relations; Records of Groups, Vol. LXII, 1955/1956.
30. "Bunche Sees Peril in African Areas," *New York Times*, May 2, 1954.
31. "Discussion Meeting Report; Colonialism," January 24, 1956, in Archives of the Council on Foreign Relations; Records of Groups, Vol. LXII, 1955/1956.
32. David Bosco, *Five to Rule Them All: The UN Security Council and the Making of the Modern World* (New York: Oxford University Press, 2009), at 72.
33. Memorandum of Discussion at the 295th Meeting of the National Security Council, Washington, DC, August 30, 1956, Foreign Relations of the United States, 1955–1957, Suez Crisis, July 26–December 31, 1956, vol. XVI. The connections between Panama and Suez were noted by many at the time; see, for example, Norman Padelford, "The Panama Canal and the Suez Crisis," *Proceedings of the American Society of International Law*, 51 (April 1957).
34. US National Security Council, Memorandum of Discussion, August 30, 1956.
35. Lipsey, *Hammarskjold*, at 297.
36. Harold Callender, "UN Occupation Offered," *New York Times*, November 3, 1956.
37. Amitav Acharya and See Sing Tan, "The Normative Relevance of the Bandung Conference for Contemporary Asian and International Order," in Amitav Acharya and Sing Tan (eds.), *Bandung Revisited* (National University of Singapore Press, 2008).
38. Laron, *Origins of the Suez Crisis*, at 107.
39. George Sokolsky, "Conference at Bandung Is Conference of Race," *Washington Post*, April 21, 1955.
40. Bandung Conference, *Final Communique*, republished in *Interventions: International Journal of Postcolonial Studies*, 11, 1 (2009), at 94.
41. Kyle, *Suez*, at 55.
42. Brenda Gayle Plummer, *Rising Wind: Black American and Foreign Affairs* (Chapel Hill: University of North Carolina Press, 1996), at 250.
43. Bunche, "The Struggle for Peace," *St. Louis Post-Dispatch*, June 8, 1955.
44. Lindsey Parrott, "UN Chief Sees a Calmer Spirit," *New York Times*, June 21, 1955.
45. Adekeye Adebajo, "From Bandung to Durban: Whither the Afro-Asian Coalition," in Acharya and Tan (eds.), *Bandung Revisited*, at 105.

46. Richard Wright, *The Color Curtain: A Report on the Bandung Conference* (New York: World Publishing, 1956), at 12, quoted in Luis Eslava, Michael Fakhri, and Vasuki Nesiah, "The Spirit of Bandung," in *Bandung, Global History, and International Law* (Cambridge, UK: Cambridge University Press, 2017), at 17.
47. Laron, *Origins of the Suez Crisis*, at 113.
48. Wested, *The Cold War*, at 271.
49. A. M. Rivera Jr., "Bunche Airs Colonialism Ills," *Pittsburgh Courier*, March 24, 1956.
50. "Bunche Sees Peril in African Areas," *New York Times*, May 2, 1954.
51. "The Suez Canal Question," *Yearbook of the United Nations* (1956).
52. UN Security Council Official Records, *S/PV 742* (October 13, 1956).
53. UN Security Council Official Records, *S/PV 736* (October 8, 1956).
54. Nichter, *The Last Brahmin*, at 150.
55. Aldridge, "The Suez Crisis," at 547.
56. Kyle, *Suez*, at 353.
57. Bunche to Hammarskjold, October 31, 1956, Dag Hammarskjold Collection, Kungliga Biblioteket, Stockholm, Sweden.
58. Bosco, *Five to Rule Them All*, at 76.
59. Note from the head of the US delegation to the UN Secretary General (September 20, 1950), at 5 UNGAOR (279th plenary meeting) Annexes (Agenda Item 68) 2–3 UN Doc A/1377.
60. UNGA Resolution 377A, November 3, 1950.
61. UNGA Resolution 997 (ES-1), November 2, 1956.
62. General Assembly, First Emergency Session Plenary Meeting, cited in Guy Sinclair, *To Reform the World* (New York: Oxford University Press, 2017), at 145.
63. Laron, *Origins of the Suez Crisis*, at 176.
64. Kyle, *Suez*, at 402.
65. Laron, *Origins of the Suez Crisis*, at 176.
66. Kyle, *Suez*, at 376.
67. *Foreign Relations of the United States*, 1955–1957, XVI, at 910.
68. Official Records of the General Assembly, ES-1, 561st Meeting, November 2, 1956 (paragraph 299).
69. Manuel Frohlich, "The Suez Story: Dag Hammarskjold, the United Nations, and the Creation of Peacekeeping," in Carsten Stahn and Henning Melber (eds.), *Peace Diplomacy, Global Justice, and International Agency* (Cambridge, UK: Cambridge University Press, 2014), at 315.
70. Kyle, *Suez*, at 389.
71. UNGA Resolution 998 (ES-1), November 4, 1956.
72. Bunche, notes, November 22, 1953, UCLA Archives, Collection 364, Box 3, Folder 1.
73. "Bunche, UN's Mr. Peace, Called on in Big Crisis," *Chicago Defender*, November 5, 1956.
74. Rovine Interview, supra.
75. Maxwell Cohen, "The Demise of UNEF," *International Journal*, 23, 1 (1967/8), at 19.
76. Lipsey, *Hammarskjold*, at 307.
77. United Nations Peacekeeping, "Our History," https://peacekeeping.un.org/en/our-history

78. Barbara Walter, Lise Howard, and Page Fortna, "The Extraordinary Relationship between Peacekeeping and Peace," *British Journal of Political Science* (2020), at 1.
79. K. Beardsley and Kristian Gleditsch, "Peacekeeping as Conflict Containment," *International Studies Review* 17 (2015).
80. Peggy Mann, *Ralph Bunche: UN Peacemaker* (New York: Coward, McCann, and Geoghegan, 1975), at 283.
81. Stanley Meisler, *United Nations: A History* (New York: Grove Press, 2011, rev. ed.), at 112.
82. "Soviet Troops Overrun Hungary," BBC, November 4, 1956. http://news.bbc.co.uk/onthisday/hi/dates/stories/november/4/newsid_2739000/2739039.stm
83. Nichter, *The Last Brahmin*, at 152.
84. Paul Kennedy, *The Parliament of Man: The Past, Present, and Future of the United Nations* (New York: Vintage Books, 2006), at 57.
85. Foreign Relations of the US, 1955–1957, Eastern Europe, Volume XXV, 153, Notes on the 42d Meeting of the Special Committee on Soviet and Related Problems, Washington, DC. November 1, 1956. https://history.state.gov/historicaldocuments/frus1955-57v25/d153
86. "The Suez Crisis, 1956," Office of the Historian, State Department of the United States. https://history.state.gov/milestones/1953-1960/suez
87. "Transcript of a Telephone Conversation between President Eisenhower in Washington and Prime Minister Eden in London," November 7, 1956, 9:55 a.m., FRUS, 1955–1957. https://history.state.gov/historicaldocuments/frus1955-57v16/d538
88. Dwight D. Eisenhower, "Radio and Television Report to the American People on Developments in the Middle East and Eastern Europe," October 31, 1956, *The American Presidency Project*. https://www.presidency.ucsb.edu/documents/radio-and-television-report-the-american-people-the-developments-eastern-europe-and-the
89. Kyle, *Suez*, at 425.

Chapter 15

1. *Public Papers of the Secretaries-General of the UN*, Vol. III (New York: Columbia University Press, 1973), at 405.
2. Manuel Frohlich, "The Suez Story: Dag Hammarskjold, the United Nations, and the Creation of Peacekeeping," in Carsten Stahn and Henning Melber (eds.), *Peace Diplomacy, Global Justice, and International Agency* (Cambridge, UK: Cambridge University Press, 2014), at 335.
3. William Frye, *A United Nations Peace Force* (New York: Oceana Publications, 1957/2021), at 24.
4. Frye, *United Nations Peace Force*, at 26.
5. "Transcript of Press Briefing," November 16, 1956, UCLA Archives, Collection 364, Box 12, Folder 5.
6. James Sloan, *The Militarization of Peacekeeping in the 21st Century* (Portland: Hart, 2011), at 22–23.

7. "UN on the Spot," *Washington Post*, November 16, 1956.
8. Meeting of the UNEF Advisory Committee, Transcript, November 20, UN Archives, Box 316/1/9 at 8.
9. Meeting of the UNEF Advisory Committee, Transcript, November 20, UN Archives, Box 316/1/9, at 12.
10. Frohlich, "The Suez Story," at 324.
11. "Ike Receives Bunche UN Reports," *Daily Defender*, November 1, 1956.
12. James Cockayne and David Malone, "The Ralph Bunche Centennial: Peace Operations Then and Now," *Global Governance*, 11, 3 (2005), at 332.
13. "Transcript of Press Briefing," November 16, 1956, UCLA Archives, Collection 364, Box 12, Folder 4.
14. UN Department of Public Information, Hammarksjold Remarks, November 14, 1956, UN Archives, Box 331/60/4.
15. Bunche to Burns, December 5, 1956, UN Archives, Box 315/1/3; Brian Urquhart, *Ralph Bunche: An American Odyssey* (New York: Norton, 1993), at 271.
16. Bunche to Hammarskjold, November 22, 1956, UCLA Archives, Collection 364, Box 12, Folder 4.
17. Dag Hammarskjold, Statement to the Press on UNEF, November 28, 1956, *Public Papers of the Secretaries-General of the UN*, Vol. III (New York: Columbia University Press, 1973), at 400.
18. "An Interview of Ralph J. Bunche by Arthur Rovine," April 13, 1966, UCLA Archives, Collection 364, Box 12, Folder 4.
19. Burns to Bunche, December 13, 1956, L 179-122, Vol. I, UNEF Incoming Cables, at 362, Dag Hammarskjold Collection, Kungliga Biblioteket, Stockholm, Sweden.
20. Bunche to Burns, December 6, 1956, UN Archives, Box 315/1/3.
21. Meeting of the Advisory Committee on UNEF, December 4, 1956, Transcript, UN Archives 316/1/11 at 11.
22. Meeting of the Advisory Committee on UNEF, December 8, 1956, Transcript, UN Archives 316/1/11 at 14.
23. Burns to Bunche, November 27, 1956, L179-122, Vol. I, UNEF Incoming Cables, at 362, Dag Hammarskjold Collection, Kungliga Biblioteket, Stockholm, Sweden.
24. "Transcript of Press Briefing," November 16, 1956, UCLA Archives, Collection 364, Box 12, Folder 4.
25. Urquhart, *Ralph Bunche*, at 273.
26. William Roger Louis and Ronald Robinson, "The Imperialism of Decolonization," *Journal of Imperial and Commonwealth History*, 17 (1994), at 480.
27. Derek Brown, "1956: Suez and the End of Empire," *The Guardian*, March 14, 2001.
28. "Foreign Policy and Domestic Politics: Leon Epstein, British Politics in the Suez Crisis—A Discussion," *Political Science Quarterly*, 80, 3 (1965), at 415.
29. Meeting of the Advisory Committee on UNEF, December 18, 1956, Transcript, UN Archives 316/1/14, at 4.
30. UN Department of Peace Operations, *First United Nations Emergency Force*, at 10.
31. b Summary Record of a Meeting between the SG and his Advisers and the Delegation of Israel (Most Secret), November 28, 156, UCLA Archives, Collection 364, Box 12, Folder 5.

32. Summary Record of a Meeting between the SG and his Advisers and the Delegation of Israel (Most Secret), November 28, 156, UCLA Archives, Collection 364, Box 12, Folder 5.

33. Burns to Bunche, January 18, 1957, L 179-122, Vol I, UNEF Incoming Cables, at 362, Dag Hammarskjold Collection, Kungliga Biblioteket, Stockholm, Sweden.

34. Odd Arne Wested, *The Cold War: A World History* (New York: Basic Books, 2017), at 273.

35. FRUS Vol XVII, "Telegram from the Mission at the UN to the Department of State," January 23, 1957, https://history.state.gov/historicaldocuments/frus1955-57v17/d32

36. Hamilton Fish Armstrong, "The UN Experience in Gaza," *Foreign Affairs*, July 1957, at 611.

37. Stavropoulos to Hammarskjold, January 25, 1957, L179-122, Vol I, UNEF Incoming Cables, at 362, Dag Hammarskjold Collection, Kungliga Biblioteket, Stockholm, Sweden.

38. UN Department of Peace Operations, *First United Nations Emergency Force*, at 16.

39. Meeting of the Advisory Committee on UNEF, March 16, 1957, Transcript, UN Archives, Box 316/2/2, at 32.

40. "Bunche Airs Danger," *Christian Science Monitor*, January 28, 1956.

41. Bunche to Hammarskjold, December 19, 1956, Dag Hammarskjold Collection, Kungliga Biblioteket, Stockholm, Sweden.

42. Peggy Mann, *Ralph Bunche: UN Peacemaker* (New York: Coward, McCann, and Geoghegan, 1975), at 284.

43. Armstrong, "The UN Experience in Gaza," at 614.

44. WGBH, "Prospects of Mankind with Eleanor Roosevelt; Africa: Revolution in Haste," 3/06/1960, WGBH Media Library & Archives, accessed October 3, 2020. http://openvault.wgbh.org/catalog/V_9749A45266AF413DBE81BFA6ED51D385 (Bunche remarks).

45. Urquhart, *Ralph Bunche*, at 277.

46. Bunche, notes, March–April 1957, UCLA Archives Box 282 Folder 12.

47. Bunche to King, February 22, 1956, Stanford Martin Luther King Jr. Research and Education Institute, King Papers. http://okra.stanford.edu/transcription/document_images/Vol03Scans/134_22-Feb-1956_From%20Ralph%20J%20Bunche.pdf

48. Charles P. Henry, "Civil Rights and National Security: The Case of Ralph Bunche," in Benjamin Rivlin (ed.), *Ralph Bunche: The Man and His Times* (New York: Holmes and Meier, 1990), at 60.

49. Paul M. Garr, " 'India's Rasputin?' V. K. Menon and American Misperceptions of Indian Foreign Policy, 1947–1964," *Diplomacy and Statecraft*, 22, 2 (2011), at 243.

50. Martin Luther King Jr., "The Birth of a New Nation," sermon delivered at Dexter Avenue Baptist Church, April 7, 1957, Stanford Martin Luther King Jr Research and Education Institute, King Papers. http://okra.stanford.edu/transcription/document_images/Vol04Scans/155_7-Apr-1957_The%20Birth%20of%20a%20New%20Nation.pdf

51. "Nationalists Rapped for Booing Bunche," *New York Amsterdam News*, August 2, 1958. Robert Vitalis, *White World Order, Black Power Politics* (Cornell University Press, 2015), at 121.

52. King Encyclopedia, "Ghana Trip," Stanford Martin Luther King Jr Research and Education Institute. https://kinginstitute.stanford.edu/encyclopedia/ghana-trip

Chapter 16

1. Brian Urquhart, *Ralph Bunche: An American Odyssey* (New York: Norton, 1998), at 277.

2. Burns to Hammarskjold, March 10, 1957, L179-122, Vol. I, UNEF Incoming Cables, at 362, Dag Hammarskjold Collection, Kungliga Biblioteket, Stockholm, Sweden; UN DPI, Press Release, "UN Undersecretary Sees President Nasser, Expresses Regret Over Gaza Death," March 13, 1957, UN Archives Box 164/3/6; Hamilton Fish Armstrong, "The UN Experience in Gaza," *Foreign Affairs* (July 1957), at 616.

3. FRUS Vol XVII, "Telegram from the Mission at the UN to the Department of State," March 11, 1957. https://history.state.gov/historicaldocuments/frus1955-57v17/d210

4. Bunche to Hammarskjold, March 11, 1957, L 179-122, Vol. I, UNEF Incoming Cables, Dag Hammarskjold Collection, Kungliga Biblioteket, Stockholm, Sweden.

5. Homer Bigart, "UN Offers Cairo Its Cooperation in Rule of Gaza," *New York Times*, March 14, 1957.

6. Armstrong, "The UN Experience in Gaza," at 617.

7. FRUS Vol. XVII, "Memorandum of a Conversation, Department of State, Washington, March 18, 1957." https://history.state.gov/historicaldocuments/frus1955-57v17/d233

8. Letter from Israel to the President of the UNSC, March 13, 1957, UN Archives, Box 164/3/6.

9. Bunche, notes, March 14 1957, UN Archives, Box 370/29/2.

10. "UNEF Helps Gaza Citrus Growers," UN Department of Public Information, EMF/123, March 13, 1957, UN Archives Box 164/3/6.

11. "Bunche Still in Gaza," *New York Times*, March 19, 1957.

12. Bunche to Hammarskjold, UNEF 598, March 15, 1957, L 179-122, Vol. I, UNEF Incoming Cables, Dag Hammarskjold Collection, Kungliga Biblioteket, Stockholm, Sweden.

13. Meeting of the Advisory Committee on UNEF, March 19, 1957, Transcript, UN Archives Box 316/2/4, at 1.

14. Urquhart, *Ralph Bunche*, at 285.

15. Meeting of the UNEF Advisory Committee, April 15, 1957, Transcript, UN Archives, Box 316/2/7, at 2.

16. Matthew Elderfield, "Rebuilding the Special Relationship: The 1957 Bermuda Talks," *Cambridge Review of International Affairs*, 3, 1 (1989).

17. Peggy Mann, *Ralph Bunche: UN Peacemaker* (New York: McCann, 1975), at 285.

18. Bunche, diary, May 10, 1957, UCLA Bunche Archives, Box 282, Folder 13.
19. Bunche, note, no date, UCLA Bunche Archives, Box 282, Folder 13.
20. Bunche, diary, May 10, 1957, UCLA Bunche Archives, Box 282, Folder 13.
21. Henry Vigier, Memo, May 28, 1959 (marked "Confidential"), UN Archives, Box 370/26/6; other notes of the encounter (unattributed) same file.
22. Bunche, diary, May 10, 1957, UCLA Bunche Archives, Box 282, Folder 13.
23. Bunche, diary, May 10, 1957, UCLA Bunche Archives, Box 282, Folder 13.
24. Bunche, diary, May 10, 1957, UCLA Bunche Archives, Box 282, Folder 13.
25. UN DPI, "UNEF in Gaza Two Months Today," Press Release EMF/166, May 7, 1957, UN Archives S-0164-0003-04 (digital version).
26. Mann, *UN Peacemaker*, at 286.
27. William Frye, *A United Nations Peace Force* (New York: Oceana Publications, 1957/2021), at 66.
28. Advisory Committee on UNEF, June 12 1957, Transcript, UN Archives, Box 316/2/10, at 1.
29. "An Interview of Ralph J. Bunche by Arthur Rovine," April 13, 1966, UCLA Archives, Collection 364, Box 12, Folder 4.
30. "Text of Hammarskjold Memorandum on Mideast Peace Force," *New York Times*, June 19, 1967.
31. Power to Bunche, September 16, 1957, UN Archives, Box 316/1/2; Meeting of the Advisory Committee on UNEF, March 5, 1958, Transcript, UN Archives Box 316/2/17, at 5.
32. Mann, *UN Peacemaker*, at 287.
33. Keith Kyle, *Suez* (London: I. B. Taurus, 1991), at 542.
34. Urquhart, *Ralph Bunche*, at 297.
35. *The Sand Dune* (UNEF monthly magazine), July 1966, UCLA Archives, Box 20, Folder 2.
36. James Cockayne and David Malone, "The Ralph Bunche Centennial: Peace Operations Then and Now," *Global Governance*, 11, 3 (2005), at 331.
37. Burns to Bunche, Cable, October 10, 1958, UN Archives Box 316/1/3.
38. William Roger Louis and Ronald Robinson, "The Imperialism of Decolonization," *Journal of Imperial and Commonwealth History* (1994), at 482.
39. Bunche, Diary, September 23, 1957, UCLA Bunche Archives, Box 282, Folder 14.
40. Bunche, Diary, October 5, 1957, UCLA Bunche Archives, Box 282, Folder 14.
41. Hammarskjold to Bunche, October 8, 1957, UN Archives, Box 370/39/18.
42. Mary Dudziak, "The Little Rock Crisis and Foreign Affairs: Race, Resistance, and the Image of American Democracy," *Southern California Law Review*, (September 1997), at 1669.
43. "Bunche Says White Power Declining," *New York Amsterdam News*, February 21, 1959.
44. King Encyclopedia, "Ghana Trip," Stanford Martin Luther King Jr Research and Education Institute. https://kinginstitute.stanford.edu/encyclopedia/ghana-trip
45. "New York Liberals Push UN Official," *Pittsburgh Courier*, February 22, 1958.
46. "The Move to Draft Dr. Bunche," *Daily Defender*, February 20, 1958.

47. Michigan State University National Poll (no date); Presidential Papers of John F. Kennedy, Folder: Polls, General, Digital Identifier JFKPOF-105-001-p0042.

48. Leonard Lyons, The Lyons Den, *Daily Defender*, August 18, 1958.

49. James Kaplan, *Sinatra: The Chairman* (New York: Penguin, 2016), at 261.

50. Stanley Hoffman, "Ralph Bunche: A Man of the World but Never at Home," *Foreign Affairs* (January–February 1995).

51. John Rogers, "Tennis Club Bars Bunche's Son: UN Aide Hits Discrimination at Forest Hills Courts," *New York Herald Tribune*, July 9, 1959.

52. Philip Benjamin, "City Investigates Tennis Club Bias," *New York Times*, July 10, 1959.

53. Robert Alden, "Pattern of Bias in Clubs Found," *New York Times*, July 13, 1959.

54. Bunche to Robinson, November 20, 1963, UCLA Archives, Box 235, Folder 7.

55. "Don't Expect Spectacular Action on Disarmament, Dr. Bunche Advises," *Los Angeles Times*, April 12, 1958.

56. Meeting of the UNEF Advisory Committee, June 2, 1959, Transcript, UN Archives, Box 316/2/21, at 3–4.

57. Meeting of the UNEF Advisory Committee, June 2, 1959, Transcript, UN Archives. Box 316/2/21, at 13.

58. Galtung, "A Pilot Project Report from Gaza," February 1964, Institute for Social Research, at 7, UN Archives, Box 316/4/8.

59. Charles P. Henry, *Model Negro or American Other?* (New York: NYU Press), at 181.

60. "You Said It," *New York Amsterdam News*, February 27, 1960.

Chapter 17

1. Bunche to Hammarskjold, July 5, 1960, UN Archives 370, Box 7, at 8.

2. Bunche to Hammarskjold, June 27, 1960, UN Archives 370, Box 3, at 6.

3. Adam Hochschild, *King Leopold's Ghost: A Story of Greed, Terrorism, and Heroism in Colonial Africa* (New York: HarperCollins, 1998).

4. David van Reybrouck, *Congo: The Epic History of a People* (New York: Ecco, 2014), at 39.

5. Bunche, "The United Nations Operation in the Congo," in Andrew Cordier and Wilder Foote (eds.), *The Quest for Peace* (New York: Columbia University Press, 1965), at 123.

6. *The United Nations at 70* (New York: Rizzoli, 2015), at 134: "the compound was built to accommodate delegates from 70 to 80 countries"; George Dudley, *A Workshop for Peace* (Cambridge, MA: MIT Press, 1994), at 54, showing plans for a UN campus seventy delegations.

7. John Hadwen and Johan Kaufman, *How United Nations Decisions Are Made*, 2nd ed. (New York: Oceana, 1962), at 128.

8. Thomas Kanza, *Conflict in the Congo: The Rise and Fall of Patrice Lumumba* (New York: Penguin, 1972), at 143.

9. Hammarskjold to Bunche, June 29, 1960, UN Archives Box 370/7/10.

10. Interview with former Assistant Secretary of State for International Organizations, Harlan Cleveland, April 22, 1960, *Yale UN Oral History Project*. https://digitallibr ary.un.org/record/466734?ln=en

11. David Kay, "The Politics of Decolonization," *International Organization* (Fall 1967), at 789.
12. Mark Mazower, *No Enchanted Palace: The End of Empire and the Ideological Origins of the United Nations* (Princeton, NJ: Princeton University Press, 2009), at 179.
13. Ruth Bunche to Ralph Bunche, January 14, 1960, UCLA Archives, Collection 364, Box 3, Folder 8.
14. Bunche, diaries, January 8, 1960, UCLA Bunche Archives, Box 283, Folder 5.
15. Roger Lipsey, *Hammarskjold: A Life* (Ann Arbor: University of Michigan Press, 2013), at 396.
16. Van Reybrouck, *Congo*, at 243.
17. Lipsey, *Hammarskjold: A Life*, at 385.
18. Rene Lamarchand, *Political Awakening in the Belgian Congo* (Berkeley: University of California Press, 1964), at 161.
19. Lise Namikas, *Battleground Africa: Cold War in the Congo, 1960–1965* (Stanford, CA: Stanford University Press, 2013), at 35.
20. WGBH, *Prospects of Mankind*, American Archive of Public Broadcasting, March 6, 1960. https://americanarchive.org/catalog/cpb-aacip_15-09w0w2sd
21. WGBH, *Prospects of Mankind*.
22. de Seynes to Bunche, June 27, 1960, UN Archives, Box 370/12/4.
23. Bunche to Hammarskjold: June 27, 1960, UN Archives 370, Box 3, at 6.
24. Lamarchand, *Political Awakening in the Belgian Congo*, at 96; Van Reybrouck, *Congo*, at 214–219.
25. "The Song of the Congo," No date or author, UN Archives 370, Box 3, at 8.
26. Crawford Young, "Ralph Bunche and Patrice Lumumba: The Fatal Encounter," in Robert Hill and Edmond Keller (eds.), *Trustee for the Human Community: Ralph Bunche, the United Nations, and the Decolonization of Africa* (Athens: Ohio University Press, 2010), at 135.
27. Bunche to Mashler, August 9, 1960, UN Archives, Box 370/12/4.
28. Kanza, *Conflict in the Congo*, at 142, 143.
29. Interview with Sture Linner, *Yale UN Oral History Project*, November 8, 1990, ST/DPI/Oral History 02/L45 10-11.
30. Bunche to Hammarskjold: June 27, 1960, UN Archives 370, Box 3, at 6.
31. Bunche, "French Educational Policy in Togoland and Dahomey," in Charles P. Henry, *Ralph Bunche: Selected Speeches and Writings* (Ann Arbor: University of Michigan Press, 1995), at 116.
32. Bunche, "The UN Operation in the Congo," Dag Hammarskjold Memorial Lecture, Columbia University, in Henry (ed.), *Ralph J. Bunche*, at 193.
33. Kay, *Politics of Decolonization*, at 789.
34. Bunche to Hammarskjold: June 27, 1960, UN Archives 370, Box 3, at 6.
35. Abdulaye Yerodia Ndombasi, interview, in *Congo Independence Crisis 1960*. https://www.youtube.com/watch?v=qkTSCcW1MDo
36. PBS, *Ralph Bunche: An American Odyssey* (Documentary, 2001).
37. Van Reybrouck, *Congo*, at 271.
38. Brian Urquhart, *Ralph Bunche: An American Odyssey* (New York: Norton, 1993), at 306.

39. Malcolm X, "OAAU Founding Rally," in George Breitman (ed.), *Malcolm X, by Any Means Necessary* (Pathfinder Press, 1970), at 64.
40. Harry Gilroy, "Lumumba Assails Colonialism as Congo Is Freed," *New York Times*, July 1, 1960.
41. For example, NPR, "Years after His Murder, Congo Leader Stirs Emotion," May 10, 2008; "The Congo: Lumumba Jumbo," *Time*, December 25, 1964, at 23.
42. Bunche to Hammarskjold (Confidential), July 4, 1960, UN Archives, 370/3/6.
43. Namikas, *Battleground Africa*, at 63.
44. "Marred: M. Lumumba's Offensive Speech in King's Presence," *The Guardian*, July 1, 1960.
45. Harry Gilroy, "Lumumba Assails Colonialism as Congo Is Freed," *New York Times*, July 1, 1960.
46. Bunche to Hammarskjold, July 4, 1960, UN Archives 370, Box 3, at 6.
47. Van Reybrouck, *Congo*, at 275.
48. Bunche to Hammarskjold (Confidential), July 4, 1960, UN Archives, 370/3/6.
49. Stephen Weissman, *American Foreign Policy in the Congo, 1960–1964* (1974), at 56.
50. de Seynes to Bunche, June 27, 1960, UN Archives, Box 370/12/4.
51. Homer Bigart, "Coalition Urged in Belgian Congo," *New York Times*, May 29, 1960.
52. Interview with Linner, at 8.
53. Transcript of press conference, September 1, 1960, UN Archives 370, Box 12, at 2.
54. Bunche, "The UN Operation in the Congo," at 197.
55. Namikas, *Battleground Africa*, at 34.
56. "Mining Congo: A Global Power Ploy," *New York Times*, November 21, 2021; Susan Williams, *Spies in the Congo: The Race for the Ore That Built the Atomic Bomb* (London: Macmillan, 2016).
57. Bunche to Hammarskjold, July 19, 1960. UN Archives 370, Box 7, at 8.
58. Frantz Fanon, *The Wretched of the Earth* (New York: Grove Press, 1963), at 35.

Chapter 18

1. Ryan Irwin, "Sovereignty in the Congo Crisis," in Elisabeth Leake and Lesley James (eds.), *Decolonization and the Cold War: Negotiating Independence* (London: Bloomsbury, 2015), at 207.
2. Bunche to Hammarskjold, July 12, 1960, UN Archives 370, Box 7, 8.
3. Bunche to Hammarskjold, July 10, 1960, UN Archives 370, Box 7, 8.
4. Madeleine Kalb, *The Congo Cables: The Cold War in Africa from Eisenhower to Kennedy* (New York: Macmillan, 1982), at 7.
5. Bunche to Hammarskjold, July 13, 1960. UN Archives 370, Box 7, 8.
6. Irwin, "Sovereignty in the Congo Crisis."
7. Elizabeth Schmidt, *Foreign Intervention in Africa: From the Cold War to the War on Terror* (Cambridge, UK: Cambridge University Press, 2013), at 60.
8. Bunche to Hammarskjold, July 12 and 13, 1960, UN Archives 370, Box 7, 8.
9. Schmidt, *Foreign Intervention in Africa*, at 59.
10. Lise Namikas, *Battleground Africa: Cold War in the Congo, 1960–1965* (Stanford University Press, 2013), at 23.

11. George C. Herring, *The American Century and Beyond: US Foreign Relations, 1893–2014* (New York: Oxford University Press, 2017), at 383.

12. "Nixon Flies to Visit Africa," *Cornell Daily Sun*, March 1, 1957.

13. UNSC Resolution 143; S/Res/143 (July 14, 1960).

14. Interview with Harlan Cleveland, Yale UN Oral History Project.

15. Kalb, *The Congo Cables*, at 22.

16. State Department, Office of the Historian, "The Congo, Decolonization, and the Cold War." https://history.state.gov/milestones/1961-1968/congo-decolonization

17. Stephen Weissman, "What Really Happened in Congo: The CIA, the Murder of Lumumba, and the Rise of Mobutu," *Foreign Affairs* (July 2014).

18. Brian Urquhart, *Hammarskjold* (New York: Norton, 1972), at 391.

19. Bunche to Hammarskjold, July 9, 1960, UN Archives 370, Box 7, 8.

20. Hammarskjold to Bunche, July 16, 1960, UN Archives 370, Box 7, 10.

21. UN Security Council Official Records, 873rd Meeting, July 13/14, 1960, S/PV 873, at 35.

22. Adam Roberts, "The So-Called 'Right' of Humanitarian Intervention," *Yearbook of International Humanitarian Law* (2001), at 33.

23. Covenant of the League of Nations, Article 22.

24. Makau Mutua, "The Complexity of Universalism in Human Rights," in Andras Sajo (ed.), *Human Rights with Modesty* (New York: Springer, 2004), at 61; see also Henry Richardson III, "Critical Perspectives on Intervention," *Maryland Journal of International Law* (2014).

25. Roberts, "The So-Called 'Right,'" at 33; see also Mark Mazower, *Governing the World* (New York: Penguin, 2012), arguing that the responsibility to protect "looks like nothing so much as the return of the civilizing mission and the 'humanitarian' interventions of previous centuries."

26. UNSC Resolution 145; S/Res/145 (July 22, 1960).

27. UN Security Council Official Records, 879th Meeting, July 22, 1960, S/PV 879.

28. Conversation notes, Bunche and Lumumba, August 12, 1960, UN Archives 370, Box 3, 6.

29. Bunche to Hammarskjold, July 21, 1960, UN Archives 370, Box 7, 8.

30. Bunche to Hammarskjold, July 17, 1960. UN Archives 370 Box 7, 8.

31. Bunche to Hammarskjold, July 21, 1960, UN Archives 370, Box 12, 2.

32. Stanley Meisler, *United Nations: A History* (New York: Grove Press, 2011), at 119.

33. Brian Urquhart, *Ralph Bunche: An American Odyssey* (New York: Norton, 1993), at 313.

34. Adam Hochschild, *King Leopold's Ghost* (New York: Mariner, 1998); Georges Nzongola-Ntalaja, *The Congo: From Leopold to Kabila* (London: Zed, 2002), at 19.

35. Bunche to Hammarskjold, July 19, 1960: UN Archives 370, Box 7, 8.

36. Irwin, "Sovereignty in the Congo Crisis," at 210.

37. Newspaper clippings, June 1, 1960; Bunche files, UN Archives Box 370/12/3.

38. David van Reybrouck, *Congo: The Epic History of a People* (New York: HarperCollins, 2014), at 259.

39. Herschelle Challenor, "The Contribution of Ralph Bunche to Trusteeship and Decolonization," in Benjamin Rivlin (ed.), *Ralph Bunche: The Man and His Times* (New York: Holmes and Meier, 1990), at 134.
40. Bunche to Hammarskjold, July 18, 1960, UN Archives, 370 Box 7, 8.
41. Urquhart, *Ralph Bunche*, at 319.
42. Bunche to Hammarskjold, July 9, 1960: UN Archives, 370, Box 7, 8.
43. Bunche "The New Concept of a United Nations 'Presence,'" March 25, 1960, Bunche Archives, Schomburg Center for Research in Black Culture, Box 15, Folder 7.
44. Meisler, *The United Nations*, at 119.
45. Andrew Cordier, quoted in Carol Collins, "The Cold War Comes to Africa: Cordier and the 1960 Congo Crisis," *Journal of International Affairs*, 47, 1 (1993), at 244.
46. Bunche to Hammarskjold, June 27, 1960, UN Archives 370, Box 3, 6.
47. Max Dorsinville, memo quoting Bunche, no date, UN Archives, Box 370/10/3.
48. Charles P. Henry, *Ralph Bunche: Model Negro or American Other?* (New York: New York University Press, 1999), at 197.
49. *First Report by the Secretary-General on the Implementation of Security Council Resolutions 2/4387 of 14 July 1960*, S/43187 14, July 1960; addendum 1.
50. Bunche to Hammarskjold, July 20, 1960 UN Archives 370, Box 7, 8.
51. Ole Wested, *The Cold War: A World History* (New York: Basic, 2017), at 282–283.
52. Dana Schmidt, "Lumumba Urges US to Aid Congo," *New York Times*, July 28, 1960.
53. Madeline Kalb, "The CIA and Lumumba," *New York Times*, August 2, 1981, at 32.
54. Adam Hochschild, "An Assassination's Long Shadow," *New York Times*, January 16, 2011; Henry, *Ralph Bunche: Model Negro or American Other?*, at 198.
55. UN Security Council Resolution 146, S/4426, August 9, 1960, paragraph 4.
56. Bunche, *Notes on Non-Military Briefing for Senior Officers of the UN Force in the Congo*, no date, labeled Not For Publication. UN Archives, 370/12/7.
57. Thomas Kanza, *Conflict in the Congo: The Rise and Fall of Lumumba* (New York: Penguin, 1972), at 179.
58. Bunche, Note cards on speech in Africa (likely Ghana), 1957, UN Archives, 370/1/4; Bunche, "The United Nations Operation in the Congo," in Andrew Cordier and Wilder Foote (eds.), *The Quest for Peace* (New York: Columbia University Press, 1965), at 133.
59. Makau wa Mutua, "Why Redraw the Map of Africa: A Moral and Legal Inquiry," *Michigan Journal of International Law*, 16, 4 (1995), at 1114–1115.
60. Ambassador Martin Kimani, "Statement during the Security Council Urgent Meeting on Ukraine," February 21, 2022. https://twitter.com/KenyaMissionUN/status/1495963864004976645/photo/1
61. Tanisha Fazal, "The Return of Conquest?" *Foreign Affairs* (May/June 2022).
62. Georges Abi-Saab, *The United Nations Operation in Congo: 1960–1964* (London: Oxford University Press, 1978), at 25.
63. Patrick O'Donovan, "Once-Tranquil Congo Gropes fore Life in Wake of Change," *Washington Post*, August 5, 1960, at A5.
64. 1960 Lodge Acceptance Speech, C-Span, www.c-span.org/video/?4011-1/1960-lodge-acceptance-speech

65. *Second Report by the Secretary-General on the Implementation of Security Council Resolutions 2/4387 of 14 July 1960 and S/4405 of 22 July 1960*, S/4417 6, August 1960; paragraph 4.

66. *Second Report by the Secretary-General on the Implementation of Security Council Resolutions 2/4387 of 14 July 1960 and S/4405 of 22 July 1960*, S/4417 6, August 1960; paragraph 8.

67. *Second Report by the Secretary-General on the Implementation of Security Council Resolutions 2/4387 of 14 July 1960 and S/4405 of 22 July 1960*, S/4417 6, August 1960; paragraph 8.

68. Henry, *Model Negro or American Other?*, at 199.

69. Bunche to Hammarskjold, August 6, 1960, UN Archives, Box 370/7/8; Urquhart, *Ralph Bunche*, at 324.

70. Charles P. Henry (ed.), *Ralph Bunche, Selected Speeches and Writings* (Ann Arbor: University of Michigan Press, 1996), at 198.

71. *Second Report by the Secretary-General on the Implementation of Security Council Resolutions 2/4387 of 14 July 1960 and S/4405 of 22 July 1960*, S/4417 6, August 1960; paragraph 8.

72. Urquhart, *Ralph Bunche*, at 328.

73. Cordier to Hammarskjold, August 4, 1960, UN Archives 370, Box 7, 10; On the Soviet role in the Congo Crisis, generally see Sergey Mazov, *A Distant Front in the Cold War: The USSR in West Africa and the Congo, 1956–1964* (Washington, DC: Woodrow Wilson Center, 2010), 81.

74. Georges Nzongola-Ntalaja, "Ralph Bunche, Patrice Lumumba, and the First Congo Crisis," in Robert Hill and Ed Keller (eds.), *Trustee for the Human Community: Ralph J. Bunche, the United Nations, and the Decolonization of Africa* (Ohio State Press, 2010), at 154.

75. Bunche to Hammarskjold, July 21 and 24, 1960, UN Archives 370, Box 7, 8.

76. Bunche, *UN Operation in Congo*, at 130.

77. Bunche to Cordier, August 21, 1960, UN Archives, Box 370/12/4.

78. Bunche to Hammarskjold, August 7, 1960, UN Archives, Box 370/7/9.

79. Bunche to Hammarskjold, August 13, 1960, UN Archives, Box 370/38/16; Henning Melber, *Dag Hammarskjold, the UN, and the Decolonization of Africa* (New York: Oxford University Press, 2019), at 79.

80. Henry, *Ralph Bunche: Model Negro or American Other?*, at 201.

81. Elizabeth Schmidt, *Foreign Intervention in Africa* (Cambridge, UK: Cambridge University Press, 2013), at 64.

82. Melber, *Decolonization of Africa*, at 79.

83. Susan Williams, *Who Killed Hammarskjold: The UN, the Cold War, and White Supremacy in Africa* (London: Hurst, 2011), at 36.

84. Namikas, *Battleground Africa*, at 105.

85. Kalb, "The CIA and Lumumba."

86. Namikas, *Battleground Africa*, at 90.

87. Memorandum from the Chief of the Africa Division, CIA, to the Assistant Secretary of State, April 18, 1960, *Foreign Relations of the United States*, Volume XXIII, Congo, 1960–1968.

88. Transcript of phone call, Bunche and Timberlake, August 24, 1960, UN Archives, Box 370/7/9.

89. Stephen Kinzer, *The Poisoner in Chief: Sidney Gottlieb and the CIA Search for Mind Control* (New York: Macmillan, 2019).
90. Nzongola-Ntalaja, *The Congo*, at 117.
91. Kinzer, *The Poisoner in Chief*; Kalb, "The CIA and Lumumba," 1981; van Reybrouck, *Congo*, at 304–305.

Chapter 19

1. "Melee in the UN," typescript from "N. Karev" of *Izvestia*, dated February 17, 1961, Dag Hammarskjold Foundation Archives.
2. Emanuel Gerard and Bruce Kuklick, *Death in the Congo: Murdering Patrice Lumumba* (Cambridge, MA: Harvard University Press, 2015), at 93.
3. Bunche to Hammarskjold, August 26, 1960, UN Archives, Box 370/7/9.
4. Bunche to Hammarskjold (Confidential), July 4, 1960, UN Archives, 370/3/6.
5. Gerard and Kuklick, *Death in the Congo*, at 96.
6. Rajeshwar Dayal, *Mission for Hammarskjold: The Congo Crisis* (Princeton, NJ: Princeton University Press, 1976), at 1.3.
7. Evan Luard, *A History of the United Nations, Volume 2: The Age of Decolonization* (New York: Macmillan, 1989), at 245.
8. David van Reybrouck, *Congo: The Epic History of a People* (New York: HarperCollins, 2014), at 248.
9. Dayal, *Mission for Hammarskjold*, at 13.
10. Madeleine Kalb, *The Congo Cables: Africa and the Cold War from Eisenhower to Kennedy* (New York: Macmillan, 1982), at 62.
11. Transcript of Press Conference, September 1, 1960, UN Archives, Box 370/12/2.
12. "At the UN: The Cold War's Biggest Battle," *Newsday*, September 17, 1960.
13. Benjamin Welles, "Khruschev Bangs His Shoe on Desk," *New York Times*, October 13, 1960.
14. Russell Howe, "UN 'Colonialism' Only Hope for Politician-Ridden Congo," *Washington Post*, September 11, 1960.
15. Adom Getachew, *Worldmaking after Empire: The Rise and Fall of Self-Determination* (Princeton, NJ: Princeton University Press, 2019), at 73.
16. Brian Urquhart, *Ralph Bunche: An American Odyssey* (Norton, 1993), at 336–337.
17. Bunche, speech at Howard University, May 14, 1964, Schomborg Center Archives Box 16/4.
18. "Bunche Notes Stand," *New York Times*, September 28, 1960.
19. Luard, *A History of the United Nations*, at 183.
20. General Assembly Resolution 1514, *Declaration on the Granting of Independence to Colonial Countries and Peoples*, 947th Plenary Meeting, December 14, 1960.
21. Resolution 1514, December 14, 1960.
22. Luard, *A History of the United Nations*, at 186.
23. General Assembly Resolution 1515, *Declaration on the Granting of Independence to Colonial Countries and Peoples*, 948th Plenary Meeting, December 15, 1960.
24. Getachew, *Worldmaking after Empire*, at 73.
25. Michael Barnett, "The New United Nations Politics of Peace: From Juridical Sovereignty to Empirical Sovereignty," *Global Governance* (Winter 1995), at 80.

26. Kalb, *The Congo Cables*, at 355.
27. Luke Nichter, *The Last Brahmin: Henry Cabot Lodge, Jr. and the Making of the Cold War* (New Haven, CT: Yale University Press, 2020), at 178.
28. "We're for Bunche," *Los Angeles Sentinel*, October 13, 1960.
29. Eric Williamson, "Unseating Segregation for a Night," *UVA Law Magazine* (Spring 2018). https://www.law.virginia.edu/uvalawyer/article/unseating-segregation-night
30. Urquhart, *Ralph Bunche*, at 303.
31. John F. Kennedy Library, Archives, Presidential Papers, Digital identifier: JFKPOF-105-001 (Poll covering Bunche as a potential primary challenger in New York Senate race, 1962); Interview, Ron Taylor, August 6, 2021.
32. Lise Namikas, *Cold War in the Congo, 1960–1965* (Stanford: Stanford University Press, 2013), at 105.
33. Dayal, *Mission for Hammarskjold*, at 72.
34. Urquhart to Bunche, September 15, 1960, UN Archives, Box 370/12/4.
35. 2D Progress Report to the Secretary-General, November 2, 1960, UN Archives, Box 219/3/16.
36. Dayal, *Mission for Hammarskjold*, at 145.
37. Ian Black, "Chronicle of a Death," *The Guardian*, June 28, 2001.
38. Henning Melber, *Dag Hammarskjold, The United Nations, and the Decolonization of Africa* (Oxford University Press, 2109), at 84.
39. van Reybrouck, *Congo*, at 308. Some accounts claim it was a different speech.
40. Ludo de Witte, *The Assassination of Lumumba*, English translation (New York: Verso, 2001), at 119.
41. Agence France-Press, "Report Reproves Belgium in Lumumba's Death," *New York Times*, November 17, 2001.
42. Stephen Weissman, "What Really Happened in Congo: The CIA, the Murder of Lumumba, and the Rise of Mobutu," *Foreign Affairs* (July/August 2014), at 17; Security Council Official Records, S/PV 933 February 13, 1961 (statement of Ambassador Stevenson); John Kent, *America, the UN, and Decolonization* (New York: Routledge, 2010), at 32–33.
43. Nzongola-Ntalaja, *The Congo*, at 121.
44. Gerard and Kuklick, *Death in the Congo*, at 2.
45. PBS, *Ralph Bunche: An American Odyssey* (Documentary 2001).
46. Security Council Official Records, S/PV 933 February 13, 1961.
47. Urquhart, *Ralph Bunche*, at 339.
48. van Reybrouck, *Congo*, at 309.
49. Constantin Katsakioris, "The Lumumba University in Moscow," *Journal of Global History* 14, 2 (2019).
50. James Baldwin, "A Negro Assays the Negro Mood," *New York Times Magazine*, March 12, 1961.
51. Bunche, note, April 17, 1967, UN Archives 370/39/14.
52. Bunche, note, date unknown but likely 1968. UN Archives 370/39/16.
53. Baldwin, "Negro Mood," 1961.

54. Bunche, "Africa Tests the UN," Oberlin College, March 24, 1961, Bunche Archives, Schomburg Center for the Study of Black Culture, Box 15/9.

55. Bunche to Mekki, June 30, 1961, UN Archives, Box 219/3/6.

56. Bunche to Hammarskjold, June 27, 1961, UN Archives Box 370/37/15.

57. James Cockayne and David Malone, "The Ralph Bunche Centennial: Peace Operations Then and Now," *Global Governance*, 11, 3 (2005), at 333b.

58. Aide Memoire, *UN Organization in the Congo, Apportionment of Costs Between the UN and Participating States*, July 22, 1960, UN Archives, Box 219/3/23.

59. Namikas, *Battleground Africa*, at 159.

60. *United Nations Financial Position and Prospects*, UN Archives, Box 219/3/23.

61. International Court of Justice, *Certain Expenses of the United Nations* (1962).

62. Bunche to Taylor, February 2, 1965, UCLA Archives, Box 20, Folder 7.

63. U Thant, *The View from the UN* (New York: Doubleday, 1978), at 49.

64. "Kanza Discusses Congo 'Tragedy'," *The Crimson*, February 17, 1961. https://www.thecrimson.com/article/1961/2/17/kanza-discusses-congo-tragedy-pan-important/

65. Bunche to Rider, January 25, 1963, UCLA Bunche Archives, Box 235, Folder 6.

66. Paul Kennedy, *The Parliament of Man: The Past, Present, and Future of the United Nations* (New York: Vintage, 2006), at 84.

67. UN Security Council Resolution 161, February 21, 1961 (Part B).

68. Luard, *A History of the United Nations*, at 269.

69. Walter Dorn, "The UN's First 'Air Force': Peacekeepers in Combat, Congo 1960–1964," *Journal of Military History*, 77, 4 (2013).

70. 33rd Meeting of the Advisory Committee on Congo, March 7, 1961 (summary record) UN Archives Box 370/3/15.

71. Susan Williams, *Who Killed Hammarskjold? The UN, The Cold War, and White Supremacy in Africa* (New York: Oxford University Press, 2014), at 40.

72. Leonard Lyons, The Lyons Den, *Chicago Defender*, June 7, 1961.

73. Brian Urquhart, Oral History, October 19, 1984.

74. Namikas, *Battleground Africa*, at 151.

75. Bunche, notes, UCLA Bunche Archives, Box 21, Folder 3, no date (but likely written in 1966).

76. Mark Mazower, *Governing the World* (New York: Penguin, 2012), at 241.

77. Brian Urquhart, *Ralph Bunche: An American Odyssey* (New York: Norton, 1993), at 353.

78. U Thant, *The View from the UN* (New York: Doubleday, 1978), at 113.

79. For example, Memo from US Ambassador to Congo Edmund Gullion to Ralph Bunche, no date (Gullion's term was 1961–1963) marked Urgent/Confidential, UN Archives Box 370/3/8, noting "of course all above is for your eyes and Bob's and not for circulation."

80. Interview with Sture Linner, *Yale UN Oral History Project*, November 8, 1990, ST/DPI/Oral History 02/L45 10–18.

81. Bunche, UCLA Bunche Archives, Box 21, Folder 3, no date (but likely written in 1966).

Chapter 20

1. Lise Namikas, *Battleground Africa: Cold War in the Congo, 1960–1965* (Stanford, CA: Stanford University Press, 2013), at 151.
2. Susan Williams, *Who Killed Hammarskjold? The UN, The Cold War, and White Supremacy in Africa* (Oxford University Press, 2014), at 79.
3. Brian Urquhart, *Ralph Bunche: An American Odyssey* (Norton, 1993), at 345.
4. Julian Borger, "Dag Hammarskjold: Nephew Calls for New Inquiry into Death of UN Chief," *The Guardian*, September 16, 2011.
5. "Was the Mysterious Death of Dag Hammarskjold Murder?" *The Economist*, September 16, 2021.
6. Barbro Alving, *Klipp ur Nuets Historia* (Stockholm: Gildlund, 1982), at 306–312; Sara Linderoth, *Världen i chock av Hammarskjölds död*, Upsala Nya Tidning, November 26, 2020. Translation by David Silverlid.
7. Barbro Alving, *Klipp ur Nuets Historia*, at 307.
8. Henning Melber, *Dag Hammarskjold, The United Nations, and the Decolonization of Africa* (New York: Oxford University Press, 2019), at 106.
9. Melber, *Dag Hammarskjold*, at 104.
10. David Halberstam, "Hammarskjold Dies in African Air Crash," *New York Times*, September 19, 1961.
11. Maurin Picard, "Stalling the Report on Dag Hammarskjold's Death is Regrettable," *PassBlue*, September 17, 2019. https://www.passblue.com/2019/09/17/stalling-the-un-report-on-dag-hammarskjolds-death-is-regrettable
12. https://undocs.org/A/73/973
13. "The UN's Acting Secretary General U Thant: Neutralist with Moral Fiber," *Time Magazine*, November 10, 1961.
14. *New Journal and Guide*, September 23, 1961.
15. Urquhart, *Ralph Bunche*, at 348.
16. Bunche, notes, UCLA Archives Box 21, Folder 3 (no date).
17. Bunche, notes, October 11, 1965, UN Archives, Box 370/39/1.
18. Bunche, notebook (January 1966), UN Archives Box 370/38/22; Notes, UN Archives, May 18, 1968, Box 370/39/16.
19. Quincy Wright, "The Goa Incident," *American Journal of International Law* (July 1962), at 619.
20. UN Doc S/PV.988.
21. Rupert Emerson, "Colonialism, Political Development and the UN," *International Organization* (Summer 1965), at 486.
22. Oliver Turner, "'Finishing the Job': the UN Special Committee on Decolonization and the Politics of Self-Governance," *Third World Quarterly*, 34, 7 (2013).
23. Emerson, "Colonialism, Political Development, and the UN," at 484.
24. Philip Geyelin, "The US and the UN: Administration Grows More Skeptical of UN As a Keeper of Peace," *Wall Street Journal*, December 22, 1961.
25. Narasimhan to Thant, January 30, 1962, UN Archives Box 219/3/7.
26. David Kay, "The Politics of Decolonization: The New Nations and the United Nations Political Process," *International Organization* (Fall 1967), at 806.

27. Kay, "The Politics of Decolonization," at 810.

28. William F. Buckley, "Must We Hate Portugal?," *National Review*, December 18, 1962.

29. Brian Urquhart, *A Life in Peace and War* (New York: Harper and Row, 1987), at 180–181.

30. Philip Geyelin, "The US and the UN: Administration Grows More Skeptical of UN as a Keeper of Peace," *Wall Street Journal*, December 22, 1961.

31. National Security Action Memorandum 97, McGeorge Bundy to Dean Rusk, September 19, 1961, FRUS Volume XX, Congo Crisis, https://history.state.gov/historicaldocuments/frus1961-63v20/d120

32. Bunche to Mekki, June 30 1961, UN Archives, Box 219/3/6.

33. Urquhart, *A Life in Peace and War*, at 187.

34. Madeline Kalb, *The Congo Cables: The Cold War in Africa from Eisenhower to Kennedy* (New York: Macmillan, 1982), at 313; U Thant, *The View from the UN* (David and Charles, 1978), at 80.

35. Walter Dorn, "UN's First Air Force: Peacekeepers in Combat, Congo 1960–1964," *Journal of Military* History, 77 (2013), at 1408.

36. Edmund Gullion, Interview, UN Oral History Project, May, 8 1990, at 32. http://dag.un.org/bitstream/handle/11176/89613/Gullion8May90TRANS.pdf?sequence=3&isAllowed=y

37. Namikas, *Battleground Africa*, at 155.

38. Kalb, *The Congo Cables*, at 301.

39. Statement of the USSR (translation), September 5, 1962, UN Archives, Box 213/6/17.

40. UNSC, 998th Meeting, S/PV 998, March 23, 1962.

41. Bunche to Dayal, October 19, 1962, UN Archives 370 Box 7, 4.

42. Bunche to Roosevelt, January 16, 1962, UCLA Archives, Box 235, Folder 8.

43. "US Flags Flying at Half-Staff As a Tribute to Mrs. Roosevelt," New *York Times*, November 9, 1962.

44. Bunche note, no date, UN Archives, Box 370/38/23.

45. Bunche note, no date, UN Archives, Box 370/38/23.

46. "Bunche Briefs Press on Congo," UN Audiovisual Library. https://www.unmultimedia.org/avlibrary/asset/2391/2391447

47. Bunche, diary, January 22, 1963, UCLA Archives Box 235, Folder 5.

48. Bunche, "Tight Spots and Close Calls in the Service of the United Nations," UCLA Bunche Archives, Box 86, Folder 5.

49. Asher Orkaby, *The International History of the Yemen Civil War, 1962–1968*, PhD dissertation, Harvard University, 2014, at 75. https://dash.harvard.edu/bitstream/handle/1/12269828/Orkaby_gsas.harvard_0084L_11420.pdf?sequence=4

50. Orkaby, *Yemen Civil War*, at 111.

51. Jesse Ferris, "Soviet Support for Egypt's Intervention in Yemen, 1962–1963," *Journal of Cold War Studies* (Fall 2008), at 13–14.

52. Bunche, notes, March 1, 1963, UN Archives 370/38/19.

53. "Bunche Ends Yemen Parley, Plans Others," *Los Angeles Times*, March 4, 1963; Bunche, notes, March 1, 1963, UN Archives 370/38/19.

54. Orkaby, *Yemen Civil War*, at 209.

55. William Oatis, "Ralph Bunche on Integration: UN Official Says Major Breakthrough Approaching," *Louisville Courier-Journal*, June 9, 1963, UCLA Archives, Digital Collection. https://digital.library.ucla.edu/catalog/ark:/21198/zz0017n1vj

56. "Africans Views on March Varied," *New York Times*, August 30, 1963.

57. Louis Menand, *The Free World* (New York: Farrar, Straus, 2021), at 382.

58. Evan Luard, *A History of the United Nations, Volume 2: The Age of Decolonization, 1955–1965* (Palgrave MacMillan, 1989), at 306.

59. Bunche to Linaberry, February 12, 1963, UCLA Archives, Box 233, Folder 7.

60. Melber, *Decolonization of Africa*, at 88; Crawford Young, "Ralph Bunche and Patrice Lumumba: The Fatal Encounter," in Robert Hill and Edmond Keller (eds.), *Trustee for the Human Community: Ralph J. Bunche, the United Nations and the Decolonization of Africa* (Athens: Ohio University Press, 2010).

61. In Congo, peacekeepers were accused of trafficking in local gold. Bunche, Memo to Alexander MacFarquhar, March 31, 1964, UN Archives, Box 219/3/9.

62. Howard French, "An Anatomy of Autocracy: Mobutu's Era," *New York Times*, May 17, 1997.

63. Bunche, Speech at International Press Institute, Tokyo, March 25, 1960, Archives, Schomburg Center for the Study of Black Culture, Box 15/7.

Chapter 21

1. John F. Kennedy, July 2, 1957. https://www.jfklibrary.org/archives/other-resources/john-f-kennedy-speeches/united-states-senate-imperialism-19570702

2. https://www.youtube.com/watch?v=-ukz3GB3W4o

3. https://geneva.usmission.gov/2013/11/22/half-a-century-ago-john-f-kennedy-addressed-united-nations/#:~:text=On%20September%2020%2C%201963%2C%20U.S.,not%20escaped%20from%20the%20darkness

4. Brian Urquhart, *Ralph Bunche: An American Odyssey* (New York: Norton, 1993), at 367.

5. Urquhart, *Ralph Bunche*, at 367.

6. Rupert Emerson, "Colonialism, Political Development, and the UN," *International Organization*, 19 (Summer 1965), at 484.

7. UN General Assembly Resolution 1761, November 6, 1962.

8. Bunche to Thant, October 9, 1963, UN Archives, Box 9/1/4.

9. Bunche to MLK, May 11, 1963, UCLA Bunche Archives, Box 233, Folder 4.

10. Andrew Kaye, Review, *Journal of American Studies* (2004), at 349, reviewing Carol Anderson, *Eyes Off the Prize: The United Nations and the African-American Struggle for Human Rights, 1944–1955* (Cambridge, UK: Cambridge University Press, 2003).

11. Charles P. Henry, *Ralph Bunche: Model Negro or American Other?* (New York: New York University Press, 1999), at 221.

12. Bunche, Press Release, June 17, 1963, UCLA Bunche Archives, Box 438, Folder 2.

13. *Vassar Miscellany News*, April 24, 1963. https://newspaperarchives.vassar.edu/?a=d&d=miscellany19630424-01.2.8&e=-------en-20--1--txt-txIN--------

14. Urquhart, *Ralph Bunche*, at 354.

15. Robinson to Bunche, November 22, 1963, UCLA Bunche Archives, Box 235, Folder 7.

16. Bunche to Robinson, November 20, 1963, UCLA Archives, Box 235, Folder 7.

17. John F. Kennedy, July 2, 1957, https://www.jfklibrary.org/archives/other-resour ces/john-f-kennedy-speeches/united-states-senate-imperialism-19570702; Gregory Cleva, *John F. Kennedy's 1957 Algeria Speech: The Politics of Anticolonialism in the Cold War Era* (Lexington, 2022).

18. Cleva, *Kennedy's Algeria Speech*, at 67.

19. For example, UN General Assembly Resolutions 1720 (1961) and 1803 (1962).

20. Brenda Gayle Plummer, *Rising Wind: Black Americans and US Foreign Affairs, 1935–1960* (Chapel Hill: University of North Carolina Press, 1996), at 51.

21. Jim Hadjin, "Bunche Spars Diplomatically with LI Pupils," *Newsday*, December 6, 1963.

22. Johnson, Speech to UNGA, December 17, 1963. https://www.unmultimedia.org/ avlibrary/asset/2547/2547251

23. Robert Caro, *The Passage of Power* (New York: Vintage, 2012), at 402.

24. Louis Menand, *The Free World* (New York: Farrar, Straus, 2021), at 687.

25. Bob Waters, "Clay: Portrait of a Young Muslim," *Newsday*, February 28, 1964.

26. Jonathan Scott Holloway, "Ralph Bunche and the Responsibilities of the Public Intellectual," *Journal of Negro Education*, 73, 2 (2004), at 125.

27. Nathaniel Nakasa, "Mr. Nakasa Goes to Harlem," *New York Times*, February 7, 1965.

28. Ben Keppel, *The Work of Democracy* (Cambridge, MA: Harvard University Press, 1995), at 61.

29. Caleb Pirtle and Jane Paganini, "Bunche Says Peace Offers No Excitement," *Austin Daily Texan*, March 25, 1964, at 1.

30. Bunche, note, March 26, 1964, UN Archives, Box 370/38/5.

31. Peggy Mann, *Ralph Bunche: UN Peacemaker* (New York: Coward, McCann, and Geoghegan, 1975), at 319.

32. UNSC Resolution 186, S/5575 (March 4. 1964).

33. Bunche, note, April 9, 1964, UN Archives, Box 370/17/3.

34. Bunche, note, April 10, 1964, UN Archives, 370/38/18.

35. "Cyprus Baffles Bunche," *Boston Globe*, April 13, 1964.

36. Urquhart, *Ralph Bunche*, at 371.

37. Urquhart, *Ralph Bunche*, at 373.

38. "Bunche Keen on Tightening UN Check in Jammu," *Times of India*, April 16, 1964, at 1.

39. Transcript of Remarks made at Departure from Nicosia Airport, July 11, 1966, UCLA Bunche Archives, Box 20, Folder 2.

40. Bunche to Thant, April 1964, UN Archives, Box 370/17/20.

41. Souad Halila, *The Intellectual Development and Diplomatic Career of Ralph Bunche: The Afro-American, Africanist, and Internationalist*, PhD Dissertation, USC, 1988, at 153.

42. Bunche, Speech at Howard University, May 14, 1964, Schomburg Center for the Study of Black Culture, Bunche Archives, Box 16, 4.

43. AP, "Fight Crowd Has Its Old Glamor," *Indianapolis Star*, February 2, 1965.

44. Reprinted in Conrad Cherry, *God's New Israel: Religious Interpretations of American Destiny* (Chapel Hill: University of North Carolina Press, 1998), at 364; Samuel Moyn, *The Last Utopia: Human Rights in History* (Cambridge, MA: Harvard University Press, 2010), at 105.

45. Steve Cady, "Clay, on 2 Hour Tour of UN, Tells of Plan to Visit Mecca," *New York Times*, March 5, 1964.

46. UN GA Resolution 1803 (1962).

47. Lawrence Finkelstein, "Bunche and the Colonial World: From Trusteeship to Decolonization" in Benjamin Rivlin (ed.), *Ralph Bunche: The Man and His Times* (New York: Holmes and Meier, 1990), supra at 109–110.

Chapter 22

1. U Thant, *A View from the UN* (New York: Doubleday, 1978), at 62.

2. Memorandum of a Conversation, White House, FRUS, August 6, 1964. https://hist ory.state.gov/historicaldocuments/frus1964-68v01/d298

3. Thant, *A View from the UN*, at 63.

4. Lady Bird Johnson, "Audio Diary and Annotated Transcript," August 6, 1964, Lyndon Johnson Library. www.discoverlbj.org/item/ctjd-19640806

5. "President Optimistic at Dinner," *New York Times*, August 7, 1964.

6. Dorothy McArdle, "Magic Dragon Triumphs at White House," *Washington Post*, August 8, 1964.

7. Brian Urquhart, *Ralph Bunche: An American Odyssey* (New York: Norton, 1993), at 379.

8. Walter Carlson, "King of Burundi Pays Visit to Fair," *New York Times*, May 22, 1964.

9. Robert Alden, "World's Fair Seizes Indonesian Pavilion," *New York Times*, April 1, 1965.

10. Bunche to Betts, January 8, 1965, UCLA Archives, Box 20, Folder 7.

11. Bunche, notes, no date, UN Archives, Box 370/38/3; February 1, 1965, UCLA Archives, Box 21, Folder 2.

12. Bunche to Betts, January 8, 1965, UCLA Archives, Box 20, Folder 7.

13. Bunche to Taylor, February 2, 1965, UCLA Archives, Box 20, Folder 7.

14. Bunche, notes, July 19, 1965, UN Archives, Box 370, 39, 1.

15. Frederic Kirgis, "United States Dues Arrearages in the United Nations and Possible Loss of Vote in the UN General Assembly," *ASIL Insights*, July 3, 1998.

16. Bunche, Remarks at NAACP Convocation on Equal Justice under Law, May 28, 1964, UCLA Archives, Box 387, Folder 1.

17. Thomas Ronan, "Liberals Caution on Senate Choice," *New York Times*, May 7, 1964.

18. The Talk of the Town, *The New Yorker*, January 1, 1972.

19. "White NAACP Pres. Tells Young Militants: Don't Give A Damn About Your Desires," *Chicago Daily Defender*, May 25, 1964.

20. The Talk of the Town, *The New Yorker*, January 1, 1972.

21. "Bunche Accuses Goldwater of 'Humbug' in Rights Talk," *The Sun*, June 6, 1964.

22. "Dr. Bunche to Join March in Alabama," *New York Times*, March 20, 1965.

23. Bunche, note, UN Archives Box 370/38/1, no date.
24. Letter, March 6, 1965, Washington, DC, to Bunche, New York, March 6, 1965, and Letter, return, March 10, 1965, Bunche Archives, UCLA, Box 249, Folder 4.
25. Jimmy Breslin, "March Begins Peacefully," *Boston Globe*, March 22, 1965.
26. "Bunche to Rejoin March Thursday," *New York Times*, March 23, 1965; Thomas Rex, "Wallace Fails to See Delegation after Rally," *Atlanta Constitution*, March 26, 1965.
27. Taylor Branch, *At Canaan's Edge: American in the King Years* (New York: Simon and Schuster, 1989), at 159–160.
28. William Chapman and Thomas Kendrick, "Rally of 3000 Climaxes Alabama Rights March," *Washington Post*, March 26, 1965; Renata Adler, "Letter from Selma," *The New Yorker*, April 10, 1965.
29. Lincoln Bloomfield, *The UN and Vietnam* (New York: Carnegie Endowment, 1968), at 7–8.
30. Bunche, notes, June 25, 1965, UN Archives, Box 21, Folder 1.
31. Walter Johnson, "The U Thant-Stevenson Peace Initiatives in Vietnam, 1964–1965," *Diplomatic History* (2007), at 286.
32. "Thant Peking-Hanoi Trip Given Sanction by US," *Boston Globe*, April 3, 1965.
33. UN Department of Political and Security Council Affairs, "Secretary-General U Thant's Efforts to Mediate the Viet-Nam Conflict," May 19, 1972, at 3. UCLA Bunche Archives, Box 20, Folder 5.
34. Bernard Firestone, "Failed Mediation: U Thant, the Johnson Administration, and the Vietnam War," *Diplomatic History*, 37, 3 (2013), at 1068.
35. Bunche to Thant, March 1, 1965, UN Archives, Box 370/42/11.
36. Urquhart, *Ralph Bunche*, at 379.
37. Benjamin Cohen, "The World's Backsliding from UN Charter," *Washington Post*, May 2, 1965.
38. On changes in territorial aggression, see Tanisha Fazal, *State Death: The Politics and Geography of Conquest, Annexation, and Occupation* (Princeton, NJ: Princeton University Press, 2007); Dominic Johnson, "Grounds for War: The Evolution of Territorial Conflict," *International Security*, 38, 3 (2013/14).
39. Bunche to Davis, February 22, 1966, UCLA Archives, Box 259.
40. "Bunche among Stevenson UN Successors," *Philadelphia Tribune*, July 17, 1965.
41. Bunche, notes, August 2, 1965, UCLA Bunche Archives, Box 21, Folder 1.
42. Bunche, notes, October 7, 1965, UCLA Bunche Archives, Box 21, Folder 2.
43. Bunche, notes, November 18, 1965, UN Archives, Box 370/38/1.
44. Bunche, notes, July 18, 1965, UCLA Bunche Archives, Box 21, Folder 1.
45. Bunche, notes, July 20, 1965, UCLA Bunche Archives, Box 21, Folder 1.
46. "Bunche Assails Nixon Charge of 'Weak' UN," *Los Angeles Times*, July 13, 1965.
47. David Stebenne, *Arthur Goldberg: New Deal Liberal* (1996), at 348.
48. Bunche, notes, July 28, 1965, UCLA Bunche Archives, Box 21, Folder 1.
49. Bunche, note, no date, UN Archives, 370/39/1.
50. Stebenne, *New Deal Liberal*, at 362.
51. "Bunche Decries Ghettoes," *New York Times*, August 18, 1965.
52. "Meeting with Ambassador Goldberg," August 24, 1965, UCLA Bunche Archives, Box 21, Folder 1.

53. "Delhi Shows No Interest in Thant's Offer," *Times of India*, August 23, 1965.

54. Peggy Mann, *Ralph Bunche: UN Peacemaker* (Coward, McCann, 1975), at 327.

55. Bunche, notes, July 10, 1967, UN Archives, Box 370/39/8.

56. Bunche to Ralph Jr., November 15, 1965, UN Archives, Box 20, Folder 5.

57. Paul Montgomery, "Margaret Unperturbed by Boycott at UN," *New York Times*, November 20, 1965.

58. Bunche, "Bad Day at the UN," April 8, 1966, UN Archives, Box 370/38/1.

59. Bunche, note, UN Archives, Box 370/38/22, November 19, 1965.

60. Bunche, notes (no date), UCLA Bunche Archives, Box 21, Folder 2.

61. Thomas Buckley, "Man, 22, Immolates Himself at Antiwar Protest at the UN," *New York Times*, November 10, 1965.

62. "Memorandum of Conversation," FRUS, 1964–1968; Vol XXXIII, December 7, 1965.

63. Bunche, notes, July 20, 1965, UCLA Bunche Archives, Box 21, Folder 1.

64. Firestone, "Failed Mediation," at 1051.

65. Bunche, notes, UCLA Bunche Archives, Box 21, Folder 3, January 18, 1966.

66. Bunche, notes, UCLA Bunche Archives, Box 21, Folder 3, February 15, 1966.

67. Bunche to Betts, UCLA Bunche Archives, Box 21, Folder 4, February 9, 1966.

68. Bunche, notes, April 20, 1966, UN Archives, Box 370/38/1.

69. Bunche, notes, April 4, 1966, UN Archives, Box 370/39/6.

70. Bunche, notes, April 20, 1966 UN Archives, Box 370/38/1

71. Viva Jeronimo, *Adapting to Change: The U.N. Security Council, Decolonization, and the Cold War*, PhD dissertation (in progress), Yale University Department of Political Science.

72. "Transcript of Remarks, Nicosia Airport," July 8, 1966, UCLA Bunche Archives, Box 20, Folder 2.

73. Bunche, notes, June 14, 1966, UN Archives, Box 370/38/1.

Chapter 23

1. Bunche, note, April 18, 1966, UN Archives, Box 370/40/11.

2. Brian Urquhart, *Ralph Bunche: An American Odyssey* (New York: Norton, 1993), at 386.

3. Bunche, note, no date, but refers to events in the winter of 1966, UN Archives 370/38/22.

4. Bunche to Davis, April 19, 1966, UCLA Bunche Archives, Box 259.

5. Milt Freudenheim, "If Thant Quits the UN, Expect Bunche to Follow," *Los Angeles Times*, June 30, 1966.

6. Bunche, notes, March 21, 1966, UCLA Bunche Archives, Box 21, Folder 5.

7. Bunche notes, April 18, 1966, UCLA Bunche Archives, Box 21, Folder 1.

8. Bunche, notes, May 19, 1966, UN Archives, Box 370/38/22.

9. Milt Freudenheim, "If Thant Quits the UN, Expect Bunche to Follow," *Los Angeles Times*, June 30, 1966.

10. Bunche notes, March 28, 1966, UCLA Bunche Archives, Box 21, Folder 2.

11. Bunche, notes, June 4, 1966, UN Archives, Box 370/39/6.
12. Bunche, notes; *Sand Dune Magazine*; both in UCLA Archives, Box 20, Folder 2.
13. Bunche to Dayan, June 1, 1966, UCLA Bunche Archives, Box 259.
14. Bull to Bunche, UCLA Bunche Archives, July 15, 1966, Box 20, Folder 2.
15. "Ireland Is One of Our Best Members—UN Official," *Irish Times*, July 18, 1966.
16. Leonard Lyons, "The Lyons Den," *Baltimore Sun*, August 2, 1966.
17. Bunche to Betts, July 28, 1966, UCLA Bunche Archives, Box 20, Folder 2.
18. Bunche, note, July 31, 1966, UN Archives, 370/38/1.
19. Bunche, note, August 16, 1966, UN Archives, 370/38/1.
20. Bunche, note, August 18, 1966, UN Archives, 370/38/1.
21. Jean White, "Two Slum Menchildren Give Stories to Senators," *Washington Post*, August 30, 1966; Marjorie Hunter, "Senators Hear of Life in the Ghetto," *New York Times*, August 30, 1966.
22. Bunche, note, September 7, 1966, UN Archives 370/38/5.
23. Urquhart, *Ralph Bunche*, at 394.
24. John Sibley, "O'Connor Urges Samuels to Be His Running Mate," *New York Times*, August 29, 1966.
25. "Is the UN Finished?" *The Observer*, October 2, 1966.
26. Bunche, notes, October 5, 1966, UN Archives, Box 370/39/1.
27. "Johnson, Thant Discuss Vietnam," *Baltimore Sun*, October 8, 1966.
28. Emanuel Perlmutter, "Bunche's Daughter Found Dead after Fall from Bronx Rooftop," *New York Times*, October 10, 1966.
29. "Dr Bunche's Daughter's Death Remains a Mystery," *New York Amsterdam News*, October 15, 1966.
30. Peggy Mann, *Ralph Bunche: UN Peacemaker* (New York: Coward, McCann, & Geoghegan, 1975), at 338.
31. Death certificate, October 11, 1966, UN Archives, Box 370/37/11.
32. Bunche, notes, November 9, 1966, UN Archives, Box 370/38/15.
33. Bunche, notes, December 3, 1966, UN Archives, Box 370/39/1.
34. Bunche, notes, December 14, 1966, UCLA Bunche Archives, Box 21, Folder 5.
35. Bunche, notes, December 12, 1966, UN Archives, Box 370/39/1.
36. Leonard Lyons, "The Lyons Den," *Baltimore Sun*, January 12, 1967.
37. Urquhart, *Ralph Bunche*, at 398.
38. Bunche, note, February 18, 1967, UCLA Bunche Archives, Box 21, Folder 5.
39. Bunche, draft statement, no date, UN Archives, Box 370/37/15; "Bunche Relents, Will Keep UN Post," *New York Times*, March 1, 1967.
40. Bunche to Harrar, March 30, 1967, UN Archives, Box 370/37/15.
41. Bunche, note, February 28, 1967, UCLA Archives, Box 21, Folder 5.
42. George Getze, "Bunche Takes Slap at Idea of UC Tuition," *Los Angeles Times*, February 11, 1967.
43. Bunche, notes, September 16, 1966, UN Archives 370/39/1.
44. Charles King, "The Fulbright Paradox," *Foreign Affairs* (July/August 2021).
45. Sam Pope Brewer, "Senate Foreign Relations Group Meets Thant for 3 Hours," *New York Times*, March 23, 1967; "Senators Impressed by UN Visit," *Washington Post*, March 27, 1967.

46. Bunche, notes, April 21, 1967, UN Archives, Box 370/39/8.

47. David Broder and William Chapman, "Secret Struggle over King: Story behind King's New Role," *Washington Post*, April 16, 1967.

48. King, "Beyond Vietnam," in the King Encyclopedia. https://kinginstitute.stanford.edu/king-papers/documents/beyond-vietnam.

49. Nikhal Singh, *Black Is a Country* (Cambridge, MA: Harvard University Press, 2004), at 1.

50. Bunche, notes, April 17, 1967, UN Archives, Box 370/39/4.

51. John Sibley, "Bunche Disputes Dr. King on Peace," *New York Times*, April 13, 1967.

52. "King Denies Trying to Merge Rights, Peace," *Los Angeles Times*, April 13, 1967.

53. "The Talk of the Town," *The New Yorker*, January 1, 1972.

54. Urquhart, *Ralph Bunche*, at 389.

55. *Washington Post*, April 14, 1967.

56. Taylor Branch, *At Canaan's Edge: America in the King Years* (New York: Simon and Schuster, 2007), at 596.

57. UN Archives, Box 370/39/14; Douglas Robinson, "100,000 Rally at UN Against Vietnam War: Many Draft Cards Burned," *New York Times*, April 16, 1967.

58. Martin Luther King at the UN. https://www.youtube.com/watch?v=YpGFOiSTs3Q

59. Bunche, notes, April 17, 1967, UN Archives, Box 370/39/14.

60. Verbatim Record of Informal Meeting of Representatives of Governments Providing Contingents for UNEF, May 17, 1967, UN Archives, Box 316/1/5, at 1.

61. US State Department, Office of the Historian, *The 1967 Arab-Israeli War*. https://history.state.gov/milestones/1961-1968/arab-israeli-war-1967

62. "An Interview of Ralph J. Bunche by Arthur Rovine," April 13, 1966, UCLA Archives, Collection 364, Box 12, Folder 4.

63. Verbatim Record of Informal Meeting of Representatives of Governments Providing Contingents for UNEF, May 17, 1967, UN Archives, Box 316/1/5, at 5.

64. Verbatim Record of Informal Meeting of Representatives of Governments Providing Contingents for UNEF, May 17, 1967, UN Archives, Box 316/1/5, at 15.

65. Urquhart, *Ralph Bunche*, at 402.

66. Leonard Lyons, "The Lyons Den," *Baltimore Sun*, May 8, 1967.

67. Dov Waxman, *The Israeli-Palestinian Conflict* (New York: Oxford University Press, 2019), Chapter 3; see also Raymond Hinnesbusch, "Revisiting the 1967 Arab-Israel War and its Consequences for the Regional System," *British Journal of Middle East Studies* (2017), examining the "calculations and miscalculations by leaders on both sides."

68. Verbatim Record of Informal Meeting of Representatives of Governments Providing Contingents for UNEF, May 18, 1967, UN Archives, Box 316/1/5, at 5.

69. Verbatim Record of Informal Meeting of Representatives of Governments Providing Contingents for UNEF, May 18, 1967, UN Archives, Box 316/1/5, at 11–12.

70. Verbatim Record of Informal Meeting of Representatives of Governments Providing Contingents for UNEF, May 18, 1967, UN Archives, Box 316/1/5, at 16.

71. Thant, *A View from the UN*, at 231.

72. Bunche to Thant, May 23, 1967, UN Archives, 370/9/18.

73. Thant to Bunche, May 24, 1967, UN Archives, 370/9/18.
74. Bunche to Thant, May 24, 1967, UN Archives, 370/9/18.
75. Marie Smith, "Tipping the Crystal to Mark UN's 25th Anniversary," *Washington Post*, July 11, 1970.
76. Thant to Eshkol, May 28, 1967; Thant to Nasser, May 28, 1967; UN Archives Box 370/39/10.
77. Security Council Official Records, S/PV 1344, May 30, 1967, at 13.
78. US State Department, *The 1967 Arab-Israeli War*.
79. Security Council Official Records, S/PV 1347, June 5, 1967, at 2.
80. Sam Pope Brewer, "Cease-Fire Steps Difficult for UN," *New York Times*, June 11, 1967.
81. UNSC Resolution 233, S/Res/233, June 6, 1967.
82. Marilyn Berger, "Can the UN Do the Job?," *Newsday*, June 17, 1967.
83. "The Talk of the Town," *The New Yorker*, July 29, 1967.
84. Lyons Den, *New York Post*, June 15, 1967; "2 Delegates Rap Bunche's UN Conduct," *Chicago Tribune*, June 15, 1967; "Arab Blasts Bunche in UN Tirade," *Newsday*, June 15, 1967. Bunche's letter of apology can be found in UN Archives, Box 370/39/5.
85. Bunche, letter to the editor, *New York Times*, June 11, 1967.
86. Max Frankel, "57 Hammarskjold Memo on Mideast Disclosed," *New York Times*, June 19, 1967.
87. Joyce Egginton, "U Thant Attack 'Inspired by US,'" *The Observer*, June 25, 1967.
88. Egginton, "U Thant Attack."
89. Frankel, "57 Hammarskjold Memo."
90. Bunche, note, June 7, 1967, UN Archives, Box 370/40/20.
91. Bunche, note, September 11, 1967, UN Archives Box 316/9/4; June 7, 1967, UN Archives, Box 370/40/20.
92. Louis Fleming, "Peacekeepers of UN Assailed for Failing to Learn Old Lessons," *Los Angeles Times*, June 5, 1967.
93. Raymond Daniell, "Thant Is Fearful of Wider Conflict," *New York Times*, May 12, 1967.
94. Associated Press, "Peace Prize Winner Hits Viet Trip," July 12, 1967.
95. Bunche, notes, July 15, 1967, UN Archives, Box 370/39/7.
96. Bunche, notes, July 9, 1967, UN Archives, Box 370/38/5.
97. Bunche, notes, September 19, 1967, UN Archives, Box 370/39/1.
98. Bunche, notes, May 15, 1967, UN Archives Box 370/47/11.
99. Bunche, notes, October 20, 1967, UN Archives, Box 370/38/5.
100. "Notes on a meeting in the Secretary-General's Office," November 22, 1967, UCLA Bunche Archives, Box 20, Folder 3.

Chapter 24

1. Lyndon Johnson, March 31, 1968. https://millercenter.org/the-presidency/presi dential-speeches/march-31-1968-remarks-decision-not-seek-re-election
2. Bunche, diary, April 1, 1968, UCLA Bunche Archives, Box 23, Folder 4.

3. Bunche, notes, February 21, 1968, UCLA Bunche Archives, Box 21, Folder 3.

4. Bunche, notes, no date, UN Archives, 370/40/6.

5. Bunche, notes, August 29, 1968, UN Archives, 370/40/8.

6. Julian Hartt, "Choose Negotiations or Holocaust, Bunche Says," *Los Angeles Times* February 21, 1968.

7. Associated Press, "Sirhan Felt Betrayed by Kennedy," *New York Times*, February 20, 1989.

8. Bunche, notes, June 10, 1968, UN Archives, 370/38/2.

9. Bunche, notes, November 3, 1969, UCLA Bunche Archives, Urquhart Collection, Box 22, Folder 5.

10. Bunche, notes, November 6, 1969, UN Archives, Box 370/37/12.

11. Nixon to Bunche, November 12, 1969, UCLA Archives, Urquhart Collection, Box 22, Folder 5.

12. Bunche to Nixon, November 20, 1969, UCLA Archives, Urquhart Collection, Box 22, Folder 5.

13. Bunche, notes, June 12, 1968, UCLA Archives. Box 21, Folder 3.

14. Bunche, notes, June 24, 1968, UN Archives, Box 370/39/16.

15. Bunche, notes, June 24, 1968, UN Archives, Box 370/39/1.

16. Bunche, notes, September 26, 1968, UCLA Bunche Archives, Box 21, Folder 3.

17. Bunche, notes, December 18, 1968, UN Archives, Box 370/39/16.

18. Bertram Johansson, "Nixon Balances Image in the UN," *Christian Science Monitor*, December 19, 1968.

19. Bunche, notes, August 12, 1968, UN Archives, Box 370/39/16.

20. Bunche, notes (likely December 18, 1968, but scrawled), UN Archives, Box 370/39/16.

21. "HHH Pays Sentimental Call at UN," *Washington Post*, November 27, 1968.

22. Bunche, notes, October 17, 1968, UN Archives, Box 370/38/2.

23. NBC Today Show, transcript, February 20, 1969, Bunche Archives, Schomburg Center, Box 19, Folder 18.

24. "Bunch as 'Idealist-Realist' Mourned by Thant and Wilkins," *New York Times*, December 12, 1971.

25. Gary Bass, *The Blood Telegram* (New York: Knopf, 2013).

26. Adam Nagourney, "In Tapes, Nixon Rails about Jews and Blacks," *New York Times*, December 10, 2010.

27. "Dr. Ralph Bunche of UN, Nobel Winner, Dies," *New York Times*, December 10, 1971.

28. "Trygve Lie Eulogized by Bunche," *New York Times*, January 7, 1969.

29. Bunche, "Nana," unpublished essay, no date, UN Archives, S-0852/1/11, at 1.

30. Bunche to Ralph Jr., January 8, 1969, UN Archives, Box 370/37/12.

31. Bunche, Remarks at the Dedication of Bunche Hall, Friday May 23, 1969, UCLA Archives, Collection 364, Box 3, Folder 7.

32. Bunche, notes, November 2, 1968, UN Archives, S-0852/1/11.

33. James Baldwin, "A Negro Assays the Negro Mood," *New York Times Magazine*, March 12, 1961.

34. Bunche, notes, no date but likely 1968–1969, UN Archives, Box 370/408.

35. Bunche, notes, no date but likely 1968–1969, UN Archives, Box 370/40/8.
36. Bunche, unpublished essay, no date but likely 1968 or 1969, UN Archives, Box 370/40/8.
37. ABC News, *Issues and Answers*, Transcript, December 28, 1969, UN Archives, Box 9/1/19.
38. Ralph Bunche, "Upheaval in the Ghettos," July 31, 1967, UN Archives, S-0852/1/13.
39. W. E. B. Du Bois, *Color and Democracy* (Harcourt, Brace, 1945).
40. This view reached its apotheosis a few years after Bunche's death in the highly influential *Theory of International Politics* by Kenneth Waltz (New York: McGraw-Hill, 1979). For an unearthing of earlier, more race-conscious thinking in the field of international relations, see Robert Vitalis, *White World Order, Black Power Politics* (Ithaca, NY: Cornell University Press, 2015).
41. Bunche, "Race and Alienation," in Charles P. Henry (ed.), *Ralph J. Bunche, Selected Speeches and Writings* (Ann Arbor: University of Michigan Press, 1995); James Manley, "Report of the Fifth East-West Philosopher's Conference," *Philosophy East and West* (October 1970).
42. Leonard Lyons, "The Lyons Den," *Minneapolis Star*, August 28, 1969.
43. Bunche, notes, "Far East Trip," UN Archives, 370/38/4.
44. Bunche, notes, no date but likely 1968, UN Archives, 370/39/16.
45. "Paisley Gets UN Greetings, Lindsay Snub," *Chicago Tribune*, September 10, 1969.
46. Bunche, notes, September 10, 1969, UN Archives, 370/39/16.
47. "Notes on UNCA Meeting with Rev. Ian Paisley" September 9, 1969, UN Archives, 370/39/16.
48. Bunche, notes, August 20, 1969, UN Archives, 370/39/16.
49. Sam Pope Brewer, "UN Mideast Debate to Go Directly to Full Assembly," *New York Times*, September 21, 1969.
50. ABC News, *Issues and Answers*, Transcript December 23, 1969 (referring to Thant's comments) UN Archives, Box 9/1/19.
51. Bunche to Winespear, March 28, 1970, UN Archives Box 350/1/1.
52. Malik to Bunche, translated from Russian, April 3, 1970, UN Archives, Box 350/1/27.
53. Powell to Topping, May 27, 1970, UN Archives, Box 350/1/15.
54. Robert Estabrook, "Age Creeping up on Top UN Officials," *Los Angeles Times*, August 9, 1970.
55. Brian Urquhart, *Ralph Bunche: An American Odyssey* (Norton, 1993), at 454.
56. "Bunche Lacks Confidence in Administration," *Atlanta Daily World*, January 1, 1970.
57. Carl Rowan, "Nixon and Racism," *Cincinnati Enquirer*, January 5, 1970.
58. "Bunche Says He Did Not Denounce Nixon," *Philadelphia Tribune*, January 10, 1970.
59. Bunche to Ralph Jr., January 16, 1970, UN Archives, Box 370/37/12.
60. Urquhart, *Ralph Bunche*, at 417.
61. Darius Jhabvala, "United Nations 25th Anniversary: A time for Appraisals," *Boston Globe*, May 31, 1970.
62. Michael Littlejohns, "The UN: 25 Years of Failure," *Jerusalem Post*, June 26, 1970.
63. Philip Jessup, "The United Nations at 25," *New York Times*, October 15, 1970.

64. Marie Smith, "Tipping the Crystal to Mark UN's 25th Anniversary," *Washington Post*, July 11, 1970.

65. "Thant Pessimistic on Peace," *The Sun*, July 10, 1970.

66. Memo from Bunche (signed by Thant), January 26, 1971, UN Archives, S-1078, Box 50/11. UCLA, and others, had been interested in and corresponded with Bunche about his papers from at least as early as 1954. See, for example, Letter from Powell to Bunche, May 13, 1955, UN Archives, S-1078/50/4. The papers were eventually acquired by UCLA.

67. "Nixon Hails Bunche," *New York Times*, October 2, 1971.

68. Israel Shenker, "Dr. Bunche, Ailing, Retires from UN: Is Back in Hospital," *New York Times*, October 1, 1971.

69. Associated Press, "UN's Ralph Bunche Dies," December 10, 1971.

70. A. S. Doc Young, "Dr. Bunche: He Transcended Race," *Los Angeles Sentinel*, December 16, 1971.

71. A. S. Doc Young, "Dr. Bunche: He Transcended Race," *Los Angeles Sentinel*, December 16, 1971.

72. "Dr. Ralph Bunche of UN, Nobel Winner, Dies," *New York Times*, December 10, 1971.

73. "The Faith of Ralph Bunche," *New York Times*, December 10, 1971.

74. "Ralph J. Bunche, 1904–1971," *Los Angeles Times*, December 10, 1971.

75. Mary Brown, "Ralph Bunche Eulogized as Endless Seeker of Peace," *Afro-American*, December 18, 1971.

76. UNGA Resolution 2625, A/Res/2625 (October 24, 1970).

Epilogue

1. The Talk of the Town, *The New Yorker*, January 1, 1972.

2. Mark Mazower, *Governing the World: The History of an Idea, 1815 to the Present* (New York: Penguin, 2012), at 251.

3. James O. Young, *Black Writers of the Thirties* (Baton Rouge: Louisiana State University Press, 1973), at 54.

4. *League of Nations Covenant*, Article XXII, signed June 28, 1919, https://avalon.law. yale.edu/20th_century/leagcov.asp

5. Samuel Zipp, "When Americans Fell in Love with the Ideal of One World," March 29, 2020, https://www.zocalopublicsquare.org/2020/03/29/true-history-wend ell-willkie-one-world/ideas/essay. On Stoddard and his influence, see gener- ally Robert Vitalis, *White World Order, Black Power Politics* (Ithaca, NY: Cornell University Press, 2015),Chapter 4.

6. Brian Urquhart, *Ralph Bunche: An American Odyssey* (New York: Norton, 1993), at 115.

7. Gregory Cleva, *John F. Kennedy's 1957 Algeria Speech: The Politics of Anticolonialism in the Cold War Era* (Lexington, 2022), at 26.

8. Hendrik Spruyt, *Ending Empire: Contested Sovereignty and Territorial Partition* (Ithaca, NY: Cornell University Press, 2005).

9. George Abi-Saab, "The Newly-Independent States and the Scope of Domestic Jurisdiction," *Proceedings of the American Society of International Law*, 54 (1960), at 87.

10. "Bunche Sees Danger in Germany, Mideast," *New York Times*, December 27, 1957.

11. Mazower, *Governing the World*, at 244.

12. Bunche, "The Role of the University in the Political Orientation of Negro Youth," *Journal of Negro Education* (October 1940), at 573, 579.

13. Bunche, "Upheaval in the Ghettos," July 31, 1967 UN Archives, S-0852/1/13.

14. Bunche to Robinson, November 20, 1963, UCLA Bunche Archives, Box 235, Folder 7.

15. Bunche, "The Role of the University," at 573; 579.

16. Bunche, notes, no date, UN Archives, Box 370/38/24.

17. The Talk of the Town, *The New Yorker*, January 1, 1972.

18. Princeton Lyman, "Ralph Bunche's International Legacy: The Middle East, Congo, and United Nations Peacekeeping," *Journal of Negro Education*, 73, 2 (Spring 2004), at 161.

19. Quoted in William Aceves, "The Watts Gang Treaty," *Harvard Civil Rights-Civil Liberties Law Review*, forthcoming 2022, at 819.

20. Aceves, "Watts Gang Treaty," at 827.

21. "An Interview of Ralph J. Bunche by Arthur Rovine," April 13, 1966, UCLA Archives, Collection 364, Box 12, Folder 4.

22. Boutros Boutros-Ghali, "Maintaining Peace and Security: The United Nations as Forum and Focal Point," *Loyola Los Angeles International and Comparative Law Journal* (1993–4), at 3.

23. Using the official United Nations list. Some of these were observer missions; the precise definition of peacekeeping is contested. but these are often seen as cognate efforts. https://peacekeeping.un.org/en/historical-timeline-of-un-peacekeeping. See also Alex J. Bellamy and Paul D. Williams, "Trends in Peace Operations, 1947–2013," in Joachim A. Koops et al. (eds.), *The Oxford Handbook of United Nations Peacekeeping Operations* (Oxford University Press, 2015).

24. Barbara Walter, Lise Howard, and Page Fortna, "The Extraordinary Relationship between Peacekeeping and Peace," *British Journal of Political Science*, 51 (2020), at 1.

25. Report of the Secretary-General, Introduction, A/70/357–S/2015/682, September 2, 2015.

26. Tanisha Fazal, *State Death: The Politics and Geography of Conquest, Occupation, and Annexation* (Princeton, NJ: Princeton University Press, 2007); Oona Hathaway and Scott Shapiro, *The Internationalists: How a Radical Plan to Outlaw War Remade the World* (New York: Simon and Schuster, 2017); Mark Zacher, "The Territorial Integrity Norm: International Boundaries and the Use of Force," *International Organization*, 55, 2 (2001).

27. Peace Research Institute Oslo, *Trends in Armed Conflict, 1946–2017* (2018). https://reliefweb.int/sites/reliefweb.int/files/resources/Dupuy%2C%20Rustad-%20Trends%20in%20Armed%20Conflict%2C%201946%E2%80%932017%2C%20Conflict%20Trends%205-2018.pdf

28. Susan Hannah Allen and Amy T. Yuen, "The Politics of Peacekeeping: UN Security Council Oversight Across Peacekeeping Missions," *International Studies Quarterly*, 58, 3 (2014), at 622.

29. "The Talk of the Town," *The New Yorker*, July 29, 1967.

30. James Cockayne and David Malone, "The Ralph Bunche Centennial: Peace Operations Then and Now," *Global Governance*, 11, 3 (2005), at 348.

31. Michael Doyle, "The John W. Holmes Lecture: Building Peace," *Global Governance*, (January/March 2007), at 6.

32. Madeline Kalb, "The UN's Embattled Peacekeeper," *New York Times Magazine*, December 19, 1982.

33. Bunche, "The United Nations Operation in the Congo," in Andrew Cordier and Wilder Foote (eds.), *The Quest for Peace* (New York: Columbia University Press, 1965), at 137.

34. Edward Luttwak, "Give War a Chance," *Foreign Affairs* (1999)

35. Arthur Larson, "Do It Through the UN," *Saturday Review*, August 28, 1962, at 10.

36. Madeline Albright, NPR Interview, December 28, 2014, https://www.npr.org/2014/12/28/373587972/albright-on-the-u-n-if-it-didnt-exist-we-would-invent-it

37. See the official UN list at https://peacekeeping.un.org/en/list-of-past-peacekeeping-operations.

38. Pankaj Mishra, "Frantz Fanon's Enduring Legacy," *The New Yorker*, November 29, 2021.

39. E.g. D. Shearer, "Africa's Great War," *Survival* (Spring 1999).

40. Bunche, "French Educational Policy in Togoland and Dahomey" (1934), in Charles P. Henry, *Ralph Bunche: Selected Speeches and Writings* (Ann Arbor: University of Michigan Press, 1995), at 116.

41. WGBH, *Prospects for Mankind*, March 6, 1960, American Archive of Public Broadcasting.

42. Bunche to Hammarskjold, June 27, 1960, UN Archives, Box 370/3/6.

43. Markus Benzing, "Midwifing a New State: The United Nations in East Timor," in *Max Planck Yearbook of United Nations Law* (Brill, 2005), at 311.

44. Many have drawn this analogy; see, for example, Jose Alvarez, "Revisiting TWAIL in Paris." http://opiniojuris.org/2010/09/28/my-summer-vacation-part-iii-revisiting-twail-in-paris

45. Adom Getachew, *World-Making After Empire: The Rise and Fall of Self-Determination* (Princeton, NJ: Princeton University Press, 2019), at 99.

46. Lawrence Finkelstein, "Bunche and the Colonial World: From Trusteeship to Decolonization," in Benjamin Rivlin, ed., *Ralph Bunche: The Man and His Times* (Holmes and Meier, 1990), at 109–110.

47. Bunche, "UN Intervention in Palestine," Philadelphia, June 6, 1949, UCLA Bunche Archives, Box 344, Folder 11.

48. "The Fight for Freedom," *New York Times*, March 12, 1954.

INDEX

For the benefit of digital users, indexed terms that span two pages (e.g., 52–53) may, on occasion, appear on only one of those pages.